A Programmer's Guide to ADO.NET in C#

MAHESH CHAND

A Programmer's Guide to ADO.NET in C#
Copyright ©2002 by Mahesh Chand

ISBN (pbk): 1-893115-39-9

Printed and bound in the United States of America 12345678910
Trademarked names may appear in this book. Rather than use a trademark symbol with every occurrence of a trademarked name, we use the names only in an editorial fashion and to the benefit of the trademark owner, with no intention of infringement of the trademark.

Technical Reviewer: Ildiko Blackburn, Boost Data Limited
Editorial Directors: Dan Appleman, Peter Blackburn, Gary Cornell, Jason Gilmore,
         Karen Watterson, John Zukowski
Managing Editor: Grace Wong
Project Manager and Developmental Editor: Tracy Brown Collins
Copy Editor: Kim Wimpsett
Production Editor: Kari Brooks
Composition: Impressions Book and Journal Services, Inc.
Artist: Cara Brunk, Blue Mud Productions
Indexer: Valerie Perry
Cover Designer: Tom Debolski
Marketing Manager: Stephanie Rodriguez

Distributed to the book trade in the United States by Springer-Verlag New York, Inc., 175 Fifth Avenue, New York, NY, 10010 and outside the United States by Springer-Verlag GmbH & Co. KG, Tiergartenstr. 17, 69112 Heidelberg, Germany.
In the United States, phone 1-800-SPRINGER, email orders@springer-ny.com, or visit http://www.springer-ny.com.
Outside the United States, fax +49 6221 345229, email orders@springer.de, or visit http://www.springer.de.

For information on translations, please contact Apress directly at 2560 9th Street, Suite 219, Berkeley, CA 94710. Phone 510-549-5930, fax: 510-549-5939, email info@apress.com, or visit http://www.apress.com.

The information in this book is distributed on an "as is" basis, without warranty. Although every precaution has been taken in the preparation of this work, neither the author nor Apress shall have any liability to any person or entity with respect to any loss or damage caused or alleged to be caused directly or indirectly by the information contained in this work.

The source code for this book is available to readers at http://www.apress.com in the Downloads section. You will need to answer questions pertaining to this book in order to successfully download the code.

To my family and friends who suffered the most.

Contents at a Glance

Foreword ....*xi*

About the Author ....*xiv*

About the Technical Reviewer ....*xv*

Acknowledgments ....*xvi*

Introduction ....*xvii*

Chapter 1: Introduction to C# *1*

Chapter 2: Introduction to Windows Forms *69*

Chapter 3: Overview of ADO.NET *123*

Chapter 4: Data Components in Visual Studio .NET *153*

Chapter 5: ADO.NET Data Providers and

           Disconnected Classes *229*

Chapter 6: Working with XML *355*

Chapter 7: Developing Web Applications Using ADO.NET *435*

Chapter 8: Using Web Services with ADO.NET *511*

Chapter 9: Handling ADO.NET Events *545*

Chapter 10: Different Flavors of ADO.NET *573*

Chapter 11: Working with the ODBC .NET Data Provider *613*

Appendix A: Relational Databases: Some Basic Concepts *653*

Appendix B: Commonly Used SQL Statements *667*

Index *685*

Contents

Foreword ....*xi*
About the Author ....*xiv*
About the Technical Reviewer ....*xv*
Acknowledgments ....*xvi*
Introduction ....*xvii*

Chapter 1: Introduction to C# *1*

Understanding the C# Language *1*
Writing Your First C# Program: "Hello, C# World!" *6*
Understanding C# Components *7*
Summary *68*

Chapter 2: Introduction to Windows Forms *69*

Design-Time versus Run-Time Development *69*
Writing a Command-Line Windows Forms Application *70*
Writing a Windows Forms Application Using
     the VS .NET IDE *78*
Windows.Forms Namespace *100*
Summary *121*

Chapter 3: Overview of ADO.NET *123*

What Is ADO.NET? *123*
Why ADO.NET Was Designed *125*
Advantages of ADO.NET *126*
Comparing ADO.NET and ADO *128*
Overview of ADO.NET Namespaces and Classes *129*
Understanding ADO.NET Components *132*
Writing ADO.NET Applications *138*
Creating a Sample ADO.NET Application *142*

Writing a Simple ADO.NET Program with
 Visual Studio .NET IDE *145*
Summary *151*

Chapter 4: Data Components in Visual Studio .NET *153*

Creating Your ADO.NET Project *153*
Using the Server Explorer *154*
Using Visual Data Components *162*
Using DataSet and DataView Components *199*
Using the Data Form Wizard *208*
Data Form Wizard: Looking under the Hood *223*
Summary *227*

Chapter 5: ADO.NET Data Providers and Disconnected Classes *229*

Looking at the ADO.NET Architecture *230*
Exploring the ADO.NET Class Hierarchy *232*
Understanding ADO.NET Disconnected Classes *237*
Using DataSet, DataView, and DataViewManager *273*
Using ADO.NET Data Providers *279*
Summary *353*

Chapter 6: Working with XML *355*

Defining XML-Related Terminology *355*
XML Overview *359*
DOM Overview *372*
Microsoft .NET and XML *375*
Reading XML *380*
The XmlWriter Classes *388*
The XmlConvert Class *393*
Understanding the DOM Implementation *393*
Transformation and XSLT *402*
ADO.NET and XML *405*
Navigation in XML *415*
Visual Studio .NET and XML Support *420*
Summary *433*

Chapter 7: Developing Web Applications Using ADO.NET 435

Introducing ASP.NET 435
Understanding Web Forms and Web Services 437
Developing Your First ASP.NET Web Application 438
Creating Your First ADO.NET Web Application 450
Using ASP.NET Server-Side Controls 455
Data Binding in ASP.NET 462
Creating a Guest Book in ASP.NET 478
Paging in DataGrid Control 490
Adding, Editing, and Deleting Data in Web Forms 496
Introducing the Table Web Control 503
Summary 509

Chapter 8: Using Web Services with ADO.NET 511

Exploring Web Services and the .NET Framework Library 512
Creating a Web Service in VS .NET 512
Testing Your Web Service 521
Creating the Web Service Consumer 525
Executing Asynchronous Web Services 539
Summary 543

Chapter 9: Handling ADO.NET Events 545

Introducing ADO.NET Events 545
Summary 570

Chapter 10: Different Flavors of ADO.NET 573

Working with Stored Procedures and Views 573
COM Interoperability 594
Using the ADO Recordset in ADO.NET 595
Using ADOX with ADO.NET 598
Accessing OLAP Server Data with ADO.NET 600
Summary 612

Chapter 11: Working with the ODBC .NET Data Provider 613

Understanding the ODBC .NET Data Provider 613
Accessing MySQL Databases 621
Accessing Text File Databases 633
Accessing Excel Databases 641
Working with Oracle Databases 644
Working with Sybase Databases 651
Summary 652

Appendix A: Relational Databases: Some Basic Concepts 653

Understanding Normalization 654
Introducing Sets, Cursors, and ADO.NET 660
Using Locking 661
References and Resources 666

Appendix B: Commonly Used SQL Statements 667

Understanding SQL References 667
Understanding Views 680
Using SQL Server's SELECT...FOR XML Clause 682
References and Resources 682

Index 685

Foreword

REMEMBER THE MASLOW TRIANGLE? According to Abraham Maslow, "self-actualization" is the pinnacle in the hierarchy of human needs. To paraphrase, he says that a musician must make music and an artist must paint if they're to be at peace with themselves.

And . . . I might add . . . a programmer must sling code.

Unfortunately, self-actualization is an elusive goal for most programmers because software development is an endless journey. There are always new technologies to learn, new techniques and tools to master, and, yes, definitely more code to write. There's always something you don't know . . . yet. Throughout this endless quest for knowledge, however, a few constants remain. Among them: the importance of data.

A truly successful programmer *must* know database programming. I've yet to write a useful application that didn't rely on data to complete its purpose. For, without data, what does an application do? Granted, I still fondly remember my somewhat unusual beginnings as a graphics programmer—doing hard-core GDI-intensive work building image-editing tools, screen savers, animations, and the like. It sure was fun while it lasted, but to be honest there are a heck of a lot more revenue-generating projects that rely on databases.

In my post-GDI beginnings, I had the luxury of progressive, incremental exposure to database programming. Pre-Win32, my first database-centric application was a two-tier application—a combination of Visual Basic 3.0 and Visual C++ 4.2 front-ends accessing a Borland Paradox database across a LAN. Connection pooling? What's that? After all, at the time, I was still earning my stripes as a programmer, and I was happy to successfully create a DSN and see that my API calls actually returned a set of records! Now, it seems like ancient history after ten years, several enterprise applications, and a variety of experiences with several DBMS platforms including Sybase, Microsoft SQL Server, and Oracle.

Those experiences taught me the value of database programming skills. But an even more important discovery I made was the value of actually leveraging the tools provided by the DBMS. Part of the job must be entrusted to the DBMS and the *database engineer* (or DBA—*not* to be confused with the *database programmer*.) The job of the database engineer is to know the capabilities of the chosen DBMS intimately. That means the best way to provide access to relational data, the capabilities of connection pooling and caching services provided by the database engine, the best uses for indexes, triggers (never, in many database engineers' eyes, but that's another story), stored procedures, relational views, and so on. The database engineer may not be a programmer, so the job of the database programmer is to work closely with the database engineer to determine how to best leverage built-in DBMS capabilities with application layer needs. In many cases, the best database design will be determined based on the needs of the application accessing the data.

Database programmers can have a tendency to want to write code "from scratch" to manage connections and improve their applications' performance. Often, this desire to control database access results from a lack of knowledge of the database and application server tools at their fingertips. Now, with XML being an integrated part of all major DBMSs, it's even more important for old-school database programmers to reinvent their approach. Those new to database programming, on the other hand, are likely to be thrown straight into the fire of distributed application development and can't afford to neglect critical design and scalability requirements.

Distributed application development today is both simple and complex. The complexity is that designing applications that support anytime/anywhere access truly puts a burden on systems engineers and programmers to handle availability and scalability needs. How many users will hit the site at once? How many connections will be needed at the application and database layer to support this potential number? These questions are particularly poignant for application service provider solutions and distributed applications leveraging Internet protocols to incorporate Web services (which is where it's at). So where's the simplicity? The simplicity is that building Web services, and integrating a myriad of applications over the Internet, is easy with today's tools, particularly with the Microsoft .NET Framework. However, that said, it becomes important for programmers to *know* what they *don't know*.

Mahesh Chand's book captures the big picture that today's database programmer needs, tailored specifically to ADO.NET. Early on, he has the reader produce simple yet complete ADO.NET applications, which gives beginners a sense of accomplishment and gives the experienced a cut-to-the-chase overview of the tools provided by the Visual Studio .NET environment. Along the way, he covers the key topics a database programmer mustn't forget relating specifically to performance, connection management, and scalability. As the book progresses, he explains how things work under the hood.

After reading this book, you'll have a clear picture of end-to-end ADO.NET programming and a well-rounded understanding of its integrated uses with XML, ASP.NET, and Web services. It's certainly a great starting point for building distributed Internet applications. In fact, the progressive way in which Chand introduces you to each subject makes this book an excellent teaching text. Of course, as with any technology, you must put in your time to get it right, but that's the beauty of a programmer's ongoing quest for self-actualization. If you acquired the knowledge without effort, how could you enjoy all of those late nights, pressing deadlines, and adrenaline rushes that accompany the process?

So, consider this book a tool to get you well on your way. If you're a seasoned programmer ready to conquer ADO.NET, or a new programmer ready to jump feet first into programming applications that fit today's model, pick up this book and start the journey. It'll show you how to get results early on through an interactive experience that won't make you wish you were writing a screen saver.

Have fun, sling great code, and prosper.

Michèle Leroux Bustamante
CIO, ConfirmNet Corporation
Associate, Idesign Inc.
`http://www.idesign.net`
`http://www.mlbtechnologies.com`

About the Author

MAHESH CHAND IS AN Indian national who has a master's degree in computer science and a bachelor's degree in mathematics and physics. He's also a Microsoft Certified Professional in VC++. He has been programming with Microsoft technologies for more than five years. His programming expertise includes VC++, MFC, ATL, COM, Visual Basic, SQL Server, Microsoft Access, .NET, C#, Visual Basic .NET, and ASP.NET.

He's currently employed as a software developer with Kruse Inc, a Downingtown, Pennsylvania, software development company. He's a founder of the Mindcracker (http://www.mindcracker.com) and C# Corner (http://www.c-sharpcorner.com) online communities. Mindcracker is a free resource community where C++ developers can share their code and knowledge, and C# Corner is one of the most active and largest .NET community Web sites.

Besides his full-time job, Mahesh spends time writing articles for C# Corner and helping the site's visitors. In his free time, he enjoys tennis, karate, and soccer.

About the Technical Reviewer

ILDIKO BLACKBURN IS AN English housewife—or that's what she might have you believe. Indeed, she may well fill the housewife role, but that description conceals the truth, which is a little more involved given that she was born and educated in Hungary as a computer scientist. So much for the English bit.

Also in common with many housewives these days, Ildiko runs and operates a number of IT consultancy companies in England, most notably Boost Data Limited (http://www.boost.net). In her role as consultant, she has been responsible for designing, developing, implementing, and project managing large client/server projects including multi-currency billing systems for UUNET and major system migrations into SAP and Siebel for WorldCom. Over the past ten years, she has worked with Oracle, Sybase, and Microsoft SQL Server on the Windows NT/2K and Unix platforms. More recently, Ildiko has been actively involved in developing and testing .NET applications. You can contact Ildiko at ib@boost.net.

Acknowledgments

First of all, I would like to thank Karen and Gary at Apress. They've been very helpful during this entire process. Second of all, thanks to Peter and Ildiko for reviewing the technical aspects of the book; Tracy for being very helpful and supportive when I missed the many deadlines; Grace and Kim for their support and understanding; and Stephanie for her marketing efforts.

I would also like to thank Michael Gold, president of Microgold Inc. for his contribution to the book. I would like to thank Melanie for being patient during the lengthy process of writing and for taking care of the C# Corner site and other issues. Finally, I would like to thank Owen Winkler, Pat Kelly, Jim Kruse, Ken McCoy and everybody at Kruse Inc., and Lana and Stacy for their motivation.

Introduction

MICROSOFT .NET IS THE NEW programming paradigm from Microsoft. The new version of Visual Studio, called the *Visual Studio .NET programming environment*, is heavily dependent on the .NET Framework. In the .NET Framework, all .NET-supported languages share a common library (the .NET Runtime Library). All compilers compile code to an Intermediate Language (IL Code) format, which the Common Language Runtime (CLR) then reads. Visual Studio .NET contains five major languages: C#, VB .NET, Managed Extensions in C++ (called *MC++*), VBScript .NET, and JScript .NET. C# (pronounced *C-sharp*) is a new language from Microsoft. After C#, VB .NET is supposed to be the most powerful language in the .NET Framework.

In the .NET Framework, the database API is ADO.NET. However, the ADO.NET model is derived from its predecessor ADO, but there's no involvement of COM or ActiveX Data Components as in ADO. The ADO.NET API is a set of managed classes that works in the same way as other classes of the .NET Framework library.

C# is one of the powerful languages used to write .NET Framework applications—both desktop applications and those on the Web. This book covers how to write database applications (desktop or Web-based applications) using ADO.NET and C# for the .NET platform.

Who Should Read This Book?

This book is for experienced developers who want to write desktop or Web-based database applications using ADO.NET in .NET and C#. This book assumes you've got prior knowledge of at least one object-oriented language and have worked with Microsoft database technologies using any of the Visual Studio languages, such as VB, C++, or Java. This book also assumes you know the basic concepts of .NET and how to install it. Knowledge of C# is a plus but not mandatory. Chapter 1 and Chapter 2 cover the basics of the C# language and Windows Forms. If you're already a C# programmer and know how to write Windows Forms applications, you can skip these two chapters.

XML is a tremendously popular language these days, and ADO.NET provides support for XML. Some knowledge of ASP is a plus to develop Web applications and Web services using ASP.NET, but it's not mandatory. I cover the basics of XML in Chapter 6. You can skip that portion of the chapter if you already know how to use XML.

What Does This Book Cover?

This book starts with introductory chapters on the C# language and Windows Forms and ends with writing Web services for the Internet.

Chapter 1 and Chapter 2 of this book cover the basics of the C# language and Windows Forms. These two chapters are a good start for beginners who have no working knowledge of C# or Windows Forms.

Chapter 3 covers the basic concepts of ADO.NET and discusses the advantages and uses of ADO.NET. After that it shows you step by step how to write simple console-based and Windows applications to access databases using ADO.NET.

Chapter 4 explores how you can take advantage of Visual Studio .NET to develop database applications quickly. This chapter also covers VS .NET tools such as the Server Explorer and the Data Form Wizard, which help you develop full-fledged database applications with only a few lines of code. The last part of this chapter shows how to use VS .NET to write XML schemas.

Chapter 5 covers ADO.NET in more depth, including different data providers, ADO.NET common classes, and ADO.NET shared classes. This chapter covers the class hierarchy models of various data providers including OleDB, Sql, and ODBC. Also, this chapter describes ADO.NET components such as connection, command, dataset, and data reader in more detail.

Chapter 6 is dedicated to XML. This chapter starts by talking about the basics of XML, its definitions, items, and DOM. Next, the chapter shows you how to read, write, search, navigate, remove, and delete data in XML documents. This chapter then shows you how ADO.NET and the XML model emerge in .NET, and it provides a scalable, high-performance solution for writing database applications.

Chapter 7 is all about ASP.NET and Web Forms and how to write database application on the Web using ASP.NET and C#. This chapter covers some real-world examples such as creating a guest book in ASP.NET for your Web site.

Chapter 8 discusses how to write database Web services and Web service consumer applications. Web services are another growing area of programming.

Chapter 9 introduces ADO.NET event handling. This chapter shows you how to use events for different objects including the connection, dataset, data table, and data adapter objects.

Chapter 10 covers some detailed issues—including stored procedures, triggers, and views—and shows you how to create and use them in VS .NET. COM interoperability is other area this chapter covers. This chapter shows how to access ADO, ADOX, and ADOMD in managed code through COM. Finally, this chapter shows how to build and use various SQL statements to create, execute, and delete new database and database objects including views, tables, and stored procedures.

Chapter 11 discusses the ODBC .NET data provider and how to access different ODBC data sources. This chapter contains ready-to-run source code samples for MySQL, Oracle 8i, Oracle 9i, Sybase, and even Excel and text databases.

Appendix A covers some basics of databases such as locking, cursors, and normalization.

Appendix B is a quick reference to SQL statements and shows you how to write various SQL statements. SQL is a vital part of database programming.

What Databases Are Used in This Book?

ADO.NET treats all databases in the same manner by using different data providers. Thus, if you know how to work with one kind of database, you can work with other kinds. The only difference is that you use different classes and connection strings. But ADO.NET takes care for that for you under the hood. For example, if you use the OleDb data provider to work with Access or other OLE DB data sources, you use `OleDbConnection`, `OleDbDataAdapter`, and `OleDbCommand` objects. If you want to work with SQL Server, you use the Sql data provider's classes `SqlConnection`, `SqlDataAdapter`, and `SqlCommand`, which work exactly in the same manner as the OleDb data provider's classes. The only thing you need to do is to change the database connection string.

To provide you with a variety, I've used multiple kinds of data sources in the sample applications in this book. You can categorize the databases as follows.

Microsoft Access

Microsoft Access is the most frequently used database among Microsoft developers. It comes with Microsoft Office and is popular on the desktop as well as the Internet. The Access database is a file with extension `*.mdb`. In this book, I'll utilize the `Northwind.mdb` database for all of the OLE DB provider examples that come with Office 2000.

Microsoft SQL Server Desktop Engine (MSDE)

This is a SQL Server–compatible database running on the desktop. It's also available in Office; further, you can use it and redistribute it for free. I'll utilize the Northwind version of this database in all of the SQL Server data provider examples.

Microsoft SQL Server 2000

Microsoft's top-of-the-line database is for high-power applications handling a lot of users who need to work with a lot of data. This database is on the level of high-end databases such as Oracle and Sybase, but it runs specifically under Windows.

You could swap in SQL Server for the Sql Server provider samples in this book, which were run using MSDE.

Oracle Data Sources

Oracle is one of the most widely used databases in Windows and Web applications. This book shows samples on how to work with the Oracle 8i and Oracle 9i databases.

Other Data Sources

Other data sources used in this book are MySQL, Sybase, Excel, and even text databases.

Overview of Microsoft Data Access Technologies

To understand the importance of ADO.NET, it's important to take a quick look at the Microsoft database access technologies that came before ADO.NET.

Since the first release of Open Database Connectivity (ODBC) to access databases for Windows applications, Microsoft has been introducing and improving ways to make a database programmer's life easier. In this series of database technologies, called Microsoft Data Access Technologies, it introduced many new and/or improved existing technologies. Each of these technologies has its own pros and cons. Some are specific to a particular kind or data source, and some of them are common to all kinds of data sources. These technologies are as follows:

- Open Database Connectivity (ODBC)

- Data Access Objects (DAO)

- Microsoft Foundation Classes (MFC) ODBC and DAO classes

- Remote Data Objects (RDO)

- Object Linking and Embedding—Database (OLE DB)

- ActiveX Data Objects (ADO)

Object Database Connectivity (ODBC)

ODBC was the first formal database access technology that Microsoft introduced a decade ago. ODBC provides a low-level C/C++ API for retrieving data from relational databases such as SQL Server, Access, or Oracle by using ODBC drivers and ODBC Administration. With the help of the ODBC drivers and ODBC Administration, you can connect to any data source using the ODBC API. Because of the relational nature of ODBC, it's difficult to use ODBC to communicate with non-relational data sources, such as object databases, network directory services, email stores, and so on.

Figure I-1 shows you ODBC connectivity with a database through ODBC drivers and ODBC Administration, also called *ODBC Driver Manager.*

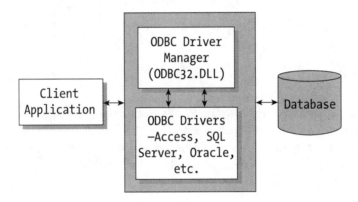

Figure I-1. ODBC architecture

Using ODBC functions is not a fun part of programming for high-level programmers. ODBC is a hierarchical model, which means you have to create environment and database objects before creating a recordset object and accessing the data. Other problems with ODBC are multiple connections and multiple data sources. An ODBC connection doesn't allow you to connect to two data sources using the same connection. Instead, you need to use two separate connection objects. Not being object-oriented in nature and its memory management were other drawbacks of ODBC.

Data Access Objects (DAO)

DAO is a set of COM interfaces for accessing databases. DAO uses the Microsoft Jet Database Engine to connect to ODBC and .mdb databases. DAO is best suited for

Jet database systems, including Access, FoxPro, and SQL Server because it can directly connect to these databases through the Jet Database Engine (see Figure I-2).

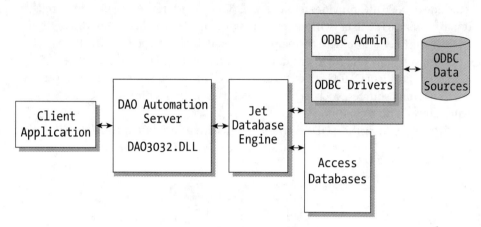

Figure I-2. DAO model

DAO is easier to use than the ODBC API, but it doesn't provide the degree of low-level control and flexibility afforded by the ODBC API. Therefore, DAO could be classified as a high-level database interface. Another problem with DAO is that it requires one more layer to work with ODBC data sources.

MFC ODBC and DAO Classes

MFC provides DAO and ODBC classes to access databases using DAO and ODBC for VC++ developers. These classes provide a high-level programming model to work with DAO and ODBC. These classes are a nice wrapper around the DAO and ODBC APIs. The only drawback of these classes is that these classes are not flexible enough and perform slowly because of too many layers.

Remote Data Objects (RDO)

RDO is an object interface for ODBC. There is an OLE layer on the top of the ODBC API. The main advantage of RDO was an object interface for ODBC developers, but the disadvantage was slow performance because of too many layers. Further, it's not well suited for nonrelational data sources.

OLE DB

OLE DB was designed to access all kinds of data including relational, nonrelational, text data, graphical data, and directory services. OLE DB components consist of data providers that expose their data, data consumers that use data, and service components that process and transport data (for example, query processors and cursor engines). OLE DB is a low-level programming model and provides the most flexibility and control over data. Figure I-3 shows the OLE DB model.

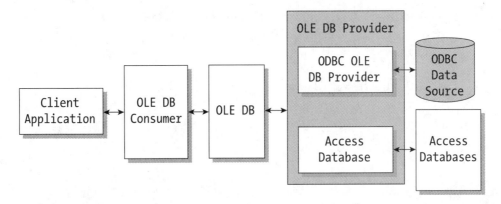

Figure I-3. OLE DB model

As you can see from Figure I-3, a client application accesses a database through the OLE DB provider and consumers. You must have an OLE DB provider installed to use OLE DB in your application, which is provided by database vendors.

> **NOTE** *OLE DB is also denoted as OLE-DB.*

ActiveX Data Objects (ADO)

ADO is a set of ActiveX controls that provide programmatic access to Microsoft's latest underlying data access technologies. In other words, ADO is a COM wrapper around OLE DB library. ADO is much simpler to use than OLE DB and can be classified as a high-level database interface. The advantages of ADO include the following:

- ADO is easy to program and is faster than ODBC and DAO with a few exceptions. ADO also provides more flexibility and control on data. You don't have to go through a hierarchy to access data as you do in DAO or ODBC.

- ADO (OLE DB) is a set of COM interfaces. This means ADO provides a binary standard to access any kind of data source. ADO can be used by any language that supports COM such as Visual Basic or C++.

- The ADO model is not hierarchical like ODBC or DAO. For instance, you can access a recordset object without going through a hierarchy of an object.

- ADO supports XML data access with the help of MSXML.

ADO.NET

ADO.NET is an evolution of ADO. ADO.NET and the XML .NET API construct a uniform model to work with relational or text-based XML data. The ADO.NET API is a managed code, which means you get all the advantages of .NET, including automatic memory management and garbage collection. Unlike DAO or ODBC, you don't have to install anything to make an ADO.NET program work if you're already running .NET applications on a machine. I'll discuss ADO.NET in more detail in Chapter 3.

What Are OLE-DB Templates?

The problem with OLE DB data access technology is that creating OLE DB providers and consumers is a pain. Because of the increasing popularity of COM, ATL, DAO, and ODBC MFC classes, Microsoft added OLE DB templates to VC++ for ATL developers. They ease the pain of creating OLE DB providers and OLE DB consumers by wrapping the functionality in C++ templates.

What Is Universal Data Access (UDA)?

As you can see from the previous discussion, many technologies work with databases. Each of these technologies has its own pros and cons. There are many occasions when a developer wants to use more than one type of technology in an application. To overcome this problem, Microsoft came up with new technology:

Universal Data Access (UDA). UDA provides access to various kinds of data sources through a single data access model.

The UDA architecture combines three basic technologies—ODBC, ADO, and OLE DB—and exposes object-oriented COM-based interfaces optimized for both low-level and high-level application development to provide a single, optimized, high-performance, and scalable solution to work with multiple data sources.

How to Contact Me

I'd like to know what you think about this book, including what you liked and what you didn't like. As a reader, you're the best judge. You can send me your comments at `mcb@mindcracker.com`. You can also find me on the C# Corner (`http://www.c-sharpcorner.com`) discussion forums.

CHAPTER 1

Introduction to C#

THIS CHAPTER WILL INTRODUCE YOU TO C#. You'll learn how to write and compile C#
programs, C# syntaxes, data types, control flow, classes and their members, interfaces, arrays, and exception handling. I'll begin with an overview of the language.

Understanding the C# Language

Microsoft developed C#, a new programming language based on the C and C++
languages. Microsoft describes C# in this way: "C# is a simple, modern, object-
oriented, and typesafe programming language derived from C and C++. C#
(pronounced C sharp) is firmly planted in the C and C++ family tree of languages
and will immediately be familiar to C and C++ programmers. C# aims to combine
the high productivity of Visual Basic and the raw power of C++."

Anders Hejlsberg, the principal architect of C#, is known for his work with
Borland on Turbo Pascal and Delphi (based on object-oriented Pascal). After
leaving Borland, Hejlsberg worked at Microsoft on Visual J++.

Some aspects of C# will be familiar to those who have programmed in C,
C++, or Java. C# incorporates the Smalltalk concept, which means everything is
an object. In other words, all types in C# are objects. C# properties are similar to
Visual Basic properties. The Rapid Application Development (RAD) goal in C# is
assisted by C#'s use of concepts and keywords, such as `class`, `struct`, `statement`,
`operator`, and `enum`. The language also utilizes the concepts contained in the
Component Object Model (COM) architecture.

Unlike Visual Basic or Delphi, events are data types in C# and can belong to
an object. Members of a class object can have variables, methods, properties, and
events. Attributes are another nice feature of the language.

> **NOTE** *C# is a case-sensitive language.*

C# and Open Source: The Mono Project

C# and Common Language Infrastructure (CLI) is under consideration at the
European Computer Manufacturers Association (ECMA). You'll probably see C#

running on Unix and Linux operating systems. It's no wonder you see many C# compilers emerging from different development tool companies.

Ximian, the Boston-based company that's well-known for its open-source product, GNOME, is working on a Linux-based, .NET open-source project called the *Mono Project*. The Mono Project incorporates key .NET-compliant components, including a C# compiler, a Common Language Runtime (CLR), a Just-In-Time (JIT) compiler, and a set of class libraries that will let developers create .NET applications that run on Windows, Linux, or Unix platforms. You'll find more information on the Mono Project at `http://www.ximian.com/mono/` or at the ECMA Web site at `http://www.ecma.ch./`.

How and Why C# Came to Be

It was a dream of developers to have a language as powerful and as fast as C++, yet as easy to program as Microsoft's Visual Basic and Borland's Delphi. Microsoft planned its .NET Framework and C# language for years.

Prior to .NET, the most popular programming languages for Web and Windows development were Visual Basic, Java, Visual C++, and Delphi. Each of these languages has its pros and cons. Visual Basic and Delphi are easy to use and simple to program; however, they're not truly object-oriented, and they lack the flexibility to develop complex programs. Java is good for Web development, but it still lacks in its object-oriented aspects and in its capability to develop complex Windows applications. Java's platform independence, however, is a plus. Visual C++ is a great tool to develop Windows- and COM-based applications, but it's not as easy to use as Visual Basic or Delphi.

Microsoft wanted to develop an integrated tool with all the positive features of these languages and more. C# is the result. C# is as easy to use and as productive as Visual Basic and Delphi. Because it's derived from C and C++, it doesn't leave the C++ programmer at the beginning of the learning curve. C# also has the power and flexibility of C++. Because of its platform-independent nature (companies are still working on supporting C# on other operating systems such as Unix and Linux), you can deploy C# applications onto any .NET-supported platform. C# also provides Web development similar to Java with the help of ASP.NET.

Characteristics and Features of C#

As explained, C# was developed as a language that would combine the best features of previously existing Web and Windows programming languages. I'll discuss some of the primary characteristics of C# in the following sections.

Modern and Object Oriented

A modern language is one that provides latest features and tools for developing scalable, reliable, and robust industry-standard applications. C# is a modern language. The current trend in programming is Web development, and C# is the best language for developing Web applications and components for the Microsoft .NET platform.

As mentioned, C# is an object-oriented language. It supports all the basic object-oriented language features: encapsulation, polymorphism, and inheritance. Unlike C++, C# doesn't support multiple inheritance; however, there are always workarounds if you really need this capability. A few articles are available on C# Corner (`http://www.c-sharpcorner.com/Language/MultipleInheritanceCB.asp`) for more information on such workarounds.

Simple and Flexible

C# is as simple to use as Visual Basic, in that everything in C# is represented as an object. All data types and components in C# are objects. C++ programmers are sometimes confused when choosing different access operators to process objects. With C#, you use a dot (.) operator to access the object members.

Programmers use C# to develop both managed and unmanaged code. *Managed code* is code managed through the CLR module. It handles garbage collection, typesafety, and platform-independent behavior. *Unmanaged code*, on the other hand, is code run outside the CLR, such as an ActiveX control.

C# provides the flexibility of using native Win 32 application programming interface (API) and unmanaged code through COM+. C# enables you to declare unsafe classes and members having pointers, COM interfaces, structures, and native APIs. Although the class and its members are not typesafe, they still can be executed from managed code using COM+. Using the N/Direct feature of C# and COM+, you can use the C language API. With the help of the COM+ run-time and the COM+ Common Language Specification (CLS), you can access the COM and COM+ API. Using the `Sysimport` attribute, you can even access native Windows API (DLLs) in C#. See the "Attributes" section of this chapter for more about attributes.

Typesafety

C# is a typesafe language. All variables and classes (including primitive types, such as integer, Boolean, and float) in C# are a type, and all types are derived from the object type.

The object type provides basic functionality, such as string conversion, and information about a type. (See "The Object Class" section of this chapter for more about the object type.) C# doesn't support unsafe type assignments. In other words, assigning a float variable directly to a Boolean variable is not permitted. If you assign a float type to a Boolean type, the compiler generates an error.

C# has two kinds of types: value types and reference types. All *value types* are initialized with a value of zero, and all *reference types* are automatically initialized with a null value (local variables need to be initialized explicitly or the compiler throws a warning). The "Types in C#" section of this chapter will discuss types in more detail.

> **NOTE** *Some books and documentation also use the word "type" to mean a class such as MSDN.*

Automatic Memory Management and Garbage Collection

Automatic memory management and garbage collection are two important features of C#. With C#, you don't need to allocate memory or release it. The *garbage collection* feature ensures that unused references are deleted and cleaned up in memory. You use the new operator to create a type object, but you never need to call a delete operator to destroy the object. If the garbage collector finds any unreferenced object hanging around in memory, it removes it for you. Although you can't call delete directly on an object, you have ways to get the garbage collector to destroy objects.

Versioning Control and Scalable

If you're a Microsoft Windows developer, you should be familiar with the expression *DLL hell*, which refers to having multiple versions of the same Dynamic Link Library (DLL) and not having backward and forward compatibility. For example, you can't run programs written in Microsoft Foundation Class (MFC) version 4.0 on systems with MFC version 3.0 or earlier. This is one of the biggest challenges for a developer, especially if you're developing MFC applications.

The C# model is based on namespaces. All interfaces and classes *must* be bundled under a namespace. A *namespace* has classes as its members. You can access all the members or just a single member of a namespace. Two separate namespaces can have the same class as their member.

C# also supports binary compatibility with a base class. Adding a new method to a base class won't cause any problems in your existing application.

.NET assemblies contain metadata called *manifest*. A manifest stores information about an assembly such as its version, locale, and signature. There is no concept of registry entries for handling compatibility. In .NET, you simply put your assembly into one global folder if you want to make it sharable; otherwise, you put it in a private folder for private use only.

Language and Cross-Platform Interoperability

C#, as with all Microsoft .NET-supported languages, shares a common .NET run-time library. The language compiler generates intermediate code, which a .NET-supported compiler can read with the help of the CLR. Therefore, you can use a C# assembly in VB .NET without any problem, and vice versa.

With the full support of COM+ and .NET Framework services, C# has the ability to run on cross-platform systems. The Web-based applications created from .NET use an Extensible Markup Language (XML) model, which can run on multiple platforms.

C# Editors

Before starting your first C# application, you should take a look at the C# editors available for creating applications. Visual Studio (VS) .NET Integrated Development Environment (IDE) is currently the best tool for developing C# applications. Installing VS .NET also installs the C# command-line compiler that comes with the .NET Software Development Kit (SDK).

If you don't have VS .NET, you can install the C# command-line compiler by installing the .NET SDK. After installing the .NET SDK, you can use any C# editor.

> **TIP** *There are many C# editors available—some are even free. Many of the editors that use the C# command-line compiler are provided with the .NET SDK. Visit the C# Corner's tools section* (http://www.c-sharpcorner.com/tools.asp) *for a list of available C# editors.*

If you can't get one of these editors, you can use a text editor, such as Notepad or WordPad. In the next sections, you'll learn how to write a Windows Forms application in Notepad, and then you'll look at the VS .NET IDE.

Writing Your First C# Program: "Hello, C# World!"

Writing a "Hello, World!" program is always the first step to learning any new programming language. In keeping with this tradition, your first C# program will write output on your console saying, "Hello, C# World!"

Before starting with the C# programming, however, you must install the C# compiler. The C# command-line compiler, `csc.exe`, comes with Microsoft's .NET SDK.

The .NET SDK supports the Windows 98, Windows ME, Windows NT 4.0, and Windows 2000 platforms. After installing the compiler, insert the code for the "Hello, C# World!" program, which is shown in Listing 1-1. Then save the file as `first.cs`.

Listing 1-1. "Hello, C# World!" code
```
using System;
class Hello
{
 static void Main() {
 Console.WriteLine("Hello, C# World!");
 }
}
```

You can compile C# code from the command line using this syntax:

```
csc C:\temp\first.cs
```

Make sure the path of your `.cs` file is correct and that the `csc` executable is included in your path. Also make sure that path of C# compiler (`csc.exe`) is correct. After compiling your code, the C# compiler creates an `.exe` file called `first.exe` under the current directory. Now you can execute the `.exe` from Windows Explorer or from the command line. Figure 1-1 shows the output.

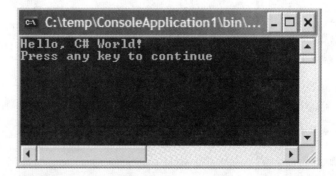

Figure 1-1. "Hello, C# World!" program output

Did you see "Hello, C# World!" on your console? If you did, then congratu-lations, you're now officially a C# programmer. If not, then you may want to check the path of your file first.cs and the path of the compiler csc.exe.

You have now written your first few lines of C# code. But what does each line of your program mean? I'll describe the various components of your "Hello, C# World!" program.

The first line of your program is this:

```
using System;
```

The .NET Framework class library is referenced in namespaces. The System namespace contains the Console class, which reads from or writes to the console.

The class keyword defines a new class that is followed by a class name, as seen in the second line of the "Hello, C# World!" code listing:

```
class Hello
{
    . . ..
}
```

The next line of code is the static void Main() function:

```
 static void Main() {
 Console.WriteLine("Hello, C# World!");
 }
}
```

In C#, every application must have a static Main() or int Main() entry point. The concept is similar to that of the main() function of C++.

The Console class is defined in the System namespace. You can access its class members by referencing them directly. WriteLine(), a method of the Console class, writes a string and a line terminator to the console.

Understanding C# Components

Now that you've finished your first C# program, it's time to talk about the intrica-cies of the C# language. In this section, I'll discuss the C# syntax and components and how to use them.

Namespaces and Assemblies

The first line of the "Hello, C# World!" program was this:

```
Using System;
```

This line adds a reference to the System namespace to the program. After adding a reference to a namespace, you can access any member of the namespace. As mentioned, in .NET library references documentation, each class belongs to a namespace. But what exactly is a namespace?

To define .NET classes in a category so they'd be easy to recognize, Microsoft used the C++ class packaging concept known as *namespaces*. A namespace is simply a grouping of related classes. The root of all namespaces is the System namespace. If you see namespaces in the .NET library, each class is defined in a group of similar category. For example, the System.Data namespace only possesses data-related classes, and System.Multithreading contains only multithreading classes.

When you create a new application using Visual C#, you see that each application is defined as a namespace and that all classes belong to that namespace. You can access these classes from other applications by referencing their namespaces.

For example, you can create a new namespace MyOtherNamespace with a method Hello defined in it. The Hello method writes "Hello, C# World!" to the console. Listing 1-2 shows the namespace.

Listing 1-2. Namespace wrapper for the Hello *class*

```
// Called namespace
namespace MyOtherNamespace
{
    class MyOtherClass
    {
        public void Hello()
        {
            Console.WriteLine("Hello, C# World!");
        }

    }
}
```

In Listing 1-3, you'll see how to reference this namespace and call MyOtherClass's Hello method from the main program.

In Listing 1-2, the MyOtherClass class and its members can be accessed from other namespaces by either placing the statement using MyOtherNamespace before the class declaration or by referring to the class as MyOtherNamespace.Hello, as shown in Listing 1-3 and Listing 1-4.

Listing 1-3. Calling MyOtherNamespace *namespace members*

```
using System;
using MyOtherNamespace;

// Caller namespace
namespace HelloWorldNamespace
{
    class Hello
    {
        static void Main()
        {
            MyOtherClass cls = new MyOtherClass();
            cls.Hello();
        }
    }
}

// Called namespace
namespace MyOtherNamespace
{
    class MyOtherClass
    {
        public void Hello()
        {
            Console.WriteLine("Hello, C# World!");
        }

    }
}
```

As you have seen in Listing 1-3, you include a namespace by adding the using directive. You can also reference a namespace direct without the using directive. Listing 1-4 shows you how to use MyOtherClass of MyOtherNamespace.

Listing 1-4. Calling the HelloWorldNamespace *member from the* MyOtherNamespace

```
// Caller namespace
namespace HelloWorldNamespace
{
    class Hello
    {
        static void Main()
        {
            MyOtherNamespace.MyOtherClass cls =
new MyOtherNamespace.MyOtherClass();
            cls.Hello();
        }
    }
}
```

Standard Input and Output Streams

The System.Console class provides the capability to read streams from and write streams to the System console. It also defines functionality for error streams. The Read operation reads data from the console to the standard input stream, and the Write operation writes data to the standard output stream. The standard error stream is responsible for storing error data. These streams are automatically associated with the system console.

The error, in, and out properties of the Console class represent standard error output, standard input, and standard output streams. In the standard output stream, the Read method reads the next character, and the ReadLine method reads the next line. The Write and WriteLine methods write the data to the standard output stream. Table 1-1 describes some of the console class methods.

Table 1-1. The System.Console *Class Methods*

METHOD	DESCRIPTION	EXAMPLE
Read	Reads a single character	int i = Console.Read();
ReadLine	Reads a line	string str = Console.ReadLine();
Write	Writes a line	Console.Write("Write: 1");
WriteLine	Writes a line followed by a line terminator	Console.WriteLine("Test Output Data with Line");

Listing 1-5 shows you how to use the Console class and its members.

Listing 1-5. Console *class example*

```
using System;

namespace ConsoleSamp
{
    class Class1
    {
        static void Main(string[] args)
        {
            Console.Write("Standard I/O Sample");
            Console.WriteLine("");
            Console.WriteLine("====================");
            Console.WriteLine("Enter your name... ");
            String name = Console.ReadLine();
            Console.WriteLine("Output: Your name is: "+ name);
        }
    }
}
```

Figure 1-2 shows the output of Listing 1-5.

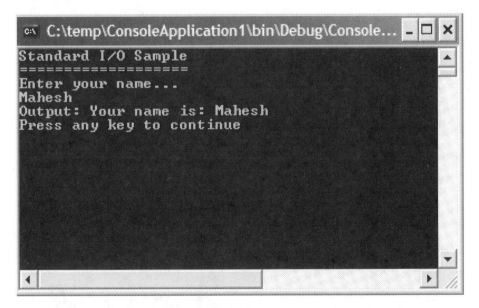

Figure 1-2. The Console *class methods output*

The Object Class

As described, in the .NET Framework, all types are represented as objects and are derived from the Object class. The Object class defines five methods: Equals, ReferenceEquals, GetHashCode, GetType, and ToString. Table 1-2 describes these methods, which are available to all types in the .NET library.

Table 1-2. Object Class Methods

METHOD	DESCRIPTION
GetType	Returns type of the object.
Equals	Compares two object instances. Returns true if they're equal; otherwise false.
ReferenceEquals	Compares two object instances. Returns true if both are same instances; othewise false.
ToString	Converts an instance to a string type.
GetHashCode	Returns hashcode for an object.

The following sections discuss the Object class methods in more detail.

The GetType Method

You can use the Type class to retrieve type information from the object. The GetType method of an object returns a type object, which you can use to get information on an object such as its name, namespace, base type, and so on. Listing 1-6 retrieves the information of objects. In Listing 1-6, you get the type of the Object and System.String classes.

Listing 1-6. GetType example

```
using System;

class TypeClass
{
    static void Main(string[] args)
    {
        // Create object of type Object and String
        Object cls1 = new Object();
        System.String cls2 = "Test String" ;
```

```
    // Call GetType to return the type
    Type type1 = cls1.GetType();
    Type type2 = cls2.GetType();

    // Object class output
    Console.WriteLine(type1.BaseType);
    Console.WriteLine(type1.Name);
    Console.WriteLine(type1.FullName);
    Console.WriteLine(type1.Namespace);

    // string output
    Console.WriteLine(type2.BaseType);
    Console.WriteLine(type2.Name);
    Console.WriteLine(type2.FullName);
    Console.WriteLine(type2.Namespace);
    }
}
```

Figure 1-3 shows the output of Listing 1-6.

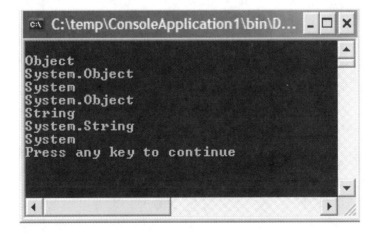

Figure 1-3. Output of Listing 1-6

The Equals and ReferenceEqual Methods

The Equals method in the Object class can compare two objects. The ReferenceEqual method can compare the two objects' instances. For example:

```
Console.WriteLine(Object.Equals(cls1, cls2));
Console.WriteLine(Object.Equals(str1, str2));
```

See Listing 1-7 for the entire code.

Listing 1-7. GetType, Equal, *and* ReferenceEquals

```
using System;

namespace TypesSamp
{

    // Define Class 1
    public class Class1 : Object
    {
        private void Method1()
        {
            Console.WriteLine("1 method" );
        }
    }

    // Define Class 2
    public class Class2 : Class1
    {
        private void Method2()
        {
            Console.WriteLine("2 method" );
        }
    }


    class TypeClass
    {
        static void Main(string[] args)
        {
            Class1 cls1 = new Class1();
            Class2 cls2 = new Class2();
```

```
Console.WriteLine("============================");
Console.WriteLine("Type Information");
Console.WriteLine("============================");

// Getting type information
Type type1 = cls1.GetType();
Type type2 = cls2.GetType();

Console.WriteLine(type1.BaseType);
Console.WriteLine(type1.Name);
Console.WriteLine(type1.FullName);
Console.WriteLine(type1.Namespace);

// Comparing two objects
string str1 = "Test";
string str2 = "Test";
Console.WriteLine("============================");
Console.WriteLine("Comparison of Two Objects");
Console.WriteLine(Object.Equals(cls1, cls2));
Console.WriteLine(Object.Equals(str1, str2));
        }
    }
}
```

Figure 1-4 shows the output of Listing 1-7.

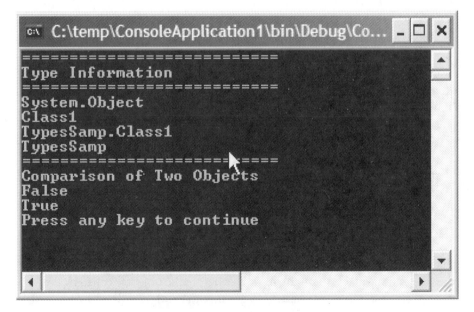

Figure 1-4. GetType *and* Compare *objects code output*

The ToString Method and String Conversion

The ToString method of the Object class converts a type to a string type. Listing 1-8 shows an example of the ToString method.

Listing 1-8. ToString *method example*

```
using System;

namespace ToStringSamp
{
    class Test
    {
        static void Main(string[] args)
        {
            int num1 = 8;
            float num2 = 162.034f;

            Console.WriteLine(num1.ToString());
            Console.WriteLine(num2.ToString());

        }
    }
}
```

The GetHashCode Method

A *hashtable* (also commonly known as a *map* or *dictionary*) is a data structure that stores one or more key-value pairs of data. Hashtables are useful when you want fast access to a list of data through a key (which can be a number, letter, string, or any object). In .NET, the Hashtable class represents a hashtable, which is implemented based on a hashing algorithm. This class also provides methods and constructors to define the size of the hashtable. You can use the Add and Remove methods to add and remove items from a hashtable. The Count property of the HashTable class returns the number of items in a hashtable.

The GetHashCode method returns the hashcode of an object. To return a hash-code for a type, you must override the GetHashCode method. An integer value is returned, which represents whether an object is available in a hashtable.

Two other useful methods of the Object class are MemberwiseClone and Finalize methods. The MemberwiseClone method creates a shallow copy of an object, which can be used as a clone of an object. The Finalize method acts as a destructor and can clean up the resources before the object is called by the garbage collector. You need to override this method and write your own code to clean up the resources. The garbage collector automatically calls the `Finalize` method if an object is no longer in use.

Types in C#

As mentioned earlier in the chapter, C# supports value types and reference types. Value types include simple data types such as `int`, `char`, and `bool`. Reference types include `object`, `class`, `interface`, and `delegate`.

   A value type contains the actual value of the object. That means the actual data is stored in the variable of a value type, whereas a reference type variable contains the reference to the actual data.

Value Types

Value types reference the actual data and are declared by using their default constructors. The default constuctor of these types return a zero-intialized instance of the variable. The value types can further be categorized into many subcategories, described in the following sections.

Simple Types

Simple types include basic data types such as `int`, `char`, and `bool`. These types have a reserved keyword corresponding to one class of a CLS type defined in the `System` class. For example, the keyword `int` aliases the `System.Int32` type, and the keywork `long` aliases the `System.Int64` type. Table 1-3 describes simple types.

Table 1-3. Simple Data Types

C# TYPE ALIAS	CLS TYPE	SIZE BITS	SUFFIX	DESCRIPTION	RANGE
sbyte	sbyte	8	n/a	Signed byte	−128 to 127
byte	byte	8	n/a	Unsigned byte	0 to 255
short	int16	16	n/a	Short integer	−32,768 to 32,767
ushort	uint16	16	n/a	Unsigned short integer	0 to 65,535
int	int32	32	n/a	Integer	−2,147,483,648 to 2,147,483,647
uint	uint32	32	u	Unsigned integer	0 to 4,294,967,295
long	int64	64	l	Long integer	−9,223,372,036,854,775,808 to 9,223,372,036,854,775,807
ulong	uint64	64	n/a	Unsigned long integer	0 to 18,446,744,073,709,551,615
char	char	16	n/a	Unicode character	Any valid character, e.g., a, *, \x0058 (hex), or \u0058 (Unicode)
float	single	32	f	Floating point number	$\pm 1.5 \times 10^{-45}$ to $\pm 3.4 \times 10^{38}$
double	double	64	d	Double floating point number	$\pm 5.0 \times 10^{-324}$ to $\pm 1.7 \times 10^{308}$
bool	boolean	1	n/a	Logical true/false value	True/false
decimal	decimal	128	m	Used for financial and monetary calculations	From approximately 1.0×10^{-28} to 7.9×10^{28} with 28 to 29 significant digits

One feature of simple types is that you can assign single direct values to these types. Listing 1-9 shows some assignment examples.

Listing 1-9. Simple type example

```
using System;

namespace ToStringSamp
{
    class Test
```

```
        {
            static void Main(string[] args)
            {
                int num1 = 12;
                float num2 = 3.05f;
                double num3 = 3.5;
                bool bl = true;

                Console.WriteLine(num1.ToString());
                Console.WriteLine(num2.ToString());
                Console.WriteLine(num3.ToString());
                Console.WriteLine(bl.ToString());


            }
        }
    }
```

Struct Types

A struct type, or *structure type,* can declare constructors, constants, fields, methods, properties, indexers, operators, and nested types. Structure types are similar to classes, but they're lightweight objects with no inheritance mechanism. However, all structures inherit from the Object class.

In Listing 1-10, your struct CarRec uses a record for a car with three members: name, model, and year.

Listing 1-10. A struct *type example*

```
using System;

struct CarRec
{
    public string Name;
    public string Model;
    public int Year;
}

class TestStructureType
{
    public static void Main()
    {
        CarRec rec;
        rec.Name = "Honda";
```

```
        rec.Model = "Accord";
        rec.Year = 1999;

        Console.WriteLine("Car Name: " +rec.Name);
        Console.WriteLine("Car Model: " +rec.Model);
        Console.WriteLine("Car Year: "+ rec.Year);
    }
}
```

Figure 1-5 shows the output of Listing 1-10.

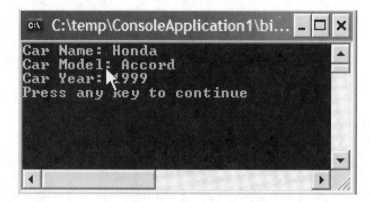

Figure 1-5. Output of Listing 1-10

Enum Data Types

The enum data types are useful when you need to represent a set of multiple values. A good example of an enumeration is a list of colors:

```
enum ColorEnum { black, red, green};
```

Enum types are limited to long, int, short, and byte.
This code declares an enum ColorEnum with members black, red, and green:

```
// black is 0, red is 1, green is 2.
enum ColorEnum { black, red, green};
```

You can also set your associated value to an enum type such as:

```
enum ColorEnum { black = 0,  red = 1, green = 2};
```

By default, enum associated value starts with 0 and increases by 1 for the next defined member. If you assign your value, the default value of the next enum type member will be the value of current member plus 1. For example, in this code the value of green is 7:

```
enum ColorEnum { black = 0,  red = 6, green };
```

Reference Types

A *reference type* is a reference to an instance type. The main reference types are class, array, interface, delegate, and event. A null value is assigned to a reference type by default. A type assigned to a null value means the absence of an instance of that type.

Class Type

A *class type* defines a data structure that can have members in the form of methods, properties, indexers, events, constructors, destructors, operators, and delegates. The class keyword is used to create a class type. You can add methods, properties, indexers, delegates, and events to the class. Listing 1-11 shows an example of a class type.

Listing 1-11. Class type example

```
// Define Class 1
public class Class1 : Object
{
    private void Method1()
    {
        Console.WriteLine("1 method" );
    }
}
```

The new keyword creates access to the class type. After creating an instance, you can use the dot (.) operator to access its members, as shown here:

```
Class1 cls1 = new Class1();
cls1. Method1();
```

I'll return to the discussion of classes later in this chapter.

Interface Type

An interface type is an abstract base class, which is a skeleton of a class and doesn't implement the members that it defines. Only the derived class of an interface can implement the members of the interface. Interfaces can contain methods, properties, events, and indexers.

In Listing 1-12, MyInterface is an interface that defines the method TestMethod. MyClass is derived from MyInterface, and you implement the MyMethod method in MyClass.

Listing 1-12. The interface *type example*

```
using System;

interface MyInterface
{
    void TestMethod();
}

class MyClass : MyInterface
{
    public static void Main()
    {
        MyClass cls = new MyClass();
        cls.TestMethod();
    }
    public void TestMethod()
    {
        Console.WriteLine("Test Method");
    }
}
```

A class can also implement multiple interfaces. Listing 1-13 defines two interfaces, MyInterface and MyInterface2. MyClass is inherited from these interfaces. You must implement these interfaces in the inherited class. If you don't implement an interface in the derived class, the compiler gives an error message.

For example, if you don't implement the method TestMethod2 of MyInterface2 in MyClass, the compiler returns this message: "MyClass does not implement the interface member 'MyInterface2.TestMethod2(int,int)'."

Listing 1-13. Multiple interfaces

```
using System;

interface MyInterface
{
    void TestMethod();
}

interface MyInterface2
{
    int TestMethod2(int a, int b);
}

class MyClass : MyInterface, MyInterface2
{


    public static void Main()
    {
        int num1 = 23;
        int num2 = 6;

        MyClass cls = new MyClass();
        cls.TestMethod();
        int tot = cls.TestMethod2(num1, num2);
        Console.WriteLine(tot.ToString());

    }
    public void TestMethod()
    {
        Console.WriteLine("Test Method");
    }
    public int TestMethod2(int a, int b)
    {
        return a + b;
    }
}
```

Delegate Types

Delegate types are mainly used with the class events. A `delegate` type encapsulates a method with a certain signature, called a *callable entity*. Delegates are the typesafe and secure versions of function pointers (callback functionality). Delegate instances are not aware of the methods they encapsulate; they're aware only if the methods are compatible in that they have the same parameter structure and return type.

There are three steps in defining and using a `delegate`: declaration, instantiation, and invocation. Delegates are declared using a `delegate` declaration syntax. For example, this code:

```
delegate void MyDelegate();
```

declares a delegate named `MyDelegate` that takes no arguments and returns void. The next step is to create an instance of delegate and call it:

```
MyDelegate del = new MyDelegate(TestMethod);
del();
```

Listing 1-14 shows an example of `delegate`.

Listing 1-14. Delegate *example*

```
delegate void MyDelegate();

class Test
{
    static void TestMethod()
    {
        System.Console.WriteLine("Test Method called");
    }
    static void Main()
    {
        MyDelegate del = new MyDelegate(TestMethod);
        del();
    }
}
```

Event Types

The event keyword defines an event. An *event type* enables an object or class to provide notifications of an event from the system. An instance of a delegate type encapsulates the callable entities. The `EventHandler` class defines a delegate definition. For example:

```
public delegate void EventHandler(object sender, System.EventArgs e);

    public event EventHandler Click;
. . . . . .
```

I'll discuss events in more detail in the "Class Members" section of this chapter.

Array Types

An *array type* is a sequential set of any of the other types. Arrays can be either single- or multidimensional. Both rectangular and jagged arrays are supported. A jagged array has elements that contain arrays that don't necessarily have the same length. A rectangular array is multidimensional, and all of its subarrays have the same length. With arrays, all of the elements must be of the same base type. In C#, the lower index of an array starts with 0, and the upper index is number of items minus 1.

You can initialize array items either during the creation of an array or later by referencing array items, as shown here:

```
int[] nums = new int[5];
int[0] = 1;
int[1] = 2;
int[2] = 3;
int[3] = 4;
int[4] = 5;
```

or here:

```
int[] nums = new int {1, 2, 3, 4, 5, };
```

Listing 1-15 shows an example of single-dimensional arrays.

Listing 1-15. Single-dimensional array example
```
class Test
{
    static void Main()
    {
        // array of integers
```

```
int[] nums = new int[5];
// array of strings
string[] names = new string[2];

for (int i = 0; i < nums.Length; i++)
    nums[i] = i + 2;
names[0] = "Mahesh";
names[1] = "Chand";

for (int i = 0; i < nums.Length; i++)
    System.Console.WriteLine("num[{0}] = {1}", i, nums[i]);
System.Console.WriteLine
    (names[0].ToString() + " " + names[1].ToString() );
        }
    }
```

The following is an example of multiple, rectangular, and jagged arrays:

```
char[] arr1 = new char[] {'a', 'b', 'c'};
int[,] arr2 = new int[,] {{2, 4}, {3, 5}};   // rectangular array declaration
int[,,] arr3 = new int[2, 4, 6];  // also rectangular
int[][] jarr = new int[3][];              // jagged array declaration
jarr[0] = new int[] {1, 2, 3};
jarr[1] = new int[] {1, 2, 3, 4, 5, 6};
jarr[2] = new int[] {1, 2, 3, 4, 5, 6, 7, 8, 9};
```

Sorting, Searching, and Copying Arrays

The array class defines functionalities for creating, manipulating, searching, sorting, and copying arrays. Table 1-4 lists and describes some of the array class properties.

Table 1-4. The array *Class Properties*

PROPERTY	DESCRIPTION
Length	Number of items in an array
Rank	Number of dimensions in an array
IsFixedLength	Indicates if an array is of fixed length
IsReadOnly	Indicates if an array is read-only

Table 1-5 describes some of the array class methods.

Table 1-5. The array *Class Methods*

METHOD	DESCRIPTION
BinarySearch	Searches for an element using BinarySearch algorithm
Clear	Removes all elements of an array and set reference to null
Copy	Copies a section of one array to another
CreateInstance	Initializes a new instance of an array
Reverse	Reverses the order of array elements
Sort	Sorts the elements of an array
Clone	Creates a shallow copy of an array
CopyTo	Copies all elements from 1D array to another
GetLength	Returns number of items in an array
GetValue	Gets a value at a specified location
SetValue	Sets a value at a specified location

The Copy method copies one array section to another array section. However, this method only works for single-dimensional arrays. Listing 1-16 shows a sample of copying array items from one array to another.

Listing 1-16. Copying array sample

```
using System;

public class ArraySample
{

    public static void Main()
    {

        // Create and initialize a new arrays
        int[] intArr = new int[5] { 1, 2, 3, 4, 5};
        Object[] objArr = new Object[5] { 10, 20, 30, 40, 50};

        foreach ( int i in intArr )
        {
            Console.Write(i);
```

```
            Console.Write(",");
        }
        Console.WriteLine();
        foreach ( Object i in objArr )
        {
            Console.Write(i);
            Console.Write(",");
        }
        Console.WriteLine();


        // Copy one first 3 elements of intArr to objArr
        Array.Copy(intArr, objArr, 3 );

        Console.WriteLine("After copying");
        foreach ( int i in intArr )
        {
            Console.Write(i);
            Console.Write(",");
        }
        Console.WriteLine();
        foreach ( Object i in objArr )
        {
            Console.Write(i);
            Console.Write(",");
        }
        Console.WriteLine();



    }
}
```

The Sort and Reverse methods of the array class are useful when you need to sort and reverse array elements. Listing 1-17 shows how to sort and reverse arrays.

Listing 1-17. Reversing and sorting array elements

```
using System;

public class ArraySample
{

    public static void Main()
```

```
    {
        // Create and initialize a new Array instance.
        Array strArr = Array.CreateInstance( typeof(String), 3 );
        strArr.SetValue( "Mahesh", 0 );
        strArr.SetValue( "Chand", 1 );
        strArr.SetValue( "Test Array", 2 );

        // Display the values of the Array.
        Console.WriteLine( "Initial Array values:" );
        for ( int i = strArr.GetLowerBound(0); i <= strArr.GetUpperBound(0); i++ )
            Console.WriteLine( strArr.GetValue( i ) );

        // Sort the values of the Array.
        Array.Sort(strArr );

        Console.WriteLine( "After sorting:" );
        for ( int i = strArr.GetLowerBound(0); i <= strArr.GetUpperBound(0); i++ )
            Console.WriteLine( strArr.GetValue( i ) );

        // Reverse values of the Array.
        Array.Reverse(strArr);

        for ( int i = strArr.GetLowerBound(0); i <= strArr.GetUpperBound(0); i++ )
            Console.WriteLine( strArr.GetValue( i ) );

    }
}
```

Type Conversions

C# supports two kinds of type conversions: implicit conversions and explicit conversions. Some of the predefined types define predefined conversions, such as converting from an int type to a long type.

Implicit conversions are conversions in which one type can directly and safely be converted to another type. Generally, small range types convert to large range types. As an example, you'll examine the process of converting from an int type to a long type. In this conversion, there is no loss of data, as shown in Listing 1-18.

Listing 1-18. Conversion example

```
using System;
class ConversionSamp
```

```
{
    static void Main()
    {
        int num1 = 123;
        long num2 = num1;
        Console.WriteLine(num1.ToString());
        Console.WriteLine(num2.ToString());
    }
}
```

Casting performs *explicit conversions*. There may be a chance of data loss or even some errors in explicit conversions. For example, converting a long value to an integer would result in data loss.

This is an example of an explicit conversion:

```
long num1 = Int64.MaxValue;
int num2 = (int)num1;
Console.WriteLine(num1.ToString());
Console.WriteLine(num2.ToString());
```

The process of converting from a value type to a reference type is called *boxing*. Boxing is an implicit conversion. Listing 1-19 shows an example of boxing.

Listing 1-19. Boxing example
```
using System;
class ConversionSamp
{
    static void Main()
    {
        int num1 = 123;
        Object obj = num1;

        Console.WriteLine(num1.ToString());
        Console.WriteLine(obj.ToString());
    }
}
```

The process of converting from a reference type to a value type is called *unboxing*. Listing 1-20 shows an example of unboxing.

Listing 1-20. Unboxing example

```
using System;
class ConversionSamp
{
    static void Main()
    {
        Object obj = 123;
        int num1 = (int)obj;

        Console.WriteLine(num1.ToString());
        Console.WriteLine(obj.ToString());
    }
}
```

Attributes

Attributes enable the programmer to give certain declarative information to the elements in their class. These elements include the class itself, the methods, the fields, and the properties. You can choose to use some of the useful built-in attributes provided with the .NET platform, or you can create your own. Attributes are specified in square brackets ([. . .]) before the class element upon which they're implemented. Table 1-6 shows some useful attributes provided with .NET.

Table 1-6. Useful Built-in Attributes

NAME	DESCRIPTION	EXAMPLE
DllImport	Imports a native DLL	`[DllImport("winmm.dll")]`
Serializable	Makes a class serializable	`[Serializable]`
Conditional	Includes/omits a method based on condition	`[Conditional("Diagnostic")]`

Variables

A variable represents a storage location. Each variable has a type that determines what values can be stored in the variable. A variable must definitely be assigned before its value can be obtained.

In C#, you declare a variable in this format:

```
[modifiers] datatype identifier;
```

In this case, the modifier is an access modifier. The "Variable Modifiers" section will discuss class member access modifiers. The data type refers to the type of value a variable can store. The identifier is the name of variable.

The next two examples are declarations of variables where `public` is the modifier, `int` is the data type, and `num1` is the name. The second variable type is a local variable. A local variable can't have a class modifier because it sits inside a method and is always private to the method. Here are the examples:

```
public int num1;
```

and:

```
int num1;
```

A value can be assigned to a variable after it's declared. You can also initialize a value during a variable declaration. For example:

```
int num1 = new Int16();
num1 = 34;
int num2 = 123;
```

Variable Modifiers

Modifiers enable you to specify a number of features that you can apply to your variables. You apply a variable modifier when you declare a variable. Keep in mind that modifiers can only be applied to fields, not to local variables.

> **NOTE**   *A local variable only has scope within its defined block in the program.*

A variable can have one or combination of more than one of the following types: `internal`, `new`, `private`, `public`, `protected`, `readonly`, and `static`.

Accessibility Modifiers

Some of the modifiers discussed in previous sections can set the accessibility level of variables. These are called *accessibility modifiers* (see Table 1-7).

Table 1-7. Accessibility Modifiers

MODIFIER	DESCRIPTION
internal	The variable can only be accessed by the current program.
public	The variable can be accessed from any where as a field.
protected	The variable can only be accessed with the class in which it's defined and its derived classes.
protected internal	The variable can only be accessed from the current program and the types derived from the current program.
private	The variable can only be accessed within the type in which it's defined.

You'll now examine access modifiers in an example. In Listing 1-21, `AccessCls` is a class accessed by the `Main` method. The `Main` method has access to `num1` because it's defined as a public variable, but not to `num2` because it's a private variable.

Listing 1-21. Variable access modifiers

```
using System;

class VarAccess
{
    class AccessCls
    {
        public int num1 = 123;
        int num2 = 54;
    }

    static void Main()
```

```
    {
        AccessCls cls = new AccessCls();
        int num1 = 98;
        num1 = cls.num1;

        //int i = cls.num2;
        Console.WriteLine(num1.ToString());
    }
}
```

When you access class members, the num2 variable is not available in the list of its members. See Figure 1-6.

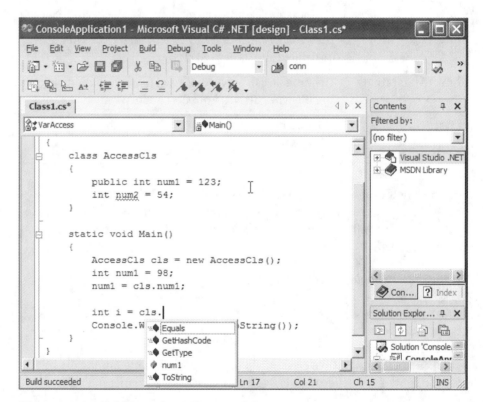

Figure 1-6. Available members of AccessCls

If you try to access num2 from the main program, the compiler gives the error shown in Figure 1-7.

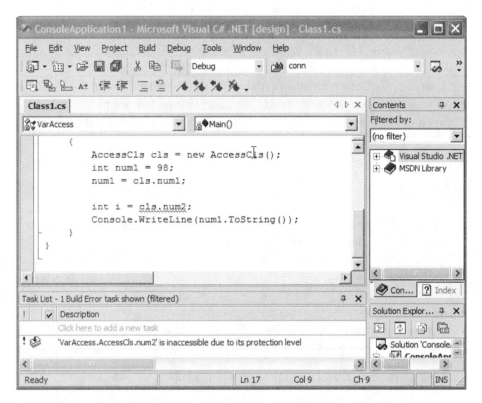

Figure 1-7. Error given when trying to access a private member of a class

Static and Read-Only Variables

By default, a field is an *instance field*. That means a new copy of a variable is created for each instance of the class to which it belongs. There are some cases where you want the variable to be shared by every instance of the class, and it's in such cases that static fields are useful. By defining the `static` keyword, you can restrict a field to create only one instance of the variable of a class and share it with all other class instances of the same type. In other words, if you change the value of a static variable in a class, all instances of the class containing the static variable know about it because it's shared at the class level rather than the instance level. You can use the `static` modifier alongside other modifiers.

For example:

```
public static int num2 = 34;
```

You can modify the value of a variable once it's initialized, but there are some cases where you don't want to change the value of a variable after it's assigned during initialization. In these cases, you can use the read-only modifier to prevent modification.

Constants

Constants are similar to read-only fields. You can't change a constant value once it's assigned. The const keyword precedes the field to define it as a constant. Assigning a value to a constant would give a compilation error. For example:

```
const int num3 = 34;
num3 = 54;
 // compilation error: The left-hand side of an assignment must
//    be a variable, property or  indexer
```

Although constants are similar to read-only fields, some differences exist. You can also declare local variables to be constants. Constants are always static, even though you don't use the static keyword explicitly, so they're shared by all instances of the class.

Expressions and Operators

An *expression* is a sequence of operators and operands that specify some sort of computation. The *operators* indicate an operation to be applied to one or two operands. For example, the operators + and – indicate adding and subtracting one object from another, respectively. Listing 1-22 is a simple example of operators and operands.

Listing 1-22. The relationship between operators and operands

```
using System;

class Test
{
    static void Main()
    {
        int num1 = 123;
        int num2 = 34;

        int res = num1 + num2;
        Console.WriteLine(res.ToString());

        res = -(res);
        Console.WriteLine(res.ToString());
    }
}
```

This example applies an operator on two objects, num1 and num2:

```
int res = num1 + num2;
```

There are three types of operators:

- The *unary* operators take one operand and use either a prefix notation (such as –x) or postfix notation (such as x++).

- The *binary* operators take two operands and all use what is called *infix* notation, where the operator appears between two objects (such as x + y).

- The *ternary* operator takes three operands and uses infix notation (such as c? x: y). Only one ternary operator, ?:, exists.

Table 1-8 categorizes the operators. The table summarizes all operators in order of precedence from highest to lowest.

Table 1-8. Operators in C#

OPERATOR CATEGORY	OPERATORS					
Primary	x.y f(x) a[x] x++ x-- new typeof					
	checked unchecked					
Unary	+ - ! ~ ++x --x (T)x					
Multiplicative	* / %					
Additive	+ -					
Shift	<< >>					
Relational and type testing	< > <= >= is as					
Equality	== !=					
Logical	AND &					
Logical	XOR ^					
Logical	OR |					
Conditional	AND &&					
Conditional	OR ||					
Conditional	?:					
Assignment	= *= /= %= += -= <<=					
	>>= &= ^= |=					

The checked and unchecked Operators

The checked and unchecked operators are two new features in C# for C++ developers. These two operators force the CLR to handle stack overflow situations. The *checked operator* enforces overflow checking through an exception if an overflow occurs. The *unchecked operator* doesn't throw an exception if an overflow occurs. Here, the code throws an exception in the case of the checked operator, whereas the unchecked part of the same code won't throw an exception:

```
checked
{
num1 += 5;
}
unchecked
{
```

```
num =+ 5;
}
```

The is Operator

The is operator is useful when you need to check whether an object is compatible with a type. For example:

```
string str = "Mahesh";
if(str is object)
{
    Console.WriteLine(str +" is an object compatible");
}
```

The sizeof Operator

The sizeof operator determines the size of a type. This operator can only be used in an unsafe context. By default, an unsafe context is false in VS .NET, so you'll need to follow the right-click on the Project ➢ Properties ➢ Build option and set Allow Unsafe Code Blocks to true to use the unsafe block in your code. Then you'll be able to compile the following code:

```
unsafe
{
Console.WriteLine(sizeof(int));
}
```

The typeof Operator

The typeof operator returns the type of a class or variable. It's an alternative to GetType, discussed earlier in the "Objects in C#" section of this chapter.
For example:

```
Type t = typeof(MyClass);
```

The GetType operator returns a Type object, which can access the type name and other type property information.

Control Flow and Program Logic

Control flow and *program logic* are two of the most important parts of a programming language's dynamic behavior. In this section, I'll cover control flow in C#. Most of the condition and looping statements in C# come from C and C++. Those who are familiar with Java will recognize most of them, as well.

The if. . .else Statement

The if. . .else statement is inherited from C and C++. The if. . .else statement is also known as a *conditional* statement. For example:

```
if(condition)
    Statement
else
    statement
```

The if. . . section of the statement or statement block is executed when the condition is true; if it's false, control goes to the else statement or statement block. You can have a nested if. . .else statement with one of more else blocks. You can also apply conditional or (||) and conditional and (&&) operators to combine more than one condition. Listing 1-23 shows you how to use the if. . .else statement.

Listing 1-23. The if. . .else *statement example*

```
using System;

public class MyClass
{
    public static void Main()
    {
        int num1 = 6;
        int num2 = 23;
        int res = num1 + num2;

        if(res > 25)
        {
            res = res - 5;
            Console.WriteLine("Result is more than 25");
        }
        else
```

```
    {
        res = 25;
        Console.WriteLine("Result is less than 25");
    }

    bool b = true;
    if ( res > 25 || b )
        Console.WriteLine("Res > 25 or b is true");
    else if ( (res>25) && !b )
        Console.WriteLine("Res > 25 and b is false");
    else
        Console.WriteLine("else condition");


    }
}
```

The switch Statement

Like the if. . . statement, the switch statement is also a conditional statement.
It executes the case part if it matches with the switch value. If the switch value
doesn't match the case value, the default option executes. The switch statement
is similar to an if. . . statement with multiple . . .else conditions, but it tends
to be more readable. Note that in C#, you can now switch on a string, which is
something C++ did not previously allow. See Listing 1-24 for an example of
a switch statement.

Listing 1-24. The switch *statement example*

```
int i = 3;
switch(i)
{
    case 1 :
        Console.WriteLine("one");
        break;
    case 2 :
        Console.WriteLine("two");
        break;
    case 3 :
        Console.WriteLine("three");
        break;
    case 4 :
        Console.WriteLine("four");
        break;
```

```
    case 5 :
        Console.WriteLine("five");
        break;
    default :
        Console.WriteLine("None of the above");
        break;
}
```

The for Loop Statement

The for loop statement is probably one of the most widely used control
statements for performing iterations in a loop. It executes a statement in the
loop until the given guard condition is true. The for loop statement is a
pretest loop, which means it first tests if a condition is true and only executes
if it is. You can use the ++ or – operators to provide forward or backward looping.
The following is an example of a for loop statement:

```
// Loop will execute 10 times from 0 to 9
for(int i=0; i<10; i++)
{
    Console.WriteLine(i.ToString());
}
```

The while Loop Statement

The while loop statement also falls in the conditional loop category. The while
loop statement executes until the while condition is true. It's also a pretest loop,
which means it first tests if a condition is true and only continues execution if it
is. In the example shown here, the while loop statement executes until the value
of i is less than 10:

```
int i = 0;
while(i<10)
{
    Console.WriteLine(i.ToString());
    i++;
}
```

The do...while Loop Statement

The do...while loop statement is a post-test loop, which means it executes a statement first and then checks if the condition is true. If the condition is true, the loop continues until the condition is false. As the name says, "*do* something *while* something is true." This is an example of a do...while loop:

```
int i = 0;
do
{
    Console.WriteLine(i.ToString());
    i++;
}while(i<10);
```

The foreach Loop Statement

The foreach loop statement is a new concept to C++ programmers but will be familiar to veteran Visual Basic programmers. The foreach loop enables you to iterate over each element of an array or each element of a collection. This is a simple example:

```
//foreach loop
string[] strArr= {"Mahesh","Chand","Test String"};

foreach(string str in strArr)
    Console.WriteLine(str);
```

In this example, the loop will continue until the items in the array are finished. Many of the collection examples in this chapter will use this loop.

The goto Statement

The goto statement is useful when you need to jump to a particular code segment. It's similar to the goto statement in Visual Basic or C++.

In the following code, if an item of array is found, the control goes to the level found and skips all code before that.

Most programmers avoid using the goto statement, but you may find a rare need for it. One such occasion is the use of fall-through on a switch statement. Fall-through is the ability for the control flow to fall from one case statement directly into another by leaving out the break statement. In C#, fall-through in a switch statement is not allowed as it was in C++. However, if you explicitly tell the switch statement to goto the next label, it will perform a jump to the next case, essentially carrying out the same function as a fall-through. Note that when using a goto in a case statement, you don't have to provide a break (in all other cases, a break statement is mandatory). In this C# example, when Bill is typed into the console, both "My name is Bill" and "Sometimes I'm called William" are displayed on the screen:

```
Console.WriteLine("What is your name? ");
string name = Console.ReadLine();
switch(name)
{
    case "Bill":
     Console.WriteLine("My name is Bill.");
      goto case "William";
    case "William":
      Console.WriteLine("Sometimes I'm called William.");
        break;
    case "Anne":
        Console.WriteLine("My name is Anne.");
        break;
    default:
        break;
}
```

The break Statement

The break statement exits from a loop or a switch immediately. The break statement is usually applicable when you need to release control of the loop after a certain condition is met, or if you want to exit from the loop without executing the rest of the loop structure. You use it in for, foreach, while, and do. . .while loop statements. The following code shows the break statement. If condition j == 0 is true, control will exit from the loop:

```
for(int i=0; i<10; i++)
{
    int j = i*i;
    Console.WriteLine(i.ToString());
    if(j == 9)
        break;
    Console.WriteLine(j.ToString());
}
```

The continue Statement

Similar to the break statement, the continue statement also works in for, foreach, while, and do. . .while statements. The continue statement causes the loop to exit from the current iteration and continue with the rest of the iterations in the loop. See the following code for an example:

```
for(int i=0; i<10; i++)
{
    int j = i*i;
    Console.WriteLine("i is"+  i.ToString());
    if(j == 9)
        continue;
    Console.WriteLine("j is "+ j.ToString());
}
```

In this code snippet, when the condition j== 9 is true, the control exits from the current iteration and moves to the next iteration.

> **NOTE**   *The* break *statement makes control exits from the entire loop, but the* continue *statement only skips the current iteration.*

The return Statement

The return statement returns from a method before the end of that method is reached. The return statement can either return a value or not, depending on the method that calls it.

This is an example of a return statement that returns nothing, and another where the return statement returns an integer value:

```
public static void Main()
{
    int output = 9 + 6;
    if( output >= 12)
        return;
    Console.WriteLine("Output less than 12");
}

public int Sum(int a, int b)
{
    return a + b;
}
```

Classes

You saw a class structure in the "Hello, C# World!" sample. In C#, you define a class by using the `class` keyword, just as you do in C++. Following the `class` keyword is the class name and curly brackets ({. . .}), as shown here:

```
class Hello
{
 static void Main() {
 Console.WriteLine("Hello, C# World!");
 }
}
```

> **NOTE**   *C# classes don't end with semicolon (;) as C++.*

Once a class is defined, you can add class members to it. Class members can include constants, fields, methods, properties, indexers, events, operators, instance constructors, static constructors, destructors, and nested type declarations. Each class member has an associated accessibility, which controls the scope of the member and defines whether these members are accessible outside the class.

Class Members

Table 1-9 describes allowable class member elements.

Table 1-9. Allowable Class Member Elements

CLASS MEMBER	INHERITANCE
Methods	Similar to C++ functions. Methods implement some action that can be performed by an object.
Properties	Provide access to a class attribute (a field). Useful for exposing fields in components.
Events	Used to provide notification.
Constants	Represents a constant value.
Fields	Represents a variable of the class.
Operators	Used to define an expression (+, *, ->, ++, [ ], and so on).
Instance Constructors	Methods called during initialization of an object.
Static Constructors	Called automatically.
Destructors	Called when an object is being destroyed.
Indexers	A new concept in C#. An indexer provides indexing on an object. It allows you to treat a class as an array.
Types	All local types used in a class.

Before examining these members in detail, you'll look at the accessibility of these members. Table 1-10 describes class member accessibility types and their scopes.

Table 1-10. Class Member Accessibility Types and Scopes

ACCESSIBILITY TYPE	SCOPE
public	Member is accessible from other programs.
protected	Member is accessible by the containing and its derived classes and types.
internal	Member is accessible only by the current program.
protected internal	Member is accessible by the current program and the class derived from the containing class.

Now you'll look at class members in more detail.

Fields

A *field* member represents a variable of a class. In this example, strClassName is a string type static public variable that can be accessed by the class instance:

```
class myClass
{
    public static string strClassName;

    public void SetClassName(string strName)
    {
        strClassName = strName;
    }

}
```

As noted earlier, you can define field members as read-only. This means the field can only be assigned in the declaration or in the constructor of the class. See the following code:

```
class myClass
{
    public static readonly string strClassName = "MyClass";

    public void SetClassName(string strName)
```

```
    {
        strClassName = strName;   // illegal assignment
    }

}
```

Note that the compiler will throw an error because of an illegal assignment.

If the field is not static, you have to access fields from the class instance. It's the same idea as accessing a public variable in C++ or structure in C. For example:

```
MyClass cls = new MyClass();
string clsName = cls.strClassName;
```

Constants

A *constant* member represents a constant value throughout the program. For example, the clsNodes is a constant that has an integer value 12. See the following code:

```
class myClass
{
    public const int clsNodes = 12;
}
```

The value of clsNodes will be 12 throughout the program and can't be reassigned.

Instance and Static Constructors

Constructors in C# are defined in the same way as in C++. C# supports two types of constructors: instance constructors and static constructors. *Instance constructors* are called every time a class is initialized. *Static constructors* are executed only once. Static constructors are useful for initializing the values of static variables. Listing 1-25 is an example of a class with a static constructor.

Listing 1-25. Calling static constructors
```
using System;
class myClass
```

```
{
    static myClass()
    {
        Console.WriteLine("Initialize Class...");
        // Do some stuff
    }
    public static void foo()
    {
        Console.WriteLine("foo");
    }
}
class Test
{
    static void Main()
    {
        myClass.foo();   // calls myClass static constructor and then foo
    }
}
```

Constructors can be overloaded, as shown in Listing 1-26.

Listing 1-26. Overloaded constructors example
```
class myClass
{
    public int iCounter, iTotal;
    public myClass () {
        iCounter = 0;
        iTotal = 0;
    }
    public myClass (int iCount, int iTot) {
        iCounter = iCount;
        iTotal = iTot;
    }
}
```

Listing 1-27 shows a full sample of calling class constructors.

Listing 1-27. Calling class constructors
```
using System;
class myClass
{
    public int iCounter, iTotal;
    public myClass ()
```

```
        {
            iCounter = 0;
            iTotal = 0;
        }
        public myClass (int iCount, int iTot)
        {
            iCounter = iCount;
            iTotal = iTot;
        }
}

class TestmyClass
{
    static void Main()
    {
        myClass cls = new myClass();
        myClass cls1 = new myClass(3, 4);

        Console.WriteLine(cls1.iCounter.ToString());
        Console.WriteLine(cls1.iTotal.ToString());
    }
}
```

Destructors

A destructor is called when it's time to destroy the object. Destructors can't take parameters. See the following code:

```
class myClass
{
    &tilde; myClass () {
    // free resources
    }
}
```

TIP *It's not compulsory—in fact it's unadvisable—to call destructors. They're called automatically by the CLR when it destroys the object during garbage collection.*

Methods

A *method* is a member that implements some functionality. It's similar in appearance to the methods found in C++ and Java. A method can return a value, have
a list of parameters, and be accessed as static or non-static. *Static* methods are
accessed through the class, whereas *non-static* methods are accessed through the
instance of the class. For example, Listing 1-28 adds a method Sum to the class
myClass and called this method from the Main method.

Listing 1-28. Class method example
```
using System;
class myClass
{
    public int Sum(int a, int b)
    {
        int res = a + b;
        return res;
    }
}


class TestmyClass
{
    static void Main()
    {
        myClass cls = new myClass();
        int total = cls.Sum(5, 8);
        Console.WriteLine(total.ToString());
    }
}
```

Methods in C# support function overloading in a similar way as C++. If
you have programmed in C++, you'll notice that C# methods are similar to C++
functions (and almost mirror those methods found in Java). So, it's not a bad
idea to call function overloading in C# *method overloading*. In Listing 1-29, I over-
load the Sum method by passing in different types of values and call each of the
overloaded Sum methods from the Main method.

Listing 1-29. Method overloading example
```
using System;
class myClass
{
    public int Sum(int a, int b)
```

```csharp
    {
        int res = a + b;
        return res;
    }

    public float Sum (float a, float b)
    {
        float res = a + b;
        return res;
    }

    public long Sum (long a, long b)
    {
        long res = a + b;
        return res;
    }

    public long Sum (long a, long b, long c)
    {
        long res = a + b + c;
        return res;
    }

    public long Sum (int[] a)
    {
      int res = 0;
      for (int i=0; i < a.Length; i++)
       {
           res += a[i];
       }
         return res;
    }

    public void Sum()
    {
        //return nothing
    }
}

class TestmyClass
{
    static void Main()
```

```
        {
            myClass cls = new myClass();
            int intTot = cls.Sum(5, 8);
            Console.WriteLine("Return integer sum:"+ intTot.ToString());
            cls.Sum();
            long longTot = cls.Sum(Int64.MaxValue - 30, 8);
            Console.WriteLine("Return long sum:"+ longTot.ToString());
            float floatTot = cls.Sum(Single.MaxValue-50, 8);
            Console.WriteLine("Return float sum:"+ floatTot.ToString());
             int[] myArray = new int[] {1, 3, 5, 7, 9};
            Console.WriteLine("Return sum of array = {0}",
             cls.Sum(myArray).ToString());


        }
    }
```

The ref and out Parameters

Did you ever need your method to return more than one value? You may need to do this occasionally, or you may need to use the same variables that you pass as an argument of the method. When you pass a reference type, such as a class instance, you don't have to worry about getting a value in a separate variable because the type is already being passed as a reference and will maintain the changes when it returns. A problem occurs when you want the value to be returned in a value type. The ref and out parameters help you to do this with value types.

The out keyword defines an out type parameter. You use the out keyword to pass a parameter to a method. This example is passing an integer type variable as an out parameter. You define a function with the out keyword as an argument with the variable type:

```
myMethod(out int iVal1)
```

The out parameter can be used to return the values in the same variable passed as a parameter of the method. Any changes made to the parameter will be reflected in the variable. Listing 1-30 shows an example of the out parameter.

Listing 1-30. Using the out *parameter*
```
using System;
public class myClass
{
    public static void ReturnData(out int iVal1, out int iVal2)
```

```
    {
        iVal1 = 2;
        iVal2 = 5;
    }

    public static void Main()
    {
        int iV1, iV2;    // variable need not be initialized
        ReturnData(out iV1, out iV2);
        Console.WriteLine(iV1);
        Console.WriteLine(iV2);
    }
}
```

The ref keyword defines a ref type parameter. You pass a parameter to a method with this keyword, as in Listing 1-31. This example passes an integer type variable as a ref parameter. This is a method definition:

```
myMethod(ref int iVal1)
```

You can use the ref parameter as a method input parameter and an output parameter. Any changes made to the parameter will be reflected in the variable. See Listing 1-31.

Listing 1-31. A ref *parameter example*

```
using System;
public class myClass
{
    public static void ReturnData(ref int iVal1, ref int iVal2, ref int iVal3 )
    {
        iVal1 += 2;
        iVal2 = iVal2*iVal2;
        iVal3 = iVal2 + iVal1;
    }

    public static void Main()
    {
        int iV1, iV2, iV3;    // variable need not be initialized
        iV1 = 3;
        iV2 = 10;
        iV3 = 1;
        ReturnData(ref iV1, ref iV2, ref iV3 );
```

```
        Console.WriteLine(iV1);
        Console.WriteLine(iV2);
        Console.WriteLine(iV3);
    }
}
```

In this method, ReturnData takes three values as input parameters, operates on the passed data, and returns the result in the same variables.

Properties

Other than methods, another important set of members of a class are variables. A *variable* is a type that stores some value. The *property* member of a class provides access to variables. Some examples of properties are font type, color, and visible properties. Basically, properties are fields. A field member can be accessed directly, but a property member is always accessed through accessor and modifier methods called get and set, respectively. If you have ever created ActiveX controls in C++ or Visual Basic, or created JavaBeans in Java, you understand.

> **NOTE** *Visual Basic programmers will note that* Let *is not available in C#. This is because all types are objects, so only the set accessor is necessary.*

In Listing 1-32, you create two properties of myClass: Age and MaleGender. Age is an integer property, and MaleGender is a Boolean type property. As you can see in the example, the get and set keywords are used to get and set property values. You're reading and writing property values from the Main method. Note that leaving out the set method in a property makes the property read-only.

Listing 1-32. Class property member example

```
using System;
class myClass
{
    private bool bGender;
    private int intAge;

    // Gender property.
    public bool MaleGender
    {
        get
```

```
        {
            return bGender;
        }
        set
        {
            bGender = value;
        }
    }
    // Age property
    public int Age
    {
        get
        {
            return intAge;
        }
        set
        {
            intAge = value;
        }
    }

}

class TestmyClass
{
    static void Main()
    {
        myClass cls = new myClass();

        // Set properties values
        cls.MaleGender = true;
        cls.Age = 25;

        if(cls.MaleGender)
        {
            Console.WriteLine("The Gender is Male");
            Console.WriteLine("Age is "+ cls.Age.ToString());
        }

    }
}
```

Why use properties if you already have the field available? First of all, properties expose fields in classes being used in components. They also provide a means for doing necessary computation before or after accessing or modifying the private fields they're representing. For example, if you're changing the color of a control in the set method, you may also want to execute an invalidate method inside the set to repaint the screen.

Events

In C#, events are a special type of delegate. An *event* member of a class provides notifications from user or machine input.

A class defines an event by providing an event declaration, which is of type delegate. The following line shows the definition of an event handler:

```
public delegate void EventHandler(object sender, System.EventArgs e);
```

The EventHandler takes two arguments: one of type Object and the other of type System.EventArgs. A class implements the EventHandler using the event keyword. In the following example, MyControl class implements the EventHandler:

```
public class MyControl
{
    public event EventHandler Click;
    public void Reset() {
       Click = null;
    }
}
```

You probably know that Windows is an event-driven operating system. In Windows programming, the system sends messages to the message queue for every action taken by a user or the system, such as mouse-click, keyboard, touch screen, and timers. Even if the operating system is doing nothing, it still sends an idle message to the message queue after a certain interval of time.

Although you usually use events in GUI applications, you can also implement events in console-based applications. You can use them when you need to notify a state of an action. You'll have a look at an example of both types.

Listing 1-33 shows you how to implement events and event handlers in a console-based application. The Boiler.cs class defines the BoilerStatus event. The SetBoilerReadings method sets the boiler temperature and pressure readings, and it writes the boiler status on the console based on the temperature and pressure readings. Boiler.cs defines BoilerStatus using the event keyword.

Listing 1-33. Boiler.cs

```csharp
namespace BoilerEvent
{
    using System;

    public class Boiler
    {
        public delegate void EngineHandler(int temp);
        public static event EngineHandler BoilerStatus;


        public Boiler()
        {
        }

        public void SetBoilerReadings(int temp, int pressure)
        {

            if ( BoilerStatus != null)
            {
                if(temp >= 50 && pressure >= 60)
                {
                    BoilerStatus(temp);
                    Console.WriteLine("Boiler Status: Temperature High");
                }
                else if(temp < 20 || pressure < 20)
                {
                    BoilerStatus(temp);
                    Console.WriteLine("Boiler Status: Temperature Low");
                }
                else
                    Console.WriteLine("Boiler Status: Temperature Normal");
            }
        }

    }

}
```

Listing 1-34 is a caller class (main application) that calls the event through BoilerEventSink. The BoilerTempoMeter method of the sink generates a warning message on the console only when the temperature of the boiler is zero.

Listing 1-34. Caller of Boiler.cs

```
namespace BoilerEvent
{
  using System;

  public class Boiler
  {
    // Boiler class here
  }

  public class BoilerEventSink
  {
    public void BoilerTempoMeter(int temp)
    {
      if (temp <= 0)
      {
        Console.WriteLine("Alarm: Boiler is switched off");
      }
    }
  }

  // Event caller mailn application
  public class BoilerCallerApp
  {
    public static int Main(string[] args)
    {
      Boiler boiler1 = new Boiler();
      BoilerEventSink bsink = new BoilerEventSink();
      Boiler.BoilerStatus +=
        new Boiler.EngineHandler(bsink.BoilerTempoMeter);
      boiler1.SetBoilerReadings(55, 74);
      boiler1.SetBoilerReadings(0, 54);
      boiler1.SetBoilerReadings(8, 23);
      return 0;
    }
  }
}
```

As you can see in Listing 1-34, I created a Boiler object that calls the BoilerStatus handler, which passes BoilerEventSink's methods as an argument when calling Boiler.EngineHandler. EngineHandler is a delegate defined in the Boiler class. Then the program calls the SetBoilerReadings method with different temperature and pressure readings. When the temperature is zero, the program displays a warning message on the console; otherwise, the program displays messages generated by the SetBoilerReadings method.

Actually, it's easier to understand events using a Windows application than it is using a console-based application. To show you an event sample in Windows Forms, you'll create a Windows application. In this application, you'll create a form and a button. The button-click event executes and displays a message box. In Chapter 2, "Introduction to Windows Forms," I'll discuss the Windows Forms and controls in more detail.

Here, the button-click event executes button1_click method:

```
button1.Click += new System.EventHandler(button1_Click);
```

and the button-click handler looks like the following:

```
private void button1_Click(object sender, System.EventArgs e)
{
        MessageBox.Show("Button is clicked");
}
```

Listing 1-35 shows a Windows Forms program with event sample. If you compile this program, the output looks like Figure 1-8.

Listing 1-35. Event handling example

```
using System;
using System.Windows.Forms;
using System.Drawing;

namespace NotePadWindowsForms
{
    public class NotePadWindowsForms : System.Windows.Forms.Form
    {
        private System.Windows.Forms.Button button1;


        public NotePadWindowsForms()
        {
            button1 = new System.Windows.Forms.Button();

            // button control and its properties
            button1.Location = new System.Drawing.Point(8, 32);
            button1.Name = "button1";
            button1.Size = new System.Drawing.Size(104, 32);
            button1.TabIndex = 0;
```

```
                    button1.Text = "Click Me";

                    // Adding controls to the form
                    Controls.AddRange(new System.Windows.Forms.Control[]
                    {    button1} );

                    button1.Click += new System.EventHandler(button1_Click);

              }


              // Button click handler
              private void button1_Click(object sender, System.EventArgs e)
              {
                    MessageBox.Show("Button is clicked");
              }

              public static int Main()
              {
                  Application.Run(new NotePadWindowsForms());
                  return 0;
              }
          }
      }
```

Figure 1-8 shows the output of Listing 1-35 after clicking the Click Me button.

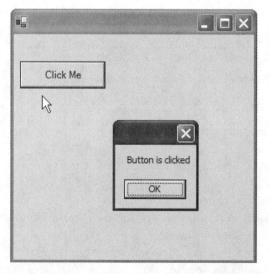

Figure 1-8. Output of Listing 1-35

Indexers

Indexers are a new concept in C#. Indexers enable a class object to function as an array. Implementing indexers is similar to implementing properties using the get and set functions. The only difference is that when you call an indexer, you pass an indexing parameter. Accessing an indexer is similar to accessing an array. Indexers are nameless, so the this keyword declares indexers.

I just said that after defining indexers, a class object can be treated as an array. What does that mean? To explain, I'll show you an example using the class called myClass. The way you treat an instance of myClass now is like this:

```
myClass cls = new myClass();
cls.MaleGender = true;
```

After defining an indexer in myClass, you could treat an instance of it as if it were an array:

```
myClass cls = new myClass();
cls[0],MaleGender = true;
cls[1].MaleGender = true;
```

You define indexer by using the this keyword as if it were an array property of type object. Listing 1-36 shows the indexer signature of myClass.

Listing 1-36. Indexers signature of myClass
```
public object this[int index]
    {
        get
        {
            if (!ValidIndex(index))
                throw new Exception("Index out of range.");
            else
                return MaleGender(index).Value;
        }
        set
        {
            if (!ValidIndex(index))
                throw new Exception("Index out of range.");
            else
                MaleGender (index).Value = value;
        }
    }
```

Inheritance

Inheritance is one of the main features of an object-oriented language. C# and the .NET class library are heavily based on inheritance. The telltale sign of this is that all .NET common library classes are derived from the Object class, discussed at the beginning of this chapter. As pointed out, C# doesn't support multiple inheritance. C# only supports single inheritance; therefore, all objects are implicitly derived from the Object class.

Implementing inheritance in C# is similar to implementing it in C++. You use a colon (:) in the definition of a class to derive it from another class. In Listing 1-37, BaseClassB is derived from BaseClassA, which later accesses the BaseClassA method in the Main method.

Listing 1-37. Inheritance example

```csharp
using System;

// Base class A
class BaseClassA
{
    public void MethodA()
    {
        Console.WriteLine("A Method Called");
    }
}
// Base class B is derived from BaseClassA
class BaseClassB: BaseClassA
{
    public void MethodB()
    {
        Console.WriteLine("B Method Called");
    }
}
class myClass
{
    static void Main()
    {
        // Base class B
        BaseClassB b = new BaseClassB();

        // BaseClassB method
        b.MethodB();
        //BaseClassA method through BaseClassB
```

```
        b.MethodA();
    }
}
```

Exception Handling

Exception handling in C# is pretty much like exception handling in C++, in which you use a try. . .catch block. If you don't catch an exception in C#, it will display it as a nasty message box to the user and then terminate the application. C# also adds the keyword finally. Exception handling works in this way: The try block executes the code within it, and if an exception occurs anywhere within that block, the code jumps directly to the catch block. If the exception in the catch block matches the exception thrown, the catch block is executed and the program continues. The finally block is similar to a catch block, except the code in the finally block is executed regardless of whether an exception is thrown. There are some built-in exception types in C#.

Table 1-11 describes a few commonly encountered ones.

Table 1-11. Exception Types in C#

EXCEPTION NAME	DESCRIPTION
Exception	Base class for all exceptions. If you want to catch any exception, use this.
SystemException	Base class for all exceptions generated at run-time. This will also catch most exceptions.
NullReferenceException	An exception thrown when you attempt to use a null reference.
IndexOutOfRangeException	Exception thrown when you attempt to use an array element that is not within the constraints of the array bounds.

Listing 1-38 is an example of a NullReference exception.

Listing 1-38. A NullReference exception

```
public void ExceptionTest1()
  {
    try
      {
        string mystring = null;
```

```
        mystring.Insert(0, "hello");
  }
  catch(Exception ex)
  {
  Console.WriteLine("Exception - {0}",
 ex.Message.ToString());
  }
 }
```

Listing 1-39 is an example of an IndexOutOfRangeException.

Listing 1-39. An IndexOutOfRange *exception*
```
public void ExceptionTest2()
  {
   try
   {
    char[] MyCharList = new char[2]{'a', 'b'};
     // remember last array index is 1
     char mychar = MyCharList[2];
   }
   catch(Exception ex)
   {
   Console.WriteLine("Exception - {0}",
 ex.Message.ToString());
   }
 }
```

Listing 1-40 is an exception-handling example.

Listing 1-40. Exception-handling example
```
    using System;
    public class myClass
    {
        public static void Main()
        {
            int aValue = 5;
            try
            {
                int[] MySequence = new int[]{3,5,6};
                aValue = MySequence[4];
            }
            catch(Exception e)
```

```
            {
                System.Console.WriteLine("Caught the exception -- {0}",
    e.Message.ToString());
            }
            finally
            {
                // do any clean up
                //      . . . . . . . . . . .
                System.Console.WriteLine("The value = {0}", aValue);
                System.Console.ReadLine();
            }


        }
    }
```

The Exception object catches all exceptions. The following code catches the overflow exception with the following output to the console:

```
Caught the Exception - An exception of type System.IndexOutOfRangeException was
thrown.
The value = 5
```

Documenting Your Source Code

Another good feature of C# language is its programmatic support of source-code documentation. The source-code documentation is a good programming practice of software development lifecycle for long-term projects. C# language supports programmatic documentation with the help of XML files. You store documentation in an XML file, tell the compiler to look for the file, and the compiler puts the documentation for you in the source code. The comments in the source code start with three slashes (///) instead of two (//).

You can even set documentation using the VS .NET IDE. You go to Project's Properties page by right-clicking on the project from Solution Explorer, going to Build Properties, and setting the XML file as XML Documentation File option. MSDN documentation has a nice tutorial on XML documentation under Visual Studio .NET/Visual Basic and Visual C#/C# Programmer's Reference/C# Language Features/XML Documentation.

Summary

This chapter offered an overview of the new Microsoft language, C#. C# takes the best features of many present-day programming languages. You became familiar with some of the language's syntax. You learned how to write and compile your first command-line program with the "Hello, C# World!" example. You also became familiar with classes and their members, their scopes, and how to use them. You learned about some unique features, such as events and indexers, which were not available in languages such as C++. You also looked at some useful objects in C#, such as arrays and exceptions.

In the next chapter, you'll examine Windows Forms and how to write Windows Forms and control-based GUI applications using Visual Studio .NET.

CHAPTER 2

Introduction to Windows Forms

IF YOU HAVE EVER PROGRAMMED IN Visual Basic, you are familiar with Windows Forms. In the Windows platform, a *form* is a window that interacts with users. Forms can receive input from users and show output in an interactive way. The nice thing about developing with Windows Forms is that you can drag and drop Windows controls to a form to develop graphical user interface (GUI) applications. In the Microsoft Visual Studio (VS) development environment, windows, dialog boxes, and Multiple Document Interface (MDI) windows are various types of forms you'll find useful in developing your applications.

In the .NET Framework, a form is a class instance. In .NET, every Windows control is an instance of a class. All the data related to a form or a control is written in the class itself. When you create an instance of a form at run-time, the framework reads the data from the class and creates a window accordingly. In .NET, these forms are *Windows Forms.*

There are many advantages to using Windows Forms. One advantage is that they're language-independent. In addition to the advantages of having Common Language Runtime (CLR) support, Windows Forms have full design-time support, are easy to use, and provide Rapid Application Development (RAD) support for developers through the Visual Studio .NET Integrated Development Environment (IDE).

This chapter will discuss how to write a Windows Forms application in a text editor and run it from the command line. Then I'll walk you through rapidly creating a simple Windows Forms application graphically using the Visual Studio .NET IDE. I'll also introduce you to a few of the powerful common controls and how to use them in your application.

Design-Time versus Run-Time Development

Every visual Windows developer is familiar with *design-time* and *run-time* development. You use a form designer to create GUI applications at design-time. Creating GUI applications is much easier when you use designers. Run-time programming enables you to write code to create Windows controls from other resources. Apparently, design-time programming is more popular among developers lately because of its Rapid Application Development (RAD) nature. The best examples of design-time IDEs are Borland's Delphi, Visual Basic, and Visual C++. By using a form designer to add a new form, drag or drop a couple of controls, and set some intrinsic properties such as colors and fonts, a large portion of your programming is done. The designer takes care of the rest.

The Microsoft Visual C++ environment was severely lacking in the RAD area, especially when you were restricted to using Microsoft Foundation Classes (MFC) and ActiveX Template Library (ATL) libraries to create Windows controls and dialogs (dialogs in MFC are similar to forms in Visual Basic). Although Visual C++ (with the help of the MFC and the ATL libraries) provides enough support to develop Windows applications and controls, programmers once had to go through the pains of writing several lines of code just to change the color and the text size of a toolbar. And don't forget all the work that went into writing event handlers for these controls!

There might be occasions when a developer doesn't have a visual IDE such as Microsoft VS .NET, or when a developer can't afford to buy VS .NET or a comparable IDE. Because the C# compiler is currently free, you can write applications in C# and compile it using the command-line compilers. Within this scenario a developer needs to know what goes on under the hood of the VS IDE.

Fortunately, it's easy to develop applications at run-time using C#. In the following sections, I'll discuss how to write code in a text editor and compile it from command line.

Writing a Command-Line Windows Forms Application

Writing Windows Forms applications in Visual Studio .NET is fairly simple. You use the New Project Wizard to create a Windows application and then use the Form Designer to drag controls on the form, set their properties, and write corresponding events. I'll discuss VS .NET later in this chapter.

You may be wondering why you would write a command-line Windows Forms application to start. A C# compiler comes with .NET SDK, but there might be cases when a developer won't have the VS .NET IDE. Even if you do have the VS .NET IDE, you might be curious to know how Windows applications work behind the scenes. These are just two possible reasons.

Writing Windows Forms applications using Notepad or a text editor is simple. You type your code in the editor and save the file with a `.cs` extension. You can then compile the `.cs` file from the command line. In the following example, save the file as `MyForm.cs`.

Creating a Form

To create a form, you need to inherit the class from System.Windows.Forms.Form class. The "Windows.Forms Namespace" section will discuss this class. You also need to call the Application.Run method with a new instance of the form so the application can create the form. This function happens within the Main method, which is the entry point of the C# application. Listing 2-1 is an example of a Windows form.

Listing 2-1. First Windows form example, MyForm.cs

```
using System;
using System.Windows.Forms;

namespace NotePadWindowsForms
{
    public class NotePadWindowsForms : System.Windows.Forms.Form
    {
        public NotePadWindowsForms()
        {
        }
        public static int Main()
        {
            Application.Run(new NotePadWindowsForms());
            return 0;
        }
    }
}
```

Now, save this program as MyForm.cs and compile it from the command line. This is the syntax:

```
C:\WINNT\Microsoft.NET\Framework\v1.0.3705\csc.exe
 /r:system.windows.forms.dll "c:\MyForm.cs"
```

The compiler creates an .exe under the bin directory in the same path as the MyForm.cs file is. Figure 2-1 shows the output of this .exe.

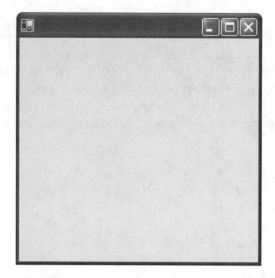

Figure 2-1. First Windows form

Setting Form Properties

You are now ready to add form properties to the form, such as background color, foreground color, and text. The System.Windows.Forms.Form class defines all form properties. You'll create properties and methods in more detail in the following section. Listing 2-2 sets the text, background color, and foreground color properties of a form.

In the listing, you'll also notice the appearance of a new namespace called System.Drawing.Windows. The Drawing namespace defines drawing functionalities such as pens, colors, and brushes. At the end of this chapter, we'll take a quick look at the Drawing namespace and its classes.

Listing 2-2. Setting form properties

```
using System;
using System.Windows.Forms;
using System.Drawing;

namespace NotePadWindowsForms
{
    public class NotePadWindowsForms : System.Windows.Forms.Form
    {
        public NotePadWindowsForms()
        {
            // Set Caption of the form
            Text = "Test WinForm";
```

```
        // Set background color
        BackColor = System.Drawing.Color.Blue;
        //Set forground color
        ForeColor = System.Drawing.Color.Yellow;


    }
    public static int Main()
    {
        Application.Run(new NotePadWindowsForms());
        return 0;
    }
  }
}
```

Adding Controls to a Form

After setting properties, the next step is to add a Button and a TextBox control to the form. I'll discuss controls later in this chapter.

To add controls to a form, first create an instance of the
`System.Windows.Forms.Button` class and set its properties (such as name, location, size, and text). After creating and setting control properties, you call the `System.Windows.Forms.Form` class's AddRange method to add controls to the form. Listing 2-3 shows you how to create and add these controls to a form. Note that you need to call this control initialization code from the constructor of your form class. As you can see from Listing 2-3, you add two control variables of Button and TextBox types at the top of the program as public variables and set these control properties in the form's constructor NotePadWindowsForms().

Listing 2-3. Creating and adding controls to a form

```
        private System.Windows.Forms.Button button1;
        private System.Windows.Forms.TextBox textBox1;

        public NotePadWindowsForms()
        {
            /* Form Properties */

            // Set Caption of the form
            Text = "Test WinForm";
            // Set background color
            BackColor = System.Drawing.Color.Blue;
            //Set forground color
```

```
                    ForeColor = System.Drawing.Color.Yellow;


// Create control objects
            button1 = new System.Windows.Forms.Button();
            textBox1 = new System.Windows.Forms.TextBox();

            // button control and its properties
            button1.Location = new System.Drawing.Point(8, 32);
            button1.Name = "button1";
            button1.Size = new System.Drawing.Size(104, 32);
            button1.TabIndex = 0;
            button1.Text = "Click Me";

            // text box control and its properties
            textBox1.Location = new System.Drawing.Point(24, 104);
            textBox1.Name = "textBox1";
            textBox1.Size = new System.Drawing.Size(184, 20);
            textBox1.TabIndex = 1;
            textBox1.Text = "textBox1";

            // Adding controls to the fomr
            Controls.AddRange(new System.Windows.Forms.Control[]
            {    textBox1, button1} );


        }
```

Adding Events

Now you'll add an event handler to the button control. In this example, upon clicking the button, you want to display the text "Button is clicked" inside the TextBox control. Adding event handlers is simple. The System.EventHandler takes one argument—the method name of the event handler—which will be executed when the button-click event is triggered. Listing 2-4 displays a message on the button click inside the event handler button1_Click.

Listing 2-4. Adding events to a form control

```
public NotePadWindowsForms()
{
 // Code here
    button1.Click += new System.EventHandler(button1_Click);


}



// Button click handler
private void button1_Click(object sender, System.EventArgs e)
{
    textBox1.Text = "Button is clicked";
}
```

In Listing 2-4, you first add the button1.Click += new
System.EventHandler(button1_Click) line in the end of the form constructor.
After that you write the button1_Click method with this signature:

```
private void button1_Click(object sender, System.EventArgs e)
```

This method sets textBox's text property to "Button is clicked" using

```
textBox1.Text = "Button is clicked";
```

Creating the Final Code

OK, now you'll combine all the previous steps and code to create the final code,
shown in Listing 2-5.

Listing 2-5. The final code of Windows Forms application

```
using System;
using System.Windows.Forms;
using System.Drawing;

namespace NotePadWindowsForms
{
    public class NotePadWindowsForms : System.Windows.Forms.Form
```

```
{
      private System.Windows.Forms.Button button1;
      private System.Windows.Forms.TextBox textBox1;

      public NotePadWindowsForms()
      {
          /* Form Properties */

          // Set Caption of the form
          Text = "Test WinForm";
          // Set background color
          BackColor = System.Drawing.Color.Blue;
          //Set forground color
          ForeColor = System.Drawing.Color.Yellow;


          button1 = new System.Windows.Forms.Button();
          textBox1 = new System.Windows.Forms.TextBox();



          // button control and its properties
          button1.Location = new System.Drawing.Point(8, 32);
          button1.Name = "button1";
          button1.Size = new System.Drawing.Size(104, 32);
          button1.TabIndex = 0;
          button1.Text = "Click Me";

          // text box control and its properties
          textBox1.Location = new System.Drawing.Point(24, 104);
          textBox1.Name = "textBox1";
          textBox1.Size = new System.Drawing.Size(184, 20);
          textBox1.TabIndex = 1;
          textBox1.Text = "textBox1";

          // Adding controls to the form
          Controls.AddRange(new System.Windows.Forms.Control[]
          {   textBox1, button1} );

      button1.Click += new System.EventHandler(button1_Click);

      }
```

```
// Button click handler
private void button1_Click(object sender,
  System.EventArgs e)
{
                textBox1.Text = "Button is clicked";
                MessageBox.Show("Button is clicked");
    }

public static int Main()
{
    Application.Run(new NotePadWindowsForms());
    return 0;
}
   }
}
```

Save this code as finalForm.cs and compile it from the command line. Figure 2-2 shows the output.

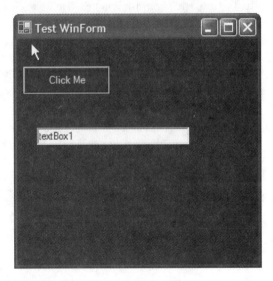

Figure 2-2. Output the Windows Forms application

You'll see a message box, like the one shown in Figure 2-2, when you click on the button. You'll also see the text of the text box change, as shown in Figure 2-3.

Figure 2-3. Output of button-click event

Writing a Windows Forms Application Using the VS .NET IDE

You'll now create a similar type of application in the VS .NET IDE. In VS .NET, you don't have to write much code when constructing your form. The VS .NET IDE takes care of that for you.

In this application, you'll create a form, a Button control, a ListBox control, and a Text control. In this sample example, you type text in the text box, and when you click on the button, the program will add the text box's contents to the ListBox control.

Just follow the steps in the forthcoming sections, and you'll be all set to go.

Selecting a Project Template

In the VS .NET IDE, the first step is to select a project type. You can create many project types, but in this sample we'll concentrate on the Windows Application template only.

Select New ➤ Project ➤ Visual C# Projects ➤ Windows Application template from the templates list, as shown in Figure 2-4.

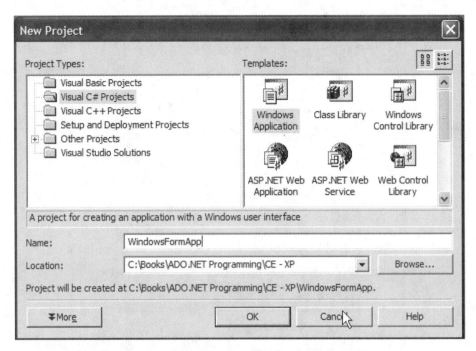

Figure 2-4. New project template selection

Click OK to create the project. The VS .NET IDE automatically adds a default form (Form1) for you.

Adding Controls to the Form

Now use the toolbox to add controls to the form. You can open the toolbox by clicking View ➢ Toolbox, as shown in Figure 2-5.

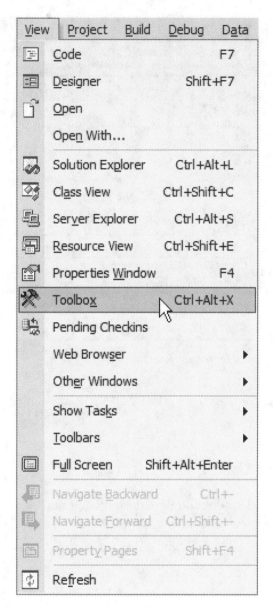

Figure 2-5. Toolbox menu item

Drag and drop controls from the toolbox (shown in Figure 2-6) to the form.

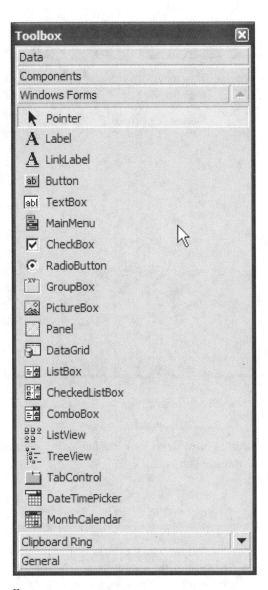

Figure 2-6. The toolbox

In your application, you'll add one Button control, one TextBox, and a ListBox control, as shown in Figure 2-7.

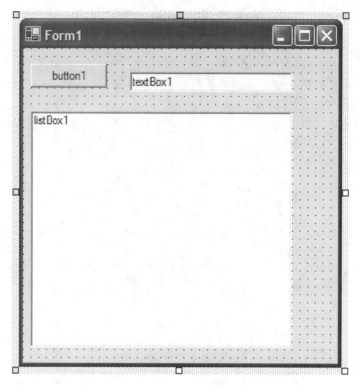

Figure 2-7. Form view with controls

Remember, your final form won't look like Figure 2-7 because you're going to set some properties of these controls.

Setting Properties

You can use the Properties windows to set the controls' properties. Right-click on the control and choose the Properties menu. For each control, the Properties window has different properties, such as text, name, background and foreground colors, font, styles, and so forth. You have changed the foreground and background color as well as the font properties of the ListBox. In Figure 2-8, you're changing the font to Verdana and bold and changing the text to "Add."

Figure 2-8. Properties window

Using the Properties window, you also set the properties of the ListBox control. You set its BackColor property to Red and ForeColor property to White. You also set the Text property of the form to Windows Forms Application.

Figure 2-9 shows the final form.

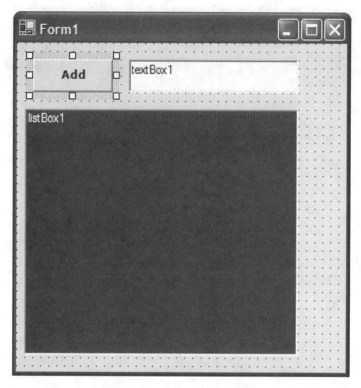

Figure 2-9. Windows Forms application in VS .NET IDE

Now right-click on the form and set these control properties by using the Properties window. Make sure you set the AutoSize property of the text box to false, so you'll be able to resize the text box to the same height as the button.

Examining the Code

You'll now take a look at what code the Form Designer has added for you. You can see the code either by right-clicking on the form and selecting View Code or by right-clicking on the Solution Explorer on the Form1.cs and selecting View Code, as shown in Figure 2-10.

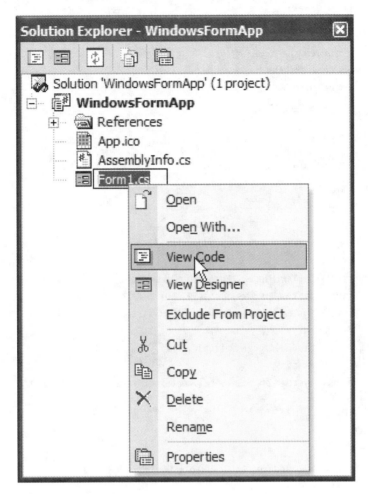

Figure 2-10. The View Code option

The View Code option opens file Form1.cs in the editor. The first things you should notice are the using namespaces. The wizard adds six namespaces. Next, you'll notice that the Form1 class is derived from the System.Windows.Forms.From class:

```
public class Form1 : System.Windows.Forms.Form
```

The rest of the code should look familiar to you, except perhaps for the Dispose method. The Dispose method is called to clean up resources. Listing 2-6 shows the source code added by VS .NET.

Listing 2-6. Windows Forms source code added by VS .NET

```csharp
using System;
using System.Drawing;
using System.Collections;
using System.ComponentModel;
using System.Windows.Forms;
using System.Data;

namespace WindowsFormApp
{
    /// <summary>
    /// Summary description for Form1.
    /// </summary>
    public class Form1 : System.Windows.Forms.Form
    {
        private System.Windows.Forms.Button button1;
        private System.Windows.Forms.TextBox textBox1;
        private System.Windows.Forms.ListBox listBox1;
        /// <summary>
        /// Required designer variable.
        /// </summary>
        private System.ComponentModel.Container components = null;

        public Form1()
        {
            //
            // Required for Windows Form Designer support
            //
            InitializeComponent();

            //
            // TODO: Add any constructor code after
            // InitializeComponent call
            //
        }

        /// <summary>
        /// Clean up any resources being used.
        /// </summary>
        protected override void Dispose( bool disposing )
        {
            if( disposing )
```

```
        {
            if (components != null)
            {
                components.Dispose();
            }
        }
        base.Dispose( disposing );
    }


    #region Windows Form Designer generated code
    /// <summary>
    /// Required method for Designer support - do not modify
    /// the contents of this method with the code editor.
    /// </summary>
    private void InitializeComponent()
    {
        this.button1 = new System.Windows.Forms.Button();
        this.textBox1 = new System.Windows.Forms.TextBox();
        this.listBox1 = new System.Windows.Forms.ListBox();
        this.SuspendLayout();
        //
        // button1
        //
this.button1.Font = new System.Drawing.Font("Verdana", 9.75F,
System.Drawing.FontStyle.Bold,
System.Drawing.GraphicsUnit.Point, ((System.Byte)(0)));
        this.button1.ForeColor = System.Drawing.Color.Black;
        this.button1.Location = new System.Drawing.Point(8, 8);
        this.button1.Name = "button1";
        this.button1.Size = new System.Drawing.Size(96, 24);
        this.button1.TabIndex = 0;
        this.button1.Text = "Add";
        //
        // textBox1
        //
        this.textBox1.AutoSize = false;
        this.textBox1.Location = new System.Drawing.Point(128, 8);
        this.textBox1.Name = "textBox1";
        this.textBox1.Size = new System.Drawing.Size(128, 32);
        this.textBox1.TabIndex = 1;
        this.textBox1.Text = "textBox1";
        //
        // listBox1
```

```
                //
                this.listBox1.BackColor = System.Drawing.Color.Red;
                this.listBox1.ForeColor =
System.Drawing.SystemColors.HighlightText;
                this.listBox1.Location = new System.Drawing.Point(8, 48);
                this.listBox1.Name = "listBox1";
                this.listBox1.Size = new System.Drawing.Size(264, 212);
                this.listBox1.TabIndex = 2;
                //
                // Form1
                //
                this.AutoScaleBaseSize = new System.Drawing.Size(5, 13);
                this.ClientSize = new System.Drawing.Size(292, 273);
                this.Controls.AddRange(new System.Windows.Forms.Control[] {

this.listBox1,

this.textBox1,

this.button1});
                this.ForeColor = System.Drawing.Color.CornflowerBlue;
                this.Name = "Form1";
                this.Text = "Windows Forms Application";
                this.ResumeLayout(false);

        }
        #endregion

        /// <summary>
        /// The main entry point for the application.
        /// </summary>
        [STAThread]
        static void Main()
        {
            Application.Run(new Form1());
        }
    }
}
```

As you can see from Listing 2-6, the Main method is the entry point of the application. This method calls the Application.Run method with the Form1 constructor as a parameter.

If you examine the InitializeComponent method, you'll see code for every action you have taken so far, including all the properties you have set, such as the controls' sizes and the form's size. The AddRange method of the Form class adds the controls to the form (see Listing 2-7).

Listing 2-7. AddRange *method of* Form *class*

```
private void InitializeComponent()
{
    this.button1 = new System.Windows.Forms.Button();
    this.textBox1 = new System.Windows.Forms.TextBox();
    this.listBox1 = new System.Windows.Forms.ListBox();
    this.SuspendLayout();
    // more source code here

  this.Controls.AddRange(new System.Windows.Forms.Control[] {
   this.listBox1, this.textBox1, this.button1});

    // more source code here
}
```

Adding Code for an Event Handler

The last thing you'll do is to add an event handler to the button-click event and create code for adding the TextBox content to the ListBox. To add an event handler, you can either double-click on the button in the form designer or use the event tab in the Properties window, shown as a lightning bolt icon in Figure 2-11. As you can see in Figure 2-11, buttons can have many events, such as Click, Paint, and DragEnter.

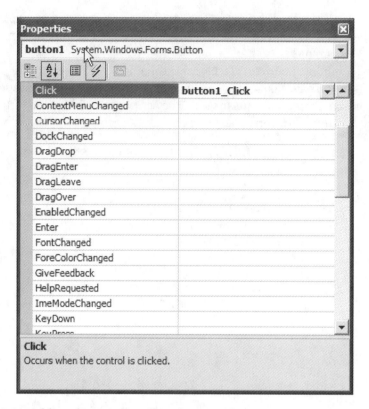

Figure 2-11. Adding the event handler of a control

You use the lightning bolt icon to add an event handler to the button-click event. Double-clicking on the Click label adds the button1_Click event handler to your code:

```
private void button1_Click(object sender, System.EventArgs e)
{
}
```

You can also manually type button1_Click as the event name (or whatever name you choose such as OnButton1Click) into the field next to the Click label. You can view the event handler placed in the code by the wizard by double-clicking on the event handler name (Click) in the Properties window or by double-clicking on the graphical button itself.

Now add one line of code to this method:

```
listBox1.Items.Add(textBox1.Text);
```

If you click on the Button, the TextBox, and the ListBox controls, you'll see their default names are button1, textBox1, and listBox1, respectively (shown in the

Properties window). The previous line calls the `listBox1.Items.Add` method to add an item to the ListBox control, which takes as an argument the `textBox1.Text`. Here `textBox1.Text` represents the text typed into the TextBox control. So in brief, this line of code adds the contents of the TextBox as the next item in the ListBox.

Now the `button1_Click` method looks like the following:

```
private void button1_Click(object sender, System.EventArgs e)
{
        listBox1.Items.Add(textBox1.Text);
}
```

The bold code represents that you've added this line manually.

Building and Running the Project

You can now proceed to run the program using Ctrl+F5 or by using the menu option from the debug menu. Figure 2-12 shows many debug options for running the program. You can debug your code lines one by one by setting these options. In this sample, you'll use the Start Without Debugging option to compile and run your program.

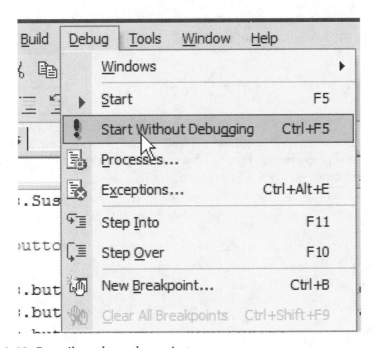

Figure 2-12. Compile and run the project

Type some text into the text box and a button-click on the Add button adds the string to the ListBox control. Figure 2-13 shows the output of the program.

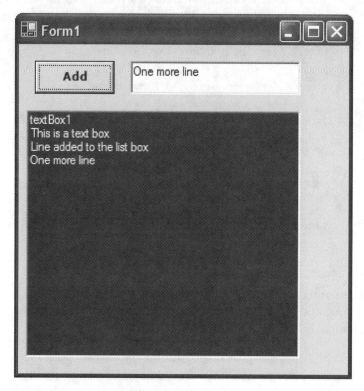

Figure 2-13. Windows form sample output

Adding a Class to a Project

The project's Class View window shows you the classes and their methods broken down in a tree structure. This window is really useful when you're adding a method or a property to a class. You can open the Class View from the View ≻ Class View menu item of VS .NET's main menu.

When you open the Class View and examine the tree, you can see all the classes and their members and properties by expanding the project and class nodes.

You can even use the Class View to add a class to your project. Right-click on your project in the Class View and click Add. Add Class calls the Class Wizard, as shown in Figure 2-14.

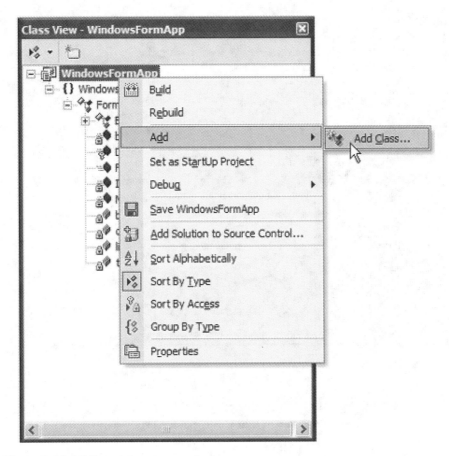

Figure 2-14. Adding a class to a project

Type your class name and other options on the first page, as shown in
Figure 2-15.

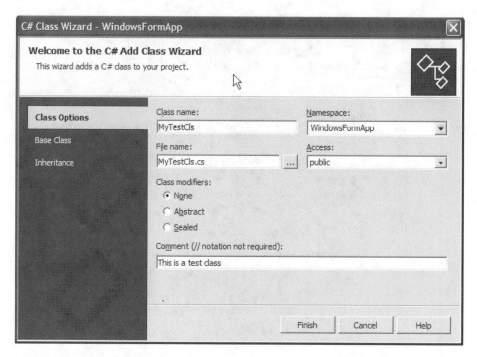

Figure 2-15. The Class Options page

The second page, Base Class, is where you choose a namespace and derive a class from the classes defined in that namespace, as shown in Figure 2-16.

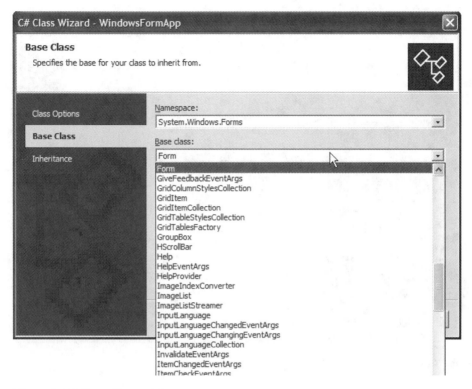

Figure 2-16. Base Class options

You derive your class from the Form class, as shown in Figure 2-16. The next page of the wizard, Inheritance, provides you available interfaces in the selected namespace. In the sample application, you selected System.Windows.forms namespace, and as you can see in Figure 2-17, the Available Interfaces list box shows you the interfaces available in that namespace.

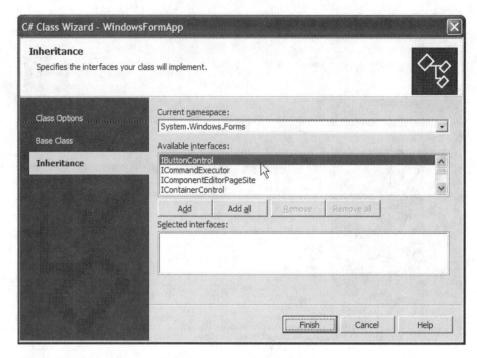

Figure 2-17. Base Class options

After you press the Finish button, the wizard adds a new class derived from the Form class, which looks like the form discussed earlier (see Listing 2-8).

Listing 2-8. myTestCls *derived from* System.Windows.Forms.Form

```csharp
using System;

namespace WindowsFormApp
{
    /// <summary>
    /// This is a test class
    /// </summary>
    public class MyTestCls : System.Windows.Forms.Form
    {
        public MyTestCls()
        {
            //
            // TODO: Add constructor logic here
            //
        }
    }
}
```

Adding Methods and Properties to a Form with Class View

You can use the Class View to add methods, properties, and fields to a form. Right-click on the `MyTestCls` class in the Class View to bring up the menu actions you can take on your class. For example, the Add pop-up menu item gives you the ability to add different members to your form class (see Figure 2-18).

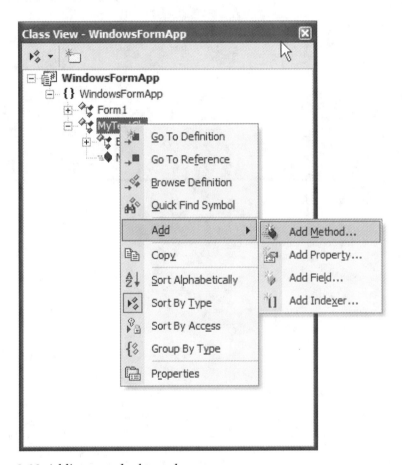

Figure 2-18. Adding a method to a class

Click the Add Method option to get to the Method Wizard. Using this wizard, you can add methods with their types and parameters (see Figure 2-19). The Method access combo gives you options to select the access type of the method. Return Type, Parameter Type, Parameter Name, Parameter List, and all other options are self-explanatory.

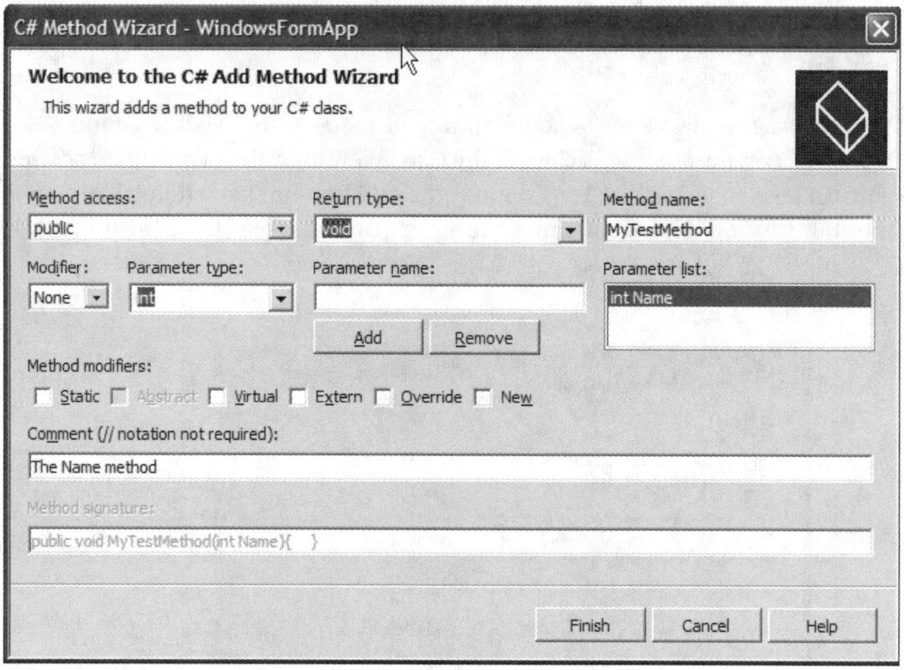

Figure 2-19. The C# Method Wizard

The results are as follows:

```
/// <summary>
/// The Name Method
/// </summary>
public void MyTestMethod(int Counter, int Name)
{

}
```

You can use the Property Wizard to add property to a form (see Figure 2-20). The property access options let you pick the access type of a property. Property Type is the type of property, and Property Name is the name.

You can also select only get, only set, or get/set both types of properties.

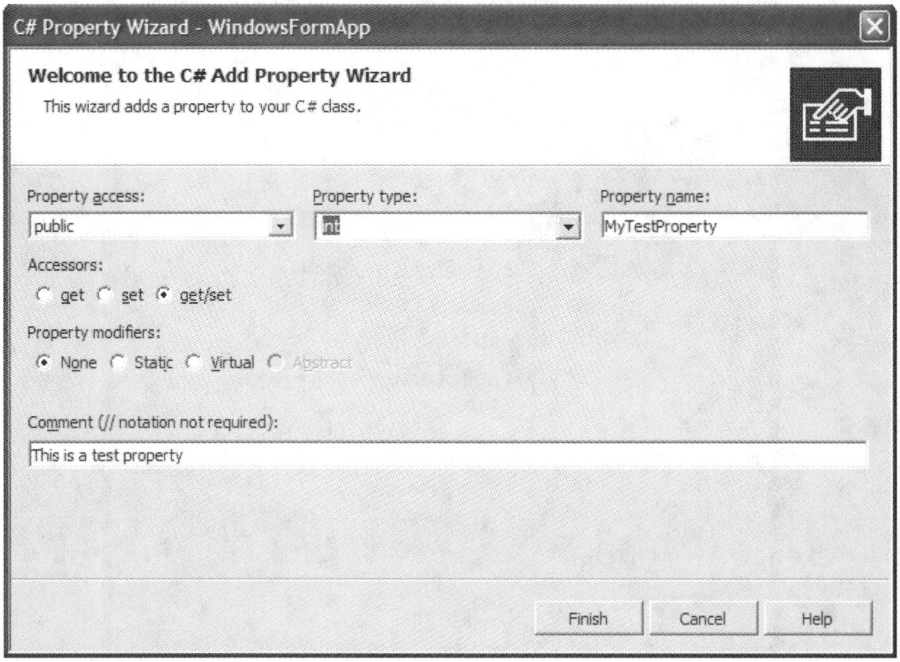

Figure 2-20. The Property Wizard

The results are as follows:

```
/// <summary>
/// // This is a test property
/// </summary>
public int MyTestProperty
{
    get
    {
        return 0;
    }
    set
    {
    }
}
```

Again, you can view these methods and properties by using your Class View (see Figure 2-21).

Figure 2-21. The Class View window

Windows.Forms Namespace

The System.Windows.Forms namespace, which resides in System.Windows.Forms (in System.Windows.Forms.dll) assembly, defines most of the Windows Forms classes. This namespace contains more than 300 classes for Windows controls and forms. Before you use any of these namespace classes, make sure you add references to these classes into your namespace.

Windows.Forms Namespace Classes

Covering the Windows.Forms namespace classes is not within the scope of this book. However, I'll introduce some common classes. Table 2-1 lists some of these classes.

Table 2-1. The System.Windows.Forms *Common Classes*

CLASS	DESCRIPTION
Application	The Application class provides application-level functionality such as starting and stopping the application.
Button, CheckBox, Label, TextBox, ListView, ListBox, ComboBox, DataGrid, Splitter, TreeView, ProgressBar, Timer, and so on	These all are Control classes. Each control in Windows Forms is associated with a class. For example, Button and TextBox classes represent a Button and a TextBox control.
ColorDialog, CommonDialog, OpenFileDialog, FileDialog, FontDialog, ColorDialog, OpenFileDialog, SaveFileDialog	Windows Forms contain common dialog classes. These classes provide access to default Windows common dialogs such as file, font, and color dialogs.
Cursor, Cursors	Cursor classes.
Form	A Form class represents a Windows Form or dialog box.
MainMenu, MenuItem, ContextMenu	Menu control classes.
MessageBox	This class wraps MessageBox functionality.
PictureBox	Represents a Windows picture box control for displaying an image.
PrintDialog, PrintPreviewDialog, PrintPreviewControl	Printing classes.

The System.Windows.Forms also contains hundreds of enumeration and delegate classes.

The Windows.Forms.Application Class

The Application class provides application-level control. It provides functionality to start or stop the application and to process Windows messages. Table 2-2 describes some of the methods and properties of the Application class.

Table 2-2. Windows.Forms.Application *Class Methods*

METHOD	DESCRIPTION
Run	Starts application's message loop for the current thread
Exit, ExitThread	Stops the message loop
CommonAppDataPath	Common application path shared by all users
UserAppDataPath	Path of the application for current user

The Control Class

The Control class implements the basic functionality of a control, including input from the keyboard and mouse, the size and position of a control, the hide and show methods, and events for these inputs. Some of its common properties are Bounds, Text, Left, Top, Bottom, Right, Visible, Width, and Height. Its common methods include Show, Hide, SetSize, SetBounds, and SetLocation. The Control class also implements the events for Mouse and Keyboards such as KeyUp, KeyDown, MouseUp, MouseDown, Enter, and Move.

The Form Class

A Form class represents a window with various functional types such as a simple form, a dialog box, or an MDI form. This class is inherited from the Control class. Its properties enable you to set the size and color of a form. The Form class also implements functionality for MDI support, Modal and Modeless dialogs, menus, and Help.

Each Windows form in .NET is derived from the Form class. The Form class *constructor* calls the InitializeComponent method, which in turn initializes the properties of the form such as a the form's size, color, caption, fonts, and so on. The Dispose method cleans up the associated resources.

Common Control Classes

Other than the classes discussed in the previous section, each control has a class in the Forms namespace. These are some of the common control classes:

Button	CheckBox	CheckListBox	ComboBox	GroupBox
HScrollBar	ImageList	Label	LinkLabel	ListBox
ListView	Panel	PictureBox	ProgressBar	RadioButton
RichTextBox	Splitter	StatusBar	TabControl	TextBox
Timer	ToolBar	ToolTip	TrackBar	TreeView
VScrollBar	ColorDialog	ContextMenu	DataGrid	DateTimePicker
DomainUp Down	FontDialog	PrintDialog	HelpProvider	OpenFile Dialog
SaveFileDialog	PageSetup Dialog	PrintPreview Control	PrintPreview Dialog	DateTimeForm
ErrorProvider	PropertyGrid	TrayIcon	TrackBar	

Adding a Toolbar to an Application

OK, now you'll go through a step-by-step tutorial on how to use a ToolBar control in your Windows application. Just follow these simple steps.

Creating a Windows Application

Create a Windows application using New ➢ Project ➢ Visual C# Projects ➢ Windows Application option in the Project Templates (see Figure 2-22).

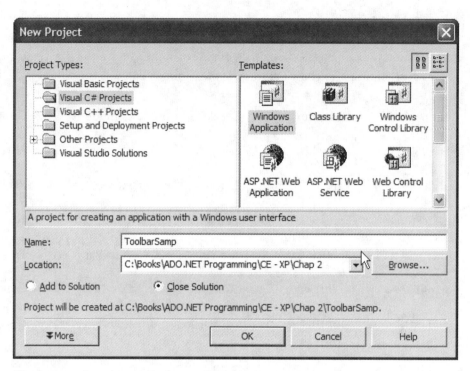

Figure 2-22. Creating a Windows application project

Now add a ToolBar control to the form by dragging a ToolBar control from the toolbox to the form (see Figure 2-23).

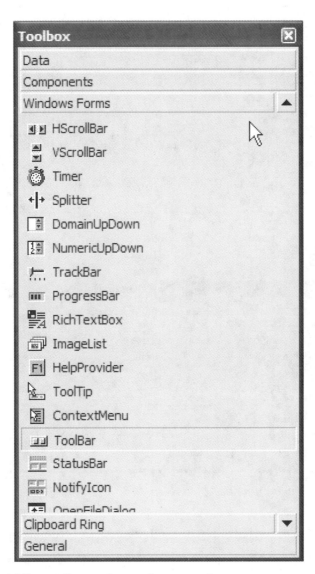

Figure 2-23. Adding toolbar and status bar controls

Now you should see an empty form with a toolbar sitting on top.

Adding Toolbar Buttons

The next step is to add toolbar buttons. You can add toolbar buttons by using the Properties window of the toolbar. Select the Buttons' properties in the Properties window and click on Collection (see Figure 2-24).

Figure 2-24. Toolbar properties

Clicking Collection launches the ToolBarButton Collection Editor, shown in Figure 2-25.

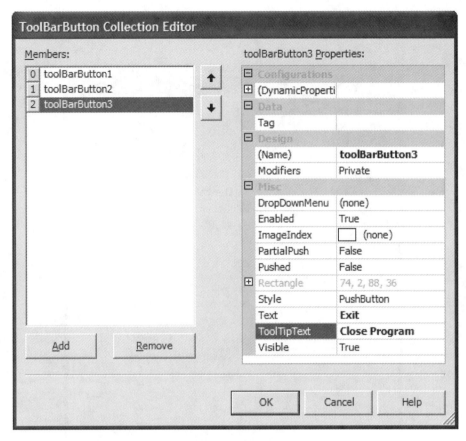

Figure 2-25. Adding and removing toolbar buttons

As you can see in Figure 2-25, you can add and remove toolbar buttons
to a toolbar using the Add and Remove buttons. You can also set toolbar
button properties such as tooltip text, style, or ImageIndex using the toolbar button Properties window in the right side of Figure 2-25.

You'll add three toolbar buttons: Open, Test, Exit, and set their ToolTipText
properties to open a file, test a button, and close a file.

Loading Images into Toolbar Buttons

To add images to a toolbar, you need to add an ImageList to the form. Open the
toolbox again and add an ImageList to the form by dragging from the toolbox to
the form. After adding an ImageList, go to the Properties window. Using the
Properties window, you can set the ImageList properties such as ColorDepth,

Transparency, and ImageSize. In this example, you're concentrating only on the Images property, which is a collection of Images (see Figure 2-26).

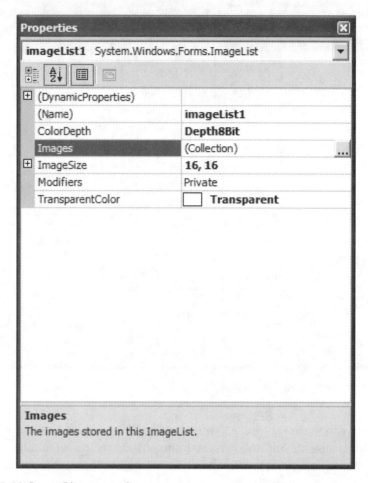

Figure 2-26. ImageList properties

Clicking the Images Collection property launches the Image Collection Editor, which lets you add and remove images to the image list using the Add and Remove buttons. You'll add three images to the image list shown in Figure 2-27.

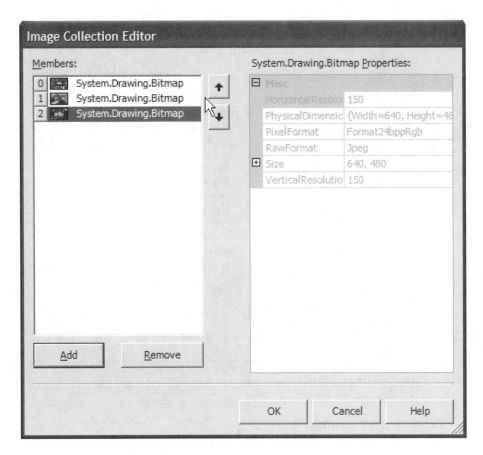

Figure 2-27. The Image Collection Editor

The Add button launches the Open dialog box, which lets you pick images
from your local machine or from any network for which you are set up
(see Figure 2-28).

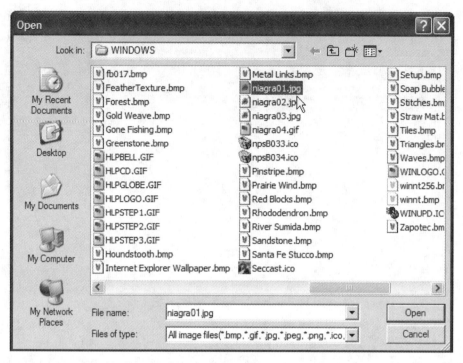

Figure 2-28. Browsing an image from the system

The next step is to attach the image list to the ToolBar by using the ToolBar's ImageList property and selecting imageList1 from the drop-down list (see Figure 2-29).

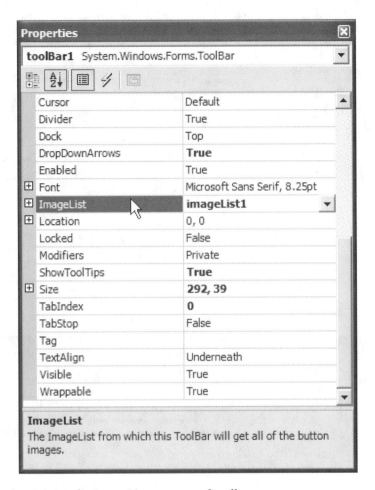

Figure 2-29. Setting the ImageList property of toolbar

Now you can go back to the ToolbarButton Collection Editor using the
Buttons property of the toolbar (Figure 2-25) and click on the ImageIndex prop-
erty of each button and set the indexes to 0, 1, and 2, consecutively (see
Figure 2-30).

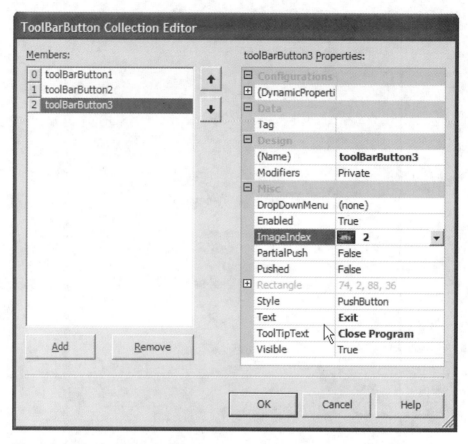

Figure 2-30. Setting ImageIndex property

This time the ImageIndex property shows you all the image list items inside a drop-down list box (see Figure 2-31).

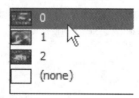

Figure 2-31. Image Index selection options

Now your toolbar looks like Figure 2-32.

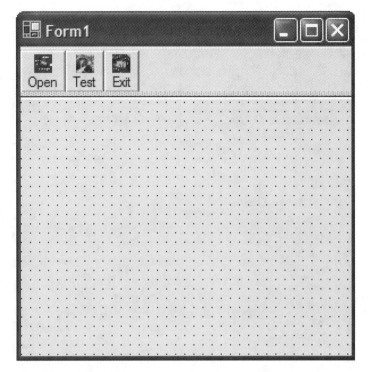

Figure 2-32. Toolbar with images

Writing Event Handlers for Toolbar Buttons

The last step is to add an event handler to the toolbar and execute some code. After this step, you are all set to run your program.

Begin by bringing up the event handler window by clicking on the event (lightning) icon in the Properties window. Type the event handler name for the ButtonClick event. In your example, the toolbar button-click handler method name is toolbar_Click (see Figure 2-33).

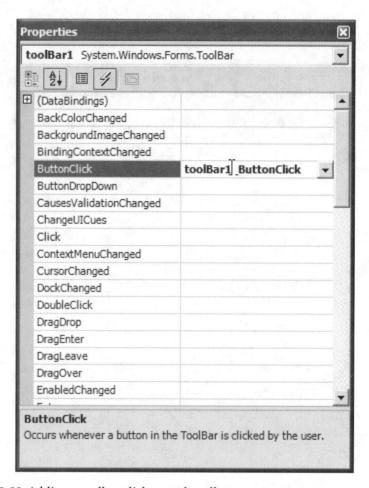

Figure 2-33. Adding a toolbar click event handler

Double-clicking on the ButtonClick label adds the event handler to your code shown here:

```
private void toolbar_Click(object sender,
System.Windows.Forms.ToolBarButtonClickEventArgs e)
{

}
```

You can use the ToolBarButtonClickEventArgs passed into the event handler to find out which button is clicked because it contains a reference to the button that was pressed.

With this knowledge, you can add code to the toolbar click event handler, which checks which button is clicked by comparing the `ToolBarButtonClickEventArgs`'s `Button` property with each of the toolbar button instances. You added the code shown in bold in the following listing to the event handler, which displays a message box corresponding to the toolbar button that was clicked:

```
private void toolbar_Click(object sender,
System.Windows.Forms.ToolBarButtonClickEventArgs e){
if ( e.Button == toolBarButton1 )
{
        MessageBox.Show( "Open Button Clicked ");
}
if ( e.Button == toolBarButton2 )
{
MessageBox.Show( "Test Button Clicked ");
}
if ( e.Button == toolBarButton3 )
{
MessageBox.Show( "Exit Button Clicked ");
}
}
```

Now compile and run your project and click on different buttons.

Adding Menu Items to an Application

Adding menus to a Windows application is somewhat easier than adding toolbars. You'll add menu items to your existing application that correspond to each of the buttons in the toolbar.

To add a menu to your application, drop a MainMenu control from the toolbox to the form. After dragging it to the form, you can edit the names of menu items by simply clicking and typing into the menu graphic. In this example, you renamed main menu to Main Menu Options and added three submenus: Open, Test, and Exit. After adding the three menu items, your form looks like Figure 2-34.

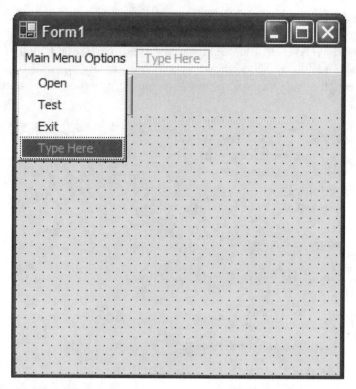

Figure 2-34. Adding menu items to a form

You can even add a radio button or check box item by setting the item's radio or checked properties in the Properties window.

The next step is to add an event handler for each menu item. You can add a click event to a menu item either by using the Properties window event icon or by double-clicking on the menu item itself.

Using the Properties window, add OpenMenuItemClick, TestMenuItemClick, and ExitMenuItemClick as click event handlers to each of the menu items (see Figure 2-35).

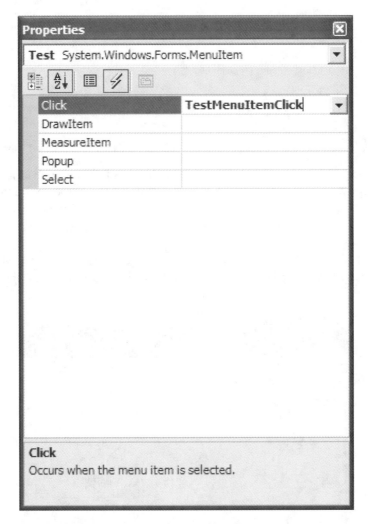

Figure 2-35. Adding a menu item click event handler

After adding event handlers, you've added a message box to these handlers that display the menu item that was clicked. After adding the message boxes, the code looks like this listing (the MessageBox calls are shown in bold):

```
private void OpenMenuItemClick(object sender, System.EventArgs e)
{
MessageBox.Show( "Open Menu ItemClicked ");
}
private void TestMenuItemClick(object sender, System.EventArgs e)
{
MessageBox.Show( "Test Menu ItemClicked ");
```

```
}
private void ExitMenuItemClick(object sender, System.EventArgs e)
{
MessageBox.Show( "Exit Menu ItemClicked ");
```

Working with Common Dialogs

Windows Forms provide classes that support common dialogs such as font, color, open and save. In this section, you'll examine some of these common dialog classes and how to use them in an application. You can either drop these controls from the toolbox into a form or create the controls at run-time using their classes.

You'll add three buttons and a text box to your existing application, which you have used in the previous two samples. Now your form looks like Figure 2-36.

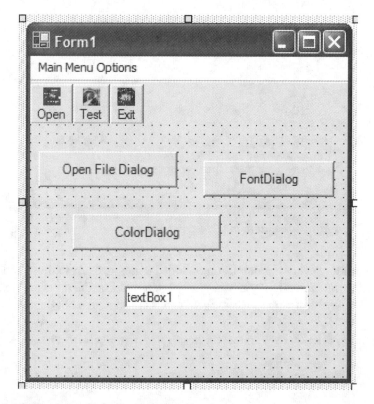

Figure 2-36. Common dialog sample application

The OpenFileDialog and SaveFileDialog classes represent the Windows open file and Windows Save File dialogs, respectively. You need to call the ShowDialog method on instances of these classes to display the dialog. The FileName property of OpenFileDialog returns the selected file name. This code shows you how to use an OpenFileDialog:

```
OpenFileDialog fdlg = new OpenFileDialog();
fdlg.Title = "C# Corner Open File Dialog" ;
fdlg.InitialDirectory = @"c:\" ;
fdlg.Filter = "All files (*.*)|*.*|All files (*.*)|*.*" ;
fdlg.FilterIndex = 2 ;
fdlg.RestoreDirectory = true ;
if(fdlg.ShowDialog() == DialogResult.OK)
{
    textBox1.Text = fdlg.FileName ;
}
```

This sample opens all file types. You can also set the Filter property to open a specific file type.

The FontDialog class represents a Windows font dialog. Figure 2-37 shows a Windows font dialog. In the FontDialog, you can select a font family, size, style, and color.

The Font, Color, and FontStyle properties represent the selected font, color, and style of the font. The listing here shows usage of a FontDialog and its members and sets textbox1's color and font to the selected color and font of the font dialog:

```
FontDialog fntDlg = new FontDialog();
fntDlg.ShowColor = true;
if(fntDlg.ShowDialog() != DialogResult.Cancel )
{
    textBox1.Font = fntDlg.Font ;
    textBox1.ForeColor = fntDlg.Color;
}
```

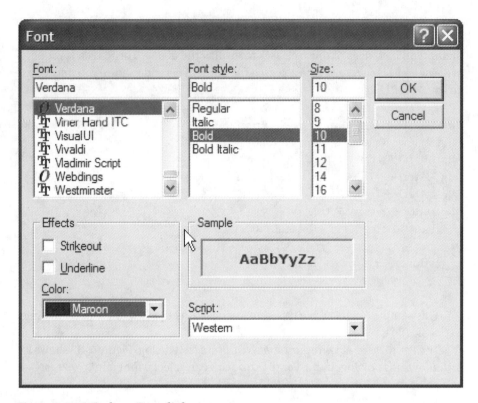

Figure 2-37. Windows Font dialog

The `ColorDialog` class represents the Windows Color dialog and looks like Figure 2-38.

The `Color` property of the `ColorDialog` represents the selected color. Here, you set the color of the text box and button controls to the selected color of the color dialog:

```
ColorDialog colorDlg = new ColorDialog();
colorDlg.ShowDialog();
textBox1.BackColor = colorDlg.Color;
button1.BackColor = colorDlg.Color;
button3.BackColor = colorDlg.Color;
```

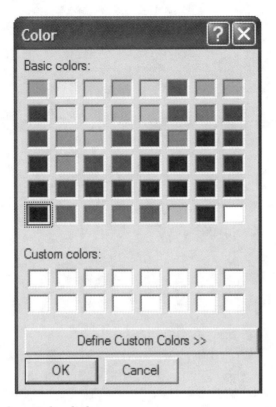

Figure 2-38. Windows Color dialog

Summary

In this chapter, you learned the basics of Windows Forms. You also learned how to write Windows applications using the command line, as well as using the VS .NET IDE, which provides design-time support to add Windows controls and set their properties and event handlers. You saw how to drag menus, toolbars, status bars, and common dialogs to a form and set their properties at design-time as well as at run-time.

All Windows Forms functionality is defined in the System.Windows.Forms namespace. You need to add a reference to the System.Windows.Forms namespace before using these classes. The System.Windows.Forms.Form class creates a form. Each Windows control has its own separate class in this namespace. In no time you can use these controls at either design-time or run-time.

CHAPTER 3

Overview of ADO.NET

ACTIVEX DATA OBJECTS FOR THE .NET Framework (ADO.NET) is the latest database access technology from Microsoft. ADO.NET addresses issues with previous database access technologies and provides future scalability. Although ADO.NET stands for *Active Data Objects .NET*, it's perhaps misnamed because ADO.NET is not an ActiveX/Component Object Model (COM) technology. As the business world is moving onto the Internet, one of the main goals of ADO.NET is to write high-performance, reliable, and scalable database applications over the Internet. ADO.NET uses .NET Common Language Runtime (CLR) services to manage the library, and it utilizes Extensible Markup Language (XML) to cache the data and exchange data among applications over the Internet as well as intranets.

This chapter will provide an overview of ADO.NET. In it, I'll provide the basics of ADO.NET, describe its advantages over current data access technologies, and briefly introduce ADO.NET classes and namespaces as well as show how to use them to write simple database applications using Visual Studio .NET. Microsoft Visual Studio .NET provides tremendous support for writing database applications in no time, using its wizards and utilities. In this chapter, you'll also take a brief look at ADO.NET components and how they fit in the model and work together. The examples in Chapters 4 and 5 will use these components. Chapter 4 will cover Visual Studio .NET and ADO.NET support. In Chapter 5, I'll cover the ADO.NET object model in more detail.

> **NOTE** *The term .NET base class library is synonymous with .NET Runtime library and .NET Framework class library.*

What Is ADO.NET?

ADO.NET is a new database access technology created by Microsoft; its .NET Framework can access any kind of data source. It's a set of object-oriented classes that provides a rich set of data components to create high-performance, reliable, and scalable database applications for client-server applications as well as distributed environments over the Internet and intranets.

In the ADO.NET model, unlike ADO (in connected state) and previous data access technologies, applications connect to the data sources when they are reading or updating the data. After that, the connection closes. This is important because in client-server or distributed applications, having connection resources open all the time is one of the most resource-consuming parts. You don't have to connect to a data source all the time; the only time you need to connect to a data source is when you are reading and writing final changes to a data source.

The old approach of having connections open all the time is problematic when considering the number of clients that access the same data source simultaneously. In larger systems, developers often used MTS/COM+ to pool ADO connections to address some of this resource consumption; however, ADO.NET provides a more optimal paradigm for large systems without needing to utilize MTS/COM+ enterprise services—unless, of course, you need to take advantage of such advanced techniques as a three-phase commit.

ADO.NET uses SQL queries and stored procedures to read, write, update, and delete data from a data source. You use SQL queries through the ADO.NET `Command` object, which returns data in the form of `DataReader` or `DataSet` objects. After that connection closes, you use `DataSet` objects to work with the data and connect to the data source again when you need to update the data source.

> **NOTE**   *SQL queries are also called SQL statements. See the Appendix for SQL query examples.*

A *dataset* is a collection of `DataTable` objects and relationships among them. It works as a container that stores returned data from a database in cached form. You can fill a dataset with the data retrieved from multiple tables of a database. Once you have a dataset (which is disconnected data, stored on your local machine), you treat the dataset as your data source and work with it. You call the `Update` method to make dataset changes final to the actual database. You can even read and update a dataset from different data sources.

You access a data source and fill a dataset via data providers. The .NET Framework provides three different types of data providers: Sql, OleDb, and ODBC. Microsoft is also working on providing a data provider for Oracle database, and other Database Management System (DBMS) suppliers may produce their own data providers. You use a `DataAdapter` object of a data provider and call its `Fill` method to fill a dataset.

XML plays a major role in ADO.NET. The ADO.NET model utilizes XML to store the data in cache and transfer the data among applications. Datasets use XML schemas to store and transfer data among applications. You can even use this XML file from other applications without interacting with the actual dataset. You can use data among all kinds of applications and components because XML is an industry standard; you can transfer data via many protocols, such as HTTP, because of XML's text-based nature.

Why ADO.NET Was Designed

To understand why ADO.NET was designed, you have to take a look at the present database access technologies. As you saw in the "Background: Microsoft Data Access Technologies" section of the Introduction, each previous data access technology has its own pros and cons. Some of them were designed specifically for a particular type of data source, some of them are not easy to program for developers, and some of them don't have good enough performance. For example, ODBC API is a set of C functions. There is no object-oriented support. So, developing applications using ODBC is a time-consuming process for developers. Another problem with ODBC is its relational nature. ODBC API is limited to relational databases, and it's difficult to use ODBC with nonrelational data sources such as network directories, email stores, ISAM data, object data, and so on. DAO is an object model but was specifically designed to work with the Microsoft Jet database engine. The MFC ODBC and DAO classes are one more wrapper for ODBC and DAO API. Because of this extra wrapper, these classes are not up to the mark performance-wise and still have some of the same limitations as ODBC and DAO.

However, OLE-DB is a solution that works with any kind of data sources using OLE-DB providers and consumers, but writing OLE-DB applications is time consuming. It's also hard for developers to program. Moreover, OLE-DB is a flat model. That means you could directly connect to a table without going through hierarchical objects of connection and databases. Because of the lower-level programming model of OLE API, OLE-DB API isn't easy to program for non-OLE programmers.

To overcome to this problem, Microsoft introduced ADO. ADO is a high-level programming model, and it was the best data access technology at that point (of course, this was before ADO.NET). It's a nice COM wrapper for OLE-DB API, and it suits most developers. The first major drawback of ADO is COM model, which isn't easy to learn and program for non-COM developers. The second drawback is the limited support for XML. You can read XML documents through ADO, but documents must have a certain format. The document must contain a root node named xml and two children. The first child of the root node describes the schema, which describes the type of each row and column, and the second node represents the serialized OLE DB rowset.

In brief, ADO.NET meets today's programming needs, including disconnected data, tight integration with XML, and a common model to work with all kinds of data sources.

To keep all these problems in mind, Microsoft wrote a set of new object-oriented classes, called ADO.NET. ADO.NET inherits its programming model from its predecessor ADO, so ADO programmers will see something common between these two APIs. It'll also take less time to jump from ADO to ADO.NET. ADO.NET classes are based on the ADO model and have some objects in common, such as `Connection` and `Command`. However, datasets replace recordsets in ADO.NET. These classes are easy to use and have solutions for all the problems discussed here.

Welcome to the ADO.NET world.

Advantages of ADO.NET

ADO.NET offers several advantages over previous Microsoft data access technologies, including ADO. The following sections will outline these advantages.

Single Object-Oriented API

As discussed in the "Background: Microsoft Data Access Technologies" section of the Introduction and previous section of this chapter, there were many ways to access various data sources. Each of these technologies has its pros and cons. Sometimes developers are confused about which technology to use. For example, to work with Microsoft Access databases, you can use ODBC, DAO, OLE-DB, ADO, DAO, and ODBC MFC classes. Which one would you choose? Again, it all depends on your requirements. The deployment of these technologies on client machines was one of the biggest problems because of the DLL hell. Believe me, because of these technology limitations, I used ODBC, DAO, and ODBC in one of my applications to get the desired result.

The ADO.NET provides a single object-oriented set of classes. There are different data providers to work with different data sources, but the programming model for all these data providers work in the same way. So, if you know how to work with one data provider, you can easily work with others. It's just a matter of changing class names and connection strings.

> **NOTE** *You can use more than one data provider to access a single data source. For example, you can use ODBC or OleDb data providers to access Microsoft Access databases.*

The ADO.NET classes are easy to use and to understand because of their object-oriented nature.

Managed Code

The ADO.NET classes are *managed classes*. They take all the advantages of .NET CLR, such as language independency and automatic resource management. All .NET languages access the same API. So, if you know how to use these classes in C#, you'll have no problem using them in VB .NET. Another big advantage is you don't have to worry about memory allocation and freeing it. The CLR will take care of it for you.

Deployment

In real life, writing database applications using ODBC, DAO, and other previous technologies and deploying on client machines was a big problem because of multiple versions of DAO and ODBC. However, this problem was somewhat taken care in ADO except that there are different versions of MDAC. Now, you don't have to worry about that. Installing distributable .NET components will take care of it.

XML Support

Today, XML is an industry standard and the most widely used method of sharing data among applications over the Internet. As discussed earlier, in ADO.NET data is cached and transferred in XML format. All components and applications can share this data, and you can transfer data via different protocols such as HTTP. You'll see this topic in more detail in Chapters 6 and 7.

Visual Data Components

Visual Studio .NET offers ADO.NET components and data-bound controls to work in visual form. That means you can use these components as you use any Windows controls. You drag and drop these components on Windows and Web Forms, set their properties, and write events. It helps programmers to write less code and develop applications in no time. VS .NET also offers the Data Form Wizard, which you can use to write full-fledged database applications without writing a single line of code. Using these components, you can directly bind these components with data-bound controls by setting these control's properties at design-time. You'll see these details in Chapter 4.

Performance and Scalability

Performance and scalability are two major factors when developing Web-based applications and services. Transferring data from one source to another is a costly affair over the Internet because of connection bandwidth limitations and rapidly increasing traffic. Using disconnected cached data in XML takes care of both of these problems.

Comparing ADO.NET and ADO

Among present Microsoft data access technologies, ADO is the most popular and powerful technology. To understand the power of ADO.NET, it's not a bad idea to compare ADO.NET with ADO.

The ADO.NET model is inherited from its predecessor ADO, but there are some key differences between ADO and ADO.NET. The following sections will describe these differences.

Connections and Disconnected Data

With ADO.NET, you use as few connections as possible and have more disconnected data.

Both the ADO and ADO.NET models support disconnected data but ADO's recordset object wasn't actually designed to work with disconnected data. So, there are performance problems with that. However, ADO.NET's dataset is specifically designed to work with disconnected data, and you can treat a dataset as a local copy of a database. In ADO.NET, you store data in a dataset and close the connection with the data source and keep it disconnected until you need to make final changes to the data source. The ADO model is not flexible enough for XML users; ADO uses OLE-DB persistence provider to support XML.

Recordset versus DataSet

In ADO, the in-memory representation of data is the recordset. A recordset is a set of records that can be an entire database table, a section of a table, or a join of more than one table. SQL statements are used to return the set of data. You use a recordset's MoveNext, MovePrevious, MoveFirst, and MoveLast methods to navigate through the data in a recordset.

In ADO.NET, the recordset is gone. The new objects introduced in ADO.NET that serve the purpose of the recordset are dataset and data reader. A DataSet object represents a dataset, and a DataReader object represents a data reader in ADO.NET. A dataset is a collection of one or more than one tables. A dataset can also contain metadata of database tables, such as their relationships, constraints, and primary and foreign keys. A DataTable object represents a table of a dataset. With the help of the DataView object, you can have multiple views of the same dataset.

A dataset doesn't have any move methods to navigate through dataset records like a recordset. In ADO.NET, a DataTable is a collection of DataRows. You use a DataRow object to navigate through the records. ADO.NET also provides DataRelation objects to navigate through master and detail records using primary and foreign keys. The DataReader object provides fast-cached, forward-only data to read data and navigate through its records.

XML Support

The ADO.NET model uses XML to store and transfer data among applications, which is not only an industry standard but also provides fast access of data for desktop and distributed applications. ADO uses *COM marshaling* to transfer data among applications, which is not only hard to program but also not as efficient or reliable as XML because of its limitations, data types and their conversions, and the nature of COM. Using XML, not only is it easy to program XML files, you can also transfer data through firewalls using HTTP, which is not possible using COM marshaling.

Overview of ADO.NET Namespaces and Classes

System.Data and its five supporting namespaces define the ADO.NET functionality. In this section, you'll take a brief look of these namespace. Chapter 5 will describe these namespaces and classes in more detail. These namespaces reside in the System.Data.dll assembly. Figure 3-1 shows the contents of this assembly in the IL DASM utility.

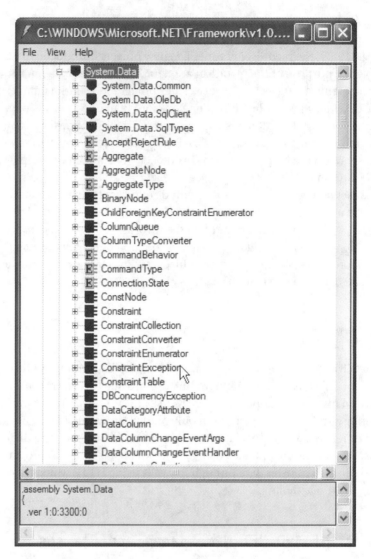

Figure 3-1. The `System.Data` *assembly contents in the IL DASM utility*

> **NOTE** *The* `Microsoft.Data.Odbc` *namespace was added to ADO.NET after it was developed. Installing it is separate, and you can find it as ODBC.NET SDK on the Microsoft site.*

The six ADO.NET namespaces are the `System.Data`, `System.Data.Common`, `System.Data.OleDb`, `Microsoft.Data.Odbc`, `System.Data.SqlClient`, and `System.Data.SqlTypes`.

The System.Data namespace is the core namespace of ADO.NET. It consists of the base classes for the ADO.NET architecture. All data providers use these classes. It defines classes that represent tables, columns, rows, and datasets. Some common classes from this namespace are DataView, DataViewManager, DataSet, DataTable, DataRow, DataColumn, and DataRelation. To use these classes in your applications, you need to add a reference to the System.Data namespace.

> **NOTE** *All classes in the .NET base class library are derived from the* Object *class and represent a type. Some authors and documentation also use word type for a .NET Framework class.*

The System.Data.Common namespace defines common classes. These classes are base classes for concrete data provider classes. These classes are shared among all data providers. DBConnection, DataAdapter, DbDataAdaper, DataColumnMapping, and DataTableMapping are some of the classed defined in this namespace. To use these classes in your application, you need to add a reference to the System.Data.Common namespace in your application.

The System.Data.OleDb namespace defines classes to work with OLE-DB data sources using .NET OleDb data providers. To work with an OLE-DB data source, you must have an OLE-DB provider for that data source. Each data provider component has a class corresponding to it. These classes start with OleDb followed by the component. For example, OleDbConnection class represents a Connection object. Some of the common classes of this namespace are OleDbDataAdapter, OleDbDataReader, OleDbCommand, OleDbCommandBuilder, OleDbError, OleDbParameter, OleDbPermission, and OleDbTransaction. To use these classes in your application, you need to add a reference to the System.Data.OleDb namespace in your application.

Similar to the System.Data.OleDb namespace, the Microsoft.Data.Odbc namespaces define ODBC .NET data provider classes to work with the ODBC data sources. To work with ODBC data sources, you need to install an ODBC driver for a database. The Microsoft.Data.Odbc namespace classes start with Odbc, followed by the component. For example, the OdbcConnection class represents a Connection object. Some of the common classes of this namespace are OdbcDataAdapter, OdbcDataReader, OdbcCommand, OdbcCommandBuilder, OdbcError, OdbcParameter, OdbcPermission, and OdbcTransaction. To use these classes in your application, you need to add a reference to the Microsoft.Data.Odbc namespace in your application.

The System.Data.SqlClient namespaces define Sql .NET data provider classes to work with SQL Server 7.0 or later databases. Similar to ODBC and OleDb classes, the classes in this namespace start with Sql. For example, common classes are SqlConnection, SqlDataAdapter, SqlCommand, SqlDataReader, and SqlTransaction.

The last namespace, System.Data.SqlTypes, provides a group of classes representing the specific types found in SQL Server. Some of these classes are SqlBinary, SqlMoney, SqlString, SqlInt32, SqlDouble, SqlDateTime, and SqlNumeric.

I'll discuss these namespaces, classes, and their members in more detail in Chapter 5.

Understanding ADO.NET Components

The ADO.NET is designed to work with multiple kinds of data sources in same fashion. You can categorize ADO.NET components in three categories: disconnected, common or shared, and the .NET data providers. The disconnected components build the basic ADO.NET architecture. You can use these components (or *classes*) with or without data providers. For example, you can use a DataTable object with or without data providers. Shared or common components are the base classes for data providers and shared by all data providers. The data provider components are specifically designed to work with different kinds of data sources. For example, ODBC data providers work with ODBC data sources, and OleDb data providers work with OLE-DB data sources.

Figure 3-2 represents the ADO.NET components model and how they work together.

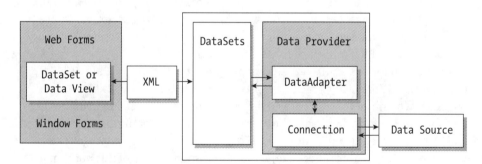

Figure 3-2. The ADO.NET components model

A data provider is a set of components, such as Connection, Command, DataAdapter, and DataReader. The Connection is the first component that talks to a data source. The Connection object establishes a connection to a data source and works as a connection reference in Command and DataAdapter objects. A Command object executes a SQL query and stored procedures to read, add, update, and delete data of a data source via a DataAdapter. The DataAdapter is a bridge between a dataset and the connection. It uses Command objects to execute SQL queries and stored procedures.

All data providers share the ADO.NET common components. These components represent the data. Some of the common components are DataSet, DataView, and DataViewManager. The DataSet uses XML to store and transfer data between the applications and the data provider. A DataSet is a set of DataTable objects. A DataTable represents a database table. The DataView and DataViewManager objects provide single or multiple views of a DataSet. You can attach a DataView or a DataViewManager directly to data-bound controls such as a DataGrid or a DataList. Other common components are DataTable, DataRow, DataColumn and so on. Now, I'll break down the ADO.NET model to show how it works.

Connection Object

The Connection object is the first component of ADO.NET that you should be looking at. A connection sets a link between a data source and ADO.NET. A Connection object sits between a data source and a DataAdapter (via Command). You need to define a data provider and a data source when you create a connection. With these two, you can also specify the user ID and password depending on the type of data source. Figure 3-3 shows the relationship between a connection, a data source, and a data adapter.

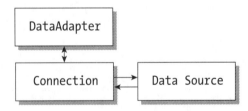

Figure 3-3. The relationship between Connection, DataAdpater, *and a data source*

Connection can also be connected to a Command object to execute SQL queries, which can be used to retrieve, add, update, and delete data to a data source. Figure 3-4 shows the relationship between the Command and Connection objects.

Figure 3-4. The relationship between the Command *object and* Connection *object*

The Connection object also plays a useful role in creating a *transaction*. Transactions are stored in Transaction objects, and Transaction classes have all those nice features for dealing with transactions such as commit and rollback. Figure 3-5 shows the relationship between the Connection object and transaction.

Figure 3-5. Creating a transaction from a Connection *object*

Each data provider has a Connection class. Table 3-1 shows the name of various connection classes for data providers.

Table 3-1. Data Provider Connection Classes

DATA PROVIDER	CONNECTION CLASS
OleDb	OleDbConnection
Sql	SqlConnection
ODBC	OdbcConnection

Command Object

The Command object can execute SQL queries and stored procedures. You can execute SQL queries to return data in a DataSet or a DataReader object. To retrieve, add, update, and delete data, you use SELECT, INSERT, UPDATE, and DELETE SQL queries. A DataAdapter generated using the VS .NET Integrated Development Environment (IDE) has these queries. Figure 3-6 shows the relationship between a DataAdapter and a Command object.

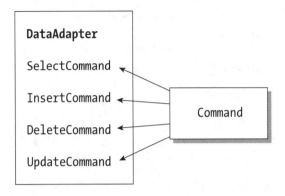

Figure 3-6. The relationship between DataAdapter *and* Command

Similar to the Connection class, each data provider has its own Command class. Table 3-2 describes command classes for .NET data providers.

Table 3-2. Data Provider Command Classes

DATA PROVIDER	COMMAND CLASS
OleDb	OleDbCommand
Sql	SqlCommand
ODBC	OdbcCommand

You call the ExecuteReader method of a Command object that executes the query and returns data in a DataReader object (see Figure 3-7).

Figure 3-7. Creating a DataReader *from a* Command *object*

The Command Builder

The SQL SELECT command is a fairly easy one to construct. Even if you don't know how to construct a SQL SELECT command, the Query Builder in Visual Studio helps you. But notice there are three other commands in Figure 3-6 to construct: InsertCommand, UpdateCommand, and DeleteCommand. These commands can get quite complicated in .NET because they require complex parameter objects and often involve large lists of columns. ADO.NET provides a nice utility known as the

CommandBuilder that automatically builds these commands for you. I'll talk about how to use this utility in Chapter 5. Figure 3-8 describes the relationship between CommandBuilder and DataAdapter. CommandBuilder is constructed with DataAdapter and immediately generates the remaining Command objects upon construction.

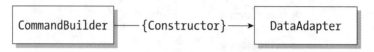

Figure 3-8. The relationship between DataAdapter *and* CommandBuilder *objects.*

The DataAdapter Object

The DataAdapter object serves as a conduit between the data source and the DataSet. The DataAdapter knows about the DataSet, and it knows how to populate it. The Adapter also knows about the connection to the data source. Figure 3-9 is a model that shows the simple relationship between the DataAdapter and the data source.

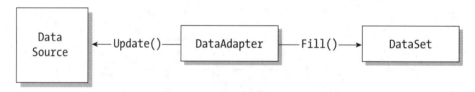

Figure 3-9. The relationship between DataAdapter *and* DataSet

As you can see from Figure 3-9, the Fill method of a DataAdapter fills data from a DataAdapter to the DataSet, and the UPDATE method makes DataSet changes to the final data source.

There is a DataAdapter available for each data provider. Table 3-3 describes data adapter classes for .NET data providers.

Table 3-3. Data Provider DataAdapter Classes

DATA PROVIDER	COMMAND CLASS
OleDb	OleDbDataAdapter
Sql	SqlDataAdapter
ODBC	OdbcDataAdapter

DataSet Structure

A DataSet object falls in disconnected components series. You can use it with or without data providers. The DataSet consists of a collection of tables, rows, columns, and relationships. Figure 3-10 illustrates these relationships, specifically that the DataSet contains a collection of DataTables and the DataTable contains a collection of DataRows, DataRelations, and DataColumns. A DataTable maps to a table in the database. The previous DataSet contains a DataTable that maps to the Orders table because you filled it with a SELECT query executed on the Orders table.

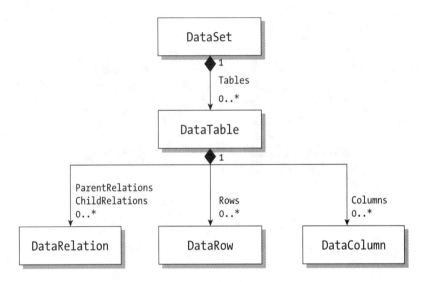

Figure 3-10. The relationship between classes in a DataSet

Well, now you see how you can look at your tables, but you still really haven't seen any hard data yet. The data in a DataSet is contained in the DataRow. A DataTable in the DataSet consists of a collection of DataRows. Each DataRow can be accessed via an index. The data in the column of the DataRow can be accessed by either an index or the column name. As you can see from Figure 3-10, a DataSet has a one-to-many relationship with DataTable. That means a DataSet can have one or more than one DataTable objects. Similarly, a DataTable can have one or more than one DataRelation, DataRow, and DataColumn objects.

DataSets in DataViews

Another thing you can do with the contents of your DataSet is sort and filter them using DataViews. You can have multiple views of a dataset. A DataView is a view of your data created according to certain criteria. Each DataView has a one-to-one mapping to a DataTable in a DataSet. For example, say you have three tables in a dataset: table1, table2, and table3. Using three different data tables and data views, you can represent this dataset in three different views. Using sort and filters, you can even sort and filter the data based on some criteria. Figure 3-11 shows three different views of a dataset in the form of three different data views.

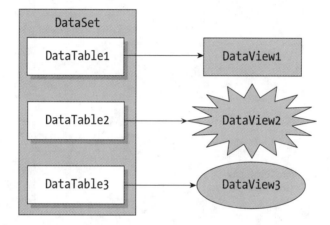

Figure 3-11. The relationship between DataSet *and* DataView *objects*

A data view can directly attach to data-bound controls such as a DataGrid, DataList, or a combo box. I'll cover this data binding in Chapter 4.

OK, enough theory. Now, you'll see how to write your first database application and get some hands-on experience with ADO.NET.

Writing ADO.NET Applications

It's now time to write your first ADO.NET application. In this section, I'll discuss the necessary steps required to write a database application using ADO.NET.

Choosing a .NET Data Provider

The first step is to decide what .NET data provider you will use in your application. As discussed in the previous section, there are many data providers that work with multiple data sources, including OleDb, Sql, and ODBC. You use OleDb data providers to access OLE-DB data sources. Sql data providers work with SQL Server 7.0 or later databases. The ODBC data providers work with ODBC data sources. You can also use more than one data provider to access the same database. For example, you can use OleDb and ODBC data providers to work with Microsoft Access databases.

I'm going to show you two sample applications. The first application uses OleDb data providers to access an Access 2000 database. The second application uses Sql data providers to access a SQL Server database.

Adding Namespace References

The second step is to add references to the assembly and include the name-spaces in your project. You can add references to the project using the Project ≻ Add Reference option. Figure 3-12 shows you how to add a reference to the System.Data.dll assembly. If you are compiling your program from the command line, you can add a reference to the assembly from the command line. I'll discuss this process in the following example.

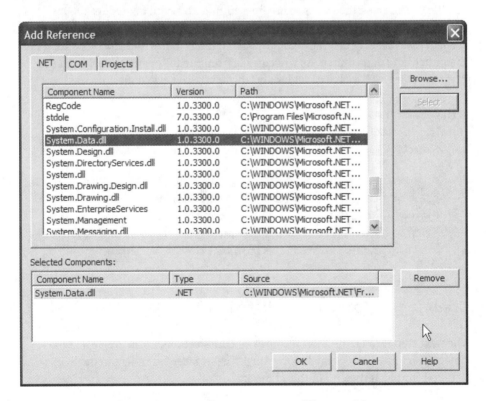

Figure 3-12. Adding a reference to the System.Data.dll *assembly*

After adding a reference to the assembly, you need to include namespaces in your project by using the using namespace. The following code shows how to include the System, System.Data, System.Data.Common, and System.Data.OleDb namespaces:

```
using System;
using System.Data;
using System.Data.Common;
using System.Data.OleDb;
```

> **NOTE** *If you are using Sql or ODBC data providers, you need to include the* System.Data.Sql *or the* Microsoft.Data.Odbc *namespaces.*

Establishing a Connection

Now, the next step is to create a Connection object. You create a Connection object using the data provider's Connection class. In the following code, you use the OleDbConnection class to create a connection with an Access 2000 database. The OleDbConnection constructor takes one parameter of a string type, connectionString, which has two parts. First, it has a provider, and second, it has the path of the data source. As you can see from the following code, I used the Microsoft.Jet.OLEDB.4.0 provider and the northwind.mdb data source:

```
string connectionString =
"Provider=Microsoft.JET.OLEDB.4.0; data source=C:\\Northwind.mdb";
OleDbConnection conn = new OleDbConnection(connectionString);
```

> **NOTE** *In this sample, the* northwind.mdb *database path is* "C:\\northwind.mdb". *You can use any database you want. You just need to change the path and name of the database and the table names you are using in SQL statements to access the data.*

Creating a Command or DataAdapter Object

The next step is to create a DataAdapter or Command object. You create a Command object by using OleDbCommand class. You'll see DataAdapter object in the SQL Server example at the end of this chapter.

The OleDbCommand constructor takes two parameters. The first is a SQL query, and the second is the Connection object. You create a SELECT SQL query from the Customers table in the Northwind database. The following code shows how to create a Command object:

```
// SELECT SQL Query
string sql = "SELECT CustomerID, ContactName, ContactTitle FROM Customers";

// Create a command object with the SELECT Query
OleDbCommand cmd = new OleDbCommand(sql, conn);
```

Filling Data to a DataSet or DataReader Object

The next step is to open the connection by calling the Open method of the Connection object and reading data from the Command object. The ExecuteReader method, OleDbCommand, returns data in an OleDbDataReader object. A DataReader object reads fast and forward only cached data. The following lines of code show this:

```
conn.Open();
OleDbDataReader reader;
reader = cmd.ExecuteReader();
```

Displaying Data

The next step is to do some operation on the data. In this example, you'll display data on the console. The Read method of OleDbDataReader reads data. The DataReader class has Getxxx methods, which return different types of data. The Getxxx methods take an index of the field you want to read data of. In the following code, you read data from two fields of the Customers table, whose indexes are 0 and 1:

```
while (reader.Read())
{
  Console.Write(reader.GetString(0).ToString() + " ," );
  Console.Write(reader.GetString(1).ToString() + " ," );
  Console.WriteLine("");
}
```

Closing the Connection

The last step is to close the reader and connection objects by calling their
Close methods:

```
reader.Close();
conn.Close();
```

Creating a Sample ADO.NET Application

Now, use all of the previous steps and write a console-based application to read
data and display it on the console. The code in Listing 3-1 reads data from the
Northwind database's Customers table and displays on the console. If you are
using Visual Studio .NET, create a console application by selecting Visual C#
Projects and then choosing the Console Application template from the Templates
listing (see Figure 3-13).

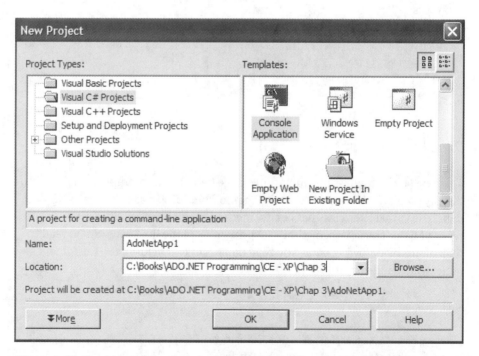

Figure 3-13. Creating a console-based application using the VS .NET IDE

After creating the project, add the Listing 3-1 source code to the project. If you are not using Visual Studio .NET, you can type the code in a text editor and save the file as AdoNetApp1.cs.

Listing 3-1. Your first ADO.NET application

```
using System;
using System.Data;
using System.Data.Common;
using System.Data.OleDb;

// First ADO.NET Application
// In this appication, I read data from Norhtwind database
// And display on the console.

namespace AdoNetApp1
{
    class AdoNetAppCls
    {
        static void Main(string[] args)
        {
            //  Form the connection string for an OleDb
            // Connection which contains the OLE-DB Provider
            // string for Access and the name of the Database,
            //  Northwind
            string connectionString = "Provider=Microsoft.JET.OLEDB.4.0;"
                +" data source=C:\\Northwind.mdb";

            //  Form the connection object to the Northwind
            // database, passing it the connection string
            OleDbConnection conn = new OleDbConnection(connectionString);

            // SELECT SQL Query
            string sql = "SELECT CustomerID, ContactName,"+
                "ContactTitle FROM Customers";

            // Create a command object with the SELECT Query
            OleDbCommand cmd = new OleDbCommand(sql, conn);

            // Open the connection to the Database
            conn.Open();

            // Create a data reader object and call
```

```
        // OleDbCommand.ExecuteReaderto return data in the reader
        OleDbDataReader reader;
        reader = cmd.ExecuteReader();

        // Display data
        Console.WriteLine("Contact Name, Contact Title");
        Console.WriteLine("=======================");

        // Read until reader has records
        while (reader.Read())
        {
            Console.Write(reader.GetString(0).ToString() + " ," );
            Console.Write(reader.GetString(1).ToString() + " ," );
            Console.WriteLine("");
        }

        // Close reader
        reader.Close();
        // Close the connection
        conn.Close();


    }
  }
}
```

Compiling C# from the Command Line

To compile the code you just examined, use the following compiler command at the command line:

```
csc.exe   ADONetApp1.cs   /r:System.Data.dll   /r:System.dll
```

> **NOTE** *You might need to supply* csc.exe *with the full path depending on the path of the .NET SDK installed on your machine.*

The output of Listing 3-1 looks like Figure 3-14.

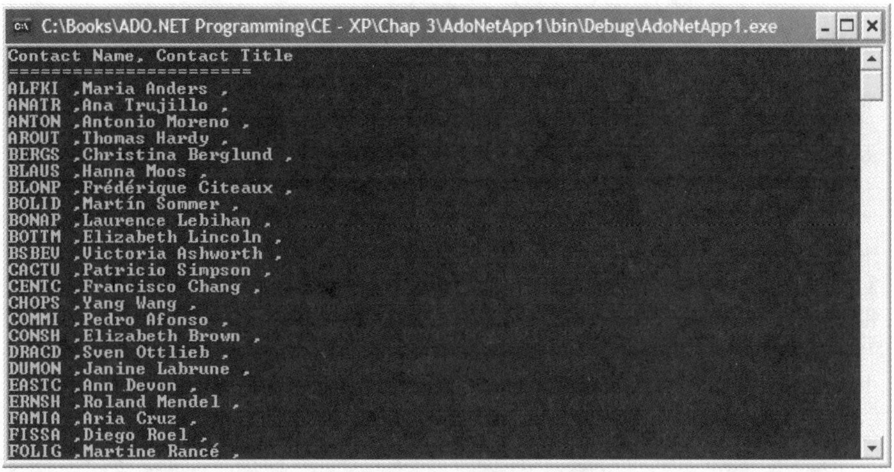

Figure 3-14. Output of your first ADO.NET application

Writing a Simple ADO.NET Program with Visual Studio .NET IDE

We just saw an example of working with an Access 2000 database. For variety, you'll see one example of a SQL Server database. In this example, you'll take a different approach. Instead of writing a console-based application, this time you'll create a Windows Forms application and use the VS .NET IDE.

This sample application uses the SQL Server Northwind database. You read data from the Customers table using the same CustomerId, ContactName, and ContactTitle columns selected in Listing 3-1.

Begin your first ADO.NET application by launching VS .NET and creating a new project using File ➢ New ➢ Project. Choose the C# Windows Application template shown in Figure 3-15 and type in your project's name.

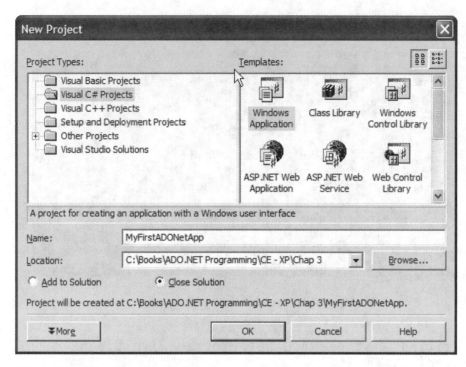

Figure 3-15. Creating a new C# Windows application

Displaying data in a DataGrid control is the simplest task. In this sample, you'll show the Customers table data in a DataGrid control.

Clicking OK brings up the blank Form View. Drag a DataGrid control from the Toolbox ➢ Window Forms onto the form and size it. Also drag a Button onto the form and assign it a Text property of Fill (see Figure 3-16).

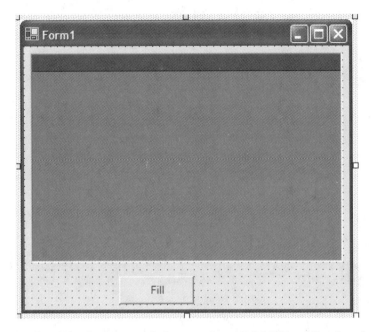

Figure 3-16. Windows form controls for your first ADO.NET application

Now you are ready to write some ADO.NET code. In the first example you'll fill your DataGrid using the SQL data provider. I'll discuss data providers in more detail in Chapter 5. This is certainly the most efficient choice of data providers for talking to a SQL Server database. First, you need to make sure you've imported all the proper namespaces for using ADO.NET and this particular data provider. This is the code you'll need at the top of the form code to bring in ADO.NET and the SQL Server data provider:

```
using System.Data;  // DataSet and related classes
using System.Data.SqlClient; // Sql Server Data Provider classes
```

Next, double-click on the Fill button to create the code for the event handler for this button. You'll implement your ADO.NET routine inside this method. In order to retrieve data from the database, you first need to connect to the database using a Connection object. The code in Listing 3-2 sets up the Connection object to the Northwind database. The server in this example is localhost.

Listing 3-2. Constructing the Sql Server `connection` *object*

```
private void button1_Click(object sender, System.EventArgs e)
{
        // Create a Connection Object
        string ConnectionString ="Integrated Security=SSPI;" +
                                  "Initial Catalog=Northwind;" +
                                  "Data Source=localhost;";

        SqlConnection myConnection = new SqlConnection();
        myConnection.ConnectionString = ConnectionString;
}
```

> **NOTE** *If you are using a remote server, then you need to pass the server name, user ID, and password in the connection string. I'll discuss this in Chapters 4 and 5.*

We have not yet connected to the database. This is done through the `SqlDataAdapter` object. The `DataAdapter` is the bridge between the data source (sql) and the `DataSet` (memory). The `DataAdapter` will be constructed with two elements in this example: a SQL `SELECT` command to tell the `DataAdapter` which data to extract into the `DataSet` and the `Connection` object to tell the `DataAdapter` how to connect to the data source. In this example, you select CustomerId, ContactName, and ContactTitle column data from the Customers table. The `DataAdapter` is constructed below in Listing 3-3. As you can see from Listing 3-3, the `sql` string is a `SELECT` statement. See Appendix B for how to construct `SELECT`, `INSERT`, `UPDATE`, and `DELETE` SQL statements.

Listing 3-3. Constructing the `DataAdapter`

```
// Creating a SQL string and data adapter object
string sql = "SELECT CustomerID, ContactName,
ContactTitle FROM Customers";
SqlDataAdapter myAdapter = new SqlDataAdapter(sql, myConnection);
```

Now you are ready to use the `DataAdapter` to transfer the desired data from the Customers table into a `DataSet`. To transfer the data, simply construct the `DataSet` and call the `Fill` method of the `DataAdapter` on the `DataSet` to fill it with the Orders table. See Listing 3-4.

Listing 3-4. Constructing the DataSet and filling it

```
// Creating a SQL string and data adapter object
 string sql = "SELECT CustomerID, ContactName, ContactTitle FROM Customers";
  SqlDataAdapter myAdapter = new SqlDataAdapter(sql, myConnection);

  // Construct the DataSet and fill it
 DataSet myDataSet = new DataSet("Customers");
 myAdapter.Fill(myDataSet, "Customers");
```

Finally, you want to display the data from the Customers table to the DataGrid control. You can do this by simply binding the DataSet to the DataGrid through its DefaultViewManager (I'll discuss DataViewManager in more detail in Chapter 5) by using DataGrid's DataSource property. You just set DataSource property of the DataSet's DefaultViewManager. For example:

```
// Bind the Listbox to the DataSet
dataGrid1.DataSource = myDataSet.DefaultViewManager;
```

The final listing of the event handler method looks like Listing 3-5.

Listing 3-5. Binding the DataSet to the ListBox control

```
private void button1_Click(object sender, System.EventArgs e)
 {
            // Create a Connection Object
            string ConnectionString ="Integrated Security=SSPI;" +
                                      "Initial Catalog=Northwind;" +
                                      "Data Source=localhost;";

            SqlConnection myConnection = new SqlConnection();
            myConnection.ConnectionString = ConnectionString;

            // Creating a SQL string and data adapter object
// Creating a SQL string and data adapter object
            string sql = "SELECT CustomerID, ContactName,"
                 +"ContactTitle FROM Customers";
SqlDataAdapter myAdapter = new SqlDataAdapter(sql, myConnection);

            // Construct the DataSet and fill it
            DataSet myDataSet = new DataSet("Customers");
            myAdapter.Fill(myDataSet, "Customers");
```

```
        // Bind the Listbox to the DataSet
        dataGrid1.DataSource = myDataSet.DefaultViewManager;
}
```

Now compile and run the project. Click the Fill button. The output of the program looks like Figure 3-17.

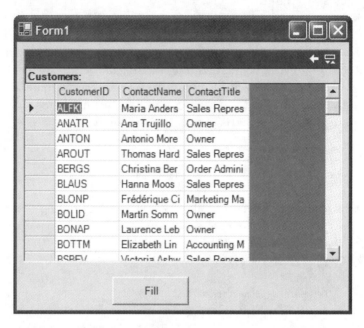

Figure 3-17. Output of ADO.NET application in a DataGrid control

CAUTION *Make sure your SQL Server is up and running. If SQL Server is not running, you'll get an exception looks like Figure 3-18.*

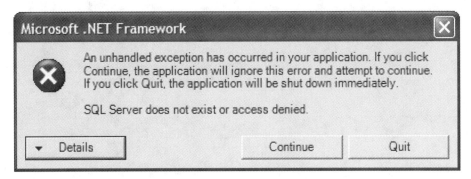

Figure 3-18. Exception when SQL Server is not running

Summary

This chapter introduced the basics of ADO.NET and its components. You learned why ADO.NET is a much better data access technology than previous technologies. ADO.NET provides data providers such as OleDb, Sql, and ODBC with the ability to work with OLE-DB, SQL Server, and ODBC data sources. ADO.NET classes come in three categories: disconnected, shared, and data providers. You can use disconnected classes with or without data providers. After that, you learned various ADO.NET objects such as Connection, Command, DataAdapter, DataReader, DataSet, and DataView as well as the relationships between them. For example, DataSet is a collection of DataTable objects. A DataTable can attach to a DataView, which can later be bound with data-bound controls. Using DataView's filter and sort properties, you can provide different views of a DataSet and DataView. At the end of this chapter, you saw how to write ADO.NET applications using VS .NET or using a text editor and compile your program from the command line.

Chapter 4 is heavily based on the VS .NET IDE. It'll cover how to take advantage of VS .NET IDE wizards and utilities to develop database applications without writing much code.

Data Components in Visual Studio .NET

IN PREVIOUS CHAPTERS, YOU'VE SEEN the basics of the ADO.NET model and its components. Visual Studio (VS) .NET provides design-time support to work with data components. In this chapter, you'll learn how to use these data components in VS .NET at design-time to create database applications. Using these components is similar to using any Windows control. You just drag the component to a form, set its properties and methods, and you're up and running.

In this chapter I'll start with the Server Explorer, a useful tool for database applications. I'll focus on developing database applications quickly, using data components in VS .NET without writing a lot of code. I'll also show you a step-by-step tutorial to help you develop and run a project. After that, I'll discuss data connection, data adapter, data command, dataset, and data view components in more detail. After finishing this chapter, you'll have a good understanding of data components and how to work with them in VS .NET.

Creating Your ADO.NET Project

Begin your project by launching VS .NET and choosing New ➤ Project from the Project menu. Choose Visual C# Projects from Project Types and then pick the Windows Application template. If you like, type an appropriate name into the Name field for your first ADO.NET application and click OK (see Figure 4-1).

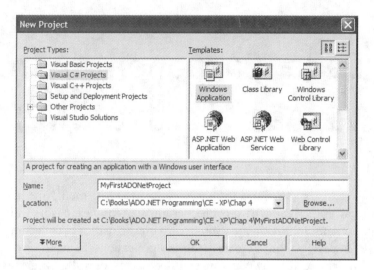

Figure 4-1. Creating a new project

Using the Server Explorer

The Server Explorer is new to Visual Studio .NET. You can open the Server Explorer by clicking the View ➤ Server Explorer menu item, as shown in Figure 4-2.

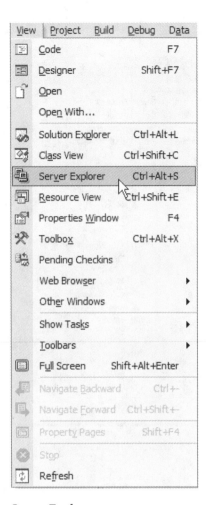

Figure 4-2. Opening the Server Explorer

The Server Explorer enables you to manage your database servers and connections. If you've ever used ODBC in your applications, then you're probably familiar with the traditional Windows ODBC Administration where you created data source names (DSNs) using ODBC drivers for a data source and then connected your application using this DSN.

Well, now you don't have to worry about it. You can use the Server Explorer to add a new server or a data connection to your list.

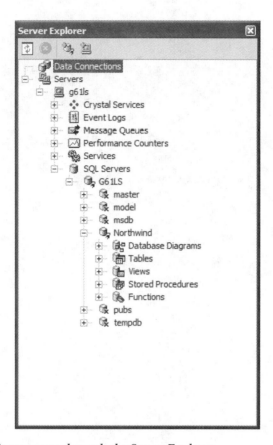

Figure 4-3. Adding a server through the Server Explorer

As you see in Figure 4-3, the Server Explorer has two root nodes: Data Connections and Servers. By right-clicking on these nodes you can add a new data connection or a new server to your list.

Specifically, to add a new server to the Server Explorer, you right-click on the Servers node, select the Add Server menu option, and enter the server name.

Adding a New Connection

Adding a new connection is the next step after adding a server (if you're using a server) to the Server Explorer. You add a new connection to your list by right-clicking on the Data Connections tree item and choosing the Add Connection option. This brings up a Data Link Properties Wizard. The first tab of this wizard, Provider, displays all the data source providers installed on your machine; this is where you select your database provider. The list could contain any OLE-DB provider, Jet OLD-DB, or other data driver available on your computer. Figure 4-4 shows you a list of providers on my machine.

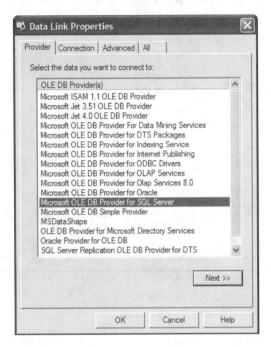

Figure 4-4. Choosing a data provider

The second tab of this wizard, Connection, lets you pick your server and corresponding data source. The drop-down list displays all the available servers. My server is a SQL Server with the default name localhost. After selecting a server, the database drop-down list displays all the available databases on the server. I'll select the Northwind database in this example. By clicking the Test Connection button, you can make sure your database connection is working. If you've provided a wrong user ID or password, the test will throw an error (see Figure 4-5).

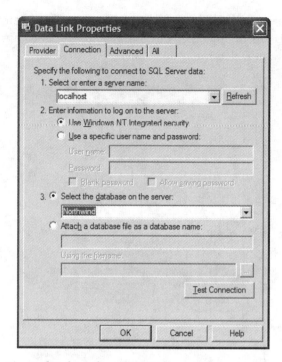

Figure 4-5. Selecting a database from SQL Server

The third tab, Advanced, is for setting connection timeout and access permissions. You can give this connection read, write, or other permissions using the Advanced tab (see Figure 4-6).

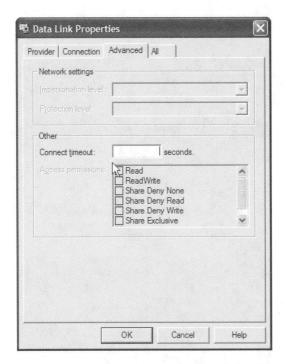

Figure 4-6. Additional options such as permissions and the connection timeout period

Managing and Viewing Data

The Server Explorer not only lets you add server and database connections, it also lets you manage and view data. You can add, update, and delete data from a database. The Server Explorer also provides options to create new databases and objects, including tables, views, stored procedures, and so on.

The Server Explorer manages database objects in a tree structure. Each database is a tree node of the server. As you expand the Northwind database node, you can see its children listed as tables, stored procedures, and views (see Figure 4-7).

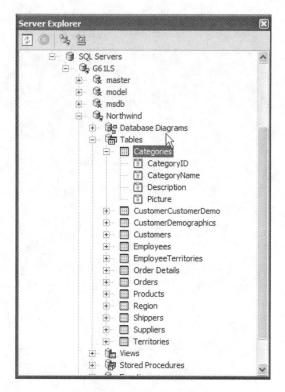

Figure 4-7. The Server Explorer with database tables

If you expand this connection by double-clicking on it, you'll notice it shows tables, views, and stored procedures. You can further expand these to see them in more detail.

Besides showing a list of database objects such as tables, views, stored procedures, and functions, the Server Explorer also lets you view, add, edit, and delete data from a data source. Figure 4-8 shows the Employees table of the Northwind database in the Server Explorer. In Figure 4-8, you see the data in a grid. You can edit this data at any time. For example, to delete a row or a collection of rows, select the rows and hit Delete, or right-click on the selected rows and hit the Delete option. The right-click option of the grid also provides you options to move to the grid's first, next, previous, and last records.

Form1.cs [Design]*	dbo.Employees...1LS.Northwind)					
EmployeeID	LastName	FirstName	Title	TitleOfCourtesy	BirthDate	HireDate
1	Davolio	Nancy	Sales Representati'	Ms.	12/8/1948	5/1/1992
2	Fuller	Andrew	Vice President, Sale	Dr.	2/19/1952	8/14/1992
3	Leverling	Janet	Sales Representati'	Ms.	8/30/1963	4/1/1992
4	Peacock	Margaret	Sales Representati'	Mrs.	9/19/1937	5/3/1993
5	Buchanan	Steven	Sales Manager	Mr.	3/4/1955	10/17/1993
6	Suyama	Michael	Sales Representati'	Mr.	7/2/1963	10/17/1993
7	King	Robert	Sales Representati'	Mr.	5/29/1960	1/2/1994
8	Callahan	Laura	Inside Sales Coo'di	Ms.	1/9/1958	3/5/1994
9	Dodsworth	Anne	Sales Representati'	Ms.	1/27/1966	11/15/1994

Figure 4-8. The Employee table in the Server Explorer

You can also right-click on a table and choose Retrieve Data from Table to retrieve data of that table, as shown in Figure 4-9.

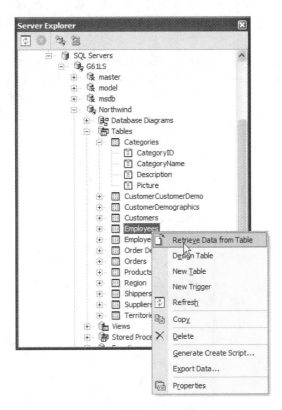

Figure 4-9. Retrieving data from a table in the Server Explorer

Using Visual Data Components

As mentioned in Chapter 2, "Introduction to Windows Forms," Microsoft .NET provides many data providers to work with different types of data sources. The class hierarchy model of these data providers remains the same, so programmers won't have any problem switching between data providers. Some of these data providers are OleDb, Sql, and Odbc. The Odbc data provider was a new addition to the .NET Framework (added after .NET Beta 2). If you don't have Odbc data providers available in your namespaces, you can install the Odbc data provider by installing Odbc .NET Software Development Kit (SDK) from the Microsoft site (http://msdn.microsoft.com/data/).

> **NOTE**   *This location may change. You can always find the updated URL in the downloads section (http://www.c-sharpcorner.com/downloads.asp) of C# Corner.*

If you're not sure, you can check the toolbox to see if you have an Odbc data provider already installed. The toolbox's Data tab shows you the available data controls in Visual Studio. These components are DataSet, DataView, SqlConnection, SqlCommand, SqlDataAdapter, OleDbConnection, OleDbCommand, and OleDbDataAdapter (see Figure 4-10).

Figure 4-10. Data components

With the OleDb and Sql data components, if you also see ODBC components, then you already have the Odbc data provider installed. Otherwise, you have to install the Odbc data provider. After installing ODBC .NET SDK, you need to go your toolbox to see the ODBC data components. After installing the ODBC .NET SDK, right-click on the toolbox and select Customize Toolbox (see Figure 4-11).

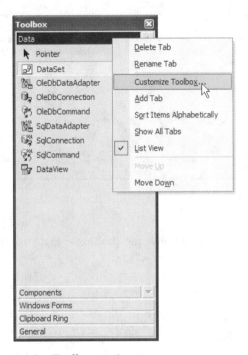

Figure 4-11. The Customize Toolbox option

Now, you'll notice a list of Component Object Model (COM) components and .NET Framework components (see Figure 4-12). Click on the .NET Framework Components tab and select the OdbcCommand, OdbcConnection, OdbcCommandBuilder, and OdbcDataAdapter components. If these components don't show up in the tab, then you need to browse for the component using the Browse button. You can usually find the ODBC components stored as \Program Files\Microsoft.NET\Odbc.NET\Microsoft.Data.Odbc.dll.

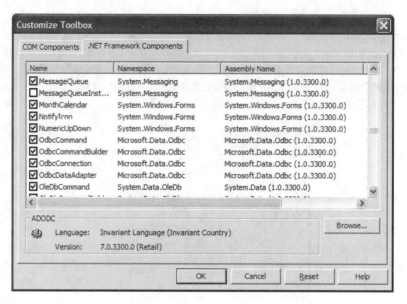

Figure 4-12. ODBC data components

After clicking the OK button, use the Toolbox ➤ Data option to see your
ODBC data components (see Figure 4-13).

> **NOTE** *If you don't see this file in your Microsoft .Net directory, the
> ODBC.NET SDK may not have installed on your machine. Try reinstalling it.*

Figure 4-13. Viewing your ODBC data components in the toolbox

As mentioned briefly in Chapter 3, "Overview of ADO.NET," the .NET Framework Library contains many ADO.NET data providers, including OleDb, Sql, and Odbc. The OleDb data provider wraps up native OLE-DB COM API to work with OLE-DB data sources. To access an OLE-DB data source, you need to install an OLE-DB data provider for that database. Sql data providers work with SQL Server 7 or later databases. Odbc data providers wrap up the ODBC API to work with ODBC data sources (with the help of ODBC Admin and ODBC drivers). Chapter 5 discusses these data providers in more detail. You can even create your own custom data providers. Microsoft and other vendors might add more data providers, which can be added to the library later.

In the .NET Framework, each of these data providers has its own name-spaces. For instance, the `System.Data.OleDb` namespace consists of classes belonging to the OleDb data providers. All of these namespace classes start with `OleDb`. The `System.Data.ODBC` and `System.Data.SqlClient` namespaces consist of classes belonging to the Odbc and Sql data providers, respectively. Similar to OleDb, classes in Odbc start with `Odbc`, and classes in SqlClient start with `Sql`.

In Visual C#, some of these classes (or objects) are available from the toolbox; you can add them to a form using drag-drop operation as any other Windows control in the toolbox. These controls are *data components*.

All of these types of components work in pretty much the same way except for the `Connection` component, whose connection string will vary based on the data source to which you're connecting.

> **NOTE**   *In the next section, I'll discuss how you can add these components to your Window Forms applications and set their properties and methods at design-time with the help of the .NET wizards.*

VS .NET also provides a set of data-bound controls. DataGrid, ListBox, and DataList are good examples of some of these data-bound controls. It's fairly easy to work with these controls. You just set a few properties, and they're ready to display your data. For example, setting a DataGrid control's DataSource property displays data from a DataSet object. You'll see these controls in the examples throughout this chapter.

Understanding Data Connections

To connect to a data source, the first thing you need to learn about is a *data connection.*

Each data provider has a connection class, and if you're using VS .NET, you can see these class objects as components in the Toolbox ➢ Data tab. For example, the SqlConnection, OdbcConnection, and OleDbConnection class objects represent a connection for the Sql, Odbc, and OleDb data providers, respectively. See the following:

- SqlConnection creates and manages SQL Server database connections.

- OdbcConnection creates and manages connections to ODBC data sources.

- OleDbConnection creates and manages connections to an OLE-DB data sources.

In VS .NET, you can create a connection component in many ways. You can use the IDE to add a connection object to a project, create it programmatically, or use data adapters that automatically create a connection object for you. In this chapter, we'll be concentrating on adding a connection through VS .NET.

The easiest way to add a connection to a project in VS .NET is to drag a connection component (SqlConnection, OleDbConnection, or OdbcConnection) from the toolbox's Data tab. This action adds a connection object to your project. After that, you can set the connection's properties using the Properties windows. For this demonstration, I'll drop a SqlConnection from the toolbox onto the form. Figure 4-14 shows the Properties window displayed after creating the SqlConnection. Note that the default connection name is the class name with a unique number appended to it. Because this is the first `Connection` object, the connection is `sqlConnection1`.

Figure 4-14. The `SqlConnection` *component's properties*

As you can see from the Properties window in Figure 4-14, a connection's properties include `Database`, `ConnectionTimeout`, `DataSource`, `PacketSize`, `WorkstationId`, `Name`, and `ConnectionString`.

> **NOTE** *The connection properties depend on the data provider. Some properties may not be available for other data providers. For example, the* `WorkstationId` *property is available in Sql data providers but not in OleDb or ODBC data providers.*

Understanding Connection Strings

The `ConnectionString` property is the main property of a connection. By clicking the drop-down list of the `ConnectionString` property, you can see all the available data connections. If you don't have a data connection, you can use its New Connection option (see Figure 4-15), which launches the Data Link Properties Wizard. Refer to the previous "Using the Server Explorer" section.

Figure 4-15. ConnectionString *property options*

After choosing the New Connection option and launching the Data Link
Properties Wizard, you choose a server in the Connection tab. On my machine,
the SQL Server's name is G61LS, the user ID and password aren't entered because
I'm using Windows NT Integrated Security. You need to enter your server name
(or select from the drop-down list), and enter your user ID and password if you're
not using Windows NT Integrated Security option (see Figure 4-16).

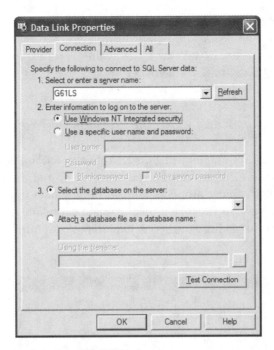

Figure 4-16. Data Link Properties Wizard

The SQLConnection string looks like following:

```
"data source=MCB;initial catalog=Northwind;persist security info=False;"+
"user id=sa;workstation id=MCB;packet size=4096"
```

> **NOTE** *In Chapter 5, I'll discuss a connection and its properties in more detail and show how to set them programmatically.*

Working with SQL Data Adapters

A *data adapter* is another important component of a data provider. Similar to the connection, each data provider has a corresponding data adapter class. All data adapters in ADO.NET work in the same way, which means if you know how to work with Sql data adapters, you can use OleDb, ODBC, and other data adapters easily. The SqlDataAdapter, OleDbDataAdapter, and OdbcDataAdaper classes represent data adapter components in Sql, OleDb, and ODBC data providers, respectively. Besides creating a data adapter programmatically (see Chapter 5 for more details), VS .NET provides you with various ways to create data adapters. Two common ways are by using the Server Explorer and by using the Data Adapter Configuration Wizard.

Creating Data Adapters with the Server Explorer

It's easy to create a data adapter using the Server Explorer. You just drag and drop database objects to a form, and the IDE takes care of everything for you. The IDE writes code that you can use programmatically or bind data controls at design-time. To add a new connection to a project, expand your database in the Server Explorer and drag a table from the Server Explorer to your form (see Figure 4-17).

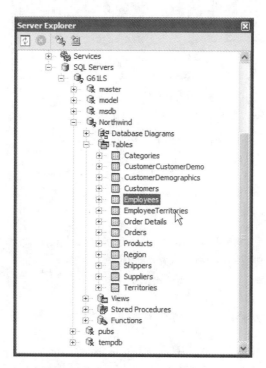

Figure 4-17. Creating an adapter using the Server Explorer

This action creates a connection and a data adapter. You can even drag selected columns or stored procedures on the form. VS .NET takes care of the rest. Right-click on the form and choose View Code to examine the code generated by the wizard; in this example, you'll see one SqlConnection component and one SqlDataAdapter component along with a set of SqlCommand components:

```
private System.Data.SqlClient.SqlConnection sqlConnection1;
private System.Data.SqlClient.SqlDataAdapter sqlDataAdapter1;
 private System.Data.SqlClient.SqlCommand sqlSelectCommand1;
 private System.Data.SqlClient.SqlCommand sqlInsertCommand1;
 private System.Data.SqlClient.SqlCommand sqlUpdateCommand1;
 private System.Data.SqlClient.SqlCommand sqlDeleteCommand1;
```

Once you have a DataAdapter, you can use it to populate datasets and work with its properties. We'll discuss DataSet basics and how to construct them manually in Chapter 5 in more detail. With VS .NET, you can even generate datasets using the visual representation of the DataAdapter. We'll discuss how to populate a DataSet using VS .NET IDE wizards in the "Generating Typed DataSets Using Data Adapter" section of this chapter.

Creating Data Adapters with the Data Adapter Configuration Wizard

The Data Adapter Configuration Wizard is a powerful tool to develop database applications. To see how you can create data adapters using the this wizard, you'll create a new Window Forms–based sample project.

In this first sample project, I'll show you how to create SQL data adapters, read data from a SQL Server data source, and display the data from a data adapter to a DataGrid control. Just follow the following simple steps in the next several sections. After completing these steps, you'll see how easy it is to develop database applications using the Data Adapter Configuration Wizard.

Step 1: Selecting a Project Template

First, create a Windows Application template as you did at the beginning of the chapter (see Figure 4-18).

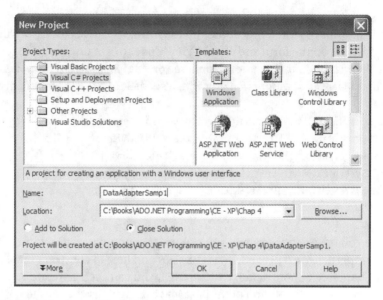

Figure 4-18. Creating a Windows Application project

Step 2: *Adding a DataGrid Control to the Form*

Now add a DataGrid control to the form by dragging a DataGrid control from the Toolbox ➤ Windows Forms category to the form.

Step 3: *Adding a Data Adapter Component*

Next, drag a SqlDataAdapter control from the Toolbox ➤ Data category to the form. As you drop the data adapter (Sql, OleDb, or ODBC), the Data Adapter Configuration Wizard pops up.

Welcome Page

The first page of this wizard is just a welcome screen (see Figure 4-19).

Figure 4-19. The Data Adapter Configuration Wizard welcome screen

Choose Your Data Connection Page

The second page of the wizard lets you create a new connection or pick from a list of available connections on your machine. In this example, I'm using the default Northwind SQL Server database that comes with Visual Studio. As you can see in Figure 4-20, the Northwind connection is available in the list. Don't confuse it with G61LS, which is specific to my machine name. This name will be different for different machines. If you don't have any connection listed, you can use the New Connection button, which launches the Data Link Properties Wizard (discussed in the "Connection Strings" section).

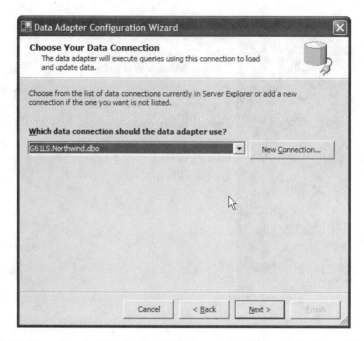

Figure 4-20. Choosing the Northwind SQL Server database in the Data Adapter Configuration Wizard

Choose a Query Type

The next page of the wizard is for command set types. A command set could consist of a SQL statement or a new or already existing stored procedure (see Figure 4-21).

Figure 4-21. Choosing a query type in the Data Adapter Configuration Wizard

Generate the SQL Statement

The next page of the Data Adapter Configuration Wizard lets you build a SQL statement or a stored procedure (see Figure 4-22).

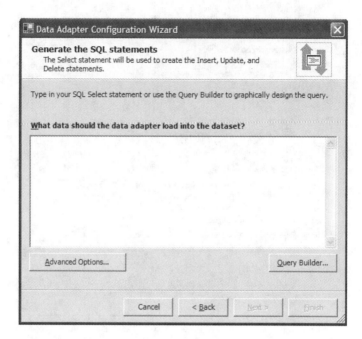

Figure 4-22. Creating a Select *statement through the Data Adapter Configuration Wizard*

Query Builder

The Query Builder option lets you pick tables from your data source. First, select the Employees table to read in the Employee data. You actually have the option of selecting as many tables as you want, but for now select only one table (see Figure 4-23) and click the Add button.

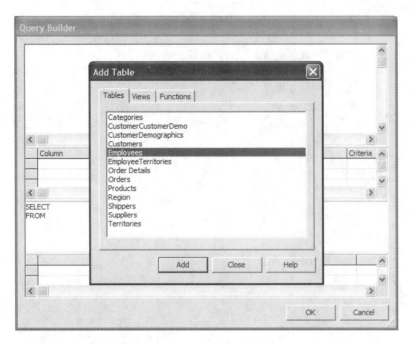

Figure 4-23. The Query Builder

If you've ever used Microsoft Access, you'll find that the Query Builder is similar to it. In Access, you can create queries by dragging tables and their columns to the grid (or checking the columns), and the Query Builder builds a SQL query for your action. In this sample, I'll select EmployeeID, FirstName, and LastName from the Employees table to build our SQL statements (see Figure 4-24).

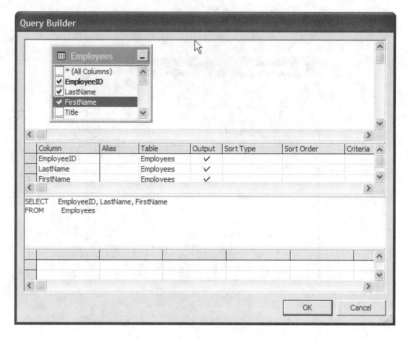

Figure 4-24. Building columns in the query

Now, I'll select three columns from the Employees table. The result looks like Figure 4-25.

Figure 4-25. The Query Builder selection

> **NOTE**   *You can even write your own SQL statement if you don't want to use the Query Builder. For performance reasons, if you only want a few columns, then use column names instead of using* SELECT * *statements.*

View Wizard Results

The View Wizard Results page shows you the action being taken by the wizard; in this example, it was successful. The Details section shows that the wizard has generated SQL Select, Insert, Update, and Delete statements and mappings (see Figure 4-26).

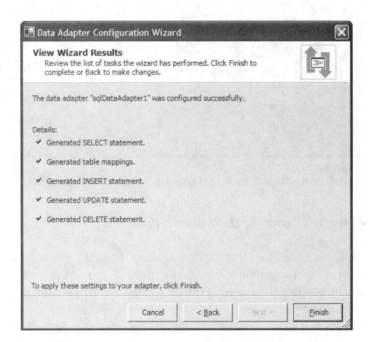

Figure 4-26. The View Wizard Results page

Now you can click the Finish button to complete the process.

Now, if you examine the form in Figure 4-27, you'll see two components: sqlConnection1 and sqlDataAdapter1. The wizard sets the properties of these components for you. Now you can use the data adapter to populate your datasets. Don't forget to resize the DataGrid you added to the project.

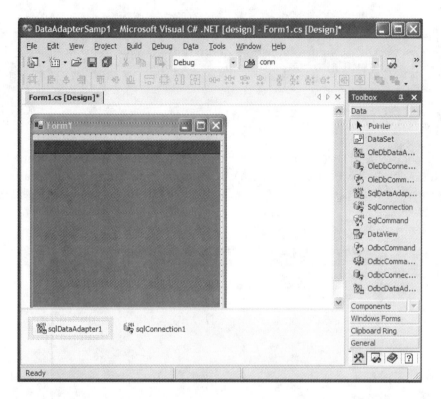

Figure 4-27. SqlConnection *and* SqlDataAdapter *shown in the form designer*

Step 4: Setting and Reviewing Data Adapter Properties

OK, now that you have a DataAdapter on your form, let's take a look at the SqlDataAdapter component properties. You can see its properties by right-clicking on the adapter and selecting the Properties menu item. The Properties window looks like Figure 4-28.

The wizard also shows the available command properties, including InsertCommand, DeleteCommand, SelectCommand, and UpdateCommand (see Figure 4-28).

Figure 4-28. The data adapter in the Properties window

You can set `DataAdapter` properties by clicking on these properties.
`SqlCommand` and `TableMappings`, for example, are important properties.
A data adapter has four `SqlCommand` properties—`SelectCommand`, `DeleteCommand`,
`InsertCommand`, and `UpdateCommand`—that all execute SQL commands on the
data source. For example, if you look at the `SelectCommand` property in
Figure 4-29, you'll see the SQL `Select` statement.

> **NOTE** *Chapter 5 covers* `SelectCommand`, `InsertCommand`, `UpdateCommand`,
> *and* `DeleteCommand` *in more detail.*

Figure 4-29. Setting the SQL SelectCommand *in the data adapter*

As you also see in Figure 4-29, you can set CommandText, CommandType, Connection, and so on using the Properties dialog box. If you double-click on CommandText, it pops up the Query Builder where you can rebuild your query (see Figure 4-30).

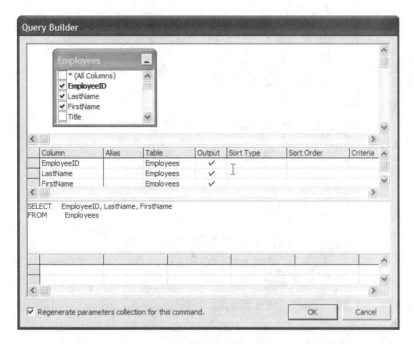

Figure 4-30. Relaunching the Query Builder from the CommandText *property*

The TableMapping class represents a mapping of DataColumns in the data source to DataColumns in the DataSet. I'll discuss DataTables and table mappings in more detail in Chapter 5. If you click on the TableMappings property (which is a collection of TableMapping objects), it brings up the Table Mappings dialog box.

As you can see from Figure 4-31, the Table Mapping dialog box has two columns: Source Table and Dataset Table. The Source Table column is a list of actual columns, and the Dataset Table column is a list of the column names used in the dataset. By default, dataset columns names are the same as the source table. This is useful when you want to use different names in a program. You can change dataset columns by editing the column itself. Of course, you can't change source columns, but you can reorder them by using the column drop-down list.

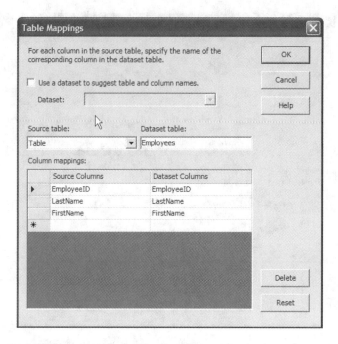

Figure 4-31. Table Mappings dialog box

By using this dialog box, you can even delete columns from your mapping using the Delete button.

Step 4: Reviewing Other Options

If you look closely at data adapter properties, you'll see three links: Configure Data Adapter, Generate Dataset, and Preview Data (see Figure 4-32).

The Configure Data Adapter option calls the Data Adapter Configuration Wizard, discussed earlier in this chapter. If you want to reset the wizard to change your options, you can use this link.

The Generate Dataset option lets you generate a dataset for this data adapter. I'll discuss how to generate datasets using data adapter properties in the "Working with OleDb Data Adapters" section of this chapter.

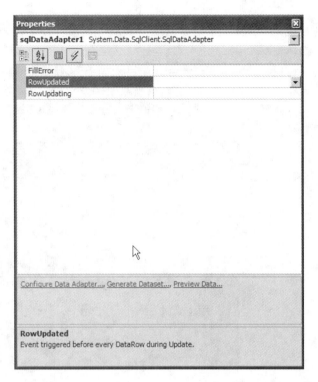

Figure 4-32. Data Adapter option links

The Preview Data option enables you to view the DataSet schema. You can even preview the data in the DataSet by clicking the Fill button. The Data Adapter Preview dialog box looks like Figure 4-33.

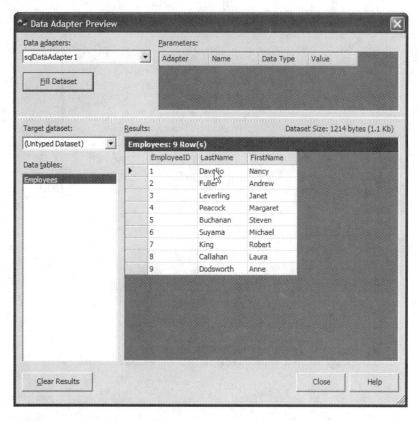

Figure 4-33. Previewing data for the data adapter

The Fill Dataset button in Figure 4-33 fills data into a grid based upon the current state of the SelectCommand in the DataAdapter.

Step 5: Reviewing the Source Code

Now it's time to examine the code and see what the wizard has done for you automatically. You can see the source code by right-clicking on the form and selecting the View Source option.

> **NOTE** *If you don't want to know what the wizard has automatically done for you, you can skip this step.*

All source code generated by the Windows form designer is defined in the InitializeComponent method of the file . Right-click on your form and choose View Code. Upon examining the source code, you'll see where the wizard has added two components, sqlConnection1 and sqlDataAdapter1, to your source file as well as four SqlCommand components. Scroll down to the Windows Designer Generated Code option and expand it. This will reveal the contents of the InitializeComponent routine (see Listing 4-1).

Listing 4-1. Added Sql Server provider components

```
namespace DataAdapterSamp1
{
    public class Form1 : System.Windows.Forms.Form
    {
        private System.Windows.Forms.DataGrid dataGrid1;
        private System.Data.SqlClient.SqlDataAdapter sqlDataAdapter1;
        private System.Data.SqlClient.SqlCommand sqlSelectCommand1;
        private System.Data.SqlClient.SqlCommand sqlInsertCommand1;
        private System.Data.SqlClient.SqlCommand sqlUpdateCommand1;
        private System.Data.SqlClient.SqlCommand sqlDeleteCommand1;
        private System.Data.SqlClient.SqlConnection sqlConnection1;
        // more Source code
        private void InitializeComponent()
        {
            this.dataGrid1 = new System.Windows.Forms.DataGrid();
            this.sqlDataAdapter1 = new System.Data.SqlClient.SqlDataAdapter();
            this.sqlSelectCommand1 = new System.Data.SqlClient.SqlCommand();
            this.sqlInsertCommand1 = new System.Data.SqlClient.SqlCommand();
            this.sqlUpdateCommand1 = new System.Data.SqlClient.SqlCommand();
            this.sqlDeleteCommand1 = new System.Data.SqlClient.SqlCommand();
            this.sqlConnection1 = new System.Data.SqlClient.SqlConnection();
...
// more code
...

    }
}
```

Do a search for the ConnectionString by hitting Ctrl+F to bring up the search dialog box. If you examine the InitializeComponent() method, you'll see that the wizard sets SqlConnection's ConnectionString property to the following:

```
this.sqlConnection1.ConnectionString = "data source=(local);initial catalog" +
"=Northwind;persist security info=False;user id" +
 "=mahesh;workstation id=7LJML01;packet size=4096";
```

It also sets the `CommandText` property of the `SqlCommand` with the corresponding `SELECT`, `INSERT`, `UPDATE`, and `DELETE` SQL statements. The `Connection` property of `SqlCommand` is set to `SqlConnection`:

```
this.sqlSelectCommand1.CommandText = "SELECT LastName, " +
 "EmployeeID, FirstName FROM Employees";
this.sqlSelectCommand1.Connection = this.sqlConnection1;
```

If you examine the Listing 4-2, you'll see that `DataAdapter` is connected to a `Connection` through data commands, and the `TableMapping` property is responsible for mapping tables and their columns. Note that the `TableMappings` between `DataSet` columns and `DataSource` columns generated by the wizard have exactly the same column names.

Listing 4-2. `DataAdapter` *connection through* `TableMapping`

```
private void InitializeComponent()
{
//
// some code here
//
this.sqlDataAdapter1.DeleteCommand = this.sqlDeleteCommand1;
this.sqlDataAdapter1.InsertCommand = this.sqlInsertCommand1;
this.sqlDataAdapter1.SelectCommand = this.sqlSelectCommand1;
Please break up code.
this.sqlDataAdapter1.TableMappings.AddRange
(new System.Data.Common.DataTableMapping[]
{new System.Data.Common.DataTableMapping
("Table", "Employees", new System.Data.Common.DataColumnMapping[]
{
    new System.Data.Common.DataColumnMapping("LastName", "LastName"),
    new System.Data.Common.DataColumnMapping("EmployeeID", "EmployeeID"),
    new System.Data.Common.DataColumnMapping("FirstName", "FirstName")})
 }
);
// . . . ..
//. . . . . ...
}
```

It looks like the wizard did a lot of the work for you!

Step 6: Filling the DataGrid Control with Data

Until now, you didn't have to write a single line of code. Now, though, you'll add a few lines of code and then you'll be all set to see the data from your data source. First, you'll create a method, `FillDBGrid`, which fills a `DataSet` object. Then you'll read data from a `DataSet` object and populate the DataGrid control.

The `Fill` method of `SqlDataAdapter` fills data from a data adapter to the `DataSet`. You call `Fill` method in `FillDBGrid` method. Once you have a `DataSet` containing data, you can do anything with it including creating views for that data. (I discussed multiple views of a `DataSet` object in the previous chapter.) In this example, you set a DataGrid control's `DataSource` property to the `DataSet.DefaultViewManager`, which binds the `DataSet` object to the DataGrid control (see Listing 4-3).

Listing 4-3. `FillDBGrid` *method*

```
private void FillDBGrid()
{
        DataSet ds = new DataSet();
        sqlDataAdapter1.Fill(ds);

        dataGrid1.DataSource = ds.DefaultViewManager;
}
```

Now you simply call `FillDBGrid` from the `Form1` constructor or the `Form_Load` event or from a button-click handler. In this example I'll call it from the form constructor just after the `InitializeComponent()` call, as you can see in Listing 4-4.

Listing 4-4. Calling the `FillDBGrid` *method from the* `Form1` *constructor*

```
public Form1()
{
    //
    // Required for Windows Form Designer support
    //
    InitializeComponent();
    FillDBGrid();
    //
    // TODO: Add any constructor code after InitializeComponent call
    //
}
```

Now build and run the project. The result looks like Figure 4-34. Easy, huh?

Figure 4-34. Output of the Employee data to a DataGrid control

Working with OleDb Data Adapters

In the previous section, I discussed Sql data adapters. Now, let's take a quick look at OleDb data adapters. Actually, all data adapters (Sql, OleDb, and ODBC) work exactly the same way. I'll take you through a quick step-by-step tutorial on how to use OldDb data adapters. To give you more of a variety, you're going to use OleDb with an Access 2000 database.

As you already know, the first step in working with ADO.NET is to add a new connection using the Server Explorer. For the purposes of consistency, I've used the Northwind Microsoft Access 2000 database for these examples. Feel free, however, to use any data source that has an OLE DB provider available on your machine.

In the Data Link Properties dialog box, choose the Microsoft Jet 4.0 OLD DB Provider (see Figure 4-35).

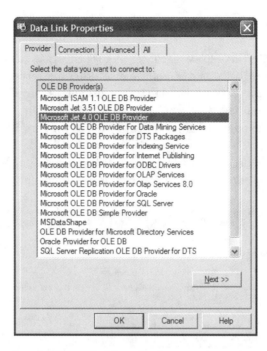

Figure 4-35. Choosing the OLE DB driver for Access

And the database is C:\Northwind.mdb, as you can see in Figure 4-36.

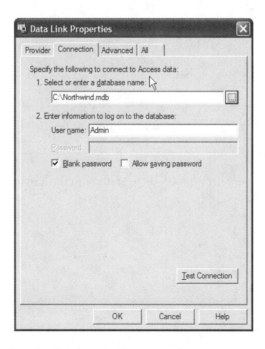

Figure 4-36. Choosing the database in Server Explorer

Adding an OleDbDataAdapter

Working with either an OleDbDataAdapter or an ODBCDataAdapter is the same as working with the SqlDataAdapter. You can use either the Server Explorer or the Data Adapter Configuration Wizard to create an OleDb data adapter. In this example, I'll use the Data Adapter Configuration Wizard. Drop an OleDbDataAdapter control from Toolbox ➤ Data to your application form. This action will bring up the Data Adapter Configuration Wizard.

On the second page of the wizard, Choose Your Data Connection, you can either create a new connection or pick an existing connection (see Figure 4-37).

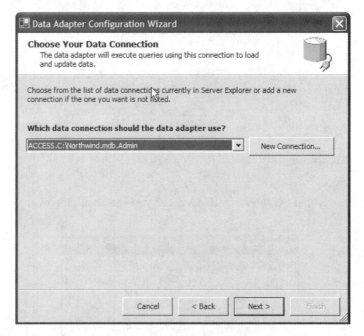

Figure 4-37. Configuring an OleDb data adapter for Access

On the next page, select the Use SQL Statement option and click the Next button (see Figure 4-38).

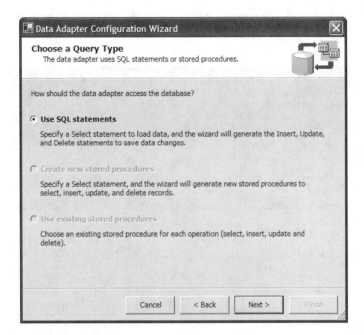

Figure 4-38. Choosing the query type in the Data Adapter Configuration Wizard

This will bring you to the Add Table selection page. As you can see from Figure 4-39, I'm picking the Orders table. Then, click the Add button.

Figure 4-39. Adding a table to the query in the Data Adapter Configuration Wizard

After clicking Add, the Query Builder brings up a table column selector, as shown in Figure 4.40.

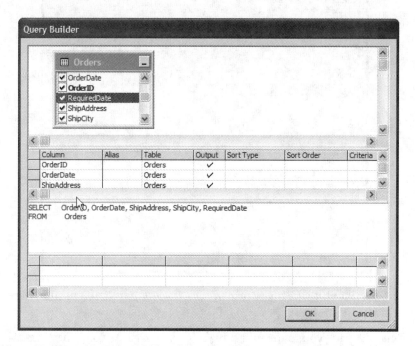

Figure 4-40. Choosing columns for the query in the Data Adapter Configuration Wizard

I chose OrderID, OrderDate, ShipAddress, ShipCity, and RequiredDate for my query by checking the columns in the Orders window. This builds the query shown in the third pane of the Query Builder. Clicking OK displays the final query, as shown in Figure 4-41.

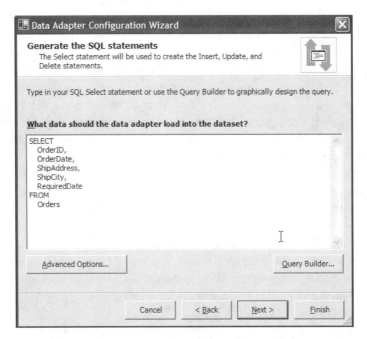

Figure 4-41. Generating the SQL statements in the Data Adapter Configuration Wizard

Clicking on the Advanced Options button brings up the Advanced SQL Generation Options dialog box, as shown in Figure 4-42.

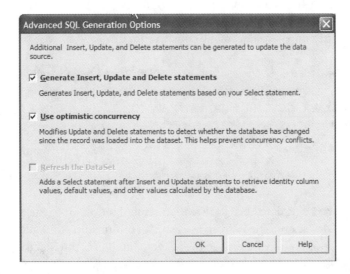

Figure 4-42. Advanced options in the Data Adapter Configuration Wizard

In this dialog box you can opt not to generate INSERT, UPDATE, or DELETE statements by turning off the first option. This is useful if you're planning on only reading the database and don't want all this extraneous code generated.

The second option, Use Optimistic Concurrency, causes the wizard to use optimistic concurrency. Optimistic concurrency checks to see if the row being updated in the database has already been changed by someone else during the update process. The data provider manages this by using a WHERE clause in the UPDATE statement that checks for the original data in the dataset. If it doesn't find the original data, it won't update the data source. A data provider maintains two sets of parameters: one with the original data and one with the current data. The current data parameters work in the UPDATE statement (this is the data you're trying to update the database with), and the original data parameters work in the WHERE clause (these parameters are the check to make sure the database hasn't been updated). If you turn off the Use Optimistic Concurrency option, the WHERE clause only contains the primary key and no original parameter data is generated. You can probably turn this off to speed things up if the application is only for a single user. Below are the differences between the Select statements generated with optimistic concurrency on and off.

This is the code with optimistic concurrency turned off:

```
dateCommand1.CommandText = @"UPDATE Orders SET OrderDate = ?,"+
"RequiredDate = ?, ShipAddress = ?, ShipCity = ? WHERE (OrderID = ?)"+
"AND (OrderDate = ? OR ? IS NULL AND OrderDate IS NULL) AND "+
"(RequiredDate = ? OR ? IS NULL AND RequiredDate IS NULL) AND "+
"(ShipAddress = ? OR ? IS NULL AND ShipAddress IS NULL) AND "+
"(ShipCity = ? OR ? IS NULL AND ShipCity IS NULL)";
```

This is the code with optimistic concurrency on:

```
this.oleDbUpdateCommand1.CommandText = @"UPDATE Orders SET OrderID = ?,"+
"OrderDate = ?, RequiredDate = ?, ShipAddress = ?, ShipCity = ?"+
"WHERE (OrderID = ?) AND (OrderDate = ?) AND (RequiredDate = ?)"+
"AND (ShipAddress = ?) AND (ShipCity = ?)" ;

"SELECT OrderID, OrderDate, RequiredDate, ShipAddress,"+
"ShipCity FROM Orders WHERE (OrderID = ?)";
```

You may also notice the SQL Select statement tacked onto the end of the SQL UPDATE statement. The Refresh the DataSet option adds this statement. Turning this option off will remove the Select statement. You had to uncheck this for the OleDb adapter or else Insert and Update don't work. This isn't true, however, for the SqlServer adapter.

Clicking Next brings up the results screen. As you can see in Figure 4-43, the Data Adapter Configuration Wizard has done quite a bit of work! It's generated all of the commands for the adapter, all of the mappings, and, although not indicated, all of the parameters.

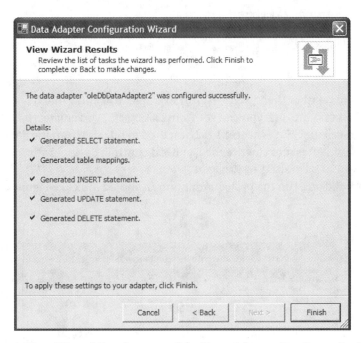

Figure 4-43. View Wizard Results page of the Data Adapter Configuration Wizard

If you examine the form designer, you'll see the wizard added two components to your form: `oleDbConnection1` and `oleDbDataAdapter1`. The source code generated by the wizard is similar to the source generated for the `SqlDataAdapter`. You'll notice differences, though, in the `ConnectionString` and the parameters if you were to go through the same process with a `SqlDataAdapter`. The `OdbcDataAdapter` will also generate similar code.

Populating DataSet and Filling the DataGrid

Now, to test whether everything went fine, create a Windows Forms application and add an `OleDataAdapter` using the previous steps. Then, add a DataGrid control to the form, as well as all the code listed in Listing 4-5 on the `Form_Load` event or a button-click handler.

Listing 4-5. Adding the code on the Form_Load *event*

```
private void Form1_Load(object sender, System.EventArgs e)
{
    DataSet ds = new DataSet();
        // Populate DataSet by calling Fill method
        oleDbDataAdapter1.Fill(ds);
        // Set DataGrid's DataSource property
        dataGrid1.DataSource = ds.DefaultViewManager;
}
```

If you remember the SqlDataAdapter example, you know that it contained almost the same code. As you can see from Listing 4-5, you create a DataSet object and call OleDbDataAdapter's Fill method to fill data from the data adapter to the dataset. After that you use the DataGrid control's DataSource property and set it as DataSet's DefaultViewManager.

Now build and run the project. Your output should look like Figure 4-44.

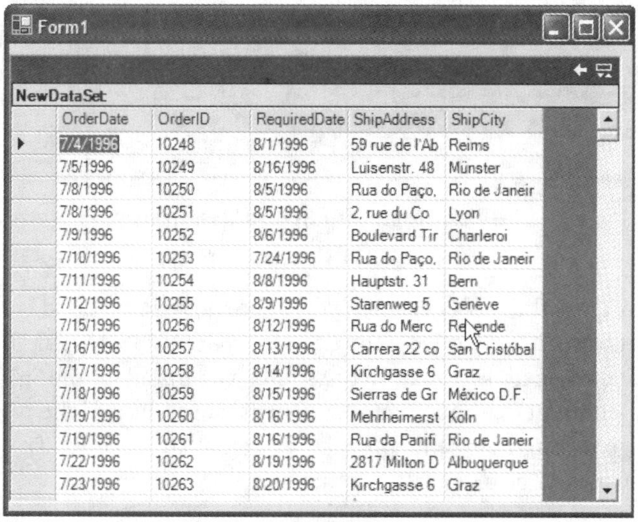

Figure 4-44. Filling a DataGrid with the Orders table

Using DataSet and DataView Components

After discussing data adapters and data connections, you got a pretty good idea of how to take advantage of VS .NET design-time support to develop data-bound Windows Form database applications.

The DataSet and DataView components are two powerful and easy-to-use components of the ADO.NET model. In this section, you'll see how to utilize DataSet and DataView components at design-time. In Chapter 5, I'll discuss their properties and methods in more detail and show how to use them programmatically. The DataSet and DataView components fall in the *disconnected* components category, which means you can use these components with or without data providers. I'll discuss connected and disconnected data components in Chapter 5 in more detail. These components work in the same way for all data providers, including Sql, OleDb, and Odbc.

Understanding Typed DataSets in Visual Studio .NET

There are two types of datasets: typed datasets and untyped datasets. As discussed in Chapter 3 (and in more detail in Chapter 5), a typed dataset has an XML schema attached to it. The XML schema defines members for a dataset corresponding to database table columns, and you can access data through these columns. Untyped datasets are ones that are created at run-time and don't have an schema attached to them. I'll now show you how you can generate typed datasets using a VS .NET wizard.

Generating Typed DataSets Using Data Adapters

You can generate typed datasets by using any of the data adapters. You can either generate a dataset by right-clicking on a data adapter and selecting the Generate Dataset menu option or by using the data adapter Properties windows. To generate a dataset from data adapter's Properties window, choose the Generate Dataset hyperlink, which generates a DataSet object, and the wizard writes the code for you (see Figure 4-45).

Figure 4-45. Generating a typed dataset from the Properties window

This action pops up a dialog box, which generates a dataset. Type your dataset name and click OK (see Figure 4-46).

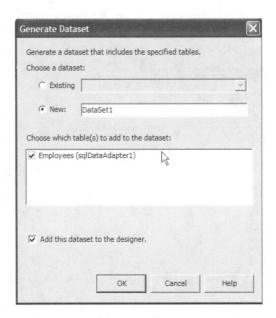

Figure 4-46. Dialog box for generating a dataset

This action adds a dataset (if you check Add This Dataset to the Designer check box) and pops up the dataset Properties dialog box (see Figure 4-47).

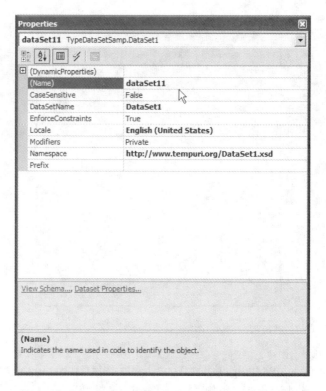

Figure 4-47. A dataset's Properties window showing a typed dataset

Every dataset generated by the IDE creates an XML schema for the dataset. Figure 4-47 provides you with two hyperlinks at the bottom of the dialog: View Schema and DataSet Properties. View Schema lets you view the DataSet schema, and the DataSet Properties hyperlink lets you set the DataSet properties. By following these links you can set the DataSet's column names and other properties (see Figure 4-48).

Figure 4-48. Setting DataSet *names and additional properties*

This action also adds one class inherited from a DataSet and one XML schema (DataSet1.xsd). The Class View of the DataSet is a derived class and looks like Figure 4-49.

Figure 4-49. A VS .NET–generated typed DataSet *class*

You can now create an instance of this class instead of creating a DataSet programmatically. This class has a member corresponding to each column of the table to which it's attached:

```
MyDataSet ds = new MyDataSet();
```

The beauty of typed datasets is that you can access the data in the columns using MyDataSet object members.

Besides creating a DataSet using the Data Adapter Configuration Wizard, there is another good way to do so. I'll discuss this alternate solution in the following section.

Adding Typed DataSets

In the previous discussion, you saw how you can generate DataSet objects from a data adapter. There are other ways to create a typed DataSet object.

You can click on the Project menu and choose Add New Item (or click Ctrl+D). This brings up the Add New Item window where you'll find the Data Set template (see Figure 4-50).

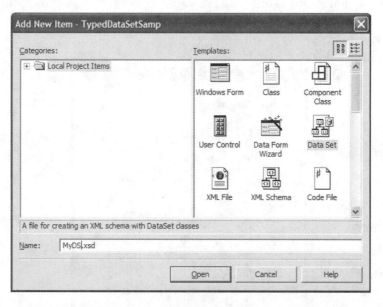

Figure 4-50. Creating a typed DataSet from the Add New Item window

After adding the DataSet, the designer creates an XSD (XML schema) file and adds it to your project area. As you can see from Figure 4-51, myDS.xsd is empty.

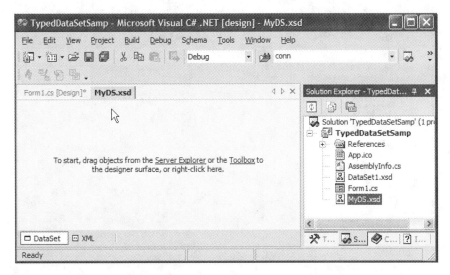

Figure 4-51. myDS.xsd *in VS .NET*

Next, drop a table (or multiple tables) from the Server Explorer to the form (see Figure 4-52).

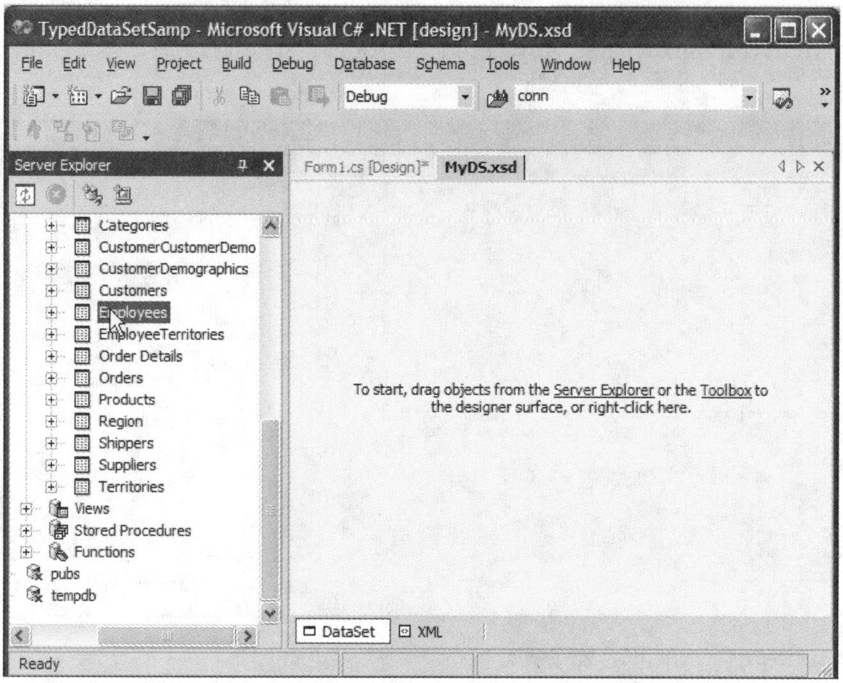
TypedDataSetSamp - Microsoft Visual C# .NET [design] - MyDS.xsd
File Edit View Project Build Debug Database Schema Tools Window Help
Debug
conn
Server Explorer
Form1.cs [Design]* MyDS.xsd
Categories
CustomerCustomerDemo
CustomerDemographics
Customers
Employees
EmployeeTerritories
Order Details
Orders
Products
Region
Shippers
Suppliers
Territories
Views
Stored Procedures
Functions
pubs
tempdb
To start, drag objects from the Server Explorer or the Toolbox to the designer surface, or right-click here.
DataSet
XML
Ready

Figure 4-52. Drag and drop tables from the Server Explorer to the form to create a typed `DataSet`

This action adds one XML schema (`MyDS.xsd`), which looks like Figure 4-53.

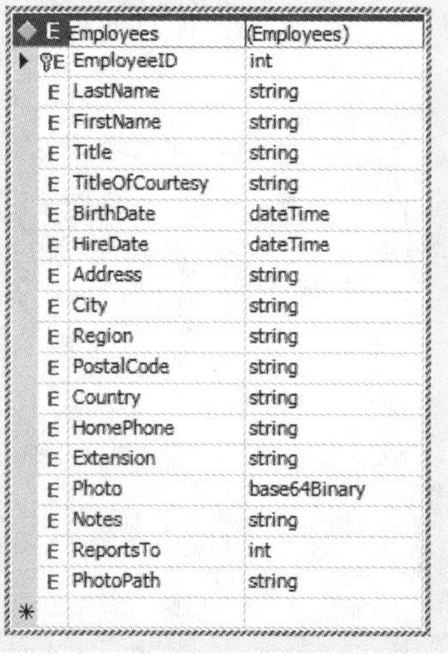
E Employees (Employees)
E EmployeeID int
E LastName string
E FirstName string
E Title string
E TitleOfCourtesy string
E BirthDate dateTime
E HireDate dateTime
E Address string
E City string
E Region string
E PostalCode string
E Country string
E HomePhone string
E Extension string
E Photo base64Binary
E Notes string
E ReportsTo int
E PhotoPath string

Figure 4-53. Design View of the XML schema of the `DataSet`

It also automatically adds the typed DataSet class that inherits from DataSet. As you can see in Figure 4-54, the myDS class contains members used to access data from the database.

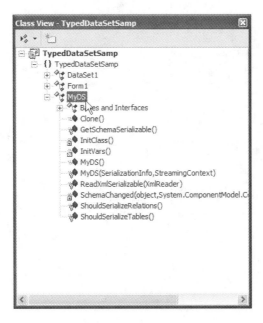

Figure 4-54. Wrapper class generated for the typed DataSet

Once you have this class, you can create an instance of this class and work with its property fields directly:

```
MyDSet ds = new MyDSet();
```

NOTE   *See Chapter 5 for a more extensive example on using datasets.*

Understanding DataView

A DataView represents a view of a DataSet object. You can set filters on the data or sort on data in the DataSet through different DataViews and produce different views of the data. For example, you can create a DataSet with three tables and create three different DataView objects for each table. Once you have a DataView object, you can attach it with any data-bound control, such as a DataGrid or a ComboBox control using data-bound control's DataSource property.

To create a DataView at design-time, drag the DataView from Toolbox ➤ Data onto your form. Then create a DataSet object and set the DataView's Table property to a table in the typed DataSet (see Figure 4-55).

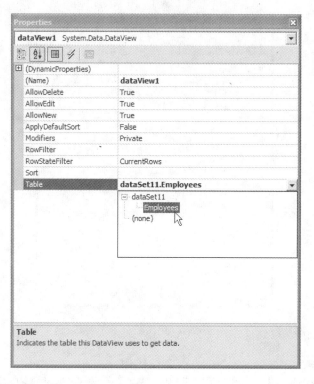

Figure 4-55. DataView *Properties window*

Using the Data Form Wizard

At the end of this chapter, I'd like to discuss Data Form Wizard, one more useful tool to develop database applications. You can use the Data Form Wizard to develop your database application with viewing, updating, and deleting capabilities. This is probably the fastest way to develop database applications in .NET (unless you're an extremely fast typist).

In this section, you'll use a Data Form Wizard to write a fully functioning database application including features such as inserting, updating, and deleting data without writing a single line of code. In this simple example, I've used the familiar Northwind database. I'll use both the Customers and Orders tables to show you a data relationship between table data.

Like many parts of this book, this topic is in the form of tutorial. Just follow the simple steps, and in a few minutes you'll be able to run a wonderful application. In this section, you're going to create a Windows application. After that you'll add a Data Form Wizard to it and call the Data Form Wizard from the main application.

Step 1: Selecting a Project Template

Create a new Windows project by selecting New Project ➤ Visual C# Projects ➤ Windows Application and typing your application name (see Figure 4-56).

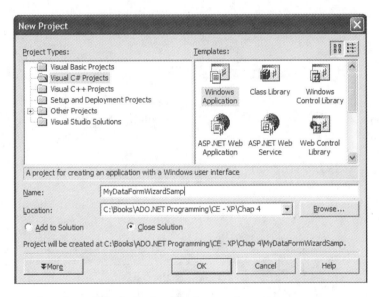

Figure 4-56. Creating a Windows Application project

Step 2: Adding a Data Form Wizard Item

Now add a Data Form Wizard by selecting Project ➤ Add New Item ➤ Data Form Wizard from the available templates. You can type the name of your DataForm class in the Name field of the dialog box (see Figure 4-57).

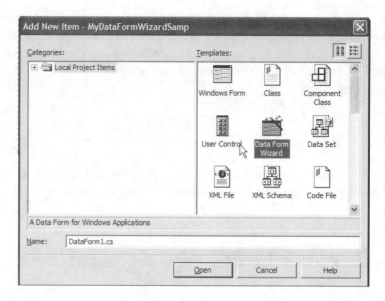

Figure 4-57. Using the Data Form Wizard

Now click Open, which calls the Data Form Wizard.

Step 3: Walking through the Data Form Wizard

The first page of the wizard is a welcome page telling you what the wizard is about to do (see Figure 4-58).

Figure 4-58. Welcome page of the Data Form Wizard

Step 4: Choosing the Dataset You Want

On the second page of the wizard, you can choose a dataset name that will later
be used to access the data. You can either create a new dataset name or select an
existing one. In this example, I'll choose MyDS as the dataset name (see in
Figure 4-59).

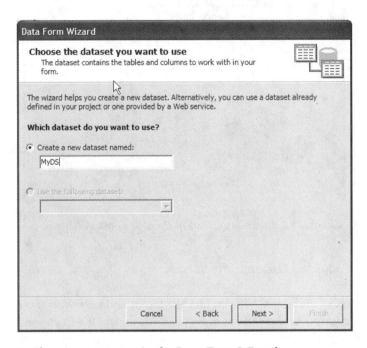

Figure 4-59. Choosing a DataSet *in the Data Form Wizard*

Step 5: Choosing a Data Connection

The next page of the wizard asks you to provide a connection. The combo box
displays your available connection. If you didn't create a connection, use the New
Connection button, which launches the Server Explorer discussed earlier in this
chapter. I'll select the usual database, Northwind (see Figure 4-60).

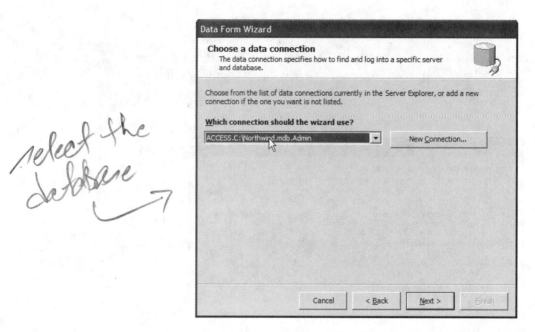

select the database →

Figure 4-60. Choosing a data connection in the Data Form Wizard

Step 6: Choosing Tables or Views

The next page of the wizard lets you pick the tables and views you want to connect to the dataset. As you can see in Figure 4-61, I select the Customers and Orders tables in the Available Items list on this page and use the > button to add these tables to the Selected Items list.

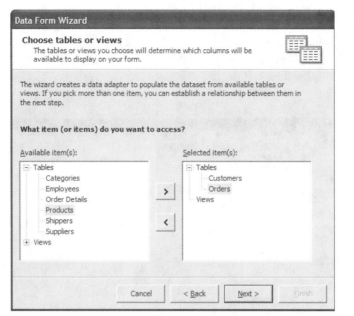

Figure 4-61. Choosing a DataTable *or* DataView *in the Data Form Wizard*

Now you're ready to create a relationship between these two tables.

Step 7: Creating a Relationship between Tables

The next page lets you define a relationship between the Customers and Orders tables. It's useful to provide a relationship between tables when you have a master-detail relationship database. In other words, a customer may have many orders associated with it, so there is a relationship through the CustomerID in the Orders table joined to information about the customer in the Customers table. Now, say you want to see all the orders of a customer based on the CustomerID. If you do this manually, you need to write code to select data from the Orders table to correspond to a CustomerID and then fill data to the form. If you use Data Form Wizard instead, it does everything for you. Neat, huh?

This is the same step you're going to see on the Create a Relationship between Tables page of the wizard. You're going to create a relationship between the Customers and Orders tables based on the CustomerID. I named the relationship between Customers and Orders table CustOrderRelation. You also need to pick the associated primary key and foreign key that links the parent to the child table. Once you've chosen the joining key (CustomerID), you have to click the > button to tell the wizard that you want to add it.

When you run the final program, you'll see how you can filter all orders for a customer based on the CustomerID. As you can see from Figure 4-62, you need to pick one table as parent and another table as a child based on the relationship between them. In this example, the Customers table is the parent table, and the Orders table is the child table.

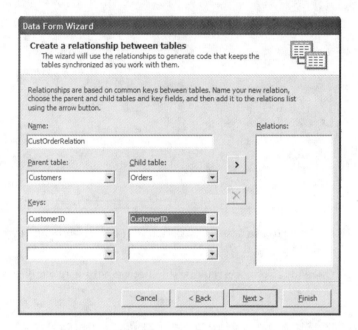

Figure 4-62. Selecting Customers as the parent and Orders as the child table to create the CustOrderRelation *relationship*

After adding the relationship to the Relations list, the wizard looks like Figure 4-63.

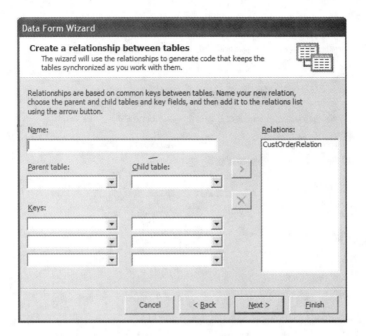

Figure 4-63. CustOrderRelation *listed in the Relations list*

Step 8: Choosing Tables and Columns to Display on the Form

The next page of the wizard lets you select which tables and columns you want to show on the form. For this example, select all the columns from both of the tables (this is the default selection). As you can see in Figure 4-64, the Customers table is the master, and the Orders table is the detail table.

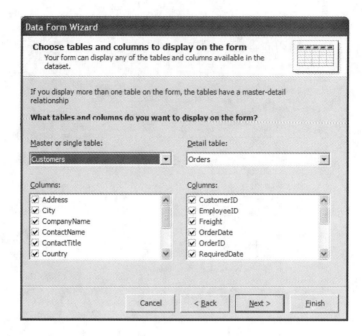

Figure 4-64. Choosing columns to display on the Data Form Wizard

Step 9: Choosing the Display Style

This page is an important part of creating your form. Actually, the Data Form Wizard adds a Windows form with some controls on it and writes code to fill, update, delete, and navigate data. There are two ways to view the data, and you choose your option on this page. These two options are:

- All Records in a Grid

- Single Record in Individual Controls

Figure 4-65 displays these options.

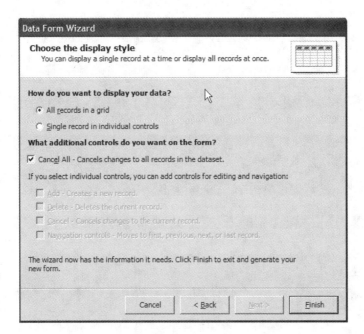

Figure 4-65. Choosing between a grid and individual controls on the Data Form Wizard

The output of All Records in a Grid looks like Figure 4-66. After that you can resize controls on the form.

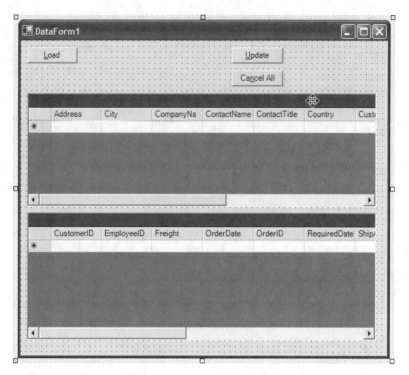

Figure 4-66. Grid DataForm *output*

The second option, Single Record in Individual Controls, shows data in text boxes and provides you with navigation controls. As you can see from Figure 4-67, the Single Record in Individual Controls option activates Add, Delete, Cancel, and Navigation controls check boxes. You can uncheck the check boxes if you don't want to add that feature in your project.

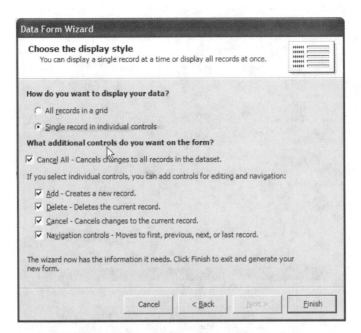

Figure 4-67. The Single Record in Individual Controls option

The form generated by this option looks like Figure 4-68. As you can see from Figure 4-68, each column of the table has a field on the form.

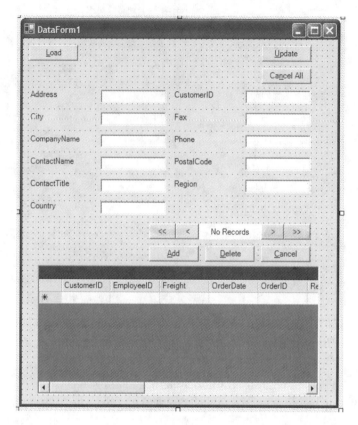

Figure 4-68. Data Form Wizard–generated form for the Single Record in Individual Control option

After your selection of data display style, you click Finish button. The Data Form Wizard adds the Windows form DataForm1 and the class DataForm1.cs corresponding to it.

Step 10: Calling the Data Form Wizard Form from the Application

Now you need to change one more thing. You need to call DataForm1 when you start your application. By default, your application calls the Form1 form on start up.

```
static void Main()
{
Application.Run(new Form1());
}
```

So, you need to replace Form1 with your Data Form Wizard's form name. In this example, Listing 4-6 replaces Form1 with DataForm1 in the Main method.

Listing 4-6. Calling DataForm1 *from the application*

```
static void Main()
  {
            Application.Run(new DataForm1());
}
```

> **NOTE**   *If you've modified the name of your Data Form Wizard–generated form, you need to call that form instead of* DataForm1.

Step 11: Viewing the Output

Now you should see the output shown in Figure 4-69 when you run your application (if you selected the grid view option).

The Load and Update buttons load and update the data, respectively, and Cancel All cancels all the operations. The neat thing is if you move into the top grid, corresponding information changes in the bottom grid. Neat, huh?

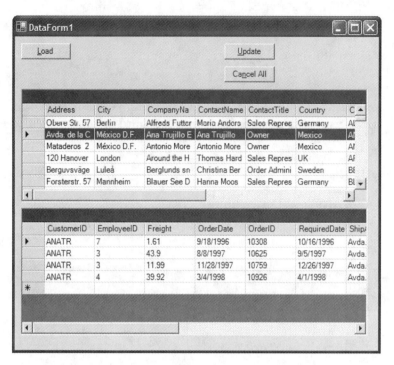

Figure 4-69. Data Form Wizard with all records in a grid option

Figure 4-70 shows the output when you select the Single Record in Individual Control option. By using this view option, you can add, edit, delete, and navigate records easily.

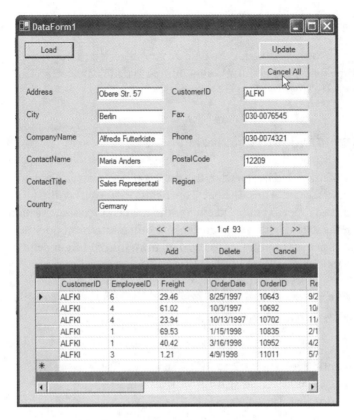

Figure 4-70. Textbox output with navigational controls

Finally, compile and run your application. Without writing a single line of code, you just created a fully functional database application.

The Load button on the individual control form loads the data, and the Add, Update, and Delete buttons on the form inserts, updates, and deletes records, respectively.

Data Form Wizard: Looking under the Hood

You just saw how you can develop fully functional database applications in no time with the help of the Data Form Wizard. Now let's see what the wizard does for you in the actual code. (The inherent beauty of VS .NET is that it magically hides all the messy code for you.) The wizard adds two items to your project: MyDS.xsd and DataForm1.cs.

Understanding MyDS.xsd

MyDS.xsd is an XML schema for the dataset you've added to the project. It's similar to the one discussed in the "Understanding Typed DataSets in Visual Studio .NET" section of this chapter.

Understanding DataForm1.cs

The second item added by the wizard is the DataForm1 class, a class derived from System.Windows.Forms.Form. The DataForm1 class defines its entire functionality. The InitializeComponent method creates the data connection, the data command, the data adapter, the dataset, and other data components.

The LoadDataSet method loads the data from the data source into the controls by calling FillDataSet (see Listing 4-7).

Listing 4-7. LoadDataSet *method generated by the Data Form Wizard*

```
public void LoadDataSet()
{
    // Create a new dataset to hold the records
    //returned from the call to FillDataSet.
    // A temporary dataset is used because filling
    //the existing dataset would
    // require the databindings to be rebound.
    MyDataFormWizardSamp.MyDS objDataSetTemp;
    objDataSetTemp = new MyDataFormWizardSamp.MyDS();
    try
    {
      // Attempt to fill the temporary dataset.
      this.FillDataSet(objDataSetTemp);
    }
    catch (System.Exception eFillDataSet)
    {
      // Add your error handling code here.
      throw eFillDataSet;
    }
    try
    {
      // Empty the old records from the dataset.
      objMyDS.Clear();
      // Merge the records into the main dataset.
      objMyDS.Merge(objDataSetTemp);
    }
```

```
catch (System.Exception eLoadMerge)
{
  // Add your error handling code here.
  throw eLoadMerge;
}
```

}

FillDataSet fills the dataset from the data adapter by calling the Fill method on each data adapter. Note that with the Data Form Wizard, a DataAdapter is created for each table, one DataAdapter for the Customers table and one DataAdapter for the Orders table. Both DataAdapters fill the same DataSet. Listing 4-8 shows the FillDataSet method.

Listing 4-8. The FillDataSet *method generated by the Data Form Wizard*

```
public void FillDataSet(MyDataFormWizardSamp.MyDS dataSet)
{
    // Turn off constraint checking before the dataset is filled.
    // This allows the adapters to fill the dataset without concern
    // for dependencies between the tables.
    dataSet.EnforceConstraints = false;
    try
    {
      // Open the connection.
      this.oleDbConnection1.Open();
      // Attempt to fill the dataset through the OleDbDataAdapter1.
      this.oleDbDataAdapter1.Fill(dataSet);
      this.oleDbDataAdapter2.Fill(dataSet);
    }
    catch (System.Exception fillException)
    {
      // Add your error handling code here.
      throw fillException;
    }
    finally
    {
      // Turn constraint checking back on.
      dataSet.EnforceConstraints = true;
      // Close the connection whether or not the exception was thrown.
      this.oleDbConnection1.Close();
    }
}
```

The UpdateDataSource method updates the data source from the DataSet. The UpdateDataSet method calls UpdateDataSource, which utilizes the Update method of the data adapters. Listing 4-9 shows the UpdateDataSource method.

Listing 4-9. The UpdateDataSource *and* UpdateDataSet *methods generated by the Data Form Wizard*

```
public void UpdateDataSource(MyDataFormWizardSamp.MyDS ChangedRows)
{
    try
    {
      // The data source only needs to be updated if there
      //are changes pending.
      if ((ChangedRows != null))
      {
        // Open the connection.
        this.oleDbConnection1.Open();
        // Attempt to update the data source.
        oleDbDataAdapter1.Update(ChangedRows);
        oleDbDataAdapter2.Update(ChangedRows);
      }
    }
    catch (System.Exception updateException)
    {
      // Add your error handling code here.
      throw updateException;
    }
    finally
    {
      // Close the connection whether or not the exception
      //was thrown.
      this.oleDbConnection1.Close();
    }

}
```

Summary

Congratulations! Now you have completed one more step toward understanding ADO.NET and its components. After completing this chapter, you should have a pretty good idea of how to write database applications using VS .NET.

In this chapter, you learned about visual data components in Visual Studio .NET. The Server Explorer is a handy utility added to VS .NET IDE to help you manage your database connections.

Data adapters let you connect to a data source a design-time and can be used to populate DataSet objects. Data adapters also allow you to add, update, and delete data through data command objects. VS .NET also lets you generate typed datasets, which create a DataSet with properties of tables and columns specific to a data source.

DataView is a bindable view of a DataSet. You can sort and filter a DataSet with a DataView and use it to bind to a graphical component in many of the Windows form controls.

Finally, the Data Form Wizard is a useful tool in which you can generate full-fledged database applications with features such as insert, delete, update in no time. In the next chapter, I'll discuss ADO.NET data providers and other ADO.NET components and show how to work with them programmatically. Chapter 5 will also cover data component's methods and properties.

CHAPTER 5

ADO.NET Data Providers and Disconnected Classes

IN CHAPTER 3 AND CHAPTER 4, you learned how to use ADO.NET components with Visual Studio (VS) .NET and by writing code manually, how to bind ADO.NET components to data-bound controls, and how to use VS .NET IDE wizards to write full-fledged database applications.

In this chapter, you'll get a broad view of the ADO.NET architecture and the basic building blocks of ADO.NET and ADO.NET data providers. I've divided this chapter into two parts: One part features ADO.NET disconnected classes, and the other focuses on ADO.NET data providers. I'll also cover base interfaces and base classes for the data provider classes.

ADO.NET *disconnected classes* are basic building blocks of the ADO.NET architecture. The classes are independent of data providers and data sources. In other words, you can use these classes with data providers as well as without data providers.

ADO.NET data providers are sets of classes designed to work with multiple data sources to provide the best out of all the database access technologies. ADO.NET provides many data providers to work with different kinds of data sources, including OleDb, ODBC, and Sql. As you can guess from their names, the OleDb data providers work with OLE DB data sources, ODBC data providers work with ODBC data sources, and Sql data providers work with SQL Server 7 or later databases.

> **NOTE** *You can access SQL Server 6.5 or previous versions using ODBC or OleDb data providers.*

> **NOTE** *In the previous versions of .NET (Beta1), data providers were known as managed providers.*

Although ADO.NET is a new programming model, it uses some of the old data access technologies to access different data sources. For example, the OleDb data provider uses the native OLE DB Application Programming Interface (API) to access OLE DB data sources. Similar to OLE DB data sources, the ODBC data provider uses ODBC drivers and ODBC Admin to access ODBC data sources. ADO.NET data providers wrap up these technologies and provide a high-level programming model to make it easier to program.

So, what's new? That is a good question. Weren't you using the ODBC and OLE DB APIs in previous data access technologies? You're right. ADO.NET still uses the same native API. The only difference is that ADO.NET provides high-level, object-oriented classes that are easy to program and understand. Further, all the data providers supply the same programming model. So, if you know how to write applications using OleDb data providers, you'll be able to write applications using ODBC or Sql providers in no time. It's just a matter of changing the class names and connection strings. To leave OleDb and ODBC data providers behind, Sql data providers supply much improvement in comparison to using ODBC. Sql data providers directly connect to the lower-level layer in the infrastructure that bypasses ODBC Admin and ODBC drivers.

Looking at the ADO.NET Architecture

You briefly looked at the ADO.NET architecture in Chapter 3. Now you'll see a broad view of the ADO.NET architecture and learn how disconnected and connected components (classes) provide access to multiple data sources. In this section, I'll talk about objects in general. The following sections of the chapter will discuss the ADO.NET components based on data providers.

Figure 5-1 shows the basic architecture of the ADO.NET model. As you can see, the entire ADO.NET model sits between the data source and client applications that can be built using Windows Forms, Web Forms, or even console-based applications. The Connection is the first component that talks to a data source. In ADO.NET, each data provider (OleDb, Sql, Odbc, or Oracle) has its own Connection class. The Connection component is a mediator between a DataAdapter (or a Command) component and a data source. The DataAdapter components create SQL INSERT, SELECT, UPDATE, and DELETE statements that add, read, update, and delete data from a data source, respectively. Not only does a DataAdapter create these SQL statements, it also executes these statements. Basically, a DataAdapter (with the help of Command) physically updates and reads data from a data source. In Figure 5-1, an arrow shows this flow of data.

You can use the Command components with or without a DataAdapter. You can directly execute SQL statements using the Command object's methods. You can also read data in a DataReader object using the Command object, which provides a read-only, forward-only fast access to data. This is best when you need to read data in applications that are not data-bound. You can also see from Figure 5-1 that all arrows are double-sided arrows except the arrow connecting a DataReader and Command. A double-sided arrow means data transfer is possible in both sides. A DataReader can only read data, which is why DataReader has only a one-sided arrow. This shows that you can fill a data reader from the command, but you can't send back data from a data reader to the command.

A DataAdapter sits between a data source and a DataSet. It provides Fill and Update methods to fill a dataset from a data source based on the SELECT statement, and the Update method saves a dataset's changes to the data source. The DataSet plays a vital role in data-bound Graphical User Interface (GUI) appli-cations to display and manipulate data. Not only does it provide fast data manipulation using XML schemas, it also provides multiple views of data that can be bound with multiple Windows Forms and Web Forms data-bound controls.

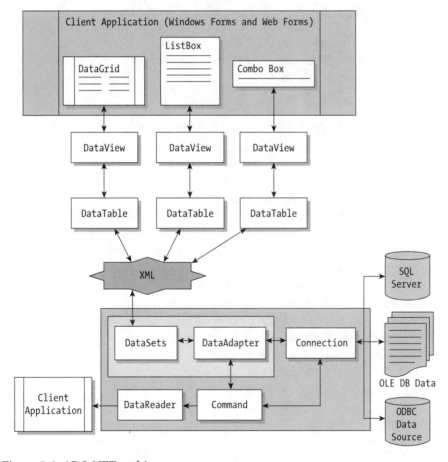

Figure 5-1. ADO.NET architecture

A DataSet is a collection of DataTable components. A DataTable represents a table in a data source. You can apply a filter or do sorts on a table. You can bind a DataTable to data-bound controls such as a DataGrid, DataList, ListBox, or ComboBox using DataView. You can also apply sorts and filters on a DataView. As you can see from Figure 5-1, there are three datasets represented as three DataTables. Each DataTable binds to different data-bound controls using different DataViews.

> **NOTE** *As you can see, some arrows are single-sided and some are double-sided. For example, you can see from the figure that you can use a data reader only to read data from a Command object, but you can use a dataset to read and write both. I'll use the same style throughout the chapter.*

This was an overview of the ADO.NET architecture. I'll discuss these controls in more detail throughout this chapter if they fall into a specific data provider category.

Exploring the ADO.NET Class Hierarchy

OK, before you start swimming in the deep ocean of ADO.NET, you need to take a quick look at the ADO.NET class hierarchy provided by the .NET Runtime class library. These classes represent ADO.NET components.

All ADO.NET functionality in the .NET Runtime class library comes in three general namespaces and *n* number of provider-specific namespaces. The three general namespaces are System.Data, System.Data.Common, and System.Data.SqlTypes. Some of the provider-specific namespaces are System.Data.OleDb, Microsoft.Data.Odbc, and System.Data.SqlClient.

The System.Data namespace defines classes that you can use with all the data providers or without data providers at all. This namespace also defines interfaces that are base classes for the data provider classes. Figure 5-2 shows the System.Data namespace's class hierarchy.

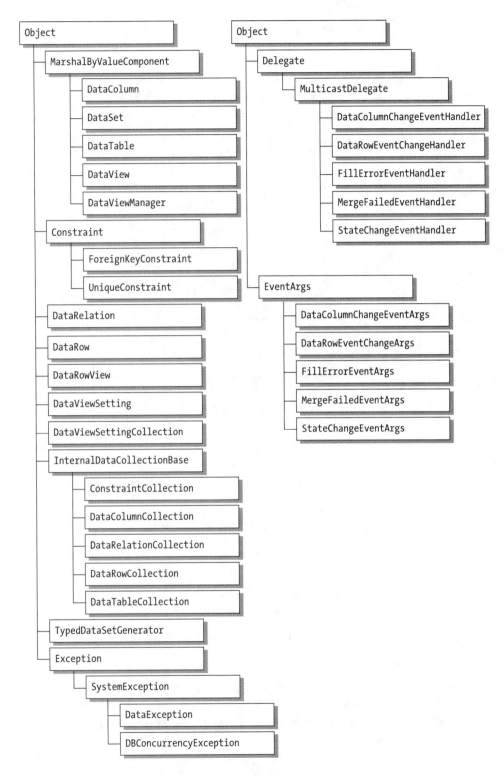

Figure 5-2. The System.Data *namespace class hierarchy*

The System.Data.Common namespace defines classes common to all data providers. Figure 5-3 shows the System.Data.Common namespace hierarchy.

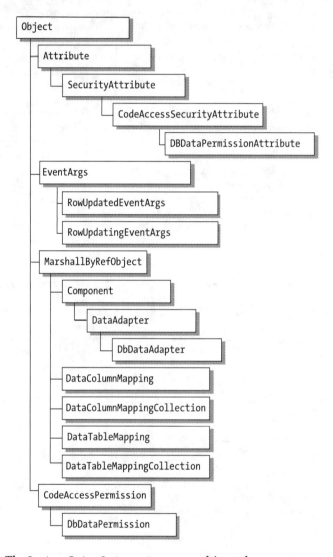

Figure 5-3. The System.Data.Common *namespace hierarchy*

The System.Data.SqlTypes namespace defines classes for native SQL Server data types that provide type-safe conversion between the .NET data types and the SQL Server native data types. Figure 5-4 shows the System.Data.SqlTypes namespace hierarchy.

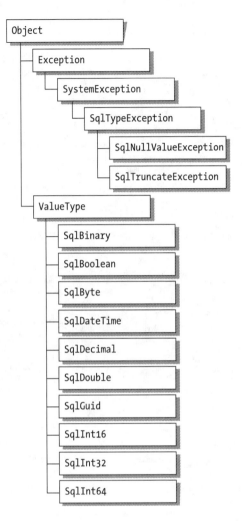

Figure 5-4. The System.Data.SqlTypes *namespace hierarchy.*

Besides these three namespaces, ADO.NET defines *n* number of provider-specific namespaces. The class hierarchy models of all of these namespaces are similar except for the name of the class. The classes defined in the provider-specific namespaces start with the data provider name. For example, the Sql data provider classes start with Sql, and the OleDb data provider classes start with OleDb. The Command object classes of the Sql and OleDb data providers are SqlCommand and OleDbCommand, respectively.

In this section, you're going to see only the System.Data.OleDb namespace class hierarchy because all the data providers (including System.Data.Sql and Microsoft.Data.Odbc) implement the same class hierarchy model. Figure 5-5 shows the System.Data.OleDb namespace hierarchy.

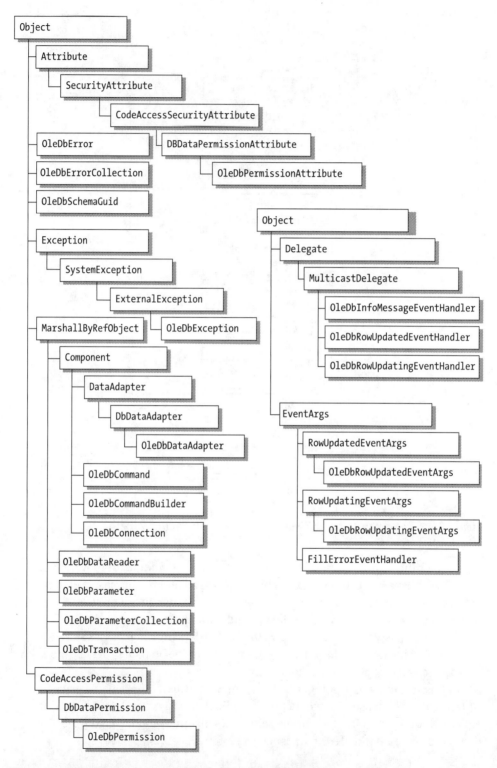

Figure 5-5. The System.Data.OleDb *namespace hierarchy*

I'll discuss these namespaces and their classes in more detail throughout this chapter.

Understanding ADO.NET Disconnected Classes

ADO.NET disconnected classes are the basic building blocks of the ADO.NET architecture. These classes are loosely coupled with data providers. The System.Data namespace defines these classes.

The System.Data Namespace

The System.Data namespace consists of classes that are the basic building blocks of the ADO.NET architecture. These classes are also known as *disconnected classes* because they store disconnected data and can work without data providers.

Table 5-1 describes some of the common classes of the System.Data namespaces. I'll discuss these classes in more detail throughout this chapter.

Table 5-1. The System.Data *Namespace Classes*

CLASS	DESCRIPTION
Constraint, ConstraintCollection, UniqueConstraint, ForeignKeyConstraint	Constraints are rules set on a database table and its columns to maintain the integrity of the data. The Constraint class object represents a constraint that you can apply on a DataColumn object. Some of these constraints are primary key, uniqueness, and foreign key. The ConstraintCollection class represents a collection of constraints for a DataTable. The UniqueConstraint and ForeignKeyConstraint represent unique and foreign key constraints.
DataColumn, DataColumnCollection	The DataColumn object represents a column of a table. The DataColumnCollection represents a collection of columns of a table.
DataRelation, DataRelationCollection	The DataRelation object represents a parent/child relationship between two DataTable objects. The DataRelationCollection represents a collection of DataRelation.
DataRow, DataRowCollection	A DataRow object represents a row of a table, and the DataRowCollection represent a collection of rows.

(continued)

Table 5-1. The System.Data *Namespace Classes (continued)*

CLASS	DESCRIPTION
DataRowView	The DataRowView represents a view of DataRow. It's useful when you want to attach a DataRow with data-bound controls such as a DataGrid.
DataSet	In ADO.NET, a DataSet object is a replacement of ADO recordset and represents an in-memory cache of data. A DataSet is a collection ofDataTable objects.
DataTable, DataTableCollection	A DataTable object represents an in-memory cache of a table, and the DataTableCollection is a collection of DataTable objects.
DataView	Represents a data bindable, customized view of a DataTable for sorting, filtering, searching, editing, and navigation.
DataViewManager	The DefaultViewManager represents the default view of a DataSet or DataTableCollection.

The System.Data namespace also defines many interfaces that are base classes for the ADO.NET data provider classes. Table 5-2 describes these namespaces.

Table 5-2. The System.Data *Namespace Interfaces*

INTERFACE	DESCRIPTION
IDataParameter	This interface represents a parameter to a Command object and is the base class of provider-specific DataParameter classes.
IDataParameterCollection	This interface represents a collection of DataParameter objects and is the base class of provider-specific DataParameterCollection classes.
IDataReader	This interface defines methods and properties to read forward-only streams and is implemented by provider-specific DataReader classes.
IDataRecord	This interface defines methods and properties that provide access to the column values within each row for a DataReader and is implemented by data providers that access relational databases.

(continued)

Table 5-2. The `System.Data` *Namespace Interfaces (continued)*

INTERFACE	DESCRIPTION
IDbCommand	This interface defines methods and properties to represent a SQL statement that is executed while connected to a data source and is implemented by data providers that access relational databases.
IDbConnection	This interface is the base class for data provider Connection classes and represents an open connection to a data source.
IDbDataAdapter	This interface is a base class for provider-specific DataAdapter classes and represents a set of command-related properties used to fill a DataSet and update a data source.
IDbDataParameter	This interface defines classes and methods that represent a parameter to a Command object and used by the Visual Basic .NET data designers.
IDbTransaction	This interface is the base class for provider-specific Transaction classes that represents a transaction.
ITableMapping	This namespace is the base class of TableMapping classes and defines methods and properties that map a data source table with a DataTable.
ITableMappingCollection	This namespace is the base class of TableMappingCollection class and defines members and properties that represent a collection of TableMapping objects.

The `System.Data` namespace also defines many enumerations and delegates that I'll be discussing throughout this chapter.

Once you have an idea of what classes the `System.Data.Common` namespace contains, you'll have no problem understanding how to use these classes in a sample application.

The `System.Data.Common` Namespace

As its name says, the `System.Data.Common` namespace contains classes shared by the .NET data providers. Some of these classes are the base classes for the .NET data provider classes. Table 5-3 defines some of these classes.

Table 5-3. The `System.Data.Common` *Namespace Classes*

CLASS	DESCRIPTION
DataAdapter	The `DataAdapter` class represents a data adapter that works as a bridge between a data source and dataset. It implements the `Fill` and `Update` methods. The `Fill` method fills data from a data source to a `DataSet` using `Command` objects. This class is a base class for the `DbDataAdapter` class, which itself is a base class for the `OleDbDataAdapter`, `SqlDataAdapter`, and ODBC `DataAdapter` classes. These classes are discussed in the "DataAdapter: Adapting to Your Environment" section in more detail.
DataColumnMapping	If you don't want to use default column names of a table columns to access these columns, you can define your own names. You map your custom names with the original column names through data adapters and use these names in your application. The `SourceColumn` and `DataSetColumn` properties of this class represent the source column name and `DataSet` column name.
DataColumnMappingCollection	Collection of `DataColumnMapping` objects.
DataTableMapping	You can even map a database table to a `DataTable` and use this `DataTable` as the source in your applications. The `ColumnMappings` property returns `DataColumnMappingCollection` for the `DataTable`. The `DataSetTable` and `SourceTable` properties represent the `DataTable` and source tables.
DataTableMappingCollection	Collection of `DataTableMapping` objects.
DbDataAdapter	Inherited from `DataAdapter`, this class implements the `IdbDataAdapter` interface. This class is used as the base class of a data provider's `DataAdapter` classes.
DBDataPermission	Ensures that data providers have security to access data. This class is a base class from the `OleDbDataPermission`, ODBC `DataPermission`, and `SqlDataPermission` classes.

The DataTable, DataColumn and DataRow Classes

A DataTable object represents a database table. A data table is a collection of columns and rows. The DataRow object represents a table row, and the DataColumn object represents a row of the table. The first step to working with these three objects is to create a data table schema, which is defined by the DataColumnCollection object. You use the Add method of the DataColumnCollection to add columns to the collection. The Columns property of the DataTable object represents the DataColumnCollection, which is a collection of DataColumn objects in a DataTable. You use a DataRow object to add data to a data table. The DataRowCollection object represents a collection of rows of a DataTable object, which can be accessed by its Rows property.

Figure 5-6 shows the relationship between the DataTable, DataRow, and DataColumn.

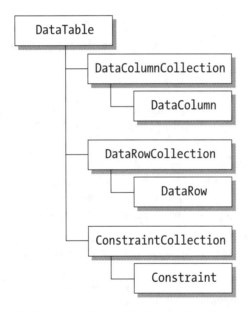

Figure 5-6. Relationship between the DataTable, *the* DataRow, *and the* DataColumn.

To understand a data table schema, take a look at Figure 5-7. Figure 5-7 shows the schema of the Customers table of Northwind database.

241

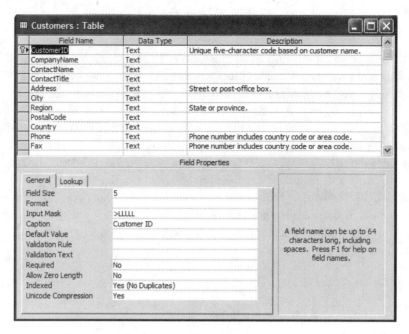

Figure 5-7. The Customers database table schema

The Field Name column represents the name of the fields, the Data Type column represents the type of data you can store in that column, and the Description column is for designers to explain a field.

The Field Properties area represents the properties of a column. If you look at the General tab, you'll notice Field Size, Caption, Allow Zero Length, Default Value, Validation Rule, Indexed fields, and others. These options are column properties. All of these properties are pretty self-explanatory. For example, field size means the number of characters you can store in a column, Allow Zero Length indicates whether a column can have zero length values, and so on.

> **NOTE** *A database table column is also called a* field.

So, when I talk about creating a data table, I mean I build a database table (in-memory, of course) and its schema using the DataTable and the DataColumn objects. Based on a column requirement, you can also apply constraints on a column. A *constraint* is a rule that restricts adding unwanted data to a column. For example, the uniqueness of a column means that a column can't have duplicate values. You'll see constraints in more detail under the "The Data Column" section.

After creating a data table schema, the second step is to add data rows to the data table. You use data rows using the DataRow object. After adding data to a database table, the filled table looks like Figure 5-8.

		Customer ID	Company Name	Contact Name	Contact Title	Address	City	
▶	+	1400	Xerox	Fred Biggles		111 Broad St	NY	▲
	+	ALFKI	Alfreds Futterkiste	Maria Anders	Sales Represen	Obere Str. 57	Berlin	
	+	ANATR	Ana Trujillo Empare	Ana Trujillo	Owner	Avda. de la C	México	
	+	ANTON	Antonio Moreno Ta	Antonio Moreno	Owner	Mataderos 2	México	
	+	AROUT	Around the Horn	Thomas Hardy	Sales Represen	120 Hanover	London	
	+	BERGS	Berglunds snabbkö	Christina Berglund	Order Administr	Berguvsväger	Luleå	
	+	BLAUS	Blauer See Delikat	Hanna Moos	Sales Represen	Forsterstr. 57	Mannhe	
	+	BLONP	Blondel père et fils	Frédérique Citeau	Marketing Mana	24, place Klé	Strasbo	
	+	BOLID	Bólido Comidas pre	Martín Sommer	Owner	C/ Araquil, 67	Madrid	
	+	BONAP	Bon app'	Laurence Lebihan	Owner	12, rue des B	Marseill	
	+	BOTTM	Bottom-Dollar Mark	Elizabeth Lincoln	Accounting Mar	23 Tsawasse	Tsawas	
	+	BSBEV	B's Beverages	Victoria Ashworth	Sales Represen	Fauntleroy Ci	London	
	+	CACTU	Cactus Comidas p	Patricio Simpson	Sales Agent	Cerrito 333	Buenos	▼

Record: 1 of 93

Figure 5-8. Filled data view of the Customers table

As you can see from Figure 5-8, the data table has data based on its column properties.

> **TIP** *To see Northwind database table schema and data, you can use Microsoft Access or VS .NET. I have used Access 2000.*

OK, now I'll show you how you can accomplish this task in ADO.NET using the DataTable, DataColumn, and DataRow objects. First I'll discuss the DataColumn and the DataRow objects followed by the DataRelation and the DataTable objects. Then, I'll show you how to build a sample project containing all these object to build a data table and add data to it programmatically.

The Data Column

To understand a data table, you must first understand data rows and data columns. As you can see from Figure 5-6, the DataColumnCollection type returns a collection of columns that can be accessed through Columns property of the DataTable. The DataColumnCollection object represents a collection of columns attached to a data table. You add a data column to the DataColumnCollection using its Add method. The DataColumn object represents

243

a column of a DataTable. For example, say you want to create a Customers table that consists of three columns: ID, Address, and Name. You create three DataColumn objects and add these columns to the DataColumnCollection using the DataTable.Column.Add method.

After creating a data table schema, the next step is to add data to the data table by using the DataRow object. I'll discuss the DataRow object in the following section.

The DataColumn has some properties. These properties describe a column, such as its uniqueness, what kind of data you can store in that column, default value, caption, name, and so on. Table 5-4 describes some of the DataColumn class members.

Table 5-4. The DataColumn Class Properties

PROPERTY	DESCRIPTION
AllowDBNull	Both read and write, represents if column can store null values or not
AutoIncrement	Represents if column's value is auto increment or not
AutoIncrementSeed	Starting value of auto increment, applicable when AutoIncrement is true
AutoIncrementStep	Indicates the increment value
Caption	Caption of the column
ColumnMapping	Represents the MappingType of the column
ColumnName	Name of the column
DataType	Data type stored by the column
DefaultValue	Default value of the column
Expression	Represents the expression used to filter rows, calculate values, and so on
MaxLength	Represents maximum length of a text column
ReadOnly	Represents if a column is read-only or not
Unique	Indicates whether the values in a column must be unique or not

Creating a DataColumn

The DataColumn class provides five overloaded constructors to create a data column. By using these constructors you can initialize a DataColumn with its name, data type, expressions, attributes, and any combination of these.

This is the format for creating a DataColumn with no arguments:

```
public DataColumn();
```

For example:

```
DataColumn dtColumn = new DataColumn();
```

This is the format for creating a DataColumn with the column name:

```
public DataColumn(string);
```

where string is the column name. For example:

```
// Create Quantity Column
DataColumn qtCol = new DataColumn("Quantity");
```

This is the format for creating a DataColumn with the column name and its type:

```
public DataColumn(string, Type);
```

where string is the column name and Type is the column data type.

This is the format for creating a DataColumn with the column name, its type, and expression:

```
public DataColumn(string, Type, string);
```

where the first string is the column name, Type is the data type, and the second string is an expression.

For example:

```
System.Type myDataType;
myDataType = System.Type.GetType("System.String");
DataColumn dtColumn = new DataColumn("Name", myDataType);
```

where string is column name, Type is data type and string is an expression.

This is the format for creating a DataColumn with the column name, expression, and MappingType:

```
public DataColumn(string, Type, string, MappingType);
```

where string is the column name, Type is the data type, string is an expression, and MappingType is an attribute.

In the following example, strExpr is an expression, which is the result of the Price and the Quantity column multiplication:

```
// Creating an expression
string strExpr = "Price * Quantity";

// Create Total Column, which is result of Price*Quantity
DataColumn totCol = new DataColumn("Total", myDataType, strExpr,
MappingType.Attribute);
```

> **NOTE**   *As you can see from the previous code, the expression* strExpr *is a multiplication of the Price and Quantity columns. The Price and Quantity columns must exist in the table before you use them in an expression. Otherwise the compiler will throw an exception of "column not found."*

Listing 5-1 summarizes all the constructors. As you can see, dcConstructorsTest creates the Price, Quantity, and Total columns of a DataTable, which later is added to a DataSet. The DataSet binds to a DataGrid using the SetDataBinding method. To test this source code, you need to create a Windows application with a form and a DataGrid control on it. After that you can call dcConstructorsTest from either Form_Load or the button-click event handler.

Listing 5-1. Creating columns using different DataColumn *constructors*

```
private void dcConstructorsTest()
{
            // Create Customers table
            DataTable custTable = new DataTable("Customers");
            DataSet dtSet = new DataSet();

            // Create Price Column
            System.Type myDataType;
            myDataType = System.Type.GetType("System.Int32");
            DataColumn priceCol = new DataColumn("Price", myDataType );
            priceCol.Caption = "Price";
            custTable.Columns.Add(priceCol);
```

```
                 // Create Quantity Column
                 DataColumn qtCol = new DataColumn();
                 qtCol.ColumnName = "Quantity";
                 qtCol.DataType = System.Type.GetType("System.Int32");
                 qtCol.Caption = "Quantity";
                 custTable.Columns.Add(qtCol);

                 // Creating an expression
                 string strExpr = "Price * Quantity";

                 // Create Total Column, which is result of Price*Quantity
                 DataColumn totCol = new DataColumn("Total", myDataType, strExpr,
                                                    MappingType.Attribute);
                 totCol.Caption = "Total";
                 // Add Name column to the table.
                 custTable.Columns.Add(totCol);

                 // Add custTable to DataSet
                 dtSet.Tables.Add(custTable);

                 // Bind dataset to the data grid
                 dataGrid1.SetDataBinding(dtSet,"Customers");

         }
```

Setting DataColumn Properties

The DataColumn class provides properties to set a column type, name, constraints, caption, and so on. Table 5-4 describes the DataColumn properties. Most of these properties are self-explanatory. After creating a DataColumn object, you set DataColumn properties.

Listing 5-2 creates a column with a name ID and sets its DataType, ReadOnly, AllowDBNull, Unique, AutoIncrement, AutoIncrementSeed, and AutoIncrementStep properties.

Listing 5-2. Creating a DataColumn *and setting its properties*

```
// Create ID Column
DataColumn IdCol = new DataColumn();
IdCol.ColumnName= "ID";
IdCol.DataType = Type.GetType("System.Int32");
IdCol.ReadOnly = true;
```

```
IdCol.AllowDBNull = false;
IdCol.Unique = true;
IdCol.AutoIncrement = true;
IdCol.AutoIncrementSeed = 1;
IdCol.AutoIncrementStep = 1;
```

As you can see from Listing 5-2, I set the `AutoIncrement` property as true along with the `AutoIncrementSeed` and `AutoIncrementStep` properties. The `AutoIncrement` property sets a column value as an auto number. When you add a new row to the table, the value of this column is assigned automatically depending on the values of `AutoIncrementStep` and `AutoIncrementSeed`. The first value of the column starts with `AutoIncrementSeed`, and the next value will be the previous column value added to the `AutoIncrementStep`. In this code, the ID number value starts with 1 and increases by 1 if you add a new row to the table. If you set the `AutoIncrementStep` value to 10, the value of the auto number column will increase by 10.

Having a primary key in a table is a common practice to maintain the integrity of the data. A primary key in a table is a unique key that identifies a data row. For example, in the Customers table, each customer should have a unique ID. So, it's always a good idea to apply primary key constraint on the ID table. The properties `AllowDBNull` as false and `Unique` as true set a key value as the primary key, and you use the `PrimaryKey` property of `DataTable` to assign a `DataTable`'s primary key. I have already set `AllowDBNull` as false and the `Unique` property as true in Listing 5-2. Now you'll set `DataTable`'s `PrimaryKey` property as the ID column (see Listing 5-3).

Listing 5-3. Setting a DataColumn *as the primary key*
```
// Make the ID column the primary key column.
DataColumn[] PrimaryKeyColumns = new DataColumn[1];
PrimaryKeyColumns[0] = custTable.Columns["ID"];
custTable.PrimaryKey = PrimaryKeyColumns;
```

Adding a DataColumn to a DataTable

You add a `DataColumn` to a `DataTable` using the `DataTable.Column.Add` method. The `Add` method takes one argument of the `DataColumn` type. Listing 5-4 creates two data columns, Id and Name, and adds them to the `DataTable` `custTable`.

Listing 5-4. Creating the Id and Name data columns of the Customers table
```
// Create a new DataTable
DataTable custTable = new DataTable("Customers");
```

```
// Create ID Column
DataColumn IdCol = new DataColumn();
// Set column properties
custTable.Columns.Add(IdCol);

// Create Name Column
DataColumn nameCol = new DataColumn();
// set column properties
custTable.Columns.Add(nameCol);
```

Now you'll put all the pieces together in Listing 5-5. In Listing 5-5, you create a Customers table with the columns ID, Name, Address, DOB, and VAR where ID is a primary key. Name and Address are string types. DOB is a date type field, and VAR is a Boolean type field.

> **NOTE**   *To test this program, create a Windows application and add a DataGrid control to the form.*

Listing 5-5. Creating a table using DataTable *and* DataColumn

```
private void CreateCustTable()
        {
            // Create a new DataTable
            DataTable custTable = new DataTable("Customers");

            // Create ID Column
            DataColumn IdCol = new DataColumn();
            IdCol.ColumnName= "ID";
            IdCol.DataType = Type.GetType("System.Int32");
            IdCol.ReadOnly = true;
            IdCol.AllowDBNull = false;
            IdCol.Unique = true;
            IdCol.AutoIncrement = true;
            IdCol.AutoIncrementSeed = 1;
            IdCol.AutoIncrementStep = 1;
            custTable.Columns.Add(IdCol);

            // Create Name Column
            DataColumn nameCol = new DataColumn();
            nameCol.ColumnName= "Name";
            nameCol.DataType = Type.GetType("System.String");
            custTable.Columns.Add(nameCol);
```

```
    // Create Address Column
    DataColumn addCol = new DataColumn();
    addCol.ColumnName= "Address";
    addCol.DataType = Type.GetType("System.String");
    custTable.Columns.Add(addCol);

    // Create DOB Column
    DataColumn dobCol = new DataColumn();
    dobCol.ColumnName= "DOB";
    dobCol.DataType = Type.GetType("System.DateTime");
    custTable.Columns.Add(dobCol);

    // VAR Column
    DataColumn fullTimeCol = new DataColumn();
    fullTimeCol.ColumnName= "VAR";
    fullTimeCol.DataType = Type.GetType("System.Boolean");
    custTable.Columns.Add(fullTimeCol);

    // Make the ID column the primary key column.
    DataColumn[] PrimaryKeyColumns = new DataColumn[1];
    PrimaryKeyColumns[0] = custTable.Columns["ID"];
    custTable.PrimaryKey = PrimaryKeyColumns;

    // Create a dataset
    DataSet ds = new DataSet("Customers");
    // Add Customers table to the dataset
    ds.Tables.Add(custTable);
    // Attach the dataset to a DataGrid
    dataGrid1.DataSource = ds.DefaultViewManager;
}
```

The output of Listing 5-5 looks like Figure 5-9, which shows empty columns in a data grid control.

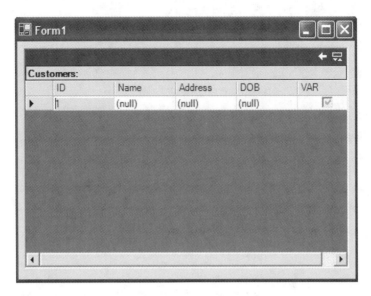

Figure 5-9. The output of Listing 5-5

The DataRow

A DataRow represents a row of data in a data table. You add data to the data table using the DataRow object. A DataRowCollection object represents a collection of data rows of a data table. You use DataTable's NewRow method to return a DataRow object of data table, add values to the data row, and add a row to the data table again by using DataRowCollection's Add method.

Before adding rows to a data table, I'll discuss the DataRow class properties and methods. Table 5-5 describes DataRow class properties, and Table 5-6 describes the DataRow class methods.

Table 5-5. The DataRow *Class Properties*

PROPERTY	DESCRIPTION
Item	Represents an item of a row
ItemArray	Represents all values in a row
RowState	Indicates the current state of a row
Table	Returns the DataTable to which this row is attached

Table 5-6. The DataRow *Class Methods*

METHOD	DESCRIPTION
AcceptChanges	Commits all the changes made to this row
BeginEdit	Starts an edit operation on a row
CancelEdit	Cancels the current edit on a row
Delete	Deletes a DataRow
EndEdit	Ends the current edit on a row
GetChildRows	Returns child rows of a DataRow
GetParentRows	Returns parent rows of a DataRow
RejectChanges	Rejects all the changes made sincez last AcceptChanges

You access DataRow members through the data table columns. A column acts as an item of the row. For example, if a data table has three columns such as Id, Name, and Address, then a row will have three members: Id, Name, and Address. You access data row members using the name of columns. For example, Listing 5-6 sets values of the Id, Name, and Address columns.

Listing 5-6. Setting values of the Id, Address, and Name columns of a DataRow

```
DataRow row1 = custTable.NewRow();
row1["id"] = 1001;
row1["Address"] = "43 Lanewood Road, Cito, CA";
row1["Name"] = "George Bishop ";
```

After setting a row member's values, you call DataTable's DataRowCollection's Add method though the DataTable.Rows property to add a row to the data table:

```
custTable.Rows.Add(row1);
```

The RejectChanges method of the DataRow rejects recent changes on that row. For example, if you have recently added row1 to the data table, calling the RejectChanges method as following:

```
row1.RejectChanges();
```

won't add the row to the data table.

You can also delete a recently added row to a data table by calling DataRow's Delete method:

```
Row1.Delete();
```

> **CAUTION** RejectChanges *and* Delete *method may not work together if you're applying both methods on the same row because* RejectChanges *doesn't add a row to the data table.*

Listing 5-7 shows a program that creates a DataTable with three columns (Id, Name, and Address) and adds three rows to the data table. At the end, this program attaches the newly created DataTable to a data grid control using a dataset.

> **CAUTION** *As you can see from Listing 5-7, the Id column of the Customers table is read-only (the* ReadOnly *property is true). That means you'll not be able to add data to the table. If you want to add data from the front-end, you need to set the* ReadOnly *property as false.*

Listing 5-7. Adding rows to a DataTable *using* DataRow

```
// This method creates Customers table
private void CreateCustomersTable()
{
// Create a new DataTable.
System.Data.DataTable custTable = new DataTable("Customers");
DataColumn dtColumn;

// Create id Column
dtColumn = new DataColumn();
dtColumn.DataType = System.Type.GetType("System.Int32");
dtColumn.ColumnName = "id";
dtColumn.Caption = "Cust ID";
dtColumn.ReadOnly = true;
dtColumn.Unique = true;
// Add id Column to the DataColumnCollection.
custTable.Columns.Add(dtColumn);

// Create Name column.
dtColumn = new DataColumn();
dtColumn.DataType = System.Type.GetType("System.String");
dtColumn.ColumnName = "Name";
dtColumn.Caption = "Cust Name";
dtColumn.AutoIncrement = false;
dtColumn.ReadOnly = false;
dtColumn.Unique = false;
```

```
// Add Name column to the table.
custTable.Columns.Add(dtColumn);

// Create Address column.
dtColumn = new DataColumn();
dtColumn.DataType = System.Type.GetType("System.String");
dtColumn.ColumnName = "Address";
dtColumn.Caption = "Address";
dtColumn.ReadOnly = false;
dtColumn.Unique = false;
// Add Address column to the table.
custTable.Columns.Add(dtColumn);

// Make the ID column the primary key column.
DataColumn[] PrimaryKeyColumns = new DataColumn[1];
PrimaryKeyColumns[0] = custTable.Columns["id"];
custTable.PrimaryKey = PrimaryKeyColumns;

// Instantiate the DataSet variable.
DataSet ds = new DataSet("Customers");
// Add the custTable to the DataSet.
ds.Tables.Add(custTable);

// Add rows to the custTable using its NewRow method
// I add three customers with their addresses, name and id
DataRow row1 = custTable.NewRow();
row1["id"] = 1001;
row1["Address"] = "43 Lanewood Road, Cito, CA";
row1["Name"] = "George Bishop ";
custTable.Rows.Add(row1);

DataRow row2 = custTable.NewRow();
row2["id"] = 1002;
row2["Name"] = "Rock Joe ";
row2["Address"] = "King of Prusssia, PA";
custTable.Rows.Add(row2);

DataRow row3 = custTable.NewRow();
row3["id"] = 1003;
row3["Name"] = "Miranda ";
row3["Address"] = "279 P. Avenue, Bridgetown, PA";
custTable.Rows.Add(row3);
```

```
//row3.RejectChanges();
//row2.Delete();

// Bind dataset to the data grid
dataGrid1.DataSource = ds.DefaultViewManager;
}
```

The output of the program looks like Figure 5-10.

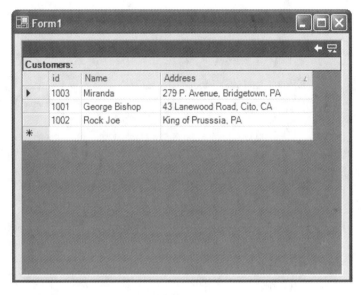

Figure 5-10. Adding rows to a DataTable

NOTE *To run this program, create a Windows application and drop a data grid control on the form. After that you can either call* CreateCustomersTable *listed in Listing 5-3 from the form load or from a button-click handler. You can write a form load event by double-clicking on the form or by opening the Properties window.*

If you uncomment the bold lines row3.RejectChanges() and row2.Delete() at the end of Listing 5-11, shown in Listing 5-8, the output looks like Figure 5-11. The RejectChanges method rejects the addition of row 3, and the Delete method deletes row 2.

Listing 5-8. Calling DataRow's RejectChanges *and* Delete *methods*

```
private void CreateCustomersTable()
{
// more code. . .
row3.RejectChanges();
row2.Delete();

// Bind dataset to the data grid
dataGrid1.DataSource = ds.DefaultViewManager;
}
```

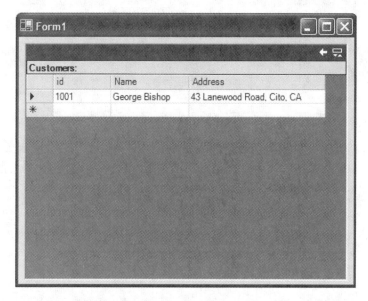

Figure 5-11. Result of the RejectChanges *and Delete DataRow methods*

The DataRowState Enumeration

The DataRowState enumeration returns the current state of a row. It's useful during operations when you want to know the current state of a row. Table 5-7 lists the values of the DataRowState enumeration.

Table 5-7. The DataRowState *Enumeration Members*

MEMBER	DESCRIPTION
Added	Row has been added and AcceptChanges has not been called.
Deleted	Row was deleted using the Delete method.
Detached	Row was created but deleted before it was added to the collection.
Modified	Row has been modified, but AcceptChanges is not called yet.
Unchanged	Row has not changed since last AcceptChanges was called.

The RowState property of a DataRow returns the DataRowState enumeration. You can use this to find out the current state of a row. For example, Listing 5-9 calls RowState just after the Delete and RejectChanges methods.

Listing 5-9. Calling the RowState *property*

```
row3.RejectChanges();
MessageBox.Show(row3.RowState.ToString());
row2.Delete();
MessageBox.Show(row2.RowState.ToString());
```

The DataRelation

To provide data integrity and consistency, you should use relationships between two tables. You achieve this relationship by defining a primary key in one table and using a foreign key in the other table. Say a customer has multiple orders; the Customers table stores the customer details, and the Orders table stores all the order details. To avoid the redundancy of data, you define the primary key of the Customers table as a foreign key in the Orders table.

> **NOTE** *In general this relationship is called the* customer/order *relationship*, parent/child, *or sometimes* master/details.

257

In this example, the Customers table is also the *parent* table, and the Orders table is also the *child* table. The ParentRelations property of DataTable represents the parent relationship, and ChildRelations represents the child relationship.

> **CAUTION** *The data type of both columns, which you're linking through a relationship in the Customers and the Orders tables, must be identical.*

You can also access this relationship through a DataSet using its Relations property. To create a relationship between two columns, you create two DataColumn objects and pass them as DataRelation arguments.

Listing 5-10 shows you how to create a customer/order relationship between the Customers and Orders table through the Customers table's id column, referenced as CustId in the Orders table. The DataRelation constructor takes three arguments: the name of the relationship, the first DataColumn, and the second DataColumn. After that you call DataTable's ParentRelation.Add method with DataRelation as an argument. (Listing 5-12 shows the full source code of this example.)

Listing 5-10. Creating a customer/order relationship using DataRelation

```
private void BindData()
{
    DataRelation dtRelation;
    DataColumn CustCol = dtSet.Tables["Customers"].Columns["id"];
    DataColumn orderCol = dtSet.Tables["Orders"].Columns["CustId"];

    dtRelation = new DataRelation("CustOrderRelation", CustCol, orderCol);
    dtSet.Tables["Orders"].ParentRelations.Add(dtRelation);

    dataGrid1.SetDataBinding(dtSet,"Customers");
}
```

The DataTable

In the previous sections you've already seen that columns and rows are the building blocks of a data table. You need to work with the DataColumn and DataRow objects to create data tables and add data to them. Besides creating a data table schema and adding rows to it, a data table has more to offer. The DataTable object represents a data table.

Before creating a data table, I'll show you the DataTable class properties and methods. Table 5-8 describes some of the common DataTable properties, and Table 5-9 summarizes some of the common DataTable methods.

Table 5-8. The DataTable *Class Properties*

PROPERTY	DESCRIPTION
Columns	Represents all table columns
Constraints	Represents all table constraints
DataSet	Returns the dataset for the table
DefaultView	Customized view of the data table
ChildRelation	Returns child relations for the data table
ParentRelation	Returns parent relations for the data table
PrimaryKey	Represents an array of columns that function as primary key for the table
Rows	All rows of the data table
TableName	Name of the table

Table 5-9. The DataTable *Class Methods*

METHOD	DESCRIPTION
AcceptChanges	Commits all the changes made since last AcceptChanges was called
Clear	Deletes all data table data
Clone	Creates a clone of a DataTable including its schema
Copy	Copies a data table including its schema
NewRow	Creates a new row, which is later added by calling the Rows.Add method
RejectChanges	Rejects all changes made after last AcceptChanges was called
Reset	Resets a data table's original state
Select	Gets an array of rows based on the criteria

The DataTable class provides methods and properties to remove, copy, and clone data tables. Not only that, but you can also apply filters on a DataTable. The

Constraints property provides access to all the constraints that a data table has. You can also access the child and parent relationship using ChildRelation and ParentRelation.

To test this theory, I'll create two data tables, Customers and Orders, and set a relationship between them. To test this application, you build a Windows Application using Visual C# and add a data grid control to the form. After that you call the CreateCustomersTable, CreateOrdersTable, and BindData methods from the form constructor after InitializeComponent. The form constructor looks like Listing 5-11.

Listing 5-11. Form's constructor calling CreateCustomersTable, CreateOrdersTable, *and* BindData

```
public Form1()
{
    InitializeComponent();

    CreateCustomersTable();
    CreateOrdersTable();
    BindData();
}
```

You also need to add a DataSet variable, dtSet, in the beginning of your form. See the following code:

```
public class Form1 : System.Windows.Forms.Form
{
// Put the next line into the Declarations section.
private System.Data.DataSet dtSet;
. . . . . . . . .
}
```

In Listing 5-12, the CreateCustomersTable method creates the Customers data table with Id, Name, and Address columns and adds three data rows to it. The CreateOrdersTable method creates the Orders table with OrderId, CustId, Name, and Description columns and adds data to it. The BindData method creates a customer/orders relationship and binds the data to a DataGrid control using DataSet.

Listing 5-12 shows all three CreateCustomerTable, CreateOrdersTable, and BindData methods.

Listing 5-12. Customer/orders relationship example

```
// This method creates Customers table
        private void CreateCustomersTable()
```

```
{
    // Create a new DataTable.
    System.Data.DataTable custTable = new DataTable("Customers");
    DataColumn dtColumn;
    DataRow myDataRow;

    // Create id Column
    dtColumn = new DataColumn();
    dtColumn.DataType = System.Type.GetType("System.Int32");
    dtColumn.ColumnName = "id";
    dtColumn.Caption = "Cust ID";
    dtColumn.ReadOnly = false;
    dtColumn.Unique = true;
    // Add id Column to the DataColumnCollection.
    custTable.Columns.Add(dtColumn);

    // Create Name column.
    dtColumn = new DataColumn();
    dtColumn.DataType = System.Type.GetType("System.String");
    dtColumn.ColumnName = "Name";
    dtColumn.Caption = "Cust Name";
    dtColumn.AutoIncrement = false;
    dtColumn.ReadOnly = false;
    dtColumn.Unique = false;
    // Add Name column to the table.
    custTable.Columns.Add(dtColumn);


    // Create Address column.
    dtColumn = new DataColumn();
    dtColumn.DataType = System.Type.GetType("System.String");
    dtColumn.ColumnName = "Address";
    dtColumn.Caption = "Address";
    dtColumn.ReadOnly = false;
    dtColumn.Unique = false;
    // Add Address column to the table.
    custTable.Columns.Add(dtColumn);

    // Make the ID column the primary key column.
    DataColumn[] PrimaryKeyColumns = new DataColumn[1];
    PrimaryKeyColumns[0] = custTable.Columns["id"];
    custTable.PrimaryKey = PrimaryKeyColumns;
```

```
                    // Instantiate the DataSet variable.
                    dtSet = new DataSet("Customers");
                    // Add the custTable to the DataSet.
                    dtSet.Tables.Add(custTable);

                    // Add rows to the custTable using its NewRow method
                    // I add three customers with thier addresses, name and id
                    myDataRow = custTable.NewRow();
                    myDataRow["id"] = 1001;
                    myDataRow["Address"] = "43 Lanewood Road, Cito, CA";
                    myDataRow["Name"] = "George Bishop ";
                    custTable.Rows.Add(myDataRow);

                    myDataRow = custTable.NewRow();
                    myDataRow["id"] = 1002;
                    myDataRow["Name"] = "Rock Joe ";
                    myDataRow["Address"] = "King of Prusssia, PA";
                    custTable.Rows.Add(myDataRow);

                    myDataRow = custTable.NewRow();
                    myDataRow["id"] = 1003;
                    myDataRow["Name"] = "Miranda ";
                    myDataRow["Address"] = "279 P. Avenue, Bridgetown, PA";
                    custTable.Rows.Add(myDataRow);

            }

// This method creates Orders table with
private void CreateOrdersTable()
{
    // Create Orders table.
    DataTable ordersTable = new DataTable("Orders");
    DataColumn dtColumn;
    DataRow dtRow;

    // Create OrderId column
    dtColumn = new DataColumn();
    dtColumn.DataType= System.Type.GetType("System.Int32");
    dtColumn.ColumnName = "OrderId";
    dtColumn.AutoIncrement = true;
    dtColumn.Caption = "Order ID";
    dtColumn.ReadOnly = true;
    dtColumn.Unique = true;
    ordersTable.Columns.Add(dtColumn);
```

```
// Create Name column.
dtColumn = new DataColumn();
dtColumn.DataType= System.Type.GetType("System.String");
dtColumn.ColumnName = "Name";
dtColumn.Caption = "Item Name";
ordersTable.Columns.Add(dtColumn);

// Create CustId column which reprence CustId from
// the custTable
dtColumn = new DataColumn();
dtColumn.DataType= System.Type.GetType("System.Int32");
dtColumn.ColumnName = "CustId";
dtColumn.AutoIncrement = false;
dtColumn.Caption = "CustId";
dtColumn.ReadOnly = false;
dtColumn.Unique = false;
ordersTable.Columns.Add(dtColumn);

// Create Description column.
dtColumn = new DataColumn();
dtColumn.DataType= System.Type.GetType("System.String");
dtColumn.ColumnName = "Description";
dtColumn.Caption = "Description Name";
ordersTable.Columns.Add(dtColumn);

// Add ordersTable to the dataset
dtSet.Tables.Add(ordersTable);

// Add two rows to Customer Id 1001
dtRow = ordersTable.NewRow();
dtRow["OrderId"] = 0;
dtRow["Name"] = "ASP Book";
dtRow["CustId"] = 1001 ;
dtRow["Description"] = "Same Day" ;
ordersTable.Rows.Add(dtRow);

dtRow = ordersTable.NewRow();
dtRow["OrderId"] = 1;
dtRow["Name"] = "C# Book";
dtRow["CustId"] = 1001 ;
dtRow["Description"] = "2 Day Air" ;
ordersTable.Rows.Add(dtRow);
```

```
        // Add two rows to Customer Id 1002
        dtRow = ordersTable.NewRow();
        dtRow["OrderId"] = 2;
        dtRow["Name"] = "Data Quest";
        dtRow["Description"] = "Monthly Magazine";
        dtRow["CustId"] = 1002 ;
        ordersTable.Rows.Add(dtRow);

        dtRow = ordersTable.NewRow();
        dtRow["OrderId"] = 3;
        dtRow["Name"] = "PC Magazine";
        dtRow["Description"] = "Monthly Magazine";
        dtRow["CustId"] = 1002 ;
        ordersTable.Rows.Add(dtRow);

        // Add two rows to Customer Id 1003
        dtRow = ordersTable.NewRow();
        dtRow["OrderId"] = 4;
        dtRow["Name"] = "PC Magazine";
        dtRow["Description"] = "Monthly Magazine";
        dtRow["CustId"] = 1003 ;
        ordersTable.Rows.Add(dtRow);

        dtRow = ordersTable.NewRow();
        dtRow["OrderId"] = 5;
        dtRow["Name"] = "C# Book";
        dtRow["CustId"] = 1003 ;
        dtRow["Description"] = "2 Day Air" ;
        ordersTable.Rows.Add(dtRow);


}


// This method creates a customer order relationship and binds data tables
// to the data grid cotnrol using dataset.
private void BindData()
{
    DataRelation dtRelation;
    DataColumn CustCol = dtSet.Tables["Customers"].Columns["id"];
    DataColumn orderCol = dtSet.Tables["Orders"].Columns["CustId"];

    dtRelation = new DataRelation("CustOrderRelation", CustCol, orderCol);
    dtSet.Tables["Orders"].ParentRelations.Add(dtRelation);
    dataGrid1.SetDataBinding(dtSet,"Customers");
}
```

As you can see from the CreateCustomersTable method in Listing 5-12, it creates the Customers table using DataTable and adds the Id, Name and Address columns to the table. You use DataColumn to add these columns. The Id column has properties such as ReadOnly and Unique. As discussed earlier, to add a column to a DataTable, you create a DataColumn object, set its properties, and then call the DataTable.Columns.Add method. Similar to the id column, you add two more columns, Name and Address, of string type to the table. After that you make the id column the primary key by setting DataTable.PrimaryKey as the id column:

```
PrimaryKeyColumns[0] = custTable.Columns["id"];
custTable.PrimaryKey = PrimaryKeyColumns;
```

After creating a DataTable you add it to a DataSet using the DataSet.Tables.Add method. This method takes one argument of type DataTable:

```
dtSet = new DataSet("Customers");
 dtSet.Tables.Add(custTable);
```

Now, the last step is to add data to DataTable. You add data using DataRow. First, you create a DataRow object using DataTable's NewRow method, add data to a DataRow's items, and add DataRow to the DataTable using the DataTable.Rows.Add method. You'll follow the same method for the second table in CreateOrdersTable to create the Orders table. The Orders table has the fields OrderId, Name, Description, and CustId. The BindData method creates a relationship by using DataRelation and binds the id column of the Customers tables to the CustId column of the Orders table. The name of the relationship is CustOrderRelation. After that you bind DataTable to the DataGrid using the SetDataBinding method.

The output of Listing 5-12 looks like Figure 5-12.

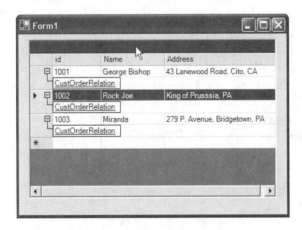

Figure 5-12. Output of Listing 5-12

If you click on the CustOrderRelation link, the output looks like Figure 5-13.

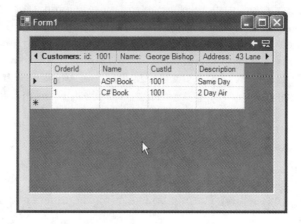

Figure 5-13. Orders record for Customers id 1001

As you can see from Figure 5-13, DataGrid shows all the orders for Customer id 1001.

More DataTable Operations

Adding and deleting data are two common operations when working with databases. You've already learned in the previous section about how to add data to a data table using DataRow. In this section you'll see how to add, delete, and search data programmatically. To test the sample application, you can create a Windows Forms application. In this sample, you'll not store data in a database. All data will be stored in memory in the form of DataTable objects.

The first step is to build a Graphical User Interface (GUI). To build this GUI, you'll create a Windows application project. After that, add a DataGrid control, three button controls, four textbox controls, three group boxes, and a couple of label controls. Then adjust them on your form. You can also change the background color of the controls, as shown in Figure 5-14. As you can see from the form, the Add button will add the name and address that you enter in the Name and Address textboxes. The Remove button will remove the row number you'll enter in the Enter Row # textbox. The Search button searches for a name in the DataTable and returns the corresponding records in the DataGrid.

> **NOTE** *You don't have to create the same form. The only thing you need to have is a DataGrid with the same number of text boxes and button controls.*

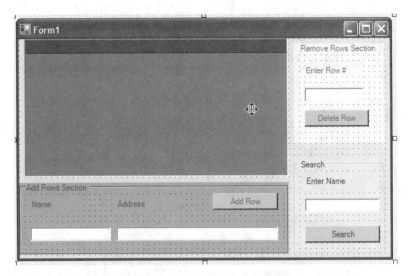

Figure 5-14. Add, delete, and search operations in DataTable

Now, you change the names of the form controls and add the DataSet variable dtSet and the DataTable variable custTable to the beginning of the form. The final control names and variables look like Listing 5-13.

Listing 5-13. Variables of Figure 5-14

```
private System.Windows.Forms.DataGrid dataGrid1;
private System.Windows.Forms.Label label1;
private System.Windows.Forms.Label label2;
private System.Windows.Forms.TextBox textBox1;
private System.Windows.Forms.TextBox textBox2;
private System.Windows.Forms.Label label3;
private System.Windows.Forms.TextBox textBox3;
private System.Windows.Forms.Button DeleteRow;
private System.Windows.Forms.Button AddRow;
private System.Data.DataTable custTable;
private System.Windows.Forms.GroupBox groupBox1;
private System.Windows.Forms.GroupBox groupBox2;
private System.Windows.Forms.GroupBox groupBox3;
private System.Windows.Forms.Label label4;
private System.Windows.Forms.Button SearchButton;
private System.Windows.Forms.TextBox SearchBox;
private System.Data.DataSet dtSet;
```

Now you create the Customers table with three columns: id, Name, and Address. I've already discussed how to add columns to a DataTable using

DataColumn and bind it to a DataGrid in the previous sections. The
CreateCustomersTable method creates the Customers table. After creating
the Customers table, you add the DataTable to the DataSet using the
DataSet.Tables.Add method. The CreateCustomersTable method looks like
Listing 5-14.

Listing 5-14. The CreateCustomersTable *method*

```
// This method creates Customers table
        private void CreateCustomersTable()
        {
            // Create a new DataTable.
            custTable = new DataTable("Customers");
            DataColumn dtColumn;

            // Create id Column
            dtColumn = new DataColumn();
            dtColumn.DataType = System.Type.GetType("System.Int32");
            dtColumn.ColumnName = "id";
            dtColumn.AutoIncrement = true;
            dtColumn.AutoIncrementSeed = 100;
            dtColumn.AutoIncrementStep = 1;
            dtColumn.Caption = "Cust ID";
            dtColumn.ReadOnly = true;
            dtColumn.Unique = true;
            // Add id Column to the DataColumnCollection.
            custTable.Columns.Add(dtColumn);

            // Create Name column.
            dtColumn = new DataColumn();
            dtColumn.DataType = System.Type.GetType("System.String");
            dtColumn.ColumnName = "Name";
            dtColumn.Caption = "Cust Name";
            dtColumn.AutoIncrement = false;
            dtColumn.ReadOnly = false;
            dtColumn.Unique = false;
            // Add Name column to the table.
            custTable.Columns.Add(dtColumn);

            // Create Address column.
            dtColumn = new DataColumn();
            dtColumn.DataType = System.Type.GetType("System.String");
            dtColumn.ColumnName = "Address";
```

```
                        dtColumn.Caption = "Address";
                        dtColumn.ReadOnly = false;
                        dtColumn.Unique = false;
                        // Add Address column to the table.
                        custTable.Columns.Add(dtColumn);

                        // Make the ID column the primary key column.
                        DataColumn[] PrimaryKeyColumns = new DataColumn[1];
                        PrimaryKeyColumns[0] = custTable.Columns["id"];
                        custTable.PrimaryKey = PrimaryKeyColumns;

                        // Instantiate the DataSet variable.
                        dtSet = new DataSet("Customers");
                        // Add the custTable to the DataSet.
                        dtSet.Tables.Add(custTable);

                        RefreshData();


            }
```

At the end of the `CreateCustomersTable` method you call the `RefreshData` method, which refreshes the DataGrid contents and fills them with the current data of the `DataTable` by setting DataGrid's `DataSource` property to DataSet's `DefaultViewManager`. The `RefreshData` method looks like the following:

```
private void RefreshData()
{
    dataGrid1.DataSource = dtSet.DefaultViewManager;
}
```

As you can see from Figure 5-14, the Add Row button adds a new row to the Customers `DataTable` with the Name and Address columns reading from Name and Address text boxes. The Delete Row button deletes the row number inserted in the Enter Row # text box. The Search button searches and returns rows that contain the name entered in the Enter Name text box of the Search group box.

OK, now it's time to write code for the button event handlers. You can write button event handlers by double-clicking on the buttons or using the Properties windows. (See Chapter 2 for more details.) First, you write the event handler for the Add Row button with the handler name `AddRow_Click` for this button. After that, write event handlers for the Remove and Search buttons; the event handler names for these buttons are `DeleteRow_Click` and `SearchButton_Click`, respectively.

Now you can write code on these handlers. First you're writing code for the Add Row button. Actually, there is nothing new about the code written for the

Add Row button handler. You add a new row to the DataTable using DataRow and call the Add and AcceptChanges methods of the DataTable. The following code snippet listed in Listing 5-15 shows the Add Row button click event handler.

As you can see from the code, I added Name as TextBox1's text and Address as TextBox2's text.

You call NewRow of DataTable to add a new row to DataTable, set its field values, and call the DataTable.Rows.Add method to add it. At the end, you call the RefreshData method to fill the DataGrid with the records.

Listing 5-15. The AddRow_Click *method*

```
private void AddRow_Click(object sender, System.EventArgs e)
{
        // Add rows to the custTable using its NewRow method
        // I add three customers with thier addresses, name and id
        DataRow myDataRow = custTable.NewRow();
        myDataRow["Name"] = textBox1.Text.ToString();
        myDataRow["Address"] = textBox2.Text.ToString();
        custTable.Rows.Add(myDataRow);
        custTable.AcceptChanges();
        RefreshData();
}
```

If you add six rows to the DataTable using the Add Row button, the result looks like Figure 5-15.

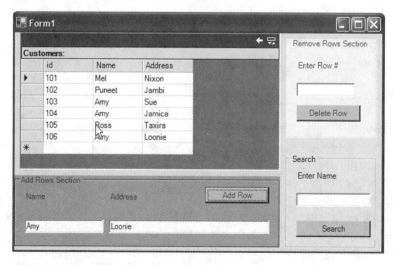

Figure 5-15. Adding rows to the DataTable

The Delete Row button deletes the row number you entered in the text box. You can delete a row from a DataTable by calling DataRow's Delete method. On the Delete Row button event handler, you call DataTable's Delete method. Before calling Delete, you need to know what row you want to delete from a DataTable. You get that from TextBox3 and return that row using DataTable.Rows(index). Once you have a DataRow, you call its Delete method and AcceptChanges method to make final changes to the DataTable. In Listing 5-16, you first call the Delete method of DataRow and call AcceptChanges to accept the changes.

Listing 5-16. The DeleteRow_Click method

```
// Deletes a row from the datatable
 private void DeleteRow_Click(object sender, System.EventArgs e)
 {
     int idx = Convert.ToInt32(textBox3.Text.ToString());
     DataRow row = custTable.Rows[idx -1];
     row.Delete();
     row.AcceptChanges();
 }
```

To test this code, you delete the second row by entering 2 in the Remove Row # text box and click Delete Row button. The result looks like Figure 5-16.

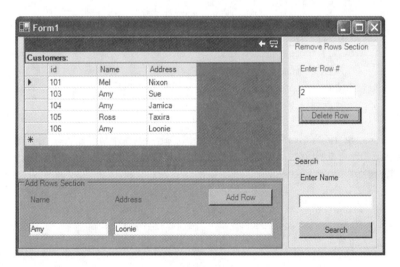

Figure 5-16. Deleting rows from the DataTable

The DataTable class also provides the Select method to select certain rows in a DataTable based on a filter. A filter is a conditional statement. All SQL conditional operators are valid in the filter string. For example, to filter rows where id is greater than 22, the filter string will be "Id>22"; for selecting records of the name Rox, the filter string will be "Name='Rox'". The SeachButton_Click method searches for the criteria and deletes all the rows from the DataTable that don't match the criteria to display only rows that match the criteria. Listing 5-17 shows the SearchButton_Click method.

Listing 5-17. The SearchButton_Click *method*

```
// Search button searches for the criteria
private void SearchButton_Click(object sender, System.EventArgs e)
{
    string str = "Name <>'"+ SearchBox.Text +"'" ;
    DataRow[] rows = custTable.Select(str);

    // If no record found
    if(rows.Length == 0)
    {
        MessageBox.Show("No records  found!");
        return;
    }
    for (int i=0; i< rows.Length; i++)
    {
        rows[i].Delete();
        rows[i].AcceptChanges();
    }
    RefreshData();
}
```

Now using the Search button and text boxes, you search for records with the name Amy by entering "Amy" in the Search text box and clicking the Search button. The result looks like Figure 5-17.

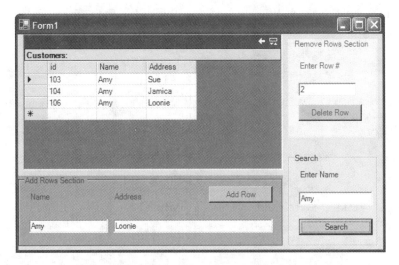

Figure 5-17. Result of clicking the Search button after entering "Amy"

Using DataSet, DataView, and DataViewManager

As you've seen in Chapter 4, ADO.NET provides components to view data in data-bound controls. These components are easy to use and provide rapid development. You just drag and drop these controls to a form, set their properties, and bind them to data-bound controls. Then you're all set to run your programs. The DataView and DataViewManager classes fall in this category. You can use these classes to represent different views of a data table based on different filter and sort criterion. You can use these classes either at design-time or run-time modes. In Chapter 4, you've seen how to use these class objects at design-time. In this chapter, you'll see how to use these classes programmatically.

A DataSet is a key component in the ADO.NET data model. It's an in-memory representation of one or multiple data tables, relations, and constraints. It provides a communication between the actual data and Windows Forms and Web Forms controls to provide the data a view through the DataView and the DataViewManager. Not only this, but a DataSet offers much more than that. (I'll discuss DataSet in more detail in "The DataSet" section.)

The DataView is useful when you need to bind a DataTable or multiple DataTable objects with data-bound controls. You can also represent multiple views of same data by applying a filter and sort on a data table, and you can bind these multiple views to different data-bound controls such as a DataGrid, DataList, Combo Box, and a ListBox control.

Figure 5-18 shows the relationship between a DataSet, DataTable, DataView, and Windows and Web Forms controls. As you can see from Figure 5-18, a DataSet contains three DataTable objects, which are represented by three different views. The three different DataView objects bind to different data-bound controls.

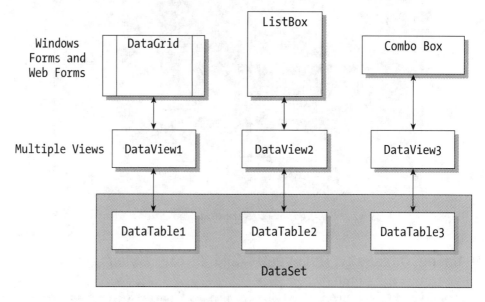

Figure 5-18. Relationship between the DataSet, DataTable, *and* DataView

The DataSet

A DataSet object plays a vital role in the ADO.NET component model. A DataSet represents a disconnected cache of data in the form of tables, rows, columns, or XML schemas. If you've ever programmed a database application in previous versions of Visual Studio, you're probably familiar with *recordsets*. A recordset object was a way to represent data in your programs. Similar to a recordset, a DataSet represents data in your applications. Once you've constructed a DataSet, you can get or set data in your application or your data source. As mentioned earlier, the DataSet works in both connected and disconnected environments. A DataSet communicates with a DataAdapter and calls DataAdapter's Fill method to fill data from a DataAdapter. You can fill a DataSet object with multiple tables or stored procedures with the aid of the DataAdapters. You'll see how a DataSet works in a connected environment to access data from multiple data sources in the "Using ADO.NET Data Providers" section. In this section, you'll see how it works with DataTable and DataView objects.

As you can see in Figure 5-19, the Fill method of data adapter fills data from a data adapter to a dataset. (I'll discuss DataAdapter in more detail in the "Using ADO.NET Data Providers" section.) Once data is filled to a DataSet from a DataAdapter, you can view it in Windows or Web applications by binding data to data-bound controls through a DataView. You can generate one or multiple views for a data tables based on the filter and sort criteria.

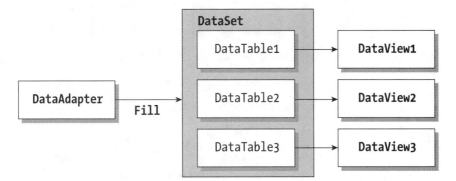

Figure 5-19. The relationship between DataSet, DataAdapter, *and* DataView *objects*

The DataSet class represents a dataset in ADO.NET. As you've seen earlier, a DataSet can have multiple DataTable objects. The DataTableCollection object represents all DataSet objects related to a DataSet. The Tables property of the DataSet represents the collection of DataTable objects. The tables relate to each other with DataRelation objects, discussed earlier in this chapter. The DataRelationCollection represents all available relations in the DataSet. The Relations property represents the DataRelationCollection of a DataSet. Table 5-10 describes some DataSet properties.

A DataSet object stores data in XML format. An XML schema represents a dataset. A DataSet also defines methods to read and write XML documents. The ReadXml method reads an XML document and fills the DataSet with the XML data, and the WriteXML method writes DataSet data to an XML document. This class also defines the methods ReadXmlSchema and WriteXmlSchema to read and write XML schema. I'll discuss these methods in more detail in Chapter 6. Table 5-11 describes some of the DataSet class members. I'll use these methods and properties throughout this chapter's examples.

Table 5-10. The DataSet *Class Properties*

PROPERTY	DESCRIPTION
DataSetName	Represents the name of the DataSet
DefaultViewManager	Default view of the data of a DataSet
Relations	Collection of relations of a DataSet that links multiple tables
Tables	Collection of tables contained in a DataSet

Table 5-11. The DataSet *Class Methods*

METHOD	DESCRIPTION
AcceptChanges	Commits all the changes made since last AcceptChanges was called
BeginInit	Begins initialization if a DataSet was used previously
Clear	Removes all data from a DataSet
Clone	Clones the structure of a DataSet
Copy	Copies a dataset's data and structure
EndInit	Ends the initialization
GetChanges	Gets a copy of dataset containing all changes made since last AcceptChanges was called or loaded
GetXml	Returns the XML representation of the data stored in a DataSet
GetXmlSchema	Returns XML schema of the data stored in a DataSet
Merge	Merges two DataSet objects
ReadXmlSchema	Reads an XML schema and fills data in a DataSet
RejectChanges	Rejects all changes made to the DataSet since it was created or AcceptChanges called
Reset	Resets a DataSet to its original state
WriteXml	Writes data of a DataSet to an XML document
WriteXmlSchema	Writes data of a DataSet to an XML schema

Typed and Untyped DataSets

As you may recall from earlier discussions, there are two kinds of a DataSet: typed or untyped. A typed DataSet first comes from the DataSet class and then uses XML schema (.xsd file) to generate a new class. You've seen how to create a typed dataset using VS.NET in Chapter 4. An untyped dataset has no built-in schema. You create an instance of a DataSet class and call its methods and properties to work with the data sources. All elements of an untyped dataset are collections. In this chapter, you'll work with untyped datasets.

Both kinds of dataset have their own advantages and disadvantages. Typed datasets take less time to write applications but offer no flexibility. They're useful when you already know the schema of a database. The biggest advantage of typed datasets is the VS.NET IDE support. As you've seen in Chapter 4, you can drag a database table, its columns, or stored procedures to a form in your application and the IDE generates typed dataset for you. After that, you can bind these datasets to the controls. There are many occasions when you don't know the schema of a database. In those cases, the untyped datasets are useful. The untyped datasets also provide the flexibility of connecting with multiple data sources. And you can use them without the VS.NET IDE.

The DataView

Another powerful feature of ADO.NET is the ability to create several different views of the same data. You can sort these views differently and filter them on different criteria. They can contain different row state information.

As you've seen in Figure 5-18, a DataView represents a customized view of data table and can bind to Windows Forms and Web Forms controls. Using DataView sort and filter features, you can also have multiple views of a single data table. Using RowFilter and Sort properties, you can apply a filter on a DataView and sort its contents before binding it to a data-bound control. The AddNew method adds a new row to a DataView, and the Delete method deletes a row from a DataView. You can use the Find and FindRows methods to search for rows based on the defined criteria.

Table 5-12 describes some of the DataView properties, and Table 5-13 describes some of its methods.

Table 5-12. The DataView Class Properties

PROPERTY	DESCRIPTION
AllowDelete	Indicates whether deletes are allowed
AllowEdit	Indicates whether edits are allowed
AddNews	Indicates whether new rows can be added
Count	Represents the number of records in a DataView after RowFilter and RowStateFilter have been applied
DataViewManager	DataViewManager associated with this view
Item	Represents an item of a row
RowFilter	Represents the expression used to filter rows to view in the DataView
Sort	Represents the sort column and sort order
Table	DataTable attached with this view

Table 5-13. The DataView *Class Methods*

METHOD	DESCRIPTION
AddNew	Adds a new row to the DataView
BeginInit	Begins the initialization if a data view was previously used
Delete	Deletes a row
Find	Finds a row in the DataView based on the specified criteria
FindRows	Returns an array of rows based on the specified criteria

The DataViewManager

A DataViewManager contains a collection of views of a dataset, one view for each data table in the dataset. The DataViewManager has a DataViewSettings property that enables the user to construct a different view for each data table in the dataset. If you want to create two views on the same data table, you need to create another instance of the DataViewManager and construct the DataViewSettings for that particular view. Then you construct a DataView using the DataViewManager. For example, in the Orders DataSet, you may want to filter out the orders with an EmployeeID of 4 and sort the orders by the date they were shipped. You can retrieve records for EmployeedId = 4 sorted on the date by when they were shipped using the sort and filter properties of the DataSet and attach the filtered and sorted data to a DataView or a DataViewManager.

To construct a DataViewManager you can either use the Default constructor or pass in a DataSet object. For example:

```
view = new DataViewManager ()
```

or

```
view = new DataSetView(myDataSet).
```

The DataViewManager has a few properties you need to know about to utilize it effectively. Table 5-14 shows the main properties.

Table 5-14. `DataSetView` *Properties*

PROPERTY	DESCRIPTION
`DataSet`	The `DataSet` being viewed of type `DataSet`.
`DataViewSettings`	Contains the collection of `Table Setting` objects for each table in the `DataSet`. The `Table Setting` object contains sorting and filtering criteria for a particular table.

The `DataViewManager` contains the `CreateDataView` method that allows you to create a `DataView` object for a particular table in your `DataSet`. You can construct the `DataView` for the table with the `DataViewManager`'s `DataViewSettings` for the particular `DataTable` of the `DataSet`. You can also adjust settings for the `DataView` by assigning filter and sort properties directly in the `DataView`.

You'll see `DataView` and `DataViewManager` objects in the sample applications in the "Using ADO.NET Data Providers" section.

Using ADO.NET Data Providers

In the previous section, you examined some of the disconnected ADO.NET classes provided by the .NET Framework. In this section, you'll examine ADO.NET data provider–specific classes.

First of all, what are the ADO.NET data providers? Technically, an ADO.NET data provider is a set of classes that enables you to connect to a data source to read and write data from a data source. A data provider also has components that serve as a conduit between the data source and the `DataSet`. In this way, the architecture isolates the manipulation of data from the source of the data. Currently, providers utilize the APIs of three main technologies that support database connectivity: the OLE-DB API, the ODBC API, and SQL Server API.

ADO.NET has a number of data providers. Some of them are the OleDb data provider for manipulating databases supporting OleDb connectivity, the Sql data provider for connecting to SQL Server 7 or later databases, and the ODBC data provider to connect to any ODBC data sources.

Figure 5-20 shows a generic class model of a data provider. The same component model applies to all of the data providers. All data providers implement the same class model, so once you're comfortable with one data provider, you can easily manipulate other data providers in no time. It's just a matter of changing class names and the connection string.

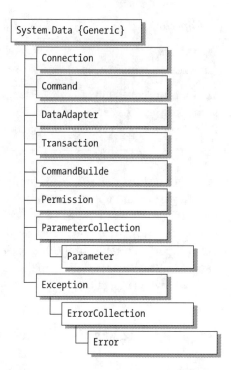

Figure 5-20. A generic data provider

You'll begin your understanding of the ADO.NET data providers by examining the different data provider namespaces contained in ADO.NET. The namespaces contain the classes necessary to manipulate the data providers.

As you've seen in the ADO.NET class hierarchy section of this chapter, ADO.NET implements *n* number of data providers. Some of them are OleDb, Sql, and ODBC.

The System.Data.OleDb namespace defines classes that work with the OLE DB data sources. These data providers use the native OLE DB API to connect with OLE DB data sources, such as Jet databases, XML files, and Microsoft Access databases. To work with a specific data source, you must have a OLE DB provider for that data source. Table 5-15 describes most of the OleDb data provider classes. I'll use these classes throughout this chapter.

Table 5-15. OleDb Data Provider Classes

CLASS	DESCRIPTION
OleDbCommand	Represents an SQL statement or stored procedure. Data can be returned in a DataReader by calling its ExecuteReader method.
OleDbCommandBuilder	Provides a mechanism to generate automatic commands for a table.
OleDbConnection you	Represents a connection object. This is the first class need to use to connect to a data source.
OleDbDataAdaper	Set of commands provides a link between OleDbConnection and DataSet.
OleDbError	Collects error and warnings returned by the data source.
OleDbErrorCollection	Collects errors generated by OLE DB data providers.
OleDbException	Exception handling class designed for OLE DB data sources.
OldDbParameter	This class represents a parameter used in OleDbCommand.
OleDbParameterCollection	A collection of parameters.
OleDbPermission	Ensures that a user has enough security to access OLE DB data sources.
OleDbPermissionAttributes	Custom attributes can be added to a security action.
OleDbTransaction	A transaction that can be processed at a data source.

Similar to the OleDb data providers, Sql and ODBC data providers provide the same class hierarchy model as in Figure 5-5. The only difference is the prefix for each data provider namespace. For example, the OleDb provider classes begins with OleDb, the Sql Server provider namespace classes start with Sql, and the ODBC provider classes begins with ODBC. This is fairly logical for a change! The System.Data classes have no prefix, of course, because they're classes used in memory and shared by all the providers.

The way ADO.NET works is that once you've connected to a database and dumped the data into the in-memory object (known as the Dataset), you can disconnect from the database and manipulate the data until you're ready to write it back to the database. The data provider classes serve as a bridge for moving data back and forth between memory and the database. In the next section I'll discuss how to initially connect to a database using these providers and then use the data provider classes to allow data to utilize this efficient bridge for your data.

In the sections that follow I'll describe how to connect to various databases with the data providers. Then I'll show you how to use the data provider classes to execute queries and stored procedures. Also, you'll see how these powerful classes work together and how the data providers differ in certain capabilities. You'll also learn how to do transaction locking, batch transactions, and transaction rollbacks. Finally, you'll learn how to capture database exceptions and information messages as well as learn how to interpret these errors.

How Do I Choose a Data Provider?

As you've seen earlier, there are many data providers available in ADO.NET. There may be cases when you can access a data source using more than one data provider. Now the question arises: Which one is better? What are the selection criteria? The main criteria of selection is performance and multiple data source connectivity.

In brief, to work with SQL Server 7 or later and MSDE databases, Sql data provider is the best choice. The Sql data provider bypasses many layers and directly connects to the internal layer of the infrastructure. Not only that, but Sql data providers provide classes that help you to convert from native SQL Server data types to the .NET data types, and vice versa.

OleDb data providers are useful when you want to access OLE DB data sources such as MS-Access, Xml, text, and other data sources. Because of the COM nature of the OLE DB API, it reduces many layers in comparison to ODBC data providers. This is also useful when you don't have an ODBC driver for a data source and have OLE DB provider.

The ODBC data providers utilize the existing way to work with data sources. ODBC is an older data access technology. Many applications still use ODBC to access data sources. ODBC data providers provide a way to access ODBC data sources through ODBC drives and ODBC Admin. Database venders generally provide the ODBC drivers. Using ODBC you can access any data source for which you have an ODBC driver installed.

In general, ODBC data provider connectivity is faster than OLE-DB because of OLE DB's COM nature, which is very "chatty." Sql data provider is faster than ODBC to work with SQL Server databases. But ODBC is useful when you need to write a generic class that can access multiple data sources through ODBC. For example, say you're writing an application that can work with multiple back-end servers including SQL Server, Oracle, Access, and MySql. When you install these back-end servers, it also installs the ODBC driver for these databases. So you can write a generic application that can access these data sources based on ODBC

DSN. You can also pass the driver and data source information in the application itself, but the user has to just create a DSN from ODBC, and the application can use that DSN as the connection string in the application for the ODBC data provider.

Adding Data Provider Namespace References

As discussed in Chapters 3 and 4, each data provider is defined in a separate namespace. The namespaces for the OleDb, Sql, and ODBC data providers are `System.Data.OleDb`, `System.Data.Sqlclient`, and `Microsoft.Data.Odbc`, respectively. Before using data adapter classes, you must add a reference of the correct namespace to your project. For example, add the following line for the OleDb data provider:

```
using System.Data.OleDb;
```

Add the following line for the Sql data provider:

```
using System.Data.SqlClient;
```

And add the following line for the ODBC data provider:

```
using Microsoft.Data.Odbc;
```

Connecting to the Database

As you've seen in Figure 5-1, the first data provider that interacts with a data source is the `Connection` object. You can bypass a `Connection` object by using a `DataProvider` directly, but in that case a `DataProvider` uses the connection internally. (I'll discuss the `DataAdapter` later in this chapter.) The `Connection` class has a different name depending upon the data provider. As you can see from Figure 5-21, the connection class for OleDb, Sql, and ODBC are `OleDbConnection`, `SqlConnection`, `OdbcConnection`, respectively. All data provider connection classes implement the `IDbConnection` interface, which represents a unique session with a data source (see Figure 5-21).

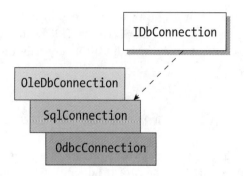

Figure 5-21. The IDbConnection *and its derived classes*

The Connection class has a connection string that opens a connection to the database. The connection string will vary depending upon the provider used. The connection string will typically contain a group of property-value pairs to describe how to connect to a database. For an OleDbConnection, you have properties such as Provider and DataSource. Table 5-16 describes the Connection class properties. Based on the data provider, some of these properties may not be applicable.

Table 5-16. Connection Object Properties

PROPERTY	DESCRIPTION
ConnectionString	Represent the connection string.
ConnectionTimeOut	Waiting time while establishing a connection.
DataBase	Name of the current database.
DataSource	Location of the file name of the data source.
Provider	Name of the OLE DB provider. This property is not available for Sql and ODBC data providers.
State	Current state of the connection of type ConnectionState. (Table 5-17 describes the ConnectionState).
PacketSize	Size of network packets. Available to only Sql data providers.
ServerVersion	SQL Server version. Available to only Sql data providers.
WorkStationId	Database client ID. Available to only Sql data providers.

The connection can have different states such as open, closed, connecting, and so on. The ConnectionType enumeration defines the members of the ConnectionState. Table 5-17 describes its members.

Table 5-17. The ConnectionType *Enumeration Members*

MEMBER	DESCRIPTION
Broken	Connection is broken after it was opened. May cause by network failure.
Closed	Connection is closed.
Connecting	Opening a new connection.
Executing	The connection is executing a command.
Fetching	Retrieving data from a data source.
Open	Connection is open and ready to use.

Table 5-18 describes the Connection object methods. You'll see some of these methods throughout this chapter. The purpose of this table is to give you an idea of available methods.

Table 5-18. The Connection *Class Members*

METHOD	DESCRIPTION
BeginTransaction	Begins a database transaction.
ChangeDatabase	Changes databases for an open connection.
Close	Closes an opened connection.
CreateCommand	Creates and returns a Command object depends on the data provider. For example, OleDbConnection returns OleDbCommand, and SqlConnection returns SqlCommand.
Open	Opens a new connection.
ReleaseObjectPool	Represents that the connection pooling can be cleared when the provider is released. Available only for OleDb data providers.

Opening and Closing a Connection

All the providers construct their connections in the same way. The thing that makes the connection construction different between the different providers is the ConnectionString. For example, the SqlClient doesn't need to specify a provider string because Sql Server is always the provider when using this class. Listing 5-18 shows how to create a Connection object using different constructors.

Listing 5-18. Creating a Connection *object using different constructors*

```
OleDbConnection conn1 = new OleDbConnection();
// Create a Connection Object
string ConnectionString = "Provider=Microsoft.Jet.OLEDB.4.0;"
+"Data Source=c:\\Northwind.mdb";

OleDbConnection conn2 = new OleDbConnection(ConnectionString);
```

> **NOTE**   *Before using data providers, you must include a namespace in your project. For example, using* System.Data.OleDb *and using* System.Data.SqlClient *will add references of OleDb and Sql data providers to your class.*

As you can see from Listing 5-18, I created two SqlConnection objects: conn1 and conn2. I created conn1 with no connection string. If you create a connection object with no connection string, you will have to set its ConnectionString property before you call Open of the connection object. I created the conn2 object with a connection string as an argument. As you can see from the connection string, it consists of a provider name and data source.

After creating a connection object, you call its Open method to open a connection. The Open method doesn't take any arguments. The following line of code opens a connection:

```
conn.Open();
```

When you're done with the connection, you call its Close method to release the connection. The Close method also doesn't take any arguments. The following line of code closes a connection:

```
conn.Close();
```

Listing 5-19 opens a connection with the Access 2000 Northwind database that resides in the C:\ dir. After opening the connection, you call its properties, and at the end you call the Close method to close the connection. As you can see from the code, you check the connection state to see if theconnection is already opened (which is impossible in this code), closed or not.

Listing 5-19. Opening and closing an OleDbConnection

```
// Create a Connection Object
string ConnectionString = "Provider=Microsoft.Jet.OLEDB.4.0;"
                +"Data Source=c:\\Northwind.mdb";
```

```
OleDbConnection conn = new OleDbConnection(ConnectionString);

// Open the connection
if( conn.State != ConnectionState.Open)
   conn.Open();

// Show the connection properties
MessageBox.Show( "Connection String :"+conn.ConnectionString
                +", DataSource :"+ conn.DataSource.ToString()
                +", Provider :"+ conn.Provider.ToString()
                +","+conn.ServerVersion.ToString()
                +"," + conn.ConnectionTimeout.ToString() );

// Close the connection
if( conn.State == ConnectionState.Open)
   conn.Close();
```

The output of program listed in Listing 5-19 looks like Figure 5-22.

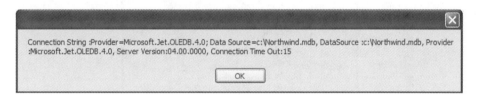

Figure 5-22. Output of Listing 5-19

You can also call the `Dispose` method to dispose the connection. The `Dispose` method tells the garbage collector to free and destroy the connection reference.

You can also use the OleDb data provider to connect to SQL Server or other databases if you have an OLE DB data provider installed for that database. Listing 5-20 shows the connection of a SQL Server using the OleDb data provider.

TIP *You can also use OleDb data providers to connect to a SQL Server database. The following code snippet shows you a connection with a SQL Server 2000 database using the OleDb data provider. You may need to access a SQL Server from a OleDb data provider when you're writing a generic class that can access multiple OLE DB data sources.*

Listing 5-20. Connecting to a SQL Server using the OleDb data provider

```
// Create a Connection Object
string ConnectionString = "Provider=SQLOLEDB.1;" +
                          "Integrated Security=SSPI;" +
                          "Persist Security Info=false;" +
                          "Initial Catalog=Northwind;" +
                          "Data Source-G61LS;";

OleDbConnection conn = new OleDbConnection(ConnectionString);
```

Now you'll connect to a SQL Server database using the Sql data providers. For this example, I'll use the SQL Server 2000 Northwind database. In the Server Explorer, my database looks like Figure 5-23.

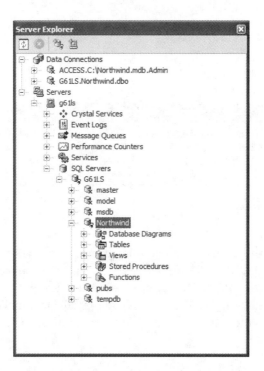

Figure 5-23. Northwind database in the Server Explorer

> **NOTE** *As you can see from the figure, G61LS is the server instance on my machine. This name will be different on your machine.*

Listing 5-21 shows the connection with SQL Server database.

Listing 5-21. Connection with SQL Server database

```
// Create a Connection Object
string ConnectionString ="Integrated Security=SSPI;" +
"Initial Catalog=Northwind;" +
"Data Source=localhost;";
SqlConnection conn = new SqlConnection(ConnectionString);

//  OleDbConnection conn = new OleDbConnection(ConnectionString);

// Open the connection
if( conn.State != ConnectionState.Open)
  conn.Open();

// Show the connection properties
MessageBox.Show( "Connection String :"+conn.ConnectionString
+ ", Workstation Id:"+ conn.WorkstationId.ToString()
+", Packet Size :"+ conn.PacketSize.ToString()
+", Server Version "+ conn.ServerVersion.ToString()
+", DataSource :"+ conn.DataSource.ToString()
+", Server Version:"+ conn.ServerVersion.ToString()
+", Connection Time Out:"+ conn.ConnectionTimeout.ToString() );

// Close the connection
if( conn.State == ConnectionState.Open)
  conn.Close();
```

The output of Listing 5-21 looks like Figure 5-24.

Connection String :Integrated Security=SSPI;Initial Catalog=Northwind;Data Source=localhost;, Workstation Id:G61LS, Packet Size :8192, Server Version 08.00.0194, DataSource :localhost, Server Version:08.00.0194, Connection Time Out:15

OK

Figure 5-24. Output of Listing 5-21

> **NOTE**   *As you can see from Listing 5-21, I've used localhost as my data source name. You can even pass your server name here.*

Connecting to Other Providers with OleDb and ODBC

Microsoft provides the capability to use specific provider strings to connect to various databases through OLE DB or ODBC providers. Table 5-19 lists the provider strings for OLE DB and some examples.

Table 5-19. Connection Strings Used for Ole Db of Various Databases

PROVIDER	DRIVER	CONNECTION	STRING
SQL Server	OLE DB	SQLOLEDB	`"Provider= SQLOLEDB.1;` `Data Source=northwind; uid=sa; pwd="`
Microsoft Jet database	OLE DB	Microsoft.Jet. OLEDB.4.0	`"Provider=Microsoft.Jet.OLEDB.4.0;` `Data Source = c:\\Northwind.mdb"`
Oracle	OLE DB	MSDAORA	`"Provider=MSDAORA;Server=serv01;` `Database=Contacts;uid=mike1;pwd=fastcar'`

Connecting with ODBC to a database is similar to connecting with OleDb. You simply pass the connection string into the ODBC Connection class. Notice that the driver string is contained in curly brackets and can often be determined by looking at the drivers in the Data Source Administrator in the control panel (see Figure 5-25).

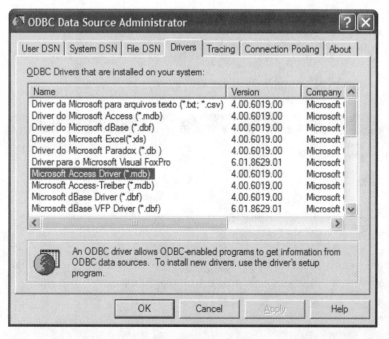

Figure 5-25. Examining drivers from the ODBC Data Source Administrator

Table 5-20 shows a list of connection strings that you can use with the ODBC provider. In the case of Access, Excel, and text, the DBQ property contains the database file. For other databases, the database name is in the DATABASE property.

Table 5-20. Connection Strings Used for Connecting with ODBC in Various Databases

DATABASE	CONNECTION STRING
Oracle	"Driver={Microsoft ODBC for Oracle}; Server=ORACLE8i7;UID=ODBC user;PWD=ODBC $5xr"
Access	"Driver={Microsoft Access Driver (*.mdb)};DBQ= Northwind.mdb"
Excel	"Driver={Microsoft Excel Driver (*.xls)}; DBQ=c:\ExcelFolder\MyExcelBook.xls"
Text	"Driver={Microsoft Text Driver (*.txt; *.csv)}; DBQ=c:\TextFilesDir"
SQLServer	"DRIVER={SQL Server};SERVER=MICROGOL-HQHJXU\\NetSDK; UID=sa;PWD=;DATABASE=northwind;"
MySQL	"Driver={MySQL};SERVER=localhost;DATABASE=menagerie;"
DSN	"DSN = MyDatabase"

So, now you actually have three ways to connect to a SQL Server database because a SQL Server Database has OleDb, ODBC, and of course direct connectivity. You must include Microsoft.Data.Odbc namespace reference when using ODBC .Net data provider to access databases.

Listing 5-22 shows you the way to use an ODBC connection to connect to a SqlServer database.

Listing 5-22. Connecting to SQL Server through ODBC

```
// Connection string for ODBC

string ConnectionString = "DRIVER={SQL  Server};"+
"SERVER=localhost;UID=sa;PWD=;DATABASE=northwind;";

// Connect to the data reader the same way you would for Sql Server or
// Ole Db Providers
OdbcConnection  conn = new OdbcConnection(ConnectionString);
conn.Open();
```

Except for the connection string, connecting to a SQL Server database is actually not that much different than with the SqlServer data provider (see Listing 5-23).

Listing 5-23. Connecting to SQL Server through the SqlClient provider
```
string ConnectionString = "Data Source = My SQLServer; user id=sa;password=;";
SqlConnection conn = new SqlConnection(ConnectionString);
```

You can also connect to a SQL Server through the SqlClient provider using this code:

```
SqlConnection conn;
conn = new SqlConnection(ConnectionString);
conn.Open();
```

Connecting to an Excel Database

The nice thing about ODBC is there are drivers for so many different databases and structures. Listing 5-24 shows how to connect to an Excel spreadsheet and retrieve data from it. As you can see, you can use the xls ODBC driver to connect to an Excel spreadsheet. The Employees.xls file is the Northwind database's Employees table exported as an .xls file from Access 2000. (I'll discuss Excel databases connectivity and working examples in Chapter 10.)

As I said earlier, you must include Microsoft.Data.Odbc namespace reference before using ODBC data provider classes.

Listing 5-24. Reading data from an Excel spreadsheet using ODBC
```
// Connection string for ODBC Excel Driver
string ConnectionString = "Driver={Microsoft Excel Driver (*.xls)};"+
"DBQ=c:\\Employees.xls";
OdbcConnection  conn = new OdbcConnection(ConnectionString);

// Tables in Excel can be thought of as sheets and are queried as shown
string sql = "Select EmployeeID, FirstName, LastName FROM Employees";
conn.Open();

OdbcDataAdapter da = new OdbcDataAdapter(sql, conn);

DataSet ds = new DataSet();
da.Fill(ds, "Employees");
```

Connecting to a Text File

You could write the same code for extracting data from a text file by simply changing the connection string and the query. The connection string simply points to the directory where the text files are stored. Each file acts as a table (see Listing 5-25).

As I said earlier, you must include `Microsoft.Data.Odbc` namespace reference before using ODBC data provider classes.

Listing 5-25. Reading data from a tab-delimited text file using ODBC

```
// Connection string for a Text File
string ConnectionString = "Driver={Microsoft Text Driver "+
"(*.txt; *.csv)};DBQ=c:\\";

// Query the TextDB.txt file as a table
OdbcConnection  conn = new OdbcConnection(ConnectionString);
conn.Open();

 OdbcDataAdapter da = new OdbcDataAdapter
("Select * FROM TextDB.txt", conn);

DataSet ds = new DataSet();
da.Fill(ds, "TextDB");

dataGrid1.DataSource = ds.DefaultViewManager;

// Close the connection
conn.Close();
```

Listing 5-25 uses `TextDB.txt`, which is a tab-delimited file of rows and columns. It looks like Table 5-21.

Table 5-21. Tab-Delimited Text File of Employee Data

EMPLOYEEID	FIRSTNAME	LASTNAME	TITLE
1	Mike	Kramer	President
2	Fred	Jones	Secretary
3	Bill	Leste	VP Sales
4	Ted	Silver	VP Manufacturing

A tab separates each element of a row; however, you could also delimit your file with commas. I'll discuss text-file connectivity in more detail in Chapter 10 with a step-by-step example.

Connecting to a Data Source

Connecting through the ODBC Data Source Name (DSN) is another option to access a database using ODBC data providers. Using DSN is useful when you need to access different kinds of ODBC data sources and you don't know the user ID and passwords. You ask the user to create a DSN, or you create a DSN pro-grammatically and ask the user to enter their UserId and password.

You can either create a DSN programmatically or create one manually using the ODBC Data Source Administrator. If you're using Windows 2000, you go to Control Panel ➤ Administrative Tools ➤ Data Source (ODBC). This brings up the ODBC Data Source Administrator. Using this Administrator, you can create data sources, reconfigure them, and remove them. The ODBC Data Source Administrator looks like Figure 5-26.

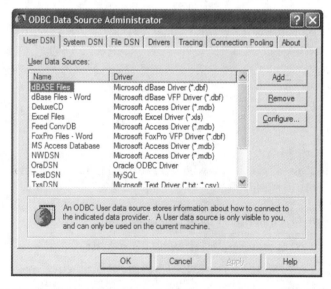

Figure 5-26. ODBC Data Source Administrator screens with add, remove, and configure options

As you can see from Figure 5-26, you can add or remove new data source names or configure existing data source names using the Add, Remove, and Configure buttons. The Add button launches the Create New Data Source Wizard.

On the first screen of this wizard, you can select the desired driver. As you can see from Figure 5-27, I picked the Microsoft Access driver because I'm going to create a DSN for the Access database.

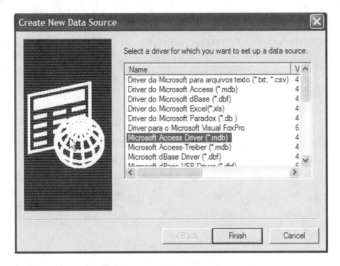

Figure 5-27. Selecting an ODBC driver for a new DSN

When you click Finish, the next step is to select a database name. On this screen, you can also create a new database or repair and compact an existing one. For this example, select the C:\Northwind Access 2000 database and give it the DSN name NWDSN (see Figure 5-28).

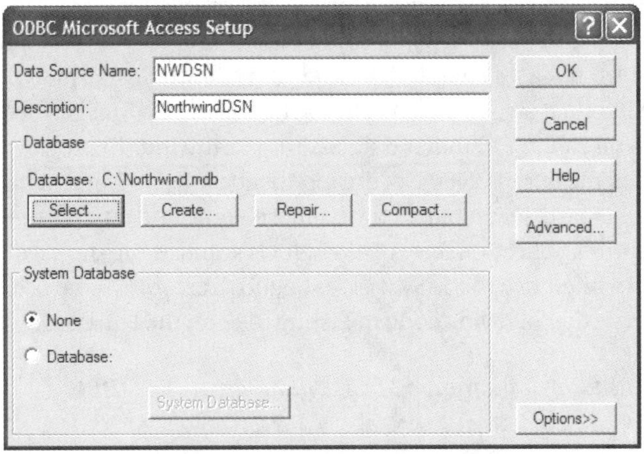

Figure 5-28. Creating a DSN using the Northwind Access database

Now you've created a DSN. Connecting to this DSN using an ODBC data provider is pretty simple. Instead of creating a connection string, you use the DSN as a connection string. Rest assured, everything is the same you've been doing so far.

As you can see from Listing 5-26, you can connect to an ODBC DSN using ODBC data providers. You'll see the full application based on ODBC DSNs in Chapter 11.

Listing 5-26. Connecting to an ODBC DSN

```
// Create the Data Source Name connection string to
// access our Data Source
string ConnectionString = @"DSN=NWDSN";
OdbcConnection  conn = new OdbcConnection(ConnectionString);
// use the SQL Query to get the Customers data
OdbcCommand cmd = new OdbcCommand("Select * FROM Customers",
conn );
conn.Open();
```

You can also access your other favorite databases, such as MySQL. You must have the MyODBC driver installed, but assuming you have everything set up that you need, you can use .NET to read this popular database. Listing 5-27 shows the code that will read the MySQL database through the TestDSN ODBC data source.

Connecting to a MySQL Database

As you can see, working with different data sources means nothing except changing the connection string. Listing 5-27 shows the connection string for the MySQL database. You access a MySQL database through Odbc data providers. (I'll discuss MySQL databases connectivity and show how to install an ODBC driver for MySQL with a step-by-step example in Chapter 11). As you can see from Listing 5-27, you can use a similar database as Northwind. To provide similar samples, I exported the Access 2000 Northwind database as a MySQL database. You can use any database. Just replace the database name and change the SQL statement. To test this application, create a Windows application, drop a data grid to the form, add a reference to the System.Data and Microsoft.Data.Odbc namespaces, and type the following code in Listing 5-27 on the Form_Load event.

Listing 5-27. Reading data from a MySQL database using ODBC

```
private void Form1_Load(object sender, System.EventArgs e)
{
string ConnectionString = "Driver={MySQL};SERVER=localhost;"+
"DATABASE=NorthwindMySQL;";
```

```
    OdbcConnection conn= new OdbcConnection(ConnectionString );
    conn.Open();

   OdbcDataAdapter da = new OdbcDataAdapter
("SELECT CustomerID, ContactName, ContactTitle FROM Customers", conn);

   DataSet ds = new DataSet("Cust");

  da.Fill(ds, "Customers");
  dataGrid1.DataSource = ds.DefaultViewManager;

  conn.Close();
}
```

Understanding Connection Pooling

After a connection has been created and placed in a connection pool, client applications can reuse these connections without performing the complete connection process. The process of reusing connection resources from a connection pool is called *connection pooling*. The connection pooling process may increase the performance of an application because an application doesn't need to open and close a connection repeatedly.

The connection pooling mechanism works different for different data providers. The Connection class defines members that allow you to pool connection resources manually.

If you've used connection pooling in ADO or OLE DB, you must be familiar with the OLE DB Services parameter. OLE DB provides automatic session pooling (also known as connection pooling), which is handled by OLE DB core components through its providers.

The OLE DB Services parameter of a connection string describes the services that are enabled for a connection. A typical connection string looks like this:

```
DSN=LocalServer;UID=sa;PWD=;OLE DB Services=-1
```

Table 5-22 shows the values and their meaning for the OLE DB Services parameter.

Table 5-22. The OLE DB Services Settings

SERVICES ENABLED	VALUE
All services (default)	`"OLE DB Services = -1;"`
All services except pooling	`"OLE DB Services = -2;"`
All services except pooling and auto enlistment	`"OLE DB Services = -4;"`
All services except client cursor	`"OLE DB Services = -5;"`
All services except client cursor and pooling	`"OLE DB Services = -6;"`
No services	`"OLE DB Services = 0;"`

The OleDb data provider uses the OLE DB API internally so it supports automatic connection pooling. You can enable and disable connection pooling programmatically in the OleDb data providers through its connection string. For example, the following string disables the connection pooling:

```
String connString = "Provider=SQLOLEDB;OLE DB Services=-2;Data Source=localhost;"+
"Integrated Security=SSPI;";
```

ADO.NET manages automatic connection pooling when you use the `Close` or `Dispose` method of a `Connection` object. A connection pool reuses the resources allocated to a connection. Once a pool is created, you can add connections to this pool until it reaches its maximum size. You can define the maximum size of a connection pool using the connection string. If a pool reaches its maximum size, the next added connection will go in the queue wait until the pool releases one existing connection.

You create a pool when you call the `Open` method of connection based on the connection string. If you're using the same database for two `Connection` objects, but the connection string is different (including spaces and single characters), both connection will be added to different pools. For example, Listing 5-28 creates two connections: `conn1` and `conn2`. The`ConnectionString1` and `ConnectionString2` connection strings are different for both connections. Because both these connections have different connection strings, they will be added to two different pools.

Listing 5-28. Creating two connections with different strings
```
// Create a Connection Object
string ConnectionString1 ="Integrated Security=SSPI;" +
    "Initial Catalog=Northwind;" +
    "Data Source=localhost;";
SqlConnection conn1 = new SqlConnection(ConnectionString1);
```

```
// Create a Connection Object
string ConnectionString2 ="Integrated Security=SSPI;" +
        "Initial Catalog=Pubs;" +
        "Data Source=localhost;";
SqlConnection conn2 = new SqlConnection(ConnectionString2);

// Open connections
conn1.Open();
conn2.Open();
// some code
conn1.Close();
conn2.Close();
```

> **CAUTION** *You must always call* Close *or* Dispose *method of* Connection *to close the connection. Connections that are not explicitly closed are not added or returned to the pool.*

You can set the behavior of connection pooling of SQL Server data providers by setting the ConnectionString values. Some of the pooling settings are in the form of key-value pairs (see Table 5-23).

Table 5-23. Connection Pooling Settings

KEY	DESCRIPTION
Connection Lifetime	Connection creation time is compared with the current time, and if time span exceeds the Connection Lifetime value, object pooler destroys the connection. The default value is 0, which will give a connection the maximum timeout.
Connection Reset	Determines whether a connection is reset after it was removed from the pool. The default value is true.
Max Pool Size	Maximum number of connections allowed in the pool. The default value is 100.
Min Pool Size	Minimum number of connections allowed in the pool. The default value is 0.
Pooling	When true, the connection is drawn from the pool or created if necessary. The default value is true.

The OleDbConnection class provides a ReleaseObjectPool method that you can use to free resources reserved for a connection. You call this method when this connection won't be used again. To call ReleaseObjectPool, first you call the Close method. Listing 5-29 shows how to use ReleaseObjectPool.

Listing 5-29. Calling ReleaseObjectPool

```
// Connection and SQL strings
string ConnectionString = @"Provider=Microsoft.Jet.OLEDB.4.0;"+
"Data Source=c:\\Northwind.mdb";
string SQL = "SELECT OrderID, Customer, CustomerID FROM Orders";

// Create connection object
OleDbConnection conn = new OleDbConnection(ConnectionString);

conn.Open();

// do something

conn.Close();
OleDbConnection.ReleaseObjectPool();
```

Taking Command

If you've ever written database applications using ODBC, DAO, or ADO, you must be familiar with the concept of manipulating data through recordsets or executing direct SQL queries. For example, in DAO and ODBC, you can use either the Execute method of a Database object to execute direct SQL commands or use a recordset to manipulate data by navigating through records one by one.

The Command object allows you to directly execute SQL statements such as INSERT, SELECT, UPDATE, and DELETE against a data source for reading, writing, and updating a database. You can also use the Command object to execute stored procedures. The SqlCommand, OleDbCommand, and OdbcCommand classes represent the Command objects in Sql, OleDb, and ODBC data providers, respectively. All of the data provider–specific command classes implement the IDbCommand interface, which implements basic functionality for these classes. Figure 5-29 shows the relationship between IDbCommand and the data provider–specific command classes.

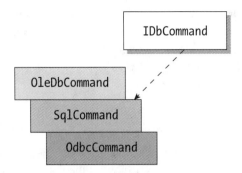

Figure 5-29. Data provider–specific classes implementing IDbCommand

Table 5-24 lists some of the more important properties of the Command class for the OleDb data provider. The CommandText listed in this table can contain either a SQL statement or a stored procedure name. The CommandType determines which one of these forms the CommandText takes on.

Table 5-24. OleDbCommand *Properties*

PROPERTY	DESCRIPTION
CommandText	Could be a SQL statement, a stored procedure, or a database table name depending on the CommandType
CommandType	An enumeration of values Text, StoredProcedure, or TableDirect
Connection	An OleDbConnection representing the ActiveConnection

Creating an OleDb Command Object

There are a number of ways to construct a command object. You can pass the command a SQL query string, you can pass it a string and a connection, or you can pass it a string, a connection, and a transaction. The following code shows you three different ways to create a command object. This code constructs a connection and a SQL string:

```
// Connection and SQL strings
string ConnectionString = @"Provider=Microsoft.Jet.OLEDB.4.0;"+
"Data Source=c:\\Northwind.mdb";
string SQL = "SELECT OrderID, CustomerID FROM Orders";
```

Now create `OleDbCommand` object using a constructor with no arguments. Later you set `OleDbCommand`'s `Connection` and `CommandText` properties to connect to a connection and set SQL statement, which this command will be executing:

```
OleDbCommand cmd = new OleDbCommand();
cmd.Connection = conn;
cmd.CommandText = SQL;
```

In the second form, you create an `OleDbCommand` object by directly passing a SQL query and the `OleDbConnection` object as the first and second arguments:

```
// Create command object
OleDbCommand cmd = new OleDbCommand(SQL, conn);
```

The third way is to create a command by just passing a SQL query as the argument and setting its `Connection` property later:

```
// Create command object
OleDbCommand cmd = new OleDbCommand(SQL);
cmd.Connection = conn;
```

Listing 5-30 shows you how to connect to the Northwind Access 2000 database, read all the records from the Orders table, and display the first and second column data to the console output. The new things you'll notice in this code are `ExecuteReader` and `OldDbDataReader`. An `OleDbDataReader` is a data reader class, and `ExecuteReader` fills data from a data source to the data reader based on the SQL query. (I'll discuss data reader classes in the next section.)

Listing 5-30. Using `OleDbCommand` *to read data from a database*
```
// Connection and SQL strings
string ConnectionString = @"Provider=Microsoft.Jet.OLEDB.4.0;"+
"Data Source=c:\\Northwind.mdb";
string SQL = "SELECT * FROM Orders";

// Create connection object
OleDbConnection conn = new OleDbConnection(ConnectionString);
// Create command object
OleDbCommand cmd = new OleDbCommand(SQL);
cmd.Connection = conn;

// Open connection
conn.Open();
```

```
// Call command's ExecuteReader
OleDbDataReader reader = cmd.ExecuteReader();

while (reader.Read())
{
    Console.Write("OrderID:"+reader.GetInt32(0).ToString() );
    Console.Write(" ,");
    Console.WriteLine("Customer:" + reader.GetString(1).ToString() );
}
// close reader and connection
reader.Close();
conn.Close();
```

The output of Listing 5-30 looks like Figure 5-30.

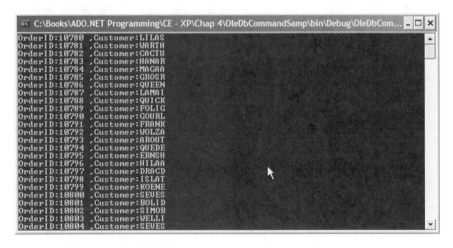

Figure 5-30. Output of Listing 5-30

Creating Sql and ODBC Command Objects

Similar to the OldDbCommand object, you create Sql and ODBC Command objects by using SqlCommand and OdbcCommand classes. You can pass the same arguments as discussed previously. The only difference is the connection string. For example, Listing 5-31 uses SqlCommand and SqlConnection to connect to a SQL Server database. As you can see from Listing 5-31, the only changes are the class prefixes and the connection string. Similarly, you can use the OdbcCommand object.

Listing 5-31. Using SqlCommand *to access a SQL Server database*

```csharp
static void Main(string[] args)
{
        // Connection and SQL strings
        string SQL = "SELECT * FROM Orders";
        // Create a Connection Object
        string ConnectionString ="Integrated Security=SSPI;" +
                 "Initial Catalog=Northwind;" +
                 "Data Source=localhost;";
        SqlConnection conn = new SqlConnection(ConnectionString);


        // Create command object
         SqlCommand cmd = new SqlCommand(SQL, conn);


        // Open connection
         conn.Open();
        // Call command's ExecuteReader
        SqlDataReader reader = cmd.ExecuteReader();
        try
        {
            while (reader.Read())
            {
                Console.Write("OrderID:"+reader.GetInt32(0).ToString() );
                Console.Write(" ,");
                Console.WriteLine("Customer:" + reader.GetString(1).ToString() );
            }
        }
        finally
        {
            // close reader and connection
             reader.Close();
            conn.Close();
        }
}
```

The output of Listing 5-31 looks like Figure 5-31.

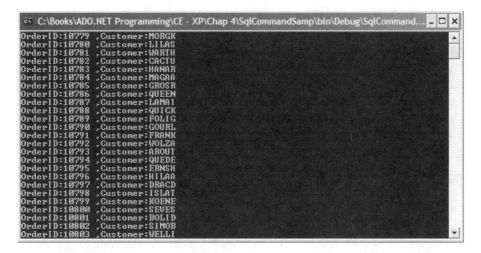

Figure 5-31. Output of Listing 5-31

The CommandType Enumeration

The CommandType enumeration decides what type of object a command will be executed as. The CommandType enumeration can have any of the three values defined in Table 5-25.

Table 5-25. The CommandType Enumeration Members

MEMBER	DESCRIPTION
StoredProcedure	The name of the stored procedure.
TableDirect	The CommandText property should be set to the table name, and all rows and columns in the table will be returned.
Text	A SQL text command.

As you can see from Table 5-25, you can call a stored procedure, use TableDirect, or execute a SQL command. I'll present these options one by one in the following sections.

Calling a Stored Procedure

Executing stored procedures using the Command object is similar to executing a SQL query. In this section you're going to see a quick overview on how to execute stored procedures. (I'll cover stored procedures in more detail in Chapter 10.)

You need to set the CommandType property of a Command object before calling a stored procedure. By default, the CommandType property is Text. If you want to call a stored procedure, you need to set the CommandType to StoredProcedure and the CommandText to the stored procedure name. After that you can call the ExecuteReader method or other methods. You can also pass parameters to the procedure by setting parameter values in the command and then calling ExecuteReader on the Command object. You can also pass a procedure name as a string when creating a Command object. Listing 5-32 shows the settings of the CommandType and CommandText properties of SqlCommand. As you can see, it calls an existing SQL Server Northwind database stored procedure, Sales By Year.

Listing 5-32. Calling a stored procedure using SqlCommand

```
// Create a SqlCommand with stored procedure as string
SqlCommand cmd =
    new SqlCommand("Sales By Year", conn);
// set Command's CommandType as StoredProcedure
cmd.CommandType = CommandType.StoredProcedure;
```

> **NOTE** *Executing stored procedures can be helpful in improving the performance of an application in multi-user and Web applications because a stored procedure executes on the server itself.*

The Northwind database in SQL Server contains a few stored procedures. One is called Sales by Year (see Listing 5-33).

Listing 5-33. Stored procedure Sales by Year *in Northwind*

```
ALTER procedure [Sales by Year]
  @Beginning_Date DateTime, @Ending_Date DateTime AS
SELECT Orders.ShippedDate, Orders.OrderID, "Order Subtotals".Subtotal,
DATENAME(yy,ShippedDate) AS Year
FROM Orders INNER JOIN "Order Subtotals" ON Orders.OrderID =
  "Order Subtotals".OrderID WHERE Orders.ShippedDate
  Between @Beginning_Date And @Ending_Date
```

This stored procedure takes two parameters, `Beginning_Date` and `Ending_Date`. The procedure will select all of the orders between these two dates. It also performs a join with the `Order Subtotals` from the Order Subtotal view, which calculates the subtotals of each. If you want to execute this stored procedure in ADO.NET, you just create a `Command` object of type `StoredProcedure` and call `ExecuteReader`. You then cycle through the results in the reader that you're looking for from your stored procedure. Listing 5-34 executes a stored procedure that selects all the orders in July and displays their order IDs.

Listing 5-34. Executing and reading the results of a stored procedure in ADO.NET

```
static void Main(string[] args)
{
// Create a Connection Object
        string ConnectionString ="Integrated Security=SSPI;" +
            "Initial Catalog=Northwind;" +
            "Data Source=localhost;";
        SqlConnection conn = new SqlConnection(ConnectionString);

        // Create a SqlCommand with stored procedure as string
        SqlCommand cmd =
            new SqlCommand("Sales By Year", conn);
        // set Command's CommandType as StoredProcedure
        cmd.CommandType = CommandType.StoredProcedure;

        // Create a SqlParameter and add a parameter
        SqlParameter parm1 = cmd.Parameters.Add
            ("@Beginning_Date", SqlDbType.DateTime, 20);
        parm1.Value = "7/1/1996";
        SqlParameter parm2 = cmd.Parameters.Add
            ("@Ending_Date", SqlDbType.DateTime, 20);
        parm2.Value = "8/1/1996";

    // Open the connection
    conn.Open();

    // Call ExecuteReader to execute the stored procedure
    SqlDataReader reader
        = cmd.ExecuteReader();
    string orderlist = "";

    // Read data from the reader
    while (reader.Read())
```

```
    {
        string result = reader["OrderID"].ToString();
        orderlist += result + '\n';
    }

    // close the connection and reader
    reader.Close();
    conn.Close();

    // Print data on the console
    Console.WriteLine("Orders in July");
    Console.WriteLine("===============");
    Console.WriteLine(orderlist);
}
```

The results of calling a stored procedure in Listing 5-34 look like Figure 5-32.

Figure 5-32. Order IDs in the month of July in Northwind

If you wanted to look at the subtotals along with the orders, you'd just add a DataReader index for dereferencing the Subtotal and concatenate with the OrderID. The new DataReader loop looks like Listing 5-35.

Listing 5-35. Adding the subtotal listing to the output of the stored procedure results

```
while (reader.Read())
{
string nextID = reader["OrderID"].ToString();
string nextSubtotal = reader["Subtotal"].ToString();
orderlist += nextID + '\t' + nextSubtotal + '\n';
}
```

The result of replacing this line of code in Listing 5-35 gives output that looks like Figure 5-33.

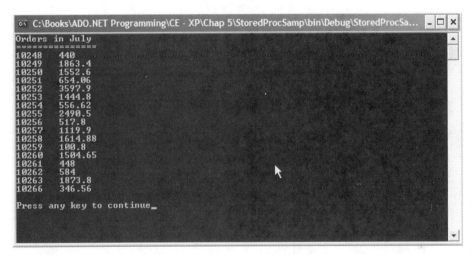

Figure 5-33. Order IDs and subtotals in the month of July in Northwind

Using TableDirect

You can also use the TableDirect CommandType to read information directly from a table. There are two changes you need to make in the example to execute a table by setting TableDirect. First, you need to set Command's CommandText property as the table name; second, set the CommandType property as CommandType.TableDirect.

The following code reads the Customers table and sets the CommandType property as CommandType.TableDirect:

```
cmd.CommandText = "Customers";
cmd.CommandType = CommandType.TableDirect;
```

Listing 5-36 reads information from the Customers table by setting the
TableDirect method and displaying it on the console.

Listing 5-36. Using TableDirect *to read a table*

```
static void Main(string[] args)
{
    // Create a Connection Object
        string ConnectionString = "Provider=Microsoft.Jet.OLEDB.4.0;"+
     "Data Source=c:\\Northwind.mdb";
  OleDbConnection conn = new OleDbConnection(ConnectionString);

            OleDbCommand cmd = new OleDbCommand();
            cmd.Connection = conn;
            cmd.CommandText = "Customers";

            cmd.CommandType = CommandType.TableDirect;

            conn.Open();
            OleDbDataReader reader = cmd.ExecuteReader();

            Console.WriteLine("Customer Id, Contact Name, Company Name");
            Console.WriteLine("=======================================");

            while (reader.Read())
            {
                Console.Write(reader["CustomerID"].ToString());
                Console.Write(", "+ reader["ContactName"].ToString());
                Console.WriteLine(", "+ reader["CompanyName"].ToString());
            }

            // release objects
            reader.Close();
            conn.Close();

        }
}
```

The output of Listing 5-36 looks like Figure 5-34.

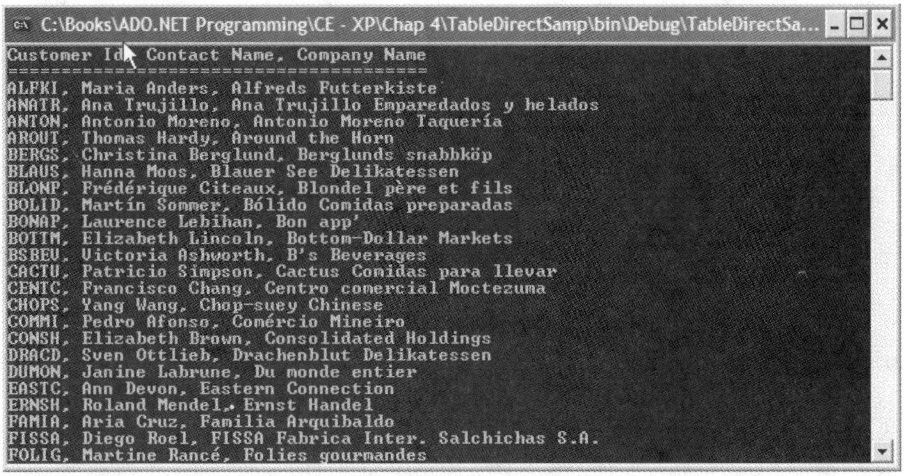

Figure 5-34. Result of the Customers table using `TableDirect`

Executing the Command

You just saw the `ExecuteReader` method, which reads data from a data source and fills the data reader object depending on the data provider. Besides the `ExecuteReader`, the `Command` object defines three more execute methods. These methods are `ExecuteNonQuery`, `ExecuteScalar`, and `ExecuteXmlReader`. The `ExecuteReader` method produces a `DataReader`. The `DataReader` is the solution for forward streaming data through ADO.NET. (I'll discuss it in more detail later in this chapter.)

The `ExecuteNonQuery` allows you to execute a SQL statement or a `Command` object with the `CommandText` property having a SQL statement without using a `DataSet`.

For example, you could have an UPDATE, INSERT, or DELETE statement in your `CommandText` and then call `ExecuteNonQuery` to execute it directly on your database.

> **NOTE** *You don't use* `ExecuteNonQuery` *to execute a* SELECT *statement because* `ExecuteNonQuery` *doesn't return data.*

Listing 5-37 is an example of inserting a row into the Northwind database using `ExecuteNonQuery`. You can even use UPDATE and DELETE SQL queries to update and delete data from a database. I'll use these statements in later examples. Here you create an INSERT query and call `ExecuteNonQuery`.

Listing 5-37. Adding records to a table using the INSERT SQL statement

```
static void Main(string[] args)
{
// Create a Connection Object
 string ConnectionString = @"Provider=Microsoft.Jet.OLEDB.4.0;"+
"Data Source=c:\\Northwind.mdb";

OleDbConnection conn = new OleDbConnection(ConnectionString);

// open an existing Connection to the Database and Create a
// Command Object with it:

conn.Open();
OleDbCommand cmd = new OleDbCommand("Customers", conn);

// Assign the SQL Insert statement we want to execute to the CommandText
cmd.CommandText = "INSERT INTO Customers"+
   "(Address, City, CompanyName, ContactName, CustomerID)"+
   "VALUES ('111 Broad St.', 'NY', 'Xerox', 'Fred Biggles', 1400)";
// Call ExecuteNonQuery on the Command Object to execute insert
cmd.ExecuteNonQuery();
// release objects
conn.Close();

}
```

The ExecuteScalar is a useful method for performing a SQL statement that retrieves a single value. A good example of this is retrieving the number of rows from a database. Listing 5-38 retrieves the number of rows from the Customers table in Northwind. Then you assign the SQL command for getting the row count in customers to the Command object, and you call ExecuteScalar to retrieve the counter.

Listing 5-38. Using the ExecuteScalar method to retrieve a single value

```
        static void Main(string[] args)
        {
// Create a Connection Object
string ConnectionString = "Provider=Microsoft.Jet.OLEDB.4.0;"+
   "Data Source=c:\\Northwind.mdb";
OleDbConnection conn = new OleDbConnection(ConnectionString);

// Creating a command object
conn.Open();
```

```
OleDbCommand cmd = new OleDbCommand();
cmd.CommandText = "SELECT Count(*) FROM Customers";
cmd.Connection = conn;

int counter = (int)cmd.ExecuteScalar();
Console.WriteLine("Total rows returned are :" + counter.ToString());

// release objects
conn.Close();

    }
```

Figure 5-35 shows the output of Listings 5-38.

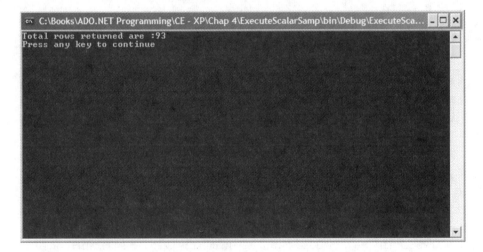

Figure 5-35. Output of an ExecuteScalar *showing the number of customers*

The ExecuteXmlReader method returns the result in an XmlReader. I'll discuss XmlReader in more detail in Chapter 6.

DataReader: An Easy Walk through the Data

As discussed earlier in this chapter, there are two ways to read and store data: one is DataSet and the other is DataReader. A data reader provides an easy way for the programmer to read data from a database as if it were coming from a stream. The DataReader is the solution for forward streaming data through ADO.NET. The data reader is also called a *firehose cursor* or *forward read-only cursor* because it moves forward through the data. The data reader not only allows you to move forward through each record of a database, but it also enables you to parse the data from each column. The DataReader class represents a data reader in ADO.NET.

Similar to other ADO.NET objects, each data provider has a data reader class. For example, OleDbDataReader is the data reader class for OleDb data providers. Similarly, SqlDataReader and ODBC DataReader are data reader classes for Sql and ODBC data providers, respectively.

The IDataReader interface defines the functionality of a data reader and works as the base class for all data provider–specific data reader classes such as OleDataReader, SqlDataReader, and OdbcDataReader. Figure 5-36 shows some of the classes that implement IDbDataReader.

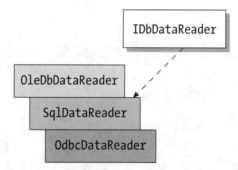

Figure 5-36. Data provider–specific classes implementing IDbDataReader

Initializing DataReader

As you've seen in the previous examples, you call the ExecuteReader method of the Command object, which returns an instance of the DataReader. For example, use the following line of code:

```
SqlCommand cmd = new SqlCommand(SQL, conn);
// Call ExecuteReader to return a DataReader
SqlDataReader reader = cmd.ExecuteReader();
```

Once you're done with a data reader, call the Close method to close a data reader:

```
reader.Close();
```

DataReader Properties and Methods

Table 5-26 describes DataReader properties, and Table 5-27 describes DataReader methods.

Table 5-26. The DataReader *Properties*

PROPERTY	DESCRIPTION
Depth	Indicates the depth of nesting for a row
FieldCount	Returns number of columns in a row
IsClosed	Indicates whether a data reader is closed
Item	Gets the value of a column in native format
RecordsAffected	Number of rows affected after a transaction

Table 5-27. The DataReader *Methods*

METHOD	DESCRIPTION
Close	Closes a DataReader object.
Read	Reads next record in the data reader.
NextResult	Advances the datareader to the next result during batch transactions.
Getxxx	There are dozens of Getxxx methods. These methods read a specific data type value from a column. For example, GetChar will return a column value as a character and GetString as a string.

Reading with the DataReader

Once the OleDbDataReader is initialized, you can utilize its various methods to read your data records. Foremost, you can use the Read method, which, when called repeatedly, continues to read each row of data into the DataReader object. The DataReader also provides a simple indexer that enables you to pull each column of data from the row. Below is an example of using the DataReader in the Northwind database for the Customers table and displaying data on the console.

As you can see from Listing 5-39, I've used similar steps as I've been using in previous examples. I created a connection object, created a command object, called the ExecuteReader method, called the DataReader's Read method until the end of the data, and then displayed the data. At the end, I released the data reader and connection objects.

Listing 5-39. DataReader *reads data from a SQL Server database*

```
static void Main(string[] args)
{
  // Create a Connection string
  string ConnectionString ="Integrated Security=SSPI;" +
              "Initial Catalog=Northwind;" +
              "Data Source=localhost;";
 string SQL = "SELECT * FROM Customers";

  // Create a Connection object
  SqlConnection conn = new SqlConnection(ConnectionString);
  // Create a Command Object
  SqlCommand cmd = new SqlCommand(SQL, conn);

  conn.Open();
  // Call ExecuteReader to return a DataReader
  SqlDataReader reader = cmd.ExecuteReader();
  Console.WriteLine("Customer ID, Contact Name,"+
"Contact Title, Address");
Console.WriteLine("===================================");

    while (reader.Read())
    {
        Console.Write(reader["CustomerID"].ToString() + ", ");
        Console.Write(reader["ContactName"].ToString() + ", ");
        Console.Write(reader["ContactTitle"].ToString()+ ", ");
        Console.WriteLine(reader["Address"].ToString()+ ", ");
    }
}
 // Release resources
  reader.Close();
  conn.Close();
}
```

Figure 5-37 shows the output of Listing 5-39.

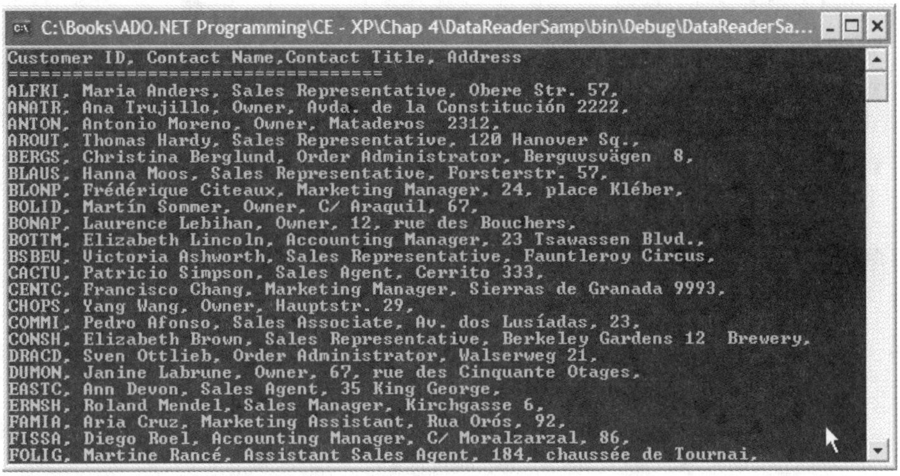

Figure 5-37. Output of the Customers table from the DataReader

Other methods in the Reader allow you to get the value of a column as a specific type. For instance, this line from the previous example:

```
string str = reader["CustomerID"].ToString();
```

could be rewritten as this:

```
string str = reader.GetString(0);
```

With the GetString method of the CustomerID, you don't need to do any conversion, but you do have to know the zero-based column number of the CustomerID (which, in this case, is zero).

Interpreting Batches of Queries

DataReader also has methods that enable you to read data from a batch of SQL queries. Below is an example of a batch transaction on the Customers and Orders tables. The NextResult method allows you to obtain each query result from the batch of queries performed on both tables. In this example, after creating a connection object, you set up your Command object to do a batch query on the Customers and the Orders tables:

```
SqlCommand cmd = new SqlCommand(
  "SELECT * FROM Customers;SELECT * FROM Orders",
  conn );
```

Now you can create the `Reader` through the `Command` object. You'll then use a result flag as an indicator to check if you've gone through all the results. Then you'll loop through each stream of results and read the data into a string until it reads 10 records. After that, you show results in a message box (see Listing 5-40).

After that you call the `NextResult` method, which gets the next query result in the batch. The result is processed again in the `Read` method loop.

Listing 5-40. Executing batches using DataReader

```
static void Main(string[] args)
        {

            // Create a Connection string
            string ConnectionString ="Integrated Security=SSPI;" +
                "Initial Catalog=Northwind;" +
                "Data Source=localhost;";
            string SQL = "SELECT * FROM Customers; SELECT * FROM Orders";

            // Create a Connection object
            SqlConnection conn = new SqlConnection(ConnectionString);
            // Create a Command Object
            SqlCommand cmd = new SqlCommand(SQL, conn);

            conn.Open();

            // Call ExecuteReader to return a DataReader
            SqlDataReader reader = cmd.ExecuteReader();

            int counter = 0;

            string str ="";
            bool bNextResult = true;
            while(bNextResult == true)
            {

                while (reader.Read())
                {
                    str += reader.GetValue(0).ToString() +"\n";
                    counter ++;
                    if (counter == 10)
                        break;
                }
                MessageBox.Show(str);
                bNextResult = reader.NextResult();
```

```
        }

        // Release resources
        reader.Close();
        conn.Close();
    }
```

Figure 5-38 shows the two MessageBoxes produced from this routine.

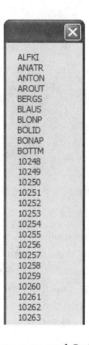

Figure 5-38. Output for the batch read of the Customers and Orders table

DataAdapter: Adapting to Your Environment

As you've seen in Figure 5-1, a `DataAdapter` plays a vital role in the ADO.NET architecture. It sits between a data source and a dataset and passes data from the data source to the dataset, and vice versa, with or without using commands. Now is the time you'll be using disconnected classes such as `DataSet`, `DataTable`, `DataView`, and `DataViewManager` to write Windows Forms– and Web Forms–based interactive database GUI applications.

The `DataAdapter` class for all data providers comes from the `DbDataAdapter` class, which in turn comes from the `DataAdapter` class.

An application doesn't create an instance of the DbDataAdapter interface directly, but instead it creates an instance of a class that inherits IdbDataAdapter and DbDataAdapter. As you can see from Figure 5-39, many data provider–specific classes implement IDbDataAdapter.

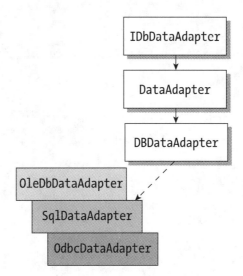

Figure 5-39. Data provider–specific classes implementing IDbDataAdapter

The DataAdapter enables you to connect to a database and specify SQL strings for retrieving data from or writing data to a DataSet. As you've seen in the beginning of this chapter, a dataset represents in-memory cached data. An in-memory object frees you from the confines of the specifics of a database and allows you to deal with the data in memory. The DataAdapter serves as an intermediary between the database and the DataSet.

Constructing a DataAdapter Object

The DataAdapter constructor has many overloaded forms. You can create a constructor with no arguments, pass a Command object, pass a Command object with Connection object as arguments, or any combination of these. You can also specify a SQL statement as a string for querying a particular table or more than one table. You can also specify the connection string or a Connection object to connect to the database.

Listing 5-41 creates a connection, builds a SQL statement using the SELECT query, and passes the SQL string and the connection objects as SqlDataAdapter constructor arguments. I've used the same Northwind SQL Server database on localhost as I've been using in the previous examples.

Listing 5-41. Executing a SELECT *statement using* SqlDataAdapter
```
string ConnectionString ="Integrated Security=SSPI;" +
                "Initial Catalog=Northwind;" +
                "Data Source=localhost;";
string SQL = "SELECT CustomerID, CompanyName FROM Customers";

SqlConnection conn = new SqlConnection(ConnectionString);

// Open the connection
conn.Open();

// Create a SqlDataAdapter object
SqlDataAdapter adapter = new SqlDataAdapter(SQL, conn);
```

As discussed earlier, there is no difference in creating OleDb, Sql, or ODBC data adapters. The only difference is the connection string. For example, the following code snippet shows you how to create an OleDbDataAdapter object. Listing 5-42 uses the Access 2000 Northwind database and accesses all records of the Orders table by using a SELECT * SQL query.

Listing 5-42. Executing a SELECT *statement using* OleDbDataAdapter
```
// Create a Connection Object
string ConnectionString = @"Provider=Microsoft.Jet.OLEDB.4.0;"+
"Data Source=c:\\Northwind.mdb";
string SQL = "SELECT * FROM Orders";

OleDbConnection conn = new OleDbConnection(ConnectionString);
// Open the connection
conn.Open();

// Create an OleDbDataAdapter object
OleDbDataAdapter adapter = new OleDbDataAdapter(SQL, conn);
```

You can also use DataAdapter's Command properties by using the Command object with OleDbDataAdaper. For example, the following code uses OleDbCommand to set the SelectCommand property of the data adapter. You can also see that OleDbDataAdapter has no arguments as its constructor:

```
// Create an OleDbDataAdapter object
OleDbDataAdapter adapter = new OleDbDataAdapter();
adapter.SelectCommand = new OleDbCommand(SQL, conn);
```

DataAdapter Properties

As you start working with data adapters, you need take a quick look at data adapter properties and methods. The DataAdapter has properties of type Command, which represent the ways it can query, insert, delete, and update the database. These properties are of type OleDbCommand.

Table 5-28 describes OleDbDataAdapter class properties.

Table 5-28. The OleDbDataAdpater *Properties*

PROPERTY	DESCRIPTION
DeleteCommand	Represents a DELETE statement or stored procedure for deleting records from the data source
InsertCommand	Represents an INSERT statement or stored procedure for inserting a new record to the data source
SelectCommand	Represents a SELECT statement or stored procedure can be used to select records from a data source
UpdateCommand	Represents an UPDATE statement or stored procedure for updating records in a data source
TableMappings	Represents a collection of mappings between actual data source table and a DataTable object

Table 5-29 shows these command properties and their examples.

Table 5-29. OleDbDataAdapter *Command Properties with Examples*

PROPERTY	EXAMPLE
SelectCommand	cmd.SelectCommand.CommandText = "SELECT * FROM Orders ORDER BY Price";
DeleteCommand	TheDataSetCommand.DeleteCommand.CommandText = "DELETE FROM Orders WHERE LastName ='Smith'";
InsertCommand	TheDataSetCommand.InsertCommand.CommandText = "INSERT INTO Orders VALUES (25,'Widget1','Smith')";
UpdateCommand	TheDataSetCommand.UpdateCommand.CommandText = "UPDATE Orders SET ZipCode='34956' WHERE OrderNum =14";

DataAdapter Methods

The DataAdapter class provides many useful methods. For instance, the Fill method of the DataAdapter fills data from a data adapter to the DataSet object, and the Update method stores data from a DataSet object to the data source.

Table 5-30 describes some of the OleDbDataAdapter methods.

Table 5-30. The OleDbDataAdapter *Methods*

METHOD	DESCRIPTION
Fill	This method fills data records from a DataAdapter to a DataSet object.
FillSchema	This method adds a DataTable to a DataSet.
GetFillParameters	This method retrieves parameters that are used when a SELECT statement is executed.
Update	This method stores data from a dataset to the data source.

Filling the DataSet

The Fill method is the primary method for bringing data into a DataSet from a data source. This command uses the SelectCommand SQL statement to fill a DataSet memory structure consisting of data tables, data rows, data columns, and data relations. The Fill method has about 10 overloaded forms. You can fill data from a data source either to a DataSet or a DataTable.

Listing 5-43 calls the Fill method to fill data to a DataSet, which later can be used to bind with data-bound controls.

Listing 5-43. Calling DataAdapter*'s* Fill *method*

```
// Create an OleDbDataAdapter object
OleDbDataAdapter adapter = new OleDbDataAdapter(SQL, conn);
DataSet ds = new DataSet("Orders");
adapter.Fill(ds);
```

DataAdapter Example

Now you'll create your first sample using data adapters. In this sample example, I'll show you how to create data adapters using Sql and OleDb data providers and fill data from data adapter to a DataGrid control.

First, create a Windows application using Visual C# Projects and add two buttons and a DataGrid control to the form by dragging the controls from the toolbox to the form. Second, set both button's Name property; use OleDbDataAdapter and SqlDataAdapter. Next, set the Text properties to OleDb DataAdapter and SQL DataAdapter. After setting these properties, the form will look like Figure 5-40. As you can see, there are two buttons, OleDb DataAdapter and SQL DataAdapter.

Now add button-click event handlers for both the OleDb DataAdapter and SQL DataAdapter buttons. You can add a button-click event handler either by double-clicking on the button or by using the Events tab of the Properties window of a button control. On the OleDb DataAdapter button-click event handler, you'll write code to read data from an OleDb data source and fill data to the

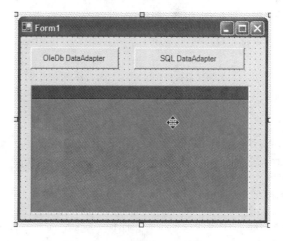

Figure 5-40. Creating a Windows Forms application and adding controls to the form

data grid. On the SQL DataAdapter button-click event handler, you'll write code to read data from a SQL Server data source and fill data to the data grid.

Listing 5-44 shows the source code for the OleDb DataAdapter button click, and Listing 5-45 shows the source code for the SQL DataAdapter button click. As you can see, you follow the same steps as before. Open a con-nection, create a data adapter object with a SELECT string, create a dataset object, call data adapter's Fill method to fill the dataset, and bind the dataset to the DataGrid control using DataGrid.DataSource property as DataSet.DefaultViewManager, which represents the default view of a DataSet object.

Listing 5-44. Displaying the Orders table data in a DataGrid
using OleDbDataAdapter

```
private void OleDbDataAdapter_Click(object sender, System.EventArgs e)
{
            // Create a Connection Object
string ConnectionString = @"Provider=Microsoft.Jet.OLEDB.4.0;"+
"Data Source=c:\\Northwind.mdb";
            string SQL = "SELECT * FROM Orders";

            OleDbConnection conn = new OleDbConnection(ConnectionString);
            // Open the connection
            conn.Open();

            // Create an OleDbDataAdapter object
            OleDbDataAdapter adapter = new OleDbDataAdapter();
            adapter.SelectCommand = new OleDbCommand(SQL, conn);

            // Create DataSet Object
            DataSet ds = new DataSet("Orders");
            // Call DataAdapter's Fill method to fill data from the
            // DataAdapter to the DataSet
            adapter.Fill(ds);

            // Bind dataset to a DataGrid control
            dataGrid1.DataSource = ds.DefaultViewManager;
}
```

The output of Listing 5-44 looks like Figure 5-41.

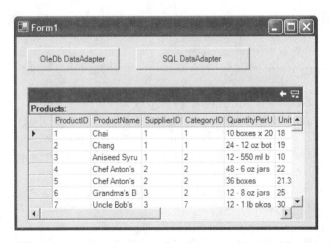

Figure 5-41. Filling data from an Access database to a DataGrid control
using OleDbDataAdapter

The output of Listing 5-45 looks like Figure 5-42.

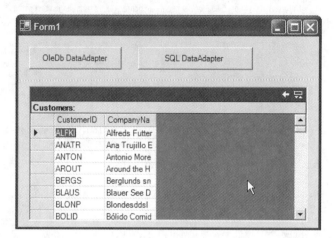

Figure 5-42. Filling data from a SQL Server database to a DataGrid control using SqlDataAdapter

Listing 5-45. Displaying the Customers tables data in a DataGrid using SqlDataAdapter

```
private void SqlDataAdapter_Click(object sender, System.EventArgs e)
{
        string ConnectionString ="Integrated Security=SSPI;" +
            "Initial Catalog=Northwind;" +
            "Data Source=localhost;";
        string SQL = "SELECT CustomerID, CompanyName FROM Customers";

        SqlConnection conn = new SqlConnection(ConnectionString);

        // Open the connection
        conn.Open();

        // Create a SqlDataAdapter object
        SqlDataAdapter adapter = new SqlDataAdapter(SQL, conn);

        // Call DataAdapter's Fill method to fill data from the
        // DataAdapter to the DataSet
        DataSet ds = new DataSet("Customers");
        adapter.Fill(ds);

        // Bind data set to a DataGrid control
        dataGrid1.DataSource = ds.DefaultViewManager;
}
```

Filling My DataAdapter from a Recordset

Because Microsoft realized it would be difficult for some developers to let go of their recordsets (or perhaps they have some legacy applications that would be difficult to convert), the DataAdapter's Fill method also allows you to fill a DataSet with a recordset. You can't, however, fill a recordset with a Dataset. The Fill method appends rows to the existing DataSet's DataTable. If a primary key exists for the DataRows in the DataSet, then the Fill method will attempt to update rows from the recordset with a matching primary key. You can call the recordset with the following code:

```
OleDbDataAdapter1.Fill(TheDataSet,  anADORecordset, SourceTableName);
```

> **NOTE**   *I'll discuss recordsets and ADO.NET in more detail in Chapter 9.*

Updating the Database Using the Update Method

The way the architecture works with the DataAdapter is that you can make any changes you want to the filled DataSet, and it won't affect the database until you call the Update method. When Update is called, the DataAdapter will attempt to execute each query (UPDATE, INSERT, DELETE) on every row of the DataSet that has been updated, inserted, and deleted. For example, if you call Delete on a row in the DataSet, then when Update is called on the DataAdapter, the DeleteCommand of the DataAdapter will be called using the particular row in the DataSet.

> **NOTE**   *Keep in mind that this* Update *is different than a* SQL UPDATE *statement.*

To insert, update, and delete data using a DataAdapter, you create an OleDbCommand object with INSERT, UPDATE, and DELETE statements and set the InsertCommand, UpdateCommand, and DeleteCommand properties of the data adapter to OleDbCommand. You can avoid building Command objects manually by using CommandBuilder.

As you saw in the DataTable, DataRow, and DataColumn sections at the beginning of this chapter, you can use the Delete method of a DataRow to delete a row. The AddNew method of the DataTable adds a row to a DataTable. To change an exisiting row's data, you can directly assign a row's value. To save data to the data source, you need to call the DataAdapter's Update method.

> **NOTE** *The* Tables *member of* DataSet *represents all* DataTable *objects attached to a* DataSet.

Listing 5-46 creates a new DataRow, sets the data of DataRow members, and adds rows to the table using the Add method of DataTable.Rows.

Listing 5-46. Adding a DataRow *to a* DataTable

```
DataRow row = ds.Tables["Customers"].NewRow();
row["CustomerId"] = "TstID";
row["ContactName"] = "Lana Jackob";
row["CompanyName"] = "Mindcracker Inc.";
ds.Tables["Customers"].Rows.Add(row);
```

Listing 5-47 deletes data by using the DataRow's Delete method.

Listing 5-47. Deleting a DataRow *from a* DataTable

```
DataRow row1 = ds.Tables["Customers"].Rows.Find("TstID");
row1.Delete();
```

In this example, I'll show you how to add, edit, and remove data from the Northwind database. I'll display the results of the Customers table in a DataGrid after adding, updating, and deleting data from the table. To test this source code, create a Windows application, drop a DataGrid, and add three buttons— InsertCommand, UpdateCommand, and DeleteCommand—to the form. Listing 5-48 shows the code on the InsertCommand button-click event. As you can see from Listing 5-48, I created a filled DataSet and created a new DataRow using the DataTable.NewRow method. After creating a DataRow, I set its column values and called the DataAdapter's Update method and displayed data in the DataGrid. I added new rows to the Customers table with CustomerId, CustomerName, and CompanyName (named TstID, Lana Jackob, and Mindcracker Inc., respectively).

Listing 5-48. Adding data using a DataAdapter's Update *method*

```
private void InsertCommand_Click(object sender, System.EventArgs e)
{
        string ConnectionString =
        "Provider=Microsoft.Jet.OLEDB.4.0;"+
            "Data Source=c:\\Northwind.mdb";
        OleDbConnection conn =
            new OleDbConnection(ConnectionString);
        DataRow row;
```

```
        DataSet ds = new DataSet();

        try
        {
            conn.Open();

            OleDbDataAdapter adapter = new OleDbDataAdapter(
                "SELECT * FROM Customers", conn);

            OleDbCommandBuilder cmdBuilder =
                new OleDbCommandBuilder(adapter);
            adapter.MissingSchemaAction =
                MissingSchemaAction.AddWithKey;

            adapter.Fill(ds, "Customers");

            row = ds.Tables["Customers"].NewRow();
            row["CustomerId"] = "TstID";
            row["ContactName"] = "Lana Jackob";
            row["CompanyName"] = "Mindcracker Inc.";
            ds.Tables["Customers"].Rows.Add(row);

            adapter.Update(ds, "Customers");
            dataGrid1.DataSource = ds.DefaultViewManager;
        }
        catch(OleDbException exp)
        {
            MessageBox.Show(exp.Message.ToString());
        }

        if(conn.State == ConnectionState.Open)
            conn.Close();

}
```

Listing 5-49 shows an example that edits row data. The Find method returns the row with CustomerId = TstID. After that I assign values of the row and call the DataAdapter's Update method.

Listing 5-49. Updating data using the DataAdapter's Update *method*

```
private void UpdateCommand_Click(object sender, System.EventArgs e)
{
        string ConnectionString =
```

```
                    "Provider=Microsoft.Jet.OLEDB.4.0;"+
                    "Data Source=c:\\Northwind.mdb";
            OleDbConnection conn =
                    new OleDbConnection(ConnectionString);
            DataSet ds = new DataSet();

            try
            {
                conn.Open();

                OleDbDataAdapter adapter = new OleDbDataAdapter(
                    "SELECT * FROM Customers", conn);

                OleDbCommandBuilder cmdBuilder =
                    new OleDbCommandBuilder(adapter);
                adapter.MissingSchemaAction =
                    MissingSchemaAction.AddWithKey;

                adapter.Fill(ds, "Customers");

                DataRow row1 = ds.Tables["Customers"].Rows.Find("TstID");
                row1["ContactName"]="Stacy Monter";
                row1["CompanyName"] = "Monter Inc.";

                adapter.Update(ds, "Customers");
                dataGrid1.DataSource = ds.DefaultViewManager;
            }
            catch(OleDbException exp)
            {
                MessageBox.Show(exp.Message.ToString());
            }

            if(conn.State == ConnectionState.Open)
                conn.Close();
        }
```

Deleting a row is simple. Listing 5-50 deletes the row with the value TstID. As you can see from the code, I called the Find method to find the row and called the Delete method of the DataRow. After that I called the DataAdapter's Update method to save the changes to the database table.

Listing 5-50. Deleting data using the DataAdapter's Update *method*

```csharp
private void DeleteCommand_Click(object sender, System.EventArgs e)
{

            string ConnectionString =
                "Provider=Microsoft.Jet.OLEDB.4.0;"+
                "Data Source=c:\\Northwind.mdb";
            OleDbConnection conn =
                new OleDbConnection(ConnectionString);
            DataSet ds = new DataSet();

            try
            {
                conn.Open();

                OleDbDataAdapter adapter = new OleDbDataAdapter(
                    "SELECT * FROM Customers", conn);

                OleDbCommandBuilder cmdBuilder =
                    new OleDbCommandBuilder(adapter);
                adapter.MissingSchemaAction =
                    MissingSchemaAction.AddWithKey;

                adapter.Fill(ds, "Customers");

                DataRow row1 = ds.Tables["Customers"].Rows.Find("TstID");
                row1.Delete();
                adapter.Update(ds, "Customers");
                dataGrid1.DataSource = ds.DefaultViewManager;
            }
            catch(OleDbException exp)
            {
                MessageBox.Show(exp.Message.ToString());
            }

            if(conn.State == ConnectionState.Open)
                conn.Close();

}
```

Table and Column Mapping

One of the important properties of the DataAdapter is the TableMappings property. This property contains a collection of the DataTableMapping objects that are found in the System.Data.Common namespace (because they're common to all providers). The DataAdapter uses the DataTableMapping object to map the table name of the data source to the DataTable name of the DataSet. In general, the names for both sources can be the same.

For example, in Listing 5-51, the Northwind database's Order Table Mapping is constructed and added to the DataAdapter.

Listing 5-51. Using DataTableMapping *to map Orders table of Northwind database*

```
private void DataMapping1()
        {
            // Create a Connection Object
            string ConnectionString ="Integrated Security=SSPI;" +
                "Initial Catalog=Northwind;" +
                "Data Source=localhost;";
            SqlConnection conn = new SqlConnection(ConnectionString);

            // Open the connection
            conn.Open();

            // Create a DataTableMapping object
            DataTableMapping myMapping =
          new DataTableMapping("Orders", "mapOrders");
        SqlDataAdapter adapter =
        new SqlDataAdapter("Select * From Orders", conn);

            // Call DataAdapter's TableMappings.Add method
            adapter.TableMappings.Add(myMapping);

            // Create a DataSet Object and call DataAdapter's Fill method
            // Make sure you use new name od DataTableMapping i.e., MayOrders
            DataSet ds = new DataSet();
            adapter.Fill(ds, "mapOrders");
            dataGrid1.DataSource = ds.DefaultViewManager;
        }
```

The default mapping for a DataTable is the Table alias. If you use this mapping name, then you don't need to mention the table in the Fill method. Listing 5-52 shows an example using DataTableMapping with the Table option.

Listing 5-52. Using DataTableMapping *with the* Table *option*

```
private void DataMapping2()
        {
                // Create a Connection Object
                string ConnectionString ="Integrated Security=SSPI;" +
                    "Initial Catalog=Northwind;" +
                    "Data Source=localhost;";
                SqlConnection conn = new SqlConnection(ConnectionString);

                // Open the connection
                conn.Open();

                // Create a DataTableMapping object
DataTableMapping myMapping =
new DataTableMapping("Table", "Orders");
SqlDataAdapter adapter =
new SqlDataAdapter("Select * From Orders", conn)

;               // Call DataAdapter's TableMappings.Add method
                adapter.TableMappings.Add(myMapping);

                // Create a DataSet Object and call DataAdapter's Fill method
                // Make sure you use new name od DataTableMapping i.e., MayOrders
                DataSet ds = new DataSet();
                adapter.Fill(ds);
                dataGrid1.DataSource = ds.DefaultViewManager;
        }
```

DataTables are not the only things aliased in .NET. You can also alias the DataColumns using DataColumnMapping objects. The DataTableMapping's ColumnMappings property contains DataColumnMappings. You construct a ColumnMapping in much the same way you do a table mapping. Listing 5-53 shows an example of DataColumnMapping. The first order is in a message box using the alias ID:

Listing 5-53. Using DataColumnMapping

```
        private void DataMapping3()
        {
                // Create a Connection Object
                string ConnectionString ="Integrated Security=SSPI;" +
                    "Initial Catalog=Northwind;" +
                    "Data Source=localhost;";
                SqlConnection conn = new SqlConnection(ConnectionString);
```

```
                // Open the connection
                conn.Open();

                // Create a DataTableMapping object
DataTableMapping myMapping =
new DataTableMapping("Table", "Orders");
SqlDataAdapter adapter =
new SqlDataAdapter("Select * From Orders", conn);
                // Call DataAdapter's TableMappings.Add method
                adapter.TableMappings.Add(myMapping);

                myMapping.ColumnMappings.Add(
new DataColumnMapping("OrderID", "mapID"));
                // Create a DataSet Object and call DataAdapter's Fill method
                // Make sure you use new name od DataTableMapping i.e., MayOrders
                DataSet ds = new DataSet();
                adapter.Fill(ds);

                MessageBox.Show( ds.Tables["Orders"].Rows[0]["mapID"].ToString());

                dataGrid1.DataSource = ds.DefaultViewManager;
        }
```

The framework automatically generates much of the mappings, so you don't have to worry about them. But, occasionally, you may want to choose your own schema names for your DataSet that map back to the data source.

CommandBuilder: Easing the Work of the Programmer

Sometimes creating SQL statements could be a lengthy job when dealing with many columns in a table. A CommandBuilder object reduces the burden of creating SQL statements for you. In other words, the CommandBuilder helps you to generate update, delete, and insert commands on a single database table for a data adapter. Similar to other objects, each data provider has a command builder class. The OleDbCommandBuilder, SqlCommandBuilder, and OdbcCommandBuilder classes represent the CommandBuilder object in the OleDb, Sql, and ODBC data providers. These classes also work in pretty similar fashion. Once you know how to use OleDbCommandBuilder, you can use SqlCommandBuilder and OdbcCommandBuilder in a similar way. I'll use OleDbCommandBuilder class in this example.

Creating a CommandBuilder Object

Creating a CommandBuilder object is pretty simple. You pass a DataAdapter as an argument of the CommandBuilder constructor. For example:

```
// Create a command builder object
SqlCommandBuilder builder = new SqlCommandBuilder(adapter);
```

SqlCommandBuilder Members

The DataAdapter property of a CommandBuilder represents the DataProvider attached to a CommandBuilder object for which automatic SQL statements are generated. The GetDeleteCommand, GetUpdateCommand, and GetInsertCommand methods return the delete, update, and insert commands in the form of a Command object. The RefreshSchema method refreshes the database schema.

Using the SqlCommandBuilder

Now you'll see how to use the SqlCommandBuilder in an application. You can use OleDbCommandBuilder and ODBC CommandBuilder classes in same way. Listing 5-54 shows how to use SqlCommandBuilder. As you can see, as usual, you create a connection to the database and use it to create the adapter object. The adapter is constructed with the initial query for the Employees table as well as with the database connection.

Next you construct the CommandBuilder by passing the DataAdapter into its constructor. The act of creating the CommandBuilder automatically causes the UPDATE, INSERT, and DELETE commands to be generated for the adapter:

```
SqlCommandBuilder builder = new
        SqlCommandBuilder(adapter);
```

Next, fill the DataSet using the adapter and create an instance of the Employee DataTable from the DataSet:

```
// Create a dataset object
DataSet ds = new DataSet("EmployeeSet");
adapter.Fill(ds, "Employees");
```

Now insert a new DataRow into the DataTable in memory and populate a row with your desired values using DataTable's AddNew method. After that you call the DataRowCollection.Add method to add the row to the DataTable:

```
// Create a data table object and add a new row
DataTable EmployeeTable = ds.Tables["Employees"];
DataRow row = EmployeeTable.NewRow();
row["FirstName"] = "Rodney";
row["LastName"] = "Dangerfield";
row["Title"] = "Comedian";
EmployeeTable.Rows.Add(row);
```

Finally you call DataAdapter's Update method to update the DataTable changes to the data source:

```
// Update data adapter
adapter.Update(ds, "Employees");
```

Listing 5-54 shows the full source code of how to create and use a CommandBuilder object.

Listing 5-54. Creating and using the SqlCommandBuilder *class*
```
// Create a Connection Object
string ConnectionString ="Integrated Security=SSPI;" +
"Initial Catalog=Northwind;" +
"Data Source=localhost;";
SqlConnection conn = new SqlConnection(ConnectionString);

// Open the connection
conn.Open();

// Create a data adapter object
SqlDataAdapter adapter = new SqlDataAdapter
("SELECT * FROM Employees ORDER BY EmployeeID", conn);

// Create a command builder object
SqlCommandBuilder builder = new SqlCommandBuilder(adapter);

// Create a dataset object
DataSet ds = new DataSet("EmployeeSet");
adapter.Fill(ds, "Employees");

// Create a data table object and add a new row
```

```
DataTable EmployeeTable = ds.Tables["Employees"];
DataRow row = EmployeeTable.NewRow();
row["FirstName"] = "Rodney";
row["LastName"] = "Dangerfield";
row["Title"] = "Comedian";
EmployeeTable.Rows.Add(row);

// Update data adapter
adapter.Update(ds, "Employees");

MessageBox.Show(row["FirstName"].ToString().Trim() + " "
+ row["LastName"].ToString().Trim() + " added to Employees");
```

As you can see from Listing 5-54, you didn't have to figure out how to create the InsertCommand for the Employees table because the CommandBuilder did it for you. All you had to do was add a row to the DataSet and invoke an Update on the DataAdapter. You may argue that the InsertCommand is automatically generated by VS.NET anyway by the DataAdapter configurer, but the CommandBuilder works with the SelectCommand you choose for the adapter, so you can change the SelectCommand on the fly and reuse the CommandBuilder at run-time.

Note that the method RefreshSchema of the CommandBuilder should be called if the SelectCommand of the associated DataAdapter changes. The RefreshSchema rebuilds the other command structures (InsertCommand, DeleteCommand, UpdateCommand) of the DataAdapter.

Staying within the Parameters

ADO.NET wraps a class around the parameters used for each column of the database. You can use the parameters in conjunction with SelectCommand to help you to select data for the DataSet. You also use it in conjunction with the other commands of the CommandDataSet (InsertCommand, UpdateCommand, DeleteCommand) to place data into the DataSet. These are generated automatically when you insert an OleDbDataAdapter component from the toolbox.

The OleDbType describes the type information for the parameter. It consists of everything from strings to Global Unique Identifiers (GUIDs). Sql data provider has a SqlDbType, and ODBC data provider has an ODBC type. These type names and definitions differ, depending upon the provider you're using; for example, the Money type is the same in ODBC and Sqldata providers, but is called Currency in OleDb data providers.

Not only does a parameter have a DbType property, but a parameter has a Direction (input, output), Size, and even a Value. Table 5-31 describes the OleDbParameter properties.

Table 5-31. The OleDbParameter *Class Properties*

PROPERTY	DESCRIPTION
DbType	Represents the DbType of the parameter.
Direction	Represents the direction of a parameter. A parameter can be input-only, output-only, bi-directional, or a stored procedure.
IsNullable	Represents whether a parameter accepts null values.
OleDbType	Represents the OleDbType of the parameter.
ParameterName	Represents the name of the parameter.
Precision	Represents the maximum number of digits used to represent the Value property.
Scale	Represents the decimal places to which Value is resolved.
Size	Represents the maximum size in bytes a column can store.
SourceColumn	Represents the source column mapped to the DataSet.
SourceVersion	Represents the DataRow version.
Value	Represents the value of the parameter.

Listing 5-55 shows the construction of an OleDbParameter generated by the framework for the Northwind database. All commands have a collection of parameters; in this example, the parameter ContactName is being added to a command used for deleting from the database.

Listing 5-55. Creating a parameter

```
this.oleDbDeleteCommand2.Parameters.Add(new
System.Data.OleDb.OleDbParameter("ContactName",
System.Data.OleDb.OleDbType.Char, 30,
System.Data.ParameterDirection.Input, false,
((System.Byte)(0)), ((System.Byte)(0)),
"ContactName", System.Data.DataRowVersion.Original,
null));
```

Luckily, you'll find that the framework will automatically generate the parameters for you because, as you can see, this is a lot of code to write for just one parameter. Imagine if you had to manually deal with a database table of 50 parameters!

You need to create and add parameters to the command for each parameter reference that appears in the SQL command. If the SQL command only describes a single row insertion or update, then you don't have parameters. But more often than not, when you're using `DataSets`, `DataTables`, and `DataRows`, you'll need parameters because these in-memory structures operate on several rows.

Parameters appear in a SQL Server `Insert` command proceeded by an @ sign, such as

```
sqlInsertCommand1.CommandText =
@"INSERT INTO Customers(CustomerID, CompanyName, ContactName)"+
" VALUES (@CustomerID, @CompanyName, @ContactName)";
```

In OleDb, parameters appear as question marks such as

```
oleDbInsertCommand2.CommandText =
"INSERT INTO Customers(Address, City, CompanyName, ContactName)"+
" VALUES (?, ?, ?, ?)";
```

To add the parameter `@CustomerID` to the `InsertCommand` of the `SqlDataAdapter`, simply call `Add` on the command's `ParameterCollection`. This will return a parameter in which you can further assign properties, such as

```
SqlParameter  workParam = theSqlServerAdapter.InsertCommand.
           Parameters.Add("@CustomerID", SqlDbType.Int);
```

Two other crucial properties are the name of the column that the parameter is mapping to and the `RowVersion`. Typically, it's good to give the parameter the same name as the column of the database:

```
    workParam.SourceColumn = "CustomerID";
    workParam.SourceVersion = DataRowVersion.Original;
```

The `SourceVersion` can take on the value `Current` or `Original`. The `SourceVersion` property helps the `DataAdapter`'s `Update` command to decide which value version to load when executing the SQL `UpdateCommand` on the database. (`InsertCommand` and `DeleteCommand` ignore the `SourceVersion`.) The `SourceVersion` property comes in handy when updating a row whose primary key you may want to change. If the value is `DataRowVersion.Original`, then the primary key will retain its original value.

Understanding Transactions and Concurrency

Transactions are groups of database commands that execute as a package and provide an ability to commit or rollback (abort) all changes made during the transaction processing. Transaction changes will be committed if there was no error during the transaction processing. If an error occurs during the transaction processing, all changes will be aborted and data will be the same as it was before any transactions started. To start a transaction processing, you call `BeginTransaction`. At the end you can call `CommitTransaction` or `Rollback Transaction` based on the status of transactions. The `CommitTransaction` reflects all changes to the databases and `Rollback` aborts all changes.

For example, say you have an application with two tables: Inventory and Orders. When a customer places an order, the Inventory table needs to be reduced. Now imagine that an update to the Orders table was successful, but an update to the Inventory table failed. This scenario will lead to data inconsistency. To maintain the integrity of data, you could package both commands into a single transaction. If one table updated successfully and the other table did not, the transaction can be rolled back; otherwise, the transaction can be committed.

Nested transactions are transactions within the scope an existing transaction. The changes made within the nested transactions are invisible to the top-level transactions until the nested transactions are committed. To create nested transactions, you call `BeginTransaction` with `CommitTransaction` and `RollbackTransaction` within the existing transactions. For example:

```
Begin Transaction A
      Begin Transaction B
                  Do something
      Commit Transaction B
Commit Transaction A
```

Savepoints are useful when you're working with nested transactions. There are occasions when you want to abort a portion of transaction, but not all of it. For example, you're processing four commands as nested transactions, but you want to commit only two commands and abort two of them. A savepoint is a temporary point in the transaction that you want to save (or back up) without aborting the entire transaction. In transaction processing, you set the savepoint call and come back later when you think it's safe to process the transaction. A unique number represents the savepoint. For example:

```
Begin Transaction A
    Do something
         SetSavePoint
    Do something
Commit or Rollback Transaction A
```

Managing and writing reliable and scalable multi-tier distributed applications is one of the most challenging jobs for database developers. Think about multiple clients accessing the same server database simultaneously. Some of them are accessing data, some of them are updating the same data, and some of them are trying to delete the same data that other clients are using in their operations.

To prevent data inconsistency, it's important to provide some kind of mechanism so other users can't update data when a user is already using the same data. The mechanism to deal with this situation is called *concurrency control*. Concurrency is the method by which multiple clients can access and update the same data simultaneously without being concerned that they're forcing data redundancy and inconsistency.

There are three common ways to manage concurrency:

- **Pessimistic concurrency control**. In this type of concurrency control, a row (or a record) is unavailable to other users from the time the record is fetched by a user until it's updated in the database.

- **Optimistic concurrency control**. In this type of concurrency control, a row is unavailable to other users only while the data is actually being updated. The update examines the row in the database and determines whether any changes have been made.

- **Last in wins concurrency control**. In this case of concurrency control, a row is unavailable to other users only while the data is actually being updated. The update overwrites the changes made by other users.

In pessimistic concurrency, the data is unavailable to other users from the time the record is fetched by a user until it's updated in the database. This is useful when a user accessing a row is going to play a major role based on the data he/she is accessing. Another advantage of pessimistic concurrency is less locking overhead. Once a row is locked, it's locked until the first user is done. The main drawback of this type of concurrency is that data is not available to other users. For example, if a user accessing data left his terminal, other users have to wait for him to release the connection.

In optimistic concurrency, data is available all the time except when a user is updating the data. In this type of concurrency, the locks are set and held only while the database is being accessed. The locks prevent other users from attempting to update records at the same instant. If other users try to update the data that is locked by the first user, the update fails.

The last in wins type of concurrency is only useful when the last user's update counts. For example, it's useful if you're keeping track of the last winner of a race. In other words, many users are updating the same data and the person who updates it last is the latest data. The data updated by other users will be lost. In this case, data could easily lead to inconsistency because of some network slowness when previously posted data arrives last.

> **NOTE** *See Appendix A for more on locking, cursors, and isolation levels.*

Transactions in ADO.NET

ADO.NET provides a transaction class that represents a transaction. All data providers provide their own version of the transaction class. The IDbTransaction interface implements the basic functionality of the transaction class. All data provider–specific classes implement this namespace. Figure 5-43 shows some of the classes that implement IDTransaction.

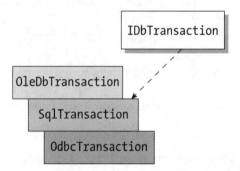

Figure 5-43. Data provider–specific classes that implement IDbTransaction

In the provider classes, a transaction is represented as an object returned after BeginTransaction is called on a Connection.

You can commit (make permanent) or roll back (cancel and return to the original state) the transactions. Table 5-32 describes the methods for the OleDb provider's Transaction class. As discussed earlier, all data provider transaction classes provides similar methods.

Table 5-32. Methods of the Transaction *Class*

METHOD	DESCRIPTION
Commit	Commits the transaction to the database
Rollback	Rollbacks a transaction to the previous database state
Begin(IsolationLevel)	Begins a nested database transaction passing the isolation level

An interesting thing to note in connecting to a database is the IsolationLevel, which allows you to lock your transaction in various ways. The default isolation level is ReadCommitted, which allows you to alter data during a transaction. If you use an isolation level of RepeatableRead, locks are placed on all the data, so you can't alter the data in this transaction. If you lock at the Serializable level, locks are placed on the entire DataSet, preventing changes to all the Data in the DataSet. Table 5-33 describes different isolation levels.

Table 5-33. Isolation Levels Available for Transactions

ISOLATION LEVEL	DESCRIPTION
ReadCommitted (default)	Locks are shared to prevent inconsistent reads between multiple users. Data can be altered during the transaction.
ReadUncommitted	Locks are not placed on the data, so a dirty read is possible.
RepeatableRead	Locks are placed on all the data of the database query, so the data can't be altered during a read.
Chaos	The changes made on transactions awaiting commitment can't be altered.
Serializable	A range lock is placed on an entire DataSet preventing changes being made to the DataSet.
Unspecified	The IsolationLevel can't be determined.

> **NOTE** *See Appendix A for more about isolation levels.*

Concurrency in ADO.NET

The ADO.NET model assumes that the optimistic concurrency is the default concurrency because of its disconnected nature of data. A user reads data in a dataset through a data adapter, and data is available to a user as a local copy of the data. The server database is available to all other users.

Even though the ADO.NET model supports optimistic concurrency by default, that doesn't mean you can't implement pessimistic concurrency in ADO.NET. The following two examples will show you both cases.

Listing 5-56 shows you how to implement optimistic concurrency. You can handle the optimistic concurrency by creating an Update command that checks the database to make sure the original data of the database row hasn't changed when an immediate update is about to be performed. It does this by creating two sets of parameters for the update command: a current set of parameters and an original set of parameters. The original parameters maintain the data that was originally read in from the DataSet. If the data has changed in the data source, when you run the Update command with the WHERE clause filter, the filter won't find the row and an update won't occur. If the data has not changed in the data source, then the WHERE clause will find the original row you're updating, and the row will be updated with the new data. Listing 5-56 has a WHERE clause on the original data built in. The framework generates the parameters such as @OrderDate and @ShippedDate. The framework even generates the Update command, but I shortened it, so you could see it more clearly.

> **NOTE** *To test these samples, create a Windows application, add a refer- ence to the* System.Data *and* System.Data.SqlClient *namespaces, add two buttons to the form, write code on the button event handlers, and make sure SQL Server is up and running.*

Listing 5-56. Optimistic concurrency example

```
void TestOptimisticConcurrency()
{
    try
    {
    string ConnectionString ="Integrated Security=SSPI;" +
        "Initial Catalog=Northwind;" +
        "Data Source=localhost;";
    SqlConnection conn = new SqlConnection(ConnectionString);
    conn.Open();
    SqlDataAdapter da = new SqlDataAdapter("SELECT * FROM Orders", conn);
    DataSet ds = new DataSet("test");
    SqlCommand updateCmd = new SqlCommand();
    updateCmd.CommandText = @"UPDATE Orders SET CustomerID = @CustomerID,"+
    "OrderDate = @OrderDate, ShippedDate = @ShippedDate WHERE "+
    "(OrderID = @Original_OrderID) AND (CustomerID = @Original_CustomerID "+
    "OR @Original_CustomerID IS NULL AND CustomerID IS NULL) AND "+
    "(OrderDate = @Original_OrderDate OR @Original_OrderDate "+
    "IS NULL AND OrderDate IS NULL) AND (ShippedDate = "+
    "@Original_ShippedDate OR @Original_ShippedDate IS NULL AND "+
    "ShippedDate IS NULL); SELECT CustomerID, OrderDate, ShippedDate, "+
    "OrderID FROM Orders WHERE (OrderID = @OrderID)";
```

```
    updateCmd.Connection = conn;
    // CustomerID parameter
    updateCmd.Parameters.Add(new SqlParameter
        ("@CustomerID", SqlDbType.NVarChar, 5, "CustomerID"));
    // OrderDate parameter
    updateCmd.Parameters.Add(new SqlParameter
        ("@OrderDate", SqlDbType.DateTime, 8, "OrderDate"));
    // ShippedDate parameter
    updateCmd.Parameters.Add(new SqlParameter
        ("@ShippedDate", SqlDbType.DateTime, 8, "ShippedDate"));
    updateCmd.Parameters.Add(new SqlParameter
        ("@Original_OrderID", SqlDbType.Int, 4,
        ParameterDirection.Input, false,
        ((System.Byte)(0)), ((System.Byte)(0)),
        "OrderID", DataRowVersion.Original, null));
    updateCmd.Parameters.Add(new SqlParameter
        ("@Original_CustomerID", SqlDbType.NVarChar,
        5, ParameterDirection.Input, false, ((System.Byte)(0)),
        ((System.Byte)(0)), "CustomerID",
        DataRowVersion.Original, null));
        updateCmd.Parameters.Add(new SqlParameter
        ("@Original_OrderDate", SqlDbType.DateTime,
        8, ParameterDirection.Input, false, ((System.Byte)(0)),
        ((System.Byte)(0)), "OrderDate",
        DataRowVersion.Original, null));
    updateCmd.Parameters.Add(new SqlParameter
        ("@Original_ShippedDate", SqlDbType.DateTime,
        8, ParameterDirection.Input, false, ((System.Byte)(0)),
        ((System.Byte)(0)), "ShippedDate",
        DataRowVersion.Original, null));
    updateCmd.Parameters.Add
        (new SqlParameter("@OrderID", SqlDbType.Int,
        4, "OrderID"));

    da.UpdateCommand = updateCmd;
    da.Fill(ds, "Orders");
    // update the row in the dataset
    ds.Tables["Orders"].Rows[0].BeginEdit();
    ds.Tables["Orders"].Rows[0]["OrderDate"] = DateTime.Now;
    ds.Tables["Orders"].Rows[0].EndEdit();
    // update the row in the data Source (Orders Table)
    da.Update(ds, "Orders");
MessageBox.Show("Finished updating first row.");
```

```
// close connection
    conn.Close();
    }
    catch(SqlException ex)
    {
        MessageBox.Show(ex.Message.ToString());
    }
}
```

Another way of handling optimistic concurrency that you may be familiar with is by checking to see if a timestamp on the data source row has changed or the row version number has changed on the row being updated.

Pessimistic locking on the database isn't really supported by the data providers because the connection to the database is not kept open, so you must perform all locking with business logic on the DataSet.

You can do a form of pessimistic concurrency, however, using ADO.NET on the data source through transactions. The way to do this is to keep the connection open on the database and create a transaction that has a certain isolation level on a row. Listing 5-57 opens a connection and creates a transaction that locks out the rows used in the update of the Orders table in the Northwind database.

Listing 5-57. Pessimistic concurrency example

```
void TestPessimisticConcurrency()
{
try
{
    // Create a Connection Object
    string ConnectionString ="Integrated Security=SSPI;" +
        "Initial Catalog=Northwind;" +
        "Data Source=localhost;";
    SqlConnection conn = new SqlConnection(ConnectionString);
    conn.Open();
    // Create a transaction that locks the records of the query
    SqlTransaction tr = conn.BeginTransaction
        (IsolationLevel.RepeatableRead, "test");
    // Create a command that updates the order of
    // the database using the transaction

    SqlCommand cmd = new SqlCommand("UPDATE Orders SET "+
        "ShippedDate = '5/10/01', ShipCity = 'Columbus' WHERE "+
        "OrderID = 10248",   conn,  tr);
```

```
        // Execute the update
        cmd.ExecuteNonQuery();

        // Generate message
        MessageBox.Show("Wait for keypress...");

        tr.Commit(); // transaction is committed
        conn.Close();
    }
    catch(SqlException ex)
    {
        MessageBox.Show(ex.Message.ToString());
    }
}
```

Rollback, Commit, and Savepoints

The Sql data provider provides some additional methods for dealing with transactions involving savepoints. Savepoints allow you to rollback to a "bookmarked" point in the transaction. Table 5-34 describes these methods.

Table 5-34. Transaction Methods in the Sql Data Provider

METHOD	DESCRIPTION
Rollback(SavePoint)	Performs a rollback on a transaction to the previous database state.
Begin(IsolationLevel)	Begins a nested database transaction passing the Isolation level.
Save(SavePointName)	Equivalent to the Transact-SQL SAVE TRANSACTION in the Sql Server database. Allows you to create a savepoint so that you can rollback to a particular saved state of the database.

Listing 5-58 shows an example of how savepoints are used in Sql Server. As you can see from Listing 5-58, first you establish a connection with the Northwind database and open the connection. After that, by calling BeginTransaction on the connection, you can return a SqlTransaction object, which you can use together with your Command object. To establish the relationship with the command object, you then pass the Transaction object in the constructor of Command.

Now that the transaction is tied to the Command object, you'll save the initial savepoint to the transaction and then execute the first insertion into the database. After that you assign a new SQL Insert to the CommandText and save the current transaction savepoint before executing the query. This Insert puts "Bob Hope" into the database.

Finally, you assign a new SQL Insert to the CommandText and save the current transaction savepoint before executing the query. This Insert puts "Fred" into the database.

Listing 5-58. Using savepoints in the Sql data provider

```
private void button1_Click(object sender, System.EventArgs e)
        {
            // Create a Connection Object
            string ConnectionString ="Integrated Security=SSPI;" +
                "Initial Catalog=Northwind;" +
                "Data Source=localhost;";

            SqlTransaction tran = null;
            SqlConnection conn = new SqlConnection(ConnectionString);


            try
            {
                conn.Open();
                tran = conn.BeginTransaction("Transaction1");
                SqlCommand cmd = new SqlCommand(
             "INSERT INTO Customers (CustomerID, ContactName, CompanyName)"+
                    "VALUES (516, 'Tim Howard', 'FireCon')", conn, tran);

                tran.Save("save1");
                cmd.ExecuteNonQuery();

                MessageBox.Show("Tim is in the Database");

                cmd.CommandText =
             "INSERT INTO Customers(CustomerID, ContactName, CompanyName)"+
                    "VALUES (517, 'Bob Hope', 'Hollywood')";
                tran.Save("save2");

                cmd.ExecuteNonQuery();

                MessageBox.Show("Bob is in the Database");
```

```
    cmd.CommandText =
"INSERT INTO Customers(CustomerID, ContactName, CompanyName)"+
 "VALUES (518, 'Fred Astaire', 'Hollywood')";
    MessageBox.Show("Fred is in the Database");

    tran.Save("save3");
    cmd.ExecuteNonQuery();
    tran.Rollback("save2");
    tran.Commit();

    MessageBox.Show("Transaction Rolledback, only Tim Made it.");
}
catch(Exception exp)
{
    if (tran != null)
        tran.Rollback();
    MessageBox.Show(exp.Message.ToString() +
        "\nTransaction Rolledback, Tim didn't make it.");
}
finally
{
    conn.Close();
}


}
```

By rolling back to the second savepoint, it's as if the second and third ExecuteNonQuery never happened, so the first ExecuteNonQuery that puts "Tim" in the database is the only one that actually gets committed. If there's an exception, then you can roll back the whole transaction (see Figure 5-44).

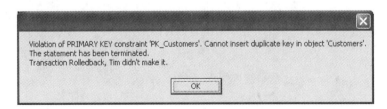

Figure 5-44. Message after rolling back the entire transaction when an exception is thrown

Catching Errors

The Error class is an aggregate of Exception and can be utilized by a try-catch block when an exception is thrown to get information about the error. The Error is populated as a collection in the Exception object. All provider Error objects have a Message property, which is a line of text describing the error. However, the SqlServer provider has a richer group of properties describing each error. For example, SqlServer has a LineNumber property that lists the line number of a stored procedure causing an error. The appendix contains a list of other useful error properties contained by Sql Server if you want to really take advantage of this property.

In the example of the OleDbException object in Listing 5-59, the Error collection of the exception is looped through after the exception is thrown, and both the error messages and the error codes are placed in a string to be printed out in a MessageBox control.

Listing 5-59. Utilizing the OleDbError *collection*

```
try
{
    . . .
}
catch(OleDbException ae)
{
    string strMessage = "";
    for (int i = 0; i < ae.Errors.Count; i++)
    {
        strMessage += ae.Errors[i].Message + " - " +
                    ae.Errors[i].SQLState  + "\n";
    }
    MessageBox.Show(strMessage);
}
```

Table 5-35 describes Message, SQLState, and other properties in OleDbError that contain information after the error that is caught.

Table 5-35. The `OleDbError` *Class Properties*

PROPERTY	DESCRIPTION
Message	Gives a brief description of the error
NativeError	Gives error information specific to the particular database being accessed through ADO.NET
Source	Name of the object producing the error
SqlState	A five-character error code representing the standard ANSI SQL error code for the particular error

Listing 5-60 used the SqlServer Exception class. You print the server name, message, and error code in a message box.

> **NOTE**   *The* `StringWriter` *class is defined in the* `System.IO` *namespace. You need to add* using `System.IO;` *to your project.*

Listing 5-60. Catching errors using the `SqlException` *class*

```
// Create a Connection Object
            string ConnectionString ="Integrated Security=SSPI;" +
                "Initial Catalog=Northwind1;" +
                "Data Source=localhost;";
            SqlConnection conn = new SqlConnection(ConnectionString);


            try
            {
                // Open the connection
                conn.Open();
            }
            catch(SqlException ae)
            {
                StringWriter sw = new StringWriter();
                sw.WriteLine("{0}: Threw an Error: ***{1}***"+
                    "with SqlServer Code {2}",
                    ae.Errors[0].Server,
                    ae.Errors[0].Message,ae.Errors[0].Number);
                MessageBox.Show(sw.GetStringBuilder().ToString());
            }
```

Table 5-36 shows a list of properties that can be accessed in the `SqlError` to give you information about your error. The `SqlError` is a bit more extensive in that it can tell you more about an error than the `OleDbError`.

Table 5-36. SqlError Properties

PROPERTY	DESCRIPTION
Message	Gives description of the error
LineNumber	Line number within the list of Sql commands or stored procedure causing the error
Source	Line of source code producing the error
State	The number modifying the error in order to provide some more information about the error
Number	Gets the number (integer) identifying the error
Procedure	Name of the stored procedure causing the error (string)

InfoMessageEventHandler: Listening to Warnings

Information or a warning message is sometimes produced after a query is executed on a database. If you need to "listen" for these messages, .NET provides a mechanism for doing this. The event for listening to information messages in the Northwind database is trapped in the `Connection` object for this database and can be delegated with the following line of code in the `InitializeComponent()` method of your .NET project:

```
this.NorthwindConnection.InfoMessage +=
new System.Data.OleDb.OleDbInfoMessageEventHandler
(this.NorthwindConnection_InfoMessage);
```

You also need to create the `NorthwindConnection_InfoMessage` method, to which the event is delegated:

```
private void NorthwindConnection_InfoMessage(object sender,
            System.Data.OleDb.OleDbInfoMessageEventArgs e)
    {
        MessageBox.Show(e.Errors[0].Message.ToString());
    }
```

The MessageBox in this code shows the first information message passed in from the InfoMessageEvent argument. This event argument contains an ErrorCollection much the same way an Exception object contains an ErrorCollection. The errors for this information message are warnings and information messages, as opposed to the more serious database errors such as bad queries.

Summary

In this chapter you saw the ADO.NET model class hierarchy. ADO.NET consists of three general and *n* data provider namespaces. General namespaces are System.Data, System.Data.Common, and System.Data.SqlTypes. The System.Data namespace defines classes that are the basic building blocks of the ADO.NET model. The System.Data.Common namespace defines classes shared by all data providers. The System.SqlTypes namespace defines classes that convert from SQL native data types to .NET data types.

You can divide ADO.NET classes into two categories: connected and disconnected. Disconnected classes can be used with or without data providers, but connected classes are designed to work with the data providers. Some of the disconnected classes are DataSet, DataTable, DataRow, DataColumn, DataView, and DataViewManager.

The connected classes are based on the data providers. There are many number of data providers. Some of them are Sql, OleDb, and ODBC. As their names represent, they're designed to work with a specific kind of data source. For example, the Sql data providers are designed to work with SQL Server databases, and OleDb data providers are designed to work with OLE DB data sources. Similarly, you can use ODBC data providers to work with any ODBC data source. Each of these data provider is best used with the proper data source. Although their names are different, all data providers work in the same way and define the same common model.

The generic data provider model consists of a common model followed by all data providers. A connection is created between the data provider and the data sources. You saw how to access different kinds of data sources using different kinds of data providers. After a connection is created, a data adapter or a command accesses and updates the data source. A data table represents an in-memory cache for a database table. A dataset is a collection of data tables. A data adapter sits between a dataset and a data source and passes data back and forth. The Fill method of a data adapter fills data from a data source to a dataset based on the SQL statement that it was created on. The Update method of a data adapter reflects dataset changes to the data source. A command can be used to execute SQL statements. You can execute direct SQL commands such as INSERT, UPDATE, and DELETE to add, update, and delete data.

A data reader is another important component used to read data from a data source through a data adapter. You can use ExecuteReader of the command to get data in a data reader. You can also execute stored procedures and views using a command. You also learned how to handle concurrency and locking issues using transactions in ADO.NET. Finally, you also learned how to use ADO.NET Error and Exception classes.

You have now learned the major concepts of the ADO.NET model and its components. I'll show more ADO.NET samples in Chapter 9 and Chapter 10.

XML plays a vital role in the entire ADO.NET model. Chapter 6 is based on XML. In this chapter you will start with basics of XML; later you'll see how ADO.NET and XML are coupled together to provide ADO.NET developers the best of both worlds.

Working with XML

THE PROGRAMMING WORLD IS moving more and more toward the Web, and Extensible Markup Language (XML) is an essential part of Web-based programming. This chapter begins with basic definitions of Hypertext Markup Language (HTML), XML, and other Web-related technologies. Then you'll take a look at the .NET Framework Library namespaces and classes that provide XML functionality in the .NET Framework.

I'll explain how to read, write, and navigate XML documents using XML and Document Object Model (DOM) .NET classes. I'll also discuss XML transformations. This chapter also covers the relationship between ADO.NET and XML and shows how to mix them up and use rich ADO.NET database components to display and manipulate XML data. At the end of this chapter I'll cover the XPathNavigator class, which you can use to navigate through XML documents.

Defining XML-Related Terminology

The ADO.NET and XML .NET Framework Application Programming Interface (API) combination provides a unified way to work with XML in the Microsoft .NET Framework. There are two ways to represent data by using XML: in a tagged-text format metalanguage similar to HTML and in a relational table format. You use ADO.NET to access relational table formats. You would use DOM to access the text format.

Before talking about the role of XML in the .NET Framework and how to work with it, it's important you understand the basic building blocks of XML and its related terminology. You'll learn the basic definitions of Standard Generalized Markup Language (SGML) and HTML in the following sections. If you're already familiar with these languages, you can skip to the "XML Overview" section.

Standard Generalized Markup Language (SGML)

In 1986, Standard Generalized Markup Language (SGML) became the international standard for representing electronic documents in a unified way. SGML provides a standard format for designing your own markup schemes. *Markup* is a way to represent some information about data.

Later, Hypertext Markup Language (HTML) became the international standard for representing documents on the Web in a unified way.

Hypertext Markup Language (HTML)

The HTML file format is a text format that contains, rather heavily, markup *tags*. A tag is a section of a program that starts with < and ends with >, such as <name>. (An *element* consists of a pair of tags, starting with <name> and ending with </name>.) The language defines all of the markup tags. All browsers support HTML tags, which tell a browser how to display the text of an HTML document. You can create an HTML file using a simple text editor such as Notepad. After typing text in a text editor, you save the file with an .htm or .html extension.

> **NOTE** *An HTML document is also called* HTML page *or* HTML file.

Listing 6-1 shows an example of an HTML file. Type the following in a text editor, and save it as myfile.htm.

Listing 6-1. A simple HTML file

```
<html>

<head>
<title>A Test HTML Page</title>
</head>

<body>
Here is the body part.
</body>

</html>
```

If you view this file in a browser, you'll see the text *Here is the body part.*

In Listing 6-1, your HTML file starts with the <html> tag and ends with the </html> tag. The <html> tag tells a browser that this is the starting point of an HTML document. The </html> tag tells a browser that this is the ending point of an HTML document. These tags are required in all HTML documents. The <head> tag is header information of a document and is not displayed in the browser. The <body> and </body> tags, which are required, make up the main content of a document. As you can see, all tags ends with a </> tag.

> **NOTE**   *HTML tags are not case sensitive. However, the World Wide Web Consortium (W3C) recommends using lowercase tags in HTML 4. The next generation of HTML, XHTML, doesn't support uppercase tags. (The W3C promotes the Web worldwide and makes it more useful. You can find more information on the W3C at* http://www.w3.org.)

Tags can have *attributes*, which provide additional information about the tags. Attributes are part of the starting tag. For example:

```
<table border="0">
```

In this example, the `<table>` tag has an attribute border and its value is 0. This value applies to the entire `<table>` tag, ending with the `</table>` tag. Table 6-1 describes some common HTML tags.

Table 6-1. Common HTML Tags

TAG	DESCRIPTION
`<html>`	Indicates start and end of an HTML document
`<title>`	Contains the title of the page
`<body>`	Contains the main content, or *body*, of the page
`<h1...h6>`	Creates headings (from level 1 to 6)
`<p>`	Starts a new paragraph
` `	Inserts a single line break
`<hr>`	Defines a horizontal rule
`<!-- >`	Defines a comment tag in a document
`<b>`	Defines bold text
`<i>`	Defines italic text
`<strong>`	Defines strong text
`<table>`	Defines a table
`<tr>`	Defines a row of a table
`<td>`	Defines a cell of a table row
`<font>`	Defines a font name and size

There are more tags beyond those described in Table 6-1. In fact, the W3C's HTML 4 specification is quite extensive. However, discussing all of the HTML tags is beyond the scope of this chapter. Before moving to the next topic, you'll take a look at one more HTML example using the tags discussed in the table. Listing 6-2 shows you another HTML document example.

Listing 6-2. HTML tags and their usage

```html
<html>

<head>
<title>A Test HTML Page</title>
</head>
<!-- This is a comment -->
<body>
<h1>Heading 1</h1>
<h2>Heading 2</h2>
<p><b><i><font size="4">Bold and Italic Text.</font></i></b></p>
<table border="1" width="43%">
  <tr>
    <td width="50%">Row1, Column1</td>
    <td width="50%">Row1, Column2</td>
  </tr>
  <tr>
    <td width="50%">Row2, Column1</td>
    <td width="50%">Row2, Column2</td>
  </tr>
</table>
</body>

</html>
```

NOTE *In Listing 6-2, the* `<font>` *and* `<td>` *tags contain size and width attributes, respectively. The* `size` *attribute tells the browser to display the size of the font, which is 4 in this example, and the* `width` *attribute tells the browser to display the table cell as 50 percent of the browser window.*

XML Overview

I'll now cover some XML-related terminology. So what exactly is XML? XML stands for Extensible Markup Language. It's a family member of SGML and an extended version of HTML. If you've ever gotten your hands dirty with HTML, then XML will be a piece of cake.

Essentially, XML extends the power and flexibility of HTML. You don't have to work with a limited number of tags as you do in HTML. You can define your own tags, and you can store your data in a structured format.

Unlike HTML, XML stores and exchanges data. By contrast, HTML represents the data. You can create separate XML files to store data, which can be used as a data source for HTML and other applications.

You'll now see an XML example. Listing 6-3 shows a simple XML file: books.xml. By default, this file comes with Visual Studio (VS) .NET. If you have VS .NET or the .NET Framework installed on your machine, you probably have this file in your samples folder.

You'll create this XML file called books.xml, which will store data about books in a bookstore. You'll create a tag for each of these properties, such as a <title> tag that will store the title of the book and so on.

You can write an XML file in any XML editor or text editor. Type the code shown in Listing 6-3 and save the file as books.xml.

This file stores information about a bookstore. The *root node* of the document is <bookstore>. Other tags follow the <bookstore> tag, and the document ends with the </bookstore> tag. Other tags defined inside the <bookstore> tag are <book>, <title>, <author>, and <price>. The tags store information on the store name, book publication date, book ISBN number, book title, author's name, and price.

Listing 6-3. Your first XML file sample

```
<?xml version='1.0'?>
<bookstore>
  <book>
    <title>The Autobiography of Benjamin Franklin</title>
    <author>
      <first-name>Benjamin</first-name>
      <last-name>Franklin</last-name>
    </author>
    <price>8.99</price>
  </book>
  <book>
    <title>The Confidence Man</title>
    <author>
      <first-name>Herman</first-name>
```

```
      <last-name>Melville</last-name>
    </author>
    <price>11.99</price>
  </book>
  <book>
    <title>The Gorgias</title>
    <author>
      <name>Plato</name>
    </author>
    <price>9.99</price>
  </book>
</bookstore>
```

The first line of an XML file looks like this: `<?xml version="1.0" ?>`. This line defines the XML version of the document. This tag tells the browser to start executing the file. You may have noticed that `<?>` doesn't have an ending `</?>` tag. Like HTML, other tags in an XML document start with `<` and are followed by a `/>` tag. For example, the `<title>` tag stores the book's title like this: `<title>The Gorgias</title>`.

In Listing 6-3, `<bookstore>` is the *root node*. Every XML document must start with a root node with the starting tag and end with the root node ending tag; otherwise the XML parser gives an error. (I'll discuss XML parsers shortly.)

Now, if you view this document in a browser, the output looks like Listing 6-4.

Listing 6-4. Output of books.xml *in the browser*

```
<?xml version="1.0" ?>
- <bookstore>
- <book>
  <title>The Autobiography of Benjamin Franklin</title>
- <author>
  <first-name>Benjamin</first-name>
  <last-name>Franklin</last-name>
  </author>
  <price>8.99</price>
  </book>
- <book>
  <title>The Confidence Man</title>
- <author>
  <first-name>Herman</first-name>
  <last-name>Melville</last-name>
  </author>
  <price>11.99</price>
  </book>
```

```
- <book>
<title>The Gorgias</title>
- <author>
<name>Plato</name>
</author>
<price>9.99</price>
</book>
</bookstore>
```

Your browser recognizes the XML and colors it appropriately.

Important Characteristics of XML

There are few things you need to know about XML. Unlike HTML, XML is case sensitive. In XML, `<Books>` and `<books>` are two different tags. All tags in XML must be *well-formed* and must have a closing tag. A language is well-formed only if it follows exact language syntaxes the way they are defined.

Improper nesting of tags in XML won't parse the document property. For example:

```
<b><i>Bold and Italic Text.</b></i>
```

is not well-formed. The well-formed version of the same code is this:

```
<b><i>Bold and Italic Text.</i></b>
```

Another difference between HTML and XML is that attributes must use double quotes in XML. *Attributes* function like HTML attributes and are extra information you can add to a tag. (I'll discuss attributes in the "An XML Document and Its Items" section later in this chapter.) Having attributes without double quotes is improper in XML. For example, Listing 6-5 is a correct example of using the attributes ISBN, genre, and publicationdate inside the `<book>` tag.

Listing 6-5. Attributes in XML files

```
<?xml version='1.0'?>
<!-- This file represents a fragment of a book store inventory database -->
<bookstore>
  <book genre="autobiography" publicationdate="1981" ISBN="1-861003-11-0">
    <title>The Autobiography of Benjamin Franklin</title>
    <author>
      <first-name>Benjamin</first-name>
      <last-name>Franklin</last-name>
```

```
      </author>
      <price>8.99</price>
    </book>
</bookstore>
```

The genre, publicationdate, and ISBN attributes store information about the category, publication date, and ISBN number of the book, respectively. Browsers won't have a problem parsing the code in Listing 6-5, but if you remove the double quotes from the attributes like this:

```
<book genre=autobiography publicationdate=1981 ISBN=1-861003-11-0>
```

then the browser will give the error message shown in Figure 6-1.

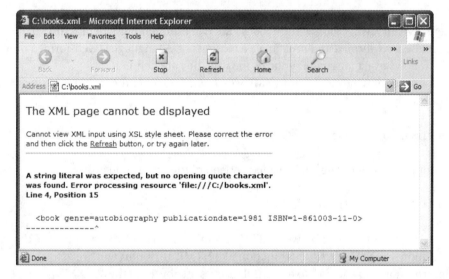

Figure 6-1. XML attribute definition error message

Another character you might notice in Listing 6-5 is the ! --, which represents a comment in XML document. (I'll cover comments in a moment. See the "Comments" section.)

Unlike HTML, XML preserves spaces, which means you'll see the white space in your document displayed in the browser.

XML Parser

An *XML parser* is a program that sits between XML documents and the application using the document. The job of a parser is to make sure the document meets the defined structures, validation, and constraints. You can define validation rules and constraints in a Document Type Definition (DTD) or schema.

An XML parser comes with Internet Explorer (IE) 4 or later and can read XML data, process it, generate a structured tree, and expose all data elements as DOM objects. The parser then makes the data available for further manipulation through scripting. After that, another application can handle this data.

MSXML parser comes with IE 5 or later and resides in the `MSXML.DLL` library. MSXML parser supports the W3C XML 1.0 and XML DOM recommendations, DTDs, schemas, and validations. You can use MSXML programmatically from languages such as JavaScript, VBScript, Visual Basic, Perl, and C++.

Universal Resource Identifier (URI)

A Universal Resource Identifier (URI) is a resource name available on the Internet. A URI contains three parts: the naming scheme (a protocol used to access the resource), the name of the machine (in the form of an Internet Protocol) upon which the resource reside, and the name of the resource (the filename). For example, `http://www.csharpcorner.com/Images/cshea1.gif` is a URI name where `http://` is a protocol, `www.csharpcorner.com` is the address of the machine (which is actually a conceptual name for the address), and `Images/afile.gif` is the filename location on that machine.

XML Namespaces

Because users define an XML document's element names, it's possible that many developers will use the same names. XML *namespaces* allow developers to write a unique name and avoid conflicts between element names with other developers. With the help of URI, a namespace ensures the uniqueness of XML elements, tags, and attributes.

To declare namespaces, you can use default or explicit names. When you define your own namespace, the W3C recommends you control the URI and point to the same location consistently.

The scope of a document's elements depends on the URI. Listing 6-6 shows an example of XML document with a namespace. In this example, `<book>` and its attributes and tags belong to the `http://www.c-sharpcorner.com/Images` URI.

Listing 6-6. XML namespace declaration example

```
<?xml version='1.0'?>
  <book xmlns="http://www.c-sharpcorner.com/Images" >
    <title>The Autobiography of Benjamin Franklin</title>
    <author>
      <first-name>Benjamin</first-name>
      <last-name>Franklin</last-name>
    </author>
    <price>8.99</price>
  </book>
```

Document Type Definition (DTD) and Schemas

A Document Type Definition (DTD) defines a document structure with a list of legal elements. You can declare DTDs inline or as a link to an external file. You can also use DTDs to validate XML documents. This an example of a DTD:

```
<!ELEMENT Two (#PCDATA)>
<!ELEMENT One (B)>
<!ATTLIST One c CDATA #REQUIRED>
```

This DTD defines a format of data. The following XML is valid because the tag <Two> is inside the tag <One>:

```
<One c="Attrib">
  <Two>Something here</Two>
</One>
```

An XML *schema* describes the relationship between a document's elements and attributes. XML schemas describe the rules, which can be applied to any XML document, for elements and attributes. If an XML document references a schema and it doesn't meet the criteria, XML parser will give an error during parsing.

You need a language to write schemas. These languages describe the syntaxes for each schema (XML document) you write. There are many schema languages, including DTD, XML Data Reduced (XDR), and Simple Object XML (SOX).

Similar to an XML document, an XML schema always starts with statement <?xml version="1.0" ?>, which specifies the XML version.

The next statement of a schema contains an xsd:schema statement, xmlns, and a target namespace. The xsd:schema indicates that the file is a schema.

A schema starts with a `<xsd:schema>` tag and ends with a `</xsd:schema>` tag. All schema items have the prefix xsd. The xmlns="http://www.w3.org/2001/XMLSchema" is a http://www.w3.org URI, which indicates the schema should be interpreted according to the default namespace of the W3C. The next piece of this line is the target namespace, which indicates the location of a machine (a URI). Listing 6-7 is a schema representation for the document in Listing 6-5.

Listing 6-7. XML schema example

```
<xsd:schema xmlns:xsd="http://www.w3.org/2001/XMLSchema">

 <xsd:element name="bookstore" type="bookstoreType"/>

 <xsd:complexType name="bookstoreType">
  <xsd:sequence maxOccurs="unbounded">
   <xsd:element name="book"  type="bookType"/>
  </xsd:sequence>
 </xsd:complexType>

 <xsd:complexType name="bookType">
  <xsd:sequence>
   <xsd:element name="title" type="xsd:string"/>
   <xsd:element name="author" type="authorName"/>
   <xsd:element name="price"  type="xsd:decimal"/>
  </xsd:sequence>
  <xsd:attribute name="genre" type="xsd:string"/>
 </xsd:complexType>

 <xsd:complexType name="authorName">
  <xsd:sequence>
   <xsd:element name="first-name"  type="xsd:string"/>
   <xsd:element name="last-name" type="xsd:string"/>
  </xsd:sequence>
 </xsd:complexType>

</xsd:schema>
```

In this listing, `<complexType>`, `<sequence>`, and `<element>` are schema elements. An *element* is a simple item with a single element. The complexType element is a set of attributes that denotes that the element has children. Some other schema items are `<all>`, `<annotation>`, `<any>`, `<anyAttribute>`, `<attribute>`, `<choice>`, `<documentation>`, `<field>`, `<group>`, `<include>`, `<key>`, `<length>`, `<maxLength>`, `<minLength>`, `<selection>`, `<pattern>`, `<simpleType>`, `<unique>`, and so on.

Elements and attributes are basic building blocks of a schema. An *element* is a tag with data. An element can have nested elements and attributes. Elements with one or more elements or attributes are complexType elements. An element contains a name and a data type. For example, the element price is of type decimal in the following line:

```
<xsd:element name="price" type="xsd:decimal" />
```

This definition of the element price makes sure that it can only store a decimal type of value. Other types of values are invalid values. For example, this is valid:

```
<price>19.95</price>
```

But this example is invalid:

```
<price>something</price>
```

Schema attributes are similar to XML attributes, but you can also define them using an xsd:attribute item. For example:

```
<xsd:complexType name="bookstoreType">
```

or

```
<xsd:attribute name=" bookstoreType" type="xsd:string" />
```

A full discussion of these items is beyond the scope of this chapter. However, I'll describe any items I use in any of the samples.

Extensible Hypertext Markup Language (XHTML)

Extensible Hypertext Markup Language (XHTML) is a next-generation language of HTML. In January 2000, XHTML 1.0 became a W3C recommendation. XHTML is a better and improved version of HTML; however, it does have some restrictions.

XHTML is a combination of XML and HTML. XHTML uses elements of HTML 4.01 and rules of XML to provide a more consistent, well-formed, and organized language.

An XML Document and Its Items

An *XML document* is a set of elements in a well-formed and valid standard format. A document is *valid* if it has a DTD associated with it and if it complies with the DTD. As mentioned earlier, a document is *well-formed* if it contains one or more elements and if it follows the exact syntaxes of the language. An XML parser will only parse a document that is a well-formed, but the document doesn't necessarily have to be valid. This means that a document must have at least one element (a root element) in it, but it doesn't matter whether it uses DTDs.

An XML document has the following parts, each described in the sections that follow:

- Prolog

- DOCTYPE declaration

- Start and end tags

- Comments

- Character and entity references

- Empty elements

- Processing instructions

- CDATA section

- Attributes

- White spaces

Prolog

The *prolog* part of a document appears before the root tag. The prolog information applies to the entire document. It can have character encoding, stylesheets, comments, and processing instructions. This is an example of a prolog:

```
<?xml version="1.0" ?>
<?xml-stylesheet type="text/xsl" href="books.xsl"?>
```

```
<!DOCTYPE StudentRecord SYSTEM "mydtd.dtd">
<!=my comments-->
```

DOCTYPE Declaration

With the help of a *DOCTYPE declaration*, you can read the structure of your root element and DTD from external files. A DOCTYPE declaration can contain a root element or a DTD (used for document validation). In a validating environment, a DOCTYPE declaration is a must. In a DOCTYPE reference, you can even use a URI reference. For example:

```
<!DOCTYPE rootElement>
```

or

```
<!DOCTYPE rootElement SYSTEM "URIreference">
```

or
```
<!DOCTYPE StudentRecord SYSTEM "mydtd.dtd">
```

Start and End Tags

Start and end tags are the heart of XML language. As mentioned earlier in the chapter, XML is nothing but a text file with start and end tags. Each tag starts with <TAG> and ends with </TAG>. If you want to add a tag called <book> to your XML file, it must start with <book> and end with </book>, as shown in this example:

```
<?xml version="1.0"  ?>
  <book xmlns="http://www.c-sharpcorner.com/XmlNet" >
    <title>The Autobiography of Benjamin Franklin</title>
    <author>
      <first-name>Benjamin</first-name>
      <last-name>Franklin</last-name>
    </author>
    <price>8.99</price>
  </book>
```

> **NOTE** Empty *elements don't have to heed this* < >. . .</ > *criteria. I'll discuss empty tags later in the "Empty Elements" section.*

> **NOTE** *An* element *is another name for a starting and ending tag pair.*

Comments

Using comments in your code is good programming practice. They help you understand your code, as well as help others to understand your code, by explaining certain code lines. You use the <!-- and --> pair to write comments in an XML document:

```
<!-- My comments here -->
<!-- This is a comment -->
```

XML parsers ignore comments.

CDATA Sections

What if you want to use < and > characters in your XML file but not as part of a tag? Well, you can't use them because the XML parser will interpret them as start and end tags. CDATA provides the following solution, so you can use XML markup characters in your documents and have the XML parser ignore them.

If you use the following line:

```
<![CDATA[I want to use < and >, characters]]>
```

the parser will treat those characters as data.

Another good example of CDATA is the following example:

```
<![CDATA[<Title>This is the title of a page</Title>
```

In this case, the parser will treat the second *title* as data, not as a markup tag.

Character and Entity Reference

In some cases, you can't use a character directly in a document because of some limitations, such as a character being treated as a markup character or a device or processor limitation.

By using character and entity references, you can include information in a document by reference rather than the character.

A *character reference* is a hexadecimal code for a character. You use the hash symbol (#) before the hexadecimal value. The XML parser takes care of the rest. For example, the character reference for the Return key is #x000d.

The reference starts with an ampersand (&) and a #, and it ends with a semi-colon (;).The syntax for decimal and hexadecimal references is &#value; and &#xvalue;, respectively. XML has some built-in entities. Use the lt, gt, and amp entities for less than, greater than, and ampersand, respectively. Table 6-2 shows five XML built-in entities and their references. For example, if you want to write *a>b* or *Jack & Jill*, you can do that by using these entities:

```
A&gt;b and Jack&amp;Jill
```

Table 6-2. XML Built-in Entities

ENTITY	REFERENCE	DESCRIPTION
lt	&lt	Less than: <
gt	&gt	Greater than: >
amp	&amp	Ampersand: &
apos	&apos	Single quote: '
quot	&quot	Double quote: "

Empty Elements

Empty elements start and end with the same tag. They start with < and end with >. The text between these two symbols is the text data. For example:

```
<Name></Name>
<IMG SRC="img.jpg" />
<tagname/>
```

are all empty element examples. The `<IMG>` specifies an inline image, and the `SRC` attribute specifies the image's location. The image can be any format, though browsers generally support only GIF, JPEG, and PNG images.

Processing Instructions

Processing instructions (PIs) play a vital role in XML parsing. A PI holds the parsing instructions, which are read by the parser and other programs. If you noticed the first line of any of the XML samples discussed earlier, a PI starts like this:

```
<?xml version="1.0" ?>.
```

All PIs start with `<?` and end with `?>`. This is another example of a PI:

```
<?xml-stylesheet type="text/xsl" href="myxsl.xsl"?>
```

This PI tells a parser to apply a stylesheet on the document.

Attributes

Attributes let you add extra information to an element without creating another element. An attribute is a name and value pair. Both the name and value must be present in an attribute. The attribute value must be in double quotes; otherwise the parser will give an error. Listing 6-8 is an example of an attribute in a `<table>` tag. In the example, the `<table>` tag has `border` and `width` attributes, and the `<td>` tag has a `width` attribute.

Listing 6-8. Attributes in the `<table>` *tag*

```
<table border="1" width="43%">
  <tr>
    <td width="50%">Row1, Column1</td>
    <td width="50%">Row1, Column2</td>
  </tr>
  <tr>
    <td width="50%">Row2, Column1</td>
    <td width="50%">Row2, Column2</td>
  </tr>
</table>
```

White Spaces

XML preserves white spaces except in attribute values. That means white space in your document will be displayed in the browser. However, white spaces are not allowed before the XML declaration. The XML parser reports all white spaces available in the document. If white spaces appear before declaration, the parser treats them as a PI.

In elements, XML 1.0 standard defines the `xml:space` attribute to insert spaces in a document. The `xml:space` attribute accepts only two values: `default` and `preserve`. The `default` value is the same as not specifying an `xml:space` attribute. It allows the parser to treat spaces as in a normal document. The `preserve` value tells the parser to preserve spaces in the document. The parser preserves spaces in attributes, but it converts line breaks into single spaces.

DOM Overview

Document Object Model (DOM) is a platform- and language-neutral interface that allows programs and scripts to dynamically access and update XML and HTML documents. The DOM API is a set of language-independent, implementation-neutral interfaces and objects based on the Object Management Group (OMG) Interface Definition Language (IDL) specification (not the COM version of IDL). See `http://www.w3.org/TR/DOM-Level-2/` for more details.

DOM defines the logical structure of a document's data. You can access the document in a structured format (generally through a tree format). Tree nodes and entities represent the document's data. DOM also helps developers build XML and HTML documents, as well as to add, modify, delete, and navigate the document's data. Figure 6-2 shows you various contents of DOM in a tree structure.

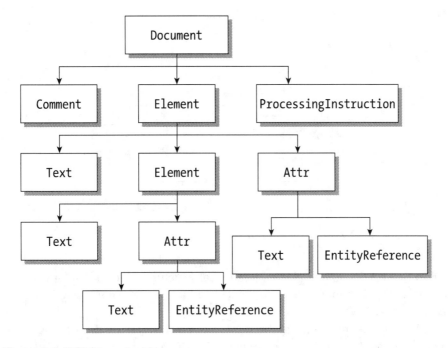

Figure 6-2. DOM tree structure

This is the tree structure implementation of an XML file:

```
<table>
  <tr>
    <td>Mahesh</td>
    <td>Testing</td>
  </tr>
  <tr>
    <td>Second Line</td>
    <td>Tested</td>
  </tr>
</table>
```

Figure 6-3 shows the DOM tree representation of this XML.

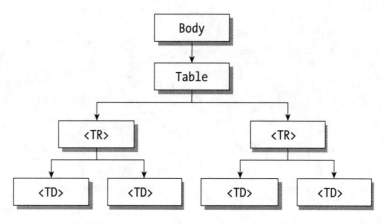

Figure 6-3. XML DOM tree representation

In DOM, a document takes a hierarchical structure, which is similar to a tree structure. The document has a root node, and the rest of the document has branches and leaves.

These nodes are defined as interfaces and objects. You use the interfaces to access and manipulate document objects. The DOM core API also allows you to create and populate documents, load documents, and save them.

Table 6-3 defines some XML document nodes and node contents.

Table 6-3. XML Nodes

NODE	DESCRIPTION	CHILDREN
Document	Represents an HTML or XML document and root of the document tree	Element, ProcessingInstruction, Document Type, Comment
DocumentType	Represents the document type attribute of a document	No children
Element	An element of the document	Element, Text, Comment, ProcessingInstruction, CDATASection, EntityReference
Attr	An attribute	Text, EntityReference
ProcessingInstruction	Represents a processing instruction; used in XML	No children

(continued)

Table 6-3. XML Nodes (continued)

NODE	DESCRIPTION	CHILDREN
Comment	Represents comments in an XML or HTML document; characters between the starting <!-- and ending -->	No children
Text	Text of a node	No children
Entity	An entity type item	Element, Text, Comment, ProcessingInstruction, CDATASection, EntityReference

Microsoft .NET and XML

Microsoft's .NET Framework utilizes XML features to internally and externally transfer data between applications. In this section, you'll see XML namespaces and classes, which I'll be using in the examples throughout this chapter. In the .NET Framework Library, the System.Xml and its four supportive namespaces define the functionality to work with XML data and documents. These namespaces are System.Xml, System.Xml.Schema, System.Xml.Serialization, System.Xml.XPath, and System.Xml.Xsl. These namespaces reside in the System.Xml.dll assembly.

Before moving to the next topic, I'll describe these namespaces and their classes. I'll also discuss some of these classes in more detail throughout this chapter.

The System.Xml Namespace

The System.Xml namespace defines common and major XML functionality. It defines classes for XML 1.0, XML namespaces and schemas, XPath, XSL Transformations (XSLT), DOM Level 2 Core, and SOAP 1.1.

The following sections define some of the Sytem.Xml namespace classes.

The XmlNode Class

The XmlNode class, an abstract base class for XmlDocument and XmlDataDocument, represents a single node in a document. This class implements methods for adding, removing, and inserting nodes into a document. This class also implements properties to get data from a node such as name, child nodes, siblings, parents, and so on.

Document Classes

The System.Xml namespace also contains classes to deal with XML documents. The XmlDocument and XmlDocumentFragment classes represent an entire XML document and a fragment of document, respectively. The XmlDocumentFragment class is useful when you deal a small fragment of a document.

The XmlDataDocument class allows you to work with relational data using the DataSet object. It provides functionality to store, retrieve, and manipulate data. The XmlDocumentType class represents the type of document.

The XmlDocument and XmlDataDocument classes come from XmlNode. Besides the methods contained in XmlNode, this class implements a series of Createxxx methods to create a document's contents such as Comment, Element, Text, and all the other contents discussed in the "DOM Overview" section of this chapter. You can even load an XML document by using its Load and LoadXml methods.

Each content type of an XML document has a corresponding class defined in this namespace. The classes are XmlAttribute, XmlCDataSection, XmlComment, XmlDeclaration, XmlEntity, XmlEntityReference, XmlProcessingInstruction, XmlText, and XmlWhitespace. All of these classes are self-explanatory. For example, the XmlAttribute and XmlComment classes represent an attribute and comment of a document. You'll see these classes in the examples.

Reader and Writer Classes

Six classes (XmlReader, XmlWriter, XmlTextWriter, XmlTextReader, XmlValidatingReader, and XmlNodeReader) represent the reading and writing XML documents.

XmlReader and XmlWriter are abstract base classes representing a reader that provides fast, non-cached, forward-only stream access to XML documents. XmlReader has three classes: XmlTextReader, XmlValidatingReader, and XmlNodeReader. As their names imply, XmlTextReader is for reading text XML documents, XmlNodeReader is for reading XML DOM trees, and XmlValidatingReader can validate data using DTDs or schemas. This reader also expands general entities and supports default attributes. XmlWriter is an abstract base class that defines functionality to write XML. It implements methods and properties to write XML contents. XmlTextWriter class comes from the XmlWriter class.

Other Classes

The XmlConvert class provides conversion in XML. It defines methods for converting Common Language Runtime (CLR), or .NET data types, and XML Schema Definition (XSD) types.

- XmlException defines functionality to represent detailed exceptions.

- XmlNamespaceManager resolves, adds, and removes namespaces to a collection and provides scope management for these namespaces.

- XmlLinkedNode returns the node immediately preceding or following this node.

- XmlNodeList represents a collection of nodes.

The System.Xml.Schema Namespace

The System.Xml.Schema namespace contains classes to work with XML schemas. These classes support XML schemas for structures and XML schemas for data types.

This namespace defines many classes to work with schemas. The discussion of these classes is beyond the scope of this book. Some of these namespace classes are XmlSchema, XmlSchemaAll, XmlSchemaXPath, and XmlSchemaType.

The System.Xml.Serialization Namespace

This namespace contains classes to serialize objects into XML format documents or streams. *Serialization* is the process of reading and writing an object to or from a persistent storage medium such as a hard drive.

You can use the main class, XmlSerializer, with TextWriter or XmlWriter to write the data to a document. Again, this namespace also defines many classes. The discussion of these classes is beyond the scope of this chapter.

The System.Xml.XPath Namespace

This namespace is pretty small in comparison to the previous three namespaces. This namespace contains only four classes: XPathDocument, XPathExression, XPathNavigator, and XPathNodeIterator.

The XPathDocument class provides fast XML document processing using XSLT. This class is optimized for XSLT processing and the XPath data model. The CreateNavigator method of this class creates an instance of XpathNavigator.

The XpathNavigator class reads data and treats a document as a tree and provides methods to traverse through a document as a tree. Its Movexxx methods let you traverse through a document.

Two other classes of this namespace are XPathExpression and XPathIterator. XPathExpression encapsulates an XPath expression, and XPathIterator provides an iterator over the set of selected nodes.

The System.Xml.Xsl Namespace

The last namespace, System.Xml.Xsl, defines functionality for XSL/T transformations. It supports XSLT 1.0. The XsltTransform class defines functionality to transform data using an XSLT stylesheet.

DOM Interfaces

As you've seen in the previous discussion, you can represent an XML document in a tree structure using DOM interfaces and objects (shown in Figure 6-3).

Microsoft .NET provides a nice wrapper around these interfaces: the DOM API. This wrapper has a class for almost every interface. These classes hide all the complexity of interface programming and provide a high-level programming model for developers. For example, the .NET class XmlDocument provides a wrapper for the Document interface.

Besides DOM, the Microsoft .NET XML API also provides corresponding classes for the XPath, XSD, and XSLT industry standards. These classes are well coupled with the .NET database models (ADO.NET) to interact with databases.

XML .NET Architecture

The XML .NET API is a nice wrapper around the XML DOM interfaces and provides a higher-level of programming over XML documents. The heart of the XML .NET architecture consists of three classes: XmlDocument, XmlReader, and XmlWriter. The XmlReader and XmlWriter classes are abstract base classes that provide fast, non-cached, forward-only cursors to read/write XML data. XmlTextReader, XmlValidatingReader, and XmlNodeReader are concrete implementations of the XmlReader class. The XmlWriter and XmlNodeWriter classes come from the XmlWriter class. XmlDocument represents an XML document in a tree structure with the help of the XmlNode, XmlElement, and XmlAttribute classes.

Figure 6-4 shows a relationship between these classes and the XML .NET architecture.

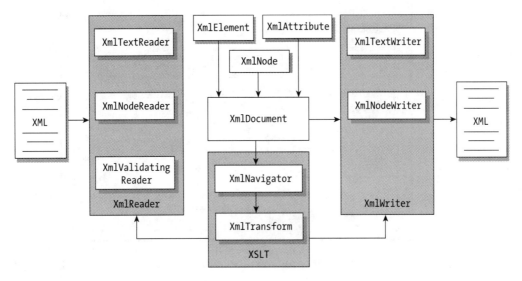

Figure 6-4. XML .NET architecture

The `System.Xml.Xsl` interface provides classes that implement XSLT. (I'll discuss XSLT in more detail later in this chapter.) The `XmlTransform` class implements XSLT. This class reads and writes XML data with the help of the `XmlReader` and `XmlWriter` classes.

The `XPathDocument` and the `XPathNavigator` classes provide read/write and navigation access to the XML documents.

Associated with these classes are some more powerful classes for working with XML. I'll discuss these classes in "Navigation in XML" and other sections of this chapter.

Adding System.Xml Namespace Reference

You're probably aware of this, but before using `System.Xml` classes in your application, you may need to add a reference to the `System.Xml.dll` assembly using Project ➤ Add Reference (see Figure 6-5) and include the `System.Xml` namespace:

```
using System.Xml;
```

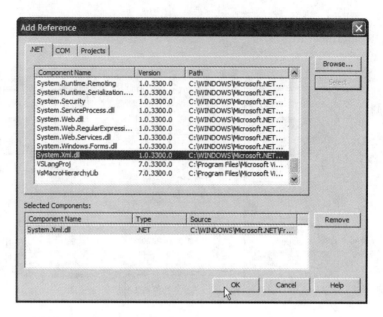

Figure 6-5. Adding a reference to the System.Xml.dll *assembly*

The abstract base classes XmlReader and XmlWriter support reading and writing XML documents in the .NET Framework.

Reading XML

The XmlReader is an abstract base class for XML reader classes. This class provides fast, non-cached, forward-only cursors to read XML documents.

The XmlTextReader, XmlNodeReader, and XmlValidatingReader classes are defined from the XmlReader class. Figure 6-6 shows XmlReader and its derived classes.

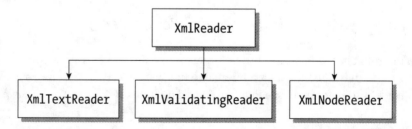

Figure 6-6. XmlReader *classes*

You use the XmlTextReader, XmlNodeReader, and XmlValidatingReader classes to read XML documents. These classes define overloaded constructors to read XML files, strings, streams, TextReader objects, XmlNameTable, and combinations of these. After creating an instance, you simply call the Read method of the class to read the document. The Read method starts reading the document from the root node and continues until Read returns false, which indicates there is no node left to read in the document. Listing 6-9 reads an XML file and displays some information about the file. In this example, I'll use the books.xml file. You can use any XML by replacing the string name.

Listing 6-9. Reading an XML file

```
XmlTextReader reader = new XmlTextReader(@"C:\books.xml");

        Console.WriteLine("General Information");
        Console.WriteLine("====================");
        Console.WriteLine(reader.Name);
        Console.WriteLine(reader.BaseURI);
        Console.WriteLine(reader.LocalName);
```

Getting Node Information

The Name property returns the name of the node with the namespace prefix, and the LocalName property returns the name of the node without the prefix.

The Item is the indexer. The Value property returns the value of a current node. You can even get the level of the node by using the Depth property, as shown in this example:

```
        XmlTextReader reader = new XmlTextReader(@"C:\books.xml");
        while (reader.Read())
        {
            if (reader.HasValue)
            {
                Console.WriteLine("Name: "+reader.Name);
                Console.WriteLine("Node Depth: " +reader.Depth.ToString());
                Console.WriteLine("Value: "+reader.Value);
            }
        }
```

The NodeType property returns the type of the current node in the form of XmlNodeType enumeration:

```
XmlNodeType type = reader.NodeType;
```

which defines the type of a node. The XmlNodeType enumeration members are Attribute, CDATA, Comment, Document, Element, WhiteSpace, and so on. These represent XML document node types.

In Listing 6-10, you read a document's nodes one by one and count them. Once reading and counting are done, you see how many comments, processing instructions, CDATAs, elements, white spaces, and so on that a document has and display them on the console. The XmlReader.NodeType property returns the type of node in the form of XmlNodeType enumeration. The XmlNodeType enumeration contains a member corresponding to each node types. You can compare the return value with XmlNodeType members to find out the type of a node.

Listing 6-10. Getting node information

```
static void Main(string[] args)
{
int DecCounter=0, PICounter=0, DocCounter=0, CommentCounter=0;
int ElementCounter=0, AttributeCounter=0, TextCounter=0, WhitespaceCounter=0;
XmlTextReader reader = new XmlTextReader(@"C:\books.xml");
    while (reader.Read())
    {

        XmlNodeType nodetype = reader.NodeType;
        switch (nodetype)
        {
            case XmlNodeType.XmlDeclaration:
                DecCounter++;
                break;
            case XmlNodeType.ProcessingInstruction:
                PICounter++;
                break;
            case XmlNodeType.DocumentType:
                DocCounter++;
                break;
```

```
            case XmlNodeType.Comment:
                CommentCounter++;
                break;
            case XmlNodeType.Element:
                ElementCounter++;
                if (reader.HasAttributes)
                    AttributeCounter += reader.AttributeCount;
                break;
            case XmlNodeType.Text:
                TextCounter++;
                break;
            case XmlNodeType.Whitespace:
                WhitespaceCounter++;
                break;
        }
    }
            // Print the info
Console.WriteLine("White Spaces:" +WhitespaceCounter.ToString());
Console.WriteLine("Process Instructions:" +PICounter.ToString());
Console.WriteLine("Declaration:" +DecCounter.ToString());
Console.WriteLine("White Spaces:" +DocCounter.ToString());
Console.WriteLine("Comments:" +CommentCounter.ToString());
Console.WriteLine("Attributes:" +AttributeCounter.ToString());

}
```

The case statement can have values XmlNodeType.XmlDeclaration, XmlNodeType.ProcessingInstruction, XmlNodeType.DocumentType, XmlNodeType.Comment, XmlNodeType.Element, XmlNodeType.Text, XmlNodeType.Whitespace, and so on.

The XmlNodeType enumeration specifies the type of node. Table 6-4 describes its members.

Table 6-4. The XmlNodeType *Enumeration's Members*

MEMBER NAME	DESCRIPTION
Attribute	Attribute node
CDATA	CDATA section
Comment	Comment node
Document	Document object
DocumentFragment	Document fragment
DocumentType	The DTD, indicated by the `<!DOCTYPE>` tag
Element	Element node
EndElement	End of element
EndEntity	End of an entity
Entity	Entity declaration
EntityReference	Reference to an entity
None	Returned if `XmlReader` is not called yet
Notation	Returned if `XmlReader` is not called yet
ProcessingInstruction	Represents a processing instruction (PI) node
SignificantWhitespace	Represents white space between markup in a mixed content model
Text	Represents the text content of an element
Whitespace	Represents white space between markup
XmlDeclaration	Represents an XML declaration node

Moving to a Content

You can use the `MoveToMethod` to move from the current node to the next content node of an XML document. A content's node is an item of the following type: text, CDATA, Element, EntityReference, or Entity. So, if you call the `MoveToContent` method, it skips other types of nodes besides the content type nodes. For example, if the next node of the current node is PI, DxlDeclaration, or DocumentType, it will skip these nodes until it finds a content type node. See the following example:

```
XmlTextReader reader = new XmlTextReader(@"C:\books.xml");

if (reader.Read())
{
      Console.WriteLine(reader.Name);
       reader.MoveToContent();
       Console.WriteLine(reader.Name);
}
```

The GetAttributes of a Node

The GetAttribute method is an overloaded method. You can use this method to return attributes with the specified name, index, local name, or namespace URI. You use the HasAttributes property to check if a node has attributes, and AttributeCount returns the number of attributes on the node. The local name is the name of the current node without prefixes. For example, if <bk:book> represents a name of a node, where bk is a namespace and : is used to refer to the namespace, the local name for the <bk:book> element is *book*. MoveToFirstAttribute moves to the first attribute. The MoveToElement method moves to the element that contains the current attribute node (see Listing 6-11).

Listing 6-11. GetAttribute *of a node*

```
using System;
using System.Xml;

class XmlReaderSamp
{
    static void Main(string[] args)
    {
        XmlTextReader reader = new XmlTextReader(@"C:\books.xml");

        reader.MoveToContent();
        reader.MoveToFirstAttribute();
        Console.WriteLine("First Attribute Value" +reader.Value);
        Console.WriteLine("First Attribute Name" +reader.Name);

        while (reader.Read())
        {
            if (reader.HasAttributes)
            {
                Console.WriteLine(reader.Name + " Attribute");
```

```
                        for (int i = 0; i < reader.AttributeCount; i++)
                        {
                            reader.MoveToAttribute(i);
                            Console.WriteLine("Nam: "+reader.Name +", Value: "
                                + reader.Value);
                        }
                        reader.MoveToElement();
                }
            }


        }
    }
```

You can move to attributes by using MoveToAttribute, MoveToFirstAttribute, and MoveToNextAttribute. MoveToFirstAttribute and MoveToNextAttribute move to the first and next attributes, respectively. After calling MoveToAttribute, the Name, Namespace, and Prefix properties will reflect the properties of the specified attribute.

Searching for a Node

The Skip method skips the current node. It's useful when you're looking for a particular node and want to skip other nodes. In Listing 6-12, you read your books.xml document and compare its XmlReader.name (through XmlTextReader) to look for a node with name bookstore and display the name, level, and value of that node using XmlReader's Name, Depth, and Value properties.

Listing 6-12. Skip *method*
```
XmlTextReader reader = new XmlTextReader(@"C:\books.xml");

while (reader.Read())
{
    // Look for a node with name bookstore
    if (reader.Name != "bookstore")
      reader.Skip();
    else
    {
        Console.WriteLine("Name: "+reader.Name);
        Console.WriteLine("Level of the node: " +reader.Depth.ToString());
        Console.WriteLine("Value: "+reader.Value);
    }
}
```

Closing the Document

Finally, use Close to close the opened XML document.

Tables 6-5 and 6-6 list the XmlReader class properties and methods. I've discussed some of them already.

Table 6-5. XmlReader *Properties*

PUBLIC INSTANCE PROPERTY	DESCRIPTION
AttributeCount	Returns the number of attributes on the current node
BaseURI	Returns the base URI of the current node
Depth	Returns the level of the current node
EOF	Indicates whether its pointer is at the end of the stream
HasAttributes	Indicates if a node has attributes or not
HasValue	Indicates if a node has a value or not
IsDefault	Indicates whether the current node is an attribute generated from the default value defined in the DTD or schema
IsEmptyTag	Returns if the current node is empty or not
Item	Returns the value of the attribute
LocalName	Name of the current node without the namespace prefix
Name	Name of the current node with the namespace prefix
NamespaceURI	Namespace Uniform Resource Name (URN) of the current namespace scope
NameTable	Returns the XmlNameTable associated with this implementation
NodeType	Returns the type of node
Prefix	Returns the namespace associated with a node
ReadState	Read state
Value	Returns the text value of a node
XmlLang	Returns the current xml:lang scope
XmlSpace	Returns the current xml:space scope

Table 6-6. XmlReader *Methods*

PUBLIC INSTANCE METHOD	DESCRIPTION
Close	Closes the stream and changes ReadState to Closed
GetAttribute	Returns the value of an attribute
IsStartElement	Checks if a node has start tag
LookupNamespace	Resolves a namespace prefix in the current element's scope
MoveToAttribute, MoveToContent, MoveToElement	Moves to specified attribute, content, and element
MoveToFirstAttribute, MoveToNextAttribute	Moves to the first and next attributes
Read	Reads a node
ReadAttributeValue	Parses the attribute value into one or more Text and/or EntityReference node types
ReadXXXX (ReadChar, ReadBoolean, ReadDate, ReadIn32, and so on)	Reads the contents of an element into the specified type including char, integer, double, string, date, and so on
ReadInnerXml	Reads all the content as a string
Skip	Skips the current element

The XmlWriter Classes

As you've seen in the "Microsoft .NET and XML" section of this chapter, the XmlWriter class contains methods and properties to write to XML documents, and XmlTextWriter and XmlNodeWriter come from the XmlWriter class (see Figure 6-7).

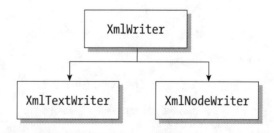

Figure 6-7. XmlWriter *classes*

Besides providing a constructor and three properties (WriteState, XmlLang, and XmlSpace), the XmlWriter classes have many Writexxx methods to write to XML documents. This section discusses some of these class methods and properties and uses them in examples of the XmlTextWriter and XmlNodeWriter classes. XmlTextWriter creates a write object and writes to the documents. The XmlTextWriter constructor can take three types of inputs: a string, a stream, or a TextWriter.

XmlWriter Properties

The XmlWriter class contains three properties: WriteState, XmlLang, and XmlSpace. The WriteState property gets the current state of the XmlWriter class. The values could be Attribute, Start, Element, Content, Closed, or Prolog. The return value WriteState.Start means the Write method is not yet called. In other cases, it represents what is being written. For example, the return value WriteState.Attibute means the Attribute value has written. WriteState.Close represents that the stream has closed by calling Close method.

Writing XML Items

As discussed earlier, an XML document can have many types of items including elements, comments, attributes, and white spaces. Although it's not possible to describe *all* the Writexxx methods here, I'll cover some of them.

The WriteStartDocument and WriteEndDocument methods open and close a document for writing, respectively. You must open a document before you start writing to it. The WriteComment method writes comment to a document. It takes only one string type of argument. The WriteString method writes a string to a document. With the help of WriteString, you can use the WriteStartElement and WriteEndElement method pair to write an element to a document. The WriteStartAttribute and WriteEndAttribute pair writes an attribute. WriteNode is another write method, which writes XmlReader to a document as a node of the document.

The following example summarizes all these methods and creates a new XML document with some items in it such as elements, attributes, strings, comments, and so on. (See Listing 6-13 in the next section.)

In this example, you create a new XML file, c:\xmlWriterText.xml, using XmlTextWriter:

```
// Create a new file c:\xmlWriterTest.xml
XmlTextWriter writer = new XmlTextWriter("C:\\xmlWriterTest.xml", null);
```

After that, add comments and elements to the document using `Writexxx` methods. After that you can read the `books.xml` xml file using `XmlTextReader` and add its elements to `xmlWriterTest.xml` using `XmlTextWriter`:

```
// Create an XmlTextReader to read books.xml
XmlTextReader reader = new XmlTextReader(@"c:\books.xml");
while ( reader.Read() )
{
        if(reader.NodeType == XmlNodeType.Element)
        {
            // Add node.xml to xmlWriterTest.xml using WriteNode
            writer.WriteNode(reader, true);
        }
}
```

XmlWriter Example

Listing 6-13 shows an example of using `XmlWriter` to create a new document and write its items. This program creates a new XML document, `xmlWriterTest`, in the `C:\` root directory.

Listing 6-13. `XmlWriter` *example*
```
static void Main(string[] args)
{

// Create a new file c:\xmlWriterTest.xml
XmlTextWriter writer = new XmlTextWriter("C:\\xmlWriterTest.xml", null);

// Opens the document
writer.WriteStartDocument();

// Write comments
writer.WriteComment("This program uses XmlTextWriter.");
writer.WriteComment("Developed By: Mahesh Chand.");
writer.WriteComment("==================================");

// Write first element
writer.WriteStartElement("root");
writer.WriteStartElement("r", "RECORD", "urn:record");
```

```
// Write next element
writer.WriteStartElement("FirstName","");
writer.WriteString("Mahesh");
writer.WriteEndElement();

// Write one more element
writer.WriteStartElement("LastName","");
writer.WriteString("Chand");
writer.WriteEndElement();


// Create an XmlTextReader to read books.xml
XmlTextReader reader = new XmlTextReader(@"c:\books.xml");
while ( reader.Read() )
{
        if(reader.NodeType == XmlNodeType.Element)
        {
              // Add node.xml to xmlWriterTest.xml using WriteNode
              writer.WriteNode(reader, true);
         }
  }


// Ends the document.
writer.WriteEndDocument();
writer.Close();
return;
}
```

> **NOTE** *In Listing 6-13, you write output of the program to a file. If you want to write your output directly on the console, pass* Console.Out *as the filename when you create an* XmlTextWriter *object. For example:*
> XmlTextWriter writer = new XmlTextWriter (Console.Out);.

When you open C: \xmlWriterTest.xml in a browser, the output of the program looks like Listing 6-14.

Listing 6-14. Output of XmlWriterSample.cs *class*

```
<?xml version="1.0" ?>
          - <!-- This program uses XmlTextWriter.
                                   -->
     - <!-- Developed By: Mahesh Chand.
```

```
                                  -->
 - <!-- ==================================
 -->
 - <root>
 - <r:RECORD xmlns:r="urn:record">
 <FirstName>Mahesh</FirstName>
 <LastName>Chand</LastName>
 - <bookstore>
 - <book genre="autobiography" publicationdate="1981" ISBN="1-861003-11-0">
 <title>The Autobiography of Benjamin Franklin</title>
 - <author>
 <first-name>Benjamin</first-name>
 <last-name>Franklin</last-name>
 </author>
 <price>8.99</price>
 </book>
 - <book genre="novel" publicationdate="1967" ISBN="0-201-63361-2">
 <title>The Confidence Man</title>
 - <author>
 <first-name>Herman</first-name>
 <last-name>Melville</last-name>
 </author>
 <price>11.99</price>
 </book>
 - <book genre="philosophy" publicationdate="1991" ISBN="1-861001-56-6">
 <title>The Gorgias</title>
 - <author>
 <name>Plato</name>
 </author>
 <price>9.99</price>
 </book>
 </bookstore>
 </r:RECORD>
 </root>
```

The Close Method

You use the Close method when you're done with the XmlWriter object, which closes the stream.

The XmlConvert Class

There are some characters that are not valid in XML documents. XML documents use XSD types, which are different than CLR (.NET) data types. The XmlConvert class contains methods to convert from CLR types to XSD types and vice versa. The DecodeName method transfers an XML name into an ADO.NET object such as DataTable. The EncodeName method is the reverse of DecodeName: It converts an ADO.NET object to a valid XSD name. It takes any invalid character and replaces it with an escape string. Another method, EncodeLocalName, converts unpermitted names to valid names.

Besides these three methods, the XmlConvert class has many methods to convert from a string object to Boolean, byte, integer, and so on. Listing 6-15 shows the conversion from a Boolean and DateTime object to XML values.

Listing 6-15. XmlConvert *example*

```
XmlTextWriter writer = new XmlTextWriter (@"c:\test.xml", null);

        writer.WriteStartElement("MyTestElements");
        bool bl = true;
        writer.WriteElementString("TestBoolean", XmlConvert.ToString(bl));

        DateTime dt = new DateTime(2000, 01, 01 );
        writer.WriteElementString("TestDate", XmlConvert.ToString(dt));

        writer.WriteEndElement();

        writer.Flush();
        writer.Close();
```

Understanding the DOM Implementation

Microsoft .NET supports the W3C DOM Level 1 and Core DOM Level 2 specifications. The .NET Framework provides DOM implementation through many classes; XmlNode and XmlDocument are two of them. By using these two classes, you can easily traverse though XML documents in the same manner you do in a tree.

The XmlNode Class

The XmlNode class is an abstract base class. It represents a tree node in a document. This tree node can be the entire document. This class defines enough methods and properties to represent a document node as a tree node and traverse though it. It also provides methods to insert, replace, and remove document nodes.

The ChildNodes property returns all the children nodes of current node. You can treat an entire document as a node and use ChildNodes to get all nodes in a document. You can use the FirstChild, LastChild, and HasChildNodes triplet to traverse from a document's first node to the last node. The ParentNode, PreviousSibling, and NextSibling properties return the parent and next sibling node of the current node. Other common properties are Attributes, BaseURI, InnerXml, InnerText, Item, NodeType, Name, Value, and so on.

You can use the CreateNavigator method of this class to create an XPathNavigator object, which provides fast navigation using XPath. The AppendChild, InsertAfter, and InsertBefore methods add nodes to the document. The RemoveAll, RemoveChild, and ReplaceChild methods remove or replace document nodes, respectively. You'll implement these methods and properties in the example after discussing a few more classes.

The XmlDocument Class

The XmlDocument class represents an XML document. Because it's derived from the XmlNode class, it supports all tree traversal, insert, remove, and replace functionality. In spite of XmlNode functionality, this class contains many useful methods.

Loading a Document

DOM is a cache tree representation of an XML document. The Load and LoadXml methods of this class load XML data and documents, and the Save method saves a document.

The Load method can load a document from a string, stream, TextReader, or XmlReader. This code example loads the document books.xml from a string:

```
XmlDocument xmlDoc = new XmlDocument();
string filename = @"C:\books.xml";
xmlDoc.Load(filename);
xmlDoc.Save(Console.Out);
```

This example uses the Load method to load a document from an XmlReader:

```
XmlDocument xmlDoc = new XmlDocument();
 XmlTextReader reader = new XmlTextReader("C:\\books.xml");
 xmlDoc.Load(reader);
xmlDoc.Save(Console.Out);
```

The LoadXml method loads a document from the specified string. For example:

```
xmlDoc.LoadXml("<Record> write something</Record>");
```

Saving a Document

The Save method saves a document to a specified location. The Save method takes a parameter of XmlWriter, XmlTextWriter, or a string type:

```
string filename = @"C:\books.xml";
 XmlDocument xmlDoc = new XmlDocument();
 xmlDoc.Load(filename);

        XmlTextWriter writer = new XmlTextWriter("C:\\domtest.xml", null);
        writer.Formatting = Formatting.Indented;
        xmlDoc.Save(writer);
```

You can also use a filename or Console.Out to save output as a file or on the console:

```
xmlDoc.Save("C:\\domtest.xml");
        xmlDoc.Save(Console.Out);
```

The XmlDocumentFragment Class

Usually, you would use this class when you need to insert a small fragment of an XML document or node into a document. This class also comes from XmlNode. Because this class is derived from XmlNode, it has the same tree node traverse, insert, remove, and replace capabilities.

You usually create this class instance by calling XmlDocument's CreateDocumentFragment method. The InnerXml property represents the children of this node. Listing 6-16 shows an example of how to create XmlDocumentFragment and load a small piece of XML data by setting its InnerXml property.

Listing 6-16. XmlDocumentFragment *sample*

```
// Open an XML file
 string filename = @"C:\books.xml";
 XmlDocument xmlDoc = new XmlDocument();
 xmlDoc.Load(filename);
 //Create a document fragment.
 XmlDocumentFragment docFrag = xmlDoc.CreateDocumentFragment();
 //Set the contents of the document fragment.
 docFrag.InnerXml ="<Record> write something</Record>";
 //Display the document fragment.
 Console.WriteLine(docFrag.InnerXml);
```

You can use XmlNode methods to add, remove, and replace data. Listing 6-17 appends a node in the document fragment.

Listing 6-17. Appending in an XML document fragment

```
XmlDocument doc = new XmlDocument();
        doc.LoadXml("<book genre='programming'>" +
            "<title>ADO.NET Programming</title>" +
            "</book>");

        // Get the root node
        XmlNode root = doc.DocumentElement;

        //Create a new node.
        XmlElement newbook = doc.CreateElement("price");
        newbook.InnerText="44.95";

        //Add the node to the document.
        root.AppendChild(newbook);

        doc.Save(Console.Out);
```

The XmlElement Class

An XmlElement class object represents an element in a document. This class comes from the XmlLinkedNode class, which comes from XmlNode (see Figure 6-8).

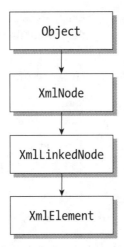

Figure 6-8. XmlElement *inheritance*

The XmlLinkedNode has two useful properties: NextSibling and PreviousSibling. As their names indicate, these properties return the next and previous nodes of an XML document's current node.

The XmlElement class implements and overrides some useful methods for adding and removing attributes and elements (see Table 6-7).

Table 6-7. Some XmlElement *Methods*

METHOD	DESCRIPTION
GetAttribute	Returns the attribute value
HasAttribute	Checks if a node has the specified attribute
RemoveAll	Removes all the children and attributes of the current node
RemoveAllAttributes, RemoveAttribute	Removes all attributes and specified attributes from an element respectively
RemoveAttributeAt	Removes the attribute node with the specified index from the attribute collection
RemoveAttributeNode	Removes an XmlAttribute
SetAttribute	Sets the value of the specified attribute
SetAttributeNode	Adds a new XmlAttribute

In the later examples, I'll show you how you can use these methods in your programs to get and set XML element attributes.

Adding Nodes to a Document

You can use the AppendChild method to add a node to an existing document. The AppendChild method takes a single parameter of XmlNode type. The XmlDocument's Createxxx methods can create different types of nodes. For example, the CreateComment and CreateElement methods create comment and element node types. Listing 6-18 shows an example of adding two nodes to a document.

Listing 6-18. Adding nodes to a document

```
XmlDocument xmlDoc = new XmlDocument();
        xmlDoc.LoadXml("<Record> Some Value </Record>");

        // Adding a new comment node to the document
        XmlNode node1 = xmlDoc.CreateComment("DOM Testing Sample");
        xmlDoc.AppendChild( node1);

        // Adding a FirstName to the document
        node1 = xmlDoc.CreateElement("FirstName");
```

```
node1.InnerText = "Mahesh";
xmlDoc.DocumentElement.AppendChild(node1);


xmlDoc.Save(Console.Out);
```

Getting the Root Node

The DocumentElement method of the XmlDocument class (inherited from XmlNode) returns the root node of a document. The following example shows you how to get the root node of a document (see Listing 6-19).

Listing 6-19. Getting the root node of a document
```
string filename = @"C:\books.xml";
 XmlDocument xmlDoc = new XmlDocument();
 xmlDoc.Load(filename);
        XmlElement root = xmlDoc.DocumentElement;
```

Removing and Replacing Nodes

The RemoveAll method of the XmlNode class can remove all elements and attributes of a node. The RemoveChild removes the specified child only. The following example calls RemoveAll to remove all elements and attributes. Listing 6-20 calls RemoveAll to remove all items of a node.

Listing 6-20. Removing all items of a node
```
public static void Main()
    {
        // Load a document fragment
        XmlDocument xmlDoc = new XmlDocument();
xmlDoc.LoadXml("<book genre='programming'>"+
"<title>ADO.NET Programming</title> </book>");
        XmlNode root = xmlDoc.DocumentElement;
        Console.WriteLine("XML Document Fragment");
        Console.WriteLine("=====================");

        xmlDoc.Save(Console.Out);
        Console.WriteLine();
        Console.WriteLine("-----------");
```

```
        Console.WriteLine("XML Document Fragment After RemoveAll");
        Console.WriteLine("=====================");
        //Remove all attribute and child nodes.
        root.RemoveAll();

        // Display the contents on the console after
        // removing elements and attributes
        xmlDoc.Save(Console.Out);
}
```

> **NOTE**   *You can apply the* RemoveAll *method on the* books.xml *files to delete all the data, but make sure to have a backup copy first!*

Listing 6-21 shows how to delete all the items of books.xml.

Listing 6-21. Calling RemoveAll *for* books.xml
```
public static void Main()
{
string filename = "C:\\books.xml";
        XmlDocument xmlDoc = new XmlDocument();
        xmlDoc.Load(filename);

        XmlNode root = xmlDoc.DocumentElement;
        Console.WriteLine("XML Document Fragment");
        Console.WriteLine("=====================");

        xmlDoc.Save(Console.Out);
        Console.WriteLine();
        Console.WriteLine("-----------");


        Console.WriteLine("XML Document Fragment After RemoveAll");
        Console.WriteLine("=====================");
        //Remove all attribute and child nodes.
        root.RemoveAll();

        // Display the contents on the console after
        // removing elements and attributes
        xmlDoc.Save(Console.Out);
}
```

The `ReplaceChild` method replaces an old child with a new child node. In Listing 6-22, `ReplaceChild` replaces `rootNode;LastChild` with `xmlDocFrag`.

Listing 6-22. `ReplaceChild` *method sample*

```
string filename = @"C:\books.xml";
 XmlDocument xmlDoc = new XmlDocument();
 xmlDoc.Load(filename);

        XmlElement root = xmlDoc.DocumentElement;

        XmlDocumentFragment xmlDocFragment = xmlDoc.CreateDocumentFragment();
xmlDocFragment.InnerXml=
"<Fragment><SomeData>Fragment Data</SomeData></Fragment>";
        XmlElement rootNode = xmlDoc.DocumentElement;

        //Replace xmlDocFragment with rootNode.LastChild
        rootNode.ReplaceChild(xmlDocFragment, rootNode.LastChild);

        xmlDoc.Save(Console.Out);
```

Inserting XML Fragments into an XML Document

As discussed previously, the `XmlNode` class is useful for navigating through the nodes of a document. It also provides other methods to insert XML fragments into a document. For instance, the `InsertAfter` method inserts a document or element after the current node. This method takes two arguments. The first argument is an `XmlDocumentFragment` object, and the second argument is the position of where you want to insert the fragment. As discussed earlier in this chapter, you create an `XmlDocumentFragment` class object by using the `CreateDocumentFragment` method of the `XmlDocument` class. Listing 6-23 inserts an XML fragment into a document after the current node using `InsertAfter`.

Listing 6-23. Inserting an XML fragment into a document

```
XmlDocument xmlDoc = new XmlDocument();
        xmlDoc.Load(@"c:\\books.xml");

        XmlDocumentFragment xmlDocFragment = xmlDoc.CreateDocumentFragment();
xmlDocFragment.InnerXml=
"<Fragment><SomeData>Fragment Data</SomeData></Fragment>";
        XmlNode aNode = xmlDoc.DocumentElement.FirstChild;
```

```
            aNode.InsertAfter(xmlDocFragment, aNode.LastChild);


            xmlDoc.Save(Console.Out);
```

Adding Attributes to a Node

You use the SetAttributeNode method of XmlElement to add attributes to an element, which is a node. The XmlAttribute represents an XML attribute. You create an instance of XmlAttribute by calling CreateAttribute of XmlDocument. After that you call an XmlElement's SetAttribute method to set the attribute of an element. Finally, you append this new item to the document (see Listing 6-24).

Listing 6-24. Adding a node with attributes
```
XmlDocument xmlDoc = new XmlDocument();
        xmlDoc.Load(@"c:\\books.xml");


        XmlElement newElem = xmlDoc.CreateElement("NewElement");
        XmlAttribute newAttr = xmlDoc.CreateAttribute("NewAttribute");
        newElem.SetAttributeNode(newAttr);
        //add the new element to the document


        XmlElement root = xmlDoc.DocumentElement;
        root.AppendChild(newElem);


        xmlDoc.Save(Console.Out);
```

Transformation and XSLT

Extensible Stylesheet Language (XSL) is a language for expressing *stylesheets.* Stylesheets format XML documents in a way so that the XML data can be presented in a certain structure in a browser or other media such as catalogs, books, and so on.

The XML stylesheet processor reads an XML document (called an *XML source tree)* and stylesheet, and it presents the document data in an XML tree format. This processing is XSL Transformation (XSLT). See Figure 6-9.

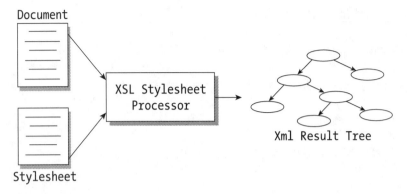

Figure 6-9. XSL transformation

The result tree generated after XML transformation contains element and attribute nodes. The result tree is also called an *element-attribute* or *tree*. In this tree, an object is an XML element, and properties are attribute-value pairs.

The XSL stylesheet plays a vital role in the XSLT process. A stylesheet contains a set of tree construction rules, which have two parts. The first part is a pattern of elements in the source tree, and the second is a template for the result tree. The XSL parser reads the pattern and elements from the source tree and then generates results according to the result tree template.

XSLT in .NET

In the .NET Framework, the XslTransform class implements the XSLT specification. This class is defined in a separate namespace called System.Xml.Xsl. Make sure you add a reference to this namespace before using the XslTransform class. You can use the XsltException class to handle exceptions thrown by an XSLT transformation.

The Transform Method

The Transform method of XslTransform transforms data using the loaded stylesheet and outputs the result depending on the argument. This method has eight overloaded forms. You can write output of Transform in the form of XmlWriter, stream, TextWriter, or XPathNavigator. (I'll discuss XPathNavigator later in this chapter.)

Transforming a Document

Follow these steps to perform the transformation:

1. First, you need to create an XslTransform object:

   ```
   XslTransform xslt  = new XslTransform();
   ```

2. Now, you load the stylesheet using the Load method:

   ```
   xslt.Load("stylesheetFrmt.xsl");
   ```

3. Finally, call the Transform method of XslTransform:

   ```
   xslt.Transform("xmlfile.xml", "file.html");
   ```

Example

Before you use XslTransform in your application, you need to add couple of namespace references to your application. These namespaces are System.Xml, System.Xml.XPath, and System.Xml.Xsl. (I'll discuss the XPath namespace in more detail in the "Navigation in XML" section of this chapter.) This example uses the books.xsl schema file that comes with the .NET SDK samples (see Listing 6-25).

Listing 6-25. XSL Transformation sample code

```
//Create a new XslTransform object and load the stylesheet
XslTransform xslt = new XslTransform();
xslt.Load(@"c:\books.xsl");

//Create a new XPathDocument and load the XML data to be transformed.
XPathDocument mydata = new XPathDocument(@"c:\books.xml");

//Create an XmlTextWriter which outputs to the console.
XmlWriter writer = new XmlTextWriter(Console.Out);

//Transform the data and send the output to the console.
xslt.Transform(mydata, null, writer);
```

ADO.NET and XML

So far in this chapter, you've seen how to work with XML documents. In this section, you'll now learn how to work with XML documents with the help of ADO.NET. There are two approaches to work with XML and ADO. First, you can use ADO.NET to access XML documents. Second, you can use XML and ADO.NET to access XML. Additionally, you can access a relational database using ADO.NET and XML .NET.

Reading XML Using DataSet

In ADO.NET, you can access the data using the DataSet class. The DataSet class implements methods and properties to work with XML documents. See Chapter 3 and Chapter 5 for more information on the DataSet object and how to work with it. The following sections discuss methods that read XML data.

The ReadXml Method

ReadXml is an overloaded method; you can use it to read a data stream, TextReader, XmlReader, or an XML file and to store into a DataSet object, which can later be used to display the data in a tabular format. The ReadXml method has eight overloaded forms. It can read a text, string, stream, TextReader, XmlReader, and their combination formats. See Chapter 4 and Chapter 5 for more details on the DataSet object.

In the following example, create a new DataSet object and call the DataSet.ReadXml method to load the books.xml file in a DataSet object:

```
// Create a DataSet Object
DataSet ds = new DataSet();
// Fill with the data
ds.ReadXml("books.xml ");
```

Once you've a DataSet object, you know how powerful it is. Make sure you provide the correct path of books.xml.

> **NOTE** *Make sure you add a reference to* System.Data *and the* System.Data.Common *namespace before using* DataSet *and other common data components.*

The ReadXmlSchema Method

The ReadXmlSchema method reads an XML schema in a DataSet object. It has four overloaded forms. You can use a TextReader, string, stream, and XmlReader. The following example shows how to use a file as direct input and call the ReadXmlSchema method to read the file:

```
DataSet ds = new DataSet();
ds.ReadXmlSchema(@"c:\books.xml");
```

The following example reads the file XmlTextReader and uses XmlTextReader as the input of ReadXmlSchema:

```
// Create a dataset object
        DataSet ds = new DataSet("New DataSet");

        // Read xsl in an XmlTextReader
        XmlTextReader myXmlReader = new XmlTextReader(@"c:\books.xml");

        // Call ReadXmlSchema
        ds.ReadXmlSchema(myXmlReader);

        myXmlReader.Close();
```

Writing XML Using DataSet

Not only for reading, the DataSet class contains methods to write XML files from a DataSet object and fill the data to the file.

The WriteXml Method

The WriteXml method writes the current data (the schema and data) of a DataSet object to an XML file. This is an overloaded method. By using this method, you can write data to a file, stream, TextWriter, or XmlWriter. This example creates a DataSet, fills the data for the DataSet, and writes the data to an XML file. Listing 6-26 shows an example of WriteXml method.

Listing 6-26. WriteXml *method*

```
using System;
using System.IO;
using System.Xml;
using System.Data;

namespace XmlAndDataSetSampB2
{
 class XmlAndDataSetSampCls
 {
  public static void Main()
  {
   try
   {
     // Create a DataSet, namespace and Student table
     //with Name and Address columns
     DataSet ds = new DataSet("DS");
     ds.Namespace = "StdNamespace";
     DataTable stdTable = new DataTable("Student");
     DataColumn col1 = new DataColumn("Name");
     DataColumn col2 = new DataColumn("Address");
     stdTable.Columns.Add(col1);
     stdTable.Columns.Add(col2);
     ds.Tables.Add(stdTable);
     // Add Student Data to the table
     DataRow newRow;newRow = stdTable.NewRow();
     newRow["Name"]= "Mahesh Chand";
     newRow["Address"]= "Meadowlake Dr, Dtown";
     stdTable.Rows.Add(newRow);
     newRow = stdTable.NewRow();
     newRow["Name"]= "Mike Gold";
     newRow["Address"]= "NewYork";
     stdTable.Rows.Add(newRow);
     ds.AcceptChanges();
     // Create a new StreamWriter
     // I'll save data in stdData.xml file
     System.IO.StreamWriter myStreamWriter = new
     System.IO.StreamWriter(@"c:\stdData.xml");
     // Writer data to DataSet which actually creates the file
     ds.WriteXml(myStreamWriter);
```

```
    myStreamWriter.Close();
  }
  catch (Exception e)
  {
    Console.WriteLine ("Exception: {0}", e.ToString());
  }
  return;
  }
}
}
```

You wouldn't believe what the WriteXml method does for you. If you see the output stdData.xml file, it generates a standard XML file that looks like Listing 6-27.

Listing 6-27. WriteXml *method output*

```
- <DS xmlns="StdNamespace">
- <Student>
<Name>Mahesh Chand</Name>
<Address>Meadowlake Dr, Dtown</Address>
</Student>
- <Student>
<Name>Mike Gold</Name>
<Address>NewYork</Address>
</Student>
</DS>
```

The WriteXmlSchema Method

This method writes DataSet structure to an XML schema. WriteXmlSchema has four overloaded methods. You can write the data to a stream, text, TextWriter, or XmlWriter. Listing 6-28 uses XmlWriter for the output.

Listing 6-28. WriteXmlSchema *sample*

```
DataSet ds = new DataSet("DS");
        ds.Namespace = "StdNamespace";
        DataTable stdTable = new DataTable("Students");
        DataColumn col1 = new DataColumn("Name");
        DataColumn col2 = new DataColumn("Address");
        stdTable.Columns.Add(col1);
        stdTable.Columns.Add(col2);
```

```
ds.Tables.Add(stdTable);
// Add Student Data to the table
DataRow newRow;newRow = stdTable.NewRow();
newRow["Name"]= "Mahesh Chand";
newRow["Address"]= "Meadowlake Dr, Dtown";
stdTable.Rows.Add(newRow);
newRow = stdTable.NewRow();
newRow["Name"]= "Mike Gold";
newRow["Address"]= "NewYork";
stdTable.Rows.Add(newRow);
ds.AcceptChanges();


XmlTextWriter writer = new XmlTextWriter(Console.Out);
ds.WriteXmlSchema(writer);
```

Refer to the previous section to see how to create an XmlTextWriter object.

XmlDataDocument and XML

As discussed earlier in this chapter, the XmlDocument class provides DOM tree structure of XML documents. The XmlDataDocument class comes from XmlDocument, which is comes from XmlNode. Figure 6-10 shows the XmlDataDocument hierarchy.

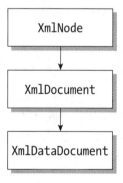

Figure 6-10. XmlDataDocument hierarchy

Besides overriding the methods of XmlNode and XmlDocument, XmlDataDocument also implements its own methods. The XmlDataDocument class lets you load relational data using the DataSet object as well as XML documents using the Load and LoadXml methods. As Figure 6-11 indicates, you can use a DataSet to load relational data to an XmlDataDocument object and use the Load or LoadXml methods to load an XML document. Figure 6-11 shows a relationship between a Reader, Writer, DataSet, and XmlDataDocument.

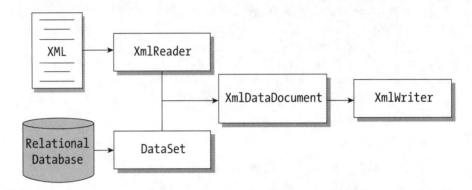

Figure 6-11. Reading and writing data using XmlDataDocument

The XmlDataDocument class extends the functionality of XmlDocument and synchronizes it with DataSet. As you know, a DataSet is a powerful object in ADO.NET. As Figure 6-11 shows, you can take data from two different sources. First, you can load data from an XML document with the help of XmlReader, and second, you can load data from relational data sources with the help of database providers and DataSet. The neat thing is the *data synchronization* between these two objects. That means if you update data in a DataSet object, you see results in the XmlDataDocument object and vice versa. For example, if you add a record to a DataSet object, the action will add one node to the XmlDataDocument object representing the newly added record.

Once the data is loaded, you're allowed to use any operations that you were able to use on XmlDocument objects. You can also use XmlReader and XmlWriter objects to read and write the data.

The XmlDataDocument class has a property called DataSet. It returns the attached DataSet object with XmlDataDocument. The DataSet property provides you a relational representation of an XML document. Once you've a DataSet object, you can do anything with it that you did in Chapter 5, such as attaching to a DataGrid.

You can use all XML read and write methods of the DataSet object through the Dataset property such as ReadXml, ReadXmlSchema, WriteXml, and WriteXmlSchema. Refer to the DataSet read and write methods in the previous section to see how these methods are used.

Loading Data Using Load and LoadXml from the XmlDataDocument

You can use either the Load method or the LoadXml method to load an XML document. The Load method takes a parameter of a filename string, a TextReader, or an XmlReader. Similarly, you can use the LoadXml method. This method passes an XML filename to load the XML file. For example:

```
XmlDataDocument doc = new XmlDataDocument();
doc.Load("C:\\Books.xml");
```

Or you can load an XML fragment, as in the following example:

```
XmlDataDocument doc = new XmlDataDocument();
doc.LoadXml("<Record> write something</Record>");
```

Loading Data Using a DataSet

As you've seen in the DataSet section of Chapter 3, a DataSet object has methods to read XML documents. These methods are ReadXmlSchema and LoadXml. You use the Load or LoadXml methods to load an XML document the same way you did directly from the XMLDataDocument. Again, the Load method takes a parameter of a filename string, TextReader, or XmlReader. Similarly, use the LoadXml method to pass an XML filename through the dataset. For example:

```
XmlDataDocument doc = new XmlDataDocument();
doc.DataSet.ReadXmlSchema("test.xsd");
```

or

```
doc.DataSet.ReadXml("<Record> write something</Record>");
```

Displaying XML Data in a DataSet Format

As mentioned previously, you can get a DataSet object from an XmlDataDocument object by using its DataSet property. OK, now it's time to see how to do that. The next sample will show you how easy is to display an XML document data in a DataSet format.

To read an XML document in a dataset, first you read to document. You can read a document using the ReadXml method of the DataSet object. The DataSet property of XmlDataDocument represents the dataset of XmlDataDocument. After reading a document in a dataset, you can create data views from the dataset, or you can also use a DataSet's DefaultViewManager property to bind to data-bound controls, as you can see in the following code:

```
XmlDataDocument xmlDatadoc = new XmlDataDocument();
xmlDatadoc.DataSet.ReadXml("C:\\XmlDataDoc.xml");
 dataGrid1.DataSource = xmlDatadoc.DataSet.DefaultViewManager;
```

Listing 6-29 shows the complete code. As you can see from Listing 6-29, I created a new dataset, Books, fill it from the books.xml, and bind to a DataGrid control using its DataSource property. To make Listing 6-29 work, you need to create a Windows application and drag a DataGrid control to the form. After doing that, you need to write the Listing 6-29 code on the Form1 constructor or Form load event.

Listing 6-29. XmlDataDocumentSample.cs

```
        public Form1()
        {
            // InitializeComponent and other code here
            // Create an XmlDataDocument object and read an XML
            XmlDataDocument xmlDatadoc = new XmlDataDocument();
            xmlDatadoc.DataSet.ReadXml("C:\\books.xml");

            // Create a DataSet object and fill it with the dataset
            // of XmlDataDocument
            DataSet ds = new DataSet("Books DataSet");
            ds = xmlDatadoc.DataSet;

            // Attach dataset view to the DataGrid control
            dataGrid1.DataSource = ds.DefaultViewManager;
        }
```

The output of this program looks like Figure 6-12. Only a few lines code, and you're all set. Neat, huh?

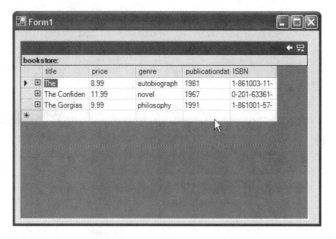

Figure 6-12. XmlDataDocumentSample.cs *output*

Saving Data from a DataSet to XML

You can save a DataSet data as an XML document using the Save method of XmlDataDocument. Actually, XmlDataDocument comes from XmlDocument, and the XmlDocument class defines the Save method. I've already discussed that you can use Save method to save your data in a string, stream, TextWriter, and XmlWriter.

First, you create a DataSet object and fill it using a DataAdapter. The following example reads the Customers table from the Northwind Access database and fills data from the table to the DataSet:

```
string SQLStmt = "SELECT * FROM Customers";
string ConnectionString =
"Provider=Microsoft.Jet.OLEDB.4.0;Data Source=C:\\Northwind.mdb" ;

        // Create data adapter
        OleDbDataAdapter da = new OleDbDataAdapter(SQLStmt,
ConnectionString);

        // Create a new dataset object and fill using data adpater's fill
method
        DataSet ds = new DataSet();
        da.Fill(ds);
```

Now, you create an instance of XmlDataDocument with the DataSet as an argument and call the Save method to save the data as an XML document:

```
XmlDataDocument doc = new XmlDataDocument(ds);
doc.Save("C:\\XmlDataDoc.xml");
```

Listing 6-30 shows a complete program listing. You create an XmlDataDocument object with dataset and call the Save method to save the dataset data in an XML file.

Listing 6-30. Saving the dataset data to an XML document
```
using System;
using System.Data;
using System.Data.OleDb;
using System.Xml;

namespace DataDocSampB2
{
class Class1
{
        static void Main(string[] args)
        {
                // Create SQL Query
            string SQLStmt = "SELECT * FROM Customers";

            // Connection string
string ConnectionString =
"Provider=Microsoft.Jet.OLEDB.4.0;Data Source=C:\\Northwind.mdb" ;

            // Create data adapter
            OleDbDataAdapter da = new OleDbDataAdapter(SQLStmt, ConnectionString);

            // Create a new dataset object and fill using data adpater's fill
method
            DataSet ds = new DataSet();
            da.Fill(ds);

            // Now use SxlDataDocument's Save method to save data as an XML file
            XmlDataDocument doc = new XmlDataDocument(ds);
            doc.Save("C:\\XmlDataDoc.xml");
        }
}
}
```

XmlDataDocument: Under the Hood

After looking at Listing 6-29, which illustrated the reading of an XML document in a DataGrid control, you must be wondering how it happened? It's all the magic of the `DataSet` object. The `DataSet` object handles everything for you under the hood:

```
doc.DataSet.ReadXml("C:\\outdata.xml");
```

As you see in this first line, you're calling `DataSet.ReadXml` method to read an XML document. The `DataSet` extracts the document and defines tables and columns for you.

Generally, the root node of the XML document becomes a table; the document's Name, Namespace, NamespaceURI, and Prefix of the XML document become the dataset's `Name`, `Namespace`, `NamespaceURI`, and `Prefix`, respectively. If an element's children have one or more children, they become another table inside the main table in a nested format. Anything left from the tables becomes columns of the table. The value of a node is added as a row in a table. `DataSet` takes care of all of this under the hood.

Navigation in XML

As you've seen, `XmlNode` provides a way to navigate DOM trees with the help of its `FirstChild`, `ChildNodes`, `LastChild`, `PreviousNode`, `NextSibling`, and `PreviousSibling` methods.

Besides `XmlNode`, the XML .NET has two more classes, which help you navigate XML documents. These classes are `XPathDocument` and `XpathNavigator`. The `System.Xml.XPath` namespace defines both of these classes.

The `XPath` namespace contains classes to provide read-only, fast access to documents. Before using these classes, you must add a reference of the `System.Xml.XPath` namespace to your application.

`XPathNodeIterator`, `XPathExpression`, and `XPathException` are other classes defined in this namespace. The `XPathNodeIterator` class provides iteration capabilities to a node. `XPathExpression` provides selection criteria to select a set of nodes from a document based on those criteria, and the `XPathException` class is an exception class. The`XpathDocument` class provides a fast cache for XML document processing using XSLT and XPath.

You use the `XPathDocument` constructor to create an instance of `XmlPathDocument`. It has many overloaded constructors. You can pass an `XmlReader`, `TextReader`, or even direct XML filenames.

The XPathNavigator Class

The XPathNavigator class implements the functionality to navigate through a document. It has easy-to-use and self-explanatory methods. You create an XPathNavigator instance by calling XPathDocument's CreateNavigator method.

You can also create a XPathNavigator object by calling XmlDocument's CreateNavigator method. For example, the following code calls XmlDocument's CreateNavigator method to create a XPathNavigator object:

```
// Load books.xml document
XmlDocument xmlDoc = new XmlDocument();
xmlDoc.Load(@"c:\books.xml");

// Create XPathNavigator object by calling CreateNavigator of XmlDocument
XPathNavigator nav = xmlDoc.CreateNavigator();
```

> **NOTE** *Don't forget to add a reference of the* System.Xml.XPath *to your project before using any of its classes.*

XPathNavigator contains methods and properties to move to the first, next, child, parent, and root nodes of the document.

XPathNavigator Move Methods

Table 6-8 describes the XPathNavigator class's Move methods. Some of these methods are MoveToFirst, MoveToNext, MoveToRoot, MoveToFirstAttribute, MoveToFirstChild, MoveToId, MoveToNamespace, MoveToPrevious, MoveToParent, and so on.

Table 6-8. XPathNavigator *Members*

MEMBER	DESCRIPTION
MoveToAttribute	Moves to an attribute
MoveToFirst	Moves to the first sibling of the current node
MoveToFirstAttribute	Moves to the first attribute
MoveToFirstChild	Moves to the first child of the current node
MoveToFirstNamespace	Moves the XPathNavigator to first namespace node of the current element
MoveToId	Moves to the node with specified ID
MoveToNamespace	Moves to the specified namespace
MoveToNext	Moves to the next node of the current node
MoveToNextAttribute	Moves to the next attribute
MoveToNextNamespace	Moves to the next namespace
MoveToParent	Moves to the parent of the current node
MoveToPrevious	Moves to the previous sibling of the current node
MoveToRoot	Moves to the root node

So, with the help of these methods, you can move through a document as a DOM tree. Listing 6-31 uses the MoveToRoot and MoveToFirstChild methods to move to the root node and first child of the root node. Once you have a root, you can display corresponding information such as name, value, node type, and so on.

Listing 6-31. Moving to root and first child nodes using XPathNavigator

```
// Load books.xml document
XmlDocument xmlDoc = new XmlDocument();
xmlDoc.Load(@"c:\books.xml");
// Create XPathNavigator object by calling CreateNavigator of XmlDocument
XPathNavigator nav = xmlDoc.CreateNavigator();

// Move to root node
nav.MoveToRoot();
string name = nav.Name;
Console.WriteLine("Root node info: ");
Console.WriteLine("Base URI" + nav.BaseURI.ToString());
Console.WriteLine("Name: " +nav.Name.ToString());
```

```
Console.WriteLine("Node Type: "+ nav.NodeType.ToString());
Console.WriteLine("Node Value: "+nav.Value.ToString());

if (nav.HasChildren)
{
        nav.MoveToFirstChild();
}
```

Now, using the MoveToNext and MoveToParent methods, you can move through the entire document. Listing 6-32 moves though an entire document and displays the data on the console. The GetNodeInfo method displays a node's information, and you call it recursively.

Listing 6-32. Reading a document using XPathNavigator

```
static void Main(string[] args)
{
// Load books.xml document
XmlDocument xmlDoc = new XmlDocument();
xmlDoc.Load(@"c:\books.xml");

// Create XPathNavigator object by calling CreateNavigator of XmlDocument
XPathNavigator nav = xmlDoc.CreateNavigator();

// Moce to root node
nav.MoveToRoot();
string name = nav.Name;
Console.WriteLine("Root node info: ");
Console.WriteLine("Base URI" + nav.BaseURI.ToString());
Console.WriteLine("Name: " +nav.Name.ToString());
Console.WriteLine("Node Type: "+ nav.NodeType.ToString());
Console.WriteLine("Node Value: "+nav.Value.ToString());

if (nav.HasChildren)
{
    nav.MoveToFirstChild();
    GetNodeInfo(nav);
}

}

        //
private static void GetNodeInfo( XPathNavigator nav1)
{
```

```
Console.WriteLine("Name: " +nav1.Name.ToString());
Console.WriteLine("Node Type: "+ nav1.NodeType.ToString());
Console.WriteLine("Node Value: "+nav1.Value.ToString());

// If node has children, move to fist child.
if (nav1.HasChildren)
{
      nav1.MoveToFirstChild();

      while( nav1.MoveToNext() )
      {
          GetNodeInfo(nav1);
          nav1.MoveToParent();
      }
}
else /* Else move to next sibling */
{
      nav1.MoveToNext();
      GetNodeInfo(nav1);
}
}
```

Searching Using XPathNavigator

Select, SelectChildren, SelectAncestors, and SelectDescendents are other useful methods. Specifically, these methods are useful when you need to select
a document's items based on an XPath expression. For example, you could use
one when selecting nodes for the author tag only and so on. Now, say you want to
search and display all <first-name> tag nodes in the books.xml document.

In Listing 6-33, you use XpathNavigator's Select method to apply
a criteria (all elements with the author-name tag) to read and display all nodes.

Listing 6-33. Use of XPathIterator *and* Select

```
// Load books.xml document
 XmlDocument xmlDoc = new XmlDocument();
xmlDoc.Load(@"c:\books.xml");

 // Create XPathNavigator object by calling CreateNavigator of XmlDocument
XPathNavigator nav = xmlDoc.CreateNavigator();
// Look for author's first name
Console.WriteLine("Author First Name");
```

```
XPathNodeIterator itrator = nav.Select("descendant::first-name");
 while( itrator.MoveNext() )
{
        Console.WriteLine(itrator.Current.Value.ToString());
}
```

Visual Studio .NET and XML Support

XML schemas play a major role in the .NET Framework, and Visual Studio .NET provides many tools and utilities to work with XML. The .NET Framework uses XML to transfer data from one application to another. XML schemas define the structure and validation rules of XML documents. You use XML Schema Definition (XSD) language to define XML schemas.

VS .NET provides an XML designer to work with schemas. In this section, you'll see how you can take advantage of the VS .NET XML designer and wizard features to work with XML documents and database.

Generating a New Schema

To generate a new schema, create a new Windows application using File ➢ New ➢Project ➢ Visual C# Projects ➢ Windows Application. Just follow the steps outlined in the following sections.

Adding an Empty Schema

First, right-click on a project and then select Add ➢ Add New Item (see Figure 6-13).

Figure 6-13. Adding a new item to the project

Now, from Templates, select the XML Schema option, type your schema name, and click Open (see Figure 6-14).

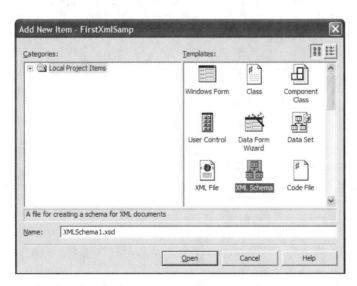

Figure 6-14. Selecting the XML Schema template to add a schema to the project

This action launches XML Designer. Now you'll see your `XmlSchema1.xsd` file, as shown in Figure 6-15.

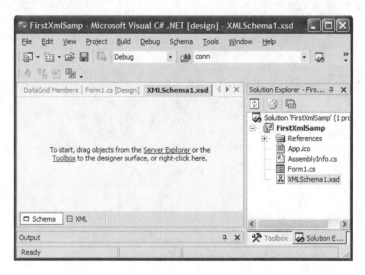

Figure 6-15. XML Designer

This action adds an empty XML schema to your project. If you click on the XML option at the bottom of screen, you'll see your XML looks like the following:

```
<?xml version="1.0" encoding="utf-8" ?>
<xs:schema id="XMLSchema1"
                targetNamespace="http://tempuri.org/XMLSchema1.xsd"
                elementFormDefault="qualified"
                xmlns="http://tempuri.org/XMLSchema1.xsd"
                xmlns:mstns="http://tempuri.org/XMLSchema1.xsd"
                xmlns:xs="http://www.w3.org/2001/XMLSchema">
</xs:schema>
```

As you see in Figure 6-15, there are two options (blue links): Server Explorer and Toolbox.

Adding Schema Items

You can add schema items using the Toolbox option. Clicking the Toolbox link launches the toolbox, as shown in Figure 6-16.

Figure 6-16. XML schema toolbox

As you can see in Figure 6-16, you can add an element, attribute, complexType, and other schema items to the form by just dragging an item to XML Designer.

OK, now you'll learn how to add XML schema items to the schema and set their properties with the help of XML Designer. First, add an element. To add an element to the schema, drag an element from the toolbox. Now you can set its name and type in the designer. The default element looks like Figure 6-17. If you click on the right-side column of the grid, you'll see a drop-down list with element types. You can either select the type of an item from the list or define your own type. Your type is called a *user-defined type*.

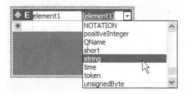

Figure 6-17. Adding a schema element and its type

Define your first element as bookstore with a custom type of bookstoretype. Figure 6-18 shows the bookstore element of bookstoretype.

Figure 6-18. Adding a new bookstore element

Now add a complexType by dragging a complexType to XML Designer (see Figure 6-19).

Figure 6-19. A complexType item

A complexType item can contain other types, too. You can add items to a complexType in many ways. You can either drag an item from the toolbox to the complexType or right-click on a complexType and use the Add option and its suboptions to add an item. Figure 6-20 shows different items you can add to a complexType.

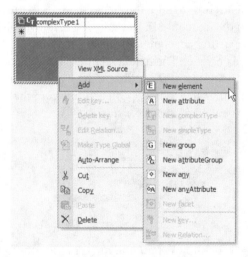

Figure 6-20. An item list can be added to a complexType

You can delete items by right-clicking and selecting Delete . You can also delete the entire complexType or other schema items by right-clicking on the header of an item or on the left side of the item.

Now, rename the added complexType name to book and add four element types: title, author, price, and category. Now your complexType book looks like Figure 6-21.

Figure 6-21. The book *complexType and its elements*

After that, add one more complexType author with two elements: first-name and last-name. Your final schema looks like Figure 6-22.

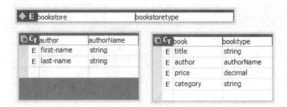

Figure 6-22. The author *and* book *complexType in an XML schema*

Now you can see XML code for this schema by clicking on the left-bottom XML button shown in Figure 6-23.

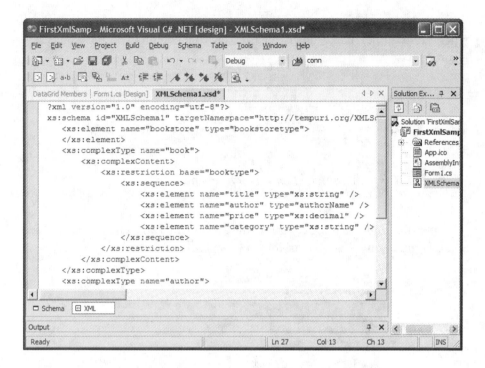

Figure 6-23. Viewing the XML for a schema

Listing 6-34 shows the schema XML code.

Listing 6-34. XML generated using XML Designer

```
<?xml version="1.0" encoding="utf-8"?>
<xs:schema id="XMLSchema1" targetNamespace
="http://tempuri.org/XMLSchema1.xsd"
elementFormDefault="qualified" xmlns="http://tempuri.org/XMLSchema1.xsd"
 xmlns:mstns="http://tempuri.org/XMLSchema1.xsd"
 xmlns:xs="http://www.w3.org/2001/XMLSchema">
    <xs:element name="bookstore" type="bookstoretype">
    </xs:element>
    <xs:complexType name="book">
```

```
    <xs:complexContent>
        <xs:restriction base="booktype">
            <xs:sequence>
                <xs:element name="title" type="xs:string">
                </xs:element>
                <xs:element name="author" type="authorName">
                </xs:element>
                <xs:element name="price" type="xs:decimal" />
                <xs:element name="category" type="xs:string">
                </xs:element>
            </xs:sequence>
        </xs:restriction>
    </xs:complexContent>
</xs:complexType>
<xs:complexType name="author">
    <xs:complexContent>
        <xs:restriction base="authorName">
            <xs:sequence>
                <xs:element name="first-name" type="xs:string">
                </xs:element>
                <xs:element name="last-name" type="xs:string" />
            </xs:sequence>
        </xs:restriction>
    </xs:complexContent>
</xs:complexType>
</xs:schema>
```

Working with DataSets

Now you'll look at the Server Explorer option of XML Designer. Clicking on Server Explorer launches Server Explorer (see Figure 6-24).

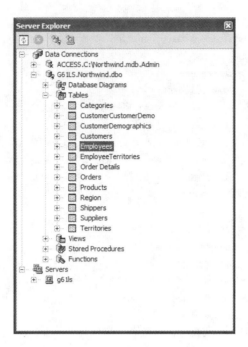

Figure 6-24. Server Explorer

In Figure 6-24, you see that you can expand a database connection and see its tables and views. You can drag these data objects (tables, views, stored procedures, columns) onto XML Designer. For this example, drag the Employees table onto the designer. After dragging, your XML Designer generates a schema for the table, which looks like Figure 6-25.

Figure 6-25. XML Designer–generated schema

Listing 6-35 shows the generated XML code.

Listing 6-35. XML schema generated for a database table

```xml
<?xml version="1.0" encoding="utf-8" ?>
<xs:schema id="XMLSchema1" targetNamespace=
"http://tempuri.org/XMLSchema1.xsd" elementFormDefault=
"qualified" xmlns="http://tempuri.org/XMLSchema1.xsd"
xmlns:mstns="http://tempuri.org/XMLSchema1.xsd"
xmlns:xs="http://www.w3.org/2001/XMLSchema" xmlns:msdata=
"urn:schemas-microsoft-com:xml-msdata">
<xs:element name="Document">
<xs:complexType>
<xs:choice maxOccurs="unbounded">
<xs:element name="Employees">
<xs:complexType>
<xs:sequence>
<xs:element name="EmployeeID" msdata:ReadOnly="true"
msdata:AutoIncrement="true" type="xs:int" />
<xs:element name="LastName" type="xs:string" />
<xs:element name="FirstName" type="xs:string" />
<xs:element name="Title" type="xs:string" minOccurs="0" />
<xs:element name="TitleOfCourtesy" type="xs:string" minOccurs="0" />
<xs:element name="BirthDate" type="xs:dateTime" minOccurs="0" />
<xs:element name="HireDate" type="xs:dateTime" minOccurs="0" />
<xs:element name="Address" type="xs:string" minOccurs="0" />
<xs:element name="City" type="xs:string" minOccurs="0" />
<xs:element name="Region" type="xs:string" minOccurs="0" />
<xs:element name="PostalCode" type="xs:string" minOccurs="0" />
<xs:element name="Country" type="xs:string" minOccurs="0" />
<xs:element name="HomePhone" type="xs:string" minOccurs="0" />
<xs:element name="Extension" type="xs:string" minOccurs="0" />
<xs:element name="Photo" type="xs:base64Binary" minOccurs="0" />
<xs:element name="Notes" type="xs:string" minOccurs="0" />
<xs:element name="ReportsTo" type="xs:int" minOccurs="0" />
<xs:element name="PhotoPath" type="xs:string" minOccurs="0" />
</xs:sequence>
</xs:complexType>
</xs:element>
</xs:choice>
</xs:complexType>
<xs:unique name="DocumentKey1" msdata:PrimaryKey="true">
<xs:selector xpath=".//mstns:Employees" />
<xs:field xpath="mstns:EmployeeID" />
</xs:unique>
</xs:element>
</xs:schema>
```

Generating ADO.NET Typed DataSet from a Schema

There may be occasions when other applications will generate XML schemas and your application needs to use them to access databases. You can generate a typed dataset from an existing schema. The Generate Dataset option generates a typed DataSet for an XML schema. But before generating a DataSet, you need to add schema to the project.

Adding an Existing Schema to a Project

Now you'll see how you can generate a DataSet object from an existing schema. To test this, I created a new Windows application project. You can use the Employees table schema generated in the previous section. To add an existing schema to the project, right-click on the project and select Add ➤ Add Existing Item and browse for the schema (see Figure 6-26).

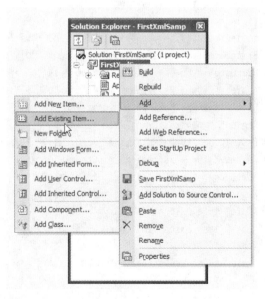

Figure 6-26. Adding an existing schema to a project

If your schema name was different, select that schema and click Open (see Figure 6-27).

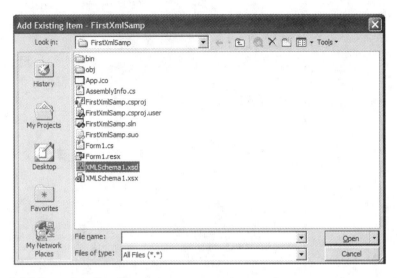

Figure 6-27. Browsing for schema

This action adds a schema to the current project. You can also add an XML schema by dragging a database table onto XML Designer.

Generating a Typed Dataset from a Schema

Generating a typed dataset from a schema is pretty simple. Right-click on XML Designer and select the Generate Dataset option (see Figure 6-28).

Figure 6-28. Generate Dataset option of XML Designer

This action generates a DataSet class and adds it to your project. If you look in your Class Wizard, you see the Document class derived from DataSet and its members. The Document class looks like Figure 6-29 in the Class View.

Figure 6-29. DataSet-derived class in the Class View

> **NOTE** *The Generate Dataset option may not generate a* DataSet *if the XML schema is not designed properly.*

Once you've a DataSet object, you can use it the way you want. I have already discussed these details in Chapter 3 and Chapter 4.

Summary

This chapter covered XML syntax as well as the uses of XML on the .NET platform. You learned about the DOM structure and DOM node types. You learned how XML is represented in .NET through classes such as XmlNode, XmlAttribute, XmlElement, and XmlDocument. You also learned how to read and write to these structures using the XmlReader and XmlWriter classes. Also discussed was the navigation in an XML node structure using XmlPathNavigator. Most importantly, you learned how XML applies to ADO.NET and how to use a DataSet to read and write data with XML. Visual Studio .NET provides XML Designer to work with XML. Using XML Designer, you can generate XML schemas, which later can be used to generate typed datasets.

Developing Web Applications Using ADO.NET

As THE PROGRAMMING WORLD moves toward the Internet these days, it's becoming important for developers to be able to create Web applications and Web services. Microsoft .NET Framework enables you to develop, maintain, and deploy reliable and high-performance Web applications and Web services.

I'll start this chapter by giving you an overview of ASP.NET, showing how to install ASP.NET, and then developing a simple Web application development using Visual Studio (VS) .NET. After that I'll discuss Web Forms controls and how to use them. Specifically, the Web Forms DataGrid control is useful to develop Web-based database applications. You can bind datasets to the DataGrid control as you did for a Windows Forms DataGrid control. I'll also discuss how to enable paging in a data grid control. I'll then show you how to develop a guest book for your Web site using ASP.NET.

Introducing ASP.NET

Writing database Web applications using ADO.NET in VS .NET is similar to writing Windows applications. The Microsoft .NET class library provides a set of server-side controls, which you can treat as Windows controls. To create a Web application, all you have to do is create a simple project, drag server-side controls onto a Web form, set their properties, and write event handlers. In this chapter, first I'll develop a simple Web application and show you how the ASP.NET model works with C# and other .NET languages. After that I'll concentrate on ASP.NET and show you how to write some real-world database Web applications using ADO.NET and C#.

ASP.NET Platform Requirements

The following operating systems support ASP.NET: Windows XP, Windows 2000 Server, and Windows NT 4 (running Service Pack 6a) with Internet Information Services (IIS) 4 or later. Also, you must have the .NET Software Development Kit (SDK) installed on the server.

ASP.NET Language Support

You can use any .NET-supported language to write ASP.NET applications, including C#, Visual Basic .NET, and JScript. Because this book is about C#, the other languages are beyond the scope of this book.

Installing ASP.NET

You can develop and run ASP.NET applications on Windows 2000 or Windows XP operating systems. ASP.NET ships with VS .NET. If you don't have Visual Studio .NET, you can install it separately from VS .NET. The ASP.NET download is available on the Microsoft Web site (http://www.microsoft.com). If you want to develop ASP.NET mobile-enabled applications for Pocket PC or cellular phones, you need to install the ASP.NET Mobile Internet Toolkit, which you can also download from Microsoft's Web site. You can also find links to these downloads in the Downloads section of C# Corner (http://www.c-sharpcorner.com).

ASP.NET Editor

I'll be using VS .NET to develop the applications in this chapter. However, you can develop ASP.NET applications using any text editor and command-line compiler. After compiling, you copy your file manually to IIS to deploy the application. The advantage of using VS .NET is that it provides you with a visual Integrated Development Environment (IDE) to drag and drop controls onto a page and view the HTML code. Other features are Intellisense and syntax checking. In sum, you can also use VS .NET to compile, debug, and deploy your application.

> **NOTE**   *ASP.NET editors, including Visual Studio .NET, provide what-you-see-is-what-you-get (WYSIWYG) support for developing applications by enabling you to drop controls on the Web Forms pages.*

ASP.NET: An Evolution of ASP

ASP.NET, previously called *ASP+*, is not just the next version of ASP. It's a new programming model based on Microsoft's .NET Framework for developing Web applications. Although ASP.NET syntaxes are taken from ASP, the ASP.NET model takes full advantage of Microsoft's Common Language Runtime (CLR) and its services. Therefore, developers have the flexibility to choose any .NET-supported language to write ASP.NET applications.

The main advantages of the ASP.NET model are the following:

ASP.NET is simple and flexible. Developing ASP.NET applications using VS .NET is similar to developing Windows applications. VS .NET offers you a set of controls to use with ASP.NET. You just need to drag and drop the controls onto a Web form, write events corresponding to the controls, and compile and run the program. Other features include simple client authentication, security, deployment, and site configuration.

ASP.NET is language independent. You can choose any language that supports .NET, including C#, Visual Basic, VBScript, and Jscript.

ASP.NET supports data binding. ASP.NET offers you a set of data-binding controls such as the DataGrid, DataList, and others. You can bind data with these controls in a similar fashion as you do in any Windows Forms application.

ASP.NET has enhanced performance and scalability. ASP.NET code is not interpreted like traditional ASP pages. ASP.NET pages compile on the server in a .NET class. It takes advantage of early binding, just-in-time compilation, native optimization, and caching services. ASP.NET also works in clustered and multiprocessor environments.

ASP.NET is browser independent. If you've ever programmed in previous versions of ASP, you're probably had problems running ASP pages in other browsers other than Internet Explorer. ASP.NET is browser independent. It automatically checks what browser you're using and produces HTML at run-time accordingly.

Understanding Web Forms and Web Services

Web Forms is a term Microsoft introduced when it released ASP+ for developing Web applications using the ASP model.

Similar to Windows applications and services, you can also write Web applications and services. A *Web application* is a distributed application, which allows you to work and distribute functionality over the Web and provides user interfaces. Using Web Forms controls, you can write Web GUI applications similar to Windows applications.

Web Forms

ASP.NET's Web Forms provide you with the ability to build Web-based GUI applications. Web Forms include Web pages (also called an *ASP.NET page* or *Web Forms page*) and *GUI components* (sometimes called *server controls*) such as text boxes, buttons, list boxes, data grids, and so on. ASP.NET provides the flexibility to add these controls to an ASP.NET page at run-time as well as at design-time. VS .NET provides design-time features to develop applications in no time. You add controls to a page by dragging controls from the toolbox to the page and then setting the controls' properties and events. Web Forms also provides a method for using the codebehind directive to separate your controls from the code. In other words, you can write code in a separate file from the controls.

Web Services

Web services are applications that perform a certain task; they can be used by a single application as well as distributed on the Web. I'll cover Web services in the next chapter of this book.

Developing Your First ASP.NET Web Application

Before I discuss the ASP.NET model in more depth, I'll show you how to develop your first ASP.NET application. In this example, I'll create a simple Web application using VS .NET. Similar to your first Windows application, I'll add a button, a text box, and a list box control to a Web page and then add text box contents to the list box on the button-click event.

Creating a Web Application Project

Creating a new ASP.NET Web application using Visual Studio .NET is simple. First create a new project using File ➤ New ➤ Project ➤ Visual C# Project and then select the ASP.NET Web Application template (see Figure 7-1).

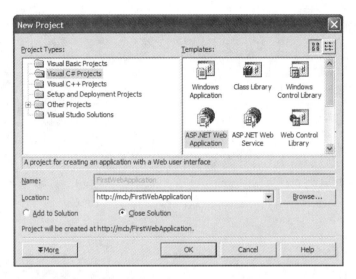

Figure 7-1. The FirstWebApplication project

The Location box will show you the default option of `http://localhost` and the application name. Here `localhost` represents the default IIS server running on your local machine. The default virtual directory for `localhost` is `C:\Inetpub\www-root`. If you're using a Web server installed on a network rather than your local machine, you need to use that server name. If you don't know the server name, you may want to contact your Web server administrator. As you can see from Figure 7-1, I'm using the MCB network Web server. So if you see the name "MCB," don't worry. Just replace it with your own server's name. You can type either **http://servername//application name** or **//servername//application name**; both formats are correct.

Clicking the OK button creates a new directory, `FirstWebApplication`, in the server's virtual directory. It also creates a new Web application and sends you to the default `WebForm1.aspx` page, as shown in Figure 7-2.

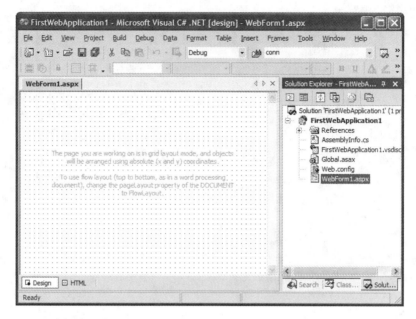

Figure 7-2. Default WebForm1.aspx *page*

From here you can edit your page's HTML. As you see in left-bottom corner of Figure 7-2, there are two modes available: Design and HTML. Click the HTML button to edit the code, as shown in Figure 7-3.

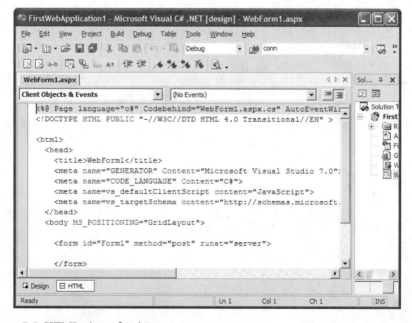

Figure 7-3. HTML view of WebForm1.aspx

The HTML view shows you the HTML code of a page, its controls, and control properties. The HTML editor also lets you edit the HTML manually.

Now if you switch the page view back to the design mode and right-click on the page, you'll get several options: View HTML Source, Build Style, View in Browser, View Code, Synchronize Document Outline, and so on (see Figure 7-4).

Figure 7-4. An ASP.NET page's right-click options

You can set a page's properties by selecting Properties from the right-click menu. The Properties menu opens the Document Property Pages window. As you can see from Figure 7-5, there are three tabs available in the Properties window: General, Color and Margins, and Keywords. Most of the properties are self-explanatory. On the General tab, the Page Layout property has two options, GridLayout and FlowLayout. GridLayout is when you want drop controls to the page and reposition them. If you want to add text to the page, you should set the page layout to FlowLayout; otherwise you won't be able to add text to the page. After setting the Page Layout property to FlowLayout, the editor works as a text editor.

Figure 7-5. An ASP.NET document's page properties

Adding Web Controls to a Web Form

Similar to the Windows control toolbox, VS .NET provides a Web Forms control toolbox. You can open the toolbox by selecting the View ➤ Toolbox main menu item. The Web Forms toolbox looks like Figure 7-6. The Web Forms category of the toolbox contains form controls, and the HTML category contains HTML controls. The Data category provides the same data components you've seen in the Windows application toolbox. It has the same connections, data adapters, datasets, data views, and `DataViewManager` components. Figures 7- 6 and 7-7 shows the Web Forms and HTML controls, respectively.

Figure 7-6. Web Forms controls

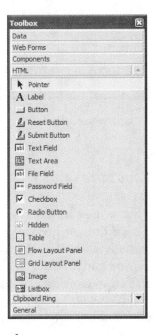

Figure 7-7. HTML Web controls

For the applications in this chapter, I'll be using the Web Forms controls.

OK, now switch the page back to the Design mode and GridLayout mode (if you changed its modes) and add a button, a text box, and a ListBox to the form by dragging these controls from the Web Forms toolbox to WebForm1.aspx. The page should now look like Figure 7-8.

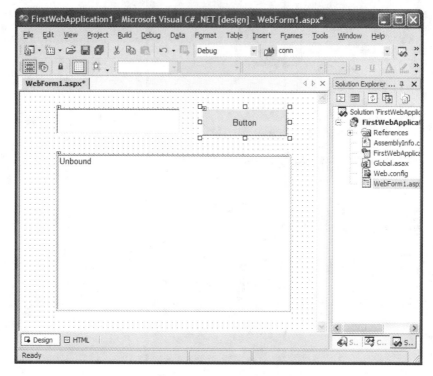

Figure 7-8. WebForms1.aspx *Design mode after adding Web Forms controls*

Setting Control Properties

The next step is to add some text to the page and change some of the controls' properties. To add text to the page, first you need to change the page layout to FlowLayout in the Properties window, which you can do by right-clicking on the page and selecting Properties. Now add a heading to the page. I added two lines to the page and set a different font and font size for these lines. The first line text is "My First ASP.NET Application," and the second line text is "Click Add button to add contents of text box to the list box." I also set some properties of the button and text box controls (see Figure 7-9).

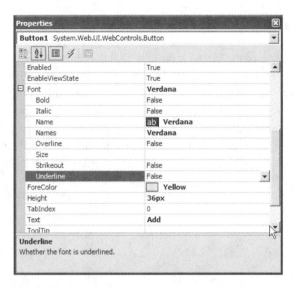

Figure 7-9. Properties window for the Web controls

Specifically, I changed the border, background color, font, and foreground color of these controls. As you can see, changing these properties is similar to changing them for Windows applications. The final page with these properties looks like Figure 7-10.

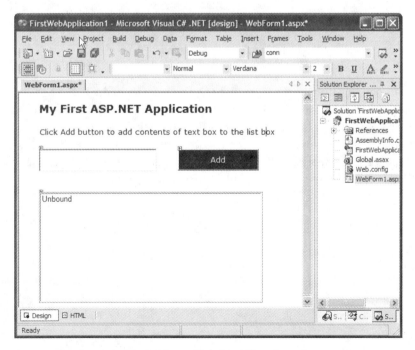

Figure 7-10. Final page of the Web application after changing some control properties

Using Document Outline

Another nice feature of the Visual Studio .NET IDE is that you can synchronize a Web page's controls with its contents in the Document Outline viewer. This is really useful when you're developing a Web application with hundreds of controls; it can be hard to keep track of all the controls, HTML tags, and other page contents. The Document Outline viewer enables you to manage a page's contents in a tree format. The tree format displays all the page elements in the order they're called in the page. You can open the Document Outline viewer by right-clicking on a page and selecting Synchronize Document Outline (see Figure 7-11).

Figure 7-11. Calling the Document Outline viewer

This action launches the Document Outline viewer in the left pane (see Figure 7-12). As you can see, the tree view displays the page contents, including the form, button, text box, and paragraph. If you click on a control in the Document Outline viewer, it selects the corresponding control in the form. And, vice versa, if you select a control in the form and make Document Outline the active window, the viewer selects that control in the tree view.

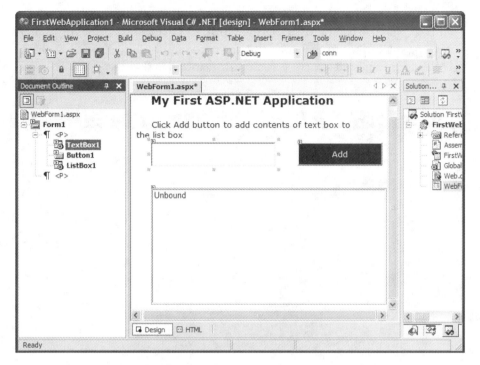

Figure 7-12. Document Outline viewer

You can also use the Document Outline viewer's right-click menu to cut, paste, delete, view the code, and view the properties of these controls (see Figure 7-13).

Figure 7-13. Document Outline viewer's right-click options

Not only that, but now I'll show you one more thing. Select the HTML view of your page, and you can move to specific HTML tags using the Document Outline viewer. As you can see from Figure 7-14, the tree view displays all the code of an HTML page in a nested structure as they're organized in the original code.

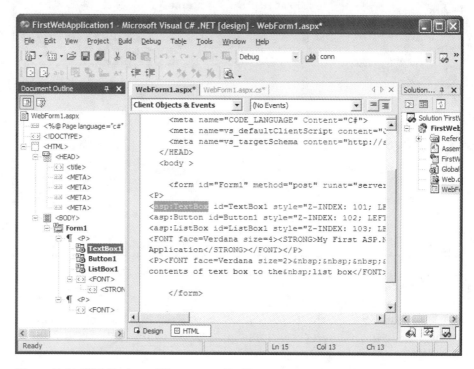

Figure 7-14. HTML view of Document Outline

So, the point is that you can find and organize your HTML code and controls from the Document Outline viewer instead of looking for a tag in the file manually.

Writing Code on the Button-Click Event Handler

The last step of this tutorial is to add an event handler for the button and write code to add some text box text to the list box. You add a control event similar to Windows applications. You can either double-click on the button or use the Properties window's lightning icon to add an event. I'll add the button's click event as Button1_Click (see Figure 7-15).

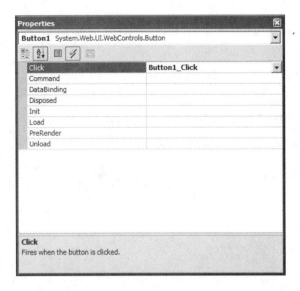

Figure 7-15. Adding an event handler to the button-click event

This action adds the `Button1_Click` method to the `WebForm1.aspx.cs` class, which hosts the code for the page controls and events. Now write a line of code to add the text box contents to the list box. Specifically, add the bold line in Listing 7-1 to the `Button1_Click` method.

Listing 7-1. Adding the text box contents to the list box
```
private void Button1_Click(object sender, System.EventArgs e)
{
    ListBox1.Items.Add(TextBox1.Text.ToString());
}
```

> **NOTE** *You can also see the code using the View Code option of the page's right-click menu.*

Now compile and run the project. The output of the program looks like Figure 7-16. Clicking the Add button adds the text box contents to the list box.

Figure 7-16. Output of our first Web application

After finishing this application, you can see the power and flexibility of ASP.NET and the VS .NET IDE. You've just developed a nice ASP.NET Web applic ation without any knowledge of ASP.NET and just by writing only one line of code.

Creating Your First ADO.NET Web Application

You've already seen how to develop an ASP.NET application using VS .NET. Now I'll show you how to develop database applications using ADO.NET and ASP.NET. To start creating your first ADO.NET application, you'll create a Web Application project as you did in the previous section. In this example you're adding only a ListBox control to the page and you're going to read data from a database and display the data in the list box.

After dragging a ListBox control from the Web Forms control toolbox and dropping it on the page, write the code in Listing 7-2 on the Page_Load event. You can add a Page_Load event either by double-clicking on the page or using the Properties window.

> **NOTE** *If you're using an Access 2000 database and OleDb data providers, don't forget to add a reference to the* System.Data.OleDb *namespace to your project.*

Listing 7-2. Filling data from a database to a ListBox control

```
private void Page_Load(object sender, System.EventArgs e)
        {
        // Create a Connection Object
        string ConnectionString = @"Provider=Microsoft.Jet.OLEDB.4.0;"+
            "Data Source=c:\\Northwind.mdb";
        OleDbConnection conn = new OleDbConnection(ConnectionString);

        // Open the connection
        if( conn.State != ConnectionState.Open)
            conn.Open();
        // create a data adapter
        OleDbDataAdapter da = new OleDbDataAdapter
            ("SELECT FirstName, LastName, Title FROM Employees", conn);

        // Create and fill a dataset
        DataSet ds = new DataSet();
        da.Fill(ds);

        // Bind dataset to the control
        // Set DataSource property of ListBox as DataSet's DefaultView
        ListBox1.DataSource = ds;
        ListBox1.SelectedIndex = 0;
        // Set Field Name you want to get data from
        ListBox1.DataTextField = "FirstName";

        DataBind();

        // Close the connection
        if( conn.State == ConnectionState.Open)
            conn.Close();
    }
```

As you can see, this code looks familiar. First you create a connection object with the Northwind.mdb database. After that you create a data adapter and select FirstName, LastName, and Title from the Employees table. Then you create a dataset object and fill it using the data adapter's Fill method. Once you have a dataset, you set the dataset as the ListBox's DataSource property and set SelectIndex as 0. The SelectIndex property represents the index of the column from a dataset you want to display in the control. The field name of your column is FirstName. At the end you call the DataBind method of the ListBox. This method binds the data to the list box.

The output looks like Figure 7-17. As you can see, the ListBox control displays data from the FirstName column of the Employees table.

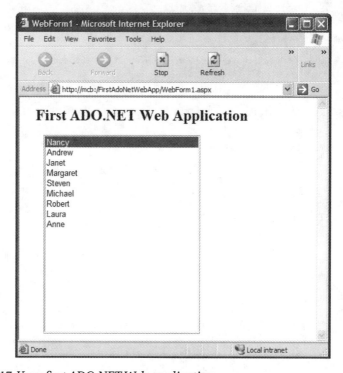

Figure 7-17. Your first ADO.NET Web application

Viewing Data in a DataGrid Control

You've already seen how to develop an ASP.NET application, connect to a database, and view data in Web Forms controls. Now you'll see one more simple example. The DataGrid control is a useful control in Web Forms. In this example, I'll show you how to connect a DataGrid control a database table and view all the table's data in the DataGrid.

First you create a Web application using the same steps you've used in two previous samples. Then you drag a button and a data grid control onto the page. Change the Text property of the button to "Fill Data," change its properties, and add some text to the page. The final Web page looks like Figure 7-18.

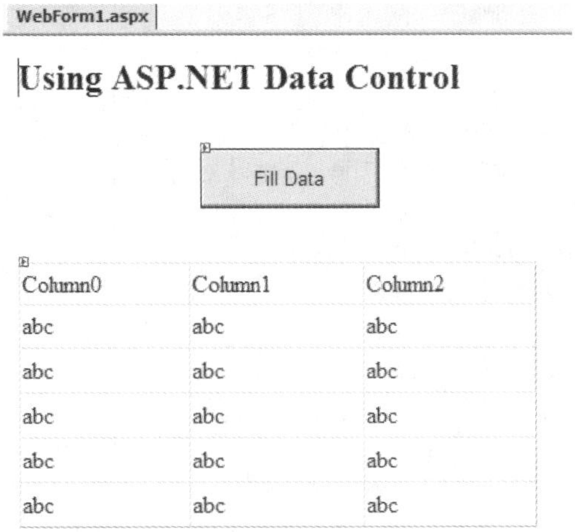

WebForm1.aspx

Using ASP.NET Data Control

Fill Data

Column0	Column1	Column2
abc	abc	abc
abc	abc	abc
abc	abc	abc
abc	abc	abc
abc	abc	abc

Figure 7-18. Database application in ASP.NET

The only thing you need to do now is write code to fill the data from a database to the list box on the Fill Data button-click event handler. I'll use the OleDb data provider with the Access 2000 Northwind database. Before using the OleDb data provider, though, don't forget to add a reference to the System.Data.OleDb namespace:

```
using System.Data.OleDb;
```

Now write a click event handler for the button and write the code from Listing 7-3 on the handler.

Listing 7-3. Filling data from a database to the DataGrid
```
private void Button1_Click(object sender, System.EventArgs e)
{
        // Create a Connection Object
        string ConnectionString = @"Provider=Microsoft.Jet.OLEDB.4.0;"+
            "Data Source=c:\\Northwind.mdb";
        OleDbConnection conn = new OleDbConnection(ConnectionString);

        // Open the connection
        if( conn.State != ConnectionState.Open)
            conn.Open();
        // create a data adapter
        OleDbDataAdapter da = new OleDbDataAdapter
            ("SELECT FirstName, LastName, Title FROM Employees", conn);
```

```
// Create and fill a dataset
DataSet ds = new DataSet();
da.Fill(ds);

// Bind dataset to the control

DataGrid1.DataSource = ds;
DataGrid1.DataBind();

// Close the connection
if( conn.State == ConnectionState.Open)
    conn.Close();
}
```

As you can see from Listing 7-3, there is nothing new except one line: `DataGrid.DataBind()`. I'll discuss the `DataBind` method in a moment. You'll follow the same steps to create a connection and data adapter objects as you've been doing in the previous chapters of the book. In this example, I'm using the Access 2000 database, `C:\Northwind.mdb`, and the OleDb data adapter to connect to the database. After creating a connection and data adapter, create and fill a dataset by calling the data adapter's `Fill` method. After that, set dataset as the DataGrid control's `DataSource` property and call DataGrid's `DataBind` method.

Now compile and run the project. The output of the Fill Data button looks like Figure 7-19.

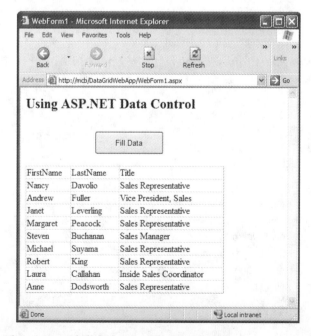

Figure 7-19. The output of clicking the Fill Data button

Neat, huh? How easy is writing database Web applications using ADO.NET?

Using ASP.NET Server-Side Controls

The Microsoft .NET Framework provides a rich set of server-side controls for developing Web applications. You can add these controls to Web Forms pages just as you add Windows controls to a form. Server-side controls are often called *server controls* or *Web Forms controls*. There are four types of server controls: HTML server controls, Web server controls, validation controls, and user controls.

HTML Server Controls

HTML developers must be familiar with old HTML controls, which they use to write GUI applications in HTML. These controls are the same HTML controls; you can run these controls on the server by defining the `runat="Server"` attribute. These control names start with `Html`. Table 7-1 defines some of these controls.

Table 7-1. HTML Server Controls

CONTROL	DESCRIPTION
HtmlForm	Creates an HTML form control, used as a placeholder of other controls
HtmlInputText	Creates an input text box control used to get input from user
HtmltextArea	Creates multiline text box control
HtmlAnchor	Creates Web navigation
HtmlButton	Creates a button control
HtmlImage	Creates an image control, which is used to display an image
HtmlInputCheckBox	Creates a check box control
HtmlInputRadioButton	Creates a radio button control
HtmlTable	Creates a table control
HtmlTableRow	Creates a row within a table
HtmlTableCell	Creates a cell within a row

Web Server Controls

Web server controls are more powerful than HTML controls because they provide more functionality and are easier to use. Besides some of the basic controls such as button, text box, label, and checkbox, ASP.NET provides some more powerful controls such as DataGrid, DataList, and Calendar. I'll use these controls throughout this chapter. Table 7-2 describes some of these controls.

Table 7-2. Web Server Controls

CONTROL	DESCRIPTION
Label	Represents a label control
ListBox	Represents a list box control
CheckBox	Represents a check box control
Calendar	Represents a calendar control
ImageButton	Represents an image button control
TableCell	Represents a table cell
Panel	Represents a panel control
DateList	Represents a data list control
TextBox	Represents a text box control
Image	Represents an image control
CheckBoxList	Represents a list box with check boxes
Button	Represents a button control
HyperLink	Represents a hyperlink control
TableRow	Represents a row of a table
RadioButtonList	Represents a list box with radio button controls
DataGrid	Represents a data grid control
DropDownList	Represents a drop-down list control
AdRotator	Represents an ad rotator control
RadioButton	Represents a radio button control
LinkButton	Represents a link button control
Table	Represents a table control
Repeater	Represents a repeater control

I'll show how to use these controls in example applications throughout this chapter.

Validation Controls

Validating user input is one of the important needs for Web applications. These controls provide features to validate user input. Using these controls you can check a required field, a value, a range, a pattern of characters, and so on. Table 7-3 describes validation controls.

Table 7-3. Validation Controls

CONTROL	DESCRIPTION
RequiredFieldValidator	Makes sure that the user doesn't skip an entry
CompareValidator	Compares user input with a value using a comparison operator such as less than, greater than, and so on
RangeValidator	Checks if the user's input falls within a certain range
RegularExpressionValidator	Checks if the user's input matches a defined pattern
CustomValidator	Creates your own custom logic

User Controls

Besides HTML server controls, Web server controls, and validation controls, you can also create your own controls by embedding Web Forms controls. These controls are called *custom controls*. You create custom controls when the available controls can't provide the functionality you need. For example, if you want to create a data grid control with check boxes, combo boxes, calendars, and date controls, you can create a custom control derived from the available controls and then write the additional functionality.

Server Controls and the .NET Framework Library

The .NET Framework library provides the System.Web and its 15 supporting namespaces to define Web classes. These namespaces reside in the

System.Web.dll assembly. Before you use any Web namespaces, though, you need to add a reference to the System.Web.dll assembly and include the required namespace in the application. Some major namespaces of the Web series are System.Web, System.Web.UI, System.Web.UI.HtmlControls, System.Web.UI.WebControls, and System.Web.Services.

The System.Web Namespace

The System.Web namespace contains browser- and server-related classes and interfaces. For example, the HTTPRequest and HTTPResponse classes provide functionality to make requests for HTTP to retrieve and post data on the server through a browser. The HttpApplication class defines the functionality of an ASP.NET application. This namespace also contains the HttpCookie and HttpCookieCollection classes for manipulating cookies. The HttpFileCollection class provides access to and organizes files uploaded by a client. You can use the HttpWriter class to write to the server through HttpResponse.

The System.Web.UI Namespace

The System.Web.UI namespace contains classes and interfaces that enable you to develop Web-based GUI applications similar to Windows GUI applications. This namespace provides classes to create Web Forms pages and controls. The control is the mother of all Web control classes and provides methods and properties for HTML, Web, or user controls. The Page class represents a Web page requested by the server in an ASP.NET application. It also has classes for data binding with the data-bound controls such as DataGrid and DataList. You'll see these classes in the examples in this chapter. In addition to these classes, it also includes state management, templates, and validation-related classes.

The System.Web.UI.HtmlControls Namespace

This namespace contains HTML control classes, which I've discussed in the "HTML Server Controls" section of this chapter. Some of these namespace classes are HtmlButton, HtmlControl, HtmlForm, HtmlImage, HtmlInputText, HtmlTable, and so on.

The System.Web.UI.WebControls Namespace

This namespace contains classes related to server controls and their supporting classes, as discussed in the "Web Server Controls" section of this chapter. Some of the classes are AddRotator, Button, Calendar, CheckBox, DataGrid, DataList, DropDownList, HyperLink, Image, Label, ListBox, ListControl, Panel, Table, TableRow, and TextBox. Besides control classes, it also contains control helper classes. For example, the DataGridItem, DataGridColumn, and DataGridColumnCollection classes are helper classes of the DataGrid control, and TableRow, TableCell, TableCellCollection, TableHeaderCell, and TableItemStyle are helper classes of the Table control.

The System.Web.Services Namespace

A Web service is an application that sits and runs on the Web server. System.Web.Service and its three helper namespaces— System.Web.Service.Description, System.Web.Service.Discovery, and System.Web.Service.Protocol—provides classes to build Web services. Chapter 8 covers Web services in more detail.

Why Are Web Forms Controls Called Server-Side Controls?

Microsoft's .NET Framework consists of powerful Web controls. By using these Web controls you can write powerful Web GUI applications similar to desktop applications. You can either write code for these controls manually or by using VS .NET, which supports the *drag-and-drop* design-time feature. In other words, you can drag and drop Web Forms controls onto a Web form, set properties by right-clicking on a control, and even write event handlers by double-clicking on the control as you'd do in Windows GUI applications such as Visual Basic.

When a client (a Web browser) makes a call for a Web control such as a Button or a DataGrid, the runat="Server" (discussed later in more detail) tells the Web server that the controls will be executed on the server and they'll send HTML data to the client at run-time after execution. Because the execution of these control events, methods, and attributes happens on the server, these controls are *server-side* Web controls. The main functionality of these controls includes rendering data from the server to the client and event handling. (The controls fire events and handle those events.)

Adding Server Side Controls to a Web Form

You have two ways to add server controls to a Web form (also referred as a *Web page*). You can either use the VS .NET IDE to add server controls or you can add controls manually by typing code using the <asp:...> syntax.

Adding Server Control Using VS .NET

Adding server controls using VS .NET is pretty simple. As you have seen in the "Developing Your First ASP.NET Web Application" section of this chapter, you create a new ASP.NET Application project, open the toolbox, drag and drop controls from the toolbox, set properties, and write event handlers for the control.

Adding Server Controls Using ASP.NET Syntax

The other method of adding server controls to an application is that you write the code manually. VS .NET writes the code in the background for you when you drop a control from the toolbox to a Web form.

To add server controls manually, you create a text file and save it with an .aspx extension. .NET utilizes XML tags to write server controls. A tag should follow XML syntaxes. Every ASP.NET control starts with asp: and a control name. For example, the following line creates a text box control:

```
<asp:textbox id=TextBox1 runat="Server" Text=""></asp:textbox>
```

In this line, I created a text box server control. Every control has a unique ID. In this sample the ID is TextBox1. The runat="Server" attribute represents that the control will run on the server.

The following code shows that you can write the same code without the closing tag:

```
<asp:textbox id=Textbox1 runat="Server" />
```

Listing 7-4 shows the ASP.NET version of your first ASP.NET application (from Figure 7-12). You can see the ASP.NET version using the HTML mode of the designer.

As you can see from Listing 7-4, asp:Button, asp:TextBox, and asp:ListBox are three server controls added using ASP.NET. In Listing 7-4, you'll see some unfamiliar items such as <%@Page, language, and codebehind. The <%@Page language is a page directive, which defines the language you're using in the page. You can use any .NET-supported language, such as C# or VB .NET. You use the codebehind directive to separate the code from the ASP.NET page. You can define a C# or VB .NET page as codebehind, which will host the code for ASP.NET controls for the page. As you can see from Listing 7-4, WebForm1.aspx.cs is a C# class, which hosts code for the WebForm1 page.

Listing 7-4. ASP.NET version of my first ASP.NET application

```
<%@ Page language="c#" Codebehind="WebForm1.aspx.cs" AutoEventWireup="false"
Inherits="FirstWebApplication.WebForm1" %>
<!DOCTYPE HTML PUBLIC "-//W3C//DTD HTML 4.0 Transitional//EN" >
<HTML>
<HEAD>
<title>WebForm1</title>
<meta content="Microsoft Visual Studio 7.0" name="GENERATOR">
<meta content="C#" name="CODE_LANGUAGE">
<meta content="JavaScript" name="vs_defaultClientScript">
<meta content="http://schemas.microsoft.com/intellisense/ie5"
name="vs_targetSchema">
</HEAD>
<body>
<form id="Form1" method="post" runat="server">
<P>
<asp:Button id="Button1" style="Z-INDEX: 101; LEFT: 20px;
 POSITION: absolute; TOP: 82px" runat="server" Text="Add "
 Width="86px" ForeColor="Yellow" BackColor="Blue"
 Font-Names="Verdana" Font-Bold="True">
 </asp:Button>

<asp:TextBox id="TextBox1" style="Z-INDEX: 102; LEFT:
127px; POSITION: absolute; TOP: 81px" runat="server"
Width="198px" Height="32px" BackColor="#FFE0C0"
BorderStyle="Groove">
</asp:TextBox>

<asp:ListBox id="ListBox1" style="Z-INDEX: 103; LEFT:
21px; POSITION: absolute; TOP: 132px" runat="server"
Width="310px" Height="209px" BackColor="#C0FFC0">
</asp:ListBox>

<FONT size="5"><STRONG>My First ASP.NET Application</STRONG>
</FONT></P>
<P><FONT face="Verdana" color="#ff3366" size="2"><STRONG>
Click Add button to add contents of text box to the list box.
</STRONG></FONT></P>
```

```
</form>
</body>
</HTML>
```

Data Binding in ASP.NET

Web Forms provides many controls that support data binding. You can connect these controls to ADO.NET components such as a `DataView`, `DataSet`, or a `DataViewManager` at design-time as well as at run-time. Data binding in Web Forms works in the same way as it does in the Windows Forms with a few exceptions. For example, to bind a dataset to a `DataGrid`, you call the `DataBind` method of the `DataGrid` control. I'll discuss all this in a moment. First let's see some basics of data-bound controls.

In this section I'll discuss data binding and how it works in ASP.NET.

Data-Bound Controls

ASP.NET provides a rich set of data-bound server-side controls. These controls are easy to use and provide a Rapid Application Development (RAD) Web development. You can categorize these controls in two groups: single-item data-bound controls and multi-item data-bound controls.

You use the single-item data-bound controls to display the value of a single item of a database table. These controls don't provide direct binding with the data source. The highlighted part of Figure 7-20 shows an *item* of a database table. You use the `Text`, `Caption`, or `Value` property of these controls to show the data of a field.

Mahesh	234, G. Road	12398
Mike	5443, NY	89433
AJ	P. Rd	54323

Figure 7-20. An item

Examples of single-item data-bound controls are textboxes, buttons, labels, images, and so on.

You use the multi-item data-bound controls to display the entire table or a partial table. These controls provide direct binding to the data source. You use the `DataSource` property of these controls to bind a database table to these controls (see Figure 7-21).

Mahesh	234, G. Road	12398
Mike	5443, NY	89433
AJ	P. Rd	54323

Figure 7-21. Multi-item controls

Some examples of multi-item data-bound controls are DataGrid, ListBox, DataList, DropDownList, and so on. Figure 7-22 shows some of the data-bound controls.

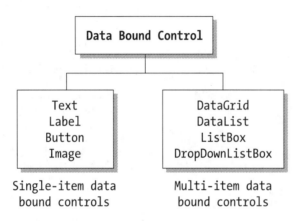

Figure 7-22. Data-bound controls

In ASP.NET, you create these controls using a `<asp:controlName>` tag. Table 7-4 describes some common data-bound server-side controls.

Table 7-4. ASP.NET Data-Bound Controls

CONTROL	ASP.NET CODE	DESCRIPTION
DataGrid	`<asp:DataGrid>`	Displays a database (through ADO.NET) in a scrollable grid format and supports selection, adding, updating, sorting, and paging
DataList	`<asp:DataList>`	Displays data in templates and style format
ListBox	`<asp:ListBox>`	Displays list box, which can be associated to ADO.NET data fields to display data in a list format

(continued)

Table 7-4. ASP.NET Data-Bound Controls (continued)

CONTROL	ASP.NET CODE	DESCRIPTION
DropDownList	`<asp:DropDownList>`	Displays DropDownList control, which can be used to display ADO.NET data source data in a drop-down combo box format
CheckBox	`<asp:CheckBox>`	Displays single check box, which can be connected to an item of the ADO.NET data source
CheckBoxList	`<asp:CheckBoxList>`	Displays list of check boxes that can be connected to the ADO.NET data source
Repeater	`<asp:Repeater>`	Displays a templated data-bound list
TextBox	`<asp:TextBox>`	Displays a text box, which can be used to display ADO.NET using its `Text` property

DataGrid and DataList Controls

A DataGrid control is one of the most powerful Web controls. By using just a DataGrid control, you can write full-fledged Web applications for your Web site. In this section, you'll learn all about the DataGrid methods and properties. The following examples are heavily based on this control.

You can use a DataGrid control to display tabular data. It also provides the ability to insert, update, sort, and scroll the data. Using and binding a DataGrid is easy with the help of the ADO.NET datasets. This grid is capable of auto-generating the columns and rows depending on which data you're connecting.

Another control worth mentioning is the DataList control. A DataList control provides a list view of the data from a data source. These controls work similarly.

DataGrid and DataList controls have similar properties. Table 7-5 describes some of the common DataGrid properties.

Table 7-5. DataGrid Control Properties

PROPERTY	DESCRIPTION
AllowPaging, AllowCustomPaging	Boolean values indicate whether paging or custom paging is allowed in the grid. Syntax: AllowPaging="true"
AllowSorting	Boolean value indicates whether sorting is allowed in the grid. Syntax: AllowSorting="true"
AutoGenerateColumns	Gets or sets a value that indicates whether columns will automatically be created for each bound data field. Syntax: AutoGenerateColumns="true"
BackColor, ForeColor, Font	Sets the background color, foreground color, and font of the grid control. Syntax: BorderColor="black"; ForeColor="green"; Font-Name="Verdana"; Font-Size="10pt"
BackImageUrl	Gets or sets the URL of an image to display in the background of the DataGrid.
BorderColor, BorderStyle, BorderWidth	Sets the border properties of the control. Syntax: BorderColor="black"; BorderWidth="1"
CellPadding, CellSpacing	Sets the cell spacing and padding. Syntax: CellPadding="10"; CellSpacing="5"
Columns	Gets a collection of column controls in the DataGrid.
CurrentPageIndex	Index of the currently displayed page.
DataKeyField	Primary key field in the data source.
DataSource	Fills the grid with the data. Syntax: DataGrid1.DataSource = ds.Tables["Student"].DefaultView;
EditItemIndex	Index of the item to be edited.
EditItemStyle	Style of the item to be edited.
HeaderStyle, FooterStyle	Header and footer styles. Syntax: HeaderStyle-BackColor="#00aaaa"; FooterStyle-BackColor="#00aaaa"
GridLines	Gets or sets the grid line style. Syntax: GridLines="Vertical"

(continued)

Table 7-5. DataGrid Control Properties (continued)

PROPERTY	DESCRIPTION
`Height, Width`	Width and height of the control.
`ID`	ID of the control.
`Page`	Returns the Page object that contains the current control. Syntax: `Page.DataBind();`
`PageCount, PageSize`	Returns the total number of pages and number of items in a page to be displayed. Syntax: `NumPages = ItemsGrid.PageCount; Items = ItemsGrid.PageCount`
`SelectedIndex`	Index of the currently selected item.
`SelectedItem`	Returns the selected item in the DataGrid.
`ShowFooter, ShowHeader`	Shows header and footer. Syntax: `ShowFooter="true";; ShowHeader="true";`
`UniqueID`	Returns the unique ID for a control.
`VirtualItemCount`	Total number of items on the page when `AllowCustomPaging` is true.

Setting DataGrid Control Properties at Design-Time

In VS .NET, you can set the DataGrid control's properties at design-time by right-clicking on the control and selecting the Properties menu item. This displays the Properties window (see Figure 7-23).

Figure 7-23. DataGrid properties

Most of these properties should look familiar to you by now. You can set the DataSource property to a data view, dataset, data view manager, or a data reader. The DataMember property represents a column of a data table if you want to display only one column in the control.

AutoFormat

Besides the general properties of a datagrid, in Figure 7-23, you see two links: Auto Format and Property Builder. The Auto Format option provides you with predefined formats for rows, columns, headers, footers, and so on (see Figure 7-24).

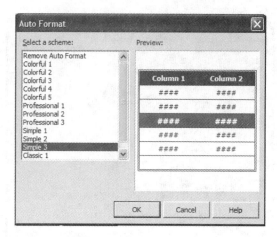

Figure 7-24. DataGrid's Auto Format dialog box

Property Builder

The Property Builder option launches the properties dialog box. The first property page is General, as shown in Figure 7-25. This page lets you set a DataSource name at design-time. For example, if you have a DataView control, you can set it as the DataSource property of a grid.

If you want to add headers and footers to the DataGrid control, you can set them by checking the Show Header and Show Footer check boxes on this page. The Allow Sorting check box enables sorting in a DataGrid control.

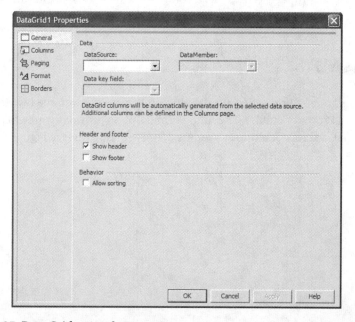

Figure 7-25. DataGrid general properties

Columns Property Page

By default, a DataGrid control adds columns at run-time depending upon the DataSource property of the grid. By using the Columns property page, you can add DataGrid columns at design-time by unchecking the Create Columns Automatically at Run Time check box (see Figure 7-26).

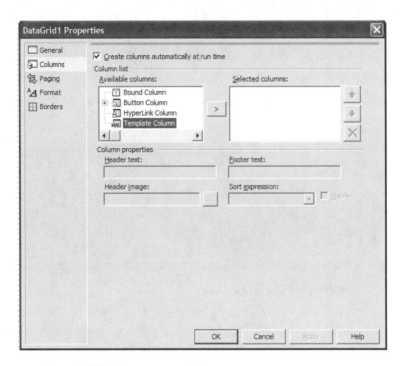

Figure 7-26. DataGrid Columns properties page

As you can see in Figure 7-26, you can even add DataGrid columns as a button, a hyperlink, or a template column.

Paging Property Page

The Paging property page enables the paging feature in the grid control. In other words, this feature allows you to set the number of records displayed per page in a data grid control. For example, if a data grid control has 50 records and you set page size to 10, the data grid will show all 50 records in five pages. The Paging property page also allows you to navigate to the first page, next page, previous page, last page, and even to a particular page number by selecting the mode of navigation for navigating pages. You can either display links to the previous and next pages or display specific page numbers (see Figure 7-27).

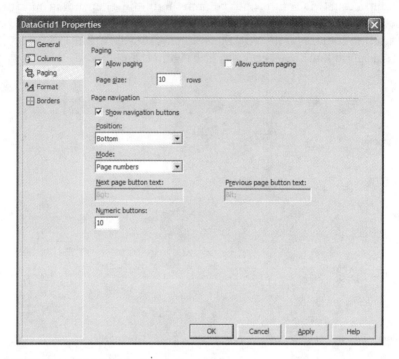

Figure 7-27. DataGrid Paging properties page

Format Property Page

If you don't want to use the Auto Format option, you can use the Format page. This page enables you to set the color and font of a DataGrid control. In fact, you can set the color and the font of the entire grid, headers, footers, and pages (see Figure 7-28).

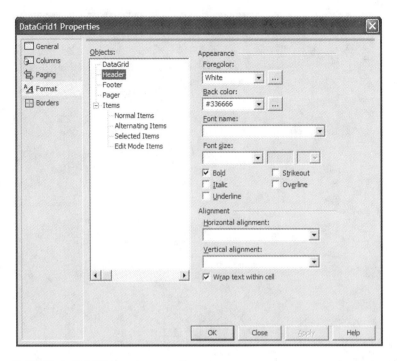

Figure 7-28. DataGrid Format properties page

Borders Property Page

The Borders page enables you to set the border, color, font, cell padding and spacing, and type of lines in the grid (see Figure 7-29).

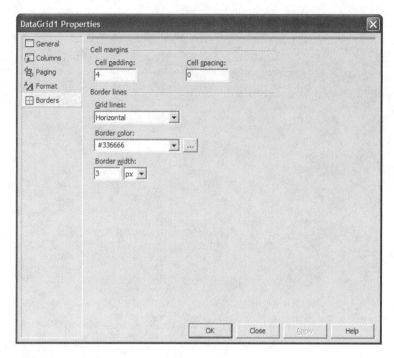

Figure 7-29. DataGrid Border properties page

You'll see how to set these properties in the sample applications throughout this chapter.

Binding Web Forms Controls at Design-Time

In the "Developing Your First ADO.NET Application" section, you saw how to bind data to Web Forms controls (ListBox and DataGrid, specifically) at run-time. Similar to Windows Forms, Web Forms also support design-time data binding. Design-time data binding helps you develop database applications with writing a few lines of code.

Binding data-bound controls at design-time using data adapters and other ADO.NET components is easy. There are many ways to create data adapters at design-time. See Chapter 4 for more details.

In this sample application, you're going to use the Data Adapter Configuration Wizard to create a data adapter. If you don't remember how to use the Data Adapter Configuration Wizard, see Chapter 4. In this example, like always, I'll use the Northwind Access 2000 database and the OleDb data provider.

Create a Data Adapter

The first step is to drag and drop an OleDbDataAdapter component from the tool-box's Data tab. As you drop the OleDbDataAdapter on the page, the Data Adapter Configuration Wizard pops up on the screen. You then follow these simple steps: At the Generate the SQL Statements page, select the EmployeeID, FirstName, LastName, Title, City, and Address fields from the Employees table, as shown in Figure 7-30.

Figure 7-30. Generating a SQL statement using the Query Builder

The Finish button adds a data adapter and a connection object to the project. Now if you view the code of your page using the View Code option, you see the wizard has added an OleDbDataAdapter, an OleDbConnection, and four OleDbCommand variables to your project. The variables look like this:

```
protected System.Data.OleDb.OleDbDataAdapter oleDbDataAdapter1;
protected System.Data.OleDb.OleDbCommand oleDbSelectCommand1;
protected System.Data.OleDb.OleDbCommand oleDbInsertCommand1;
protected System.Data.OleDb.OleDbCommand oleDbUpdateCommand1;
protected System.Data.OleDb.OleDbCommand oleDbDeleteCommand1;
protected System.Data.OleDb.OleDbConnection oleDbConnection1;
```

Generating a DataSet from Data Adapter

The next step is to generate a dataset from the data adapter. To generate a dataset from the OleDbDataAdapter, right-click on the OleDbDataAdapter, and click the Generate Dataset menu option. This option brings up the Generate Dataset page, as shown in Figure 7-31. The default name of the dataset is DataSet1.

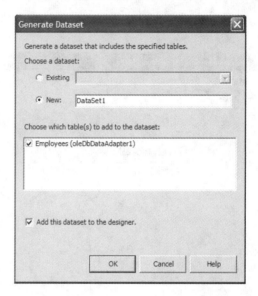

Figure 7-31. Generating a dataset using the data adapter's Generate Dataset option

This page actually generates a class called DataSet1, which comes from the DataSet class. This class looks like Figure 7-32 in Class View.

Figure 7-32. The Class View representation of the DataSet1 *class*

This action also adds one DataSet variable, named dataSet11, to your project (see Figure 7-33).

Figure 7-33. The DataSet11 *variable generated by the data adapter*

You'll be using this dataSet11 in your application; it represents a dataset having data from the Employees table (the SQL statement you saw in Figure 7-30).

Creating a DataView and Connecting It with a Dataset

The next step is to connect the dataset to a data view. To do so, drop a DataView from the toolbox's Data tab onto the page and set its Table property to dataSet11.Employees, as shown in Figure 7-34.

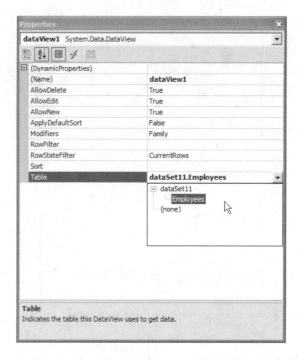

Figure 7-34. Setting the Table *property of a* DataView

Dropping a data view control to the page adds a data view control named as dataView1.

Binding a DataGrid

Now set the data grid control's DataSource property to the data view. I set DataGrid.DataSource property to dataView1, as shown in Figure 7-35.

Figure 7-35. Setting the DataGrid's DataSource *property*

Filling DataSet

You're almost there. Now the only thing you need to do is to call the data adapter's Fill method and fill the dataset, and you're all set. Call the oldDbDataAdapter1.Fill method with dataSet11 as the only argument on the Page_Load event and then call the DataGrid1.DataBind method to bind data grid with the data. Listing 7-5 shows how do to this.

Listing 7-5. Filling the DataSet *from* DataAdapter

```
private void Page_Load(object sender, System.EventArgs e)
{
        // Put user code to initialize the page here
        oleDbDataAdapter1.Fill(dataSet11);
        DataGrid1.DataBind();
}
```

Now run the project. The output of the project looks like Figure 7-36.

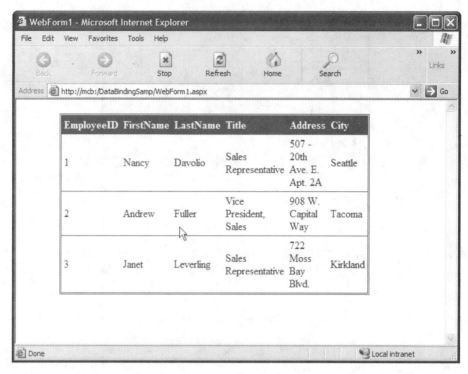

Figure 7-36. Viewing data in a data grid using the design-time data binding method

As you can see from the previous discussion, by writing only two lines of code, you've developed a database application.

Creating a Guest Book in ASP.NET

Today, a guest book is one of the basic requirements of a Webmaster to gather information from a Web site about its visitors. In this example, I'll show you how to create a guest book using ASP.NET and C#. In this application, I'll use a Microsoft Access 2000 database to store the data submitted by site visitors. The database's name is GuestBook.mdb. You can create this database in Access 2000. This database has only one table, Guest. Figure 7-37 shows the table schema. As you can see, ID is a unique autonumber field. The Name, Address, Email, and Comments fields represent the name, address, e-mail address, and comments of a visitor.

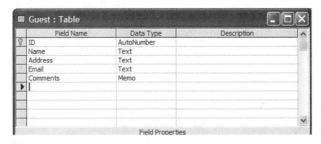

Figure 7-37. Table schema of Guest table of GuestBook.mdb

This is a simple tutorial that will guide you through creating a guest book for your Web site step by step.

To create a guest book, first you create an ASP.NET Web Application project using the Visual C# ➢ Web Application template from the available templates, as shown in Figure 7-38.

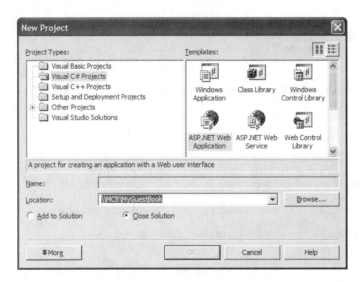

Figure 7-38. Creating the MyGuestBook ASP.NET Web Application project

Default Web Form: MyGuestBook.aspx

When you create a new Web Application project, the wizard adds one default Web form to your project called WebForm1.aspx. You can see this page when you run your application. In this application, I've renamed WebForm1.aspx to MyGuestBook.aspx. You can rename a page by right-clicking on the .aspx file in the Solution Explorer and selecting the Rename option, as shown in Figure 7-39.

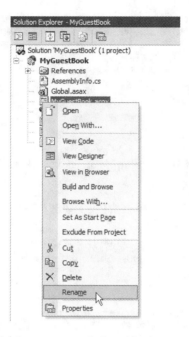

Figure 7-39. Renaming WebForm.aspx *to* MyGuestBook.aspx

Next, add a few Web controls to the form. In my form, I've added the controls listed in Table 7-6.

Table 7-6. Web Controls on My Guest Book Page

CONTROL	TYPE	DESCRIPTION
NameTextBox	`<asp:TextBox>`	Name text box
AddressTextBox	`<asp:TextBox>`	Address text box
EmailTextBox	`<asp:TextBox>`	Email text box
CommentsTextBox	`<asp:TextBox>`	Comments text box
Button1	`<asp:Button>`	Button control saves data to the database and calls Thanks.aspx
Button2	`<asp:Button>`	Calls ViewGuestBook.aspx
Label1–Label4	`<asp:Label>`	Four label controls

As you can see from Table 7-6, I added four text boxes, two buttons, and four labels and renamed them accordingly by setting each one's properties. For example, I set the CommentsTextBox control's `TextMode` property to `Multiple`. By changing the properties of the controls, `MyGuestBook.aspx` form looks like Figure 7-40.

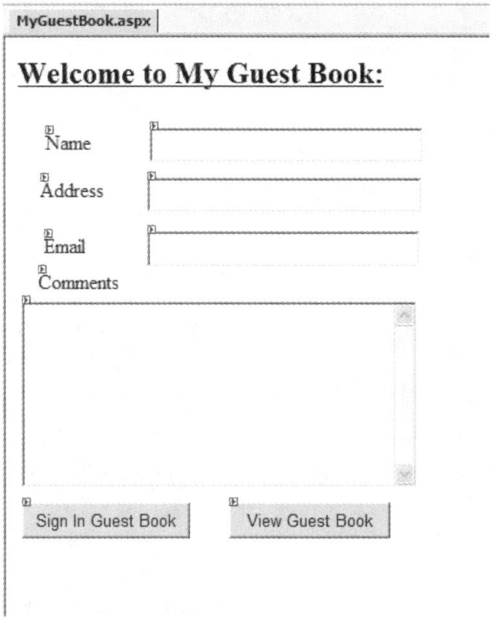

Figure 7-40. My Guest book submission page

Now double-click on the Sign In Guest Book button and write the code in Listing 7-6.

Listing 7-6. Source code for adding guest data to the database

```
private void Button1_Click(object sender, System.EventArgs e)
        {
            // set Access connection and select strings
            string strDSN = "Provider=Microsoft.Jet.OLEDB.4.0;"+
                "Data Source=C:\\GuestBook.mdb";
            string strSQL = "INSERT INTO Guest"+
                "(Name, Address, Email, Comments )"+
                "VALUES('"+NameTextBox.Text.ToString()+"','"
                +AddressTextBox.Text.ToString() +"','"
                +EmailTextBox.Text.ToString()
                +"','"+CommentsTextBox.Text.ToString()+"')" ;
```

```
// create OleDbDataAdapter
OleDbConnection myConn = new OleDbConnection(strDSN);

// Create OleDbCommand and call ExecuteNonQuery to execute
// a SQL statement

OleDbCommand myCmd = new OleDbCommand(strSQL, myConn );
try
{
    myConn.Open();
    myCmd.ExecuteNonQuery();
}
catch (Exception exp)
{
    Console.WriteLine("Error: {0}", exp.Message);
}
myConn.Close();

// Open Thanks.aspx page after adding entries to the guest book
Response.Redirect("Thanks.aspx");
}
```

As you can see from Listing 7-6, you write the data entered into the Web form to an Access database. My database resides in the C:\ root dir. Obviously, if your database is somewhere else, you need to change this database path. After writing to the database's Guest table you continue the program by opening the Thanks.aspx page in your browser. I'll discuss this page a little bit further along in the "Thanks.aspx" section.

Now add the code in Listing 7-7 to the click event of the View Guest Book button. The View Guest Book click event opens the ViewGuestBook.aspx page in the browser.

Listing 7-7. Source code for opening ViewGuestBook.aspx
```
private void Button2_Click(object sender, System.EventArgs e)
    {
        // View ViewGuestBook.aspx page
        Response.Redirect("ViewGuestBook.aspx");
    }
```

Adding Forms to the Guest Book

Other than the MyGuestBook.aspx page, I'll add two more Web forms to the project. The first form I'll add is called ViewGuestBook.aspx, and the second form is Thanks.aspx. The ViewGuestBook.aspx form reads the data from the database and enables you to view the contents in a DataGrid on a Web page. The Thanks.aspx form is, as you may have guessed, a simple "thank you" Web page shown to the guest, thanking them for registering on the site.

To add a new Web form, right-click on your project and select Add ➢ Add Web Form (see Figure 7-41).

Figure 7-41. Adding a new Web page to the project

Clicking on this menu item opens a form, which lets you pick different types of items for your project. Choose the Web Form template and type **Thanks.aspx** and then click Open. Then do the same for the ViewGuestBook.aspx page to add these two Web forms to the project (see Figures 7-42 and 7-43).

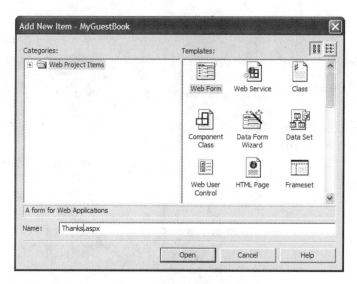

Figure 7-42. Adding Thanks.aspx *to the project*

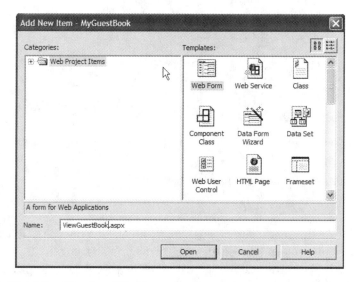

Figure 7-43. Adding ViewGuestBook.aspx *to the project*

ViewGuestBook.aspx

The ViewGuestBook.aspx form contains two controls, a DataGrid control and a button control (see Table 7-7).

Table 7-7. Web Controls of ViewGuestBook.aspx

CONTROL	TYPE	DESCRIPTION
DataGrid1	<asp:DataGrid>	Displays guest book entries from the database
Button1	<asp:button>	Navigates to the home page

The DataGrid control displays the guest book entries from the database. The code for populating the DataGrid from the database is on the Page_Load event of the form.

I've used OleDbDataAdapter and DataSet to get the data from the database. As discussed, the DataSource property of the DataGrid takes care of rest. You just need to set the DataSource property as the DefaultView of the DataSet, like so:

```
DataGrid1.DataSource = ds.Tables["Guest"].DefaultView;
```

Listing 7-8 shows the Page_Load event code.

Listing 7-8. PageLoad *event handler code of* ViewGuestBook.aspx

```
private void Page_Load(object sender, System.EventArgs e)
{
        // Create a connection object
        OleDbConnection conn = new OleDbConnection();
        conn.ConnectionString =
            "Provider=Microsoft.Jet.OLEDB.4.0;"+
            "Data Source=C:\\GuestBook.mdb";
        string sql = "SELECT * FROM Guest";

        // Create a data adapter
        OleDbDataAdapter da = new OleDbDataAdapter(sql, conn);

        // Create and fill dataset and bind it to the data grid
        DataSet ds = new DataSet();
        da.Fill(ds, "Guest");
        DataGrid1.DataSource = ds.Tables["Guest"].DefaultView;
        DataGrid1.DataBind();

}
```

The button-click event handler opens the home page, and the code looks like the following:

```
private void Button1_Click(object sender, System.EventArgs e)
{
Response.Redirect("http://www.c-sharpcorner.com/");
}
```

Thanks.aspx

The Thanks.aspx page is merely a confirmation page that the user receives after adding data to the guest book. It has two buttons and a simple message. The buttons are responsible for navigating you through the ViewGuestBook.aspx page or the site home page. Table 7-8 lists the controls for Thanks.aspx.

Table 7-8. Controls of Thanks.aspx *Page*

CONTROL	TYPE	DESCRIPTION
ViewGuestBookButton	`<asp:button>`	Calls ViewGuestBook.aspx page
GoHomeButton	`<asp:button>`	Navigates the browser to the site home page

The Thanks.aspx page looks like Figure 7-44.

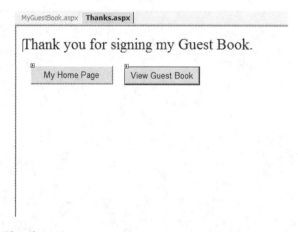

Figure 7-44. Thank you!

Listing 7-9 shows the My Home Page button and the View Guest Book button-click code. As you can see from the listing, the My Home Page button click calls http://www.c-sharpcorner.com. Obviously, you can call your Web site's home page. The View Guest Book button click calls ViewGuestBook.aspx.

Listing 7-9. The Go Home and View Guest Book buttons' code

```
private void ViewGuestBookButton_Click(object sender, System.EventArgs e)
    {
        Response.Redirect("ViewGuestBook.aspx");
    }


    private void GoHomeButton_Click(object sender, System.EventArgs e)
    {
        Response.Redirect("http://www.c-sharpcorner.com/");
    }
```

> **NOTE**   *Don't forget to add a reference to the* System.Data.OleDb *namespace in the* ViewGuestBook.aspx *and* MyGuestBook.aspx *pages*

Compiling and Running the Guest Book Project

Now you're all set to compile and run the project. You should be able to do everything that you usually do in a guest book. The output of the program looks like Figure 7-45.

Figure 7-45. Welcome to my guest book

As you can see from Figure 7-45, I added a new record by filling data in the fields and clicking the Sign In Guest Book button. The next page displayed is the Thanks page, which looks like Figure 7-46.

Figure 7-46. The Thanks page of the guest book

Now, if you view the Guest Book, it looks like Figure 7-47. As you'll notice, I have couple of extra records in my guest book.

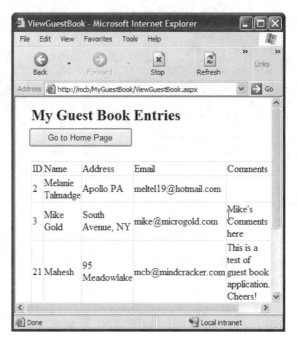

Figure 7-47. My guest book entries

Paging in DataGrid Control

As I discussed earlier in the "Paging Property Page" section, the Paging page of
the Property Builder for a DataGrid control lets you set a DataGrid's paging properties. In this example I'll show you how you can write applications with paging
and navigate through pages in a DataGrid control. You can set a DataGrid's paging properties in the Property Builder at design-time as well as programmatically.
In this section I'll walk you through both methods.

> **NOTE** *To test my samples, I'll use the Northwind database.*

To test this application, create an ASP.NET Web application and add
a DataGrid control to the Web form from the toolbox.

Enabling Paging at Design-Time

You can set paging options at design-time by right-clicking on the DataGrid's Properties menu item. The Paging page looks like Figure 7-48. This page lets you set the number of rows per page and the type of navigation you want to show. If you want to provide your own custom paging, click on the Allow Custom Paging check box.

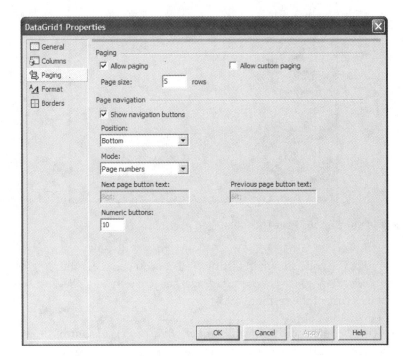

i.e., put 1 2 3 4 @ the bottom of the page.

Figure 7-48. DataGrid paging properties

As you can see from Figure 7-48, I set the Page Size to 5 rows and Mode to Page Numbers. So, when a browser displays the first page of a table in the DataGrid, it will show five rows. Additionally, it will display page numbers at the bottom of the page so that users can navigate through the pages. The next step for enabling paging in a data grid is to write a PageIndexChanged event handler. You can add the PageIndexChanged handler from the data grid's Properties window, as shown in Figure 7-49.

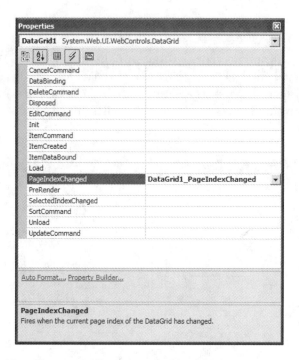

Figure 7-49. Adding the PageIndexChanged *event handler*

Now write the code shown in Listing 7-10. As you can see, I set
DataGrid.CurrentPageIndex as DataGridPageChangedEventArgs's NewPageIndex.
VS .NET takes care of the rest for you.

Listing 7-10. The PageIndexChanged *handler of the data grid control*

```
private void DataGrid1_PageIndexChanged(object source,
System.Web.UI.WebControls.DataGridPageChangedEventArgs e){
DataGrid1.CurrentPageIndex = e.NewPageIndex;
DataGrid1.DataBind();
}
```

The next thing I'm going to do is to fill data from a database. Listing 7-11
shows the code that fills the data from the Northwind database on the form load.
The code should look familiar. I created a connection and data adapter objects
and filled a dataset from the Employees table.

Listing 7-11. Source code of DataGrid *paging sample*

```
private void Page_Load(object sender, System.EventArgs e)
        {
            // Create a Connection Object
            string ConnectionString = @"Provider=Microsoft.Jet.OLEDB.4.0;"+
```

```
            "Data Source=c:\\Northwind.mdb";
        OleDbConnection conn = new OleDbConnection(ConnectionString);

        // Open the connection
        if( conn.State != ConnectionState.Open)
            conn.Open();
        // create a data adapter
        OleDbDataAdapter da = new OleDbDataAdapter
            ("SELECT FirstName, LastName, Title FROM Employees", conn);

        // Create and fill a dataset
        DataSet ds = new DataSet();
        da.Fill(ds);

        // Bind dataset to the control

        DataGrid1.DataSource = ds;
        DataGrid1.DataBind();

        // Close the connection
        if( conn.State == ConnectionState.Open)
            conn.Close();

    }
```

Now if you run the program, you'll see that the first page looks like Figure 7-50.

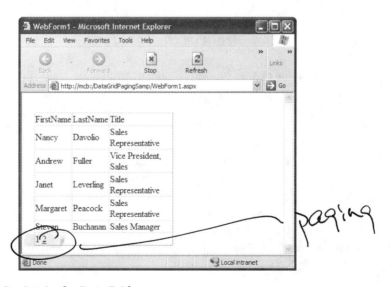

Figure 7-50. Paging in the DataGrid

As you can see from Figure 7-50, there are five rows displayed in the grid and there are two pages available. If you click on the 2 link, the result looks like Figure 7-51.

Figure 7-51. The second page of DataGrid paging sample

Enabling Paging Programmatically

You can also enable paging programmatically from your .aspx file. Listing 7-12 shows the HTML code for a data grid control and its properties.

Listing 7-12. HTML view of DataGrid

```
<asp:DataGrid id="DataGrid1" style="Z-INDEX: 101; LEFT: 204px;
POSITION: absolute; TOP: 174px" runat="server" Width="279px"
Height="212px" BorderStyle="None" BorderWidth="1px"
BorderColor="#CC9966" BackColor="White" CellPadding="4"
PageSize="5" AllowPaging="True">
<FooterStyle ForeColor="#330099" BackColor="#FFFFCC"></FooterStyle>
<HeaderStyle Font-Bold="True" ForeColor="#FFFFCC"
```

```
BackColor="#990000"></HeaderStyle>
<PagerStyle HorizontalAlign="Center" ForeColor="#330099"
BackColor="#FFFFCC"></PagerStyle>
<SelectedItemStyle Font-Bold="True" ForeColor="#663399"
BackColor="#FFCC66"></SelectedItemStyle>
<ItemStyle ForeColor="#330099" BackColor="White"></ItemStyle>
</asp:DataGrid>
```

The general paging properties include AllowPaging and PageSize. Both are pretty self-explanatory. Basically, `AllowPaging` enables paging, and `PageSize` sets the number of pages in a page. You can set these properties programmatically, as shown in Listing 7-13.

Listing 7-13. Setting the AllowPaging, PageSize, *and* AllowSorting *properties*
```
DataGrid1.AllowPaging = true;
DataGrid1.PageSize = 5;
DataGrid1.AllowSorting = true;
```

Like the Property Builder, you can choose to have either the numeric page mode or the previous/next page mode. The numeric mode option shows you the number of pages to move to the previous or next pages (1, 2, and so on), and the previous/next mode displays angle brackets (< and >) to move to previous and next pages. Listing 7-14 shows how to set the DataGrid's pager style modes to the Numeric and NextPrev styles.

Listing 7-14. Setting DataGrid's PagerStyle *modes*
```
DataGrid1.PagerStyle.Mode = PagerMode.NumericPages;
DataGrid1.PagerStyle.Mode = PagerMode.NextPrev;
```

You can even change the text of your previous/next mode from angle brackets to the text you want (see Listing 7-15).

Listing 7-15. Setting DataGrid's PageStyle *text*
```
DataGrid1.PagerStyle.NextPageText = "Go to Next Page";
DataGrid1.PagerStyle.PrevPageText = "Go to Prev Page";
```

If you want to put your own images for the next and previous buttons, you can do that as well. Just use the simple HTML <IMG> tag (see Listing 7-16).

Listing 7-16. Setting an image as DataGrid's next and previous page text
```
DataGrid1.PagerStyle.NextPageText = "<img srv=next.gif>";
DataGrid1.PagerStyle.PrevPageText = "<img srv=prev.gif>";
```

Adding, Editing, and Deleting Data in Web Forms

In this example, I'll show you various database operations such as adding, updating, and deleting data from a database using ADO.NET. I've used a Microsoft Access 2000 database in this application to add, edit, and delete data; however, working with other data sources such as SQL Server is similar to Microsoft Access. The only difference is creating data adapters objects, which I discussed in Chapter 4.

Creating the Application

This application is a Web application developed in Visual C# (see Figure 7-52). It displays the contents of the Employees table of the Northwind database. You can set the color, fonts, headers, and footers of a DataGrid by using its Properties window at design-time as well as at run-time.

Besides the GridControl, the page has three buttons, three text boxes, and three labels. The Add button adds a record to the database, the Edit button updates a record, and the Delete button deletes a record from the database.

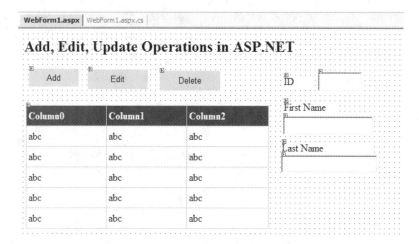

Figure 7-52. Adding, editing, and deleting in an ASP.NET application

Creating the Data Source

Similar to the previous samples, I'll use the same Northwind database in this application. Listing 7-17 shows the code for the `FillDataGrid` method. As you can see, you create a data adapter and a dataset and then fill the dataset using the

Fill method of the data adapter. After that you set the DataSource property of the data grid and call the DataGrid.DataBind method.

Listing 7-17. The FillDataGrid *method to fill a datagrid*

```
private void FillDataGrid()
{
        // Creating a connection
        OleDbConnection conn = new OleDbConnection();
        conn.ConnectionString = "Provider=Microsoft.Jet.OLEDB.4.0;"+
            "Data Source = C:\\Northwind.mdb";
        string sql = "SELECT EmployeeID, FirstName,"+
            "LastName, Title FROM Employees";

        conn.Open();

        // Creating a data adapter
        OleDbDataAdapter da = new OleDbDataAdapter(sql, conn);



        // Create a DataSet Object
        DataSet ds = new DataSet();

        // Fill DataSet with the data
        da.Fill(ds, "Employees");
        DataGrid1.DataSource =  ds.Tables["Employees"].DefaultView;
        DataGrid1.DataBind();

        conn.Close();
}
```

Executing SQL Queries

As discussed in Chapter 3 and Chapter 5, you can use the OleDbCommand or SqlCommand object's Execute and ExecuteNonQuery methods to execute SQL queries. If you want to add, update, or delete data from a database, executing SQL queries is one of the easiest ways to do so. It's fast and requires a minimum of code to write.

You use the OleDbCommand object to execute a SQL command. The Execute and ExecuteNonQuery methods of OleDbCommand execute a SQL query. The OleDbCommand.Execute method executes the CommandText property and returns data in the OleDbDataReader object. As you can see from Listing 7-18, the CreateMyOleDbCommand method executes a SQL statement.

Listing 7-18. Calling the Execute *method to execute a SQL statement*

```
public void CreateMyOleDbCommand(string sqlQuery, string myCon)
{
    OleDbCommand cmd = new OleDbCommand(sqlQuery, AdoCon);
    OleDbCommand myCom = (OleDbCommand) cmd.Clone();
    OleDbDataReader reader;
    myCom.ActiveConnection.Open();
    myCom.Execute(out reader);
}
```

Listing 7-19 shows how to construct OleDbCommand and set the OleDbCommand.CommandText property for performing a SELECT from the database's Employees table.

Listing 7-19. The Commandtext *property of the command object*

```
OleDbCommand cmd = new OleDbCommand();
cmd.CommandText = "SELECT * FROM Employees";
```

The OleDbCommand.ExecuteNonQuery method executes CommandText and doesn't return any data. The logical time to use this method is when you're writing to the database or executing SQL statements that don't return any data (see Listing 7-20).

Listing 7-20. Calling the ExecuteNonQuery *method*

```
public void CreateMyOleDbCommand(string sqlQuery, string AdoCon)
{
    OleDbCommand cmd = new OleDbCommand(sqlQuery, AdoCon);
    cmd.ActiveConnection.Open();
    cmd.ExecuteNonQuery();
}
```

> **NOTE** *Listing 7-21 shows the complete code for using the* ExecuteNonQuery *method to execute SQL statements.*

In this example, I used the OleDbCommnad.ExecuteNonQuery() method to execute the INSERT, UPDATE, and DELETE SQL queries because I don't need to return any data. My ExecuteSQL method wraps the execution of a SQL query (see Listing 7-21).

Listing 7-21. The ExecuteSQL *method executes a SQL statement using the* ExecuteNonQuery *method*

```
public bool ExecuteSQL ( string strSQL )
{
            // Creating a connection
            OleDbConnection conn = new OleDbConnection();
            conn.ConnectionString = "Provider=Microsoft.Jet.OLEDB.4.0;"+
                "Data Source = C:\\Northwind.mdb";

            OleDbCommand myCmd = new OleDbCommand( strSQL, conn );

            try
            {
                conn.Open();
                myCmd.ExecuteNonQuery();
            }
            catch (Exception exp)
            {
                Console.WriteLine("SQL Query Failed! {0}", exp.Message);
                return false;
            }
            finally
            {
                // clean up here
                conn.Close();
            }
            return true;
}
```

Adding Data

The Add button adds a new record to the database and calls the FillDataGrid method, which rebinds the data source and fills the DataGrid control with the updated data. Because the ID column of the database table is AutoNumber, you don't have to enter it. You only need to enter the first name and last name. Listing 7-22 shows the Add button click event handler. As you can see, you create an INSERT SQL statement, call ExecuteSQL, and refill the data using the FillDataGrid method.

Listing 7-22. Add button click event handler

```
// Add Button click event handler
private void Button1_Click(object sender, System.EventArgs e)
{
        // Build a SQL Statement
        string SQL = "INSERT INTO Employees(FirstName, LastName)"+
        " VALUES('"+TextBox2.Text.ToString()+"', '"+
        TextBox3.Text.ToString()+ "')" ;

        // Execute SQL and refresh the data grid
        ExecuteSQL(SQL);
        FillDataGrid();
}
```

In Figure 7-53, I add a new record with first name as "Amy" and the last name as "Sue."

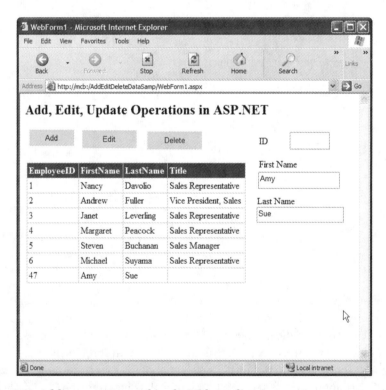

Figure 7-53. Adding a new record in the Web application

Editing Data

The Edit button updates a record corresponding to an ID. This is where you build an UPDATE...SET SQL statement and execute it by calling the ExecuteSQL method, as shown in Listing 7-23.

Listing 7-23. Updating data on the Edit button click

```
// Edit Button click event handler
private void Button2_Click(object sender, System.EventArgs e)
{
        // Build a SQL Statement
        string SQL = "UPDATE Employees SET FirstName='"+
            TextBox2.Text+"', LastName='"+TextBox3.Text
            +"' WHERE EmployeeID="+TextBox1.Text ;

        // Execute SQL and refresh the data grid
        ExecuteSQL(SQL);
        FillDataGrid();
}
```

Now to test the code, I type **Mel** in the First Name box, **Tel** in the Last Name box, and **10** in the ID box. Then I click the Edit button. The result updates the row with ID=10 and the output looks like Figure 7-54. As you can see, that record is updated as Mel Tel.

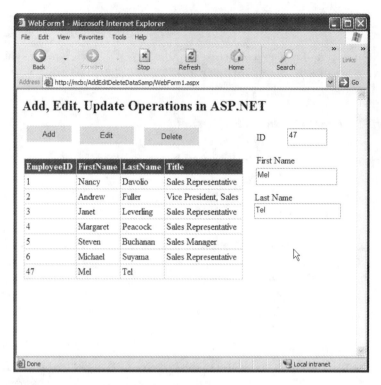

Figure 7-54. Editing records in a Web application

Deleting Data

The Delete button deletes a record corresponding with the ID from the database. I then build a DELETE SQL statement and execute it by calling the ExecuteSQL method, as shown in Listing 7-24.

Listing 7-24. Deleting data on the Delete button click

```
// Delete Button click event handler
private void Button3_Click(object sender, System.EventArgs e)
{
        // Build a SQL Statement
        string SQL = "DELETE * FROM Employees"+
            "WHERE EmployeeID= "+TextBox1.Text ;

        // Execute SQL and refresh the data grid
        ExecuteSQL(SQL);
        FillDataGrid();


}
```

To delete the newly added record, just enter 10 in the ID field or the ID of the record you want to delete and click the Delete button.

By using these insert, update and delete data operations, you can write a full-fledged database application for your Web site.

Introducing the Table Web Control

As I approach the end of this chapter, I'd like to take a quick look at one other widely used Web control: the Table control. A Table Web control creates an HTML table in simple HTML with the help of the <tr> and <td> tags.

You can use the <table>, <tr>, and <td> tags to create a table and its rows in HTML. For example, the HTML code in Listing 7-25 creates a table with two rows and three columns with their values.

Listing 7-25. HTML code for a Table control

```
<table border="1" width="39%">
  <tr>
    <td width="33%">Row1,Col1</td>
    <td width="33%">Row1,Col2</td>
    <td width="34%">Row1,Col3</td>
  </tr>
  <tr>
    <td width="33%">Row2,Col1</td>
    <td width="33%">Row2,Col2</td>
    <td width="34%">Row2,Col3</td>
  </tr>
</table>
```

In the .NET Framework, the Table class enables you to build an HTML table. The System.Web.UI.Controls namespace defines the Table class, along with the other Web controls. You can create tables in .NET using a Table control and its helper controls TableRow and TableCell. As with all Web controls, you can create a Table control at run-time as well as at design-time using the VS .NET IDE. Table 7-9 describes the Table control and its helper controls.

Table 7-9. ASP.NET Table and Its Helper Control Classes

CONTROL	CODE	DESCRIPTION
Table	`<asp:Table>`	The `System.Web.UI.Table` class encapsulates an HTML table. An HTML Table control, used to create a table with the help of `TableRow` and `TableCell`.
TableRow	`<asp:TableRow>`	The `System.Web.UI.TableRow` class encapsulates a row within a table, which later can be used to get or set row's cells values using `TableCell`.
TableCell	`<asp:TableCell>`	The `System.Web.UI.TableCell` class encapsulates a cell within a table.
TableRowCollection	`<asp:TableRowCollection>`	The `System.Web.UI.TableRowCollection` encapsulates a table row collection and is used to manage a collection of table rows such as adding a row to a collection or removing a row from it.
TableCellCollection	`<asp:TableCellCollection>`	Manages a collection of table cells such as adding a cell to a row or removing a cell from it.
TableHeaderCell	`<asp:TableHeaderCell>`	Encapsulates a table header cell.

Creating a Table at Design-Time

You can create a table at design-time as well as run-time. To add a Table control to your form at design-time, just drag and drop a Table control from the Web Control toolbox to a Web form. Then use the Properties window to add the rows and cells to the table.

The Rows property of a Table control adds rows to a table (see Figure 7-55).

Developing Web Applications Using ADO.NET

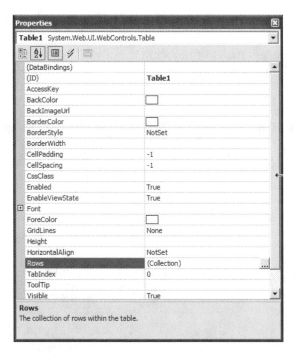

Figure 7-55. Table control properties

In this example, I added three rows to the table by using the Add button of the TableRow Collection Editor. (Clicking on the Collection of Rows property launches the TableRow Collection Editor; see Figure 7-56).

Figure 7-56. Adding rows with the TableRow Collection Editor

Now simply add cells to the rows by using the `Cells` property of a row. Use the `Text` property of a cell to add a value to the cell, and use the Add and Remove buttons of the TableCell Collection Editor to add and remove cells from a row. (You can launch the TableCell Collection Editor by clicking on the Collection of Cells property; see Figure 7-57).

Figure 7-57. TableCell Collection Editor

After taking this action, the IDE writes the ASP code for you, which looks like Listing 7-26.

Listing 7-26. ASP.NET code for a table control

```
<asp:Table id=Table2 runat="server" width="228" height="71">
<asp:TableRow>
<asp:TableCell Text="Row1,Col1"></asp:TableCell>
<asp:TableCell Text="Row1,Col2"></asp:TableCell>
<asp:TableCell Text="Row1,Col3"></asp:TableCell>
</asp:TableRow>
<asp:TableRow>
<asp:TableCell Text="Row2,Col1"></asp:TableCell>
<asp:TableCell Text="Row2,Col2"></asp:TableCell>
<asp:TableCell Text="Row2,Col3"></asp:TableCell>
</asp:TableRow>
<asp:TableRow>
```

```
<asp:TableCell Text="Row3,Col1"></asp:TableCell>
<asp:TableCell Text="Row3,Col2"></asp:TableCell>
<asp:TableCell Text="Row3,Col3"></asp:TableCell>
</asp:TableRow>
</asp:Table>
```

Creating a Table Programmatically

You can even create a table and add its cells and cell values programmatically.
First, create a table using the `<asp:Table>` tag and then add rows to it (see
Listing 7-27).

Listing 7-27. Creating a table's rows programmatically
```
<asp:Table id=Table1 runat="server" Width="439" Height="117" BackColor="#FFFFC0">
<asp:TableRow></asp:TableRow>
<asp:TableRow></asp:TableRow>
<asp:TableRow></asp:TableRow>
<asp:TableRow></asp:TableRow>
<asp:TableRow></asp:TableRow>
</asp:Table>
```

Now you add cells and their values at run-time using the `TableRow` and
`TableCell` class object (see Listing 7-28).

Listing 7-28. Adding table rows and cells programmatically
```
int rows = 3;
int cols = 2;
for (int j=0; j<rows; j++)
{
   TableRow r = new TableRow();
   for (int i=0; i<cols; i++)
   {
     TableCell c = new TableCell();
c.Controls.Add(new LiteralControl("row " +
j.ToString() + ", cell " +i.ToString()));
r.Cells.Add(c);
   }
   Table1.Rows.Add(r);
}
```

The example you saw in Listing 7-28 creates a table with three rows and two
columns. You can also add rows and columns to a table programmatically. This

program, which looks like Figure 7-58, adds rows and columns to a table at run-time based on the values entered in the text boxes. You create a Web application and add a control, two labels, and two text boxes to the page.

First, you create one <asp:Table> control to your .aspx page:

```
<asp:Table id="Table1" style="Z-INDEX: 104; LEFT: 119px;
POSITION: absolute; TOP: 291px" runat="server"></asp:Table>
```

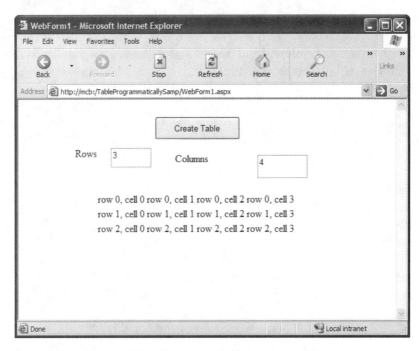

Figure 7-58. Creating a table programmatically

Next, add the code in Listing 7-29 on the button-click handler.

Listing 7-29. Button-click handler creates a table programmatically
```
public void Button1_Click (object sender, System.EventArgs e)
{
        int rows = Convert.ToInt16(TextBox1.Text);
          int cols = Convert.ToInt16(TextBox2.Text);

        for (int j=0; j<rows; j++)
        {
                TableRow r = new TableRow();
                for (int i=0; i<cols; i++)
                {
```

```
            TableCell c = new TableCell();
          c.Controls.Add(new LiteralControl("row " +
             j.ToString() +", cell " + i.ToString()));
          r.Cells.Add(c);
      }
      Table1.Rows.Add(r);
   }
}
```

Finally, run the application and enter the number of rows and the number of columns to the text boxes and then click the Create Table button to create a table.

Summary

ASP.NET is a new framework to write Web applications for Microsoft's .NET platform. ASP.NET supports a rich set of Web Forms controls. You can use these controls at run-time as well as design-time. In Visual Studio .NET, you can just drag these controls onto a Web form, set their properties and methods, and your application is ready to run on the Web.

You can also use ADO.NET components in Web Forms in the same way you use them in desktop applications. All ADO.NET components including data reader, dataset, data view, and data commands work in the same way as they would in a desktop application. ASP.NET provides many data-bound controls that you can directly bind to a data source with the help of `DataSet` and `DataView`. For example, DataGrid and ListBox are two common data-bound controls. You can use the `DataSource` property of these controls to bind to a dataset.

The DataGrid is the most versatile control among all the Web controls. By using the DataGrid control, you can write full-fledged database applications for your Web sites. The `DataTable` of the `DataSet` provides the programmer a means of working with the data in these controls. A table is a collection of rows and columns. A data table represents a database table. With the help of the `DataView` class, you can bind a data table to a DataGrid or other data-bound controls.

In next chapter I'll show you how to use ADO.NET to develop a Web service that accesses a database.

CHAPTER 8

Using Web Services with ADO.NET

WEB SERVICES PROVIDE A way to run a service on the Web and access its methods using standard protocols, including Simple Object Access Protocol (SOAP), Extensible Markup Language (XML), Web Service Description Language (WSDL), and Hypertext Transfer Protocol (HTTP). Technically, a Web service is nothing more than an application that exposes its interface to a client who wants to access the service's abilities. The uses of a Web service include validating credit cards, searching for data in a database, inserting an order into a shopping cart, and updating a guest list. The sky is the limit on what you can have your Web service do on your server. In the past, JavaBeans, ActiveX/Component Object Model (COM) controls, and other nonstandard service components handled these services, which required specialized formats to exchange data with the client. But Web services under .NET run by invoking methods in the service directly through HTTP or SOAP, so someone wanting to run your Web service from their computer at home can simply send an HTTP call to your service, passing the parameters in a standard Uniform Resource Locator (URL). I'll show you how to do this later in the chapter.

Three attributes make up a Web service:

- **Discovery**: First, you need to locate the Web service. You locate Web services through the Discovery Service Protocol. The `*.disco` file stores the protocol in your Visual Studio (VS) .NET project. This file contains references to all the Web services under your Web site's virtual directory. VS can automatically generate this file for you. The discovery file (`.vsdisco`), an XML file, is used to identify searchable paths on the Web server used by discovery process.

- **Description**: Once you've discovered your service, you need a way to tell the client what methods, classes, and so on the Web service has and what wiring protocol (SOAP, HTTP, and so on) the services are using. You do this through WSDL, an XML format. VS provides tools for generating WSDL files automatically from your services.

- **Wiring protocol**: Web services under .NET use two main protocols, HTTP-post/HTTP-get and SOAP. HTTP-post and HTTP-get enable you to send and receive information via a URL by passing and receiving name-value pair strings. Unfortunately, HTTP can only pass strings that repre sent different data types. SOAP allows you to pass a richer type of information, such as datasets.

Exploring Web Services and the .NET Framework Library

The .NET Framework class library provides four namespaces that contain Web services classes. These namespaces are System.Web.Services, System.Web.Services.Description, System.Web.Services.Discovery, and System.Web.Services.Protocol.

The System.Web.Services namespace provides classes that enable you to build and use Web services. It has four classes. The WebService class defines the optional base class for Web services, which provides direct access to an ASP .NET application. Server, Session, User, and Context are some of its properties. WebMethodAttribute, WebServiceAttribute, and WebServiceBindingAttribute are other classes of this namespace.

The System.Web.Services.Description namespace provides classes that enable you to describe a WSDL.

The System.Web.Services.Discovery namespace provides classes that enable Web service consumers to locate a Web service through discovery.

The System.Web.Services.Protocols namespace provides classes that define the protocols used to transmit data between a client and a Web service.

Creating a Web Service in VS .NET

To understand Web services better, I'll show you how to build a simple Web service. The Web service will receive an order ID and then query the Northwind database's Orders table for the correct order. It'll then return the order in a DataSet.

The first step in creating the Web service is to select File ➢ New ➢ Project and choose the ASP .NET Web Service template, as shown in Figure 8-1.

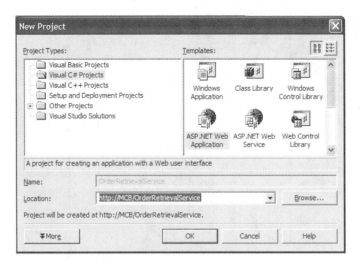

Figure 8-1. Creating a new Web service project

This creates a Web service project on the MCB Web server. By default, local-host is available as a Web server on your development machine. After the server name, you give it a project name. In this sample, the project name is OrderRetrievalService. VS .NET creates a new folder with the project name on the Web server and keeps all project files under that folder. Clicking the OK button creates the project.

If you look at the Solution Explorer, you'll notice a list of files created automatically for the project, as shown in Figure 8-2. You won't be able to see some code and resource files by default; they're hidden. You need to click on the Show All Files button of the Solution Explorer to view all the files (see Figure 8-2).

Figure 8-2. Files included in the Web service project

First, the Web.config file is an XML file containing information on how to run the service under ASP .NET. Second, the Global.asax and Global.asax.cs files enable you to handle application-level events for the service. These event handlers include event-handling pairs such as Application_Start-Application_End, Session_Start-Session_End, and Begin_Request-EndRequest. You can view Global.asax.cs by right-clicking on the Global.asax file in the Solution Explorer and choosing View Code. Next, OrderRetrievalService.vsdisco is an XML file containing information for discovery of the service. You'll actually need to generate an OrderRetrievalService.disco file for your client to see the service (more on this later).

Finally, the Service1.asmx file serves as the entry point into the service. The code behind the service, Service1.asmx.cs is where you'll place the method for retrieving the order. Right-click on the Service1.asmx file in the Solution Explorer and choose View Code from the pop-up menu, as shown in Figure 8-3.

Figure 8-3. Viewing the code in the Web service

See Listing 8-1 for the Web service code. Note that it looks like any other C# component; it has a constructor, an InitializeComponent method, and a Dispose method.

Listing 8-1. Initial Web service code in OrderRetrievalService.asmx.cs

```csharp
public class Service1 : System.Web.Services.WebService
{
        public Service1()
        {
        //CODEGEN: This call is required by the ASP.NET Web Services Designer
         InitializeComponent();
        }

        #region Component Designer generated code

        //Required by the Web Services Designer
        private IContainer components = null;

        /// <summary>
        /// Required method for Designer support - do not modify
        /// the contents of this method with the code editor.
        /// </summary>
```

```
        private void InitializeComponent()
        {
        }


        /// <summary>
        /// Clean up any resources being used.
        /// </summary>
        protected override void Dispose( bool disposing )
        {
            if(disposing && components != null)
            {
                components.Dispose();
            }
            base.Dispose(disposing);
        }

        #endregion

    // WEB SERVICE EXAMPLE
    // The HelloWorld() example service returns the string Hello World
    // To build, uncomment the following lines then save and build the project
    // To test this web service, press F5

//      [WebMethod]
//      public string HelloWorld()
//      {
//          return "Hello World";
//      }
}
```

Now I'll add database support to the Web service. Actually adding database support to a Web service is quite easy using ADO.NET. You can add ADO.NET data components to a Web service by just dragging ADO.NET components from the toolbox's Data tab to Web Forms. Similar to Windows Forms, you can also use the Server Explorer to add database components to a Web service.

As I've discussed in Chapters 3, 4, and 5, you can access different kinds of data sources in a similar fashion. The only thing you change is the data provider and the connection string.

In this example, I'll use the Access 2000 Northwind database. I simply create a connection and a data adapter to the Orders table in the Northwind database. You can do this automatically through the .NET Framework by simply dragging the Orders table from the Server Explorer onto the `Service1.asmx.cs` Design View, as shown in Figure 8-4. In fact, as you can see from the figure, you can drag any database table to the Web page.

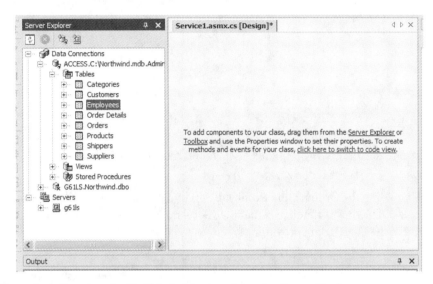

Figure 8-4. Creating the `OleDbDataAdapter` *from the Server Explorer*

Drag the Orders table to the page. This action adds a connection, data adapter, and four command objects as follows:

```
private System.Data.OleDb.OleDbCommand oleDbSelectCommand1;
private System.Data.OleDb.OleDbCommand oleDbInsertCommand1;
private System.Data.OleDb.OleDbCommand oleDbUpdateCommand1;
private System.Data.OleDb.OleDbCommand oleDbDeleteCommand1;
private System.Data.OleDb.OleDbConnection oleDbConnection1;
private System.Data.OleDb.OleDbDataAdapter oleDbDataAdapter1;
```

Figure 8-5 shows the results in Design View.

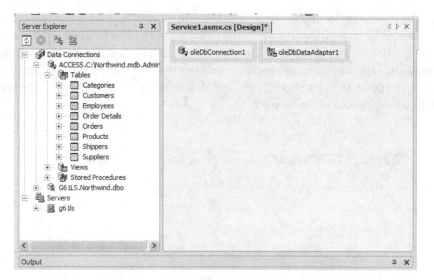

Figure 8-5. Results of dragging the Orders table from the Server Explorer

If you drag the Orders table from SQL Server database, the result will look like Figure 8-6. The only difference is that SQL Server uses the Sql data provider instead of the OleDb data provider.

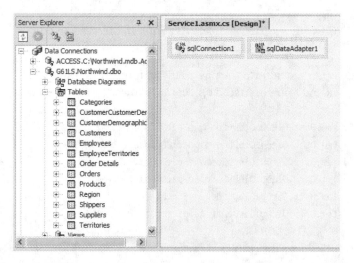

Figure 8-6. Results of dragging the SQL Server Orders table from the Server Explorer

Now, the next step is to add a Web method to the project. You can use the Class Wizard to add a method, or you can also add a method manually. For this example, I'll use the Class Wizard to add a method.

To add a method to the project, open the Class View from main menu's View ➤ Class View option and right-click on the Service1 class and select Add ➤ Add Method, as shown in Figure 8-7.

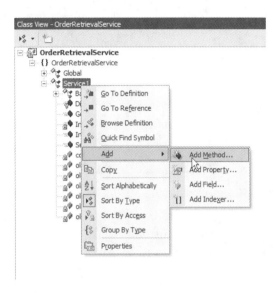

Figure 8-7. Adding a new method to a Web service

The Add Method option opens the C# Method Wizard, which lets you add a method. As you can see from Figure 8-8, I added a GetOrderFromDatabase method, which returns a DataSet (type "DataSet" in the Return Type text box). This method also takes one argument of integer type. You type the parameter name "OrderId" of integer type and use the Add button to add the parameter. Now click Finish. This process adds a method to the class, which looks like following:

```
public DataSet GetOrderFromDatabase(int OrderId)
{
     return null;
}
```

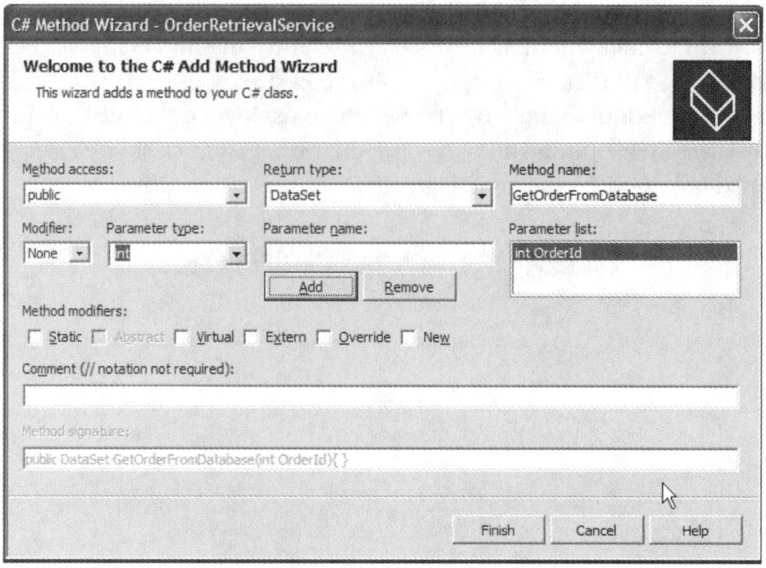

Figure 8-8. Adding GetOrderFromDatabase *using the C# Method Wizard*

Wait, this method is not a Web method yet. Before you write any code, you need to add the [WebMethod] attribute at the beginning of this method to recognize it as a Web method.

Now you're going to add some code to the method. This method returns a DataSet that will have records from the Orders table corresponding to an OrderId. Listing 8-2 shows the GetOrdersFromDatabase method.

Listing 8-2. The Web Service *method for obtaining an order from an* OrderId

```
[WebMethod]
public DataSet GetOrderFromDatabase(int OrderId)
{
    DataSet ds = new DataSet("OrderSet");
    oleDbDataAdapter1.SelectCommand.CommandText =
        "Select * from Orders WHERE OrderID = " +
    OrderId.ToString();
    oleDbDataAdapter1.Fill(ds, "Orders");
    return ds;
}
```

As you can see from Listing 8-2, the method receives an OrderId from a client and returns a DataSet to the client. It uses the DataAdapter to fill a DataSet with the row containing that OrderId.

> **NOTE** *You have to add a* WHERE *clause onto* SelectCommand *to filter the single row of data. Also, you must make all exposed methods in the Web service public, and they must contain a [* WebMethod *] attribute; otherwise, the client won't see them.*

Testing Your Web Service

Now you're actually ready to build and test your Web service. First, build the service using the Build menu option and then start it in Debug mode. This will bring up the Web service in your browser, as shown in Figure 8-9.

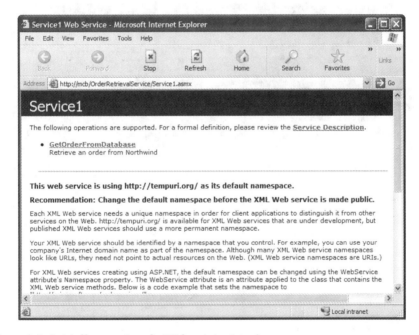

Figure 8-9. Initially running the Web service Service1.asmx

As you can see in Figure 8-9, one method GetOrderFromDatabase is available in the browser.

You can make this screen a bit more descriptive by adding a WebService attribute to the top of the class and then adding descriptions to both the WebService attribute and the WebMethod attribute. As you can see from Listing 8-3, I added a description to both.

Listing 8-3. Adding descriptions to the WebService *and* WebMethod *attributes*

```
[WebService(Description = "Working with Orders in Northwind")]
public class Service1 : System.Web.Services.WebService
{
      . . ..
    [WebMethod(Description = "Retrieve an order from Northwind")]
    public DataSet GetOrderFromDatabase(int orderID)
    {
        . . ..
    }
```

The service now looks like Figure 8-10.

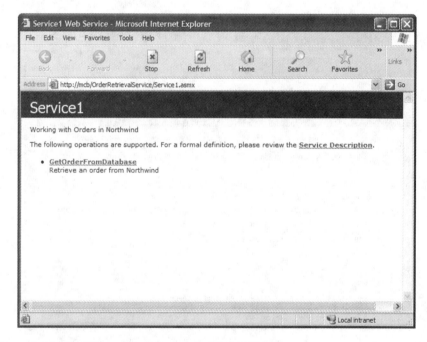

Figure 8-10. The Web service after you add attributes

If you click on the link for the `GetOrderFromDatabase` method, you see the screen in Figure 8-11. This browser screen enables you to test the method by entering an OrderID.

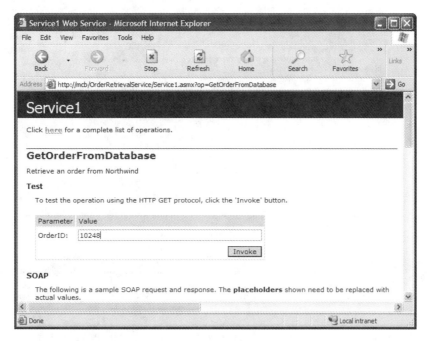

Figure 8-11. Testing the Web service's `GetOrderFromDatabase` *method*

After you click the Invoke button, the browser returns the XML data representing the `DataSet`, which contains the order with the order ID of 10248. Figure 8-12 shows a piece of the XML data representing the order and displayed by the browser.

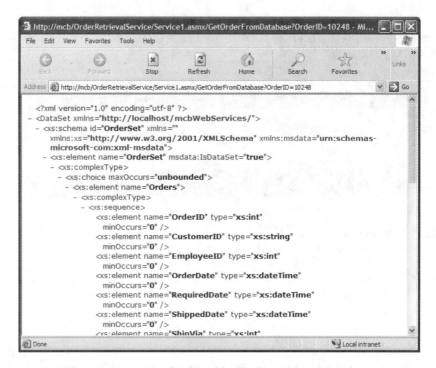

Figure 8-12. The Order DataSet *displayed by the browser in XML format*

Note that because you're using a complex structure such as a DataSet for the return parameter, you need to use SOAP with an XSD schema (which happens to be the default wiring protocol) to transfer the data back to the client. The encoding of the SOAP format is beyond the scope of this book, but if you're interested, you can visit the World Wide Web Consortium (http://www.w3.org).

As you can see from Figure 8-12, the default namespace for the DataSet xmlns is http://tempuri.org. You can use the WebService attribute to specify the namespace and description text for the XML Web service. As you can see, VS .NET doesn't generate this attribute by default. You have to write it manually. If you are specifying more than one property, you can separate them with a comma. For example, the following code sets the namespace and the description properties of the WebService attribute:

```
[WebService(Namespace="http://servername/xmlwebservices/",
        Description="My Web Service")]
public class Service1 : System.Web.Services.WebService
{
    // Implementation code.
}
```

Creating the Web Service Consumer

Now that you've created a Web service, you should create a client to use it. In this tutorial, you'll create an ASP .NET Web Form application that accesses the Web service to retrieve an order. The client will then display the order in a DataGrid.

First, create an ASP .NET Web project by going to File ➤ New ➤ Project and choosing the ASP.NET Web Application template, as shown in Figure 8-13. As you can see in Figure 8-13, I'm creating my application on the MCB Web server. Your default server may be localhost, so you can keep your server name as localhost and type your project name after the server.

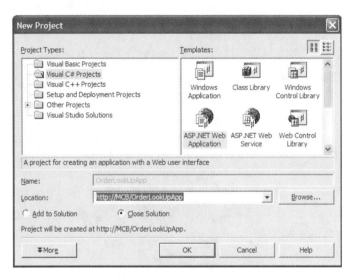

Figure 8-13. Creating a new Web-based client application

Creating a Web application adds a Web page to the project, which is the default gateway when VS .NET is done creating the project. As you saw in Chapter 7, you can use Web pages as Windows forms. You can add Web and HTML controls to Web pages by simply dragging controls from the toolbox to the Web page.

In my sample, I add a label, a text box, a button, and a data grid by dragging them from ToolBox ➤ Web Forms to the WebForm1.aspx Design View. Next, set the controls' properties. Figure 8-14 shows the final page after setting the properties.

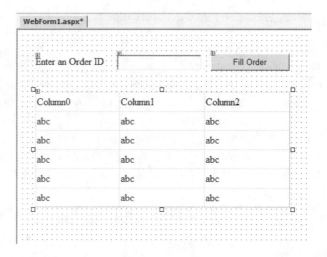

Figure 8-14. Design View for searching for and displaying an order

To use the Web service in the client application, you need to add a Web reference to the service. In the Solution Explorer, right-click on the References option and choose Add Web Reference, as shown in Figure 8-15.

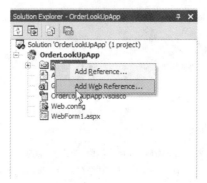

Figure 8-15. Adding a Web reference

This brings up the Add Web Reference page, as shown in Figure 8-16.

Figure 8-16. The Add Web Reference locator

As you can see from Figure 8-16, you can choose from any existing Web service. Those Web services can exist on your localhost drive in the Microsoft Universal Description, Discovery, and Integration Business Registry (UDDI) or somewhere on the Internet. You just need to provide the URL of the service in the Address text box. In this case, you need to provide the URL of OrderRetrievalService's .asmx page and then you need to add "?wsdl" at the end of URL. You can specify the .asmx file and URL path where the service entry point is located in the Address field of the wizard. As you can see in Figure 8-17, I passed the URL of the service with the MCB server. You need to replace MCB with localhost if you're using your local development machine as the default Web server. Figure 8-17 shows the contents of the service.

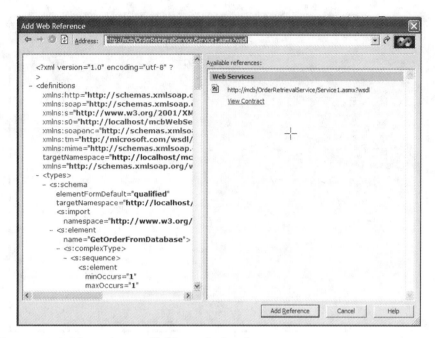

Figure 8-17. Web services available on the local server

Now click the Add Reference button, which adds a reference of the service to the project. As you can see in Figure 8-18, the Web reference "mcb" is added to the project. To access Web services on this server, you need to use this namespace. You can even rename the namespace by right-clicking and choosing Rename.

Figure 8-18. Viewing OrderRetrievalService *with the Add Reference button*

Clicking the Add Reference button causes VS .NET to generate three files for referencing the service:

- A discovery file (Service1.disco)

- A WSDL file (Service1.wsdl)

- A proxy file (Service1.cs)

As already discussed, the discovery file is an XML file that helps the client to find the service. The WSDL file describes the methods and classes supplied by the service in XML and defines the format that messages need to adhere to when exchanging information with the client. The proxy file, although not displayed in the Solution Explorer, is a C# stub file generated so that the programmer can call the methods in the Web service with the same exact method names and method parameter structure as the Web service contains. You may know about proxies used with the Interface Definition Language (IDL) or Java Remote Method Invocation (RMI).

These proxies wrap the method calls to the Web service so that the convoluted exchange of parameter passing and method invocation to the remote service are transparent to the programmer. If you expand the Web References node, you can see the files belong to a service (see Figure 8-19).

Figure 8-19. Files generated by the Web References Wizard to access the Web service

Now, everything is all set, and you're ready to call the Web service's method. You can access a Web service by either adding the mcb namespace (or localhost if you're using localhost as your default Web server) to the project or referencing the namespace directly in the project. In our sample, we're going to call the GetOrderFromDatabase method from the Fill Order button click. Now double-click on the button to write a click event handler for the button. As you probably noticed, the class in this example is Service1. So, that's the class of which you'll be creating an instance. You're going to use Service1 through the mcb namespace, which represents the Web server.

> **NOTE** *You need to add the* localhost *namespace if you're using localhost as your default Web server.*

Once you have an instance to the service, you can call GetAnOrderFromDatabase in the service and assign it to a DataSet reference. To display the DataSet in a DataGrid, simply assign the DataSet to the DataGrid's DataSource, and call DataBind on the Grid. Listing 8-4 shows the code for Fill Order button-click handler.

Listing 8-4. Button-click event handler that calls the order retrieval Web service

```
private void Button1_Click(object sender, System.EventArgs e)
{
// construct and call the web service with the order id in the textbox
mcb.Service1 myWebService = new mcb.Service1();
DataSet ds = myWebService.GetOrderFromDatabase
(Convert.ToInt32(this.TextBox1.Text));
// bind the data to the grid
DataGrid1.DataSource = ds;
DataGrid1.DataBind();
```

As you can see from Listing 8-4, I called GetOrderFromDatabase through mcb.Service1, which returns a DataSet. You use this database and bind to the data grid control and call DataGrid's DataBind method.

Compile and run the Web application. Enter an order ID of 10248 and click the Fill Order button. Figure 8-20 shows the resulting output in Internet Explorer.

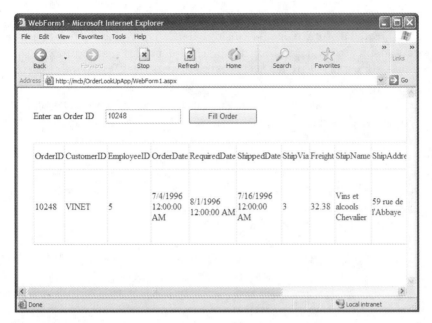

Figure 8-20. Result of the Fill *method in a DataGrid*

There's not much to it, huh? Actually, VS .NET takes away a lot of the WSDL, proxy, and discovery file coding so that you can concentrate on what you do best: coding the service. The truth is that without knowing anything about SOAP, XML, or even HTTP, you were able to develop this Web service. In the next section you'll create a Web service for entering an order into the database using this knowledge and what you know about ADO.NET.

Adding More Functionality to the Service

Now, why don't you ask the Web service to do some more work than just return-ing data from a database table?

This time I'm going to write to the database. I read data from a client in the form of an array, place it in a dataset, and then add the data to the Orders table of the Northwind database.

To do so, I open the OrderRetrievalService project and generate a dataset by using right-click ➤ Generate DataSet option of the data adapter. (See Chapter 4 for more details on how to generate a dataset from a data adapter.) The Generate DataSet option of the data adapter generates a typed dataset and adds the class DataSet1, which comes from the dataset.

Now I add a new Web method called `InsertOrder` (see Listing 8-5). In this method, I read data from a database using a data adapter and filled data from the data adapter to a dataset using the data adapter's `Fill` method. As you can see from Listing 8-5, I've used a `SELECT *` query with `ORDER BY` for the OrderId column value.

It gets the last OrderID in the table to determine what is the next available OrderID value. Then it creates a new `DataRow` in the dataset and populates the row with data passed in from the client. Finally, it calls the `Update` method of the data adapter to save the new row into the database.

Listing 8-5. Web service method for populating an order in the database

```
[WebMethod(Description = "Insert Order from Array")]
    public int  InsertOrder(string[] OrderInfo)
    {
        DataSet1 ds = new DataSet1();
        oleDbDataAdapter1.SelectCommand.CommandText =
            "Select * From Orders ORDER BY OrderID";
        oleDbDataAdapter1.Fill(ds, "Orders");
        DataRow drLast = ds.Orders.Rows[ds.Orders.Rows.Count - 1];
        int LastOrderID = Convert.ToInt32(drLast["OrderID"]);
        DataSet1.OrdersRow  dr = ds.Orders.NewOrdersRow();
        dr.OrderID = LastOrderID + 1;
        dr.OrderDate  = Convert.ToDateTime(OrderInfo[0]);
        dr.ShipName   = OrderInfo[1];
        dr.ShipAddress   = OrderInfo[2];
        dr.ShipCity = OrderInfo[3];
        dr.ShipCountry = OrderInfo[4];
        dr.ShipPostalCode = OrderInfo[5];
        ds.Orders.AddOrdersRow(dr);
        oleDbDataAdapter1.Update(ds, "Orders");
        return dr.OrderID;
    }
```

Now build and test the service. This service now has two methods, as shown in Figure 8-21.

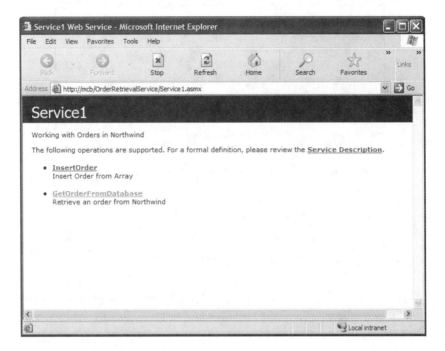

Figure 8-21. The InsertOrder *and* GetOrderFromDatabase *methods of*
OrderRetrievalService

Now it's time to test your newly added Web method InsertOrder. To test this
service, follow the same steps as in the previous section when testing your
GetOrderFromDataset method.

Create a Web application project using VS .NET. You can even use the same
client you used to test the GetOrderFromDatabase method. Create a new project
called AddOrderClientApp (see Figure 8-22).

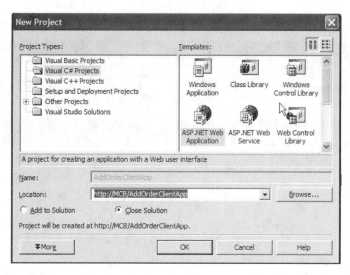

Figure 8-22. Creating a client to test the `InsertOrder` *Web method*

The next step is to add a Web reference to the Web service by right-clicking on the References node of a project in the Solution Explorer and clicking on the Add Web Reference option.

> **NOTE** *If you're using same client application you used last time, you need to remove the namespace and then add it again by using the Add Web Reference option to get the latest updated Web service contents.*

Again, follow the same steps as in the last sample. Type the URL of your service in the Address text box and click the Add Reference button, which adds the `mcb` namespace (or `localhost` if you're using default localhost as the Web server) to the project. Add Reference also generates the `*.disco`, `*.wsdl`, and proxy files. Now you can call your Web service. Add some controls to the page to make it look like Figure 8-23. I added six text boxes to accept the order date, name, address, city, country, and zip of a customer. The Enter Order button submits the order to the service.

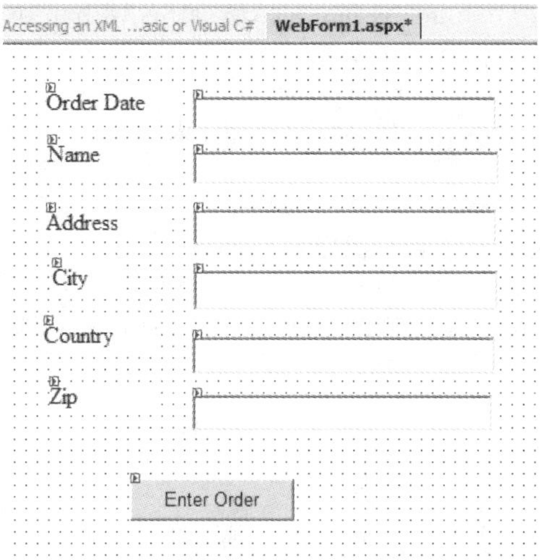

Figure 8-23. Design View of the order customer entry Web service

Again, double-click on the Enter Order button and use the code in Listing 8-6 to populate the order array and pass it to the Web service. The Enter Order button event handler looks like Listing 8-6.

Listing 8-6. Client event handler for executing the Web service

```
private void Button1_Click(object sender, System.EventArgs e)
        {
            string[] orderData = new string[6];
            orderData[0] = TextBox1.Text;
            orderData[1] = TextBox2.Text;
            orderData[2] = TextBox3.Text;
            orderData[3] = TextBox4.Text;
            orderData[4] = TextBox5.Text;
            orderData[5] = TextBox6.Text;

            mcb.Service1 myWebService = new mcb.Service1();
            myWebService.InsertOrder(orderData);
        }
```

The button event handler assigns a string array with information typed into the order form. You can create an instance of the service by directly using mcb.Service1 and calling the InsertOrder method. If you're using localhost as your Web server, the code would look like the following:

```
localhost.Service1 myWebService = new localhost.Service1();
    myWebService.InsertOrder(orderData);
```

As you can see from Figure 8-24, the InsertOrder method is available in the list.

Figure 8-24. The InsertOrder *method available in the list*

Now build and run the application. The output looks like Figure 8-25. Now you enter customer data and clicking the Enter Order button adds the data to the Orders table.

Figure 8-25. Adding an order to the database using Enter Order

Passing XML to the Web Service

One more interesting and practical approach to passing an order entry is to pass it using an XML node. SOAP enables you to pass an XML node of data. This way the data will have more useful node names such as OrderName rather than a constant representing the order name. You won't have to worry so much about tracking integer constants. Listing 8-7 shows InsertOrderFromNode method for taking an XmlNode with your customer order information. You populate the new DataRow by extracting InnerText from each ChildNode of XmlNode.

> **NOTE** *You'll need to include the using* System.Xml *namespace to utilize* XmlNode.

Listing 8-7. Web service method populating an order from XML

```
[WebMethod(Description = "Insert Order from XML")]
    public int InsertOrderFromNode(XmlNode aNode)
    {
        DataSet1 ds = new DataSet1();
        oleDbDataAdapter1.SelectCommand.CommandText =
            "Select * From Orders ORDER BY OrderID";
        oleDbDataAdapter1.Fill(ds, "Orders"); 
        DataRow drLast = ds.Orders.Rows[ds.Orders.Rows.Count - 1];
        int LastOrderID = Convert.ToInt32(drLast["OrderID"]);
        DataSet1.OrdersRow  dr = ds.Orders.NewOrdersRow();
        dr.OrderID = LastOrderID + 1;
        dr.OrderDate  = Convert.ToDateTime(aNode["OrderDate"].InnerText);
        dr.ShipName  = aNode["ShipName"].InnerText;
        dr.ShipAddress  = aNode["ShipAddress"].InnerText;
        dr.ShipCity = aNode["ShipCity"].InnerText;
        dr.ShipCountry = aNode["ShipCountry"].InnerText;
        dr.ShipPostalCode = aNode["ShipPostalCode"].InnerText;
        ds.Orders.AddOrdersRow(dr);
        oleDbDataAdapter1.Update(ds, "Orders");
        return dr.OrderID;
    }
```

Now you add the InsertOrderFormNode method to your existing Web service and test the method as you've been doing in the previous two samples.

Then, on the client side, you use the same client as in the previous sample. You add one more button to the page, so now it looks like Figure 8-26.

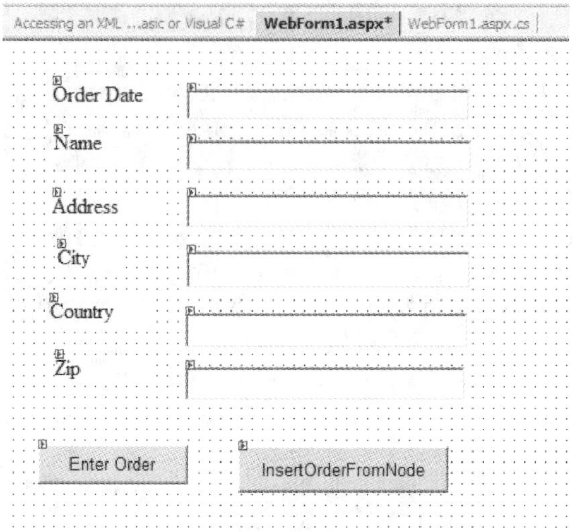

Figure 8-26. Calling the InsertOrderFromNode *Web method*

This time, instead of passing an array to your Web service, you can simply pass an XML node with the named nodes of the customer order. You use the XmlDocument class to create the initial node and then populate it with the LoadXml method. The node passes to your new Web method, which takes an XmlNode instead of a string array. Listing 8-8 shows how to pass XmlDocument as an input for the InsertOrderFromNode method.

Listing 8-8. Client event handler for executing the Web service

```
private void Button2_Click(object sender, System.EventArgs e)
{
    XmlDocument node = new XmlDocument();
    node.LoadXml(
        "<Order>" +
        "<OrderDate>" + TextBox1.Text + "</OrderDate>" +
        "<ShipName>" + TextBox2.Text + "</ShipName>" +
        "<ShipAddress>" + TextBox3.Text + "</ShipAddress>" +
        "<ShipCity> "+ TextBox4.Text + "</ShipCity>" +
        "<ShipCountry>" + TextBox5.Text + "</ShipCountry>" +
        "<ShipPostalCode>" + TextBox6.Text + "</ShipPostalCode>" +
        "</Order>");
     mcb.Service1 myWebService = new mcb.Service1();
    myWebService.InsertOrderFromNode(node);
}
```

> **NOTE** *The Web service automatically strips out the root node <#document>*
> *when it receives the node, so the root element node on the Web service side*
> *is <Order>.*

Now compile and run application. Insert data to the text boxes and click the
InsertOrderFromNode button. To see if program worked, see the Orders table of
the database.

Executing Asynchronous Web Services

There are two ways to access Web services from a client application—synchronously and asynchronously. A *synchronous* Web service is like the one we just
executed in our client applications. When a client is accessing a Web service synchronously, a client has to wait until it gets a response from the Web service. As
we saw in our client applications in the previous sections, we're accessing
OrderRetrievalService synchronously. What if a Web method takes a long time in
response? For instance, what if our InsertOrderFromNode method takes 10 minutes in response and client has many other things to process? In the present case,
the client has to wait for 10 minutes and can't execute any thing else until getting
a response from the Web service. In other words, a client's main thread is busy
with the Web service if the client is accessing a Web service synchronously.
Executing a Web service *asynchronously* allows client applications to execute
more than one thread simultaneously. In other words, by calling accessing Web
services asynchronously, a client can continue to use the calling thread while
waiting for the XML Web service to respond. To access Web services asynchronously doesn't require any special configuration.

When adding a Web reference to a client application, VS .NET generates
a proxy class capable of calling an XML Web service both synchronously and
asynchronously. You can see the proxy reference of OrderRetrievalService by
expanding the mcb node in the Solution Explorer; the reference filename is
Reference.cs (see Figure 8-27).

Figure 8-27. Proxy reference file for OrderRetrievalService

To view the contents of the proxy file, right-click and select View Code. This file stores information related to the Web service and its methods. It also contains the URL of the Web service. You can find the following code in Reference.cs as OrderRetrievalService:

```
/// <remarks/>
public Service1() {
this.Url = "http://mcb/OrderRetrievalService/Service1.asmx";
}
```

Other information this file stores is asynchronous methods for every Web method published by a Web service. For each Web method, there are two contains a corresponding Begin and End method. Therefore, for Web method InsertOrderFromNode, asynchronous calls are BeginInsertOrderFromNode and EndInsertOrderFromNode. You can find the following methods in Reference.cs file:

```
/// <remarks/>
public System.IAsyncResult BeginInsertOrderFromNode
(System.Xml.XmlNode aNode,
System.AsyncCallback callback, object asyncState) {
    return this.BeginInvoke("InsertOrderFromNode", new object[] {
                aNode}, callback, asyncState);
}
```

```
/// <remarks/>
public int EndInsertOrderFromNode(System.IAsyncResult asyncResult) {
        object[] results = this.EndInvoke(asyncResult);
      return ((int)(results[0]));
}
```

Asynchronous Web service execution requires a two-step process. First, you tell the Web service to begin execution by calling the `Begin` method. The second step, calling the `End` method, completes the Web service call and returns the response.

To call a Web service asynchronously, a client thread can use a `WaitHandle`. When you get to a place in your client code when you are required to wait for the service to end, you call a `WaitHandle` there. Listing 8-9 is an example of how to use the `WaitHandle`. You can also assign a `WaitHandle` a timeout period in case the Web service takes to long.

In Listing 8-9, the code is adding two customer orders, so it need to call the Web service twice. The code starts by calling `BeginInsertOrderFromNode` on the first order, which returns an `AsynchronousResult` object. You can also use the same method, `BeginInsertOrderFromNode`, to begin the service for inserting a second order. You can use the `WaitHandles` returned from these calls to create the `WaitHandle` instance. When you require the client to wait for the service to finish, you execute the `WaitHandle`'s `WaitAll` method. The `WaitAll` method waits for all the asynchronous threads to complete before continuing execution of the code in the client. In this method you also pass a timeout period of 15 minutes, so you don't have to wait forever. When the `Wait` has completed, you call the `EndInsertOrderFromNode` for both asynchronous threads. In the case where you were waiting for a return value, the `End<Method>` call would also return the data.

> **NOTE** *You need to add a reference of the* `System.Threading` *namespace to the application because the* `WaitHandle` *class is defined in the* `System.Threading` *namespace.*

Listing 8-9. Using `WaitHandle` *to make synchronous calls*
```
private void Button3_Click(object sender, System.EventArgs e)
{
    // create the Order Information in Xml from the Client TextBoxes
    XmlDocument OrderInfo = new XmlDocument();
    OrderInfo.LoadXml(
        "<Order>" +
        "<OrderDate>" + TextBox1.Text + "</OrderDate>" +
```

```
           "<ShipName>" + TextBox2.Text + "</ShipName>" +
           "<ShipAddress>" + TextBox3.Text + "</ShipAddress>" +
           "<ShipCity>" + TextBox4.Text + "</ShipCity>" +
           "<ShipCountry>" + TextBox5.Text + "</ShipCountry>" +
           "<ShipPostalCode>" + TextBox6.Text + "</ShipPostalCode>" +
           "</Order>");

    // construct the Web Service for entering an Order
    mcb.Service1 OrderEntry = new mcb.Service1();

    // Call the Asynchronous InsertOrderFromNode
    IAsyncResult ws1 = OrderEntry.BeginInsertOrderFromNode(
           OrderInfo, null, null);

    // Change the Order Information slightly
    OrderInfo["Order"]["ShipName"].InnerText   = "Fred Estaire";

    // Call another Asynchronous InsertOrderFromNode Call
    IAsyncResult ws2 = OrderEntry.BeginInsertOrderFromNode(OrderInfo,
      null, null);

    // Construct an array of Wait Handles and call WaitHandle for a
    // maximum of 15 minutes
    WaitHandle[] TheWaitHandles = {ws1.AsyncWaitHandle ,
                                      ws2.AsyncWaitHandle};
    WaitHandle.WaitAll(TheWaitHandles, new TimeSpan(0, 15, 0), true);

    // All the Web Services have returned (or timed out)
    //  call End Order on both Web Service Threads
    int orderid1 = OrderEntry.EndInsertOrder(ws1);
    int orderid2 =  OrderEntry.EndInsertOrder(ws2);
}
```

WaitHandles has a few modes. In the previous mode, WaitAll, the command will wait until all services are completed (wait until ws1 *and* ws2 are completed). You can also call WaitAny. In the case of WaitAny, the method will wait until any of the services complete (wait until ws1 *or* ws2 is complete).

Summary

In this chapter you learned what a Web service is and how you can set it up to perform services on the Web. You worked through a tutorial for creating a simple Web service for retrieving an order using ADO.NET and ASP .NET. You then created a Web service that allowed you to enter a customer for the order using XML and ADO.NET. Finally, you learned how to use asynchronous Web service calls to give you some flexibility in accessing your Web service. Now you have much of the knowledge you need to begin programming database applications for the Web.

The next chapter discusses ADO.NET events. You'll learn how to use different ADO.NET data component events.

CHAPTER 9

Handling ADO.NET Events

EVENTS ARE USEFUL FOR NOTIFYING a program of when an action happens to an object. An event can have a method associated with it. This method is an *event handler*. When an event occurs, the associated method executes. An event can have multiple event handlers.

In Chapters 1 and 2, I discussed events in C# and Windows Forms. As I explained in Chapter 1, a class defines an event by providing an event declaration, which is of type delegate. The following defines an event handler:

```
public delegate void EventHandler(object sender, System.EventArgs e);
```

EventHandler takes two arguments: one of type Object and the other of type System.EventArgs. As you can see from Figure 9-1, each of the event handlers has an event argument type that corresponds to it. The event argument class contains the data related to the event, which can be accessed through event argument class members.

In this chapter, I'll show you how you can handle events for ADO.NET objects.

Introducing ADO.NET Events

As I discussed in Chapter 5, you can divide ADO.NET classes into two groups: disconnected classes and data provider classes. The System.Data namespace defines the common event handlers and event argument classes for all data providers. As you can see from Figure 9-1, event handler classes come from the Delegate class, and event argument classes come from the EventArgs class.

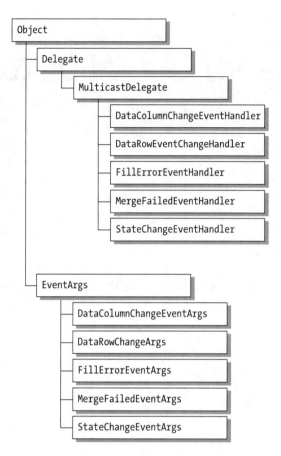

Figure 9-1. Event handler and event argument classes defined in the
System.Data *namespace*

You use the DataColumnChangeEventHandler as an event handler for
DataColumn when you are changing a value for a column in a DataRow. You use
DataRowChangeEventHandler as an event handler that handles the RowChanging,
RowChanged, RowDeleting, and RowDeleted events of a DataTable. You use the
FillErrorEventHandler as an event handler that handles a data adapter's Fill
event. If an error occurs during the fill operation, then FillError fires, which executes FillErrorEventHandler. MergeFailedEventHandler handles a dataset's
MergeFailed event, which occurs when a dataset's merge operation fails.
StateChangeEventHandler handles the StateChange event, which occurs when the
connection state changes. Besides the Data namespace defining the event handler and event argument classes, the data provider–specific namespaces also
define the data provider event handler and event argument classes. Some of
these classes and their usage may vary from provider to provider. Figure 9-2
shows the OleDb data provider event handlers and event argument classes.

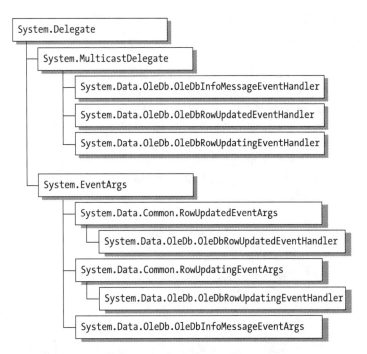

Figure 9-2. OleDb data provider event handler and event arguments

OleDbInfoMessageEventHandler handles the InfoMessage event of OleDbConnection. An InfoMessage event occurs when a provider sends a warning or an informational message to the application.

OleDbRowUpdatedEventHandler handles the RowUpdated event of OleDbDataAdapter. The RowUpdated event occurs when you call an Update method on a data adapter.

OleDbRowUpdatingEventHandler handles the RowUpdating event of OleDbDataAdapter. The RowUpdating event occurs before a command executes against the data source.

Working with Connection Events

The Connection object has two events that notify the application if a connection state changes. You can use these events to retrieve informational messages from a data source or to determine if the state of Connection changes. These two events are InfoMessage and StateChange. The InfoMessage event occurs when an informational message is returned from a data source. The exception handling doesn't catch these messages. The StateChange event occurs only when the state of a connection changes.

The `InfoMessage` event receives an `InfoMessageEventArgs` object. The `InfoMessageEventArgs` is as follows:

```
public delegate void OleDbInfoMessageEventHandler(
    object sender,
    OleDbInfoMessageEventArgs e
);
```

where `sender` is the source of the event and `e` is an `OleDbInfoMessageEventArgs` object that contains the event data. Table 9-1 defines the `InfoMessageEventArgs` properties.

Table 9-1. The `InfoMessageEventArgs` *Properties*

PROPERTY	DESCRIPTION
ErrorCode	Returns HRESULT following the ANSI SQL standard for the database
Errors	Returns the collection of warnings sent from the data source
Message	Returns the full text of the error
Source	Returns the name of the object that generated the error

> **CAUTION** *Some of these members may vary for other data providers. For example, the Sql data provider doesn't have an* `ErrorCode` *property.*

The `StateChange` event occurs when the state of `Connection` changes. The `StateChange` event receives `StateChangeEventArgs`, which enables you to determine the change in state of `Connection` using the `OriginalState` and `CurrentState` properties. The `OriginalState` property represents the original state of the connection, and the `CurrentState` property represents the current state of the connection. The `ConnectionState` enumeration defines properties for connection states (see Table 9-2).

Table 9-2. The ConnectionState *Properties*

PROPERTY	DESCRIPTION
Broken	This state occurs when the connection is broken after it was opened.
Closed	The connection is closed.
Connecting	The connection is connecting to a data source.
Executing	The connection object is executing a command.
Fetching	The connection object is retrieving data.
Open	The connection is open.

To test the connection events, I created a Windows application and added two buttons to the form. I then set the name of the button controls to StateChangeEventBtn and InfoMessageEventBtn. I also set the text of the buttons to "StateChange Event" and "InfoMessage Event." The final form looks like Figure 9-3.

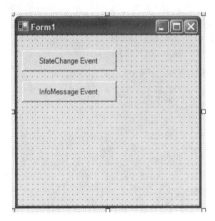

Figure 9-3. Windows application for testing connection events

You can add both connection events programmatically as well as at design-time. To add these events from VS .NET, just drag a SqlConnection (or OleDbConnection) from toolbox's Data tab to a form and write events from the Properties windows. As you can see in Figure 9-4, you merely double-click the InfoMessage and StateChange events to write event handlers for them.

Figure 9-4. Adding the InfoMessage *and* StateChange *events*

Write the code in Listing 9-1 for both the events.

Listing 9-1. Writing event handlers for the InfoMessage *and* StateChange *events*

```
// Connection InfoMessage Event Handler
    private void sqlConnection1_InfoMessage
        (object sender, System.Data.SqlClient.SqlInfoMessageEventArgs e)
    {
        int i;
        for (i=0; i < e.Errors.Count; i++ )
        {
            MessageBox.Show(e.Errors[i].Message);
        }
    }

    // Connection StateChange Event Handler
    private void sqlConnection1_StateChange
        (object sender, System.Data.StateChangeEventArgs e)
    {
        MessageBox.Show("Original State:" + e.OriginalState.ToString()
            + ", New state = " + e.CurrentState.ToString() );
    }
```

NOTE   *Don't forget to add a reference to the data provider namespace.*

To test these events, write code on the `StateChange` event and `InfoMessage` event button-click handlers (see Listing 9-2). As you can see, the `StateChangeEventBtn _Click` handler opens a connection and then closes the connection. Opening and closing a connection invokes the `StateChange` event and executes code written on the `StateChange` event handler.

On the `InfoMessageBtn _Click` handler, I opened a connection, called the `ChangeDatabase` method of `SqlConnection` and then closed the connection. The `ChangeDatabase` method invokes `InfoMessageEvent`.

Listing 9-2. Writing code that executes connection events

```
private void StateChangeEventBtn_Click(object sender, System.EventArgs e)
    {
        try
        {
            // Create a Connection Object
            string ConnectionString ="Integrated Security=SSPI;" +
                "Initial Catalog=Northwind;" +
                "Data Source=localhost;";

            sqlConnection1.ConnectionString = ConnectionString;
            // Open the connection
            if( sqlConnection1.State != ConnectionState.Open)
                sqlConnection1.Open();


            // Close the connection
            sqlConnection1.Close();

        }
        catch( Exception ex )
        {
            MessageBox.Show(ex.Message);
        }

    }

    private void InfoMessageBtn_Click(object sender, System.EventArgs e)
    {
        try
        {
            // Create a Connection Object
            string ConnectionString ="Integrated Security=SSPI;" +
```

```
                    "Initial Catalog=Northwind;" +
                    "Data Source=localhost;";

            sqlConnection1.ConnectionString = ConnectionString;
            // Open the connection
            if( sqlConnection1.State != ConnectionState.Open)
                sqlConnection1.Open();

            // Change database
            sqlConnection1.ChangeDatabase("Master");

            // Close the connection
            sqlConnection1.Close();

        }
        catch( Exception ex )
        {
            MessageBox.Show(ex.Message);
        }
    }
```

The output of the StateChange event's button-click handler looks like Figure 9-5 and Figure 9-6. The StateChangeEventBtn_Click method fires the StateChange event two times—first when you call the Open method and the connection state changes from closed to open and, second, when you call the Close method and the connection state changes from open to closed.

Figure 9-5. The StateChangeEvent *output when you call the* Open *method*

Figure 9-6. The StateChangeEvent *output when you call the* Close *method*

The output of `InfoMessageBtn` click looks like Figure 9-7, which shows the database changing to master as a result of the `ChangeDatabase` method.

Figure 9-7. The InfoMessage *event output when you call the* ChangeDatabase *method*

Working with DataAdapter Events

The data adapter has a `FillError` event that occurs during a fill method. It allows a user to determine whether a fill operation should continue. For example, `FillError` could occur when you can't convert data from a database to Common Language Runtime (CLR) type without losing precision or when data type casting is not valid.

`FillErrorEventHandler` handles the `FillError` event. The event handler receives an argument of type `FillErrorEventArgs`, which contains data related to this event. The `FillErrorEventHandler` is as follows:

```
public delegate void FillErrorEventHandler(
    object sender,
    FillErrorEventArgs e
);
```

where `sender` is the source of the event and e is `FillErrorEventArgs`, which contains the event data. Table 9-3 defines the `FillErrorEventArgs` properties.

Table 9-3. The FillErrorEventArgs *Members*

PROPERTY	DESCRIPTION
Continue	Represents a value indicating whether to continue the fill operator
DataTable	Returns the data table being updated when the error occurred
Errors	Returns the errors
Values	Returns the rows being updated when error occurred

RowUpdated and RowUpdating are two more events that a data adapter supports. The RowUpdating event occurs when an Update method is called before a command executes against the data source. The RowUpdated event occurs when a command executes.

The RowUpdated event handler receives an argument of type OleDbRowUpdatedEventArgs that contains data related to this event. Table 9-4 describes the OleDbRowUpdateEventArgs members.

Table 9-4. The OleDbRowUpdatedEventArgs *Members*

PROPERTY	DESCRIPTION
Command	Returns the command object executed when Update is called
Errors	Returns errors generated during the update operation
RecordsAffected	Returns the number of rows affected during insert, update, and delete operations
Row	Returns the data row sent through an Update
StatementType	Returns the SQL statement type
Status	Returns the UpdateStatus of a command
TableMapping	Returns the DataTableMapping sent through an Update

Similar to RowUpdated, the RowUpdating event handler receives an argument of type OleDbRowUpdatingdEventArgs that defines the same properties as OleDbRowUpdated with the same meaning.

OK, now it's time to write an application to test the data adapter events. I created a Windows application and added a button control to the form. After that I changed the button's name property to DataAdapterEventsTestBtn and wrote a button-click event handler by double-clicking on the button control.

Next, I added a data adapter control to the form by dragging the OleDbDataAdapter component from the toolbox's Data tab to the form. As you drop the OleDbDataAdapter component to the form, the Data Adapter Configuration Wizard pops up. (I discussed the Data Adapter Configuration Wizard in Chapter 4.) In this application, I added the Customers table to the Query Builder and selected the CompanyName, ContactName, and CustomerID columns from the Customers table. As you can see from Figure 9-8, the Query Builder shows the SQL statement.

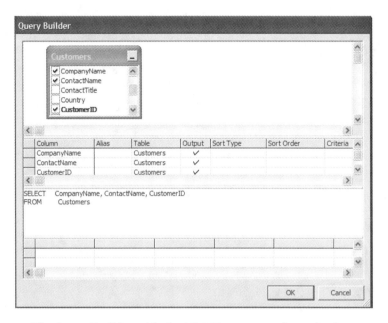

Figure 9-8. The Query Builder with the SELECT *statement from the Customers table*

Next, I used the Properties ➤ Events (the lightning bolt) button of the data adapter to add the event handlers. I added all three FillError, RowUpdating and RowUpdated event handlers, as shown in Figure 9-9.

Figure 9-9. Adding DataAdapter *events from the Properties window*

Now you can write code on the FillError event handler. You call the FillError event handler when the Fill method of data adapter fails. Listing 9-3 shows the code for the FillError event handler. As you can see from Listing 9-3, I used DataFillErrorEventArgs's members to get information about the error.

Listing 9-3. DataAdapter FillError *event handler code*

```
// FillError Event Handler
    private void oleDbDataAdapter1_FillError(object sender,
        System.Data.FillErrorEventArgs e)
    {
        if (e.Errors.GetType() == typeof(System.OverflowException))
        {
            MessageBox.Show("Error in Fill operation for table "+
                e.DataTable.TableName +
                ", Error Message: "+e.Errors.Message.ToString() +
                ", Source: "+ e.Errors.Source.ToString() );
            e.Continue = true;
        }
    }
```

Listings 9-4 and 9-5 show the code for the RowUpdated and RowUpdating event handlers. You call the RowUpdated event handler when a row is updated using the Update method of a data adapter, and you call RowUpdating when a row is updating.

Listing 9-4. The RowUpdated *event handler*

```
    // RowUpdated Event Handler
    private void oleDbDataAdapter1_RowUpdated(object sender,
        System.Data.OleDb.OleDbRowUpdatedEventArgs e)
    {
        if (e.Status == UpdateStatus.ErrorsOccurred)
        {
            MessageBox.Show("Error Message: "+e.Errors.Message.ToString()+
                ", Source: "+ e.Errors.Source.ToString() );

            e.Row.RowError = e.Errors.Message;
            e.Status = UpdateStatus.SkipCurrentRow;
        }
        else
        {
            MessageBox.Show("Updated");
        }
    }
```

As you can see from Listing 9-5, you can compare the StatementType member of OleDbRowUpdatingEventArgs to the StatementType enumeration to find out the statement type. The StatementType enumeration defines Select, Insert, Update, and Delete members.

Listing 9-5. The RowUpdating *event handler*

```
// RowUpdating Event Handler
        private void oleDbDataAdapter1_RowUpdating(object sender,
            System.Data.OleDb.OleDbRowUpdatingEventArgs e)
        {
            // Inserting
            if (e.StatementType == StatementType.Insert)
            {
                MessageBox.Show("Inserting");
            }
            // Updating
            else if (e.StatementType == StatementType.Update)
            {
                MessageBox.Show("Updating");
            }
            // Deleting
            else if (e.StatementType == StatementType.Delete)
            {
                MessageBox.Show("Deleting");
            }
            // Selecting
            else if (e.StatementType == StatementType.Select)
            {
                MessageBox.Show("Selecting");
            }
        }
```

Now, to test these events you can write code that fills a dataset and calls the Update method of data adapter. I added an event handler for the button by double-clicking on it and writing the code shown in Listing 9-6. As you can see, I created a new OleDbDataAdapter object and copied oleDbDataAdapter1 to it (the framework added oleDbDataAdapter1).

Listing 9-6. Calling DataAdapter*'s* Fill *and* Update *methods*

```
private void DataAdapterEventsTestBtn_Click(object sender,
        System.EventArgs e)
    {
        OleDbConnection conn = new OleDbConnection();
```

```
        string strDSN = "Provider=Microsoft.Jet.OLEDB.4.0;"+
            "Data Source=C:\\Northwind.mdb";
        conn.ConnectionString = strDSN;


        OleDbDataAdapter da = new OleDbDataAdapter();
        da = oleDbDataAdapter1;

        // Create InsertCommand
        da.InsertCommand = new OleDbCommand
            ("INSERT INTO Customers (CustomerID, CompanyName)"+
            "VALUES(?, ?)", conn);

        da.InsertCommand.Parameters.Add
            ("@CustomerID", OleDbType.VarChar, 5, "CustomerID");
        da.InsertCommand.Parameters.Add
            ("@CompanyName", OleDbType.VarChar, 30, "CompanyName");

        // Opening Connection
        conn.Open();

        // Create and Fill DataSet
        DataSet custDS = new DataSet();
        da.Fill(custDS, "Customers");

        // Add a new data row and call Update method
        // of data adapter
        DataRow custRow = custDS.Tables["Customers"].NewRow();
        custRow["CustomerID"] = "NEWCO";
        custRow["CompanyName"] = "New Company";
        custDS.Tables["Customers"].Rows.Add(custRow);

        da.Update(custDS, "Customers");

        // Close the connection
        conn.Close();
    }
```

> **NOTE** *Don't forget to add a reference to the* System.Data.OleDb *namespace.*

You can also use the SelectCommand, UpdateCommand, and DeleteCommand objects to select, update, and delete data from the table. (See Chapter 5 for how to use these commands.)

Now, if you run the application, you'll see an insert message; if you click the button more than once, you'll get the error shown in Figure 9-10.

Figure 9-10. The error message generated by the RowUpdated *event handler when trying to add duplicate employee records*

Working with DataSet Events

A dataset has a MergeFailed event that occurs when merging two datasets fails. MergeFailedEventHandler handles the MergeFailed event, which receives an argument of type MergeFailedEventArgs that contains data related to this event. The MergeFailedEventHandler is as follows:

```
public delegate void MergeFailedEventHandler(
    object sender,
    MergeFailedEventArgs e
);
```

where sender is the source of the event and e is the MergeFailedEventArgs object that contains the event data.

The MergeFailedEventArgs has Conflict and Table properties. The Conflict property returns a description of the merge conflict, and the Table property returns the name of the data table. Listing 9-7 shows an example of the MergeFailed event handler. As you can see, the MergerFailedBtn_Click method creates a connection and a data adapter and then fills a dataset using the Fill method of the data adapter. After that the code creates a second dataset, calls the Fill method to fill it, and then calls the Merge method of the dataset.

Listing 9-7. Writing code to call the MergeFailed *event handler*
```
private void MergedFailedBtn_Click(object sender, System.EventArgs e)
{
  OleDbConnection conn = new OleDbConnection();
  string strDSN = "Provider=Microsoft.Jet.OLEDB.4.0;"+
```

```
        "Data Source=C:\\Northwind.mdb";
    conn.ConnectionString = strDSN;
    conn.Open();

    string sql = "SELECT * FROM Employees";
    OleDbDataAdapter da = new OleDbDataAdapter(sql, conn);
    DataSet ds1 = new DataSet("ds1");
    da.Fill(ds1);

    sql = "SELECT * FROM Customers";
    da = new OleDbDataAdapter(sql, conn);
    DataSet ds2 = new DataSet("ds2");
    da.Fill(ds2);

    ds1.MergeFailed += new MergeFailedEventHandler
        (OnMergeFailed);


     ds1.Merge(ds2);

}

protected static void OnMergeFailed
    (object sender, MergeFailedEventArgs args)
{
    MessageBox.Show(args.Conflict.ToString());
}
```

Working with DataTable Events

A DataTable represents a table of a dataset. DataTable provides many events that an application can track down (see Table 9-5).

Table 9-5. The DataTable *Events*

EVENT	DESCRIPTION
ColumnChanged	This event occurs when a value of a column has been changed.
ColumnChanging	This event occurs when a new value is being added to a column.
RowChanged	This event occurs when a value of a row in the table has been changed.

(continued)

Table 9-5. The DataTable *Events (continued)*

EVENT	DESCRIPTION
RowChanging	This event occurs when a row in a table is changing.
RowDeleted	This event occurs when a row in a table has been deleted.
RowDeleting	This event occurs when a row is being deleted.

ColumnChangedEventHandler handles the ColumnChanged event; it's as follows:

```
public delegate void DataColumnChangeEventHandler(
    object sender,
    DataColumnChangeEventArgs e
);
```

where sender is the source of the event and e is DataColumnChangedEventArgs, which contains the event data.

ColumnChangingEventHandler handles the ColumnChanging event; it's as follows:

```
public delegate void DataColumnChangeEventHandler(
    object sender,
    DataColumnChangeEventArgs e
);
```

where sender is the source of the event and e is DataColumnChangingEventArgs, which contains the event data.

Similar to these two event handlers, RowChangedEventHandler, RowChangingEventHandler, RowDeletingEventHandler, and RowDeletedEventHandler handle the RowChanged, RowChanging, RowDeleted, and RowDeleting events, respectively. Definitions of these event handlers are similar to DataColumnChangingEventHandler and DataColumnChangedEventHandler.

To test these events I'll create a data table, add data rows to the table, and then update and delete rows from the table.

Listing 9-8 creates a data table, adds three columns (id, name, and address), adds data to the table, and changes the column of the table. It also calls the ColumnChanged and ColumnChanging event handlers. You write the code for the ColumnChanged and ColumnChanging event handlers in the Column_changed and Column_Changing methods. Specifically, you can write this code on a button-click event handler.

Listing 9-8. Writing the ColumnChanging *and* ColumnChanged *event handlers*

```
private void ColumnChange_Click(object sender, System.EventArgs e)
    {
        DataTable custTable = new DataTable("Customers");
        // add columns
        custTable.Columns.Add( "id", typeof(int) );
        custTable.Columns.Add( "name", typeof(string) );
        custTable.Columns.Add( "address", typeof(string) );

        // Add ColumnChanging and ColumnChanged event handlers
        custTable.ColumnChanging +=
            new DataColumnChangeEventHandler( Column_Changing );
        custTable.ColumnChanged +=
            new DataColumnChangeEventHandler( Column_Changed );

        // add Two rows
        custTable.Rows.Add(
            new object[] { 1, "name1", "address1"} );
        custTable.Rows.Add(
            new object[] { 2, "name2", "address2"} );

        custTable.AcceptChanges();

        // change the name column in all the rows
        foreach( DataRow row in custTable.Rows )
        {
            row["name"] = "new name";
        }
    }
private static void Column_Changed
    ( object sender, DataColumnChangeEventArgs e )
{
    MessageBox.Show("Column_Changed Event: " + " ," +
        e.Row["name"] +" ," +e.Column.ColumnName + " ,"+
        e.Row["name", DataRowVersion.Original] );
}
private static void Column_Changing
    ( object sender, DataColumnChangeEventArgs e )
{
    MessageBox.Show("Column_Changing Event: " + " ," +
        e.Row["name"] +" ," +e.Column.ColumnName + " ,"+
        e.Row["name", DataRowVersion.Original] );
}
```

Listing 9-9 creates a data table, adds three columns (id, name, and address), adds data to the table, and changes the column of the table. It also calls the RowChanging and RowChanged event handlers.

Listing 9-9. Writing the RowChanging *and* RowChanged *event handlers*

```
private void UpdateRow_Click(object sender, System.EventArgs e)
{
        DataTable custTable = new DataTable("Customers");
        // add columns
        custTable.Columns.Add( "id", typeof(int) );
        custTable.Columns.Add( "name", typeof(string) );
        custTable.Columns.Add( "address", typeof(string) );


        // add Two rows
        custTable.Rows.Add(
          new object[] { 1, "name1", "address1"} );
        custTable.Rows.Add(
          new object[] { 2, "name2", "address2"} );

        custTable.AcceptChanges();

        foreach( DataRow row in custTable.Rows )
        {
          row["name"] = "new name";

          // Adding RowChanged and RowChanging event handlers
          custTable.RowChanged +=
            new DataRowChangeEventHandler( Row_Changed );
          custTable.RowChanging +=
            new DataRowChangeEventHandler( Row_Changing );
        }


}



        private static void Row_Changed
            ( object sender, DataRowChangeEventArgs e )
        {
            MessageBox.Show("Row_Changed Event:" +
                e.Row["name", DataRowVersion.Original].ToString() +
                e.Action.ToString() );
        }
```

```
private static void Row_Changing
    ( object sender, DataRowChangeEventArgs e )
{
    MessageBox.Show("Row_Changing Event:" +
        e.Row["name", DataRowVersion.Original].ToString() +
        e.Action.ToString() );
}
```

Listing 9-10 creates a data table, adds three columns (id, name, and address), adds data to the table, and changes the column of the table. It also calls the RowDeleting and RowDeleted event handlers.

Listing 9-10. Writing the RowDeleting *and* RowDeleted *event handlers*

```
private void DeleteRow_Click(object sender, System.EventArgs e)
{
    DataTable custTable = new DataTable("Customers");
    // add columns
    custTable.Columns.Add( "id", typeof(int) );
    custTable.Columns.Add( "name", typeof(string) );
    custTable.Columns.Add( "address", typeof(string) );

    // Adding RowDeleting and RowDeleted events
    custTable.RowDeleting +=
        new DataRowChangeEventHandler( Row_Deleting );
    custTable.RowDeleted +=
        new DataRowChangeEventHandler( Row_Deleted );


    // add Two rows
    custTable.Rows.Add(
        new object[] { 1, "name1", "address1"} );
    custTable.Rows.Add(
        new object[] { 2, "name2", "address2"} );

    custTable.AcceptChanges();

    // Delete all the rows
    foreach( DataRow row in custTable.Rows )
        row.Delete();
}


private static void Row_Deleting
    ( object sender, DataRowChangeEventArgs e )
```

```
    {
        MessageBox.Show("Row_Deleting Event:" +
            e.Row["name", DataRowVersion.Original].ToString() +
            e.Action.ToString() );
    }
    private static void Row_Deleted
        ( object sender, DataRowChangeEventArgs e )
    {
        MessageBox.Show("Row_Deleted Event:" +
            e.Row["name", DataRowVersion.Original].ToString() +
            e.Action.ToString() );
    }
```

Working with XmlDataDocument Events

The XmlDataDocument events are useful when your application needs to notify you when changes are being made to an XmlDataDocument object. XmlDocument defines XmlDataDocument events (see Table 9-6).

Table 9-6. XmlDataDocument *Events*

EVENT	DESCRIPTION
NodeChanged	Occurs when the value of a node has been changed
NodeChanging	Occurs when the value of a node is changing
NodeInserted	Occurs when a node inserted into another node
NodeInserting	Occurs when a node is inserting to another node
NodeRemoved	Occurs when a node has been removed
NodeRemoving	Occurs when a node is being removed

The XmlNodeChangedEventHandler method handles the events listed in Table 9-6. The XmlNodeChangedEventHandler is as follows:

```
public delegate void XmlNodeChangedEventHandler(
    object sender,
    XmlNodeChangedEventArgs e
);
```

where sender is the source of the event and e is an XmlNodeChangedEventArgs that contains the event data. XmlNodeChangedEventArgs defines properties (see Table 9-7).

Table 9-7. The XmlNodeChangedEventArgs *Properties*

PROPERTY	DESCRIPTION
Action	Returns a value indicating the type of node changed event
NewParent	Returns the value of parent node after the operation is finished
Node	Returns the node that is being added, removed, or changed
OldParent	Returns the value of the parent node before operation started

Listing 9-11 handles XmlDataDocument events. The XmlDocumentBtn_Click method creates event handlers for the NodeChanged, NodeInserted, and NodeRemoved events. The MyNodeChangedEvent, MyNodeInsertedEvent, and MyNodeRemoved event handlers execute when these events fire. I used LoadXml to load an XML fragment and then used the ReplaceChild and RemoveChild methods to replace and remove document nodes.

Listing 9-11. The XmlDataDocument *event handling sample*

```
private void XmlDocumentBtn_Click(object sender, System.EventArgs e)
        {
            XmlDocument xmlDoc = new XmlDocument();
            xmlDoc.LoadXml("<Record> Some Value </Record>");

            //Create the event handlers.
            xmlDoc.NodeChanged +=
                new XmlNodeChangedEventHandler(this.MyNodeChangedEvent);
            xmlDoc.NodeInserted +=
                new XmlNodeChangedEventHandler(this.MyNodeInsertedEvent);
            xmlDoc.NodeRemoved +=
                new XmlNodeChangedEventHandler(this.MyNodeRemovedEvent);


            XmlElement root = xmlDoc.DocumentElement;
            string str = root.ToString();

            XmlDocumentFragment xmlDocFragment =
                xmlDoc.CreateDocumentFragment();
            xmlDocFragment.InnerXml=
            "<Fragment><SomeData>Fragment Data</SomeData></Fragment>";
```

```
    // Replace Node
    XmlElement rootNode = xmlDoc.DocumentElement;
    rootNode.ReplaceChild(xmlDocFragment, rootNode.LastChild);

    // Remove Node
    XmlNode node = xmlDoc.LastChild;
    xmlDoc.RemoveChild(node);
}
```

Listing 9-12 shows the NodeChangedEvent handler. The Node property of XmlNodeChangedEventArgs returns XmlNode. Using the Node property you can get more information about a node such as its parent node, value, name, namespace, and so on. (See Chapter 6 to learn more about XmlNode.)

Listing 9-12. The NodeChanged *event handler*

```
public void MyNodeChangedEvent(Object src,
    XmlNodeChangedEventArgs args)
{
    MessageBox.Show
        ("Node Changed Event Fired for node "+ args.Node.Name);
    if (args.Node.Value != null)
    {
        MessageBox.Show(args.Node.Value);
    }
}
```

Similar to Listing 9-12, Listings 9-13 and 9-14 show event handlers for the NodeInserted and NodeRemoved events.

Listing 9-13. The NodeInserted *event handler*

```
public void MyNodeInsertedEvent(Object src,
    XmlNodeChangedEventArgs args)
{
    MessageBox.Show
        ("Node Inserted Event Fired for node "+ args.Node.Name);
    if (args.Node.Value != null)
    {
        MessageBox.Show(args.Node.Value);
    }
}
```

Listing 9-14. The NodeRemoved *event handler*

```
public void MyNodeRemovedEvent(Object src,
    XmlNodeChangedEventArgs args)
{
    MessageBox.Show
        ("Node Removed Event Fired for node "+ args.Node.Name);
    if (args.Node.Value != null)
    {
        MessageBox.Show(args.Node.Value);
    }
}
```

Working with DataView and DataViewManager Events

DataView and DataViewManager define the ListChanged event, which occurs when a row is added to or deleted from a DataView or DataViewManager object. The ListChangedEventHandler method handles the ListChanged event; it's as follows:

```
public delegate void ListChangedEventHandler(
    object sender,
    ListChangedEventArgs e
);
```

where sender is the source of the event and e is ListChangedEventArgs, which contains the event data. Table 9-8 defines the ListChangedEventArgs members.

Table 9-8. The ListChangedEventArgs *Members*

MEMBER	DESCRIPTION
ListChangedType	Returns the way that list changed
NewIndex	Returns the new index of the item in the list
OldIndex	Returns the old index of the item in the list

Listing 9-15 shows the OnListChanged event handler.

Listing 9-15. The OnListChanged *event handler*

```
protected static void OnListChanged(object sender,
        System.ComponentModel.ListChangedEventArgs args)
{
        MessageBox.Show("ListChanged: Type = " + args.ListChangedType
```

```
            + ", OldIndex = " + args.OldIndex
            + ", NewIndex = " + args.NewIndex );
}
```

To test this application, you can create a Windows application and write the code in Listing 9-16 on the form load or a button-click event handler. As you can see from Listing 9-16, the code creates a DataView object, adds a new row to DataView, and then removes the first row from DataView. The adding and removing of rows is responsible for firing the OnListChanged event handler.

Listing 9-16. Adding, updating, and deleting rows of a DataView

```
private void Form1_Load(object sender, System.EventArgs e)
{
            OleDbConnection conn = new OleDbConnection();
            string strDSN = "Provider=Microsoft.Jet.OLEDB.4.0;"+
                "Data Source=C:\\Northwind.mdb";
            conn.ConnectionString = strDSN;
            string sql =
            "SELECT EmployeeId, LastName, FirstName FROM Employees";
            // Opening Connection
            conn.Open();

            // Create a data adapter
            OleDbDataAdapter da = new OleDbDataAdapter(sql, conn);

            // Create and Fill DataSet
            DataSet ds = new DataSet();
            da.Fill(ds, "Employees");

            DataView dv = ds.Tables["Employees"].DefaultView;

            // Add DataView Event Handlers
            dv.ListChanged   += new
                System.ComponentModel.ListChangedEventHandler
                (OnListChanged);

            // Add a row to the DataView
            dv.AllowEdit = true;
            DataRowView rw = dv.AddNew();
            rw.BeginEdit();
            rw["FirstName"] = "FName";
            rw["LastName"] = "LName";
            rw.EndEdit();
```

```
                    // Remove a row from the DataView
                    if(dv.Count > 0)
                    {
                        dv.Delete(0);
                        dv[0].Row.AcceptChanges();
                    }

                    // Close the connection
                    conn.Close();
}
```

> **CAUTION**   *As you can see from Listing 9-16, the* AcceptChanges() *method removes a row permanently from the database. If you don't want to remove the row, call the* RejectChanges() *method.*

The output of Listing 9-16 looks like Figures 9-11 and 9-12.

Figure 9-11. The ListChanged *events output after adding a new row*

Figure 9-12. The ListChanged *events output after deleting a row*

Summary

In this chapter, you learned about ADO.NET object events and how to handle them. Events are useful to notify a program of when an object takes an action. The connection object has two events: InfoMessage and StateChange. The DataAdapter provides FillError and the UpdateChanging and UpdateChanged events. DataSet has only one event: MergeFailed. DataTable provides events raises during column and row changes and row deletions. XmlDataDocument provides events that enable you to add, change, and remove an XML document's nodes. `DataView` and `DataViewManager` define the `ListChanged` event, which occurs when a row is added to or deleted from a `DataView` or from a `DataViewManager`.

In next chapter, I'll cover ADO.NET topics including working with stored procedures, triggers, and views. I'll also discuss COM interoperability issues.

Different Flavors of ADO.NET

IN PREVIOUS CHAPTERS, YOU saw how to use ADO.NET in Windows Forms, Web Forms, XML, and Web services. In this chapter, I'll show you how to write database applications utilizing the power of stored procedures and views. In this chapter, I'll also show how you can use unmanaged data access technologies such as ActiveX Data Objects (ADO), ADO Extensions for Data Definition Language and Security (ADOX), and ActiveX Data Objects Multi-Dimensional Library (ADOMD) in managed code with ADO.NET.

Working with Stored Procedures and Views

In this section, I'll discuss how to create and execute stored procedures and views using VS .NET. For most of the examples in this chapter, I'll use SQL Server's copy of Northwind as the sample database, not the Microsoft Access version. (Access doesn't support stored procedures, which are used to group multiple SQL statements to perform complex activities associated with transactions, security, and so on. Microsoft SQL Server has a variety of stored procedures, including *system* and *extended* stored procedures that you can read about in its *Books Online* help, for example, but I'll talk about user-defined stored procedures in this chapter.)

Creating a Stored Procedure

There are different ways you can create stored procedures. As a database administrator, you can use a database server to create and manage stored procedures. As a programmer, you can create stored procedures programmatically by using the CREATE PROCEDURE SQL statement. You can also create and manage stored procedures using Server Explorer in VS .NET. In this chapter, you'll see how to create and manage stored procedures using VS .NET.

In VS .NET, the Server Explorer enables you to create, update, and delete stored procedures. I've already discussed the Server Explorer in Chapter 4. You can launch the Server Explorer by selecting View ➤ Server Explorer (see Figure 10-1).

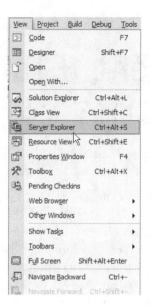

Figure 10-1. Launching the Server Explorer from the View menu

As you can see from Figure 10-2, you can expand a database's Stored Procedures node to manage stored procedures. You can view stored procedures by double-clicking on the stored procedure's name.

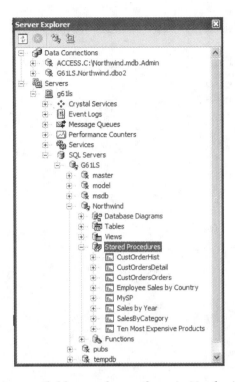

Figure 10-2. Viewing available stored procedures in Northwind database

The right-click menu option allows you to create a new stored procedure and edit, delete, and execute existing stored procedures (see Figure 10-3).

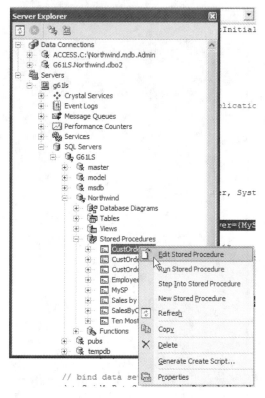

Figure 10-3. Creating, editing, deleting, and running stored procedures

The Edit Stored Procedure option lets you edit a stored procedure. The stored procedure editor looks like Figure 10-4.

```
ALTER PROCEDURE CustOrderHist @CustomerID nchar(5)
AS
SELECT ProductName, Total=SUM(Quantity)
FROM Products P, [Order Details] OD, Orders O, Customers C
WHERE C.CustomerID = @CustomerID AND
AND C.CustomerID = O.CustomerID AND
O.OrderID = OD.OrderID AND OD.ProductID = P.ProductID
GROUP BY ProductName
```

Figure 10-4. Stored procedure editor

You can create a new stored procedure by using the New Stored Procedure menu option after right-clicking the Stored Procedures node (see Figure 10-5).

Figure 10-5. Creating a new stored procedure from the Server Explorer

The New Stored Procedure menu option launches the stored procedure editor, which is used to write stored procedures.

As you can see from Figure 10-6, the stored procedure editor lets you edit the stored procedure. In SQL Server, dbo is for the database owner. In Figure 10-6, the syntax CREATE PROCEDURE dbo.StoredProcedure1 creates a stored procedure where StoredProcedure1 is the name of the stored procedure and dbo is the owner of the stored procedure.

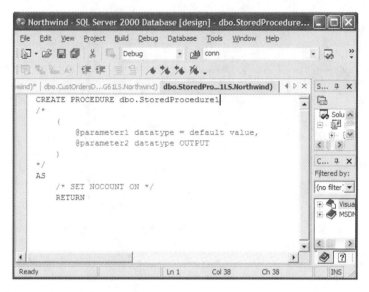

Figure 10-6. The stored procedure editor

A stored procedure can return data as a result of a SELECT statement, a return code (an integer value), or an output parameter. As you can see from Figure 10-6, the section after CREATE PROCEDURE closed with comments (/* and */) is the parameters section. If you have no requirement of using parameters in a stored procedure, you can skip this area. The section after AS is the actual SQL statement, and the section after RETURN is to return a value when you execute a stored procedure.

OK, now you can write a simple SELECT statement and save it as a stored procedure. Use this SQL statement:

```
SELECT CustomerId, CompanyName, ContactName
FROM Customers WHERE Country ='USA'
```

to select three columns values for the customers from the United States. I changed the stored procedure name to mySP. The final stored procedure looks like Figure 10-7.

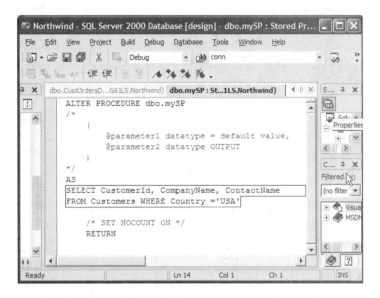

Figure 10-7. The mySP *stored procedure in the editor*

You can save a stored procedure by using File ➢ Save mySP or the Save All menu option or toolbar button. The Save option is also available on the right-click menu on the stored procedure editor (see Figure 10-8).

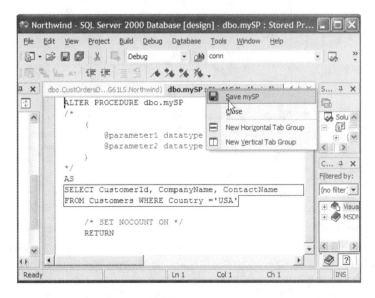

Figure 10-8. Saving a stored procedure

> **NOTE**   *The Save option not only creates a stored procedure, but it also changes the* CREATE PROCEDURE *statement to* ALTER PROCEDURE *because the stored procedure is already created.*

Now, if you go to the Server Explorer and see all the stored procedures for the Northwind database, you'll see your stored procedure listed. As you can see from Figure 10-9, stored procedure mySP has three fields listed under it that appear in the SELECT statement.

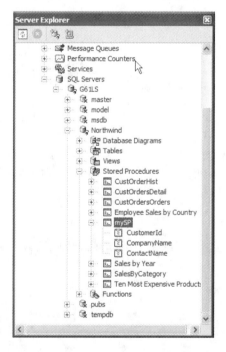

Figure 10-9. Stored procedures list for the Northwind database

Executing a Stored Procedure from VS .NET

As you've seen in Figure 10-3, you can execute a stored procedure by right-clicking on the stored procedure and selecting the Run Stored Procedure option. You can also run a stored procedure by right-clicking on the stored procedure editor and selecting Run Stored Procedure.

The output of stored procedure mySP looks like Figure 10-10.

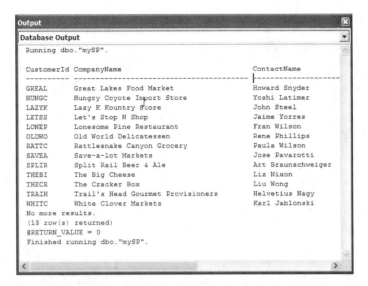

```
Output                                                                          ☒
Database Output                                                                 ▼
  Running dbo."mySP".

  CustomerId CompanyName                                ContactName
  ---------- ----------------------------------------   |-------------------
  GREAL      Great Lakes Food Market                    Howard Snyder
  HUNGC      Hungry Coyote Import Store                  Yoshi Latimer
  LAZYK      Lazy K Kountry Store                        John Steel
  LETSS      Let's Stop N Shop                           Jaime Yorres
  LONEP      Lonesome Pine Restaurant                    Fran Wilson
  OLDWO      Old World Delicatessen                      Rene Phillips
  RATTC      Rattlesnake Canyon Grocery                  Paula Wilson
  SAVEA      Save-a-lot Markets                          Jose Pavarotti
  SPLIR      Split Rail Beer & Ale                       Art Braunschweiger
  THEBI      The Big Cheese                              Liz Nixon
  THECR      The Cracker Box                             Liu Wong
  TRAIH      Trail's Head Gourmet Provisioners           Helvetius Nagy
  WHITC      White Clover Markets                        Karl Jablonski
  No more results.
  (13 row(s) returned)
  @RETURN_VALUE = 0
  Finished running dbo."mySP".
```

Figure 10-10. The output of mySP *stored procedure in VS .NET*

> **NOTE** *Similar to your* SELECT *SQL statement in the stored procedure, you can use any SQL statement, such as* UPDATE *and* DELETE.

A stored procedure can also accept input parameters. For example, if you view the CustOrdersDetail stored procedure (see Figure 10-11), which takes a value of parameter of OrderId based on the OrderID value, it returns ProductName and calculates Discount and ExtendedPrice.

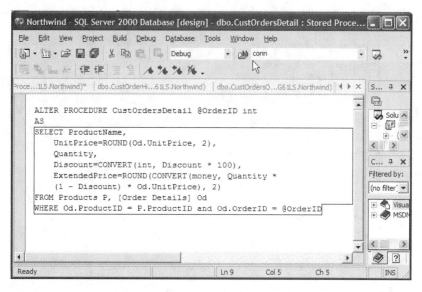

Figure 10-11. Stored procedure with input parameter

When you run the stored procedure it asks you the value for OrderId parameter, as shown in Figure 10-12.

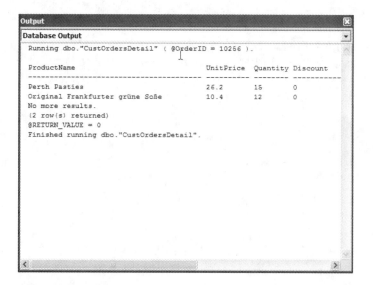

Figure 10-12. Stored procedure parameter

The output of the stored procedure CustOrdersDetail looks like Figure 10-13.

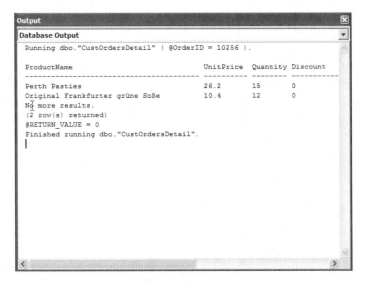

```
Output                                                        ⊠
Database Output                                               ▼
  Running dbo."CustOrdersDetail" ( @OrderID = 10256 ).

  ProductName                               UnitPrice Quantity Discount
  ----------------------------------------- --------- -------- -----------
  Perth Pasties                             26.2      15       0
  Original Frankfurter grüne Soße           10.4      12       0
  No more results.
  (2 row(s) returned)
  @RETURN_VALUE = 0
  Finished running dbo."CustOrdersDetail".
```

Figure 10-13. The output of stored procedure CustOrdersDetail

Executing a Stored Procedure Programmatically

As an application developer, most of the time you'll be executing stored procedures programmatically. You can execute a stored procedure programmatically using the command object. Instead of passing a SQL statement, you pass the stored procedure name as the SQL statement to execute a stored procedure. As you saw in Chapter 5, each data provider provides a command object to execute SQL statements. The command classes for the OleDb, Odbc, and Sql data providers are OleDbCommand, OdbcCommand, and SqlCommand, respectively. In Listing 10-1, I'll use SqlCommand to execute a stored procedure programmatically against a SQL Server database.

There are two steps involved in executing a stored procedure from your program. First, you set the command object property CommandText as the stored procedure name; second, you set the CommandType property as CommandType.StoredProcedure. Listing 10-1 executes the mySP stored procedure you created in the previous section. To test Listing 10-1, I created a console application and typed Listing 10-1 on the Main method. Don't forget to add a reference to the System.Data.dll assembly and add the following two namespaces to the project before using the Sql data provider classes:

```
using System.Data;
using System.Data.SqlClient;
```

Listing 10-1. Executing mySP *stored procedure using Sql data provider*

```
static void Main(string[] args)
{
// Create a Connection Object
            string ConnectionString ="Integrated Security=SSPI;" +
                "Initial Catalog=Northwind;" +
                "Data Source=localhost;";
            SqlConnection conn = new SqlConnection(ConnectionString);

            conn.Open();

            SqlCommand cmd = new SqlCommand("mySP", conn);
            cmd.CommandType = CommandType.StoredProcedure;

            SqlDataReader reader = cmd.ExecuteReader();

            while (reader.Read())
            {
                Console.Write(reader[0].ToString());
                Console.Write(reader[1].ToString());
                Console.WriteLine(reader[2].ToString());
            }

            Console.Read();

            // Close reader and connection
            reader.Close();
            conn.Close(); }
```

As you can see from Listing 10-1, I created a SqlCommand object by passing the stored procedure as the first parameter of the SqlCommand constructor and then set the CommandType property CommandType.StoredProcedure. The result of Listing 10-1 looks like Figure 10-14.

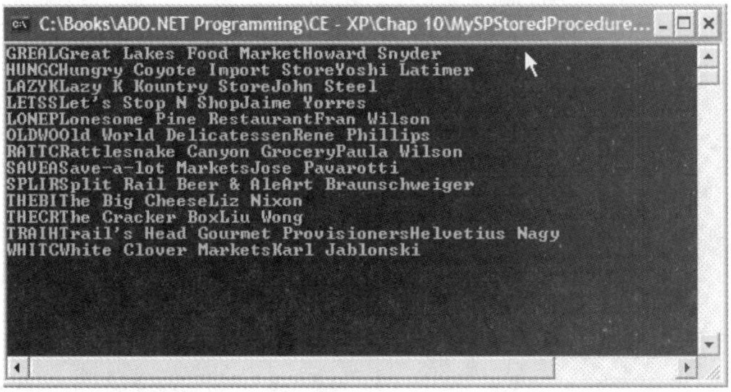

Figure 10-14. Output of stored procedure mySP

A stored procedure can also accept input, output, and both types of parameters. Now I'll modify the mySP stored procedure a little bit. This time I'll give the user an option to select the customers based on their country. Figure 10-15 shows the modified stored procedure.

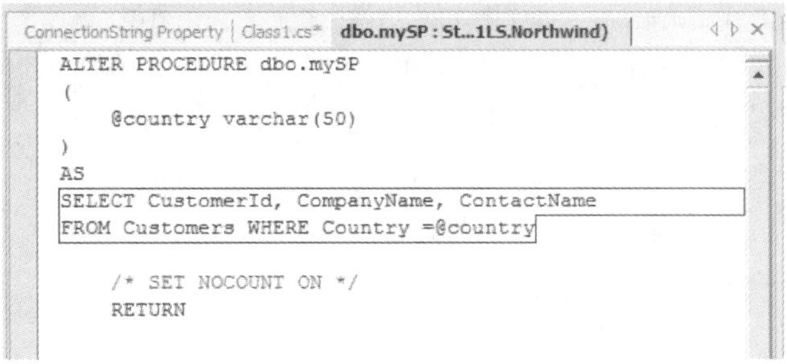

Figure 10-15. Stored procedure with parameters

As you can see from Figure 10-15, I selected customers based on the country entered by the user. You can use the SqlParameter class to create a parameter. The SqlParameter class has properties such as Direction and Value. The Direction property defines the direction if the stored procedure is an input or output (or both) or has a return value. The ParameterDirection enumeration defines values of Direction (see Table 10-1).

Table 10-1. *The* ParameterDirection *Members*

MEMBER	DESCRIPTION
Input	Input parameter.
InputOutput	Both input and output parameter.
Output	Output only.
ReturnValue	The parameter returns a value returned by the stored procedure.

The Value property sets the value of the parameter. The following code adds a parameter with the value UK. After you execute the mySP stored procedure, it'll return customers from the United Kingdom only:

```
SqlParameter param = new SqlParameter();
param = StoredProcedureCommand.Parameters.Add("@country", SqlDbType.VarChar, 50);
param.Direction = ParameterDirection.Input;
param.Value = "UK";
```

The updated source code looks like Listing 10-2, and the output of Listing 10-2 looks like Figure 10-16. In Listing 10-2, I created SqlParameter as the country and set its value to UK. ExecuteReader only returns rows where Country = "UK".

Listing 10-2. Using parameters in a stored procedure

```
// Create a Connection Object
            string ConnectionString ="Integrated Security=SSPI;" +
                "Initial Catalog=Northwind;" +
                "Data Source=localhost;";
            SqlConnection conn = new SqlConnection(ConnectionString);

            SqlCommand StoredProcedureCommand = new SqlCommand("mySP", conn);
            StoredProcedureCommand.CommandType = CommandType.StoredProcedure;

            SqlParameter param = new SqlParameter();
         param = StoredProcedureCommand.Parameters.Add("@country", SqlDbType.VarChar, 50);
            param.Direction = ParameterDirection.Input;
            param.Value = "UK";

            conn.Open();
            SqlDataReader reader = StoredProcedureCommand.ExecuteReader();

            while (reader.Read())
```

```
    {
        Console.Write(reader[0].ToString());
        Console.Write(reader[1].ToString());
        Console.WriteLine(reader[2].ToString());
    }

    Console.Read();

    // Close reader and connection
    reader.Close();
    conn.Close();
```

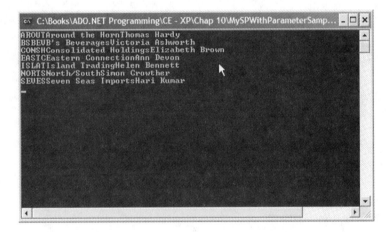

Figure 10-16. Output of Listing 10-2

To return a value from a stored procedure, the only thing you need to do is change the stored procedure, which will store and return a value as a parameter, and set the parameter's Direction property as follows:

```
SqlParameter param = new SqlParameter();
param.Direction = ParameterDirection.ReturnValue;
```

Also, store the command execute results in a number variable like this:

```
param = StoredProcedureCommand.Parameters.Add("@counter", SqlDbType.Int);
```

> **NOTE** *See the following example for the complete source code.*

Now I'll show you an example of using ParameterDirection.Output. To test this source code, create a console application and the following namespace references:

```
using System;
using System.Data;
using System.Data.Common;
using System.Data.SqlClient;
```

Now create a stored procedure called AddCat1 that adds a row to the Categories table and returns the row count (see Listing 10-3).

Listing 10-3. AddCat1 stored procedure
```
CREATE PROCEDURE AddCat1
   @CategoryName nchar(15),
   @Description char(16),
   @Identity int OUT
AS
INSERT INTO Categories (CategoryName, Description)
VALUES(@CategoryName, @Description)
SET @Identity = @@Identity
RETURN @@ROWCOUNT
```

Listing 10-4 shows how to use output parameters. Everything is similar to the previous samples except that I used the parameter direction ParameterDirection.Output.

Listing 10-4. Executing a stored procedure with output parameter
```
string connString =
            "Data Source=localhost;Integrated Security=SSPI;"
            + "Initial Catalog=northwind";
        string sql =
        "SELECT CategoryID, CategoryName, Description FROM Categories";

        SqlConnection conn = new SqlConnection(connString);
        SqlDataAdapter da = new SqlDataAdapter(sql, conn);

        da.InsertCommand = new SqlCommand("AddCat1", conn);
        da.InsertCommand.CommandType = CommandType.StoredProcedure;

        SqlParameter myParm =
            da.InsertCommand.Parameters.Add("@RowCount", SqlDbType.Int);
        myParm.Direction = ParameterDirection.ReturnValue;
```

```
da.InsertCommand.Parameters.Add
    ("@CategoryName", SqlDbType.NChar, 15, "CategoryName");
da.InsertCommand.Parameters.Add
    ("@Description", SqlDbType.Char, 16, "Description");
myParm = da.InsertCommand.Parameters.Add
    ("@Identity", SqlDbType.Int, 0, "CategoryID");
myParm.Direction = ParameterDirection.Output;

DataSet ds = new DataSet();
da.Fill(ds, "Categories");

DataRow row = ds.Tables["Categories"].NewRow();
row["CategoryName"] = "Beverages";
row["Description"] = "Chai";
ds.Tables["Categories"].Rows.Add(row);

da.Update(ds, "Categories");

Console.WriteLine(
    da.InsertCommand.Parameters["@RowCount"].Value.ToString() );
```

Working with Views

A *view* is a virtual table that represents data from one or more than one database table. You can select data from a single or multiple tables based on the sort and filter criteria (using the WHERE and GROUP BY clauses) and save data as a view. You can also set permissions on views. For example, a manager, an accountant, and a clerk of a company share the same database. The manager can access all data from different tables of the database. The accountant can access partial data from multiple tables, and the clerk can access partial data from a single table. You can create three different views based on these user rights and let the users access these views based on their rights.

Creating a View

Similar to stored procedures, you can create and manage views from the Server Explorer. To create a view, you can expand a database, right-click on the Views leaf, and select the New View option. This action launches the wizard, which lets you pick tables. The Add button adds tables to the view designer (see Figure 10-17).

Figure 10-17. Adding tables to the view designer

I added three tables to the designer: Customers, Orders, and Employees. I selected only a few columns from each table (see Figure 10-18).

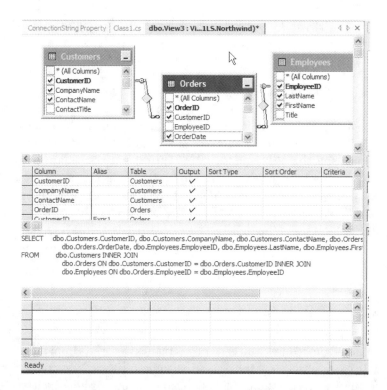

Figure 10-18. Creating a view after selecting columns from three tables

Now you can save a view by using the Save button or menu or by right-clicking on the view and selecting the Save option (see Figure 10-19).

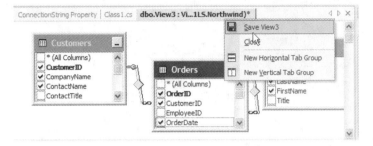

Figure 10-19. Saving a view

I called the view `CustEmpView` and clicked OK (see Figure 10-20).

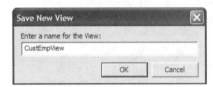

Figure 10-20. Click OK to save a view.

Now when you see the Server Explorer views, you'll see `CustEmpView` listed (see Figure 10-21).

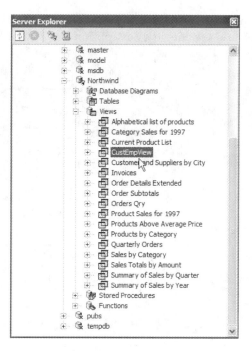

Figure 10-21. Available views in the Server Explorer

Executing Views from VS .NET

Now you can execute a view by right-clicking on one in the Server Explorer and selecting the Retrieve Data from the View option. The output of the CustEmpView looks like Figure 10-22.

CustomerID	CompanyName	ContactName	OrderID	Expr 1	OrderD
VINET	Vins et alcools Chev	Paul Henriot	10248	VINET	7/4/19
TOMSP	Toms Spezialitäten	Karin Josephs	10249	TOMSP	7/5/19
HANAR	Hanari Carnes	Mario Pontes	10250	HANAR	7/8/19
VICTE	Victuailles en stock	Mary Saveley	10251	VICTE	7/8/19
SUPRD	Suprêmes délices	Pascale Cartrain	10252	SUPRD	7/9/19
HANAR	Hanari Carnes	Mario Pontes	10253	HANAR	7/10/1
CHOPS	Chop-suey Chinese	Yang Wang	10254	CHOPS	7/11/1
RICSU	Richter Supermarkt	Michael Holz	10255	RICSU	//12/1
WELLI	Wellington Importa	Paula Parente	10256	WELLI	7/15/1
HILAA	HILARION-Abastos	Carlos Hernández	10257	HILAA	7/16/1

Figure 10-22. Results of the CustEmpView after executing it from the Server Explorer

Retrieving Data from a View Programmatically

Similar to the stored procedures, the command object executes a view. You can retrieve data from a view programmatically by replacing the view name as the table name in a SQL statement. Listing 10-5 shows you how to use the CustEmpView in an application. As you can see from the code, I've used the CustEmpView view as table name in the SELECT statement:

```
SELECT * FROM CustEmpView
```

To test this code, create a Windows application in VS .NET, add a DataGrid control to the form, and write the code in Listing 10-5 on the Form_Load event. Also don't forget to add a reference to the System.Data.SqlClient namespace in the project.

Listing 10-5. Executing a view programmatically

```
private void Form1_Load(object sender, System.EventArgs e)
{

            // Create a Connection Object
            string ConnectionString ="Integrated Security=SSPI;" +
                "Initial Catalog=Northwind;" +
                "Data Source=localhost;";
            SqlConnection conn = new SqlConnection(ConnectionString);

        SqlDataAdapter adapter = new SqlDataAdapter("SELECT * FROM CustEmpView", conn);

            DataSet ds = new DataSet("CustEmpView");
            adapter.Fill(ds, "CustEmpView");

            dataGrid1.DataSource = ds.DefaultViewManager;

}
```

The output of Listing 10-5 looks like Figure 10-23.

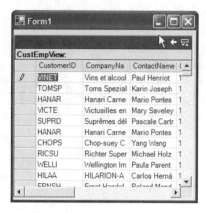

Figure 10-23. The output the CustEmpView view from a program

COM Interoperability

The code written for the .NET Framework is also referred to as *managed code,* and the code written for traditional Windows applications (previous to the .NET Framework) is called *unmanaged code.* Managed code contains metadata used by the Common Language Runtime (CLR).

The Component Object Model (COM) has been around for many years and is used by many Windows applications. Eventually the .NET platform will replace COM, but until then you may need to develop COM components from .NET and access them from unmanaged code, or you may want to use COM components in .NET applications. *COM interoperability* (also referred as *COM interop*) enables you to use existing COM components in .NET applications or use .NET components in unmanaged code.

In COM, type libraries stored metadata for a COM component and described the characteristics of a COM component. In .NET, an *assembly* is the primary building block of a .NET application. An assembly is a collection of functionality that is built, versioned, and deployed as a component. Similar to COM type libraries, an assembly contains an assembly manifest. The assembly manifest includes information about an assembly such as the identity, version, culture, digital signature, compile-time dependencies, files that make up the assembly implementation, and permissions required to run the assembly properly.

In brief, COM understands the language of type libraries, and the .NET Framework understands the language of assembly manifests. So converting a type library into an assembly manifest provides accessibility of COM components from the managed code, and converting an assembly manifest to a COM type library provides accessibility of .NET assemblies in unmanaged code.

Interop assemblies are .NET assemblies that act as a bridge between managed and unmanaged code. Internet assemblies provide mapping of COM object members to equivalent .NET managed members.

The .NET Framework defines a common set of data types. All .NET programming languages use these common data types. During the import process of a COM type library, there may be cases when the parameters and return values of COM objects use different data types than .NET data types. The interop marshaler handles these conversions for you. *Interoperability marshaling* is the process of packaging parameters and returning values into equivalent data types during conversion of a COM type library to an assembly manifest and an assembly manifest to a COM type library.

In the following sections, I'll show you how to use unmanaged libraries in managed code through COM interoperability.

Using the ADO Recordset in ADO.NET

Using Visual Studio .NET, you can import a type library in an application using the Project ➢ Add Reference menu option. The Add Reference option adds the assembly namespace to your project.

In this sample, you'll see how to import the ADO type library and use the ADO recordset to access a database. After that, you'll fill data to a DataSet from the ADO recordset using a data adapter.

To test this application, create a Windows application and drag a DataGrid control to the form from the toolbox. To add a reference to a COM type library, go to the Add Reference option from the Project menu and select the COM tab in the Add Reference dialog box. As you can see from Figure 10-24, I selected Microsoft ActiveX Data Objects 2.7 Library. Click Select to add the selection to the Selected Components list. Now click OK.

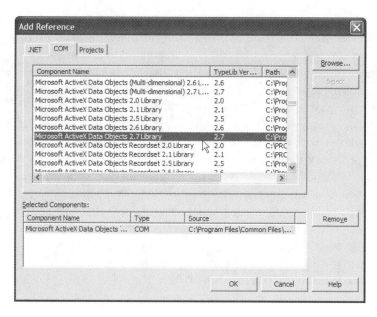

Figure 10-24. Adding a reference to a COM library

This action adds the ADODB namespace to the project. You can see this namespace from the project namespaces (see Figure 10-25).

Figure 10-25. Namespace after adding ADODB namespace to the project

After adding a reference of a namespace to a project, its members are available for use in your project. You include this namespace in your application by calling using. You also should add a reference to the System.Data.OleDb

namespace because you'll use the OleDb data adapter to fill a dataset. So, add
these two namespace references to the project with this:

```
using System.Data.OleDb;
using ADODB;
```

Now you can use the ADO recordset and connection to access a database. As
you can see from Listing 10-6, I created a Connection object and set the connection mode and cursor location. After that I called the connection's Execute
method to execute a SQL statement that returns the _Recordset object. The
Fill method of data adapter reads data from a recordset and fills data to
a dataset. As you can see, I also created a dataset and data adapter and called the
data adapter's Fill method. The Fill method takes three parameters: a dataset,
a recordset, and a dataset name. After that, bind the dataset to a data grid in
order to fill data from the dataset to the data grid.

Listing 10-6. Using ADODB namespace to access a database

```
private void Form1_Load(object sender, System.EventArgs e)
        {

                // Create SQL and Connection strings
                string ConnectionString = @"Provider=Microsoft.Jet.OLEDB.4.0; Data
                  Source=c:\Northwind.mdb";
                string sql = "SELECT CustomerId, CompanyName, ContactName From Customers";

                // Create a Connection object and open it
                Connection conn = new Connection();
                int connMode = (int)ConnectModeEnum.adModeUnknown;
                conn.CursorLocation = CursorLocationEnum.adUseServer;
                conn.Open(ConnectionString, "", "", connMode);

                object recAffected = null;
                int cmdType = (int)CommandTypeEnum.adCmdText;
                _Recordset rs = conn.Execute(sql, out recAffected, cmdType);

                // Create dataset and data adpater objects
                DataSet ds = new DataSet("Recordset");
                OleDbDataAdapter da = new OleDbDataAdapter();

                // Call data adapter's Fill method to fill data from ADO
                // Recordset to the dataset
                da.Fill(ds, rs, "Customers");
```

```
        // Now use dataset
        dataGrid1.DataSource = ds.DefaultViewManager;
    }
```

The output of Listing 10-6 looks like Figure 10-26.

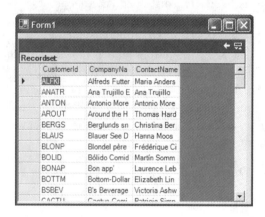

Figure 10-26. Displaying data from an ADO recordset to a data grid

Using ADOX with ADO.NET

Microsoft ActiveX Data Objects Extensions for Data Definition Language and Security (ADOX) is an extension to ADO and provides an object model to manipulate data definition and security.

You can use ADOX in managed code in a pretty similar way to how you used an ADO recordset in the previous section. Just add a reference to ADOX type library using VS .NET's Add Reference option and use the namespace and its members as you would in unmanaged code.

To test this, create a new Windows application. After that add a reference to the Microsoft ADO Ext. 2.7 for DLL and Security component to the project (see Figure 10-27).

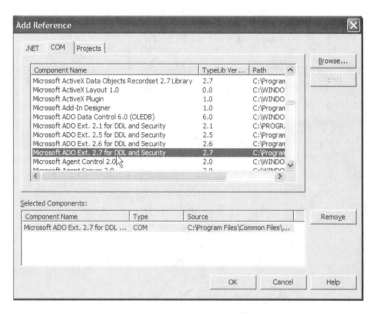

Figure 10-27. Adding a reference to ADOX library

Now if you add references in your project, you'll see that ADOX namespace is listed (see Figure 10-28).

Figure 10-28. ADOX namespace listed in project references

Now the only thing you need to do is to use the namespace and its members. The ADOX classes should be available in your application after adding using ADOX to the project. ADOX provides objects that you can use to create databases, tables, and columns. The Catalog object represents a database and its create method creates a new database. The Table object represents a database table. You can add columns to a table using the Columns collection's Append method.

Listing 10-7 creates a new Microsoft Access database called Test.mdb with the table MyTable and two columns, col1 and col2, in it.

Listing 10-7. Using ADOX from managed code

```
private void Form1_Load(object sender, System.EventArgs e)
    {
        // Create SQL and Connection strings
        string ConnectionString =
            @"Provider=Microsoft.Jet.OLEDB.4.0; Data Source=c:\Test.mdb";

        try
        {
            // Create a Catalog object
            Catalog ct = new Catalog();
            ct.Create(ConnectionString);

            // Create a table and two columns
            Table dt = new Table();
            dt.Name = "MyTable";
            dt.Columns.Append("col1", DataTypeEnum.adInteger, 4);
            dt.Columns.Append("col2", DataTypeEnum.adVarWChar, 255);

            // Add table to the tables collection
            ct.Tables.Append((object)dt);
        }
        catch(Exception exp)
        {
            MessageBox.Show(exp.Message.ToString());
        }
    }
```

Accessing OLAP Server Data with ADO.NET

The ActiveX Data Objects Multi-Dimensional Library (ADOMD) provides access to Online Analytical Processing (OLAP) Server data from applications. OLAP services extract, summarize, organize, and store data warehouses in multi-dimensional structures, also known as OLAP *server cubes*.

To test the OLAP sample, I'll use the FoodMart 2000 database that comes with the Microsoft SQL Server Analysis Server. Before testing this sample, you must have SQL Server 2000 Analysis Server running. If you don't have SQL Server 2000 Analysis Server running, you can install it from Microsoft SQL Server

CD by selecting SQL Server 2000 Components ➣ Install Analysis Services. This option will install SQL Server Analysis Service on your machine.

> **NOTE** *Installing Analysis Services may not install the FoodMart 2000 database. On my machine I needed to restore the database from the* C:\Program Files\Microsoft Analysis Services\Samples\ foodmart 2000.cab *file. You can restore a database by using Analysis Manager ➣ Meta Data ➣ Restore option.*

ADOMD functionality is defined in the msadomd.dll library. If this library is not listed in your COM components list, you can use the Browse button in the Add Reference dialog box to browse it. The default path for this library is C:\Program Files\Common Files\System\ADO (see Figure 10-29).

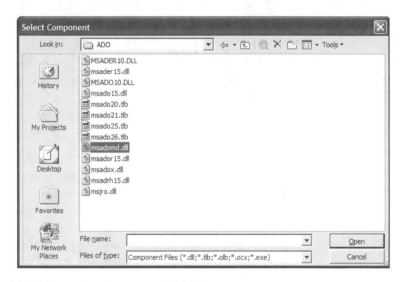

Figure 10-29. Browsing the msadomd.dll *library*

After adding a reference to the msadomd.dll, the Add Reference dialog box looks like Figure 10-30.

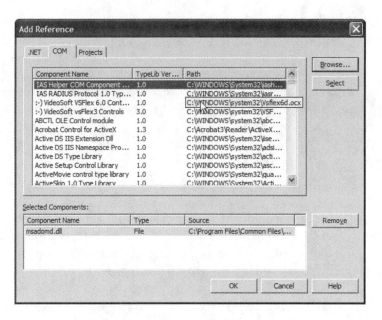

Figure 10-30. Adding a reference to `msadomd.dll` *library*

Now click the OK button to add the reference. This action adds the ADOMD namespace to the project (see Figure 10-31).

Figure 10-31. ADOMD namespace listed in the project namespaces

Now you can use the `using` directive to include the ADOMD namespace in your project and use ADOMD classes.

> **NOTE** *I added a reference to the ADOMD and ADODB (described in the "Using the ADO Recordset in ADO.NET" section) because I'll also use the* Connection *object of ADO.*

To test the source code, create a Windows application and add two list boxes, two buttons, a text box, and a label and set their properties (see Figure 10-32).

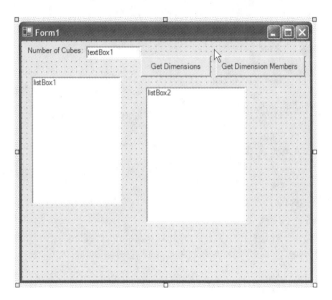

Figure 10-32. Windows Form to test ADOMD

Now add references to ADOMD and ADODB in the application as follows:

```
using ADOMD;
using ADODB;
```

Also add the following variables in the beginning of the form class.

```
// Define variables
private string strConn;
private Connection dbConn;
private Catalog dtCatalog;
private CubeDefs cubes;
```

After that, create Connection and Catalog objects on the Form_Load event and use CubeDefs of Catalog to get all the cubes. As you can see from Listing 10-8, I added all cubes to the list box and the number of cubes to the text box.

Listing 10-8. Getting all available cubes from the FoodMart 2000 database

```
private void Form1_Load(object sender, System.EventArgs e)
{
    strConn = "Provider=msolap; Data Source = localhost;" +
    "Initial Catalog = FoodMart 2000; User ID =sa; Pwd=";

    // Create and open a connection
    dbConn = new Connection ();
    dbConn.Open (strConn, "", "",
      (int)ConnectModeEnum.adModeUnknown);

    // Create a Catalog object and set it's active connection
        // as connection
        dtCatalog = new Catalog ();
        dtCatalog.ActiveConnection = (object)dbConn;

        // Get all cubes
        cubes = dtCatalog.CubeDefs;
        // Set text box text as total number of cubes
        textBox1.Text = cubes.Count.ToString();

        foreach (CubeDef cube in cubes)
        {
            string str = "";
            listBox1.Items.Add(cube.Name.ToString());

            str = "Cube Name :"+ cube.Name.ToString() + ", ";
            str += "Description :"+ cube.Description.ToString() + ", ";
            str += "Dimensions :"+ cube.Dimensions.ToString();
        }

        listBox1.SetSelected(0, true);

}
```

Now if you run the application, the output looks like Figure 10-33.

Figure 10-33. All available cubes in the FoodMart 2000 database

The Get Dimensions button gets the dimensions of the selected cube in the left list box in Figure 10-33. Listing 10-9 returns the dimensions of a cube and adds it to the right list box of Figure 10-33.

Listing 10-9. Getting all the dimensions of a cube

```
private void button1_Click(object sender, System.EventArgs e)
{

    // Get the selected cube
    CubeDef cube = cubes[listBox1.SelectedItem.ToString()];

    // Get all the dimensions of the selected cube
    for (int i=0; i< cube.Dimensions.Count; i++)
    {
        Dimension dim = cube.Dimensions[i];
        listBox2.Items.Add(dim.Name.ToString());
    }
    listBox2.SetSelected(0, true);
}
```

The output of the Get Dimensions button fills the right list box with the dimensions (see Figure 10-34).

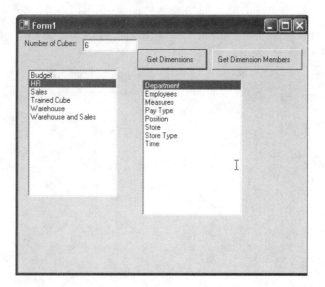

Figure 10-34. Getting dimensions of a cube

The Get Dimension Members button returns the properties of a dimension such as name, hierarchies, UniqueName, and Properties (see Listing 10-10).

Listing 10-10. Getting dimension members

```
private void button2_Click(object sender, System.EventArgs e)
{
    // Get the selected cube
    CubeDef cube = cubes[listBox1.SelectedItem.ToString()];
    // Get the selected Dimension
    Dimension dim = cube.Dimensions[listBox2.SelectedItem.ToString()];

    MessageBox.Show("Dimension Properties :: Name="+dim.Name.ToString()
        +", Description="+ dim.Description.ToString() +", Hierarchies="
        + dim.Hierarchies.ToString() +", Unique Name="
        + dim.UniqueName.ToString());
}
```

The output of Listing 10-10 looks like Figure 10-35.

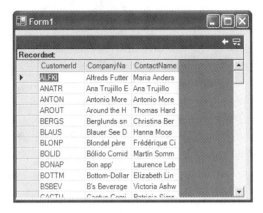

Figure 10-35. Viewing dimension properties

Getting a Database Schema

Usually when you work with databases, you already know the database schema such as database tables, table columns, and the column properties. What if you don't know the database schema, and you need to know database tables, their columns, and column properties programmatically?

In this sample I'll show you how to access a database schema programmatically. As you can see from Figure 10-36, I created a Windows application with one text box, three buttons, and two list boxes. The Browse button lets you browse .mdb databases on your machine. The GetTables button then reads the database tables and adds them to the first list box. The Get Table Schema button returns table columns and their properties of the selected table in list box.

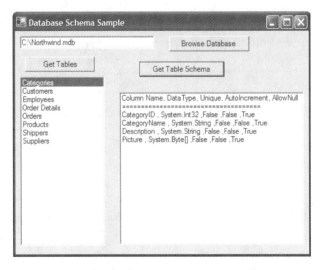

Figure 10-36. Getting a database schema programmatically

Listing 10-11 shows the source code for this application. As you can see, the `BrowseBtn_Click` handler browses Access databases on the machine, fills the selected database name to the text box, and sets `dbName` as the database name, which is a string type of variable defined as follows:

```
private string dbName = "";
```

Listing 10-11. Reading a database schema programmatically

```
private void BrowseBtn_Click(object sender, System.EventArgs e)
{
  OpenFileDialog fdlg = new OpenFileDialog();
  fdlg.Title = "C# Corner Open File Dialog" ;
  fdlg.InitialDirectory = @"c:\" ;
  fdlg.Filter = "All files (*.*)|*.mdb|"+
  "MS-Access Database files (*.mdb)|*.mdb" ;
  fdlg.FilterIndex = 2 ;
  fdlg.RestoreDirectory = true ;
  if(fdlg.ShowDialog() == DialogResult.OK)
  {
     textBox1.Text = fdlg.FileName ;
     dbName = fdlg.FileName;
  }
}
```

The `GetOleDbSchemaTable` method of `OleDbConnection` returns a data table object containing database tables. As you can see from the `GetTableBtn_Click` handler in Listing 10-12, I set the dataset to the left list box with the `DisplayMember` property as `TABLE_NAME`. I set `DisplayMember` because I want to show only one column of the data table in the list box.

Listing 10-12. Getting database tables from a SQL Server database

```
private void GetTablesBtn_Click(object sender, System.EventArgs e)
 {
// Connection string
        string strDSN = "Provider=Microsoft.Jet.OLEDB.4.0;"+
            "Data Source="+ dbName;

        try
        {
            // Create a connection and open it
            OleDbConnection conn = new OleDbConnection(strDSN);
            conn.Open();
```

```
                // Call GetOleDbSchemaTable to get the schema data table
                DataTable dt = conn.GetOleDbSchemaTable
                (OleDbSchemaGuid.Tables, new object[]
                    {null, null, null, "TABLE"});

                // Set DataSource and DisplayMember properties
                // of the list box control
                listBox1.DataSource = dt.DefaultView;
                listBox1.DisplayMember = "TABLE_NAME";

                // Close the connection
                conn.Close();
            }
            catch(Exception exp)
            {
                MessageBox.Show(exp.Message.ToString());
            }
        }
}
```

GetSchemaBn_Click listed in Listing 10-13 is the event handler that returns the columns and their properties of a database table. You read the database table using SELECT * and use DataTable to get columns. The DataColumn class defines the member for the table column's properties such as allow null, autonumber, unique, column data type, column name, and so on.

NOTE *See Chapter 5 for more details on* DataTable *and* DataColumn *class members.*

Listing 10-13. Getting a database table schema

```
private void GetSchemaBtn_Click(object sender, System.EventArgs e)
        {
            // Get the selected item text of list box
            string selTable = listBox1.GetItemText(listBox1.SelectedItem);

            // Connection string
            string strDSN = "Provider=Microsoft.Jet.OLEDB.4.0;"+
                "Data Source="+ dbName;

            try
            {
```

```
                    // Create and open connection
                    OleDbConnection conn = new OleDbConnection(strDSN);
                    conn.Open();

                    string strSQL = "SELECT * FROM "+selTable;

                    // Create data adapter
                    OleDbDataAdapter myCmd = new OleDbDataAdapter
                        (strSQL, conn );


                    // Create and fill dataset
                    DataSet dtSet = new DataSet();
                    myCmd.Fill( dtSet);
                    DataTable dt = dtSet.Tables[0];

                    // Add items to the list box control
                    listBox2.Items.Add("Column Name, DataType, Unique,"+
                        " AutoIncrement, AllowNull");
                    listBox2.Items.Add("=====================================");

                    foreach( DataColumn dc in dt.Columns )
                    {
                        listBox2.Items.Add(dc.ColumnName+" , "+dc.DataType +
                            " ,"+dc.Unique +" ,"+dc.AutoIncrement+" ,"+dc.AllowDBNull );
                     }
                    // close connection
                    conn.Close();
                }
                catch(Exception exp)
                {
                    MessageBox.Show(exp.Message.ToString());
                }
            }
```

Selecting Distinct Records

It isn't hard to select unique rows from a database table using SELECT DISTINCT, but sometimes people get stuck on this. So, it's not a bad idea to talk about the procedure.

You can use the SELECT DISTINCT SQL statement to select distinct records from a database. This is useful when you want to return only one record corresponding to a criterion. Listing 10-14 returns distinct records from the Employees table ordered by the LastName.

Listing 10-14. Selecting distinct rows from a database table

```
private void button1_Click(object sender, System.EventArgs e)
    {

        // Create a Connection Object
        string ConnectionString = @"Provider=Microsoft.Jet.OLEDB.4.0;"+
            "Data Source=c:\\Northwind.mdb";
        OleDbConnection conn = new OleDbConnection(ConnectionString);

        // Open the connection
        if( conn.State != ConnectionState.Open)
            conn.Open();


        string sql = "SELECT DISTINCT(LastName)"+

            "FROM Employees ORDER BY LastName";
        OleDbDataAdapter da = new OleDbDataAdapter(sql, conn);

        DataSet ds = new DataSet();
        da.Fill(ds, "Employees");

        dataGrid1.DataSource = ds.DefaultViewManager;

        // Close the connection
        if( conn.State == ConnectionState.Open)
            conn.Close();
    }
```

Summary

In this chapter you learned about using stored procedures and views. You also saw how to use COM type libraries in managed code using COM interoperability. After that you learned about the `OleDbConnection`'s `GetOleDbSchemaTable` method, which you can use to return a database's schema programmatically.

I used SQL Server and Access databases in my samples. ADO.NET accesses other data sources in a similar way. In the next chapter, you'll see how to use ODBC data providers to work with different kinds of data sources, including MySQL, Oracle, Sybase, Excel and even text files.

CHAPTER 11

Working with the ODBC .NET Data Provider

IN PREVIOUS CHAPTERS, YOU were using SQL Server and Microsoft Access in the sample applications. In this chapter, I'll show you how to work with different data sources (or databases) using the ODBC .NET data provider. You'll see how you can use the ODBC .NET data provider to work with MySQL, Oracle, Excel, and even text data files.

Understanding the ODBC .NET Data Provider

You read a brief discussion on the ODBC .NET data provider in Chapter 4. The ODBC .NET data provider provides access to ODBC data sources with the help of native ODBC drivers in the same way that the OleDb .NET data provider accesses native OLE DB providers. One of the best things about working with ADO.NET data providers is that all data providers define the similar class hierarchy. The only things you need to change are the classes and the connection string.

Installing the ODBC .NET Data Provider

Unlike the Sql and OleDb data providers, the ODBC data provider is an add-on component to the .NET Framework. If the ODBC .NET provider isn't installed on your system, you can download it from the .NET Software Development Kit (SDK) and Visual Studio .NET. You can find the ODBC .NET data provider on the Microsoft site (http://www.microsoft.com/data). Alternatively, you can find the latest links of the ODBC .NET SDK on C# Corner's Downloads section (http://www.c-sharpcorner.com/downloads.asp).

   After installing ODBC .NET, you need to customize the toolbox to add the ODBC data components to it. You can customize the toolbox by right-clicking on the toolbox's Data tab and selecting Customize Toolbox (see Figure 11-1).

Figure 11-1. The Customize Toolbox option

NOTE *Make sure the Data tab is selected when you select Customize Toolbox. Otherwise new components will be added to the active tab.*

Next, you click on the .NET Framework Components tab (not the default COM components) and look for ODBC components. Check the appropriate boxes, and click the OK button (see Figure 11-2).

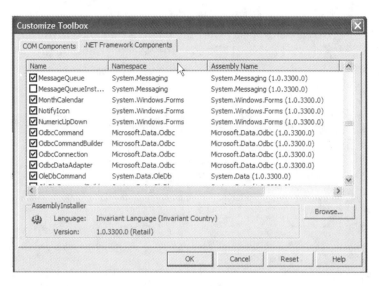

Figure 11-2. Adding ODBC components to the project

Next, you need to add a reference to the `Microsoft.Data.Odbc.dll` assembly using the Project ➢ Add Reference. You can use the Browse button to browse the directory. The `Microsoft.Data.Odbc.dll` resides in the `\Program Files\Microsoft.NET\Odbc.NET` directory (see Figure 11-3).

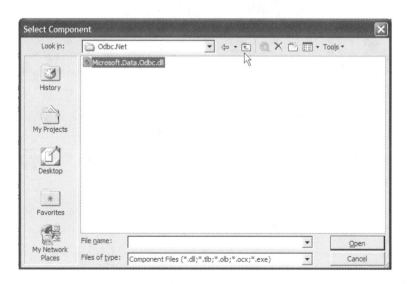

Figure 11-3. Browsing the Odbc.Net folder

Select the component and then click Open to add the reference to the `Microsoft.Data.Odbc` namespace. The Add Reference dialog box will appear and you'll see `Microsoft.Odbc.dll` listed in the Selected Components list (see Figure 11-4).

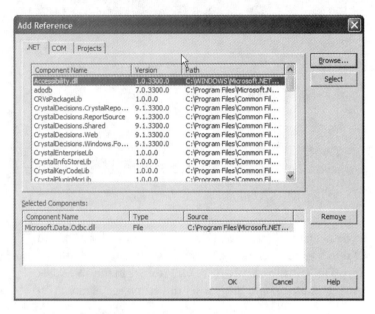

Figure 11-4. Adding reference to `Microsoft.Data.Odbc.dll`

Click OK. Using the Solution Explorer, click your project and then expand the References node. You'll see that the `Microsoft.Data.Odbc` reference has been added to your project (see Figure 11-5).

Figure 11-5. The `Microsoft.Data.Odbc` *namespace*

To make sure the ODBC data provider is installed and added to your project, you can also look at the toolbox (see Figure 11-6). If the toolbox has the ODBC data components listed, that means the ODBC data provider is installed on your system and the reference to the data provider has been added to your project.

Figure 11-6. ODBC data provider components

> **NOTE** *The toolbox's Data tab is not available for console applications.*

Now you can use ODBC components in a similar way that you've used the Sql and OleDb data provider components.

The ODBC .NET data provider installation adds the `Microsoft.Data.Odbc` namespace to the namespace, which defines the classes for ODBC data providers. To use the ODBC .NET data provider, you must add a `using` statement for the `Microsoft.Data.Odbc` namespace to your application:

```
using Microsoft.Data.Odbc;
```

Using the ODBC .NET Data Provider

You've seen how to use the SQL and OleDb data providers in previous chapters. Working with the ODBC data provider is no different from working with the Sql and OleDb data providers. Unlike the Sql and OleDb data providers, however, the ODBC data provider is defined in the `Microsoft.Data.Odbc` namespace. You must add a reference to this namespace before you start using the ODBC data provider classes.

The ODBC data provider defines similar classes and a class hierarchy as the Sql and OleDb data providers. Further, you can use the ODBC classes as you've used the SQL and OleDb classes. Table 11-1 defines the ODBC .NET data provider classes (discussed in more detail in Chapter 5).

Table 11-1. The ODBC .NET Data Provider Classes

CLASS	DESCRIPTION
OdbcCommand	Similar to OleDbCommand and SqlCommand, this class represents an SQL statement or stored procedure to execute against a data source.
OdbcCommandBuilder	Similar to OleDbCommandBuilder and SqlCommandBuilder, this class automatically generates select, insert, update, and delete SQL commands.
OdbcConnection	Represents a connection.
OdbcDataAdapter	Represents a data adapter.
OdbcDataReader	Represents a data reader.
OdbcError	Represents errors and warnings.
OdbcErrorCollection	Represents collection of errors and warnings.
OdbcException	Represents an ODBC exception class.
OdbcParameter	Represents an ODBC parameter.
OdbcParameterCollection	Represents a parameter collection.
OdbcTransaction	Represents a transaction.

As you can see from Table 11-1, the ODBC data provider has connection, command, data adapter, parameter, exception and errors, command builder, data reader, transaction, and other classes similar to the Sql and OleDb data providers. To use the ODBC data provider classes, you create a connection object, fill data from the connection to a data adapter or a data reader, and then display the data.

Now I'll show you an example of how to access data from a data source using the ODBC data provider. In this example, I'll use the Access 2000 Northwind database as the data source.

Before creating a connection, the first thing you need to understand is the connection string. The connection string for OdbcConnection contains a data source driver and the data source path with an optional user ID and password. Optionally, you can also use an ODBC Data Source Name (DSN) as a connection string. You create a DSN from the ODBC Administration.

The connection string for an Oracle database looks like the following:

```
Driver={Microsoft ODBC for Oracle};Server=ORACLE8i7;UID=odbcuser;PWD=odbc$5xr
```

The connection string for a Microsoft Access database looks like the following:

```
Driver={Microsoft Access Driver (*.mdb)};DBQ=c:\Northwind.mdb
```

The connection string for an Excel database looks like the following:

```
Driver={Microsoft Excel Driver (*.xls)};DBQ=c:\bin\book1.xls
```

The connection string for a text database looks like the following:

```
Driver={Microsoft Text Driver (*.txt; *.csv)};DBQ=c:\
```

You can use any data source name (DSN) by using the following connection string:

```
DSN=dsnname
```

The connection string for a SQL Server database looks like the following:

```
"DRIVER={SQL Server};SERVER=MyServer;UID=sa;PWD=Qvr&77xk;DATABASE=northwind;";
```

Listing 11-1 reads data from Northwind database and shows the results on the console. In this sample, I created a console application to test the code. As you can see from Listing 11-1, first I included the Microsoft.Data.Odbc namespace. After that I created an OdbcConnection object with the Microsoft Access ODBC driver and the Northwind database. The next step was to create an OdbcCommand object and call the ExecuteReader method, which returns OdbcDataReader. After that I read data from the data reader and displayed the results on the console.

Listing 11-1. Reading data from Northwind using the ODBC data provider

```csharp
using System;
using Microsoft.Data.Odbc;

namespace FirstODBCSamp
{
    class Class1
    {
        static void Main(string[] args)
        {
            // Build a connection and SQL strings
            string connectionString
                = @"Driver={Microsoft Access Driver (*.mdb)};DBQ=c:\Northwind.mdb";
            string SQL = "SELECT * FROM Orders";


            // Create connection object
            OdbcConnection  conn = new OdbcConnection(connectionString);
            // Create command object
            OdbcCommand cmd = new OdbcCommand(SQL);
            cmd.Connection = conn;
            // Open connection
            conn.Open();
            // Call command's ExecuteReader
            OdbcDataReader reader = cmd.ExecuteReader();
            // Read the reader and display results on the console
            while (reader.Read())
            {
                Console.Write("OrderID:"+reader.GetInt32(0).ToString() );
                Console.Write(" ,");
                Console.WriteLine("Customer:" + reader.GetString(1).ToString() );
            }
            // close reader and connection
            reader.Close();
            conn.Close();
        }
    }
}
```

The output of Listing 11-1 looks like Figure 11-7.

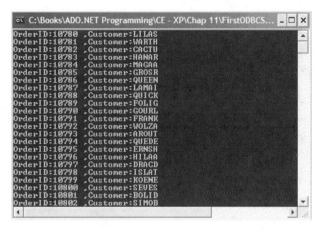

Figure 11-7. The output of Listing 11-1

Accessing MySQL Databases

MySQL is a widely used multithreaded, multi-user, robust SQL database server. You can use MySQL free of charge under the GNU General Public License. You can download the MySQL database and its tools from `http://www.mysql.com`. Specifically, the Downloads section of the site contains downloads (`http://www.mysql.com/downloads/index.html`). After downloading the zip file, you unzip it in a folder and run `Setup.exe`. By default the setup installs MySQL in your `C:/mysql` folder. The documentation section of `http://www.mysql.com` has detailed instructions on how to install and register the MySQL server and its services.

> **NOTE** *You may need Administrator rights to install and register MySQL server and its services.*

After installing MySQL, make sure it's running. If the service is not running, you may need to start it manually. You can start it from Control Panel ➤ Administrative Tools ➤ Services and look for the MySql service, right-click, and select the Start menu option. This action will start MySql as a service (see Figure 11-8).

Now you're all set to use the server.

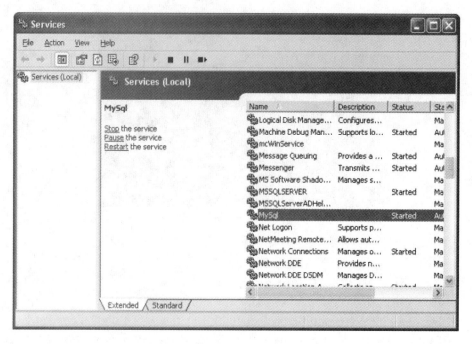

Figure 11-8. Starting MySQL as a service

Because you'll be using ODBC to connect to a MySQL database, you need to install an ODBC driver for it. You can find the most widely used ODBC driver for MySQL, called MyODBC, at the following URL:

```
http://www.mysql.com/downloads/api-myodbc.html
```

After downloading the zip file, the obvious action is to unzip it and install it. If the driver is installed properly, you can see it from ODBC Data Source Administrator from Control Panel ➢ Data Source (ODBC) option (see Figure 11-9).

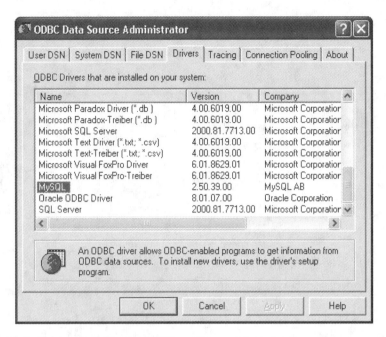

Figure 11-9. Drivers listed in ODBC Data Source Administrator

You can use any database, but this example will use the Northwind database. First you'll import the Access 2000 Northwind database into the MySQL server, and then you'll set it up as a data source.

To import the Access Northwind database, I used a free tool called DBTools. This tool provides many handy functions for MySQL developers. You can download DBTools at the following URL:

```
http://www.dbtools.com.br/
```

After installing it, run DBTools (see Figure 11-10). The Servers node on the left side lists the servers. You can expand the Servers node to see databases, users, and database objects.

> **NOTE** *If you don't see any servers listed under the Servers node, you can register a server using the Server Manager option. The Server Manager screen will display your server name, host, database name, and password. The default server name, host name, user ID, password, and database are MySql, localhost, root, null, and mysql, respectively.*

Figure 11-10. Using DBTools

> **NOTE** *Thanks to Levent Camlibel for providing the links and steps to download this utility.*

Registering the server adds a server to the Servers list and a database to the Database list. Now right-click on the server and click Connect. After that you can expand the server and database roots to see the database contents (see Figure 11-11).

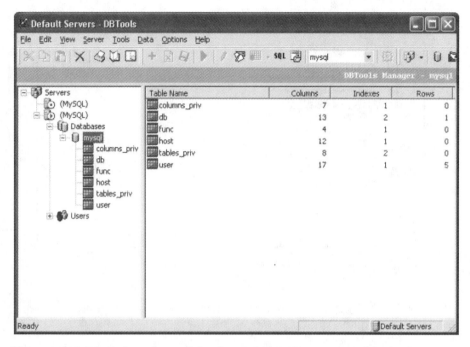

Figure 11-11. Data view of mysql database of MySQL server in DBTools

Now, by right-clicking on the nodes of databases, you can create new database, tables, users, and other database objects.

Importing the Northwind Database into MySQL Server

The next step is to import the Northwind Microsoft Access 2000 database into MySQL. You can do so using the DBTools utility. To import an Access 2000 database, first you need to set the preferences of DBTools, which you can find under the Options menu. Check the External Data Connections item: Use DAO 3.6 (requires MSOffice 2000). See Figure 11-12.

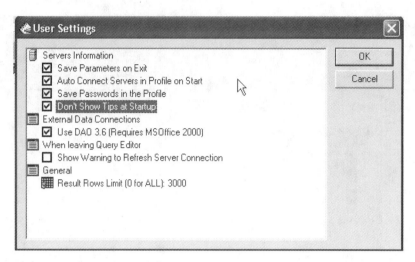

Figure 11-12. Setting external data connections of DBTools

Click OK. Then click the Import Data toolbar button to import a database (see Figure 11-13).

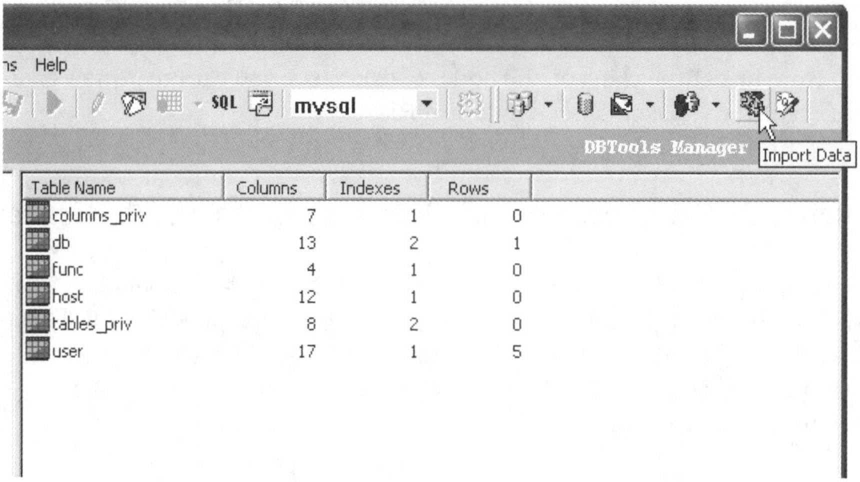

Figure 11-13. Import Data option of DBTools

The Import Data option lets you select the type of data source you want to import. You can select many different files, including .mdb, .xls, and .dbf, from the list. For this example, select the Microsoft Access (*.mdb) option and click Next (see Figure 11-14).

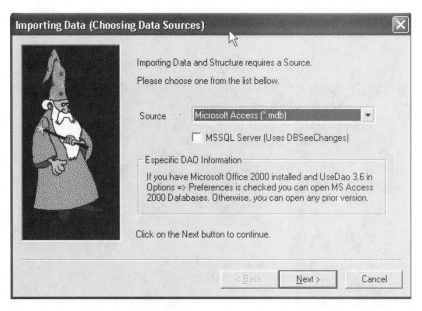

Figure 11-14. Selecting the Microsoft Access option

The next step is to select the database. You can use the browse button (a folder icon in Figure 11-15) to browse a folder. As you can see from Figure 11-15, I selected the Northwind database from the `C:\` root folder.

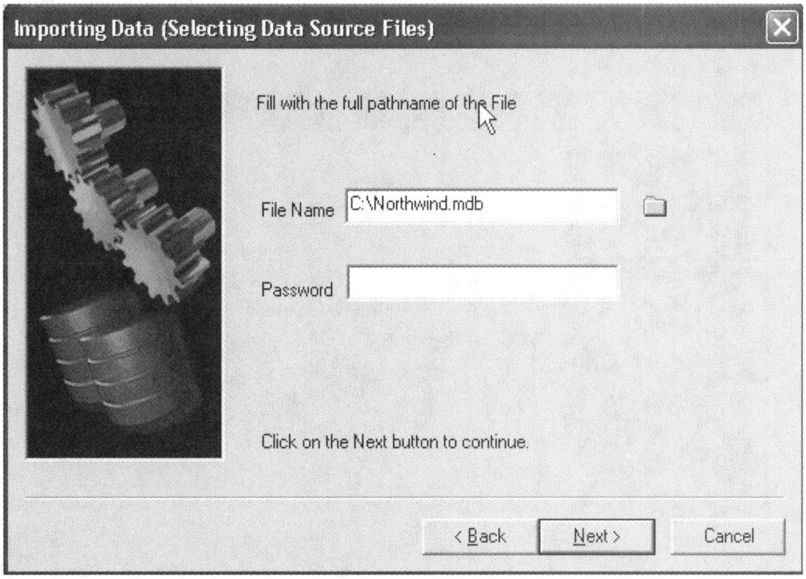

Figure 11-15. Selecting database to import data

Click Next and the next screen of the wizard lets you select the data you want to import. You can import the selected tables and all the data by setting these options (see Figure 11-16).

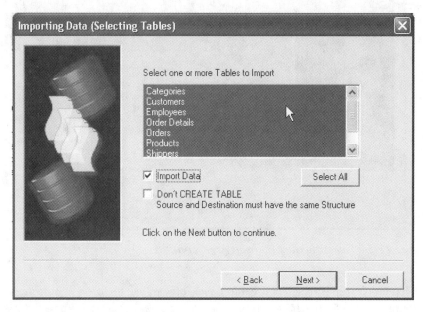

Figure 11-16. Selecting data and tables

You can even change table names in the imported database on the next page of the wizard (see Figure 11-17).

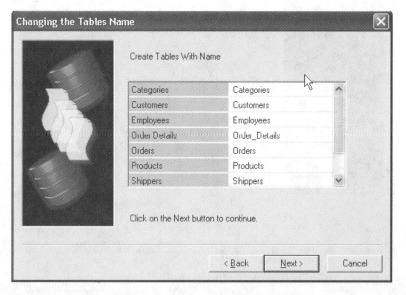

Figure 11-17. Changing table names in the imported database

The next page lets you create a new database on the MySql server, which will contain all the imported data. I created a new database named NorthwindMySQL (see Figure 11-18).

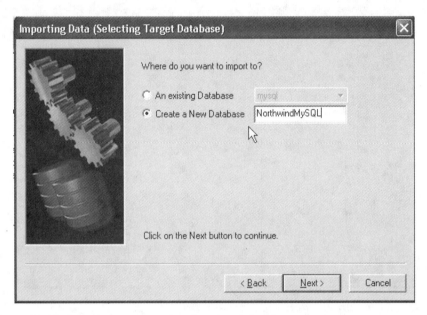

Figure 11-18. Selecting a name of an imported database

> **NOTE** *You can even use an existing database by selecting the An Existing Database option.*

Now click Next and then click the Finish button. This action imports data from the Northwind database. If you go to MySQL, you can see the new NorthwindMySQL database and its tables. If you click on the Get Data button, it fills data to the table (see Figure 11-19).

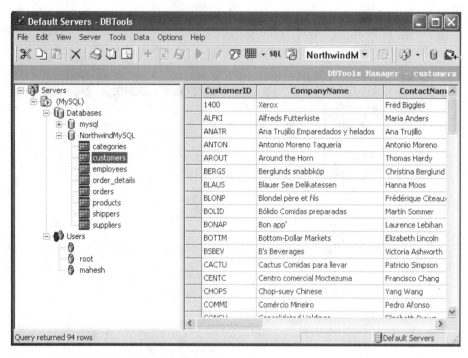

Figure 11-19. NorthwindMySQL database view

Creating an ODBC DSN

You can connect a MySQL database either using an ODBC DSN or by passing a
database name. The good thing about using a DSN is that you don't have to pass
the driver name and other parameters because they're already defined in the
DSN. This option is also useful when you don't know the database path on
a client's machine, but you can ask the client to create a DSN.

You can create a DSN by selecting Control Panel ➤ Data Source (ODBC) on
Windows 2000, Windows NT, and Windows 98. On Windows XP, select Control
Panel ➤ Administrative Tools ➤ Data Source (ODBC). You use the Add button to
add a new DSN entry and select MySQL as the driver (see Figure 11-20).

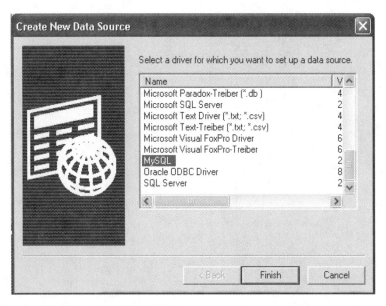

Figure 11-20. Selecting the MySQL driver

The next page asks you to add the server settings and database name. As you can see from Figure 11-21, I set the DSN name as TestDSN, the host as local-host, the database name as NorthwindMySQL, the user ID as root, and the password blank.

> **NOTE** *You need to use your own password if you set one previously.*

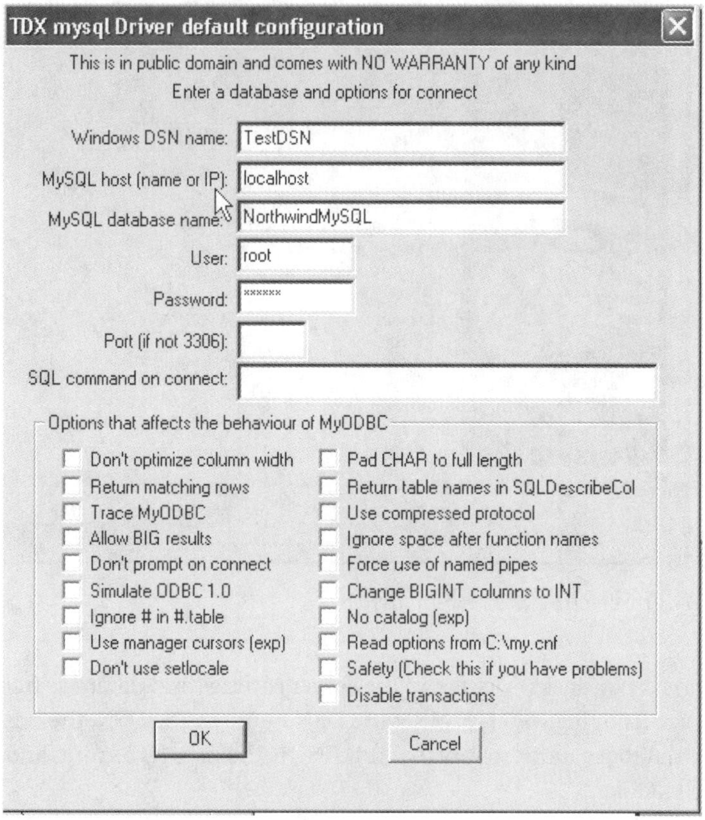

Figure 11-21. Setting MySQL DSN configurations

Using a MySQL Database

As I've been saying, working with different data sources is only a matter of changing the connection string. You can access a MySQL database either using a DSN
or using the direct database name in the connection string. You can use a database name directly as shown in the following code:

```
string connectionString =
@"Driver={MySQL};SERVER=localhost;DATABASE=NorthwindMySQL;";
```

Or you can use an ODBC DSN. As you can see from the following code, I've
used TestDSN DSN to connect to the data source:

```
OdbcConnection conn= new OdbcConnection("DSN=TestDSN");
```

To test this code, create a Windows application, add a DataGrid control to the form, and add the code in Listing 11-2 to the Form_Load event. This code is similar to the code you saw previously. It creates a connection, creates a data adapter, fills the dataset from the data adapter, and sets the dataset's DefaultViewManager as the DataGrid control's DataSource property.

Listing 11-2. Accessing a MySQL database
```
private void Form1_Load(object sender, System.EventArgs e)
{
    string connectionString = @"Driver={MySQL};SERVER=localhost;DATABASE=NorthwindMySQL;";
OdbcConnection conn= new OdbcConnection(connectionString);

    conn.Open();

OdbcDataAdapter da = new OdbcDataAdapter
("SELECT CustomerID, ContactName, ContactTitle FROM Customers", conn);
   DataSet ds = new DataSet("Cust");

  da.Fill(ds, "Customers");
  dataGrid1.DataSource = ds.DefaultViewManager;

  conn.Close();
}
```

Accessing Text File Databases

To test text database connectivity, you can export the Employees table of the Northwind database using the File ➤ Export option of Access 2000. In this section, I'll export a table to a text file, and I'll show you how to use it using the ODBC data adapter.

Exporting an Access Table to a Text File

You can export an Access database table to a text file using the Export option. As you can see from Figure 11-22, I selected the Employees table and chose File ➤ Export.

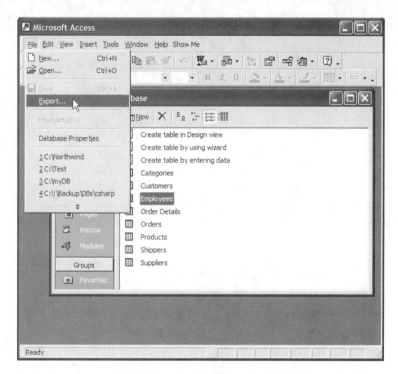

Figure 11-22. Exporting the Employees table of Northwind.mdb

The next dialog box lets you pick a path and filename you want to export. There are many export options are available. As you can see from Figure 11-23, I selected the Text Files option, left the exported filename as Employees, and saved the file to the C:\ root directory.

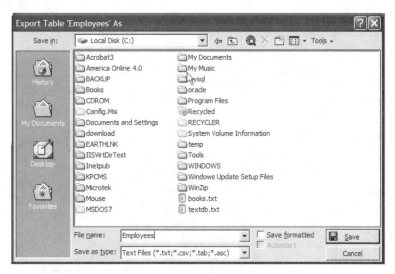

Figure 11-23. Selecting a path of exported file

Now, the Export Text Wizard lets you define the format of the text file. A dialog box lets you select either delimited or fixed width (see Figure 11-24).

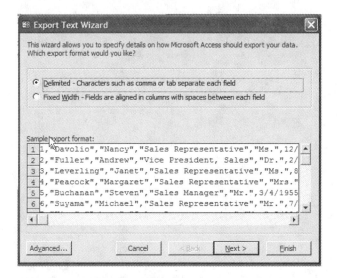

Figure 11-24. Export Text Wizard options

You can also select the Advanced option to set more options (see Figure 11-25).

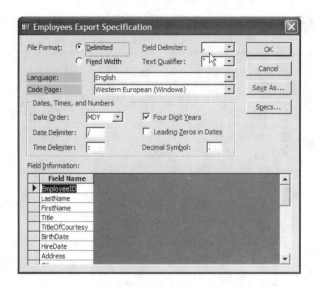

Figure 11-25. The Advanced option of Export Text Wizard

The next screen lets you pick the delimiter including comma, tab, semicolon, space, and others. I left the Comma option checked (see Figure 11-26).

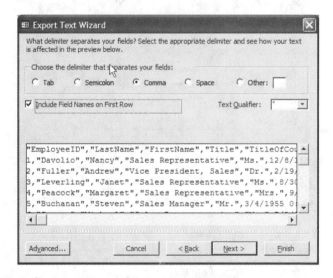

Figure 11-26. Delimiter options of Export Text Wizard

I also checked the Include Field Names on First Row check box. This option adds the first row of the text file as field names.

The last page asks you the filename (see Figure 11-27).

Figure 11-27. Filename page of the Export Text Wizard

Now click the Finish button. When the wizard is done exporting, you'll see a message saying the export is finished. Click OK and close Access.

Now view C:\Employees.txt (see Figure 11-28).

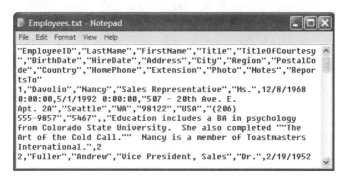

Figure 11-28. Exported Employees.txt *file from* Northwind.mdb

Accessing a Text File

You can access a text file using the ODBC data provider. There are two ways to access text files. Either you can create a DSN from the ODBC Data Source Administrator or you access the text file directly in your application. To create a data source for a text file, you go to the ODBC Data Source Admin, click the New button (or the Add button if you're using Windows XP), and select the Microsoft Text Driver (*.txt, *.csv) option (see Figure 11-29).

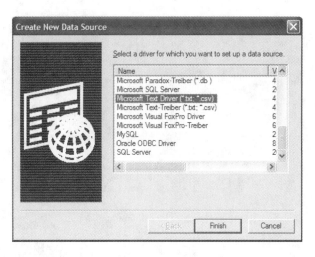

Figure 11-29. Selecting the Microsoft Text Driver (*.txt, *.csv) option

You define the DSN name and description in the ODBC Text Setup dialog box. Uncheck the Use Current Directory option to enable the Select Directory button and click on Options to see more options (see Figure 11-30).

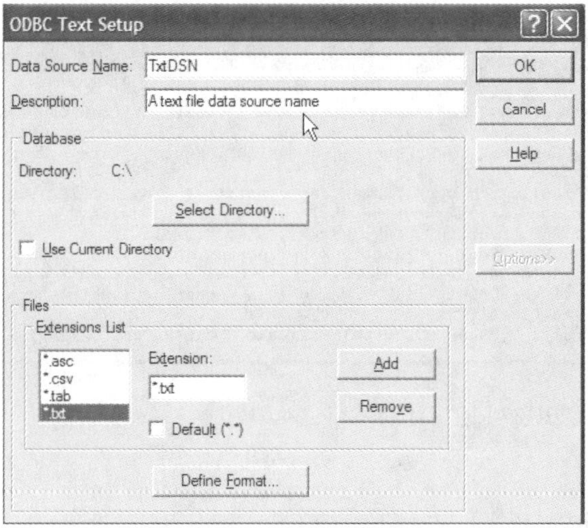

Figure 11-30. Setting the DSN name and description

After that you select your DSN name. You can select any directory you want to use. An entire text file is used as a database table (see Figure 11-31).

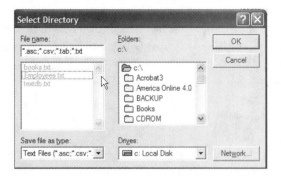

Figure 11-31. Selecting directory and file types

You can even define different formats by using the Define Format button. As you can see from Figure 11-32, all files are treated as a database table. From the Format drop-down box, you can select the type of format you want, such as comma-delimited or tab-delimited. The Guess button guesses the column names for you. If it doesn't find a proper format file, it creates F1 . . . Fn columns for you. You can also add, modify, and remove columns and their types.

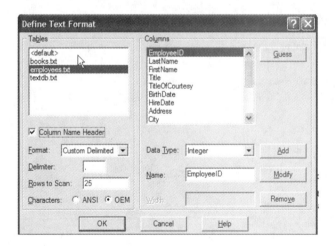

Figure 11-32. Defining a text file format and column settings

After creating a DSN, you can use DSN as a connection source for your connection:

```
OdbcConnection  conn = new OdbcConnection("DSN=TxtDSN");
```

Another way to access text files is directly using the text ODBC driver in the connection string. For example, ConnectionString in the following code defines a connection having the Microsoft Text Driver and source directory as C:\.

```
// Connection string for a Text File
string ConnectionString =
    @"Driver={Microsoft Text Driver (*.txt; *.csv)};DBQ=c:\";
```

Every text or .csv file in the C:\ directory will be treated as a database table, which you pass in your SQL string:

```
OdbcConnection  conn = new OdbcConnection(ConnectionString);
OdbcDataAdapter da = new OdbcDataAdapter
("Select * FROM Employees.txt", conn
```

To test this code, I created a Windows application, dropped a DataGrid control on the form, and used the code shown in Listing 11-3 on the Form_Load event.

Listing 11-3. Accessing the TextDB.txt file
```
private void Form1_Load(object sender, System.EventArgs e)
{
// Connection string for a Text File
string ConnectionString =
    @"Driver={Microsoft Text Driver (*.txt; *.csv)};DBQ=c:\";
// Query the Employees.txt file as a table
OdbcConnection  conn = new OdbcConnection(ConnectionString);
conn.Open();

OdbcDataAdapter da = new OdbcDataAdapter
("Select * FROM Employees.txt", conn);

DataSet ds = new DataSet();
da.Fill(ds, "TextDB");

dataGrid1.DataSource = ds.DefaultViewManager;

// Close the connection
conn.Close();

}
```

> **NOTE**   *Don't forget to add a reference to the* Microsoft.Data.Odbc *namespace.*

Now compile and run the application, and you should see data in the DataGrid.

Accessing Excel Databases

The next example will show you how to connect with Excel databases. To test this sample, if you don't have an Excel database, you can export data from your Northwind database. As you can see from Figure 11-33, you can export the Employees table from Microsoft Access by right-clicking on the table and selecting the Export option or by selecting File ➢ Export.

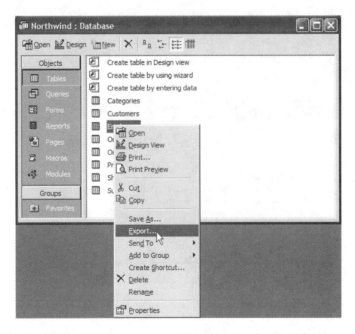

Figure 11-33. Exporting the Employees table as an Excel spreadsheet

When you export, make sure you have selected the Microsoft Excel 97-2000 (*.xls) option in the Save as Type drop-down list (see Figure 11-34).

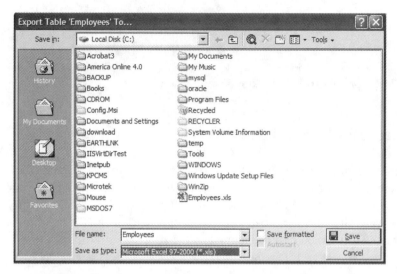

Figure 11-34. Saving the Employees table as an Excel spreadsheet

Now if you open Employees.xls, it looks like Figure 11-35.

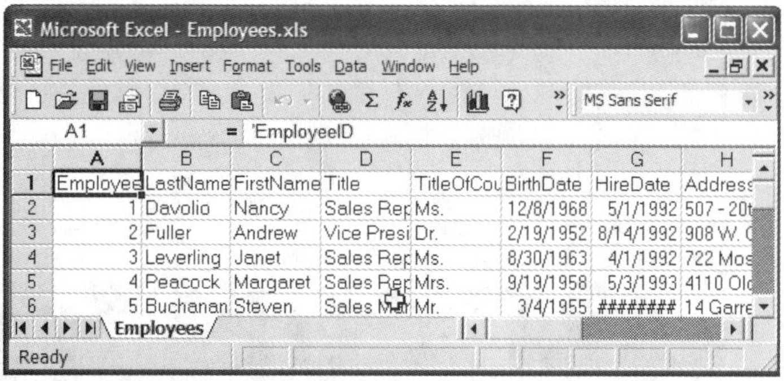

Figure 11-35. Employees.xls *data view*

Again, you can access the Excel database either using an ODBC DSN or by passing the database name directly in the connection string. In this sample, you're passing the database name directly:

```
string ConnectionString =
@"Driver={Microsoft Excel Driver (*.xls)};DBQ=c:\Employees.xls";
```

After that, the code should be familiar to you. It's the same steps as creating a data adapter, selecting some fields of the table, filling a dataset from data adapter, and binding data with the data-bound controls. Listing 11-4 shows the full source code.

Listing 11-4. Accessing Employees.xls using the ODBC data provider

```
private void Form1_Load(object sender, System.EventArgs e)
{
 // Connection string for ODBC Excel Driver
 string ConnectionString =
 @"Driver={Microsoft Excel Driver (*.xls)};DBQ=c:\Employees.xls";
 OdbcConnection  conn = new OdbcConnection(ConnectionString);

 // Tables in Excel can be thought of as sheets and are queried as shown
 string sql = "Select EmployeeID, FirstName, LastName FROM Employees";
 conn.Open();

 OdbcDataAdapter da = new OdbcDataAdapter(sql, conn);

 DataSet ds = new DataSet();
 da.Fill(ds, "Employees");

 dataGrid1.DataSource = ds.DefaultViewManager;
 listBox1.DataSource = ds.DefaultViewManager;
 listBox1.DisplayMember = "Employees.FirstName";
}
```

The output of Listing 11-4 looks like Figure 11-36.

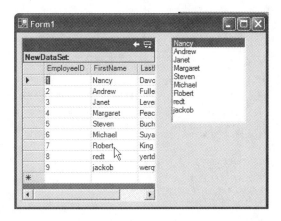

Figure 11-36. Output of Listing 11-4

Working with Oracle Databases

As discussed earlier, working with Oracle databases is no different from working with SQL Server or other databases. The only difference is the connection string. You can use the OleDb or ODBC data providers to connect to an Oracle database. In this section, I'll show you both ways (OleDb and ODBC) to access Oracle 8i and 9i databases.

Accessing an Oracle 8i Database Using the ODBC Data Provider

To use an ODBC data provider, the first thing you need to do is add a reference to the ODBC data provider and include the using statement in your application to add the `Microsoft.Data.Odbc` namespace as follows:

```
using Microsoft.Data.Odbc;
```

After that you follow same familiar steps: creating a connection string, adding data from database to a data adapter, and filling a dataset. To test this sample application, I created a Windows application, added a DataGrid control to the form, and added the code in Listing 11-5 to the `Form_Load` event.

Listing 11-5 Accessing an Oracle database using the ODBC data provider

```
private void Form1_Load(object sender, System.EventArgs e)
{
        string connString = "Driver={Oracle ODBC Driver};"+
            "Server=localhost;UID=system;PWD=manager;";
        OdbcConnection conn = new OdbcConnection(connString);

        if( conn.State != ConnectionState.Open)
            conn.Open();

        OdbcDataAdapter da =
            new OdbcDataAdapter("SELECT * FROM STDTABLE", conn);
        DataSet ds = new DataSet("STDTABLE");
        da.Fill(ds,"STDTABLE");

        dataGrid1.DataSource = ds.DefaultViewManager;

        // Close connection
        if( conn.State == ConnectionState.Open)
            conn.Close();
}
```

As you can see from Listing 11-5, I created a connection with the Oracle ODBC driver with the server as localhost, the user ID as system, and the password as manager.

You may want to change the user ID and password if you're using something different from those used in Listing 11-5. After that I created a data adapter by selecting data from STDTABLE, created a dataset, and filled the dataset by calling the Fill method of OdbcDataAdapter. The last step was to bind the dataset to a data grid.

The output of Listing 11-5 looks like Figure 11-37.

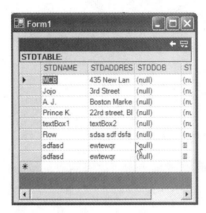

Figure 11-37. Data view in a data grid from an Oracle database

Accessing an Oracle 8i Database Using the OleDb Data Provider

If you don't have an ODBC driver for the Oracle database, OLE DB is another way to access the database. You use the Oracle provider MSDAORA (see Listing 11-6). The DSN name is oracle, the user ID is system, and the password is manager. You may want to change the user ID and password if you're not using the default. I also created an instance of OleDbConnection in Listing 11-6. You can add these variables either publicly or privately in your class.

Listing 11-6. The connection string from the Oracle OleDb data provider
```
string connString = "Provider=MSDAORA;DSN=oracle;"
+"User ID=system;Password=manager";
OleDbConnection conn = new OleDbConnection();
```

Once you have the connection string, you use this string to open a connection. You work with the connection in the same way as before: creating a data adapter or command, executing commands, filling datasets, and so on.

As you can see from Listing 11-7, I simply set the connection string and opened the connection. After that I used connection as I've been doing with all the other databases. It's the same steps as creating an OleDbDataAdapter: creating a dataset, filling data from a database table STDTABLE, and binding the dataset to data grid to display the data.

Listing 11-7. Viewing data from an Oracle database table

```
private void ViewDataBtn_Click(object sender, System.EventArgs e)
    {
        // Open connection if not already open
        conn.ConnectionString = connString;
        if( conn.State != ConnectionState.Open)
            conn.Open();

        OleDbDataAdapter da =
            new OleDbDataAdapter("SELECT * FROM STDTABLE", conn);
        DataSet ds = new DataSet("STDTABLE");
        da.Fill(ds,"STDTABLE");

        dataGrid1.DataSource = ds.DefaultViewManager;

        // Close connection
        if( conn.State == ConnectionState.Open)
            conn.Close();

    }
```

As you've been doing in the other samples, you can create a SQL statement and execute it against an Oracle database. As you can see from Listing 11-8, I created an INSERT statement to insert data into STDTABLE with three columns (MyId, myName, and myAddress) with values and then called the OleDbCommand.ExecuteNonQuery method to execute the command.

Listing 11-8. Executing an INSERT statement

```
string sql ="";
sql = "INSERT INTO STDTABLE(MyId, myName, myAddress) "
    +"VALUES(1001,'new name', 'new address')" ;




        try
        {
            // Create Command object and Execute SQL statement
```

```
        OleDbCommand cmd = new OleDbCommand(sql, conn);
        cmd.ExecuteNonQuery();
    }
    catch(OleDbException ae)
    {
        string strMessage = "";
        for (int i = 0; i < ae.Errors.Count; i++)
        {
            strMessage += ae.Errors[i].Message + " - " +
                ae.Errors[i].SQLState  + "\n";
        }
        MessageBox.Show(strMessage);
    }


        // Close connection
        if( conn.State == ConnectionState.Open)
            conn.Close();
```

Similar to Listing 11-8, you can create UPDATE and DELETE commands to update and delete data from the database.

Working with an Oracle 9i Database

In the previous section, you saw a sample of the Oracle 8i database. In this section, I'll show you how to work with Oracle 9i databases using ODBC data providers.

The Oracle 9i connection string looks like this:

```
string connString = "Driver={Oracle in OraHome90};"+
"Server=localhost;UID=system;PWD=mahesh;";
```

where Oracle in OraHome90 is the Oracle ODBC driver. I've used the user ID system and the password mahesh. You need to change these to your user ID and password. If you're using the default user ID and password, you can use the system/manager or scott/tiger pairs as the user ID and password.

In this sample application, I'll create a database table called myTable with four columns (Id, Name, Address, and Zip) of type integer, string, string, and integer, respectively. The Id column is the primary key column.

To test this application, I created a Windows application and added a DataGrid control and three buttons to the form by dragging the controls from the toolbox to the form and changing the name of the buttons to Create Table,

Fill Data, and Delete Table. The Create Table button creates myTable and adds data to the table. The Fill Data button reads the table and views the data in the DataGrid control, and the Delete Table button removes the table from the database.

First, I added a reference to the `Microsoft.Data.Odbc` namespace and then added the following variables in the beginning of my form class:

```
// Connection string for Oracle 9i
string connString = "Driver={Oracle in OraHome90};"+
"Server=localhost;UID=system;PWD=mahesh;";

string sql = "SELECT * FROM OraTable";
// Create a connection
OdbcConnection conn = null;
// Create a command
OdbcCommand cmd = null;
OdbcDataAdapter da = null;
```

Now I create connection and command objects on the form load, as shown here:

```
private void Form1_Load(object sender, System.EventArgs e)
{
// Create a connection and command
conn = new OdbcConnection(connString);
cmd = new OdbcCommand(sql, conn);
}
```

The Create Table button handler creates a new table. The code of this button handler looks like Listing 11-9. Listing 11-9 also creates myTable and adds data to the table.

Listing 11-9. Creating a new database table and adding data to it

```
private void button1_Click(object sender, System.EventArgs e)
    {

        try
        {

            if( conn.State != ConnectionState.Open)
                conn.Open();
```

```
string sql = "CREATE TABLE myTable"+
  "(Id INTEGER CONSTRAINT PKeyMyId PRIMARY KEY,"+
  "Name CHAR(50), Address CHAR(255), Zip INTEGER)" ;


cmd = new OdbcCommand(sql, conn);
cmd.ExecuteNonQuery();

// Adding records the table
sql = "INSERT INTO myTable(Id, Name, Address, Zip) "+
  "VALUES (1001, 'Mr. Galler Hall', "+
  "'23 Church Street, Pace City, NY', 32432 ) " ;
cmd = new OdbcCommand(sql, conn);
cmd.ExecuteNonQuery();

sql = "INSERT INTO myTable(Id, Name, Address, Zip) "+
  "VALUES (1002, 'Dr. Dex Leech',"+
  "'3rd Aven, President Road, NJ', 743623) " ;
cmd = new OdbcCommand(sql, conn);
cmd.ExecuteNonQuery();


sql = "INSERT INTO myTable(Id, Name, Address, Zip) "+
  "VALUES (1003, 'Lambert Mart', "+
  "'45 Petersburgh Ave, Jacksonville, GA', 53492) " ;
cmd = new OdbcCommand(sql, conn);
cmd.ExecuteNonQuery();

sql = "INSERT INTO myTable(Id, Name, Address, Zip) "+
  "VALUES (1004, 'Moann Texur', "+
  "'4th Street, Lane 3, Packville, PA', 23433) " ;
cmd = new OdbcCommand(sql, conn);
cmd.ExecuteNonQuery();

// Close connection
if( conn.State == ConnectionState.Open)
  conn.Close();

}
catch(OdbcException ae)
{
  MessageBox.Show(ae.Message.ToString());
}
}
```

The View Data button handler reads data from myTable and views it in a DataGrid control. Listing 11-10, which should look familiar, shows the View Data button-click handler. I created a data adapter, filled a DataSet using the OdbcDataAdapter's Fill method, and bound the DataSet to the DataGrid control using DataGrid.DefaultViewManager.

Listing 11-10. Viewing myTable data in a DataGrid

```
private void button2_Click(object sender, System.EventArgs e)
    {

      try
      {
        if( conn.State != ConnectionState.Open)
          conn.Open();

        da = new OdbcDataAdapter("SELECT * FROM myTable", conn);
        DataSet ds = new DataSet("ds");
        da.Fill(ds,"myTable");

        dataGrid1.DataSource = ds.DefaultViewManager;

        // Close connection
        if( conn.State == ConnectionState.Open)
          conn.Close();
      }
      catch(OdbcException ae)
      {
        MessageBox.Show(ae.Message.ToString());
      }

    }
```

The Delete Table button handler removes myTable from the database. As you can see from Listing 11-11, I simply constructed a DROP TABLE SQL statement and executed it using the OdbcCommand.Execute method.

Listing 11-11. Executing a DROP TABLE SQL statement using OdbcCommand

```
private void button3_Click(object sender, System.EventArgs e)
{
    try
    {
```

```
                 if( conn.State != ConnectionState.Open)
                    conn.Open();

                 // Construct DROP TABLE query and execute it
                 string sql = "DROP TABLE myTable";
                 cmd = new OdbcCommand(sql, conn);
                 cmd.ExecuteNonQuery();

                 // Close connection
                 if( conn.State == ConnectionState.Open)
                    conn.Close();

              }
              catch(OdbcException ae)
              {
                 MessageBox.Show(ae.Message.ToString());
              }
}
```

Working with Sybase Databases

You can access a Sybase database using the OleDb data provider. The only thing you need to do is to set up an ASO OLE DB provider data source. As you can see from Listing 11-12, I created a data source called sydev with the user ID tiraspr and the password tiraspr. After creating a connection, you use the same steps to access the database as described previously. I selected data from the user_tree_start table and used it to create a command object. After that I called ExecuteReader to execute the string and fill data in a reader.

Listing 11-12. Accessing a Sybase database

```
using System;
using System.Data;
using System.Data.OleDb;

namespace AccessSybase
{
    class Class1
    {
        static void Main(string[] args)
        {
            string connectionString, sql;
```

```
            OleDbConnection conn;
            OleDbDataReader rdr;
            OleDbCommand cmd;

            connectionString =
            "Provider=Sybase ASE OLE DB Provider;Datasource=sydev;" +
                "User ID=tiraspr;Password=tiraspr";
            conn = new OleDbConnection(connectionString);

            conn.Open();

            sql = "select * from user_tree_start";
            cmd = new OleDbCommand(sql, conn);
            cmd.CommandType = CommandType.Text;
            rdr = cmd.ExecuteReader();

            while (rdr.Read())
                Console.WriteLine(rdr["user_id"].ToString() +
                    " " + rdr["tree_start"] + " " + rdr["strategy_group"]);

            Console.WriteLine("DONE");
            Console.Read();
        }
    }
}
```

NOTE   *Thanks to Roman Tirapolsky for contributing the code in Listing 11-12.*

Summary

The best thing about ADO.NET is that it treats all types of data sources similarly. As I've stated repeatedly, the only difference is the connection string and the class names. So, if you know how to build a connection string, you can use the same code to work with multiple data sources. Based on the same theory, in this chapter you saw how to work with the MySQL, Oracle, and Sybase databases. You also saw how to work with Excel spreadsheets and text files.

APPENDIX A

Relational Databases: Some Basic Concepts

THIS APPENDIX DISCUSSES SOME key concepts of relational databases, including normalization, sets, cursors, and locking.

A *relational database* is a collection of tables, and a *table* is a set of columns and rows. A table's columns can be referred to as *columns*, *fields*, or *attributes*, and each column in a table requires a unique name and a data type. The data in a given row are generally referred to as a *record*. (The term *recordset* refers to a set of records, reminding you that relational databases use set-based operations rather than row-at-a-time, pointer-based operations.)

In relational databases, each table needs to have a key, which is associated with a column. There are two important types of keys: primary keys and foreign keys. A *primary key* is a column of a table with a unique value for each row, which helps ensure data integrity by (theoretically) eliminating duplicate records. A *foreign key* takes care of the *relational* in relational databases and provides a link between related data that are contained in more than one table. For example, in a classic parent/child relationship such as customers and orders, if CustomerId is the primary key in the Customers table, it'll need to occur in the Orders table as a foreign key to associate each order with an individual customer. The customer/order relationship is a one-to-many relationship because each *one* customer can have *many* orders. That relationship is sometimes depicted as 1:n.

> **NOTE** *A primary key can also be a combination of several columns of a table, where one of those columns is a foreign key. For example, in one of my database tables, one table has a primary key, which is a combination of the Path and File columns, to avoid duplicate file records. The File column is a foreign key.*

A database is collection of tables, indexes, constraints, and other objects. The definition of these objects is known as the database's *schema*, which can be represented in a graphical way using various diagrams.

    Metadata refers to the collection of data about data that describes the content, quality, relations, and other characteristics of data. A database's metadata includes information that ranges from table definitions to users and their permissions.

Understanding Normalization

If you've been working with databases for a while, you're probably familiar with the term *normalization*. Database designers or developers often ask whether a database is normalized. So, what's normalization? Normalization is a process of eliminating data redundancy (except for the redundancy required by foreign keys) in multiple relational tables, and it ensures that data is organized efficiently. When you normalize a database, you basically have three goals:

- Ensuring you've organized the data correctly into groups that minimize the amount of duplicate data stored in a database

- Organizing the data such that, when you (or your users) modify data in it (such as a person's address or email), the change only has to be made once

- Designing a database in which you can access and manipulate the data quickly and efficiently without compromising the integrity of the data in storage

    E. F. Codd first proposed the normalization process way back in 1972. Initially, he proposed three normal forms, which he called *first, second,* and *third normal forms* (1NF, 2NF, and 3NF). Subsequently, he proposed a stronger definition of 3NF, which is known as *Boyce-Codd normal form* (BCNF). Later, others proposed forth and fifth normal forms. Most people agree that a database that's 3NF is probably good enough—in other words, normalized enough.

First Normal Form (1NF)

A table is in first normal form (1NF) if the values of its columns are *atomic*, containing no repeating values. Applying 1NF on a table eliminates duplicate columns from the same table, which creates separate tables for each group of related data, and adds a primary key to the table to identify table rows with a unique value. For example, say you have a table called Customers (see Figure A-1). The Customers table is designed to store data about customer orders. The columns store data about a customer such as name, address, and order description.

Customers : Table

Field Name	Data Type
CustomerName	Text
Address	Text
City	Text
Order1	Text
Order2	Text
Order3	Text
OrderDes1	Text
OrderDes2	Text
OrderDes3	Text

Figure A-1. Customers table as it might appear in Microsoft Access before normalization

The data of the Customers table looks like Figure A-2.

CustomerName	Address	City	Order1	Order2	Order3	OrderDes1	OrderDes2	OrderDes
Jack	ABC Road	Jacksonville	001	002	003	Books	Paper	Copies
Mr. X	X Avenue	Exton	004	005	006	Paper	Books	Magazine

Figure A-2. Two rows of data from the Customers table

Figure A-1 shows the design of a Customers table. As you can see, it's been designed to store up to three orders for any customer—sort of mimicking an array structure in spreadsheet format. There are obvious problems with this design. As you can see from Figure A-2, there are many columns related to orders (that's a classic giveaway of a poorly designed table—mixing two or more *entities*, or kinds of data.) Whenever a customer posts a new order, a new column will be added to the table. Not only that, if the same customer posts more than one order, the duplicate Address and City column data will be added to the table. This scenario adds duplicate data to the table. This table is not in 1NF because the 1NF rule says that a table is in 1NF if and only if a table's columns have no repeating values.

You apply 1NF on this table by eliminating the details about the orders, providing just enough relational information to link the Customers table with a new Orders table. The new format of this table after 1NF would look like Figure A-3. You still have some information about orders in this Customers table but only basic link information: OrderNumber. You've fixed the repeating fields problem by jamming all the other order information into a single OrderDescription field.

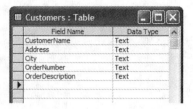

Figure A-3. Customers table schema after 1NF

The data of the table now looks like Figure A-4.

CustomerName	Address	City	OrderNumber	OrderDescription
Jack	ABC Road	Jacksonville	001	Books
Jack	ABC Road	Jacksonville	002	002
Jack	ABC Road	Jacksonville	003	Copies
Mr. X	X Avenue	Exton	004	Paper
Mr. X	X Avenue	Exton	005	Books
Mr. X	X Avenue	Exton	006	Magazine

Figure A-4. Data of Customers table after 1NF

Second Normal Form (2NF)

Second normal form (2NF) eliminates redundant data. A table is in 2NF if it's in 1NF and every non-key column (not a key column—primary or foreign) is fully dependent upon the primary key.

Applying 2NF on a table removes duplicate data on multiple rows, places data in separate rows, places grouped data in new tables, and creates relationships between the original tables and new tables through foreign keys. As you can see from Figure A-4, there are six records for two customers and three columns—CustomerName, Address, and City has the same information three times. 2NF eliminate these cases. Under 2NF, you separate data into two different tables and relate these tables using a foreign key. Records in tables should not depend on anything other than the table's primary key.

In this example, you now create a separate table called Orders. As you can probably guess, the Orders table stores information related to customer orders. It *relates* back to the correct customer via the CustomerId column. Now the two tables, Customers and Orders, look like Figure A-5 and Figure A-6.

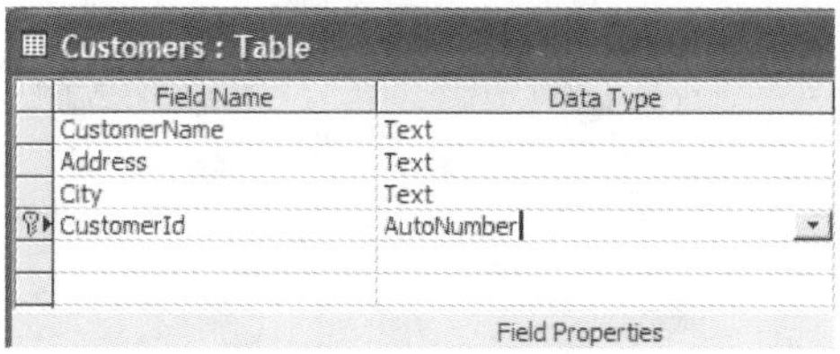

Customers : Table
Field Name
Data Type
CustomerName
Text
Address
Text
City
Text
CustomerId
AutoNumber
Field Properties

Figure A-5. Customers table after 2NF

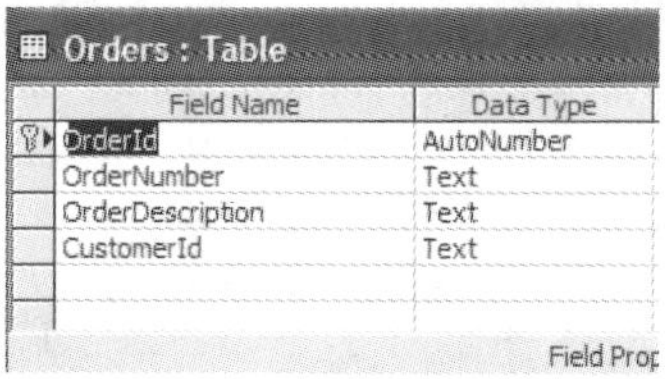

Orders : Table
Field Name
Data Type
OrderId
AutoNumber
OrderNumber
Text
OrderDescription
Text
CustomerId
Text
Field Prop

Figure A-6. Orders table after 2NF

As you can see from Figures A-5 and A-6, both tables now have a primary key—denoted by the key icon to the left of the column name. This key will be unique for each record. The CustomerId column of the Customers table is mapped to the CustomerId column of the Orders table. The CustomerId column of the Orders table is a foreign key. The relationship between the Customers and Orders table looks like Figure A-7.

Orders
OrderId
CustomerId
UnitPrice
Quantity
Customers
CustomerName
Address
City
CustomerId

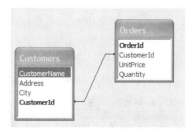

Figure A-7. Relationship between the Customers and Orders table

Now the data in these tables look like Figure A-8 and Figure A-9.

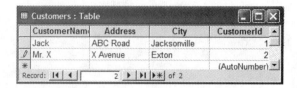

Figure A-8. Customers table after 2NF

	OrderId	OrderNumber	OrderDescripti	CustomerId
	1	001	Books	1
	2	002	Paper	1
	3	003	Copies	1
	4	004	Paper	2
	5	005	Books	2
	6	006	Magazine	2
*	(AutoNumber)			

Record: ◄◄ ◄ 6 ► ►► ►* of 6

Figure A-9. Orders table after 2NF

Third Normal Form (3NF)

A table is in third normal form (3NF) if all columns of a table depend upon the primary key. 3NF eliminates columns that do not depend on the table's primary key. (Note that primary keys don't have to be single columns as shown in these simple examples.)

For example, as you can see from Figure A-10, CustomerId, UnitPrice, and Quantity depend on OrderId (the primary key). But the Total column doesn't depend on the OrderId column; it depends upon the UnitPrice and the Quantity columns.

	OrderId	CustomerId	UnitPrice	Quantity	Total
	1	1001	$3.00	6	$18.00
	2	1002	$2.50	4	$10.00
	3	1002	$4.00	2	$8.00
	4	1003	$12.00	2	$24.00
►	(AutoNumber)		$0.00	0	$0.00

Record: ◄◄ ◄ 5 ► ►► ►* of 5

Figure A-10. Orders table before 3NF

The data of the Orders table look like Figure A-11 after applying the 3NF rule on it, and you can calculate Total as the multiplication of UnitPrice and Quantity in your SQL statement.

For example:

```
SELECT UnitPrice * Quantity AS Total FROM Orders
```

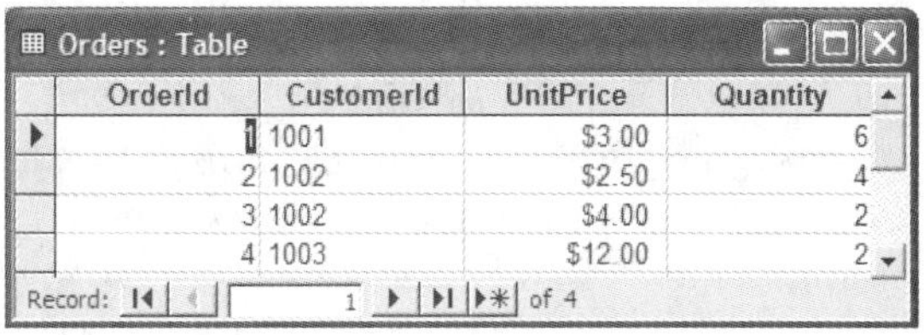

OrderId	CustomerId	UnitPrice	Quantity
1	1001	$3.00	6
2	1002	$2.50	4
3	1002	$4.00	2
4	1003	$12.00	2

Figure A-11. Orders table after 3NF

Boyce-Codd Normal Form (BCNF)

A determinant column is the column on which other columns are fully dependent. The Boyce-Codd normal form (BCNF) is an extended version of 3NF. A database is in BCNF if and only if every determinant is a candidate key. A *candidate key* is a combination of columns that can be uniquely used to identify a row. Each table may have one or more candidate keys.

Fourth Normal Form (4NF)

Fourth normal form (4NF) and fifth normal form (5NF) seem only to be of interest in Computer Science classes and in the academic world in general. But, if you're really interested, a database is in 4NF if and only if it's in BCNF and all multivalued dependencies are also functional dependencies. For example, a customer can have multiple orders and multiple addresses. This data (customer having multiple addresses and multiple orders) can be stored in a single table, but after applying 4NF, the data will be stored in two tables. The first table will store the CustomerId with addresses, and the second table will store the CustomerId with orders.

Fifth Normal Forms (5NF or PJ/NF)

A database is in 5NF (or PJ/NF) if it can't have a lossless decomposition into any number of smaller tables. In other words, this means a table that has been decomposed into three or more smaller tables must be capable of being joined again on common keys to form the original table.

This ends the quick overview of normal forms. *SQL Server Magazine* has numerous articles about database design and normal forms that you might find helpful at `http://www.sqlmag.com/Articles/Index.cfm?AuthorID=436`.

> **NOTE** *If you've heard about database normal forms and normalization, chances are you've also heard about* denormalization, *which basically refers to the process of embracing a less than rigorously perfect relational design in favor of performance. You might, for example, include calculated fields or aggregations in your design. By including redundant information in your design, you* denormalize *it.*

Introducing Sets, Cursors, and ADO.NET

Cursors were basically added to SQL to accommodate programmers who preferred row-at-a-time, pointer-style processing. *Real* relational databases don't even have a notion of record number, for example; you use a SELECT statement to obtain record sets.

The ADO.NET model is redesigned from scratch. There's no explicit support for cursors in ADO.NET. Why do you need cursors? This is a good question. To get your answer, first you have to find out what cursors do.

In ADO, a recordset represents the set of rows returned from a data source after executing a SQL statement. A recordset uses a *cursor* to keep track of the current location and navigate through rows.

ADO supports four types of cursors: static, forward-only, keyset, and dynamic. The static cursors are a static copy of records on the client side. Static cursors are either read-only or read/write and provider both backward and forward navigation by using the MoveFirst, MoveNext, MovePrevious, MoveLast, and Move methods of the recordset. Also, you can bookmark records using this type of cursor. The AbsolutePosition property provides the row number of a cursor.

Forward-only cursors are similar to static cursors except they support forward-only navigation from the first to the last record in the cursor. You can update records, insert new records, and delete records, but you can't move backward. Only the MoveNext method of the recordset is supported for the forward-only cursor.

Keyset cursors support both backward and forward navigation through the recordset object's Move methods. In addition to that, they also reflect changes made by other users. Dynamic cursors provide dynamic navigation and reflect all changes immediately. They're useful when your application allows multiple users to add, update, delete, and navigate records simultaneously. Dynamic cursors are flexible, but they don't support absolute positioning and bookmarks.

In ADO, when you create a recordset, you can specify the type of cursors to use. Table A-1 represents the cursor types and their values.

Table A-1. Recordset Cursor Type and Their Values in ADO

CONSTANT	VALUE	DESCRIPTION
adOpenForwardOnly	0	Forward-only recordset cursor (the default)
adOpenKeyset	1	Keyset recordset cursor
AdOpenDynamic	2	Dynamic recordset cursor
AdOpenStatic	3	Static recordset cursor

As you can see, ADO uses cursors to navigate, to position, and to bookmark records in a recordset. ADO.NET represents a new approach. To be blunt, record-sets are history! They've been replaced by the DataTable and DataReader. Under ADO.NET, a DataReader enables you to perform the function of the forward-only, server-side cursor. However, a DataReader doesn't have a MoveNext method, which is used to move to the next record of a recordset. But it provides a Read method, which reads all the records until the end of the records. A DataReader is useful when you need to read data fast with no updates and you're not using data-bound controls.

The DataSet and command objects enable you to work with data as a discon-nected source, which is similar to ADO client-side behavior. This method is useful when you need to write data-bound, control-based applications.

ADO.NET doesn't support server-side cursors. However, you can use server-side cursors through ADO by adding a reference to the ADODB type library by generating a .NET wrapper for its objects.

Using Locking

In database terms, *locking* is a mechanism used to avoid inconsistency when multiple users access and update data simultaneously. Using the locking tech-nique, you can lock records or a database table when a user is modifying the records or table, and the data will be unavailable for other users until the current user calls the update method to make final changes. For example, say user A is updating a record. During this operation user B deletes that record. This scenario may lead to inconsistency in the table. You can avoid this scenario by making that record unavailable when user A is updating it and make it available when user A is done updating it. The only drawback of this is user B has to wait until user A is done updating the record. Oh well, waiting is better than having inconsistencies and inaccurate data.

Isolation Levels

An *isolation level* represents a particular locking strategy applied on a database. It's basically a way of representing the stages of locking depending on the complexity of locking. There are four isolation levels, starting from level 0 to 3. Applying these levels on transactions is also called determining *transaction isolation levels (TILs)*.

TILs provide consistency during data manipulation when multiple users are accessing data simultaneously. There are three cases that apply to the transactions:

- **Dirty read**: A dirty read occurs when a user reads data that have not yet been committed. For example, user 1 changes a row. User 2 reads the row before user 1 commits the changes. What if user 1 rolls back the changes? User 2 will have data that never existed.

- **Nonrepeatable read**: A nonrepeatable read occurs when a user reads the same record twice but gets different data each time. The simple case for this situation is when user 1 reads a record. User 2 goes and either changes a record or deletes a record and commits the changes. Now if user 1 tries to read the same records again, user 1 gets different data.

- **Phantom**: A phantom is a record that matches the search criteria but is not initially seen. For example, say user 1 searches for records and gets some records. Now user 2 adds new rows with having user 1's search criteria. Now if user 1 searches again using the same criteria, user 1 gets different results than the previous one.

Table A-2 lists the isolation levels defined by OLE DB.

Table A-2. Isolation Levels

LEVEL	DEFINITION
Read Uncommitted	A user can read uncommitted changes made by other users. At this level all three cases (dirty reads, nonrepeatable reads, and phantoms) are possible.
Read Committed	A user can't see changes made by other users until the changes are committed. At this level of isolation, dirty reads aren't possible, but nonrepeatable reads and phantoms are possible.
Repeatable Read	A user can't see the changes made by other users. At this level of isolation, dirty reads and nonrepeatable reads aren't possible, but phantoms are possible.
Serializable	A user sees only changes that are finalized and committed to the database. At this isolation level, dirty reads, nonrepeatable reads, and phantoms aren't possible.

> **NOTE** *The definitive book on transaction processing,* Concurrency Control and Recovery in Database Systems *by Philip A. Bernstein, Vassos Hadzilacos, and Nathan Goodman, is available in its entirety as a 22.9MB self-extracting ZIP from* http://research.microsoft.com/pubs/ccontrol/. *You can also find related information at* http://research.microsoft.com/~philbe/.

Table A-3 summarizes the data consistency behaviors and isolation level relationship. (Read Committed is SQL Server's default isolation level.)

Table A-3. Isolation Levels and Data Consistency

LEVEL	DIRTY READ	NONREPEATABLE READ	PHANTOM
0, Read Uncommitted	Yes	Yes	Yes
1, Read Committed	No	Yes	Yes
2, Repeatable Read	No	No	Yes
3, Serializable	No	No	No

Locking Modes

In general, locking avoids the consequences of multiple users accessing the same data simultaneously and tries to maintain the data's consistency and integrity. There are two locking modes: shared and exclusive. The shared mode lets multiple users access the same data simultaneously. However, an exclusive mode won't let user 2 access the data until user 1 unlocks the data. Depending on the database, locking can be done on a record, a table, or a page level. In table locking, a user can lock the entire table until he commits the changes and unlocks the table. The same method applies on a page as well as on a record for page-level and record-level locking.

> **NOTE** *Chapters 4 and 5 discuss ADO.NET concurrency.*

Based on these general locking modes, ADO provides two different types of locking on recordsets and the combination of them: optimistic locking and pessimistic locking. Optimistic locking is based on the assumption that there won't be any other users when a user is accessing some records of a table.

In optimistic locking, locking only occurs during the final update of records. If any changes were made to the data since it was last accessed, the application must read data again and update the data.

In pessimistic locking, records are unavailable to other users when a user is accessing records until the final changes are done by the user.

You can pass an argument when you create a recordset to specify the type of locking. Table A-4 describes these values.

Table A-4. Locking Types

CONSTANT	VALUE	DESCRIPTION
adLockReadOnly	1	Read-only
adLockPessimistic	2	Pessimistic locking
adLockOptimistic	3	Optimistic locking
adLockBatchOptimistic	4	Optimistic locking with batch updates

You set the LockType variable in the recordset to 1 when you need to read data. It doesn't allow you to add or update data.

You use LockType=3, or optimistic locking, when you need to lock records and only when ADO physically updates the record. Otherwise, records are available when you're editing them. In contrast to the optimistic locking, pessimistic locking locks the records when you start editing records. You set LockType=2 in that case. Before applying optimistic locking, you need to make sure that database manufacturer supports it. Some database manufacturers don't support optimistic locking.

Optimistic locking with batch updates, LockType=4, enables you to access multiple records, update them locally, and update the database as a single batch operation. Again, before using this type of locking, you need to make sure that database manufacturer supports this type of locking. Many don't.

> **NOTE** *For more information on locking and concurrency levels, you may want to read Jim Gray's article on isolation levels at* `http://research.microsoft.com/~gray/Isolation.doc` *or his 1993 classic book, coauthored with Andreas Reuter,* Transaction Processing: Concepts and Techniques.

What Are Deadlocks?

If you've heard about concurrency and different kinds of locks, you've probably also heard about *deadlocks*. Unfortunately, they're an inevitable fact of life in the database world. But, fortunately, today's Database Management Systems are typically designed to handle deadlocks—usually by selecting a "victim" whose transaction gets rolled back (or undone).

When users share access to database tables, they may prevent each other from completing transactions. That's because a user who locks a table or a single record during an update may prevent other transactions from acquiring the locks they need to complete their task. As a result, the other transactions enter a wait state, waiting their turn. Sometimes, the locks are unresolvable, though. For example, if transaction A can't complete until it acquires a lock being used by transaction B, and transaction B can't complete until it acquires a lock being used by transaction A, the transactions enter a deadlock state and neither can complete unless the other is terminated.

Microsoft's *SQL Server Books Online* describes deadlocks by noting, "A deadlock occurs when there is a cyclic dependency between two or more threads for some set of resources" and adding that deadlocks can occur on any system with multiple threads, not just on a relational database management system.

References and Resources

Here's a list of further references and resources that you can access online:

- "Normalization Is a Nice Theory" by David Adams and Dan Beckett:
  http://www.4dcompanion.com/downloads/papers/normalization.html

- *Concurrency Control and Recovery in Database Systems* by Philip A. Bernstein, Vassos Hadzilacos, and Nathan Goodman:
  http://research.microsoft.com/pubs/ccontrol/

- "Denormalization Guidelines" by Craig S. Mullins:
  http://www.tdan.com/i001fe02.htm

- "Fundamentals of Relational Database Design" presented by Paul Litwin:
  http://www.microsoft.com/technet/treeview/default.asp?url=
  /TechNet/prodtechnol/office/plan/sysplan/ac101.asp

- "Transaction Isolation Levels" by Kalen Delaney:
  http://www.sqlmag.com/Articles/Index.cfm?ArticleID=5336

- "Responsible Denormalization" by Michelle A. Poolet:
  http://www.sqlmag.com/Articles/Index.cfm?ArticleID=9785

Commonly Used SQL Statements

STRUCTURED QUERY LANGUAGE (SQL) is a language to work with relational databases. In this appendix, I'll discuss some commonly used SQL queries and how to construct them. To test the SQL statements, I'll use the familiar Northwind database, specifically its Customers and Orders tables.

> **NOTE** *SQL queries are also referred to as* SQL statements.

Understanding SQL References

For the most part, I've used Access 2000's Northwind database to illustrate the SQL statements discussed in this appendix, but you can also use the Northwind database that's in SQL Server. (I use the SQL Server version in my examples on views because Access doesn't support the SQL concept of views as virtual tables.) To test SQL statements, you can open Northwind database in Access and create a new query by selecting Queries and the New button (see Figure B-1).

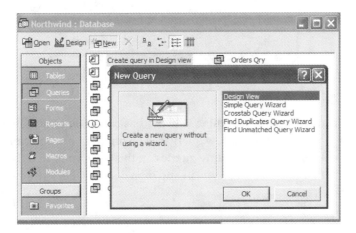

Figure B-1. Creating a new query in Access 2000

Figure B-2 shows all the tables in the database and lets you pick the tables with which you want to work. Click the Close button.

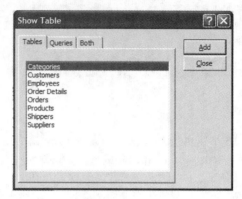

Figure B-2. Selecting database tables

Now, right-click on the query pane and click on the SQL View menu option (see Figure B-3).

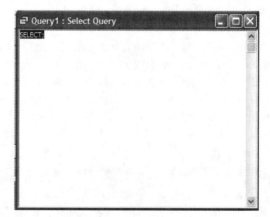

Figure B-3. Selecting the SQL View option

This will launch the Query Editor, which is basically a blank screen that appears when you're creating a new query (see Figure B-4), but you can also use it to examine the contents of existing queries. In this case, you can either type in a SQL statement directly or paste one in and then choose Query ➤ Run Query to execute the statement.

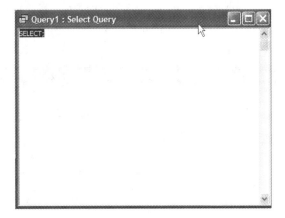

Figure B-4. The Query Editor of Access 2000

Now let's take a look at Northwind's Customers table. Figure B-5 shows the table schema (the structure) with its column names and their data types (all of type Text in this case). Note that the CustomerID field is the primary key field.

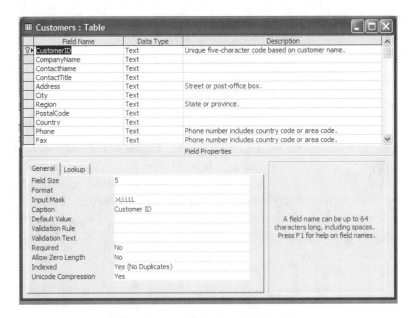

Figure B-5. Customers table schema of Northwind database

The Orders table columns and their data types look like Figure B-6. OrderID is the primary key in the Orders table. CustomerID and EmployeeID function as foreign keys and provide the "glue" that links data in the Customers table to data that are stored in Orders and Employees. (Employees is another table in the Northwind database that stores employees records.)

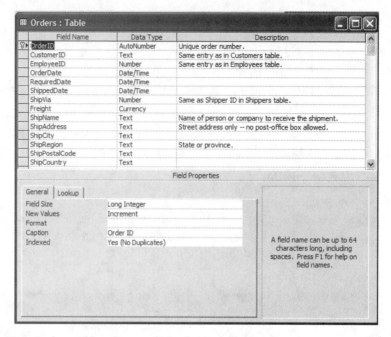

Figure B-6. Orders table schema of Northwind database

The SELECT Statement

The SELECT statement is the workhorse of the SQL language and enables you to retrieve data from a single or multiple database tables and/or views. If you only want to retrieve data from selected columns, you list the column names in the SELECT statement. You use the WHERE clause to retrieve data only from selected rows.

The simplest form of the SELECT statement is SELECT. . .FROM, which returns records from a table defined after FROM. This is the syntax:

```
SELECT column1, column2, .., FROM table
```

For example, the following SELECT statement returns all records from the CustomerID, Company Name, Address, and City columns of the Customers table:

```
SELECT CustomerID, CompanyName, Address, City FROM Customers
```

The output looks like Figure B-7.

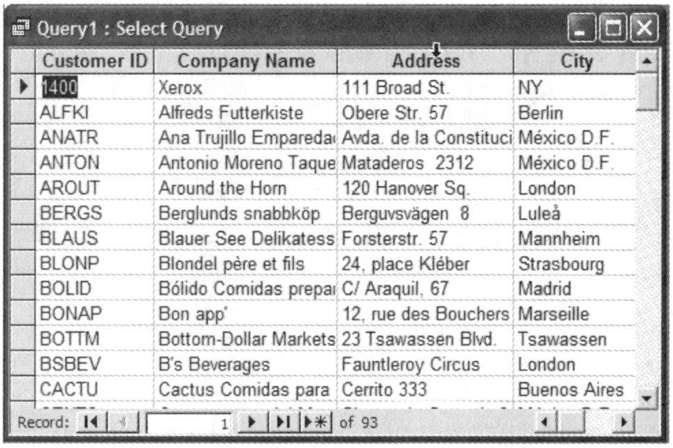

Query1 : Select Query

Customer ID	Company Name	Address	City
1400	Xerox	111 Broad St.	NY
ALFKI	Alfreds Futterkiste	Obere Str. 57	Berlin
ANATR	Ana Trujillo Empareda	Avda. de la Constituci	México D.F.
ANTON	Antonio Moreno Taque	Mataderos 2312	México D.F.
AROUT	Around the Horn	120 Hanover Sq.	London
BERGS	Berglunds snabbköp	Berguvsvägen 8	Luleå
BLAUS	Blauer See Delikatess	Forsterstr. 57	Mannheim
BLONP	Blondel père et fils	24, place Kléber	Strasbourg
BOLID	Bólido Comidas prepa	C/ Araquil, 67	Madrid
BONAP	Bon app'	12, rue des Bouchers	Marseille
BOTTM	Bottom-Dollar Markets	23 Tsawassen Blvd.	Tsawassen
BSBEV	B's Beverages	Fauntleroy Circus	London
CACTU	Cactus Comidas para	Cerrito 333	Buenos Aires

Record: 1 of 93

Figure B-7. Output of the `SELECT` *statement*

> **NOTE** *You can go back to the SQL view using View ➢ SQL View.*

You use `SELECT *` to return all columns from a table (* is a handy wildcard character in most dialects of SQL). For example, the following statement returns all records from the Customers table:

```
SELECT * FROM Customers
```

The output looks like Figure B-8.

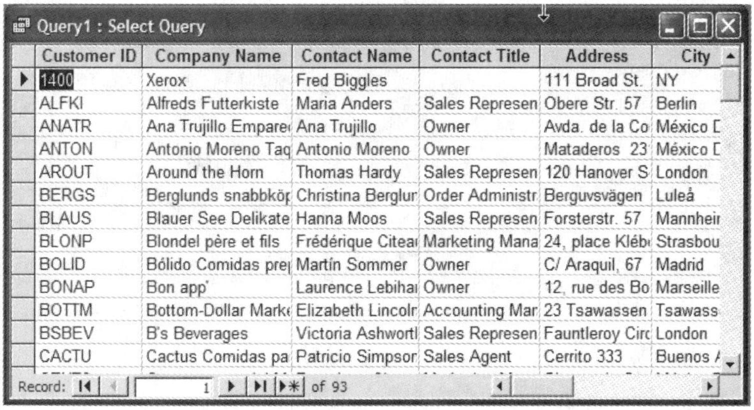

Query1 : Select Query

Customer ID	Company Name	Contact Name	Contact Title	Address	City
1400	Xerox	Fred Biggles		111 Broad St.	NY
ALFKI	Alfreds Futterkiste	Maria Anders	Sales Represen	Obere Str. 57	Berlin
ANATR	Ana Trujillo Empare	Ana Trujillo	Owner	Avda. de la Co	México D
ANTON	Antonio Moreno Taq	Antonio Moreno	Owner	Mataderos 23	México D
AROUT	Around the Horn	Thomas Hardy	Sales Represen	120 Hanover S	London
BERGS	Berglunds snabbköp	Christina Berglur	Order Administr	Berguvsvägen	Luleå
BLAUS	Blauer See Delikate	Hanna Moos	Sales Represen	Forsterstr. 57	Mannheir
BLONP	Blondel père et fils	Frédérique Citea	Marketing Mana	24, place Kléb	Strasbou
BOLID	Bólido Comidas pre	Martín Sommer	Owner	C/ Araquil, 67	Madrid
BONAP	Bon app'	Laurence Lebiha	Owner	12, rue des Bo	Marseille
BOTTM	Bottom-Dollar Mark	Elizabeth Lincoln	Accounting Mar	23 Tsawassen	Tsawass
BSBEV	B's Beverages	Victoria Ashwort	Sales Represen	Fauntleroy Circ	London
CACTU	Cactus Comidas pa	Patricio Simpsor	Sales Agent	Cerrito 333	Buenos /

Record: 1 of 93

Figure B-8. Output of `SELECT * FROM Customers` *statement*

There are some occasions when the database table stores redundant records, but you generally don't want duplicate records returned. You can use the SELECT DISTINCT statement for this purpose:

```
SELECT DISTINCT column1, column2, .., FROM table
```

For example, the following statement returns only unique records from the Customers table:

```
SELECT DISTINCT CompanyName FROM Customers
```

In addition to restricting columns to those you're interested in, you can also restrict rows by using the SELECT. . .FROM. . .WHERE statement. The WHERE clause takes a conditional statement:

```
SELECT column1, column2, .., FROM table WHERE condition
```

For example, the following query:

```
SELECT * FROM Customers WHERE CustomerID = "BOTTM"
```

returns records only having CustomerID = "BOTTM". The output of Northwind's Customers table looks like Figure B-9.

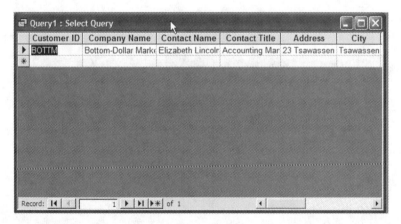

Figure B-9. Output of SELECT. . .WHERE *statement*

Table B-1 summarizes the conditional statement used in SQL.

Table B-1. Conditional Statements Used in SQL

OPERATOR	MEANING
<	Less Than
>	Greater Than
<>	Not Equal To
=	Equal To

You can also use the SUM and AVG functions to return the sum and average of numeric columns, respectively:

```
SELECT function(column) FROM table
```

For example, the following query returns the sum of the Freight column in the Orders table:

```
SELECT SUM(Freight) FROM Orders
```

See Figure B-10 for the output of this statement.

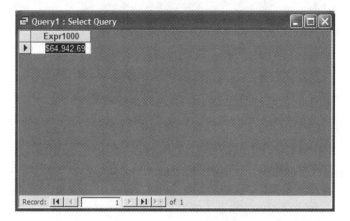

Figure B-10. Output of a query that uses the SQL SUM function

The following query returns the average of the Freight column:

```
SELECT AVG (Freight) FROM Orders
```

You can use SELECT COUNT to return the number of rows in a table (based on a column). This is the syntax:

```
SELECT COUNT(column) FROM table
```

For example, the following statement returns the number of rows in the Customers table:

```
SELECT COUNT(CustomerID) FROM Customers;
```

The output of this statement looks like Figure B-11.

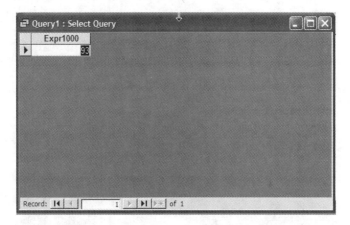

Figure B-11. Output of COUNT

GROUP BY is another handy clause that returns results grouped by the mentioned column. This is the syntax:

```
SELECT column1, SUM(column2) FROM table GROUP BY column1
```

For example, the following statement returns the number of rows grouped by OrderDate from the Orders table:

```
SELECT OrderDate, SUM(Freight) FROM Orders GROUP BY(OrderDate)
```

The output of the query looks like Figure B-12.

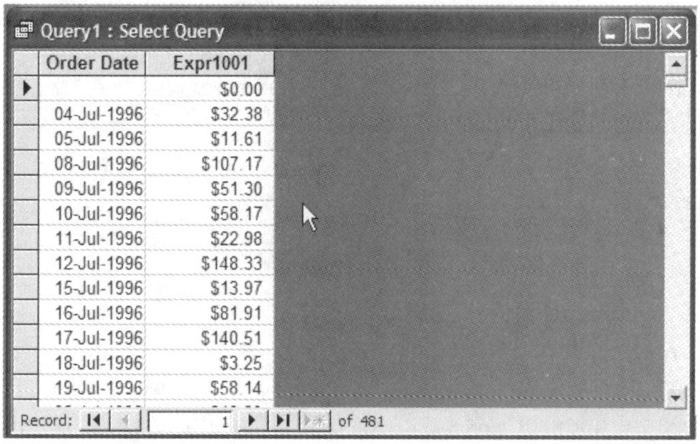

Figure B-12. Output of GROUP BY

The HAVING clause limits output based on a criterion. You can use it with or without the GROUP BY clause. This is the syntax:

```
SELECT column1, column2 FROM table GROUP BY column1 HAVING condition
```

For example, the following statement returns records of the OrderDate column having total freight more than 900:

```
SELECT OrderDate FROM Orders GROUP BY(OrderDate) HAVING SUM(Freight) > 900
```

The UPDATE Statement

The UPDATE statement makes changes to existing records in a database table. The UPDATE statement takes database table names and table columns and their values.

The syntax for UPDATE statement is as follows:

```
UPDATE table SET column1 = [new value],  column2 =[new value],...
WHERE {condition}
```

For example, the following query updates the Freight column value to 500 in the Orders table where OrderId is 10248:

```
UPDATE Orders SET Freight = 500 WHERE OrderId = 10248
```

Using a comma (,), you can update as many as columns as you want. If you want to update all the rows of a column or more than one column, you don't use the WHERE clause. For example, the following query updates all the rows of the Freight column with the value of 500:

```
UPDATE Orders SET Freight = 500
```

The DELETE Statement

The DELETE statement removes records from a database table. Using the DELETE statement is dangerously simple. Using the DELETE statement, you can either delete records based on certain criteria or delete *all* the records of a database table.

The syntax of the DELETE statement is as follows:

```
DELETE FROM table WHERE {condition}
```

For example, the following statement deletes all rows of OrderId 10248 (there should only be one because OrderID is the primary key):

```
DELETE FROM Orders WHERE OrderID = 10248
```

If you want to delete all of a table's rows, retaining an empty table, you can use the following statement:

```
DELETE FROM Orders
```

(In Access, DELETE statements can impact more than one table's rows depending on whether cascading deletes are enabled.)

The CREATE TABLE Statement

A database table is a collection of rows and columns. Each field in a table is represented as a column. Each field of a table must have a defined data type and a unique name. You can use the CREATE TABLE statement to create database tables programmatically.

The syntax for CREATE TABLE is as follows:

```
CREATE TABLE table (column1 column1_datatype,
column2 column2_datetype, ..., column column_datatype)
```

The following statement creates a table called myTable with columns myId, myName, myAddress, and myBalance, which can store integer, character 50, character 255, and floating values, respectively. The CONSTRAINT ...PRIMARY KEY syntax makes a column a primary key column:

```
CREATE TABLE myTable (myId INTEGER CONSTRAINT PKeyMyId PRIMARY KEY,
myName CHAR(50), myAddress CHAR(255), myBalance FLOAT)
```

The DROP TABLE Statement

There might be some occasions when either you need to delete a table permanently or you need to create temporary, *scratch* tables and then delete them. The DROP TABLE statement deletes a database table.

The syntax for DROP TABLE is as follows:

```
DROP TABLE table
```

For example, the following statement deletes myTable from the database:

```
DROP TABLE myTable
```

The TRUNCATE TABLE Statement

DROP TABLE deletes all records of a table and the table itself from the database. What if you don't want to delete the table, just its records? One way of doing this is using the DELETE FROM query. TRUNCATE TABLE is another way to remove data of a table without getting rid of the table itself. TRUNCATE TABLE removes all records from a table without logging the individual record deletes. The DELETE statement removes records one at a time and records an entry in the transaction log for each deleted record. TRUNCATE TABLE is faster than DELETE because it removes the data by deallocating the database table data pages, and only deallocations of the pages are recorded in the transaction log.

TRUNCATE TABLE doesn't remove the table structure, columns, constraints, or indexes. If you want to remove a table definition and its data, use DROP TABLE instead.

The syntax of this statement is simple:

```
TRUNCATE TABLE table
```

For example, the following statement will truncate the Customers table:

```
TRUNCATE TABLE Customers
```

> **NOTE**   `TRUNCATE TABLE` *is not supported natively in Access databases.*

The INSERT Statement

In the previous sections, you saw how to retrieve information out of tables. But how do these rows of data get into the tables in the first place? This is what this section, covering `INSERT INTO`, and the next section, covering `UPDATE`, are about.

There are basically two ways to insert data into a table. One is to insert them one row at a time, and the other is to insert the data several rows at a time. First let's look at how you can insert data one row at a time.

The syntax for inserting data into a table one row at a time is as follows:

```
INSERT INTO table (column1, column2, .., columnn)
VALUES (value1, value2, ..., valunen)
```

For example, the following query will add a new record to the Customers table columns with their corresponding values.

```
INSERT INTO Customers(CompanyName, ContactName, ContactTitle,
Address, City, Phone) VALUES ('New Name','New Contact','New Title',
'New Address', 'New City', 'New Phone' )
```

You can also insert records in a table by selecting records from another table. You can do that by mixing `INSERT INTO` and `SELECT` statements. The only condition is that the data type of the columns must match in both tables.

The syntax for this is as follows:

```
INSERT INTO table1 (column1, column2, ...)
 SELECT column1, column2, ... FROM table2
```

The previous syntax selects data from table2 and inserts it in table1. The data types of column1 in table1 must match with the data type of column1 in table2 and so on.

The following query reads CustName and ContName from the NewTable and inserts data to the Customers table:

```
INSERT INTO Customers (CustomerName, ContactName)
SELECT CustName, ContName FROM NewTable
```

You can also apply `WHERE` and other clauses on this query as you have applied them on the previous `SELECT` statements.

JOINs and Aliases

A table and column can be represented in a SQL statement using their alias names. Aliases are frequently used as shorthand—especially in JOIN queries. This is the syntax:

```
SELECT aliastable.column1 aliascolumn FROM table aliastable
```

For example, this code uses A1 as the alias for the Customers table:

```
SELECT A1.CustomerID FROM Customers A1;
```

Figure B-13 shows the output of this statement. You can use the same syntax for multiple tables by separating them with commas.

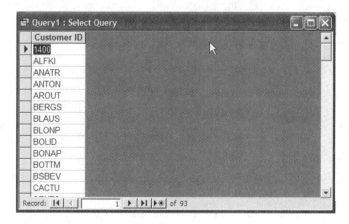

Figure B-13. Output of the Alias *statement*

JOINs are useful when you need to select data from multiple tables based on selection criteria from more than one table. For example, you want to select data from the Orders and Customers tables where the CustomerID column in the Customers table exists in the CustomerID column of the Orders table as a foreign key. The following statement will return you the result:

```
SELECT DISTINCT Orders.OrderID, Orders.CustomerID, Orders.EmployeeID,
Customers.CompanyName, Customers.Address, Customers.City
FROM Customers INNER JOIN Orders ON Customers.CustomerID = Orders.CustomerID;
```

The output of this statement looks like Figure B-14.

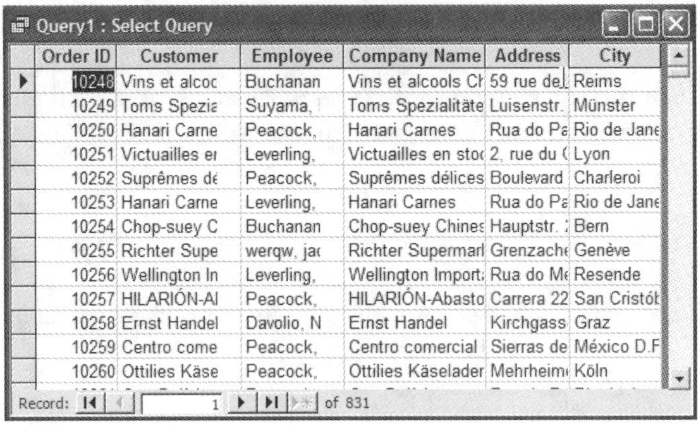

Order ID	Customer	Employee	Company Name	Address	City
10248	Vins et alcoc	Buchanan	Vins et alcools Ch	59 rue de l	Reims
10249	Toms Spezia	Suyama,	Toms Spezialitäte	Luisenstr.	Münster
10250	Hanari Carne	Peacock,	Hanari Carnes	Rua do Pa	Rio de Jane
10251	Victuailles er	Leverling,	Victuailles en stoc	2, rue du (	Lyon
10252	Suprêmes dé	Peacock,	Suprêmes délices	Boulevard	Charleroi
10253	Hanari Carne	Leverling,	Hanari Carnes	Rua do Pa	Rio de Jane
10254	Chop-suey C	Buchanan	Chop-suey Chines	Hauptstr. :	Bern
10255	Richter Supe	werqw, jac	Richter Supermarl	Grenzache	Genève
10256	Wellington In	Leverling,	Wellington Import:	Rua do Me	Resende
10257	HILARIÓN-Al	Peacock,	HILARIÓN-Abasto	Carrera 22	San Cristót
10258	Ernst Handel	Davolio, N	Ernst Handel	Kirchgass	Graz
10259	Centro come	Peacock,	Centro comercial	Sierras de	México D.F
10260	Ottilies Käse	Peacock,	Ottilies Käselader	Mehrheim	Köln

Figure B-14. Output of the JOIN statement

There are a handful of different types of JOINs, the most important of which are INNER JOINs, OUTER JOINs, and CROSS JOINs.

INNER JOINs are used to return records when both tables have at least one row that satisfies the JOIN condition.

OUTER JOINs work with `LEFT (OUTER) JOIN`, `RIGHT (OUTER) JOIN`, and `FULL (OUTER) JOIN` clauses. The `OUTER JOIN` with `RIGHT JOIN` returns all records from the right table and null values for the unmatched records in the left table. The `OUTER JOIN` with `LEFT JOIN` clause is the reverse of the `OUTER JOIN` with `RIGHT JOIN`. It returns all records from the left table and null values for the unmatched records in the right table. The `OUTER JOIN` with the `FULL JOIN` clause returns all records from both tables. If there's no match for a record of left table in the right table, the right table returns null values and vice versa.

CROSS JOINs return all records from the left table, and each row of the left table is combined with all records of the right table.

Understanding Views

A *view* is a virtual table that represents data from one or more than one database table. You can select data from single or multiple tables based on the sort and filter criteria (using `WHERE` and `GROUP BY` clauses) and save data as a view. You can also set permissions on views to control access to sensitive data. For example, a manager, an accountant, and a clerk of a company may all use the same database. The manager can access all data from different tables of the database, the accountant can only access some of the data from multiple tables, but the clerk can only access some of a single table's data. The easiest way to do this is with SQL views; you create three different views based on the user rights and let the user access these views based on their rights.

> **NOTE** *SQL views aren't natively supported in Access databases. You'll need to use a "true" relational database to explore views. I use SQL Server and its copy of Northwind.*

The CREATE VIEW SQL statement creates a view. The simple format of CREATE VIEW statement is as follows:

```
CREATE VIEW viewname AS selectstatement
```

where viewname is the name of the view and selectstatement is the SELECT statement used to select data from one or more tables.

Here's a simple CREATE VIEW statement. The following statement creates a myView with records as a result of SELECT myName FROM myTable:

```
CREATE VIEW myView AS SELECT myName FROM myTable
```

The following two CREATE VIEW statements create two different views: View1 and View2 from the Orders table based on different criteria:

```
CREATE VIEW "View1" AS
SELECT OrderID, OrderDate, ShippedDate
FROM Orders
WHERE (Freight < 10)
```

```
CREATE VIEW "View2" AS
SELECT OrderID, OrderDate, ShippedDate
FROM Orders
WHERE (Freight > 1000)
```

You can also create views by selecting data from multiple tables. For example, the following view selects data from the Products and Categories tables. By using views this way, you can essentially "save" frequently used queries.

```
CREATE VIEW "Products by Category" AS
SELECT Categories.CategoryName, Products.ProductName, Products.QuantityPerUnit,
Products.UnitsInStock, Products.Discontinued
FROM Categories INNER JOIN Products ON Categories.CategoryID
= Products.CategoryID
WHERE Products.Discontinued <> 1
ORDER BY Categories.CategoryName, Products.ProductName
```

Using SQL Server's SELECT...FOR XML Clause

Most of today's databases support Extensible Markup Language (XML). In SQL Server, for example, you can execute SQL queries to return results as XML rather than standard rowsets. These queries can be executed directly or from within stored procedures. To retrieve results directly, you use the FOR XML clause of the SELECT statement. Within the FOR XML clause, you specify one of three XML modes: RAW, AUTO, or EXPLICIT. (You can also work with XML data in Access, Oracle, MySQL, and other databases, but the techniques vary.)

For example, this SQL Server SELECT statement retrieves information from the Customers and Orders tables in the Northwind database:

```
SELECT Customers.CustomerID, ContactName, CompanyName,
       Orders.CustomerID, OrderDate
FROM Customers, Orders
WHERE Customers.CustomerID = Orders.CustomerID
AND (Customers.CustomerID = N'ALFKI'
    OR Customers.CustomerID = N'XYZAA')
ORDER BY Customers.CustomerID
FOR XML AUTO
```

References and Resources

Here's a list of further references and resources that you can access online:

- *Code Centric: T-SQL Programming with Stored Procedures and Triggers* by Garth Wells: http://www.sqlbook.com/

- "A Gentle Introduction to SQL" by Andrew Cumming: http://www.dcs.napier.ac.uk/~andrew/sql/

- Microsoft SQL Server Product Documentation:
  `http://www.microsoft.com/sql/techinfo/productdoc/2000/default.asp`

- MSDN Library, Transact SQL:
  `http://msdn.microsoft.com/library/default.asp?url=/library`
  `/en-us/tsqlref/ts_ra-rz_9oj7.asp`

Index

Symbols and Numbers

/ / / (three slashes), using with comments in source code, 67

<!-- > tag, description of, 357, 362

- (unary) operators, using with for loop statements, 42

& (ampersand), role XML-document references, 370

, (comma), using with UPDATE statement in SQL, 676

&& (conditional and) operator, using with if . . . else statement, 40–41

" (double quote) entity in XML, representing, 370

; (semicolon)
   advisory about, 46
   role in XML-document references, 370

' (single quote) entity in XML, representing, 370

(hash symbol), role in XML-document character references, 370

++ (unary) operators, using with for loop statements, 42

<-- and --> pairs, role in XML comments, 369

< and > characters in XML documents, advisory about, 369

< (less than)
   entity in XML, 370
   operator in SQL, 673

<> (not equal to) operator in SQL, 673

= (equal to) operator in SQL, 673

> (greater than)
   entity in XML, 370
   operator in SQL, 673

@ (at) sign, appearance in SQL Server Insert commands, 339

|| (conditional or) operators, using with if . . . else statements, 40–41

0-3 isolation levels, details of, 663

1-4 values for locking types, descriptions of, 664

1NF (first normal form), explanation of, 654–656

2NF (second normal form), explanation of, 656–658

3NF (third normal form), explanation of, 658–659

4NF (fourth normal form), explanation of, 659

5NF (fifth normal form), explanation of, 659–660

A

AcceptChanges method
   of ADO.NET DataRow class, 252
   of ADO.NET DataSet class, 276
   of ADO.NET DataTable class, 259

Access connection string for ODBC, displaying, 291

Access tables, exporting to text files, 633–637

accessibility modifiers
   example of, 32
   functionality of, 33–35

Action property of XmlNodeChangedEventsArgs, description of, 566

AddCat1 stored procedure, code for, 588

Added member of ADO.NET DataRowState enumeration, 257

additive operators, examples of, 38

AddNew method of ADO.NET DataView class, description of, 278

AddNews property of ADO.NET DataView class, description of, 277

AddRange method of Form class, code for, 89

AddRow_Click method, code for, 270

ADO (ActiveX Data Objects)
   versus ADO.NET, 128–129
   recordset cursor types and values in, 661

ADO recordsets, using in ADO.NET, 595–598

ADODB namespace
   accessing databases with, 597–598
   adding references to, 603
   including in projects, 596–597
   viewing, 596

ADOMD (ActiveX Data Objects Multi-Dimensional Library)
   adding references to, 603
   functionality of, 601
   testing, 603

ADOMD namespaces, adding to projects, 602

ADO.NET (ActiveX Data Objects .NET)
   accessing OLAP server data with, 600–611
   adding database support to Web services with, 516–517
   adding parameters to stored procedures with, 585–587
   versus ADO, 128–129
   advantages of, 126–128
   and COM interoperability, 594–595
   CommandBuilder utility in, 135–136
   concurrency control in, 343–347
   creating Command objects for, 140–141

creating DataAdapter objects for, 140–141
creating OleDb Command objects for, 301–303
creating stored procedures with, 573–580, 576–577
DataViewManager class, 278–279
deployment of, 127
editing, deleting, and executing stored procedures with, 575–578
executing and reading results of stored procedures in, 307–308
executing stored procedures with programmatically, 583–589
explanation of, 123–124
filling data to DataSets or DataReader objects in, 141
getting database schemas from, 607–610
introduction to, 123
and ODBC, 125–126
and OLE-DB, 125–126
overview of namespaces and classes in, 129–132
performance and scalability of, 128
pessimistic concurrency in, 346–347
purpose of, 125–126
and relational databases, 660–661
returning data from stored procedures with, 578
returning values from stored procedures with, 586
role of Command components in, 230–231
role of Command object in, 133–135
role of Command objects in, 300–301
role of Connection components in, 230–231
role of Connection object in, 133–134
role of DataAdapter components in, 230–231
role of DataSet class in, 273
role of DataSet components in, 231–232
role of DataSets in, 124, 274–277
role of DataTable components in, 232
role of DataView class in, 273
role of DataViews in, 277–278
role of managed class in, 127
role of managed code in, 127
role of parameters in, 337–339
role of XML in, 124
saving SELECT statements as stored procedures with, 578–579
selecting records with, 610–611
support for XML, 127
System.Data namespace class, 237–238
transactions in, 342–343
typed and untyped DataSets in, 276–277
using ADO recordsets in, 595–598
using ADOX with, 598–600
using DataReaders with, 313–314
using output parameters and stored procedures with, 588

using views with, 588–594
viewing stored procedures with, 574
visual data components of, 127
ADO.NET applications
adding namespace references to, 139–140
choosing .NET data providers for, 138–139
closing connections to, 142
constructing SQL Server Connection objects for, 148
creating in VS .NET, 153–154
displaying data in, 141
establishing connections in, 140
writing, 138–145
writing with Visual Studio .NET IDE, 145–151
ADO.NET architecture, examining, 230–232
ADO.NET class hierarchy, exploring, 232–237
ADO.NET components, understanding, 132–138
ADO.NET data provider namespace references, adding to projects, 283
ADO.NET data providers
choosing, 282–283
connecting to databases, 283–285
explanation of, 229
introduction to, 279–283
opening and closing connections for, 285–289
ADO.NET disconnected classes
DataRelation, 257–258
DataRows, 251–256
DataRowState, 256–257
DataTable, DataColumn, and DataRow, 241–243
DataTables, 258–273
explanation of, 229
introduction to, 237
role of DataColumns in, 241–243
System.Data namespaces, 237
System.Data.Common namespaces, 239–240
ADO.NET events
calling Fill and Update methods of DataAdapter for, 557–558
introduction to, 545–546
role of FillError property of data adapters in, 553
testing data adapter events used with, 554–559
using connection events with, 547–553
using DataAdapter events with, 553–559
using DataSet events with, 559–560
using DataTable events with, 560–565
using DataView and DataViewManager events with, 568–570
using XmlDataDocument events with, 565–568
ADO.NET objects, transferring XML names to, 393
AdoNetApp1.cs application, code for, 143–144

ADOX (ActiveX Data Objects Extensions for
    Data Definition Language and
    Security)
    using from managed code, 600
    using with ADO.NET, 598–600
aliases, using with SQL, 679–680
AllowCustomPaging property of ASP.NET
    DataGrid control, description of,
    465
AllowDBNull property of ADO.NET
    DataColumn disconnected class,
    description of, 244
AllowDelete property of ADO.NET DataView
    class, description of, 277
AllowEdit property of ADO.NET DataView
    class, description of, 277
AllowPaging property
    of ASP.NET DataGrid control, 465
    example of, 495
    setting, 495
AllowSorting property
    of ASP.NET DataGrid control, 465
    setting, 495
amp XML built-in entities and references,
    description of, 370
ampersand (&), role XML-document refer-
    ences, 370
apos XML built-in entities and references,
    description of, 370
AppendChild XML method, functionality of,
    398–399
Application class of System.Windows.Forms,
    description of, 101–102
array elements, iterating with foreach loop
    statement, 43–44
array types, explanation of, 25–29
arrays
    imitating with indexer class members, 63
    sorting, searching, and copying, 26–29
ASP.NET
    adding even handlers to button-click
        events with, 448–449
    adding server-side controls with, 460–462
    advantages of, 437
    binding Web Forms controls at design-
        time with, 472–478
    creating data views and connecting to
        datasets with, 475–476
    creating guest books with, 478–490
    creating tables at design-time with,
        504–507
    creating tables programmatically with,
        507–509
    creating Web applications with, 438–442
    data binding in, 462
    installing, 436
    introduction to, 435
    platform requirements of, 436
    setting control properties for, 444–448
    setting page properties for, 441–442
    table controls for, 504

    using data-bound controls with, 462–464
    using DataGrid and DataList controls
        with, 464–469
    viewing data in DataGrid controls with,
        452–455
    viewing page options for, 441
ASP.NET applications
    adding, editing, and deleting data in,
        496–503
    adding new records to, 499–500
    developing with VS .NET, 450–455
    enabling automatic paging in, 494–495
    enabling paging at design-time in,
        491–494
    executing SQL queries in, 497–499
    filling data to ListBox controls with,
        451–452
    MyGuestBook example, 479–490
    updating data in, 501
    using ExecuteNonQuery method with, 498
    using ExecuteSQL method with, 499
    using SQL SELECT statements with, 498
ASP.NET server-side controls
    explanation of, 455
    and .NET Framework library, 457–459
    types of, 455–457
assemblies
    definition of, 594
    understanding, 8–10
assignment operators, examples of, 38
asynchronous Web services, executing,
    539–542
at (@) sign, appearance in SQL Server Insert
    commands, 339
atomic columns, role in 1NF, 654
Attr node in XML, description of, 374
Attribute member of XmlNodeType
    enumeration, description of, 384
AttributeCount property of XmlReader class,
    description of, 387
attributes
    adding to XML nodes, 402
    explanation of, 31
    returning for XML nodes, 385–386
    role in XML documents, 371
    in XML, 361–362
AutoGenerateColumns property of ASP.NET
    DataGrid control, description of,
    465
AutoIncrement property of ADO.NET
    DataColumn disconnected class,
    description of, 244
AutoIncrementSeed property of ADO.NET
    DataColumn disconnected class,
    description of, 244
AutoIncrementStep property of ADO.NET
    DataColumn disconnected class,
    description of, 244
automatic memory management feature of
    C#, explanation of, 4
AVG function, using in SQL, 673

B

\<b\> tag, description of, 357

BackColor property of ASP.NET DataGrid control, description of, 465

BackImageUrl property of ASP.NET DataGrid control, description of, 465

BaseURI property of XmlReader class, description of, 387

BCNF (Boyce-Codd normal form), explanation of, 659

BCNI (Boyce-Codd normal form), explanation of, 654

BeginEdit method of ADO.NET DataRow class, description of, 252

BeginInit method
of ADO.NET DataSet class, 276
of ADO.NET DataView class, 278

Begin(IsolationLevel) method
of Transaction class, description of, 342
in Sql data providers, 347

BeginTransaction method of ADO.NET Connection class, description of, 285

binary compatibility with base classes, C# support for, 4–5

binary operators, definition of, 37

BinarySearch property of array class, description of, 27

BindData method, example of, 260–264

\<body\> tag, description of, 357

Boiler.cs class example, implementing events and event handlers with, 58–60

bookstore elements, adding to XML schemas, 423–424

books.xml
deleting all items in, 400–401
loading from strings, 394–395
output of, 360–361

bool C# type alias, details of, 18

BorderColor property of ASP.NET DataGrid control, description of, 465

BorderStyle property of ASP.NET DataGrid control, description of, 465

BorderWidth property of ASP.NET DataGrid control, description of, 465

boxing, definition of, 30

\<br\> tag, description of, 357

break statement, functionality of, 44

Broken member of ADO.NET ConnectionType enumerations, description of, 285

Broken property of ConnectionState enumeration, description of, 549

Button class of System.Windows.Forms, description of, 101

button-click handlers, creating ASP.NET tables with programmatically, 508–509

button event handlers, writing code for, 269

byte C# type alias, details of, 18

C

C#
automatic memory management feature of, 4
background of, 1
case-sensitivity of, 1
characteristics and features of, 2–5
compiling from command line, 144–145
and DLLs, 4
evolution of, 2
exception types in, 65
garbage collection in, 4
lack of support for inheritance, 3
language and cross-platform interoperability in, 5
as modern language, 3
as object-oriented language, 3
and open source, 1–2
operators in, 38
performing type conversions in, 29–31
role of manifests in, 5
role of namespaces in, 4, 7
role of object types in, 3–4
scalability of, 4–5
simplicity and flexibility of, 3
standard input and output streams in, 10–11
support for binary compatibility with base classes, 4–5
support for function overloading, 52–54
typesafety of, 3–4
versioning control in, 4–5

C# code, compiling from command line, 6

C# components, understanding, 7–10

C# Corner Web site, 3

C# editors, availability of, 5

C# types
explanation of, 4
introduction to, 17–18

CancelEdit method of ADO.NET DataRow class, description of, 252

candidate key, role in BCNF, 659

Caption property of ADO.NET DataColumn disconnected class, description of, 244

CarRec struct type example, 19–20

Catalog object of ADOX, functionality of, 599

CDATA member of XmlNodeType enumeration, description of, 384

CDATA sections, role in XML documents, 369

CellPadding property of ASP.NET DataGrid control, description of, 465

cells, adding to rows of ASP.NET tables at design-time, 506–507

CellSpacing property of ASP.NET DataGrid control, description of, 465

ChangeDatabase method of ADO.NET Connection class, description of, 285

Chaos isolation level for transactions, descriptions, 343

char C# type alias, details of, 18

character and entity references, role in XML documents, 370

CheckBox ASP.NET data-bound control, description of, 464

CheckBox class of System.Windows.Forms, description of, 101

CheckBoxList ASP.NET data-bound control, description of, 464

checked operators, explanation of, 38–39

child nodes, moving to, 417–418

ChildNodes property of XmlNode class, functionality of, 394

ChildRelation property of ADO.NET DataTable class, description of, 259

class constructors, calling, 50–51

class events, using delegate reference types with, 24

class keyword, definition of, 7

class members, elements of, 46

class method example, 52

class objects, using indexer class members with, 63

class property member example, 56–58

class reference types, explanation of, 21–22

Class View window, displaying Windows Forms classes in, 92–100

classes

    adding to VS .NET IDE Windows Forms application, 92–96

    in ADO.NET, 129–132

    functionality of, 46

    implementing multiple interfaces with, 22–23

    for ODBC .NET data providers, 618

Clear method

    of ADO.NET DataSet class, 276

    of ADO.NET DataTable class, 259

Clear property of array class, description of, 27

CLI (Common Language Infrastructure) and C#, 1–2

clients, creating for Web services, 525–539

Clone method

    of ADO.NET DataSet class, 276

    of ADO.NET DataTable class, 259

Clone property of array class, description of, 27

Close method

    of ADO.NET Connection class, 285

    of ADO.NET DataReaders, 315

    using with XML documents, 392

Close property of XmlReader class, description of, 388

Closed member of ADO.NET ConnectionType enumerations, description of, 285

Closed property of ConnectionState enumeration, description of, 549

CLR (Common Language Runtime)

    handling stack overflow with, 38–39

    incorporation into Mono Project, 2

CLR types, converting to XSD types, 393

code segments, using goto statement with, 43–44

ColorDialog class, functionality of, 101, 120–121

ColumnChanged event of DataTable event, description of, 560, 562

ColumnChanging event of DataTable event, description of, 560, 562

ColumnMapping property of ADO.NET DataColumn disconnected class, description of, 244

ColumnName property of ADO.NET DataColumn disconnected class, description of, 244

columns, displaying with Data Form Wizard, 215–216

Columns object of ADOX, functionality of, 599

Columns property

    of ADO.NET DataTable class, 259

    of ASP.NET DataGrid control, 465

COM (Component Object Model) and ADO.NET, 594–595

COM libraries, adding references to, 595–596

ComboBox class of System.Windows.Forms, description of, 101

comma (,), using with UPDATE statement in SQL, 676

Command components, role in ADO.NET, 230–231

command line, compiling C# from, 144–145

command-line Windows forms applications, writing, 70–78

Command object, role in ADO.NET, 134–135

Command objects

    calling stored procedures with, 306–309

    creating for ADO.NET applications, 140–141

    functionality of, 300–301

    role in ADO.NET, 133–134

Command property of OleDbRowUpdatedEventArgs, description of, 554

CommandBuilder objects

    creating, 335–336

    functionality of, 334–335

CommandBuilder utility, using with ADO.NET, 135–136

CommandText property of OledDbCommand, description of, 301

CommandType item

    functionality of, 305

    of OledDbCommand, 301

Comment member of XmlNodeType
      enumeration, description of, 384
Comment node in XML, description of, 375
comments
      role in XML, 369
      using /// (three slashes) with, 67
Commit method of Transaction class,
      description of, 342
CommitTransaction, functionality of, 340
common dialogs, creating with
      Windows.Forms namespace,
      118–121
CommonAppDataPath method of
      Windows.Forms.Application
      class, description of, 102
CommonDialog class of
      System.Windows.Forms,
      description of, 101
Compare objects, sample output of, 15
CompareValidator ASP.NET server-side
      control, description of, 457
complexType items, adding to XML schemas,
      424–425
concurrency control
      in ADO.NET, 343–347
      definition of, 341
      Web site for, 665
conditional and (&&) operators, using with if
      . . . else statements, 40–41
Conditional built-in attribute, description
      of, 31
conditional operators, examples of, 38
conditional or (||) operators, using with if . . .
      else statements, 40–41
Configure Data Adapter option, using with
      SQL data adapters, 184
Connecting member of ADO.NET
      ConnectionType enumerations,
      description of, 285
Connecting property of ConnectionState
      enumer-ation, description
      of, 549
Connection class, using with ADO.NET data
      providers, 283–285
Connection components, role in ADO.NET,
      230–231
connection events
      adding programmatically at design-time,
      549
      testing, 549
      writing code for execution of, 551–552
connection events, using with ADO.NET
      events, 547–553
Connection Lifetime connection pooling set-
      ting, description of, 299
Connection objects
      creating for ADO.NET applications, 140
      creating with different constructors, 286
      role in ADO.NET, 133–134
connection pooling, understanding, 297–300
Connection property of OledDbCommand,
      description of, 301

Connection Reset connection pooling setting,
      description of, 299
connection strings
      for ODBC with various databases, 291
      for Ole Db with various databases, 290
      role in VS .NET, 167–169
connections
      adding with Server Explorer, 156–159
      creating with different strings, 298–299
      establishing for ADO.NET data providers,
            283–285
      establishing in ADO.NET applications, 140
      opening and closing for ADO.NET data
            providers, 285–289
connections and disconnected data, manage-
      ment by ADO.NET versus ADO,
      128
ConnectionState enumeration properties, list
      of, 548–549
ConnectionString class, searching, 187
ConnectionString property of ADO.NET
      Connection objects,
      description of, 284
ConnectionTimeOut property of ADO.NET
      Connection objects, description
      of, 284
console-based ADO.NET applications,
      creating, 142–145
Console class and members
      accessing, 7
      displaying, 11
constant class member
      functionality of, 49
      and inheritance, 46
constants, definition of, 36
Constraint class in ADO.NET System.Data
      namespaces, description of, 237
ConstraintCollection class in ADO.NET
      System.Data namespaces,
      description of, 237
constraints, definition of, 242
Constraints property of ADO.NET DataTable
      class, description of, 259
constructors, overloading, 50
ContextMenu class of
      System.Windows.Forms, descrip-
      tion of, 101
Continue property of FillErrorEventArgs,
      description of, 553
continue statement, functionality of, 45
Control class of Windows.Forms namespace,
      functionality of, 102
Control classes of System.Windows.Forms,
      description of, 101
control flow, explanation of, 40
controls
      adding to VS .NET IDE Windows Forms
            application, 79–82
      adding to Windows Forms, 73–74
Copy method
      of ADO.NET DataSet class, 276
      of ADO.NET DataTable class, 259

Copy property of array class, description of, 27

CopyTo property of array class, description of of array class, 27

Count property of ADO.NET DataView class, description of, 277

CREATE TABLE statement, using with SQL, 676–677

CREATE VIEW statement, using with SQL, 681

CreateCommand method of ADO.NET Connection class, description of, 285

CreateCustomersTable, calling with form's constructor, 260

CreateCustomersTable method, code for, 268–269

CreateCustomerTable method, example of, 260–265

CreateInstance property of array class, description of, 27

CreateNavigator method of XmlNode class, functionality of, 394

CreateOrdersTable method, example of, 260–264

CROSS JOINs, using with SQL, 680

.cs extension, adding to Windows Forms applications, 70

Ctrl+F keyboard shortcut, searching ConnectionString class with, 187

Ctrl+F5 keyboard shortcut, running VS .NET IDE Windows Forms application with, 91

cubes
getting dimensions of, 605–607
getting from FoodMart 2000 database, 604–605
role in OLAP, 600

CurrentPageIndex property of ASP.NET DataGrid control, description of, 465

Cursor classes of System.Windows.Forms, description of, 101

cursors, role in relational databases, 660–661

CustEmpView, displaying, 592–593

custom ASP.NET server-side controls, explanation of, 457

customer/order relationship
example of, 260–264
explanation of, 257–258

CustomValidator ASP.NET server-side control, description of, 457

CustOrderRelation relationship, creating with Data Form Wizard, 214–215

CustOrdersDetail stored procedure, displaying output of, 582–583

D

data
displaying in ADO.NET applications, 141
managing and viewing with Server Explorer, 159–161

reading and storing, 313–314
retrieving from views programmatically, 593–594

Data Adapter Configuration Wizard
binding ASP.NET Web Forms controls at design-time with, 472–478
binding DataGrid controls with, 476–477
filling datasets with, 477–478

Data Adapter Configuration Wizard, creating SQL adapters with, 171

data adapters, generating DataSet objects from, 474–475

data-bound controls, using with ASP.NET, 462–464

data columns, understanding, 243–244

data components, using with VS .NET, 162–166

data connection pages, choosing for SQL data adapters, 173

data connections
choosing with Data Form Wizard, 211–212
role in VS .NET, 166–169

Data Form Wizard
adding items to, 209–210
calling from applications, 220–221
choosing data connections with, 211–212
choosing DataSet objects with, 211
choosing display style for, 216–220
choosing project templates for, 209
choosing tables and columns to display with, 215–216
choosing tables with, 212
choosing views with, 212
creating relationships between tables with, 213–215
examining functionality of, 223–226
generating FillDataSet method with, 225
generating LoadDataSet method with, 224–225
generating UpdateDataSet method with, 226
generating UpdateDataSource method with, 226
Grid DataForm sample output in, 218
role of DataForm1.cs class in, 224–226
role of MyDS.xsd in, 224
viewing output from, 221–223
walking through, 210

data providers
choosing for ADO.NET applications, 138–139
choosing with Server Explorer, 157
Connection class for, 134

data sources, connecting through ODBC DSN, 294–296

data synchronization, definition of, 410

DataAdapter class
description of, 240
methods of, 323

DataAdapter components
adding for SQL data adapters, 172–173
role in ADO.NET, 230–231

DataAdapter constructors, overloaded forms of, 320
DataAdapter events
adding from Properties Window of Query Builder, 554–555
using with ADO.NET events, 553–559
DataAdapter objects
connecting through TableMapping property, 188
constructing, 320–321
constructing for SqlDataAdapter objects, 148
creating for ADO.NET applications, 140–141
example of, 323–326
functionality of, 319–320
generating typed DataSets with, 199–204
inserting, updating, and deleting data with, 327
performing table and column mapping with, 332–334
properties of, 322
relationship to Command objects in ADO.NET, 134–135
relationship to DataSet and DataView objects, 275
role in ADO.NET, 136
using FillError event handlers with, 556
DataAdapter properties, setting and reviewing for SQL data adapters, 180–184
DataBase property of ADO.NET Connection objects, description of, 284
database schemas
explanation of, 653
getting from ADO.NET, 607–610
database table columns versus fields, 242
database tables. *See* tables
DataColumn class
in ADO.NET System.Data namespaces, 237
creating for ADO.NET applications, 245–247
properties of, 244
relationship to DataRow and DataTable classes, 241
DataColumn constructors, creating columns with, 246–247
DataColumn properties, setting, 247–248
DataColumnChangeEventHandler ADO.NET event, functionality of, 546
DataColumnCollection class in ADO.NET System.Data namespaces, description of, 237
DataColumnMapping class in ADO.NET System.Data.Common namespaces, description of, 240
DataColumnMapping example, 333–334
DataColumnMappingCollection class in ADO.NET System.Data.Common namespaces, description of, 240
DataColumns, adding to DataTables, 248–251

DataForm1.cs class, role in Data Form Wizard, 224–226
DataGrid ASP.NET data-bound control, description of, 463
DataGrid control properties, setting at design-time, 466–467
DataGrid controls
adding to forms for SQL data adapters, 172
creating with Data Adapter Configuration Wizard, 476–477
displaying HTML view of, 494–495
displaying Orders table data in, 325
filling in VS .NET, 197–198
filling with data, 189–190
paging in, 490–493
setting images as next and previous page text for, 495
using AutoFormat option with, 467–468
using Borders property page with, 471–472
using Columns property page with, 469
using Format property page with, 470–471
using Paging property page with, 469–470
using Property Builder with, 468
using with ASP.NET, 464–469
viewing ASP.NET data in, 452–455
DataKeyField property of ASP.NET DataGrid control, description of, 465
DataList ASP.NET data-bound control, description of, 463
DataList controls, using with ASP.NET, 464–466
DataReaders
filling data to, 141
functionality of, 313–314
initializing and closing, 314–315
properties and methods of, 315
reading with, 315–317
using with SQL Server databases, 316–317
DataRelation class in ADO.NET System.Data namespaces, description of, 237
DataRelation constructor, functionality of, 257–258
DataRelationCollection class in ADO.NET System.Data namespaces, description of, 237
DataRow class
in ADO.NET System.Data namespaces, 237
explanation of, 251–256
relationship to DataColumn and DataTable classes, 241
DataRow objects
adding rows to DataTables with, 253–255
adding to DataTables, 328
functionality of, 241
DataRowChangeEventHandler ADO.NET event, functionality of, 546
DataRowCollection class in ADO.NET System.Data namespaces, description of, 237

DataRowState enumeration, functionality of, 256–257
DataRowView class in ADO.NET System.Data namespaces, description of, 238
DataSet class
in ADO.NET System.Data namespaces, 238
reading XML documents with, 405–406
relationship to DataTable and DataView classes, 274
role in ADO.NET, 273
writing XML documents with, 406–409
DataSet components
role in ADO.NET, 231–232
using with VS .NET, 199–208
dataset data, saving to XML documents, 414
DataSet events, using with ADO.NET events, 559–560
DataSet format, displaying XML data in, 411–413
DataSet objects
adding DataTables to, 265
choosing with Data Form Wizard, 211
connecting to data views in ASP.NET, 475–476
constructing and filling for ADO.NET applications, 149
in DataView objects in, 138
filling data to, 141, 323, 477–478
functionality of, 137, 274–276
generating from data adapters, 474–475
generating from existing XML schemas, 430–432
loading XML data with, 411
populating in VS .NET, 197–198
relationship to DataAdapter and DataView objects, 275
role in ADO.NET, 124
using Server Explorer with, 427–429
using with DataAdapter objects in ADO.NET, 136
DataSet property
of ADO.NET DataSetView class, 279
of ADO.NET DataTable class, 259
DataSet1 class, generating with Data Adapter Configuration Wizard, 474–475
DataSetName property of ADO.NET DataSet class, description of, 275
DataSource property
of ADO.NET Connection objects, 284
of ASP.NET DataGrid control, 465
DataTable class
in ADO.NET System.Data namespaces, 238
properties of, 259
relationship to DataColumn and DataRow classes, 241
relationship to DataSet and DataView classes, 274
DataTable components, role in ADO.NET, 232
DataTable events, using with ADO.NET events, 560–565

DataTable objects, functionality of, 241
DataTable property of FillErrorEventArgs, description of, 553
DataTableCollection class in ADO.NET System.Data namespaces, description of, 238
DataTableMapping class in ADO.NET System.Data.Common namespace, description of, 240
DataTableMapping objects, using with DataAdapters, 332–333
DataTableMappingCollection class in ADO.NET System.Data.Common namespaces, description of, 240
DataTable objects
adding DataColumns to, 248–251
adding DataRows to, 328
adding rows to, 253–255, 270
DataType property of ADO.NET DataColumn disconnected class, description of, 244
DataView and DataViewManager events, using with ADO.NET events, 568–570
DataView class
in ADO.NET System.Data namespaces, 238
relationship to DataSet and DataTable classes, 274
role in ADO.NET, 273
DataView components, using with VS .NET, 199–208
DataView objects
adding, updating, and deleting rows of, 569–570
DataSet objects in, 138
relationship to DataAdapter and DataSet objects, 275
role in ADO.NET, 277–278
role in VS .NET, 207–208
DataViewManager class
in ADO.NET System.Data namespaces, 238
role in ADO.NET, 278–279
DataViewManager property of ADO.NET DataView class, description of, 277
DataViewSettings property of ADO.NET DataSetView class, description of, 279
DbDataAdapter class in ADO.NET System.Data.Common namespaces, description of, 240
DBDataPermission class in ADO.NET System.Data.Common namespaces, description of, 240
DBTools
importing Access Northwind database with, 623–625
setting internal data connections of, 626
DbType property of OleDbParameter class, description of, 338

deadlocks, explanation of, 665
decimal C# type alias, details of, 18
DecodeName method, using with XML documents, 393
DefaultValue property of ADO.NET DataColumn disconnected class, description of, 244
DefaultView property of ADO.NET DataTable class, description of, 259
DefaultViewManager property of ADO.NET DataSet class, description of, 275
delegate reference types
    explanation of, 24
    using with event class members, 58
Delete method
    of ADO.NET DataRow class, 252–253, 255–256
    of ADO.NET DataView class, 278
DELETE statement, using with SQL, 676
DeleteCommand property
    of OleDbDataAdapter Command, 322
    of OleDbDataAdapters, 322
Deleted member of ADO.NET DataRowState enumeration, 257
DeleteRow_Click method, code for, 271
delimiters, choosing with Export Text Wizard, 636
Depth property
    of ADO.NET DataReaders, 315
    of XmlReader class, 387
description, role in Web services, 511
design-time versus run-time development, role in creating Windows forms, 69–70
Design View, displaying orders for Web services in, 525–526, 535
destructor class member
    advisory about, 51
    functionality of, 51
    and inheritance, 46
Detached member of ADO.NET DataRowState enumeration, 257
dialog classes of System.Windows.Forms, description of, 101
dialogs, creating with Windows.Forms namespace, 118–121
Direction property of OleDbParameter class, description of, 338
dirty reads, role in relational database isolation levels, 662
*.disco files, role in Web services, 511, 529
disconnected components, definition of, 199
discovery files, using with Web services, 529
discovery, role in Web services, 511
Dispose method, functionality of, 85, 287
DllImport built-in attribute, description of, 31
DLLs (dynamic link libraries) and C#, relationship between, 4
DOCTYPE declaration, role in XML documents, 368
document classes in System.Xml namespace, explanation of, 376

Document member of XmlNodeType enumeration, description of, 384
Document node in XML, description of, 374
Document Outline viewer, synchronizing Web-page controls with, 446–448
DocumentElement XML method, functionality of, 399
DocumentFragment member of XmlNodeType enumeration, description of, 384
documenting source code, 67
documents, loading with XmlDocument class, 394–395
DocumentType member of XmlNodeType enumeration, description of, 384
DocumentType node in XML, description of, 374
DOM API (application programming interface), explanation of, 378
DOM (Document Object Model), overview of, 372–375
DOM implementation
    role of Load methods in, 394–395
    role of Save methods in, 395
    role of XmlDocument class in, 394–395
    role of XmlDocumentFragment class in, 395–396
    role of XmlElement class in, 397–402
    role of XmlNode class in, 394
double C# type alias, details of, 18
double quote (") entity in XML, representing, 370
do . . . while loop statement, functionality of, 43
drag-and-drop design-time feature in VS .NET, advantages of, 459
DROP TABLE statement
    executing with OdbcCommand, 650–651
    using with SQL, 677
DropDownList ASP.NET data-bound control, description of, 464
DSNs (Data Source Names)
    connecting to data sources through, 294–296
    creating, 630
    defining when accessing text files, 638
DTD (Document Type Definition), explanation of, 364–366
dynamic cursors, explanation of, 660

E

ECMA (European Computer Manufacturers Association), 1–2
EditItemIndex property of ASP.NET DataGrid control, description of, 465
EditItemStyle property of ASP.NET DataGrid control, description of, 465
element-attributes in XSLT, definition of, 403
Element member of XmlNodeType enumeration, description of, 384
Element node in XML, description of, 374

elements
in HTML, 356
in XML, 365–366, 369
Employees table, saving as Excel spreadsheet, 642
empty elements in XML documents, explanation of, 370–371
EndEdit method of ADO.NET DataRow class, description of, 252
EndElement member of XmlNodeType enumeration, description of, 384
EndEntity member of XmlNodeType enumeration, description of, 384
EndInit method of ADO.NET DataSet class, description of, 276
entity and character references, role in XML documents, 370
Entity member of XmlNodeType enumeration, description of, 384
Entity node in XML, description of, 375
EntityReference member of XmlNodeType enumeration, description of, 384
enum data types, explanation of, 20–21
EOF property of XmlReader class, description of, 387
equal to (=) operator in SQL, 673
equality operators, examples of, 38
Equals method of Object class, explanation of, 12, 14–15
Error class, functionality of, 350–352
ErrorCode property of InfoMessageEvents, description of, 548
errors, catching with SqlException class, 351–352
Errors property
of FillErrorEventArgs, 553
of OleDbRowUpdatedEventArgs, 554
Errors property of InfoMessageEvents, description of, 548
event class member
functionality of, 58–62
and inheritance, 46
event handlers
adding code to VS .NET IDE Windows Forms application, 89–91
adding to button-click events with ASP.NET, 448–449
adding to button controls in Windows Forms, 74–75
adding to menu items with Windows.Forms namespace, 116–117
defining, 58
implementing with Boiler.cs class, 58–59
writing for toolbar buttons with Windows.Forms namespace, 113–115
event handling, example of, 61–62
event reference types, explanation of, 24–25
events
adding to Windows Forms, 74–75

implementing with Boiler.cs class, 58–59
understanding, 61
Excel connection string for ODBC, displaying, 291
Excel databases
accessing, 641–643
connecting to, 292
exception handling, functionality of, 65–67
Exception type in C#, description of, 65
Execute method, using with SQL statements in ASP.NET applications, 498
ExecuteNonQuery method
of Command object, 311
using with ASP.NET applications, 498
ExecuteScalar method of Command object, description of, 312–313
ExecuteSQL method, using with ASP.NET applications, 499
Executing member of ADO.NET ConnectionType enumerations, description of, 285
Executing property of ConnectionState enumeration, description of, 549
Exit, ExitThread methods of Windows.Forms.Application class, description of, 102
explicit type conversions, explanation of, 30
Export Text Wizard, exporting Access tables to text files with, 635
Expression property of ADO.NET DataColumn disconnected class, description of, 244
expressions, definition of, 36–39

F
Fetching property
of ADO.NET ConnectionType enumerations, 285
of ConnectionState enumeration, 549
field class member and inheritance, relationship between, 46
FieldCount property of ADO.NET DataReaders, description of, 315
fields class member, functionality of, 48–49
fields versus database table columns, 242
FileDialog class of System.Windows.Forms, description of, 101
Fill Data button, effect in ASP.NET, 454
Fill method
of DataAdapter, 557–558
of OleDbDataAdapters, 323
FillDataGrid method, example of, 496–497
FillDataSet method, generating with Data Form Wizard, 225
FillDBGrid method, calling from Form1 constructor, 189
FillError event handler code, using DataAdapter with, 556
FillError property of data adapters, role in ADO.NET events, 553
FillErrorEventHandler ADO.NET event, functionality of, 546

FillSchema method of OleDbDataAdapters, description of, 323
Finalize method of Object class, use of, 16–17
Find method of ADO.NET DataView class, description of, 278
FindRows method of ADO.NET DataView class, description of, 278
firehose cursors, definition of, 313
first child nodes, moving to, 417–418
first.exe file, creation of, 6
FirstWebApplication project, creating with ASP.NET, 439
float C# type alias, details of, 18
Font dialog box, displaying, 119–120
Font property of ASP.NET DataGrid control, description of, 465
<font> tag, description of, 357–358
FontDialog class of System.Windows.Forms, description of, 101
FoodMart 2000 database, getting all available cubes from, 604–605
FooterStyle property of ASP.NET DataGrid control, description of, 465
for loop statement, functionality of, 42
foreach loop statement, functionality of, 43
ForeColor property of ASP.NET DataGrid control, description of, 465
foreign keys, role in relational databases, 653
ForeignKeyConstraint class in ADO.NET System.Data namespaces, description of, 237
Form class of Windows.Forms namespace, functionality of, 102–103
Form classes of System.Windows.Forms, description of, 101
form controls, adding events with Windows Forms, 74–75
Form Designer, examining code in, 84–89
form properties, adding to Windows Forms, 72–78
Form_Load event, adding code on, 198
forms, definition of, 69
forward read-only cursors, definition of, 313, 660
function overloading, C# support for, 52

G
garbage collection in C#, explanation of, 4
Generate Dataset option, using with SQL data adapters, 184
GetAttribute method
    using with XML nodes, 385–386
    of XmlElement class, 398
GetAttribute property of XmlReader class, description of, 388
GetChanges method of ADO.NET DataSet class, description of, 276
GetChildRows method of ADO.NET DataRow class, description of, 252
GetFillParameters method of OleDbDataAdapters, description of, 323

GetHashCode method of Object class, description of, 12, 16–17
GetLength property of array class, description of, 27
GetOrderFromDatabase method
    adding to sample Web service, 519–520
    testing in sample Web service, 523
GetParentRows method of ADO.NET DataRow class, description of, 252
GetType method of Object class, description of, 12–15
GetType operator versus typeof operator, 39
GetValue property of array class, description of, 27
GetXml method of ADO.NET DataSet class, description of, 276
GetXmlSchema method of ADO.NET DataSet class, description of, 276
Getxxx method of ADO.NET DataReader, description of, 315
Global.asax files in Web services, explanations of, 514
goto statement, functionality of, 43–44
greater than (>)
    entity in XML, 370
    operator in SQL, 673
Grid DataForm sample output in Data Form Wizard, 218
GridLines property of ASP.NET DataGrid control, description of, 465
GROUP BY clause, using with SQL, 674–675
gt XML built-in entities and references, description of, 370
guest books, creating in ASP.NET, 478–490
GuestBook.mdb, table schema of Guest table in, 479
GUI components, role in Web Forms, 438
GUI (Graphical User Interface), building for DataTable operations, 266–267

H
<h1 . . . h6> tag, description of, 357
HasAttribute method of XmlElement class, description of, 398
HasAttributes property of XmlReader class, description of, 387
hash symbol (#), role in XML-document character references, 370
hashtables, definition of, 16
HasValue property of XmlReader class, description of, 387
HAVING clause, using with SQL, 675
HeaderStyle property of ASP.NET DataGrid control, description of, 465
Height property of ASP.NET DataGrid control,, 466
"Hello, C# World!" program, writing, 6–7
Hello class, creating namespace wrapper for, 8
HelloWorldNamespace member, calling from MyOtherNamespace, 10

<hr> tag, description of, 357
HTML ASP.NET server-side controls, list of, 455
HTML files, simple example of, 356
HTML (HyperText Markup Language)
    explanation of, 356–358
    versus XML, 359, 361
HTML tags
    examples of, 358
    explanation of, 356
    list of, 357
    navigating with Document Outline viewer, 448
<html> tag, description of, 357

I
<i> tag, description of, 357
ID property of ASP.NET DataGrid control, description of, 466
IDataParameter interfaces of ADO.NET System.Data namespaces, description of, 238
IDataParameterCollection interfaces of ADO.NET System.Data namespaces, description of, 238
IDataReader interfaces of ADO.NET System.Data namespaces, description of, 238
IDataRecord interfaces of ADO.NET System.Data namespaces, description of, 238
IDbCommand interfaces of ADO.NET System.Data namespaces, description of, 239
IDbConnection interfaces of ADO.NET System.Data namespaces, description of, 239
IdbDataAdapter interfaces of ADO.NET System.Data namespaces, description of, 239
IDbDataAdapters, implementing with data provider-specific classes, 320
IDbDataParameter interfaces of ADO.NET System.Data namespaces, description of, 239
IDbTransaction, implementing with data provider-specific classes, 342
IDbTransaction interfaces of ADO.NET System.Data namespaces, description of, 239
if . . . else statement, functionality of, 40–41
images, adding to toolbar buttons with Windows.Forms namespace, 107–113
implicit type conversions, explanation of, 29–30
indexer class member
    functionality of, 63
    and inheritance, 46
IndexOutOfRangeException type in C#, description of, 65–66
InfoMessage ADO.NET event
    testing, 551, 553
    using with Connection object and ADO.NET events, 547–548
    writing event handlers for, 550
InfoMessageEventHandlers, functionality of, 352–353
inheritance, functionality of, 64–65
InitializeComponent routine, code for, 187
INNER JOINs, using with SQL, 680
input and output streams in C#, explanation of, 10–11
Input member of ParameterDirection enumeration, description of, 586
input parameters, accepting with stored procedures, 581–582
InputOutput member of ParameterDirection enumeration, description of, 586
INSERT statement
    adding records to tables with, 311–313
    using with Oracle databases and OleDb data providers, 646–647
    using with SQL, 678–679
InsertAfter XML method, functionality of, 401
InsertCommand property
    of OleDbDataAdapter Command, 322
    of OleDbDataAdapters, 322
InsertOrder method of OrderRetrievalService project, testing, 533–536
InsertOrderFromNode Web method, calling for sample Web service, 538
instance constructor class member
    functionality of, 49–51
    and inheritance, 46
instance fields, definition of, 35
int C# type alias, details of, 18
interface reference types, explanation of, 22–23
internal accessibility modifier, description of, 33
internal accessibility type for class members, 47
interoperability marshaling, definition of, 595
is operator, explanation of, 39
IsClosed property of ADO.NET DataReaders, description of, 315
IsDefault property of XmlReader class, description of, 387
IsEmptyTag property of XmlReader class, description of, 387
IsFixedLength property of array class, description of, 26
IsNullable property of OleDbParameter class, description of, 338
isolation levels
    and data consistency, 663
    role in relational databases, 662–663
IsolationLevel, role in database connections, 343
IsReadOnly property of array class, description of, 26
IsStartElement property of XmlReader class, description of, 388

ITableMapping interfaces of ADO.NET System.Data namespaces, description of, 239
ITableMappingCollection interfaces of ADO.NET System.Data namespaces, description of, 239
Item property
    of ADO.NET DataReaders, 315
    of ADO.NET DataRow disconnected class, 251
    of ADO.NET DataView class, 277
    role in getting XML node information, 381–382
    of XmlReader class, 387
ItemArray property of ADO.NET DataRow disconnected class, description of, 251

J

jagged arrays, example of, 26
JIT (Just-In-Time) compiler, incorporation into Mono Project, 2
JOIN queries, using with SQL, 679–680

K

keyset cursors, explanation of, 660–661

L

Label class of System.Windows.Forms, description of, 101
last in wins concurrency control, definition of, 341
Length property of array class, description of, 26
less than (<)
    entity in XML, 370
    operator in SQL, 673
LineNumber property of SqlError class, description of, 352
ListBox ASP.NET data-bound control, description of, 463
ListBox class of System.Windows.Forms, description of, 101
ListBox controls, filling data to, 451–452
ListChanged event, components of, 568, 570
ListChangedType member of ListChangedEventArgs, description of, 568
ListView class of System.Windows.Forms, description of, 101
Load methods, role in DOM implementation, 394–395
LoadDataSet method, generating with Data Form Wizard, 224–225
local variables, explanation of, 32
LocalName property of XmlReader class, description of, 387
locking modes, role in relational databases, 664–665
locking, role in relational databases, 661–665

logical operators, examples of, 38
long C# type alias, details of, 18
LookupNamespace property of XmlReader class, description of, 388
loops
    exiting with break statement, 44
    exiting with continue statement, 45
lt XML built-in entities and references, description of, 370

M

MainMenu class of System.Windows.Forms, description of, 101
managed classes, role in ADO.NET, 127
managed code
    definition of, 3
    role in ADO.NET, 127
    using ADOX from, 600
managed code, definition of, 594
manifests, role in C#, 5
markup, definition of, 355
master/details relationship, explanation of, 257–258
Max Pool Size connection pooling setting, description of, 299
MaxLength property of ADO.NET DataColumn disconnected class, description of, 244
MemberwiseClone method of Object class, use of, 16–17
Menu control classes of System.Windows.Forms, description of, 101
menu items, adding to Windows applications with Windows.Forms namespace, 115–118
MenuItem class of System.Windows.Forms, description of, 101
Merge method of ADO.NET DataSet class, description of, 276
MergeFailed dataset event, explanation of, 559–560
MergefailedEventHandler ADO.NET event, functionality of, 546
Message property
    of InfoMessageEvents, 548
    of OleDbError class, 351
    of SqlError class, 352
MessageBox control classes of System.Windows.Forms, description of, 101
metadata, role in relational databases, 654
method class member
    functionality of, 52–56
    and inheritance, 46
method overloading example, 52–54
methods
    adding to VS .NET IDE Windows Forms application, 97–100
    of Windows.Forms.Application class, 102
Microsoft .NET and XML, functionality of, 375–380

Microsoft.Data.Odbc namespace
    displaying, 616
    locating, 130
Microsoft.Data.Odbc.dll assembly, adding
        references to, 615–616
Min Pool Size connection pooling setting,
        description of, 299
modern language, C# as, 3
Modified member of ADO.NET DataRowState
        enumeration, 257
modifiers, definition of, 32
Mono Project, explanation of, 2
Move methods of XPathNavigator class,
        descriptions of, 417
MoveToAttribute property of XmlReader
        class, description of, 388
MoveToContent method, navigating nodes
        in XML documents with,
        384–385
MoveToContent property of XmlReader class,
        description of, 388
MoveToElement property of XmlReader class,
        description of, 388
MoveToFirstAttribute property of XmlReader
        class, description of, 388
MoveToMethod, navigating nodes in XML
        documents with, 384–385
MoveToNextAttribute property of XmlReader
        class, description of, 388
msadomd.dll library
    adding references to, 602
    locating, 601
MSXML parser, description of, 363
multi-item data-bound controls, using with
        ASP.N ET, 462–463
multiple arrays, example of, 26
multiplicative operators, examples of, 38
myClass, indexers signature of, 63
MyDS.xsd XML schema, role in Data Form
        Wizard, 224
MyForm.cs example, creating with Windows
        Forms, 71–72
MyGuestBook ASP.NET application
    adding forms to, 483–487
    compiling and running, 487–490
    controls on, 480
    creating, 479–482
    source code for adding guest data to data-
        base, 481–482
    submission page for, 481
MyOtherNamespace namespace members,
        calling, 9
mySP stored procedure
    displaying output of, 580–581
    executing using SQL data providers, 584
MySQL database
    connecting through Odbc data providers,
        296–297
    downloading, 621
    finding ODBC drivers for, 622–623
    starting as service, 621–622
    using, 632–633

MySQL Server, importing Northwind data-
        base into, 625–630
MyTable data, viewing in DataGrid control,
        650
myTestCls derived from
        System.Windows.Forms.Form
        example, 96

N
Name property of XmlReader class, descrip-
        tion of, 387
Name property, reading XML node informa-
        tion with, 381–384
namespace references, adding to ADO.NET
        applications, 139–140
namespaces
    in ADO.NET, 129–132
    role in C#, 4, 7
    understanding, 8–10
NamespaceURI property of XmlReader class,
        description of, 387
NameTable property of XmlReader class,
        description of, 387
NativeError property of OleDbError class,
        description of, 351
nested transactions, definition of, 340
.NET base class library, terminology advisory,
        123
.NET data providers, choosing for ADO.NET
        applications, 138–139
.NET Framework and Web services, relation-
        ship between, 512
.NET Framework library and ASP.NET server-
        side controls, relationship
        between, 457–459
.NET Framework, using XslTransformation
        class with, 403–404
NewIndex member of ListChangedEventArgs,
        description of, 568
NewParent property of
        XmlNodeChangedEventsArgs,
        description of, 566
NewRow method of ADO.NET DataTable
        class, description of, 259
NextResult method of ADO.NET
        DataReaders, description of, 315
Node property of
        XmlNodeChangedEventsArgs,
        description of, 566
NodeChanged event handler, code for, 567
NodeInserted event handler, code for, 567
NodeRemoved event handler, code for, 568
nodes. *See* XML nodes
NodeType property of XmlReader class,
        description of, 387
NodeType property, role in getting XML node
        information, 382
non-static methods, definition of, 52
None member of XmlNodeType enumera-
        tion, description of, 384
nonrepeatable reads, role in relational data-
        base isolation levels, 662

normalization, role in relational databases, 654

Northwind database
  choosing in Server Explorer for use with OleDb data adapters, 191
  Customers database table schema in, 241–242
  displaying in Server Explorer, 288
  displaying Orders table schema of, 670
  importing into MySQL Server, 625–630, 625–630
  importing with DBTools, 623–625
  listing stored procedures for, 580
  using ODBC .NET data providers to read data from, 620–621
  viewing Employee table with Server Explorer, 160–161
  viewing table schema and data in, 243

not equal to (<>) operator in SQL, 673

Notation member of XmlNodeType enumeration, description of, 384

NullReferenceException type in C#, description of, 65–66

Number property of SqlError class, description of, 352

O

Object class
  explanation of, 12–17
  Finalize method of, 16–17
  getting type of, 12–13
  MemberwiseClone method of, 16–17

object types, role in C#, 3–4

objects
  comparing with Equals method in Object class, 14–15
  destroying with destructor class member, 51

ODBC Command objects, creating, 303–305

ODBC data components, viewing in toolbox, 164–165

ODBC data provider for ADO.NET
  Command class for, 135
  connecting to Excel databases with, 292
  connecting to other providers with, 290–292
  connecting to SQL Server databases with, 291
  connecting to text files with, 293–294
  Connection class for, 134
  for DataAdapter class, 136

Odbc data providers
  connecting to MySQL databases through, 296–297
  downloading, 162

ODBC Data Source Administrator, examining drivers from, 290

ODBC drivers
  accessing text files with, 640
  finding for MySQL database, 622–623

ODBC DSNs (Data Source Names)
  connecting to data sources through, 294–296
  creating, 630–632

ODBC .NET data providers
  accessing data from data sources with, 619–621
  accessing Excel databases with, 641–643
  accessing text files with, 637–641
  customizing toolbox for, 613–614
  finding components for, 614–615, 617
  installing, 613–617
  introduction to, 613
  using, 617–621
  using with Oracle 9i databases, 647–651
  using with Oracle databases, 644–651
  using with Sybase databases, 651–652
  verifying presence of, 617

ODBC (Open Data Base Connectivity) and ADO.NET, 125–126

OdbcCommand, executing DROP TABLE SQL statement with, 650–651

OdbcConnection class object, role in VS .NET, 166

Odbc.Net folder, browsing, 615

OLAP (Online Analytical Processing) Server data, accessing with ADO.NET, 600–611

OldIndex member of ListChangedEventArgs, description of, 568

OldParent property of XmlNodeChangedEventsArgs, description of, 566

OLE-DB (Object Linking and Embedding Data Base) and ADO.NET, 125–126

OLE DB Services settings, details of, 298

OleDb Command objects, creating, 301–303

OleDb data adapters, working with, 190–191

OleDb data providers
  accessing Oracle 8i databases with, 645–647
  Command class for, 135
  connecting to a SQL Server with, 288
  connecting to other providers with, 290–292
  Connection class for, 134
  for DataAdapter class, 136
  using with VS .NET, 165

OleDb data provider classes, list of, 281–282

OleDb data provider event handlers and event argument classes for ADO.NET events, diagram of, 546–547

OleDbCommand constructor, functionality of, 141

OleDbCommand objects reading data from databases with, description of, 302–303

OleDbConnection class object, role in VS .NET, 166

OleDbConnections, opening and closing, 286–287
OleDbDataAdapter class, properties of, 322
OleDbDataAdapter Command properties, list of, 322
OleDbDataAdapters
    creating for VS .NET applications, 192–197
    creating for Web services with Server Explorer, 517–519
    displaying Orders table data in DataGrids with, 325
    executing SELECT statements with, 321
OleDbError class properties, list of, 351
OleDbError collection, utilizing, 350
OleDbInfoMessageEventHandler OleDb data provider event handler for ADO.NET events, functionality of, 547
OleDbRowUpdatedEventArgs members, list of, 554
OleDbRowUpdatedEventHandler OleDb data provider event handler for ADO.NET events, functionality of, 547
OleDbRowUpdatingEventHandler OleDb data provider event handler for ADO.NET events, functionality of, 547
OleDbType property of OleDbParameter class, description of, 338
OnListChanged event handler, code for, 568–569
Open method of ADO.NET Connection class, description of, 285
Open property of ConnectionState enumeration, description of, 549
OpenFileDialog class, functionality of, 119
OpenfileDialog class of System.Windows.Forms, description of, 101
operands versus operators, 37
operator class member and inheritance, relationship between, 46
operators
    definition of, 36–39
    versus operands, 37
    types of, 37
optimistic concurrency
    in ADO.NET, 343–347
    definition of, 341
    role in OleDbDataAdapters and VS .NET, 196
optimistic locking, explanation of, 664–665
Oracle 8i databases, accessing with OleDb data providers, 645–647
Oracle 9i databases, using ODBC .NET data providers with, 647–651
Oracle connection string for ODBC, displaying, 291
Oracle databases, using ODBC .NET data providers with, 644–651

Order DataSet object, displaying for sample Web service, 524
OrderRetrievalService project
    displaying proxy reference file for, 540
    testing, 533
OrderRetrievalService reference, viewing for sample Web service, 528
OrderRetrievalService.asmx.cs sample Web service, displaying, 515–516
out parameters, using with methods, 54–56
OUTER JOINs, using with SQL, 680
Output member of ParameterDirection enumeration, description of, 586
output parameters, using with stored procedures, 588–589

P
<p> tag, description of, 357
PacketSize property of ADO.NET Connection objects, description of, 284
Page property of ASP.NET DataGrid control, description of, 466
Page_Load event, displaying for ViewGuestBook.aspx, 485–486
PageCount property of ASP.NET DataGrid control, description of, 466
PageIndexChanged event handler, adding to ASP.NET DataGrid controls, 491–492
PagerStyle modes, setting for DataGrid controls, 495
PageSize property
    of ASP.NET DataGrid control, 466
    setting, 495
paging, enabling at design-time, 491–494
ParameterDirection enumeration, members of, 585–586
ParameterDirection.Output, example of, 588
ParameterName property of OleDbParameter class, description of, 338
parameters
    creating, 338
    role in ADO.NET, 337–339
parent/child relationship, explanation of, 257–258
ParentRelation property of ADO.NET DataTable class, description of, 259
pessimistic concurrency
    definition of, 341
    example in ADO.NET, 346
pessimistic locking, explanation of, 664
phantoms, role in relational database isolation levels, 662
PictureBox class of System.Windows.Forms, description of, 101
PIs (processing instructions), role in XML documents, 371
PJ/NF, explanation of, 659–660

Precision property of OleDbParameter class, description of, 338
Prefix property of XmlReader class, description of, 387
Preview Data option, using with SQL data adapters, 185
primary keys
    role in relational databases, 653
    role in setting DataColumn properties, 248
primary operators, examples of, 38
PrimaryKey property of ADO.NET DataTable class, description of, 259
printing classes of System.Windows.Forms, description of, 101
private accessibility modifier, description of, 33
Procedure property of SqlError class, description of, 352
ProcessingInstruction member of XmlNodeType enumeration, description of, 384
ProcessingInstruction node in XML, description of, 374
program logic, explanation of, 40
ProgressBar class of System.Windows.Forms, description of, 101
project templates
    choosing for Data Form Wizard, 209
    selecting for SQL data adapters, 171–172
    selecting for Windows Forms application written in VS .NET IDE, 78–79
prologs, role in XML documents, 367–368
properties
    adding to VS .NET IDE Windows Forms application, 97–100
    setting for Windows Forms, 72–78
    setting in VS .NET IDE Windows Forms application, 82–84
Property Builder, using with DataGrid controls, 468
property class member
    functionality of, 56–58
    and inheritance, 46
protected accessibility modifier, description of, 33
protected accessibility type for class members, 47
protected internal accessibility modifier, description of, 33
protected internal accessibility type for class members, 47
Provider property of ADO.NET Connection objects, description of, 284
proxy files
    using with Web services, 529
    viewing contents of, 540
public accessibility modifier, description of, 33

public accessibility type for class members, accessibility types and scopes for, 47

Q

queries, reading batches with DataReaders, 317–319
Query Builder
    relaunching from CommandText property, 183
    using with SQL data adapters, 176–178
Query Editor, launching, 668–669
query types, choosing for SQL data adapters, 174
quot XML built-in entities and references, description of, 370

R

radio buttons, adding to Windows applications with Windows.Forms namespace, 116
RangeValidator ASP.NET server-side control, description of, 457
Rank property of array class, description of, 26
Read Committed isolation level, definition of, 663
Read method
    of ADO.NET DataReaders, 315
    of System.Console class, 10
read-only variables, explanation of, 35–36
Read property of XmlReader class, description of, 388
Read Uncommitted isolation level, definition of, 663
ReadAttributeValue property of XmlReader class, description of, 388
ReadCommitted isolation level for transactions, descriptions, 343
reader and writer classes, role in System.Xml namespace, 376
ReadInnerXml property of XmlReader class, description of, 388
ReadLine method of System.Console class, description of, 10
ReadOnly property of ADO.NET DataColumn disconnected class, description of, 244
ReadState property of XmlReader class, description of, 387
ReadUncommitted isolation level for transactions, descriptions, 343
ReadXml method, functionality of, 405
ReadXmlSchema method
    of ADO.NET DataSet class, 276
    functionality of, 406
ReadXXXX property of XmlReader class, description of, 388
records
    adding to tables with INSERT SQL statement, 311–313

selecting, 610–611
RecordsAffected property
    of ADO.NET DataReaders, 315
    of OleDbRowUpdatedEventArgs, 554
recordsets
    versus DataSets, 128–129, 274
    filling DataAdapters with, 327
rectangular arrays, example of, 26
ref parameters, using with methods, 54–56
reference types, explanation of, 4, 21–25
Reference.cs file, contents of, 540–541
ReferenceEquals method of Object class,
        description of, 12, 14–15
references
    adding to ADOMD, 603
    adding to ADOX libraries, 599
    adding to COM libraries, 595–596
    adding to Microsoft.Data.Odbc.dll assem-
        bly, 615–616
    adding to msadomd.dll library, 602
RegularExpressionValidator ASP.NET server-
        side control, description of, 457
RejectChanges method
    of ADO.NET DataRow class, 252–253, 256
    of ADO.NET DataSet class, 276
    of ADO.NET DataTable class, 259
relational databases
    and ADO.NET, 660–661
    details of, 653–654
    dirty reads in, 662
    effect of deadlocks on, 665
    nonrepeatable reads in, 662
    and normalization, 654–660
    phantoms in, 662
    resources for, 666
    role of cursors in, 660–661
    role of isolation levels in, 662–663
    role of locking in, 661–665
    role of locking modes in, 664–665
    role of sets in, 660–661
relational operators, examples of, 38
Relations property of ADO.NET DataSet class,
        description of, 275
relationships between tables, creating with
        Data Form Wizard, 213–215
ReleaseObjectPool method
    of ADO.NET Connection class, 285
    calling, 300
RemoveAll methods of XmlElement class,
        description of, 398–400
RemoveAllAttributes methods of XmlElement
        class, description of, 398
RemoveAttribute methods of XmlElement
        class, description of, 398
RemoveAttributeAt methods of XmlElement
        class, description of, 398
RemoveAttributeNode methods of
        XmlElement class,
        description of, 398
Repeatable Read isolation level, definition of,
        663

RepeatableRead isolation level for transac-
        tions, descriptions, 343
Repeater ASP.NET data-bound control,
        description of, 464
ReplaceChild XML method, functionality of,
        401
RequiredFieldValidator ASP.NET server-side
        control, description of, 457
Reset method
    of ADO.NET DataSet class, 276
    of ADO.NET DataTable class, 259
return statement, functionality of, 45
ReturnValue member of ParameterDirection
        enumer-ation, description of, 586
Reverse property of array class,
        description of, 27–29
Rollback method of Transaction class,
        description of, 342
Rollback Transaction, functionality of, 340
Rollback(SavePoint) transaction method in
        Sql data providers, 347
root nodes
    getting for XML documents, 399
    moving to, 417–418
    role in XML, 359
Row property of
        OleDbRowUpdatedEventArgs,
        description of, 554
RowChanged event of DataTable event,
        description of, 560, 563–564
RowChanging event of DataTable event,
        description of, 561, 563–564
RowDeleted event of DataTable event,
        description of, 561, 564–565
RowDeleting event of DataTable event,
        description of, 561, 564–565
RowFilter property of ADO.NET DataView
        class, description of, 277
rows
    adding to ASP.NET tables at design-time,
        504–505, 507
    adding to DataTables, 270
    deleting from DataTables, 271
    using SELECT DISTINCT SQL statement
        with, 611
Rows property of ADO.NET DataTable class,
        description of, 259
RowState property of ADO.NET DataRow dis-
        connected class, description of,
        251
RowUpdated event handler, code for, 556–557
RowUpdating event handler, code for, 557
Run method of Windows.Forms.Application
        class, description of, 102

S
Sales by Year stored procedures in Northwind
        database, code for, 306–307
Save methods, role in DOM implementa-
        tions, 395
SaveFileDialog class, functionality of, 119

SaveFileDialog class of System.Windows.Forms, description of, 101
savepoints
definition of, 340
using in SQL Server, 347–349
Save(SavePointName) transaction method in Sql data providers, 347
sbyte C# type alias, details of, 18
scalability in C#, explanation of, 4–5
Scale property of OleDbParameter class, description of, 338
schemas, role in XML, 364–366
SearchButton_Click method, code for, 272
SELECT COUNT statement, using with SQL, 674
SELECT DISTINCT SQL statement, selecting records with, 611, 672
Select method
of ADO.NET DataTable class, 259
using with XPathNavigator class, 419–420
SELECT statements
examples of, 670–675
executing with SqlDataAdapters, 321
saving as stored procedures with ADO.NET, 578–579
SelectCommand property
of OleDbDataAdapter Command, 322
of OleDbDataAdapters, 322
setting in SQL data adapters, 182
SelectedIndex property of ASP.NET DataGrid control, description of, 466
SelectedItem property of ASP.NET DataGrid control, description of, 466
SELECT . . . FORM XML clause, using with SQL, 682
semicolon (;)
advisory about, 46
role in XML-document references, 370
Serializable built-in attribute, description of, 31
Serializable isolation level, explanation of, 343, 663
serialization, explanation of, 377
server controls, role in Web Forms, 438
server cubes
getting dimensions of, 605–607
getting from FoodMart 2000 database, 604–605
role in OLAP, 600
Server Explorer
adding connections with, 156–159
creating SQL data adapters with, 170–171
displaying Northwind database in, 288
displaying views available in, 592
introduction to, 154–156
launching, 427
launching to create stored procedures, 573–574
managing and viewing data with, 159–161
using DataSet objects with, 430–432
servers, adding to Server Explorer, 156

ServerVersion property of ADO.NET Connection objects, description of, 284
Service1.asmx file in Web services
explanation of, 514
running, 521
SetAttribute method of XmlElement class, description of, 398
SetAttributeNode method of XmlElement class, description of, 398
sets, role in relational databases, 660–661
SetValue property of array class, description of, 27
SGML (Standard Generalized Markup Language), explanation of, 355–356
shift operators, examples of, 38
short C# type alias, details of, 18
ShowFooter property of ASP.NET DataGrid control, description of, 466
ShowHeader property of ASP.NET DataGrid control, description of, 466
SignificantWhitespace member of XmlNodeType enumeration, description of, 384
simple types, explanation of, 17–19
single-dimenisional array example, 25–26
single quote (') entity in XML, representing, 370
Size property of OleDbParameter class, description of, 338
sizeof operator, explanation of, 39
Skip method, using with XML nodes, 386
Skip property of XmlReader class, description of, 388
SOAP (Simple Object Access Protocol), passing XML nodes with, 537–539
Solution Explorer, using with Web services, 513
Sort property
of ADO.NET DataView class, 277
of array class, 27–29
source code
documenting, 67
reviewing for SQL data adapters, 186–189
Source property
of OleDbError class, 351
of SqlError class, 352
Source property of InfoMessageEvents, description of, 548
SourceColumn property of OleDbParameter class, description of, 338
SourceVersion property of OleDbParameter class, description of, 338
Splitter class of System.Windows.Forms, description of, 101
Sql Command objects, creating, 303–305
SQL data adapters
adding DataAdapter components to, 172–173
adding DataGrid controls to forms for, 172
choosing data connection pages for, 173

choosing query types for, 174
creating with Data Adapter Configuration Wizard, 171
creating with Server Explorer, 170–171
generating SQL statements for, 175
introduction to, 169–170
previewing data for, 186
reviewing source code for, 186–189
selecting project templates for, 171–172
setting and reviewing DataAdapter properties for, 180–184
setting SelectCommand in, 182
using Query Builder with, 176–178
Sql data provider for ADO.NET
Command class for, 135
connecting to SQL Server databases with, 288–289
Connection class for, 134
for DataAdapter class, 136
transaction methods in, 347
using savepoints with, 347–349
SQL data providers, executing mySP stored procedure with, 584–585
SQL queries
executing in Web Forms, 497–499
executing with ADO.NET Command object, 134–135
SQL Server
connecting through ODBC, 291–292
connecting through SqlClient data provider, 292
connecting with OleDb data provider, 288
using savepoints with, 347–349
SQL Server Connection objects, constructing for ADO.NET applications, 148
SQL Server databases
accessing with SqlCommand, 304–305
getting tables from, 608–609
using DataReaders with, 316–317
SQL Server exception, advisory about, 150–151
SQL statements
generating for SQL data adapters, 175
testing, 667
SQL (Structured Query Language)
aliases, 679–680
conditional statements used in, 673
CREATE TABLE statement with, 676–677
CREATE VIEW statement, 681
CROSS JOINs, 680
DELETE statement with, 676
DROP TABLE statement with, 677
GROUP BY clause, 674–675
HAVING clause with, 675
INNER JOINs, 680
INSERT statement, 678–679
JOIN queries with, 679–680
OUTER JOINs, 680
resources for, 682–683
SELECT COUNT statement, 674
SELECT statements, 670–675

SELECT . . . FORM XML clause, 682
SUM and AVG functions, 673
TRUNCATE TABLE statement with, 677–678
UPDATE statement with, 675–676
using views with, 680–682
SQL View option, choosing, 668
SqlClient data provider, connecting to SQL Server through, 292
SqlCommand
accessing SQL Server databases with, 304–305
calling stored procedures with, 306
SqlCommandBuilder, using, 335–337
SqlConnection class object
role in VS .NET, 166, 169, 171
viewing in form designer, 180
SqlDataAdapters
connecting to ADO.NET databases with, 148
displaying Customers tables data in DataGrids with, 326
executing SELECT statements with, 321
viewing in form designer, 180
SqlError class, properties of, 352
SqlException class, catching errors with, 351–352
SqlParameter class, using with ADO.NET stored procedures, 585
SqlState property of OleDbError class, description of, 351
start and end tags, role in XML documents, 368–369
State property
of ADO.NET Connection objects, 284
of SqlError class, 352
StateChange ADO.NET event
testing, 551–552
writing event handlers for, 550
StateChange event, using with Connection object and ADO.NET events, 547–548
StateChangeEventHandler ADO.NET event, functionality of, 546
StatementType property of OleDbRowUpdatedEventArgs, description of, 554
static constructor class member
functionality of, 49–51
and inheritance, 46
static cursors, explanation of, 660
static methods, definition of, 52
static variables, explanation of, 35–36
Status property of OleDbRowUpdatedEventArgs, description of, 554
stored procedures
accepting input parameters with, 581–582
adding parameters to, 585–587
adding subtotal listings to, 309
calling with Command objects, 306–309
creating with ADO.NET, 573–580, 576–577

stored procedures *(continued)*
    editing, deleting, and executing with
        ADO.NET, 575–578
    executing with ADO.NET Command
        object, 134–135
    executing and reading results in ADO.NET,
        307–308
    executing from VS.NET, 580–583
    executing programmatically with
        ADO.NET, 583–589
    returning data with, 578
    returning values from, 586
    using output parameters with, 588–589
    viewing, 574
StoredProcedure member of CommandType
        enumeration, description of, 305
string conversion, performing with ToString
        method of Object class, 16
StringWriter class, definition of, 351
<strong> tag, description of, 357
struct types, explanation of, 19–20
stylesheets, expressing with XSL, 402–404
SUM function, using in SQL, 673
switch statement
    functionality of, 41–42
    versus goto statement, 44
switches, exiting with break statement, 44
Sybase databases, using ODBC .NET data
        providers with, 651–652
synchronous Web services, explanation of,
        539
System.Console class, functionality of, 10–11
System.Data assembly in ADO.NET, contents
        in IL DASM utility, 129–131
System.Data namespace
    event handler and event argument classes
        defined in, 546
    hierarchy in ADO.NET, 232–233
    interfaces in ADO.NE, 238–239
System.Data.Common namespace in
        ADO.NET
    diagram of, 234
    functionality of, 131, 237, 239–240
System.Data.dll assembly adding namespace
        references to, 139
System.Data.OleDb namespace
    functionality of, 131
    hierarchy in ADO.NET, 235–236
SystemData.SqlClient namespace in
        ADO.NET, functionality of,
        131–132
System.Data.SqlTypes namespace hierarchy
        in ADO.NET, diagram of, 234–235
SystemException type in C#, description of,
        65
System.String class, getting type of, 12–13
SystemWeb namespace, role in .NET
        Framework library, 457–458
System.Web.Services namespace, role
        in .NET Framework library, 459
System.Web.UI namespace, role in .NET
        Framework library, 458

System.Web.UI.HtmlControls namespace,
        role in .NET Framework library,
        458
SystemWeb.UI.WebControls namespace, role
        in .NET Framework library, 459
System.Windows.Forms common classes, list
        of, 101
System.Windows.Forms namespace
    adding menu items to applications with,
        115–118
    adding toolbars to applications with,
        103–115
    common Control class in, 103
    creating dialogs with, 118–121
    functionality of, 100
System.Xml namespace
    adding reference for System.Xml.dll
        assembly to, 379–380
    role in Microsoft .NET and XML, 375–377
System.Xml.dll assembly, adding reference to
        System.Xml namespace, 379–380
System.Xml.Schema namespace, role in
        Microsoft .NET and XML, 377
System.Xml.Serialization namespace, role in
        Microsoft .NET and XML, 377
System.Xml.XPath namespace, role in
        Microsoft .NET and XML, 377–378
System.Xml.Xsl namespace, role in Microsoft
        .NET and XML, 378

T

tab-delimited text files, using ODBC to read
        data from, 293
Table control, introduction to, 503–509
table information, reading with TableDirect
        CommandType, 309–311
Table Mappings dialog box, displaying for
        SQL data adapters, 183–184
Table object of ADOX, functionality of, 599
Table property
    of ADO.NET DataRow disconnected class,
        251
    of ADO.NET DataView class, 277
table schemas, getting, 609–610
<table> tag, description of, 357
TableDirect CommandType, reading table
        information with, 309–311
TableDirect member
    of CommandType enumeration, 305
TableMapping property
    of OleDbRowUpdatedEventArgs, 554
TableMapping property, making DataAdapter
        connections through, 188
TableMappings property
    of DataAdapter class, 332
    of OleDbDataAdapters, 322
TableName property of ADO.NET DataTable
        class, description of, 259
tables
    adding records with INSERT SQL state-
        ment, 311–313
    adding to View Designer, 590

choosing with Data Form Wizard, 212
creating and adding data to, 648–649
creating at design-time with ASP.NET, 504–507
creating with DataTables and DataColumns, 249–250
displaying with Data Form Wizard, 215–216
getting from SQL Server databases, 608–609
Tables property of ADO.NET DataSet class, description of, 275
tags in HTML
    examples of, 358
    explanation of, 356
    list of, 357
    navigating with Document Outline viewer, 448
<td> tag, description of, 357–358
ternary operators, definition of, 37
text file databases, accessing, 633–641
text files
    accessing, 637–641
    connecting with ODBC data providers for ADO.NET, 293–294
    defining formats and column settings for, 639
    exporting to Access tables, 633–637
Text member
    of CommandType enumeration, 305
    of XmlNodeType enumeration, 384
Text node in XML, description of, 375
TextBox ASP.NET data-bound control, description of, 464
TextBox class of System.Windows.Forms, description of, 101
TextDB.txt file, accessing, 640
Thanks.aspx item, adding to MyGuestBook ASP.NET application, 484, 486–487
three slashes (///), using with comments in source code, 67
TILs (transaction isolation levels), determining for relational databases, 662–663
Timer class of System.Windows.Forms, description of, 101
<title> tag, description of, 357
toolbar buttons
    adding images with Windows.Forms namespace, 107–113
    writing event handlers with Windows.Forms namespace, 113–115
ToolBar controls, adding with Windows.Forms namespace, 104–105
toolbars, adding to applications with Windows.Forms namespace, 103–115
ToString method of Object class, description of, 12, 16

<tr> tag, description of, 357
Transaction classes, methods of, 342
transaction processing, beginning, 340
transactions
    in ADO.NET, 342–343
    introduction to, 339–341
Transform XSL method, functionality of, 403–404
trees in XSLT, definition of, 403
TreeView class of System.Windows.Forms, description of, 101
TRUNCATE TABLE statement, using with SQL, 677–678
try . . . catch blocks, using, 65
Type class
    and inheritance, 46
    usage of, 12
type conversions, performing in C#, 29–31
type testing operators, examples of, 38
typed DataSet objects, using in VS .NET, 199–207
typed DataSets
    in ADO.NET, 276–277
    advantages of, 204
    generating from existing XML schemas, 430–432
typeof operator, explanation of, 39
types
    definition of, 4
    introduction to, 17–18
typesafety feature of C#, explanation of, 3–4

U

uint C# type alias, details of, 18
ulong C# type alias, details of, 18
unary (-) operators, using with for loop statements, 42
unary (++) operators, using with for loop statements, 42
unary operators
    definition of, 37
    examples of, 38
unboxing, definition of, 30–31
Unchanged member of ADO.NET DataRowState enumeration, 257
unchecked operators, explanation of, 38–39
Unique property of ADO.NET DataColumn disconnected class, description of, 244
UniqueConstraint class in ADO.NET System.Data namespaces, description of, 237
UniqueID property of ASP.NET DataGrid control, description of, 466
unmanaged code, definition of, 3, 594
Unspecified isolation level for transactions, descriptions, 343
untyped DataSets in ADO.NET, description of, 276–277
Update method
    adding data with, 328–330
    calling for ADO.NET events, 557–558

Update method *(continued)*
　deleting data with, 331
　of OleDbDataAdapters, 323
　using with databases, 327–331
UPDATE statement, using with SQL, 675–676
UpdateCommand property
　of OleDbDataAdapter Command, 322
　of OleDbDataAdapters, 322
UpdateDataSet method, generating with
　　Data Form Wizard, 226
UpdateDataSource method, generating with
　　Data Form Wizard, 226
URI (Universal Resource Identifier),
　　explanation of, 363
User ASP.NET server-side controls,
　　explanation of, 457
UserAppDataPath method of
　　Windows.Forms.Application
　　class, description of, 102
ushort C# type alias, details of, 18
Using System; line of "Hello, C# World!") pro-
　　gram, examining, 8

V

valid XML documents, explanation of, 367–372
Validation ASP.NET server-side controls, list
　　of, 457
Value property
　　of OleDbParameter class, 338
　　role in getting XML node infor-mation,
　　　381–382
　　of XmlReader class, 387
value types, explanation of, 4, 17
values
　　assigning to variables, 32
　　representing with enum data types, 20–21
Values property of FillErrorEventArgs,
　　description of, 553
variable access modifiers, explanation of,
　　32–33
variables
　　explanation of, 32–36
　　using with property members, 56
versioning control in C#, explanation of, 4–5
View Code option in Form Designer, using,
　　84–85
View Wizard Results page, displaying for SQL
　　adapters, 179
ViewGuestBook.aspx item, adding to
　　MyGuestBook ASP.NET applica-
　　tion, 484–486
ViewGuestBook.aspx, source code for open-
　　ing of, 482
views
　　choosing with Data Form Wizard, 212
　　creating, 589–592
　　executing from VS.NET, 592
　　retrieving data from programmatically,
　　　593–594
　　saving, 591
　　using with ADO.NET, 588–594
　　using with SQL, 680–682

VirtualItemCount property of ASP.NET
　　DataGrid control, description of,
　　466
visual data components, 162–166
VS .NET IDE Windows Forms
　　application
　　adding classes to, 92–96
　　adding controls to, 79–82
　　adding event handlers to, 89–91
　　adding methods and properties to, 97–100
　　building and running, 91–92
　　examining code in, 84–89
　　selecting project template for, 78–79
　　setting properties in, 82–84
VS (Visual Studio) .NET
　　adding connection events at design-time
　　　with, 549
　　adding OleDbDataAdapters to, 192–197
　　adding server-side controls with, 460
　　benefits of using with ASP.NET, 436
　　creating ADO.NET projects in, 153–154
　　creating connection components with,
　　　166–167
　　creating console-based applications with,
　　　142–145
　　creating stored procedures with, 573–574
　　creating Web services in, 512–521
　　developing ASP.NET applications with,
　　　450–455
　　executing stored procedures from, 580–583
　　executing views from, 592
　　filling DataGrid controls in, 197–198
　　generating typed DataSets with, 199–204
　　populating DataSet objects in, 197–198
　　returning values from stored procedures
　　　with, 586
　　role of connection strings in, 167–169
　　role of data connections in, 166–169
　　role of DataView objects in, 207–208
　　understanding typed DataSets in,
　　　199–207
　　using Data Form Wizard with, 208–223
　　using DataSet components with, 199–208
　　using DataView components with,
　　　199–208
　　using OleDb data provider with, 165
　　using Server Explorer with, 154–159
　　using visual data components with,
　　　162–166
　　writing ADO.NET applications with,
　　　145–151

W

W3C, Web site for, 357
WaitHandle method, making asynchronous
　　calls to Web services with,
　　541–542
warnings, listening to, 352–353
Web applications
　　creating with ASP.NET, 438–442
　　definition of, 438
Web-based client applications, creating, 525

Web Forms
  adding, editing, and deleting data in, 496–503
  adding new records to, 499–500
  adding server-side controls to, 460
  adding Web controls to, 442–444
  binding at design-time, 472–478
  executing SQL queries in, 497–499
  explanation of, 437–438
Web Forms controls as server-side controls, explanation of, 459–462
Web methods, adding to Web services, 519
Web services
  accessing, 530
  adding database support to, 516–517
  adding Web methods to, 519
  adding Web references to, 526–527
  attributes of, 511–512
  creating clients for, 525–539
  creating consumers for, 525–539
  creating in VS .NET, 512–521
  creating method for populating database orders in, 532
  displaying client event handler for execution of, 538
  displaying client event handlers for execution of, 535
  displaying files in, 514
  displaying for local servers, 528
  executing asynchronously, 539–542
  explanation of, 438, 511
  increasing functionality of, 531–536
  and .NET Framework, 512
  order retrieval example of, 530
  passing XML to, 537–539
  testing, 521–524
  using discovery files with, 529
  using proxy files with, 529
  using WSDL files with, 529
  viewing code in, 515
  viewing OrderRetrievalService reference for, 528
  writing to databases with, 531
Web sites
  C# Corner, 3
  C# editors, 5
  for DOM, 372
  locking and concurrency levels, 665
  Mono Project, 2
  MySQL database, 621
  normal forms, 660
  ODBC .NET data providers, 613
  Odbc .NET Software Development Kit, 162
  relational databases, 666
  role of design-time versus run-time development in, 69–70
  SQL (Structured Query Language), 682–683
  W3C, 357
Web.config file in Web services, explan-ation of, 514
WebForm1.aspx page, displaying, 440

WebService and WebMethod attributes, adding descriptions to, 522
WebService attribute, setting namespace and description properties for, 524
Weight property of ASP.NET DataGrid control, description of, 466
well-formed XML documents, explan-ation of, 361, 367
while loop statement, functionality of, 42
white spaces, role in XML documents, 372
Whitespace member of XmlNodeType enumeration, description of, 384
Windows applications
  adding menu items with Windows.Forms namespace, 115–118
  creating for toolbar example in Windows.Forms namespace, 103–104
Windows Forms
  adding controls to, 73–74
  adding events to, 74–75
  advantages of, 69
  creating, 71–72
  creating final code for example of, 75–78
  sample output of, 77–78
  setting properties for, 72–78
  writing applications from command line, 70–78
Windows Forms application written with VS .NET IDE
  adding classes to, 92–96
  adding controls to, 79–82
  adding event handlers to, 89–91
  adding methods and properties to, 97–100
  building and running, 91–92
  examining code in, 84–89
  selecting project template for, 78–79
  setting properties in, 82–84
Windows.Forms namespace
  adding menu items to applications with, 115–118
  adding toolbars to applications with, 103–115
  common Control class in, 103
  creating dialogs with, 118–121
  functionality of, 100
Windows.Forms.Application class, methods of, 102
wiring protocol, role in Web services, 512
WorkStationId property of ADO.NET Connection objects, description of, 284
Write method of System.Console class, description of, 10
WriteLine method of System.Console class, description of, 10
WriteNode XML method, functionality of, 389
WriteXml method
  of ADO.NET DataSet class, 276
  functionality of, 406–408

WriteXmlSchema method
  of ADO.NET DataSet class, 276
  functionality of, 408–409
WSDL (Web Services Description Language)
        files, using with Web services, 529

X

XHTML (Extensible Hypertext Markup
        Language), explanation of, 366
XlLang property of XmlReader class,
        description of, 387
XML data
  displaying in DataSet format, 411–413
  loading with DataSet objects, 411
XML Designer
  generating XML with, 426–427
  using Generate Dataset option of,
        431–432
XML Designer, launching, 422
XML documents
  adding nodes, 398–399
  adding to projects, 420–421
  closing, 387–388
  components of, 367–372
  generating ADO.NET typed DataSets
        from, 430–432
  getting node information about, 381–384
  getting root nodes for, 399
  inserting fragments of, 395–396
  inserting XML fragments into, 401–402
  loading with Load and LoadXml methods,
        411
  navigating nodes in, 384–385
  reading, 412
  reading with DataSet class, 405–406
  reading with XmlReader class, 381
  reading with XPathNavigator class,
        418–419
  removing and replacing nodes in, 399–401
  role of attributes in, 371
  role of CDATA sections in, 369
  role of character and entity references in,
        370
  role of DOCTYPE declaration in, 368
  role of empty elements in, 370–371
  role of processing instructions in, 371
  role of prologs in, 367–368
  role of start and end tags in, 368–369
  role white spaces in, 372
  sample tree structure implement-ation of,
        373
  saving data from DataSets to, 413–414
  transforming, 404
  using Close method with, 392
  validating with DTDs, 364–366
  writing attributes for, 389
  writing comments to, 389
  writing elements to, 389
  writing strings to, 389
  writing to console, 391
  writing with DataSet class, 406–409

XML DOM tree representation, diagram of,
        374
XML elements, explanation of, 365–366, 369
XML (eXtensible Markup Language)
  attributes in, 361–362
  case-sensitivity of, 361
  characteristics of, 361–362
  example of, 359–360
  functionality of, 359
  and Microsoft .NET, 375–380
  navigating in, 415–420
  passing to Web services, 537–539
  role in ADO.NET, 124, 127
  role of comments in, 369
  role of DTDs and schemas in, 364–366
  role of URIs in, 363
XML items, writing, 389–390
XML names, transferring to ADO.NET
        objects, 393
XML namespaces, explanation of, 363–364
XML .NET API, explanation of, 378–379
XML nodes
  adding attributes to, 402
  description of, 374–375
  navigating, 384–385
  reading and displaying, 419–420
  reading for XML documents, 382–383
  removing and replacing, 399–401
  searching for, 386
  using GetAttributes method with, 385–386
XML parser, explanation of, 363–366
XML-related technology, defining, 355–358
XML schema items
  adding to projects, 422–427
  deleting from projects, 424
XML schema toolbox, displaying, 422–423
XML schemas
  browsing for, 431
  creating, 406
  explanation of, 364–366
  generating, 420
  generating DataSet objects from, 430–432
  generating for database tables, 429
XML source trees, definition of, 402–403
XML support, management by ADO.NET ver-
        sus ADO, 129
XML trees, opening documents as, 402–403
XML versions of documents, defining, 360
XmlConvert class in System.Xml namespace,
        explanation of, 377
XmlConvert class, example of, 393
XmlDataDocument class
  diagram of, 409
  explanation of, 376
  functionality of, 415
  loading data from, 411
  reading and writing data with, 410
XmlDataDocument events, using with
        ADO.NET events, 565–568
XmlDataDocumentSample.cs, code and out-
        put for, 412–413

XmlDeclaration member of XmlNodeType
  enumeration, description of, 384
XmlDocument class
  role in DOM implementation, 394–395
  role in XML .NET API, 378
  in System.Xml namespace, 376
XmlDocumentFragment class
  role in DOM implementation, 395–396
  in System.Xml namespace, 376
XmlDocumentType class in System.Xml
  namespace, explanation of, 376
XmlElement class, role in DOM
  implementation, 397–402
XmlException class, role in System.Xml
  namespace, 377
XmlLinkedNode class, role in System.Xml
  namespace, 377
XmlNamespaceManager class, role in
  System.Xml namespace, 377
XmlNode class in System.Xml namespace,
  explanation of, 375–376
XmlNode class
  functionality of, 401
  role in DOM implementation, 394
XmlNode methods, functionality of, 396
XmlNodeChangedEventHandler, code for,
  565–566
XmlNodeList class, role in System.Xml name-
  space, 377
XmlNodeType enumeration, role in getting
  XML node information, 382–384
XmlReader and XmlWriter classes, role in
  System.Xml namespace, 376
XmlReader class
  diagram of, 380

properties of, 387–388
  role in XML .NET API, 378
XmlSpace property of XmlReader class,
  description of, 387
XmlTextWriter method, example of, 389–390
XmlWriter class
  diagram of, 388
  example of, 390–392
  properties of, 389
  role in XML .NET API, 378
XmlWriterSample.cs class, output of,
  391–392
xmlWriterTest document, code for, 390–392
XPathDocument class in System.Xml.XPath
  namespace, explanation of, 378
XPathExpression class in System.Xml.XPath
  namespace, explanation of, 378
XPathIterator class in System.Xml.XPath
  namespace, explanation of, 378
XPathNavigator class
  functionality of, 416
  Move methods of, 416–417
  reading XML documents with, 418–419
  searching with, 419–420
  in System.Xml.XPath namespace, 378
XSD (XML Schema Definition) types versus
  CLR data types, 393
xsd:schema statements, explanation of,
  364–365
XSL (Extensible Stylesheet Language), functionality of, 402
XSLT (XSL Transformation), explanation of,
  402–404
XslTransformation class in .NET Framework,
  functionality of, 403–404

Announcing *About VS.NET*—
the *free* Apress .NET e-newsletter with great .NET news, information, code—and attitude

We guarantee that this isn't going to be your typical boring e-newsletter with just a list of URLs (though it will have them as well).

Instead, *About VS.NET* will contain contributions from a whole slate of top .NET gurus, edited by award-winning, best-selling authors Gary Cornell and Dan Appleman. Upcoming issues will feature articles on:

- Best coding practices in ADO.NET

- The hidden "gotchas" in doing thread programming in VB.NET

- Why C# is (not) a better choice than VB.NET

- What Java can learn from C# and vice versa

About VS.NET will cover it all!

This *free* e-newsletter will be the easiest way for you to get up-to-date .NET information delivered to your Inbox every two weeks—more often if there's breaking news!

Books for professionals by professionals™
www.apress.com

apress™

Apress Titles

ISBN	PRICE	AUTHOR	TITLE
1-893115-73-9	$34.95	Abbott	Voice Enabling Web Applications: VoiceXML and Beyond
1-893115-01-1	$39.95	Appleman	Dan Appleman's Win32 API Puzzle Book and Tutorial for Visual Basic Programmers
1-893115-23-2	$29.95	Appleman	How Computer Programming Works
1-893115-97-6	$39.95	Appleman	Moving to VB. NET: Strategies, Concepts, and Code
1-59059-023-6	$39.95	Baker	Adobe Acrobat 5: The Professional User's Guide
1-893115-09-7	$29.95	Baum	Dave Baum's Definitive Guide to LEGO MINDSTORMS
1-893115-84-4	$29.95	Baum, Gasperi, Hempel, and Villa	Extreme MINDSTORMS: An Advanced Guide to LEGO MINDSTORMS
1-893115-82-8	$59.95	Ben-Gan/Moreau	Advanced Transact-SQL for SQL Server 2000
1-893115-91-7	$39.95	Birmingham/Perry	Software Development on a Leash
1-893115-48-8	$29.95	Bischof	The .NET Languages: A Quick Translation Guide
1-893115-67-4	$49.95	Borge	Managing Enterprise Systems with the Windows Script Host
1-893115-28-3	$44.95	Challa/Laksberg	Essential Guide to Managed Extensions for C++
1-893115-39-9	$44.95	Chand	A Programmer's Guide to ADO.NET in C#
1-893115-44-5	$29.95	Cook	Robot Building for Beginners
1-893115-99-2	$39.95	Cornell/Morrison	Programming VB .NET: A Guide for Experienced Programmers
1-893115-72-0	$39.95	Curtin	Developing Trust: Online Privacy and Security
1-59059-008-2	$29.95	Duncan	The Career Programmer: Guerilla Tactics for an Imperfect World
1-893115-71-2	$39.95	Ferguson	Mobile .NET
1-893115-90-9	$49.95	Finsel	The Handbook for Reluctant Database Administrators
1-59059-024-4	$49.95	Fraser	Real World ASP.NET: Building a Content Management System
1-893115-42-9	$44.95	Foo/Lee	XML Programming Using the Microsoft XML Parser
1-893115-55-0	$34.95	Frenz	Visual Basic and Visual Basic .NET for Scientists and Engineers
1-893115-85-2	$34.95	Gilmore	A Programmer's Introduction to PHP 4.0
1-893115-36-4	$34.95	Goodwill	Apache Jakarta-Tomcat
1-893115-17-8	$59.95	Gross	A Programmer's Introduction to Windows DNA
1-893115-62-3	$39.95	Gunnerson	A Programmer's Introduction to C#, Second Edition
1-59059-009-0	$49.95	Harris/Macdonald	Moving to ASP.NET: Web Development with VB .NET
1-893115-30-5	$49.95	Harkins/Reid	SQL: Access to SQL Server
1-893115-10-0	$34.95	Holub	Taming Java Threads
1-893115-04-6	$34.95	Hyman/Vaddadi	Mike and Phani's Essential C++ Techniques
1-893115-96-8	$59.95	Jorelid	J2EE FrontEnd Technologies: A Programmer's Guide to Servlets, JavaServer Pages, and Enterprise JavaBeans
1-893115-49-6	$39.95	Kilburn	Palm Programming in Basic
1-893115-50-X	$34.95	Knudsen	Wireless Java: Developing with Java 2, Micro Edition
1-893115-79-8	$49.95	Kofler	Definitive Guide to Excel VBA
1-893115-57-7	$39.95	Kofler	MySQL
1-893115-87-9	$39.95	Kurata	Doing Web Development: Client-Side Techniques
1-893115-75-5	$44.95	Kurniawan	Internet Programming with VB

ISBN	PRICE	AUTHOR	TITLE
1-893115-38-0	$24.95	Lafler	Power AOL: A Survival Guide
1-893115-46-1	$36.95	Lathrop	Linux in Small Business: A Practical User's Guide
1-893115-19-4	$49.95	Macdonald	Serious ADO: Universal Data Access with Visual Basic
1-893115-06-2	$39.95	Marquis/Smith	A Visual Basic 6.0 Programmer's Toolkit
1-893115-22-4	$27.95	McCarter	David McCarter's VB Tips and Techniques
1-59059-021-X	$34.95	Moore	Karl Moore's Visual Basic .NET: The Tutorials
1-893115-76-3	$49.95	Morrison	C++ For VB Programmers
1-893115-80-1	$39.95	Newmarch	A Programmer's Guide to Jini Technology
1-893115-58-5	$49.95	Oellermann	Architecting Web Services
1-59059-020-1	$44.95	Patzer	JSP Examples and Best Practices
1-893115-81-X	$39.95	Pike	SQL Server: Common Problems, Tested Solutions
1-59059-017-1	$34.95	Rainwater	Herding Cats: A Primer for Programmers Who Lead Programmers
1-59059-025-2	$49.95	Rammer	Advanced .NET Remoting
1-893115-20-8	$34.95	Rischpater	Wireless Web Development
1-893115-93-3	$34.95	Rischpater	Wireless Web Development with PHP and WAP
1-893115-89-5	$59.95	Shemitz	Kylix: The Professional Developer's Guide and Reference
1-893115-40-2	$39.95	Sill	The qmail Handbook
1-893115-24-0	$49.95	Sinclair	From Access to SQL Server
1-893115-94-1	$29.95	Spolsky	User Interface Design for Programmers
1-893115-53-4	$44.95	Sweeney	Visual Basic for Testers
1-59059-002-3	$44.95	Symmonds	Internationalization and Localization Using Microsoft .NET
1-59059-010-4	$54.95	Thomsen	Database Programming with C#
1-893115-29-1	$44.95	Thomsen	Database Programming with Visual Basic .NET
1-893115-65-8	$39.95	Tiffany	Pocket PC Database Development with eMbedded Visual Basic
1-893115-59-3	$59.95	Troelsen	C# and the .NET Platform
1-59059-011-2	$59.95	Troelsen	COM and .NET Interoperability
1-893115-26-7	$59.95	Troelsen	Visual Basic .NET and the .NET Platform
1-893115-54-2	$49.95	Trueblood/Lovett	Data Mining and Statistical Analysis Using SQL
1-893115-68-2	$54.95	Vaughn	ADO.NET and ADO Examples and Best Practices for VB Programmers, Second Edition
1-59059-012-0	$49.95	Vaughn/Blackburn	ADO.NET Examples and Best Practices for C# Programmers
1-893115-83-6	$44.95	Wells	Code Centric: T-SQL Programming with Stored Procedures and Triggers
1-893115-95-X	$49.95	Welschenbach	Cryptography in C and C++
1-893115-05-4	$39.95	Williamson	Writing Cross-Browser Dynamic HTML
1-893115-78-X	$49.95	Zukowski	Definitive Guide to Swing for Java 2, Second Edition
1-893115-92-5	$49.95	Zukowski	Java Collections
1-893115-98-4	$54.95	Zukowski	Learn Java with JBuilder 6

Available at bookstores nationwide or from Springer Verlag New York, Inc. at 1-800-777-4643; fax 1-212-533-3503. Contact us for more information at sales@apress.com.

Apress Titles Publishing SOON!

ISBN	AUTHOR	TITLE
1-59059-022-8	Alapati	Expert Oracle 9i Database Administration
1-59059-039-2	Barnaby	Distributed .NET Programming
1-59059-019-8	Cagle	The Graphical Web
1-59059-015-5	Clark	An Introduction to Object Oriented Programming with Visual Basic .NET
1-59059-000-7	Cornell	Programming C#
1-59059-014-7	Drol	Object-Oriented Flash MX
1-59059-033-3	Fraser	Managed C++ and .NET Development
1-59059-038-4	Gibbons	Java Development to .NET Development
1-59059-030-9	Habibi/Camerlengo/Patterson	Java 1.4 and the Sun Certified Developer Exam
1-59059-006-6	Hetland	Practical Python
1-59059-003-1	Nakhimovsky/Meyers	XML Programming: Web Applications and Web Services with JSP and ASP
1-59059-001-5	McMahon	Serious ASP.NET
1-893115-27-5	Morrill	Tuning and Customizing a Linux System
1-59059-028-7	Rischpater	Wireless Web Development, 2nd Edition
1-59059-026-0	Smith	Writing Add-Ins for .NET
1-893115-43-7	Stephenson	Standard VB: An Enterprise Developer's Reference for VB 6 and VB .NET
1-59059-032-5	Thomsen	Database Programming with Visual Basic .NET, 2nd Edition
1-59059-007-4	Thomsen	Building Web Services with VB .NET
1-59059-027-9	Torkelson/Petersen/Torkelson	Programming the Web with Visual Basic .NET
1-59059-018-X	Tregar	Writing Perl Modules for CPAN
1-59059-004-X	Valiaveedu	SQL Server 2000 and Business Intelligence in an XML/.NET World

Available at bookstores nationwide or from Springer Verlag New York, Inc. at 1-800-777-4643; fax 1-212-533-3503. Contact us for more information at sales@apress.com.

books for professionals by professionals™

apress™

About Apress

Apress, located in Berkeley, CA, is a fast-growing, innovative publishing company devoted to meeting the needs of existing and potential programming professionals. Simply put, the "A" in Apress stands for *"The Author's Press™"* and its books have *"The Expert's Voice™"*. Apress' unique approach to publishing grew out of conversations between its founders Gary Cornell and Dan Appleman, authors of numerous best-selling, highly regarded books for programming professionals. In 1998 they set out to create a publishing company that emphasized quality above all else. Gary and Dan's vision has resulted in the publication of over 50 titles by leading software professionals, all of which have *The Expert's Voice™*.

Do You Have What It Takes to Write for Apress?

Apress is rapidly expanding its publishing program. If you can write and refuse to compromise on the quality of your work, if you believe in doing more than rehashing existing documentation, and if you're looking for opportunities and rewards that go far beyond those offered by traditional publishing houses, we want to hear from you!

Consider these innovations that we offer all of our authors:

- **Top royalties with *no* hidden switch statements**
  Authors typically only receive half of their normal royalty rate on foreign sales. In contrast, Apress' royalty rate remains the same for both foreign and domestic sales.

- **A mechanism for authors to obtain equity in Apress**
  Unlike the software industry, where stock options are essential to motivate and retain software professionals, the publishing industry has adhered to an outdated compensation model based on royalties alone. In the spirit of most software companies, Apress reserves a significant portion of its equity for authors.

- **Serious treatment of the technical review process**
  Each Apress book has a technical reviewing team whose remuneration depends in part on the success of the book since they too receive royalties.

Moreover, through a partnership with Springer-Verlag, New York, Inc., one of the world's major publishing houses, Apress has significant venture capital behind it. Thus, we have the resources to produce the highest quality books *and* market them aggressively.

If you fit the model of the Apress author who can write a book that gives the "professional what he or she needs to know™," then please contact one of our Editorial Directors, Gary Cornell (gary_cornell@apress.com), Dan Appleman (dan_appleman@apress.com), Peter Blackburn (peter_blackburn@apress.com), Jason Gilmore (jason_gilmore@apress.com), Karen Watterson (karen_watterson@apress.com), or John Zukowski (john_zukowski@apress.com) for more information.